What Do We Know about War?

What Do We Know about War?

Edited by
John A. Vasquez

ROWMAN & LITTLEFIELD PUBLISHERS, INC.
Lanham • Boulder • New York • Oxford

ROWMAN & LITTLEFIELD PUBLISHERS, INC.

Published in the United States of America
by Rowman & Littlefield Publishers, Inc.
4720 Boston Way, Lanham, Maryland 20706
http://www.rowmanlittlefield.com

12 Hid's Copse Road, Cumnor Hill, Oxford OX2 9JJ, England

British Library Cataloguing in Publication Information Available

Library of Congress Cataloging-in-Publication Data

What do we know about war? / John A. Vasquez, [editor].
    p. cm.
    Includes bibliographical references and indexes.
    ISBN 0-8476-9926-9 (alk. : cloth)—ISBN 0-8476-9927-7 (alk. : paper)
    1. War. 2. Peace. I. Vasquez, John A., 1945–
U21.2.W477   2000
355.02—dc21   00-030980

Printed in the United States of America

♾ ™ The paper used in this publication meets the minimum requirements of American
National Standard for Information Sciences—Permanence of Paper for Printed Library
Materials, ANSI/NISO Z39.48-1992.

To My Mother,
Helen J. Vasquez

Contents

Preface

It seems that war is always with us. Yet, as Ecclesiastes reminds us, a time of war will eventually give way to a time of peace. The struggle of humanity has been to break this cycle so that the time of peace lasts. The foundation of this struggle has always rested on the shoulders of those who could provide answers to why war occurs and how it can be prevented. Studying war, for many, has been a way to peace, not a way to perfect the *ultima ratio regum* of coercion, as Louis XIV referred to his cannons of war. Even though knowledge does not guarantee a political solution to public problems, without knowledge there can be little reasonable expectation for the amelioration of perennial problems such as war.

This book reports on one approach to the study of peace and war: the use of the scientific method to identify those factors that promote the outbreak of interstate war and those factors that promote peace. Within contemporary society this has become an important and fairly widespread movement among international relations scholars, especially political scientists. This movement is one of the best hopes of humanity for solving the intellectual puzzle of war because it replaces the solitary efforts of past great thinkers, such as Thucydides and Freud, with a large number of researchers committed to using the best method of inquiry humanity has invented. Their approach permits a division of labor and the creation of a body of research findings that will provide a cumulation of knowledge. Having many minds work on the same problem in a sustained manner may have payoffs that have eluded previous efforts.

This book serves as a report of what we know to date. Such a goal is ambitious, and to have any hope of achieving it, scholars would have to have sustained interaction and discussion. Fortunately, much of this discussion had already taken place before the contributors to this book were invited to meet for four days in the spring of 1997 at Vanderbilt University to see what we had learned as a community of peace researchers. Except for two new Ph.D.s who were invited, all of the scholars had known each other for a number of years and had regularly seen each other at annual meetings, especially that of the Peace Science Society (International), which has provided an important forum for discussion and the exchange of research. A number had also participated in a conference hosted by

Stuart Bremer (1995a) and Thomas Cusack that set out a common research
agenda seeking to enhance the field's progress.

Many but not all of the scholars have either been associated with or used data
from the Correlates of War project. Since that project is now in its thirty-sixth
year, the time seemed ripe to assess the question that J. David Singer had started
out with: What have we learned about the correlates of war? The conference was
organized around a set of factors that research in the field had identified as important in bringing about war or in bringing about peace. The majority of participants were asked to focus on a specific factor. Is this variable a factor (or correlate) of war? In light of existing research, can a pattern be documented? If there
is disagreement about whether a pattern exists, what research designs can be constructed that would resolve the empirical disagreement? If there is a pattern, how
do we explain it? Can alternate explanations be found in the literature? Which of
these have been tested and/or supported by empirical evidence?

Not all scholars take the same tack on these factors, so sometimes more than
one scholar was invited to discuss the same variable. This was the case with the
questions of territory, alliances, and rivalry. Similarly, not all researchers think
that the focus should be on correlates per se—some wish to distinguish correlates
from "causes"; others prefer to look at factors that increase the probability of
war or of peace.

Several scholars were also invited to provide a general overview of what we
have learned. These were of two sorts. Some were asked to review research on
all of the factors under discussion with an eye to their relative importance and
how they might fit together. Others were asked to reflect on the lessons of this
conference. Each of the papers was discussed and sometimes even debated. The
chapters were then prepared in light of the conference and subsequent criticisms.
The end result is a fairly detailed report of what has been learned about those
factors that are probably most related to the onset of war and the creation of
peace.

A number of individuals helped make the conference and the book possible.
The most important was Mary Lynn Armistead, a 1922 graduate of Vanderbilt
University who had a lifelong interest in public affairs. She provided a bequest
for the establishment of a series of lectures and forums that would promote the
free exchange of ideas and honor the values of Norman Thomas, the great American socialist. Norman Thomas hated the scourge of war and devoted much of his
life to the achievement of peace. We hope that he would have found the ideas and
research in this book useful to his struggle to end war.

I would also like to extend my thanks to several scholars who attended the
conference and helped stimulate the discussion and provided useful criticisms:
Nils Petter Gleditsch, Marie Henehan, Paul Senese, and Dina Zinnes. Special
thanks go to Douglas Gibler, who helped me with arranging all the details of the
conference, and to Chris Leskiw, who helped prepare the manuscript, especially
the disks, for submission. Each of them eased my burden at busy times and did

a professional job. Vanderbilt University and the Department of Political Science provided a congenial venue for the conference. My thanks to Erwin Hargrove, Donna Bahry, and James Lee Ray for placing the Norman Thomas fund at my disposal for both running the conference and publishing the book. Publishing the book with Rowman & Littlefield and working with Jennifer Knerr have been a distinct pleasure. From the time I first broached the idea of the book with her to the last detail, she and other staff smoothed the way and made this process go much faster than it would have at any other press. Let me also acknowledge Matthew Melko, who a number of years ago organized a panel entitled "What Do We Know about War?" The title and the search for answers have stuck with me.

Lastly, I wish to express my appreciation to two people. The first, Marie Henehan—my lifelong colleague and partner—has always provided emotional support (even during times that were very pressing for her) and has always been someone with whom I could share and test out ideas, including many of those in this book. The second is my mother, Helen J. Vasquez, to whom I dedicate this book. Born in the year the United States entered World War I, married shortly after Pearl Harbor, and keeping the peace in the family during the sixties, she like millions of other Americans has been touched by war, even though she has avoided its worst scourges. She has always been supportive of me and helped instill a sense of work that has been immensely useful in my academic life. More important, she has provided a sense of love without which no life would be worth living.

John A. Vasquez

Introduction

John A. Vasquez

For most of history, intellectuals and scholars have pondered what causes war, owing in no small part to the horrors of war. Despite this long intellectual history of inquiry, it has been only relatively recently that a group of scholars has come together to study the factors related to the onset of war through the application of the scientific method and the use of data analysis to delineate patterns. In 1964, J. David Singer founded the Correlates of War project with the intention of collecting reproducible data that would serve as the foundation for creating a body of scientific knowledge on war.[1]

Since the mid-1960s, a very large number of scientific studies on war have been published using correlates-of-war data by numerous scholars. Indeed, one of the things that separates the Correlates of War project from the early efforts of Richardson (1939), Sorokin (1937), and Wright (1942) has been its ability to bring together a community of scholars to focus on researching the onset of war even when they have not been part of the project. The project itself has helped sustain a wider peace research community dedicated to the use of scientific analysis to study war and the conditions of peace. It is not an exaggeration to say that in the last thirty-five years, more social scientists have been working on this set of related research questions than at any other time in history. What have they learned?

This book has been written to answer this question. Rather than producing a secondary study of that research, this book brings together those scholars who are actively engaged in research to answer the question themselves. The emphasis here is on international relations scholars. Many of the contributors are associated with the Correlates of War project, but a number of other scholars reflecting different theoretical approaches, projects, or research programs have been included. This book, however, is not just another compendium that reports the results of various projects; rather, it attempts to provide a systematic discussion of what we think we know about the onset of war after all this research and what we need to do to confirm this knowledge and extend it.

Of course, the knowledge we have about war is not as definitive as knowledge produced in physics. Nonetheless, that does not mean that we know nothing or that everything is a matter of perspective. The word *knowledge* is used in this book to indicate that certain hypotheses have passed at least a modicum of rigorous tests using reproducible data—in other words, that the knowledge claims are based on some sort of rigorous examination of evidence and are not just based on speculation or intellectual argument. This does not mean that further inspection may not lead to different conclusions. Science is a process, not necessarily an end product. This is especially the case when one is working at the frontiers of knowledge in a young science, as are the contributors to this book. In a sense, this is a book about what we know *now*, what we have learned about war within international relations inquiry in the last thirty-five years or so.

The book is divided into three parts. Part I provides an overview of what has been learned by the scientific study of peace and war. In chapter 1, J. David Singer, the founder of the Correlates of War project, provides a history and rationale of the project. In chapter 2, Stuart A. Bremer attempts to integrate findings on correlates of war to see how they might fit together to bring about the onset of war. He does this by identifying the factors that determine "who will fight whom, when, where, and why." In chapter 3, Michael Brecher, Patrick James, and Jonathan Wilkenfeld compare the findings of the International Crisis Behavior project with those of the Correlates of War project to show that there is a certain amount of convergence as to what the most important factors seem to be, even though the two projects are based on different data.

Part II devotes a chapter to each of the factors that have been thought to be important in bringing about war. Each author reviews and presents research to see whether the factor in question is a correlate of war and/or responsible for increasing the probability of war. Each author then goes on to discuss the theoretical implications of the relevant research for explaining the onset of war. Almost all of the research discussed in this section shares a common research design and perspective—each piece of research tries to identify what factors distinguish the comparatively few militarized disputes that go to war from the overwhelming number that do not.

Chapters 4 and 5 examine whether the issue at stake in a dispute is a key element in distinguishing which disputes go to war and which do not. Both chapters focus on whether territorial disputes increase the probability of war. In chapter 4, Paul R. Hensel starts with data on militarized interstate disputes and sees whether territorial disputes are more war prone than nonterritorial disputes and more likely to be associated with a set of behaviors that encourages the outbreak of war. He then reviews various explanations for these findings and concludes that the territorial explanation of war receives the most support from existing evidence. In chapter 5, Paul K. Huth (focusing on his own data on territorial claims) examines the factors associated with states initiating territorial claims and analyzes what factors make territorial claims escalate to militarized disputes and to war. His research provides several insights as to what distinguishes the territorial disputes that go to war from those that do not. Both of these chapters go a long way in providing evidence that disputes over territory are an important factor increasing the probability of war.

Chapters 6 and 7 focus on the role of alliances in bringing about war. In chapter 6, Zeev Maoz reviews the literature and presents original research to see whether alliances are associated with the outbreak of war. He finds that the relationship will vary depending on whether the alliance involves major states or democratic states. In chapter 7, Douglas M. Gibler tries to resolve this question by developing a typology of alliances that theoretically distinguishes those that can be expected to be followed by war from those that can be expected to be followed by peace. He then tests his claim using data going back to 1815 and is very successful in discriminating the war-prone alliances from those followed by peace.

Chapter 8 is devoted to the role of military buildups and arms races in bringing about war. Susan G. Sample looks at the debate over whether military buildups and arms races are associated with the escalation of militarized disputes to war. Using various measures, she is able to resolve a number of contentious questions in this debate and provide evidence that shows that arms races that occur in the context of ongoing militarized disputes do increase the probability of these disputes' escalating to war in the prenuclear period.

Chapters 9 and 10 look at how interstate rivalry in the form of recurring disputes is associated with the onset of war. These chapters show that states that are rivals have a much higher probability of going to war than other types of states. In chapter 9, Gary Goertz and Paul F. Diehl examine the research that shows that recurring conflict leads to war. They then explore the internal dynamics of a rivalry that make it go to war. In chapter 10, Frank Whelon Wayman presents additional findings on recurrent conflict and the outbreak of war. He then outlines how recurrent disputes are an important component in constructing an explanation of war. Both of these chapters show that pairs of states that have repeated disputes with one another have a higher probability of going to war than states whose disputes do not recur as frequently. This conclusion confirms the general notions that violence encourages violence and that war is often the outcome of a process whereby lower levels of coercion fail and give rise to higher levels of coercion that often escalate to war.

In chapter 11, Russell J. Leng looks at whether the bargaining behavior of states within a crisis plays an important role in whether the crisis escalates to war. He reviews existing evidence that shows that there is an association between certain kinds of bargaining strategies and the outbreak of war. He assesses these findings in light of two competing perspectives—the psychological and the realist. He then further examines the research and the alternative explanations by looking in depth at the Cuban Missile Crisis and the pre–Six Day War crisis.

From these cases, he concludes that the rate and intensity of the escalation appear to generate nonrational responses in leaders.

In chapter 12, Daniel S. Geller focuses on capability balances between pairs of states and the onset of war. His review shows that differences in capability are most likely to play a role when there is a dispute between those who are trying to change the status quo (revisionist actors) and those who are defending it, and the balance is unstable. Geller also explores a number of other relationships, including what kinds of indicators of capability (economic, demographic, or military) are most able to predict the onset of war, and concludes that the military component may be more critical than the other factors.

Part III shifts the focus to the conditions of peace. Wallensteen (1984) has identified the major peaceful eras since 1815. What factors are associated with these eras? As the work on correlates of war begins to be integrated, more attention can be expected to be given to identifying the correlates of peaceful eras. Not a great deal of research has been done on the factors related to peace, but two major areas of inquiry appear promising: the work on norms and the research on the democratic peace. In chapter 13, Gregory A. Raymond looks at the place international norms play in bringing about and sustaining peace. He reviews the existing evidence to show that restrictive normative orders lower the probability of militarized disputes and wars. In chapter 14, James Lee Ray examines the findings on the democratic peace. He extends his analysis to the question of whether democratic states are generally more peaceful, even if they are facing nondemocratic opponents and if the system as a whole will become more peaceful as the number of democratic states increases.

Part IV assesses what lessons and conclusions can be drawn from the attempt to identify correlates of war and peaceful eras. In chapter 15, Jack S. Levy uses the previous chapters as a basis for examining how much and what kind of progress has been made in the scientific study of peace and war. In chapter 16, Manus I. Midlarsky looks at the question of "mature theories" (i.e., theories that have significant empirical validation) and the criteria one uses in evaluating them. In chapter 17, John Vasquez draws on the chapters in the first three parts of the book to see what we know about war and delineate what questions we need to research to expand that knowledge.

The analyses presented in this book show that the early strategy J. David Singer took in the Correlates of War project of trying to identify and document patterns through empirical analysis has borne fruit. Such an investigation has been inductive, but not blindly inductive in the sense of being theory-free (see the early theoretical statements of Singer, reprinted in Singer [1979]). Singer has never said that research should be conducted without any guidance from theoretical analyses. How can one test hypotheses, for example, without some kind of theory producing the hypotheses in the first place? What he has maintained in reaction to the data-free traditionalist-dominated fifties is that theory in the absence of systematic evidence is really speculation. Research and theory construction must go hand in hand. As findings become clearer, we begin to learn what is and is not related to the onset of war. Not everything is a correlate of war, and not all correlates are of equal theoretical significance.

The research reviewed in this volume has presented a road map of what we know to date. While we still have a long way to go, it is clear that we know a great deal more today than we did thirty-five years ago. All of the factors analyzed in this book appear to play some role in the onset of war. States that dispute territorial issues have a higher probability of going to war than other states. Certain kinds of alliances increase the probability of war involvement. Building up one's military in the context of ongoing militarized disputes makes it more likely that this dispute or one within a few years will escalate to war. As disputes recur between the same parties, the probability that one will escalate to war increases substantially. Crises that exhibit certain kinds of bargaining between the parties will be more likely to escalate to war than other crises. Certain kinds of capability balances between revisionist and status quo states increase the likelihood that a militarized dispute will escalate to war. In addition, we have learned that norms can reduce the likelihood of militarized disputes and their escalation to war and that democratic states seem to be able to better manage their disputes with other democratic states so as to avoid war, at least in the post–World War II period.

While other factors may promote or inhibit the onset of war, these appear to be among the major ones for which some systematic evidence exists. These research findings will enrich our attempts at explanation, which then will give rise to new research that will further refine our knowledge about war and about peace. Scientific knowledge is not so much an end as it is a process that produces usable bits of information along the way. We hope that this volume has produced some usable bits of information as we search for the "causes" of war.

NOTE

1. This occurred in the context of several other attempts to study war either through investigating crises that lead to war (e.g., the 1914 studies of Robert North [Holsti, North, and Brody 1968; Choucri and North 1975] and the later International Crisis Behavior project [Brecher and Wilkenfeld 1989, 1997b]) or through analyzing the dynamics of international conflict (e.g., Rummel 1979 and Guetzkow 1968).

PART I

OVERVIEW

1

The Etiology of Interstate War
A Natural History Approach

J. David Singer

Some may disagree, but I subscribe to the proposition that a field of study suffers when there is little awareness of its historical past. Somewhere between obeisance to Thucydides and Machiavelli, on the one hand, and reference only to the hot button arguments that surfaced while in graduate school, on the other, there would seem to be a prudent attention to some "relevant" historical background. One virtue, of course, is to reduce the frequency with which the social science discipline reinvents the wheel, wasting many student-hours and research-hours working through a line of reasoning that has already been nicely and clearly articulated by one or more of our predecessors. Another is to help avoid repeating errors that have been made—and often rectified—in the past, ranging from matters methodological to those of an empirical or conceptual sort. Yet a third virtue is to permit taking advantage of some painstaking and incremental gains that have been made and then all too often forgotten. A fourth and frequently needed virtue is to be able to recall how a certain concept was understood at its inception or earlier use. While there is little that we can do to prevent slippage, if not corruption, in the natural language of everyday practice, the scientific community might want to attend more diligently to matters of semantic clarity, continuity, and precision.

One way to take advantage of our intellectual legacies and to avoid these problems is to pay closer attention to the education of graduate students, many of whom will be academic colleagues in less than a decade. They should be spared the presence of very recent Ph.D.s in gateway and other graduate-level seminars, especially since the odds are good that the latter's own graduate education was also excessively at the hands of new and immature young scholars. It is, of course, desirable that graduate students be exposed to the latest ideas, methods, and findings, but it is equally desirable that they learn more about the field's intellectual origins and turning points. My advice would be to give the first- and second-year graduate students—in world politics and elsewhere—*some* exposure to very junior professors, but 50 to 75 percent of their courses might well be taught by those of greater experience in their first two years.

A second and equally effective way to avoid the loss-of-memory problem is to see to it that the courses we teach, panels and conferences that we organize, articles that we write, and books that we publish and edit take sufficient efforts to preserve and build on the more helpful work that has gone before. This anthology serves as an excellent example of how we may benefit from a rich mix of scientists who span and represent a goodly range of cohort groups. In this connection, with such founding fathers as Lewis Richardson and Quincy Wright and such powerful reference figures as Kenneth Boulding and Karl Deutsch no longer alive, it looks as if I now find myself one of the more senior perpetrators of the scientific study of world politics. Thus, it is an honor and a responsibility to contribute the opening chapter to this exciting and valuable collection.

STAGES IN THE EVOLUTION OF OUR INVESTIGATION

It might be useful to begin by suggesting one possible way of differentiating the stages that mark the development of a particular field of study—in our case, the search for an explanation of war between territorial actors, usually states.

The First Stage: Speculation

The first and longest stage is that of intelligent speculation—ranging perhaps from Thucydides to Morgenthau or Aron—in which we observe contemporary wars and near-wars, invent some plausible explanations, and then ransack history for those cases that seem to support our hypotheses. The opposite side of the same coin has us form certain generalizations from our recollection of the salient past and then try to apply them to more recent or contemporary events.

The Second Stage: Demonstration of Possibilities

The second stage—a very long time in coming—is nicely marked by Lewis Richardson's studies following his grim experience as a conscientious objector and ambulance driver with the Sixteenth French Infantry Division during World War I. As the cartoonist Bill Mauldin quipped, "If this is the war to end all war, why did they give it a number?" Deeply moved by the mindless slaughter in Flanders and other killing fields, on returning home to England Richardson began to read the military and diplomatic historians and concluded that he could do considerably better. While probably unaware of these names, he followed the urgings of Buckle (1857–1861), Quetelet (1848), Condorcet (1795), Durkheim (1895), and other apostles of quantitative social analysis who had gone largely unnoticed in European intellectual circles. In any event, Richardson—who was by profession a meteorologist—began to work on the etiology of "deadly quarrels," invoking mathematical models, operational coding rules, and statistical analysis. As is well known, few of his many papers were accepted by the scholarly journals, and it was not until seven years after his death that a group of his admirers published *The Statistics of Deadly Quarrels* and *Arms and Insecurity* (both 1960).

I would add three other scholars to this second stage. Just as important as Richardson, in my judgment, was Quincy Wright, an American professor of international law whose father was a mathematician and whose older brother Sewell had been a pioneer in the development of mathematical biology. The story has it that the latter admired Quincy's scholarship and his preoccupation with the scourge of war but lamented the lack of methodological rigor in his work and thus introduced him to scientific method—hence the fifteen-year project that culminated in the monumental *Study of War* (1942). Then there was Pitirim Sorokin, whose volume 3 of *Social and Cultural Dynamics* (1937) contains a rigorous and remarkably prescient body of data and discussion on armed conflict going back to the Roman legions. Finally, I would include as the fourth horseman of the second stage the Polish economist, Jean de Bloch, whose six-volume *Future of War* (1899) is really a quantitative and highly operational history of warfare over several centuries. His extraordinary rich and detailed study led to three major conclusions. First, the appearance of the machine gun would permit a small number of men in trenches behind barbed wire to hold a long defensive line indefinitely against numerically superior infantry and cavalry forces. Written in the 1890s, this observation was an uncanny prediction of what Richardson observed in the battles at the Marne, Somme, and Verdun. Second, he predicted that the cost of preparing to fight and then conducting such a war would be monumental. Finally, being an economist, with that discipline's touching faith in the rationality of those in power, Block believed that the European elites would thus turn to other means of interstate conflict resolution!

Others also come to mind, but these four scholars mark that four decades or so in which the basic ideas of scientific method were first brought to bear on the explanation of war. Unfortunately, World War II intervened not only to put a halt to this promising systematic research but to demonstrate beyond a doubt how desperately we needed it. Worse yet, with the end of that tragic set of episodes, the victorious major powers quickly turned on one another, easily mobilizing what Halberstam (1969) might have called the "best and the brightest" on both sides of the Cold War.

The Third Stage: Correlates of War and Natural History

As a result, the beginning of the third stage was delayed by more than a decade, until a "critical mass" of social scientists came together at the Stanford Center for Advanced Study in the Behavioral Sciences and put together plans that culminated in the establishment of the Center for Research on Conflict Resolution at the University of Michigan in 1957. The group was, in any intellectual sense, quite revolutionary. They were explicitly committed to the proposition that rigorous social science research could generate knowledge about individual and collective behavior that could tell the elites and the attentive publics not only what sorts of behavior were conducive to the onset and escalation of disputes but also what sorts of decisions and behaviors might help to head off serious disputes between and among states (as well as in other social settings). Without getting too autobiographical (Singer 1988), I found this focus irresistible, and after a postdoctoral year in the Harvard Department of Social Relations, I eagerly accepted an offer to join the Department of Political Science at the University of Michigan in 1958. Working alongside of Robert Angell and Kenneth Boulding and tremendously stimulated by them and the others around the center, I began to lay out the research strategy that would mark the third, correlates-of-war stage. Despite our eagerness to come up with findings that could, as soon as possible, help turn the Soviets and Americans away from the menacing road to Armageddon, our sense was that a more modest and incremental research strategy was the responsible way to go. We saw the writing and thinking of the first stage as heuristically valuable, brimming with possible insights, and the work of the second stage as evidence that the war question could indeed be researched in the scientific mode. The time seemed appropriate to blend the traditional with the behavioral, and rather than succumb to physics envy and suffer from premature explanation, my/our decision was to pursue systematic description and empirical generalization. In short, we would embark on the natural history stage in war-peace research, much as did Charles Darwin in biology. He never stopped observing and he never stopped thinking, and—despite occasional suggestions of barefoot or dustbin empiricism—our Correlates of War colleagues continue to think, observe, and count now, thirty-five years after the birth of the project.

As I look at the work of my former graduate students from the beginnings in the early 1960s through the late 1990s, as well as others in that social scientific cohort (Vasquez 1993), it seems that the third stage is still with us. Quite clearly, the emphasis is to articulate interesting queries about war and peace, summarize earlier speculation and research findings, lay out a sensible research design, and put to the test a well-formulated model that embraces the central query. Furthermore, it is neither desirable nor likely that we try to move too rapidly out of this stage and the research paradigm that it entails. We still know so little about "what goes with what," even where we have seen a respectable body of research, that it often shows more inconsistency than a cumulative process should tolerate. But as this natural history/correlates-of-war work goes on, we need to attend to two key issues. One is the distinction between additive and integrative cumulation; as all of us keep repeating, just piling up more and more findings on related questions may strengthen the case for one or another important generalization, but it may not carry us very far toward understanding how these generalizations mesh together. To tinker with a metaphor used by Guetzkow back in 1976, we are certainly moving ahead in producing atolls of knowledge (he called them, prematurely, "islands of theory") but are not doing as well in bridging them together into an integrated archipelago. As I see it, advances on that front will mark the gradual transition to our fourth stage. It will rest heavily on natural history, but the emphasis will be somewhat less on descriptive generalization and somewhat more on explanatory interpretation that rests on such generalization.

From a detached scientific perspective, we need not be in a hurry; the more solid and numerous our generalizations, the more likely we are to get our explanations right. On the other hand, most of us are not only committed to the generation of knowledge in the best scientific tradition; we are also committed not to what I call an "applied science" but to an *applicable science*. To that extent, it seems perfectly reasonable to begin thinking ahead a bit toward the possibility of one or more explanatory models that offer sufficiently compelling stories about how interstate disputes go from minor to militarized to all-out war. To contribute effectively to more adaptive policies and behaviors on the part of those whom we generously call statesmen, we must have such stories, and they need to be pretty credible to us before we offer them to those who decide the fate of nations.

The Fourth Stage: Beyond Covariation

What sorts of research can help us move beyond the correlates-of-war/natural history stage, and how far along might we already be? As I see it, several convergent research paradigms are worth considering in this context. Quite clearly, the leading candidates for shaping the next stage are—and ought to be—models that reflect the formal—deductive—mathematical mode. This orientation reflects the reasonable view that the sooner we can use formal and well-specified models that can both integrate recent findings and suggest the next steps in empirical investigation, the better. Whether expressed in game theory, structural equations, or computer simulations, this orientation reminds us that we need to be thinking of how we move from empirical descriptions of what goes with what to the question of "How come?" In more sophisticated terms, this is the impending transition from the third stage—the correlates of war and the natural history by which disputes escalated to war—to more aggressive efforts to *explain* these processes.

Quite clearly, the stages that I suggest are not quite operationally distinct at their borders nor are they now mutually exclusive. The overlap is impressive, given that different research programs are under way at different times and in different places. For example, the really valuable systematic natural history type of research is today very strong in the public universities of the Midwest and South of the United States, and it is just beginning to surface on the West and East Coasts of North America and isolated locales in Scandinavia and Japan. At the same time, we find a handful of studies under way in these same places, as well as in continental Europe, that seem to leapfrog the data-based, empirical generalization program and move beyond that to the articulation of formal "theories" that purport to explain and account for the research results generated by those colleagues of a more incremental turn of mind.

Having suggested that the natural history/correlation stage must not be the final one, let me nevertheless urge that it is probably the most crucial one, providing a powerful link between the anecdotal and the explanatory. Let me now turn to a few considerations that might be kept in mind as we seek to make this stage more productive than it has been over the last three decades or so.

SOME RELEVANT ASSUMPTIONS

In any scholarly endeavor, one begins with certain assumptions, but all too often these are unknown, unnoticed, and unarticulated. Those that will shape any investigation are of three sorts: *ethical*, or what the authors and researchers consider to be morally right, wrong, or in between; *epistemological*, or what criteria we use to evaluate knowledge claims; and *empirical*, or what we assume about the way that the world works, used to work, and is likely to work in the future.

Ethical Assumptions

If not for the awesome volume of hot air on the topic, we could pass this dimension with a genuflection or two; but a look at the book titles, fellowship themes, conference announcements, and the content of the journal of the same name (*Ethics and International Affairs*) reminds us of the confusion—and, yes, the ethical confusion—surrounding the study of war and peace. From my perspective, the confusion emerges out of the distinction in the West between facts and values or, worse yet, between empirical or positive theory and "normative theory." Typically, we treat ethical questions as if the answers are, and always will be, matters of subjective personal opinion, beyond the ken of scientific inquiry, and thus in the realm of "normative theory." This approach ignores the consequential dimension of ethics and illuminates another of the ways in which economic and mathematical reasoning have muddied the political waters. That is, individuals and groups are rarely able to select and automatically get their preferred outcome; what we do is select one or another preferred outcome and *then go on to select a strategy* by which we hope to achieve that outcome. To poke fun at some of our game theory and economics colleagues, life is more than preferring vanilla to chocolate and strawberry to both, and the global system is not just another ice cream parlor. Put simply, we make ethical choices not only on the basis of—inter alia—the likely consequences of such choices, based on our understanding of that connection, but also in light of our understanding of their achievability. Both of these are a function of our *knowledge* and thus very much a scientific matter.

Having said this, we need to confront the link between our research and teaching, on the one hand, and our normative stance on war, on the other hand. To come at the question indirectly, scholars in the United States who were doing systematic research on interstate war during the half century or so of Soviet-American armed rivalry were viewed with suspicion from at least two sides. The more evident criticism came from the "left"—those who opposed, for example, the U.S. role in the Vietnam War saw that role as a creature of the Pentagon's (and Rand's) quantitative "whiz kids" and often believed that any quantitative research was inspired and funded by the Department of Defense (DOD). Perhaps there was a germ of truth in their assertion, given the links to Project Camelot, the counterinsurgency work of some, the largesse of the Advanced Research Project Agency (ARPA), and the Office of Naval Research. However, a list of those doing (and publishing) scientific work on international conflict as revealed in the abstract books of *Beyond Conjecture* (Jones and Singer 1972) and *Empirical Knowledge* (Gibbs and Singer 1993) would show only a handful of co-opted Cold Warriors.

More to the point—and without for a moment suggesting that scientific method will single-handedly save humanity from the scourge of war or any other evil—we need to note that if we merely rely on the forces of light to overcome the forces of darkness, we are doomed to repeat most of the evils of our past. Wealth, power, prestige, and arrogance will usually carry the day against innocence, altruism, and humaneness. The defenses of the weak, and the most powerful weapon of decency, rest on knowledge and evidence. Most human beings live in a state of partial thralldom, manipulated, cajoled, and conscripted by the politicians and the priests who legitimize the tribalisms and the superstitions. They and we are the victims of our collective ignorance, an ignorance shared by the governors and the governed, even when the former wrap themselves in the garb of patriotism, throw up a smokescreen of alleged expertise, and hide behind a veil of confidentiality, classified information, top-secret double talk, and the mystique of "the national interest." Nor is more education of the sort we still dispense likely to do much good; those who decide for war or peace (and those who act and speak for them) are usually the better educated in any society, and our grief is no less for that. In sum, the ignorant of the reformers are seldom a match for the ignorant of the establishment, and until we know much more about the etiology of war and can make that knowledge accessible and credible to the national security establishments and their critics, our efforts will remain largely academic.

Less evident but equally naive and more destructive was the skepticism from the "right": those who saw peace researchers as questioning not only the wisdom but the morality of the national security establishments. More than one of them would ask, "Don't you think that we know what we're doing?" That is, if we trusted the wisdom, competence, and values of those people, we'd have no need to do research into the questions of war and peace. Reconsidering those Cold War experiences from the perspective of a moderately dovish and quantoid consultant with a "top secret" and a "Q" clearance from my naval intelligence days until about 1970, I can give voice to these ethical issues. Quite simply, the answer should be "No, we trust neither your competence nor your ethics." Some examples: the United States using the atomic bomb on the cities of Hiroshima and Nagasaki, when the Japanese were ready to surrender (according to Hap Arnold, Curtis LeMay, Tooey Spatz, Douglas MacArthur, Chester Nimitz, William Leahy, William Halsey, Ernest King, and probably Dwight Eisenhower, inter alia); carpet bombing in Vietnam; training and funding state terrorism in Central America; the Japanese using bacterial weapons on Chinese villages; the Iraqis using poison gas on the Kurds; the Russians assaulting Chechnya; the Serbs engaging in "ethnic cleansing"; and, of course, the Germans and the Holocaust. The list is tragically long and does not even mention the superpowers and their genocidal "deterrence" capabilities and doctrines during the Cold War.

While the list of items on the ethical agenda can be quite lengthy, let me wrap up for the time being with one more item. One has to do with how we finance our more resource-dependent investigations, especially when the generation or acquisition of data is involved. Some of us have been criticized for relying on the National Science Foundation (NSF) for support on the grounds that we thus become beholden to the U.S. government, if not to the Pentagon or Central Intelligence Agency (CIA), and are no longer free to arrive at our scientific conclusions. The critics need to know two things in this context. First, the NSF is the least politicized of any of the major foundations and consistently funds work in world politics that runs the gamut from left to right and from hawk to dove. Nor does it impose any restrictions when it comes to publishing results.

By contrast, the large private foundations (Ford, Carnegie, Rockefeller, MacArthur, Social Science Research Council, and, by extension, the U.S. Institute of Peace) all tend to recruit from the same pool, read the same magazines, and go to the same conferences. Not only is it rare to find a bona fide social scientist on their staffs (despite many Ph.D.s), but worse yet, they seldom support scientific work in world politics. Their board members, senior officers, and professional staff members *are* (or are alarmingly close to) the foreign policy establishment. Thus, whether we seek and accept funding from the NSF, CIA, DOD, AID, ACDA, ONR, or the White House or from the nongovernmental sector, it does not really matter. My early conclusion was that there is no such thing as "dirty money" for the simple reason that there is no "clean money." The federal government gets its money through means that range from misinformation to extortion and from enticement to coercion, while the foundations rest largely on the fortunes of the robber barons of the nineteenth century and the buccaneers of today's "free market" jungle. If we raise it honestly and use it rigorously and openly, it should be clean enough for the most finicky among us.

Epistemological Assumptions

While I see the ethical dimensions of our research and teaching roles as relatively clear-cut, the same cannot be said of those of an epistemological sort. We have a range of interesting and important differences among ourselves, and the other chapters will make this point abundantly clear. Let me lay bare several of those premises that I would like to see in evidence as our enterprise continues to move forward.

I begin with the one that will cause little grief in these precincts but could lead to howls of anguish within the Modern Language Association. Reference is, of course, to the syndrome know as "deconstruction," and it is usually associated with those schools of thought that could be called "the posties," embracing the postmodern, poststructural, postbehavioral, and, most germane to scientific researchers, the postpositivist outlook. I make no pretense of being on intimate terms with colleagues of those persuasions or familiar with the distinctions among them. As I understand this fairly recent orientation (and it may go back to Karl Mannheim), developing a science of human behavior just is not possible for several reasons: (1) there may not even *be* any empirical social reality; it is nothing more than imaginings given credibility by the language we use to describe these fictitious happenings; (2) even if there *is* a social reality, we can never apprehend it because every human being is the product of his or her cultural identity, gender, age, profession, education, and accumulated personal experiences; and (3) the representations of reality that we generally accept are "socially constructed," created and imposed on societies by the elites as an instrument of control.

A milder—and less nihilistic—version of the "mission impossible" school doesn't deny the existence of an empirical reality but argues that we positivists define it too narrowly. For example, Alker (1996) suggests that our "data" must include not only the alleged historical and empirical phenomenon that we attempt to describe and explain but also the reports about alleged observations of such phenomena, sometimes referred to as a call for more hermeneutics and less exegesis, as in biblical studies. Coming closer to the perspective of our small but growing "epistemic community" (Haas 1989) are those in the tradition of Bull (1966) who—with a touching faith in their own observational accuracy and perfect recall—question the need for all this scientific paraphernalia and assure us that the classical methods of the historian will do just fine. These traditionalists might want to listen to Mannheim more attentively; a good scientist attends to rigorous methods of observation, measurement, analysis, and inference simply because we *do* take some of the latter's warnings seriously.

To rectify all these failings of the contemporary scientific scene, quite a variety of dubious epistemology is offered. Already familiar to the quantitative world politics community is Dessler's (1991) effort to borrow from meteorology the idea that we need to, and can, "identify the mechanisms through which specified outcomes occur" or "the real structures that produce the observed phenomena" (343 and 345). But at the end of this thoughtful essay, we are left with no guidance toward this end beyond the strictures of "scientific realism" and the belief that causality does indeed obtain in the referent world. This line of reasoning will, of course, lead to the articulation of increasingly ambitious "theories" that are, in truth, little more than speculative models that rest on problematic and far from operational premises. In my view, causality is a chimera invented to help persuade us that we really can *know* how the world works, and it might best be replaced with the concept of *explanation*. That is, as we uncover more and more regularities and covariations—and thus generate an increasingly rich and credible description of the ways in which all sorts of events and conditions go together empirically—we will arrive at increasingly accepted *explanations*. As these persuasive "stories" are combined with what we think we know about individual and group behavior, the closer we will come to legitimate theories—in the sense of codified knowledge that commands the assent of our most capable colleagues.

Considerably more unnerving, and further down the self-styled "realist" path, is an approach that is called "evolutionary epistemology" intended to resolve the realist versus relativist impasse that arose out of the alleged passing of positivist and empiricist methodologies (Azevedo 1997). These recurrent debates over epistemology in the social sciences need not be surprising, given how poorly scientific method is taught and how dubious the status of the social sciences in the academic world. Furthermore, when we read those philosophers who tend to support and illuminate the scientific approach to social phenomena, we find that many of them are as confused as they are inaccessible; I find Hempel (1966) and Popper (1959), not to mention Harre (1970) and Lakatos (1970), not very helpful. Like religion, philosophy of science should be kept out of reach until we are sufficiently mature and experienced to be adequately immune to their all-too-plausible blandishments!

Turning from the doubters to the doers, let me lay out in telegraphic form some of the more relevant empirical-epistemic assumptions about the "nature of" the universe and the social systems—sometimes called "artificial" for reasons that still baffle me (H. Simon 1969)—of concern to us and ways of comprehending these systems:

1. The global system and the social groups that it comprises evince highly regular and thus recurring patterns, but we have only begun to discover them and confirm their existence. There are lawlike regularities, but we still have only a dim view of them.
2. Despite the existence of all these regularities, they are far from deterministic; while certain types of states respond over and over to the same stimuli

in the same context in the same way, there are plenty of exceptions, giving us statistical distributions rather than deterministic and perfectly uniform laws.

3. Even when we find extraordinary regularities, it is worth noting that the "causal path" between background conditions and behavioral outcomes can vary considerably; there are several ways to go from a given set of initial conditions to a well-specified outcome.

4. Regularities can take several forms, of which the simplest is a trend line in the magnitude of a given attribute of a given system; inasmuch as every social system is an evolving one, rates of change in such an attribute are also subject to change over time.

5. Cyclical patterns are often found, usually not in fixed intervals of real time but in the form of recurring sequences or the order in which events and conditions follow one another.

6. We are not likely to uncover fully deterministic regularities not only because all the systems and subsystems that we study are evolving, and in sequences that may well be irregular, but also because there is an *inherent randomness* in their behaviors and interactions vis-à-vis one another.

7. While the magnitude of such stochastic phenomena will diminish as we reduce (inter alia) measurement error, erroneous simplifying assumptions, misspecifications of our models, and the factors subsumed under the error term, it will never be reduced to zero; as asserted earlier, this residual randomness is inherent in the universe.

8. Our search for the lawlike regularities in matters of war and peace will advance erratically as a result of both empirical findings and theoretical insights; we will not get very far relying on only one or the other, despite pendulum-like fashions; systematic, data-based investigations are rarely "barefoot" or "dustbin" empiricism, nor is the construction of formal models merely "intellectual gymnastics."

9. In our search for an explanation of interstate war, we may discover empirically that two, three, or more subtypes arise out of systematically different conditions and processes, but we can always increase the goodness of fit by adding more differentiating variables; if not careful, we end up with a different model for each of the eighty-odd interstate wars since 1816, and we can leave case studies to colleagues of the "no two wars are alike!" school.

Empirical Assumptions

From my perspective, the single most crucial assumption we make in developing an explanation for war is not whether the interstate system is anarchic or hierarchical, constant or evolving, ordered or random, nor is it whether the states in conflict are democratic, equal in capabilities, or quarreling over territory for example. It is *how we conceive of the national security decision process*. I say this so bluntly to emphasize my rock-bottom commitment to a "reductionist" model of world politics, in which the human beings who make the decisions for war and peace are the central actors in the narrative that is supposed to describe how certain conditions and events at several levels of social aggregation combine to move one or more of the states toward or away from the precipice. The decision process can be thought of as the funnel through which must pass all those global, regional, and domestic factors that will affect the behavior of the state vis-à-vis its neighbors, allies, and adversaries; nothing happens in the way of a state's behavior until the stimuli have passed through the decision process. Several interesting questions are embedded in this process: (1) Which individuals and groups are involved, in the fairly direct sense of the word? (2) How discrete and distinct are their decisions? (3) How do they define the "national interest" (if I may use one of the most ambiguous and self-serving phrases in the lexicon)? and (4) What are the general decision rules?

While appreciating that there will be some variation across cultures and nationalities, historical epochs, and issues on the agenda and that crises will not be addressed in the same way as day-to-day routine matters, the similarities are quite overwhelming. Thus, my general model—applicable to most bureaucratized and politicized societies, ranging in size and modernity from Belgium to China, from Bolivia to India, and from Ghana to Russia—begins with the assumption that the decision process involves a lot of people from several ministries, numerous offices, and various parliamentary factions, not to mention domestic and foreign interest groups, each with somewhat different priorities. Coalition formation is ever present. Second, and partly for the above reason, the process is not only lengthy but also continuous with all sorts of feedback loops, erratic change of pace, and frequent redefinition of the problem. Not only do the players and the agenda change, but even when it appears that a move has been agreed to, it can often be eroded or reversed; worth noting, too, is that such closure at the decisional level can be questioned, altered, and sabotaged in its execution.

From this set of assumptions, it readily follows that, no matter how we try (Clinton 1996), there is no way to define "the national interest" objectively or specify the criteria by which we identify its role in the foreign policy and national security sectors. Each player brings his or her own factional, bureaucratic, and personal preferences, perceptions, and predictions to the process. Furthermore, as I have urged on several occasions (Singer 1972b, 1991b), in the absence of a solid, shared, and credible body of knowledge as to which types of states behave in which manner under which conditions and in response to which stimuli, there is no quickly recognized consensus as to which policies are most likely to produce which results, and thus no alternative to the loose and shifting coalitions as they (gradually or rapidly) move toward a decision. This, incidentally, is why almost every policy decision must be explained in terms of more than one consideration, as each contributing person or group signs on for somewhat different reasons. Illustrative in U.S. policy are dropping the atomic bombs on Japan in

1945 and attacking the Iraqis in 1991. My students recognize this as "Singer's First Law," in which it is pointed out that *nothing* can be explained by one variable alone.

All of this, in turn, suggests the difficulty of identifying the operational code or decision rules: it can be done only—whether in more autocratic or more democratic societies—via very careful inferences based on fairly detailed and disparate bodies of evidence. Again, by way of illustration in the U.S. context, consider the reluctance to intervene militarily in foreign disputes, crises, and disasters in light of such alleged "doctrines" as those of Nixon, Weinberger, Powell, and, in due course, others. This leads, in turn, to the need for extreme caution in our embracing any single model of national security decision making, even in the more restricted case of initiation or entering into interstate war. One thinks of such widely accepted explanations as the "realpolitik" of Morgenthau (1948), Kaplan (1957), or Blainey (1973) or the more sophisticated expected utility model of Bueno de Mesquita and Lalman (1992). We need usually to ask *whose* utilities, whose subjective probabilities, whose expected gains and losses, and so forth.

To be sure—and scholars as knowledgeable as H. Simon (1969) and Riker (1962) have made this point—we can adopt the "as if" strategy, also known as the teleonomic, versus teleological, approach; rather than claim that a small group of competent, highly informed, and unambiguously patriotic experts actually sit down and calculate expected utilities, we merely assume that the policy behaviors that emerge out of the decision process are remarkably close to what might have emerged *if* such a calculus *had* been followed. Worth noting is that some researchers, notably Bueno de Mesquita (1996), have done a rather successful job in postdicting as well as predicting on the basis of such a strategy; but the jury is still out.

One consequence of this point of view is that we need to return, but with greater rigor, to research on the decision process. On the one hand, it made perfect sense during the first three decades of systematic research on war and peace to "black box" the process. It gave us the time to better understand the input–output association: under what ecological and interactional conditions which types of states and societies showed which types of behavior. We know quite a bit more about the conditions of state behavior now than we did in the late sixties (Geller and Singer 1998) and are thus in a better position to infer which sets of decision rules—throughput—are more, or less, likely to be at work. On the other hand, much of the work to date (whether by psychologists or political scientists) has tended to be fairly casual, not only quite speculative but perhaps too simplistic as well.

Of course, any serious effort to get at the decision process will call into question our assumptions regarding "human nature." What sorts of people do we think are involved in the separate foreign policy establishments, the public and private interest groups, the regional and global organizations, the opinion makers, and, not to be neglected, the attentive and not-so-attentive publics? Whereas Morgenthau (1948) and his "realist" brethren buy into the rather unrealistic premise that the dominant drive in *Homo sapiens* is not so much knowing as it is power, control, and dominance, a little introspection as well as a lot of research should tell us that we are far less single-minded than that. Those of us who are normal are capable of subordination as well as dominance, cooperation as well as conflict, altruism as well as selfishness, and of course ludic as well as purposive behavior. Or, to put it in the language of motivational psychology (McClelland and Winter 1981), we respond to the need for achievement and for affiliation as well as the need for power.

In addition to this diversity of drives, my psychological assumptions embrace lability and plasticity; we find not only different drives in differing circumstances and moods but also a marked—but not unlimited—malleability. We differ in this respect from culture to culture and epoch to epoch and in the same vein are vulnerable to indoctrinability in the sense that propaganda, education, and acculturation are all at work. On the other hand, this is not to embrace too eagerly the "nurture over nature" perspective. For example, Somit and Peterson (1997) make a persuasive case for the biological and genetically induced preference for hierarchical as distinct from egalitarian social arrangements, and the same may probably be said for pugnacity vis-à-vis pacifism.

To put it simply, any alleged theory of social behavior, especially concerning matters of war and peace, that rests on some simple, constant, and universal human drive or propensity needs to be looked at askance. Whether the presumed single drive is for wealth, food, land, sex, progeny, or power, it neglects a vast body of evidence and is thus likely to eventuate in foolish—and in our case, dangerous—explanations. Having said this, however, one can always retreat into the aforementioned teleonomic position leading to "as if" predictions; these can be treated as *null* models, and the discrepancy between empirically observed regularities and those predicted by the null model can turn out to be heuristically useful.

Let us move now from some of the simpler empirical assumptions to the more complex questions of which types of metamodel might best guide us in pursuit of those specific queries that might lead to a compelling and powerful explanation of interstate war.

SOME METATHEORETICAL CONSIDERATIONS

While the line between empirical assumptions and those of a metatheoretical sort is far from clear and precise, the distinction is probably worth preserving. Mostly it is the difference between one well-defined cluster of phenomena such as decision making, public opinion, or personality, as opposed to a more complex interplay of several sets of phenomena and how they might be assumed to interact with one another. Where one comes out on some of these metatheoretical questions will rarely *determine* the sorts of models that we put forward for empirical investigation, but it will certainly bias our tendencies.

Deterministic or Stochastic

At this level of abstraction, considering the range of metamodels, we encounter some critical issues that have drawn insufficient attention from the scientific peace research community. Unless we are quite clear and specific on these issues, we are likely to flounder as we examine and evaluate the more persuasive alternative explanations of interstate war. Perhaps the most pertinent is the eternal issue in all of the sciences: what is the mix of the stochastic and the deterministic in the stories that we invoke to account for the patterns and regularities that we turn up—or *believe* that we turn up?

Let me begin with the assertion that war is hardly ever inevitable, no matter how far down the road the protagonists have come. Whereas some of the more popular models come close to the monocausal end of the spectrum (Blainey 1973) and some look like a laundry list (Snyder, Bruck, and Sapin 1962), almost all of them seem to assume that war is overdetermined; my inclination is to see it as underdetermined. The metaphor that comes to mind is that of the log floating down the river and getting caught against a boulder, thus deflecting the current against the shore and gradually producing a small channel that eventually joins another river and so forth. While each of these events and processes can be explained in terms of a fairly deterministic principle, the likelihood of the ultimate outcome was far from inevitable. It required an intricate co-incidence of fairly improbable events. The research implication is nicely captured by Bremer's (1995b) metaphor that the lock that conceals the explanation for war is not the kind that opens with a single key; rather, it is a complex combination lock that requires us to know which of several sets of numbers must be entered in which sequence and following which movements.

Poisson or Periodic

A second metatheoretical question is whether it pays to assume—or to look for—periodicity or cycles or waves in the onset of interstate wars. Given the lively debates and the moderate successes in economics and demographics, political scientists have from time to time gone off in pursuit of one or another of these possible regularities. Semantically, it might be useful to differentiate between them such that we define waves or cycles as the repeated unfolding of certain conditions and events that typically culminate in some recurrent outcome such as war; were these culminations to occur at constant (or nearly so) real-time intervals, we would speak of periodicity and begin to apply such techniques as spectral or Fourier analysis to ascertain the length of the intervals.

At the other end of this spectrum we find the premise that while certain classes of events appear and reappear from time to time, the intervals are rarely the same; their magnitudes are best generalized by the Poisson distribution (Singer and Cusack 1981). In the cited study, we looked for the possibility that the intervals between major power wars, measured in several ways, might turn out to be fairly consistent; they are not, as demonstrated by their goodness of fit to the Poisson distribution. These and other findings lead to the conclusion that the interesting regularities in interstate conflict are best understood in the more varied recurrent sequence mode. For example, while the evidence is not yet in, we hypothesize a systematically repetitive sequence that might be called the "from war to war" cycle. That model postulates the termination of each major war as marking a new and well-defined hierarchy among the major powers. Usually, this settlement is unsatisfactory to one or another of the powers—not necessarily on the defeated side—and to redress the arrangement, the dissatisfied state begins to increase its military capabilities. This, in turn, induces a gradual shift in domestic influence toward the beneficiaries of the military buildup who, in conformity with the well-established cognitive dissonance model, press regularly for heavier reliance on the military as a foreign policy instrument. As a result, they get into militarized disputes (Jones, Bremer, and Singer 1996) more frequently, and, given their increased clout at home plus their touching faith in the threat and use of force, find these disputes escalating to war more often than might be expected.

Similarities or Compatibilities

Yet a third and rather vexatious metatheoretical issue is that of the connection between intergroup similarities and their friendliness, as well as intergroup differences and hostility. This presumed correlation seems to arise from time to time and place to place as a sort of folklore, with the current decade providing an especially pernicious example. Following the demise of the Soviet empire and the passing of the Cold War, we have witnessed a remarkable upsurge in violent conflict between large groups marked by differences in nationality, religion, language, and, especially, ethnic identity. Journalists, politicians, and even academics seem to be accepting the proposition that these bloody conflicts not only can be explained by such cultural dissimilarities but also are a part of their inexorable histories.

It used to be Russian and Turk, German and French, Chinese and Malay, but today it is Bosnian and Serb, Hutu and Tutsi, and Armenian and Azeri. The mere mention of some of these legendary hostilities is enough to remind us that they are far from permanent and require a lot more than cultural dissimilarity to bring them to war or genocide. As a matter of fact, some preliminary studies in the Correlates of War project suggest that most such dissimilarities rarely go to bloodshed and typically require conditions of a serious scarcity and the agitations of ruthless politicians. More than a century ago, we were treated to the racial simplicities of Gobineau (1874), and today we have the dire but dubious speculations of Huntington (1996), and while the former tended to magnify and make more permanent these intergroup differences, the latter sees them as the root of some approaching clash of civilization—yet another crusade of Christians against Moslems?

Another side of this question is illuminated by some emerging empirical generalizations. First, we typically find that formal alliances are more likely to be consummated between societies that are fairly dissimilar in terms of regime type, religion, language, and ethnicity; to some extent this tendency is driven by the fact that disputes are ordinarily between contiguous neighbors amplified by the dictum that the enemy of my enemy should be my friend—even though he is several boundaries and cultures away. Second, as already implied, is that geographic proximity tends to correlate with political, cultural, and economic similarity, while at the same time that very proximity is a frequent source of conflict. Out of this conflict arises the proposition that whereas immediate neighbors are likely to be similar in political, cultural, and perhaps even economic terms, neighbors of an indirect and interrupted sort are likely to be relatively dissimilar. As Richardson (1960a, 296) observed in regard to cultural factors, "no general pacifying effect was found for either common language or common religion," but he did conclude that Chinese-speaking groups experienced less war than expected, while Spanish-speaking groups experienced more war than expected.

Moving from the cultural to the political and economic, our field is now awash in generalizations to the effect that the democratic dyad tends to be quite—if not absolutely—combat-free, but an interesting and credible variation suggests that it is not as much that these regional neighbors both have democratic or market economy regimes as that—whether democratic or autocratic, market or planned economy—they merely enjoy highly similar systems.

Looking at similarities in industrial or military capabilities, however, the story seems to be quite different. In the long-running debate between "peace through parity" and "peace through preponderance," the latter seems to be coming out to be more historically accurate. Further reinforcing this generalization at the interstate level is the evidence for the capability transition hypothesis, suggesting that as two rivals or potential rivals move closer to that similarity known as "power parity," their likelihood of a militarized dispute or war itself appears to increase.

In sum, the evidence so far is that the myriad similarities and differences between states provide too simple and nondifferentiating a basis for helping to explain interstate war.

THE ROADS TO WAR

One way to illustrate this underdetermined and complex process is to note that there are quite a few roads to interstate war, and all of them have fairly frequent exit ramps. On the other hand, some of these exits are not clearly marked, and even when they are, the protagonists fail to see them because (1) they are not interested in looking for them, (2) they are moving too fast, (3) they are anxious as to what lies beyond them, or (4) they fear an ambush from their own country-men as soon as they slow down. As social scientists pursuing an improved under-standing of the etiology of war, you might say that our central mission is to dis-cover the location of these exits, improve their visibility, find out how to make them safer, and then go on to map the roads to which they lead.

It might not be so crucial that we concentrate on exit research were it not for the seldom-noticed reality that just about every state in the system is *always* on one or another of the roads to war. What justifies this rash assertion? It sounds rash because we are all so habituated to those war preparation activities that we no longer notice them. First, every country socializes its children to think in terms of "we" and "they"; the world is full of foreigners, and by and large we are better or stronger or richer or nobler or more virtuous than they, especially if they are adjacent neighbors. Second, almost every state has an army, if not a navy and air force, usually recruited through conscription. Third, to encourage us to salute the flag, sing the anthem, pay for the armed forces and their equipment, deliver our young people to the tender mercy of the military, tolerate a lot of secrecy, and accept lethal doses of toxicity in the air, water, and soil, we are often being reminded of the vices and threats of one or another foreign state and thus pushed along into a hostile frame of mind. Thus, all are moving, at different rates, down the road to war, and our self-appointed task is to find out how to get them off that road, if not demolish that road entirely.

A more modest and interim task emerges from a more general perspective on the etiology of war. This begins with the theoretical proposition that armed con-flict can be reduced or perhaps even eliminated through the existence and inter-play of three sets of conditions. One of the more obvious is the existence of *effec-tive institutions* for peaceful settlement and enforcement of agreed legal norms. Not only is the United Nations system a far cry from these desiderata, but most of the auguries seem to proceed at a snail's pace, with almost as many steps backward as forward, especially in regard to the major powers. A second peace-inducing element might be a widely shared global outlook embracing *agreed views* on justice, reason, and nonviolence. Despite some isolated oases in the in-ternational desert and some occasional intimations of emotional and cognitive growth (Inglehart 1997), trends in this direction are depressingly weak and er-ratic. The third ingredient—and the one that poses the more relevant short-run challenge—is that of *incentives and constraints* vis-à-vis the behavior of foreign policy and national security elites around the world. In the near-absence of the political institutions and ethical norms, can we come up with some pragmatic inducements for getting off the roads to interstate war—or at least paying more attention to the exit ramps?

Obviously, most of us would not be engaged in the sort of research that we do if we did not think so. Let me try to make the connection by adumbrating a few illustrative research (and even researchable) questions, only a few of which have received serious treatment.

1. In a dispute that has not yet become militarized, what sorts of moves are likely to convey a willingness to make concessions while at the same time reducing the likelihood that the adversary will exploit this putative sign of weakness and resisting the domestic hawks' (a breed whose life expectancy seems unlimited) efforts to erode the credibility of the regime?
2. When the regime of an adjacent state begins to respond positively to a domestic irredentist group and expresses "our responsibility to protect our brothers and sisters across the border," what sorts of moves might prevent this familiar process from escalating?
3. When two states are involved in a militarized dispute over a piece of territory, are there any compromises, such as redefining the boundaries or sharing the same piece of turf by using it at different times of the day, week, or month?
4. As interest in preventive diplomacy increases, what are the indicators of early warning and timely assurance (Singer and Wallace 1979; Singer and Stoll 1984) that might improve the ability of regional or global third parties to anticipate which types of conflict are most (and least) likely to escalate?

This list of research questions could be expanded, but it is worth noting that these brief examples suggest that domestic politics may be the frequent catalyst of dispute escalation, which raises the question of whether this conflict-inducing consideration existed in the predemocratic epoch when royalty of seventeenth- and eighteenth-century systems nevertheless found it difficult to extricate themselves from foreign conflicts even without the tormentors from within.

CONCLUSION

One of the assignments to participants in this enterprise was to spell out what we considered to be the correlates of war, and most of the chapters here do a fine job on that score. But I have decided to finesse that assignment, for two reasons. First, I am reluctant to privilege a small handful of our findings, while ignoring many others. Second, a reasonably solid and highly detailed answer will be found in our recently completed *Nations at War* (Geller and Singer 1998). I hope that I have thus paid my dues and will not be cast out as a free rider!

2

Who Fights Whom, When, Where, and Why?

Stuart A. Bremer

As I survey the history of the field of international relations (and its distant cousin, diplomatic history), it appears to me that its central concern has been to provide an answer to the question "Who fights whom, when, where, and why?" This is, of course, a paraphrase of Harold Lasswell's (1958) famous definition of politics as the study of "who gets what, when, how." International relations embraces the study of other questions as well, and in the last ten years or so the research agenda has broadened as the subfield of international political economy has matured. Still, I would maintain that, while not as dominant as it used to be, the question posed in the title of this chapter remains the single most important one in international politics. Clearly I do not share the optimism of those like Mueller (1989) who believe that war is like a bad habit that we're learning to break or Fukuyama (1992) who see the end of the Cold War as ushering in a "brave new world" in which wars will not occur. I would like to believe that either or both of these opinions are true, but my reading of history leads me to conclude that contemporary observers tend to overstate the import of changes they experience. We may have to wait several decades before we can judge the impact of the recent changes in the global political system.

Before attempting to answer this chapter's central question, I need to declare one important limitation to this enterprise: I will only be concerned with interstate fights. By this I mean the "who" and "whom" in the question refer to states as they are conventionally defined (Russett, Singer, and Small 1968). I recognize that interstate wars are not the only kind of war we need to worry about (the death toll from civil wars in the last two hundred years probably exceeds that of interstate wars in the same period, but these lie outside the scope of this chapter and my area of expertise). It may be possible that interstate wars are becoming a thing of the past and that future wars will be mostly internal, what Holsti (1996) calls "wars of the third kind." If so, then my focus on interstate wars may be misplaced. I do not share this judgment for several reasons. First, over the last two centuries interstate and intrastate wars have been about equally frequent but with notable fluctuation in their frequency from time period to time period and region to region (Small and Singer 1982). Hence, it is too early to determine whether a fundamental shift along the lines postulated by Holsti has taken place. Second, a discernible but ill-understood connection exists between interstate and intrastate wars. Intrastate wars can become internationalized, but they can also indirectly foster interstate wars by upsetting balances of power. And interstate wars in turn can promote intrastate wars directly by undermining existing governments or indirectly by resulting in the creation of new, weak states. While we are far from a good understanding of the connections between interstate and intrastate wars, I think the evidence will ultimately show that they are related to one another in important ways.[1]

With these preliminary matters dealt with, let me turn to the question at hand: "Who fights whom, when, where, and why?" To organize my remarks I will draw on an analogy. Suppose, for the sake of exposition, that the interstate system is like a small political community that lacks law enforcement—a town on the American western frontier in the previous century, perhaps. Fights break out between members (states) of the (interstate) community (named Interstate System) with some regularity but not all that frequently.[2] To understand the conditions that promote fighting in Interstate System, we need to answer the question "Who fights whom, when, where, and why?" Let us take the question apart and see the degree to which our empirical knowledge about militarized interstate conflict can shed light on fighting behavior in our lawless community.

WHO-WHOM?

The first thing we observe is that most members of the community very rarely, if ever, engage in fighting. In fact, most fights involve citizens drawn from the same 20 or so percent of the community. The second thing to be observed is that the pairing of opponents is decidedly nonrandom; that is, the "who" and the "whom" are not independent of one another. In other words, knowing the "who" tells one a lot about who the "whom" is likely to be. This characteristic argues that a dyadic focus is likely to be the most useful one to adopt.

After further observing Interstate System, we would come to the not surprising conclusion that most of those who fight are neighbors. Few would dispute that geographic proximity plays an important role in interstate fights, for the evidence is quite convincing (Bremer 1992; Vasquez 1993). It is not clear, however, whether this effect is due primarily to enhanced opportunities to fight (physical proximity of some sort being a requisite for fighting) or increased willingness to fight (proximity implies a degree of interdependence that almost inevitably leads to sharp conflicts of interest). More than likely some combination of the two effects operates, but untangling their individual contributions looks to be a very difficult task. Moreover, proximity appears to be neither a sufficient nor a necessary condition for fighting since most neighbors in Interstate System never fight and a few nonneighbors do fight.

A second not surprising characteristic of those who fight one another is that they tend to have a history of fighting one another (Small and Singer 1982). Hence, a fight breaking out between states A and B appears to significantly increase the likelihood that they will fight again in the future, leading to what some call "enduring rivalries" (Goertz and Diehl 1992a, 1993). There are two explanations for this phenomenon. One asserts that fights take place over issues, which are rarely settled by a single fight, and so as long as the issues remain unresolved, fighting continues to periodically occur. In addition, fighting itself can give rise to new issues and lay the basis for future fighting. A second perspective focuses less on tangible issues and more on intangible psychological processes. In this view, the mere act of fighting produces feelings of grievance and hostility, even hatred, for the opponent that lead in turn to cognitive distortions such as stereotyping and enemy imaging (Boulding 1956; Jervis 1976). The outcome of this is that small differences of opinion are easily transformed into major reasons to fight and conflicts take on the nature of irrational feuds. The two perspectives are not inconsistent with one another, for they both may be operating in the propensity of fighting to beget fighting. In these times when the assumption that all state behavior is rational seems to be in ascendance there is a danger that we will underestimate the importance of social-psychological factors.

A third characteristic of those who fight is that in Interstate System the strong tend to fight the strong and the weak tend to fight the weak (Garnham 1976b; Bremer 1992; Geller 1993). While exceptions occur, it is somewhat unusual for fighters to be mismatched in terms of strength. The commonly accepted explanation for this is that the strong can prevail over the weak without fighting through intimidation, while evenly matched opponents may each believe that they can best their opponent in a fight and conclude that fighting is a viable option. This does not mean that strong-strong and weak-weak confrontations are equally likely, for some evidence suggests that the stronger two states are, the greater the likelihood of a fight between them (Bremer 1995a).

Ideological differences are present in Interstate System, and these appear to influence patterns of fighting behavior. The ideological spectrum runs from very democratic to very authoritarian, and it appears to have two effects. The first is that town members that are ideologically similar tend not to fight one another, and the likelihood of fighting seems to be at least partly determined by the degree of ideological dissimilarity between two potential opponents (Bremer 1995a; Mousseau 1998). The second is that the inhibition about fighting ideologically similar town members appears to be stronger among the more democratic than among the more authoritarian ones (Bremer 1992; Russett 1993; Ray 1995; Mousseau 1998). The first effect may be due to a more general tendency for those with different value systems to have difficulty communicating and understanding one another and to look on each other with fear and suspicion. The second effect is commonly attributed to unique features of the democratic ideology that allow those that embrace it to resolve conflicts more readily without resorting to fighting.

The evidence in support of the previously discussed characteristics of fighters is reasonably strong, and I feel fairly confident about these generalizations. I suspect that some other factors are operative, but the evidence is weaker. Among those is the tendency for those who fight to be socially unconnected. This means that they tend to belong to different groups and to have few friends in common. Alliances or gangs tend to develop within Interstate System, and it appears that members of the same gang are less likely to fight one another than members of different gangs (Weede 1975; Bremer 1992). But the effect is not as strong as we would expect it to be, perhaps due to the fact that some gangs are a lot more cohesive than others. More research is clearly needed here before we have confidence in this generalization. In the meantime, it may be postulated that such an effect, if it is found to be operative, grows out of the tendency for gangs to form to promote common interests and group dynamics that inhibit intragroup conflict but promote intergroup conflict (Coser 1964).

Another characteristic of those who fight that I suspect is relevant is that at least one of the fighters is typically a community leader. These town members, who call themselves the "major powers" and have great influence over town matters, are involved in a disproportionate number of fights (Bremer 1980; Small and Singer 1982; Eberwein 1982). It is difficult to disentangle this effect from other confounding factors, however, because these community leaders tend to have other characteristics that place them in the fight-prone category (e.g., superior strength). If further research supports this generalization, this would not come as a surprise since in a lawless community, a leader achieves and maintains his or her position, in part, by fighting.

Virtually all members of Interstate System are armed to one degree or another. Some are very well armed, while most cannot or will not pay the price of being well armed. Controversy simmers in the community about whether armaments inhibit or promote fighting. Those who believe in deterrence feel strongly that weapons offer protection and reduce the likelihood of fighting,[3] while others believe that weapons in the community make fights more likely and certainly more deadly. I am uncertain about the overall impact of weapons on the community. I see a slight tendency for one or both fighters to be drawn from the ranks of the well armed rather than the poorly armed, but, again, because of confounding factors, it is difficult to see the independent effect of armaments. My personal opinion is that the maxim "If you seek peace, prepare for war" is off the mark. On the contrary, I believe that "If you prepare to war, chances are pretty good that you're going to get it."

I suspect that another set of citizens in Interstate System is disproportionately involved in fights, for there appears to be a tendency for at least one of the fighters to be a "young rebel" (Maoz 1996). These community members are immature and come from violent backgrounds, but it does not appear that their young age is the critical factor since young states that do not have violent backgrounds do not appear to be disproportionately involved in fights. Hence, early socialization and exposure to violence seem to play a critical role in accounting for this tendency.

Like any community, residents of Interstate System belong to different economic classes. Some states are highly skilled and well-off, what we might call "white collar," but the majority are "blue collar" or even "shirtless" by virtue of the fact that they are less educated and skilled. As a consequence, these latter states are relatively poor. It is unclear to me precisely what the impact of economic class is on fighting behavior, for the evidence on this factor is less than conclusive. I suspect that there is a disproportionate tendency for at least one of the fighters to be blue-collar or shirtless states, but white-collar states also engage in fights, so the pattern is not all that clear. It does appear that fights between white-collar states occur less often than one would expect by chance (Bremer 1992). Still, potentially confounding factors make it difficult to sort out the unique effect of economic class on fighting behavior, so I remain uncertain about the importance of this factor.

Another characteristic that seems to distinguish pairs of states that fight is that at least one of the states involved behaves like a "bully" (Leng 1993). With this style of interaction, resistance on the part of an opponent is met by escalation and increased intimidation to make the other side back down. This differs from what has been called the "tit-for-tat" style of interaction in which actions by an opponent prompt responses that are comparable (i.e., nonescalatory). Although the evidence is far from complete, I believe that fights between those who have a tit-for-tat style of interaction are relatively rare. It is not clear, however, to what degree the choice of interaction style is situationally determined or an inherent characteristic of the "personality" of the state. That is, it may be that some states habitually employ a bully strategy, regardless of the situation, or it may be that all states sometimes adopt such a strategy, depending on the situation. Further research is clearly needed in this area.

Interstate System is very heterogeneous, culturally speaking, for its citizens possess quite different ethnic, linguistic, and religious characteristics. Evidence from social psychology suggests strongly that cultural differences such as these should lead to misunderstandings, stereotyping, clashes of values, and so forth, which in turn promote intercultural fights (Rubin, Pruitt, and Kim 1994). I suspect that those who fight one another tend to come from different cultures, but I have little systemic evidence that bears directly on this question.[4] The measurement of cultural differences and similarities is far from easy, and perhaps for that reason the impact of cultural factors on fighting behavior has had a low priority on the conflict research agenda. I think the importance of the cultural dimension has been underestimated by conflict researchers, and more of our attention should be directed to cultural factors.

The economy of Interstate System is characterized by a division of labor, so its inhabitants are not economically self-sufficient (or, more accurately, they choose not be self-sufficient because of the economic gains they obtain from a division of labor). This means that they must engage in exchange to obtain the things they need or want. These exchanges create economic interdependencies that many believe inhibit fighting behavior between those involved. That is, states that trade a lot with one another should refrain from fighting one another because, to the degree that fighting interferes with exchange (Barbieri and Levy 1998), it will adversely affect their economic well-being. Recent evidence on this subject offers us a confusing picture. Some studies suggest that states that trade a lot with one another fight each other less frequently than one would expect (e.g., Oneal and Russett 1997b), while other studies present evidence that this is not so (e.g., Barbieri 1996a). Measurement problems abound in this area, particularly with respect to assessing trade in the more distant past. As with the cultural area, comparatively little research has been done on the effects of exchange on fighting behavior, and we may not have a clearer understanding of the effect of trade on conflict for some time. At a more general level, social psychologists tell us that "close" or "intimate" relationships have a dual nature; they can produce the strongest bonds of amity but can also lead to high degrees of enmity (Rubin et al. 1994). My own suspicion is that we will not understand which of these will prevail in a relationship until we discover those critical factors that play an intervening role.

Most fights in Interstate System are small affairs involving only two states. Occasionally, however, other states do join one or both sides of the fight, and a few of these grow into large brawls involving a large number of the town's residents. These brawls, although rare, are very dangerous situations, but the conditions that trigger them are not well understood. We do know a few things about who is likely to join an ongoing fight, however. Neighbors of fighting states have a significantly higher probability of joining the fight, as do states that are allied with fighters (Siverson and Starr 1991). Beyond these basic facts, very little is known about fight joining, and it remains an area where much work needs to be done if we want to prevent devastating brawls. Evidence suggests that the larger a fight becomes, the greater the likelihood that still more states will join (Yamamoto and Bremer 1980). This self-aggravating process may be similar to what is observed in hockey, a sport in which fighting is not uncommon. Officials observed that if fights between players remain one-on-one conflicts, they were generally brief distractions. But if a third player enters the fight, the odds that other players will join in go up significantly, and a brawl involving all the players becomes much more likely. For this reason, officials impose a heavy penalty on the "third person in." Perhaps the town of Interstate System would benefit from such a rule.

There is obviously a lot we don't know about the "who-whom" part of our central question, but we know even less about the next part of the question, "When?"

WHEN?

The frequency and intensity of fighting in Interstate System has varied significantly over time, but it is not clear why this so. Some wonder why the "big fight of 1914" didn't start in 1913 or 1915 or some other year, for example, but little research has been explicitly focused on this kind of question. Many studies have examined the question of whether fighting exhibits some kind of cyclical pattern (Singer and Cusack 1981; Bremer 1982; Levy and Morgan 1986), but these have not revealed strong or consistent temporal regularities. Still, a few things can be surmised to make those with a predisposition to fight more likely to fight at one time rather than another.

One factor that has received a lot of attention and that may provide us with a partial answer to "When?" is the distribution of power across the community as a whole. This has varied over time in Interstate System, and some find it useful to distinguish among unipolar periods, when one state is considerably more powerful than all the rest; bipolar periods, when two states are significantly more powerful than the rest; and multipolar periods, when a half a dozen or so states are roughly equal in power but noticeably more powerful than the rest. Great debates have raged over which of these periods should be the most peaceful—hegemonic stability theorists argue that unipolar periods should have that distinction (Gilpin 1981; Thompson 1988), structural realists tend to award that honor to bipolarity (Waltz 1979), and old-fashioned balance-of-power theorists credit multipolarity with being the most peaceful (Morganthau 1966; Gulick 1955). Empirical efforts to test these contentions have not been notably successful because of the difficulties of measuring polarity.

Studies that focus on the concentration of power among the major powers rather than polarity have revealed an interesting pattern.[5] Fighting occurs less often when power is highly concentrated in the hands of one major power or when power is more evenly distributed across all the major powers (Mansfield 1994; Bremer 1995a). Fighting tends to be more frequent, then, when the distribution of power is somewhere in between these high and low values of concentration. It may be that there are two ways by which some degree of order is brought to Interstate System. When power is highly concentrated, then the dominant state acts as a kind of police officer who prevents some (but not all) fights from taking place. But fighting appears also to be inhibited by checks and balances that are alleged to be operative when power is distributed more evenly across the powers. Under this interpretation, then, fights will be more frequent when both of these ordering principles are weak; that is, when power concentration is in the medium range.

Although essentially lawless, Interstate System is not without a normative order, and the normative order has been observed to vary over time. Sometimes this order is permissive, allowing states to behave pretty much as they like, while at other times it is more restrictive. During the restrictive periods states are expected to behave in a more honest and honorable fashion, and it comes as no surprise that fights are more frequent when the normative order is permissive (Kegley and Raymond 1990). How strong these normative constraints are remains an open question.

One final item that may be relevant to the "when" part of our question is the general state of Interstate System's economy. We don't know too much about the effect of this factor, but some evidence suggests that fighting is more prevalent during periods of prosperity rather than periods of stagnation or depression (Goldstein 1988). The explanation for this is that during prosperous periods states are more optimistic and expansionistic, leading them, perhaps, to adopt more aggressive foreign policies that in turn lead to more fighting (Blainey 1988). But the overall effect of this factor does not appear to be all that strong with respect to individual states (Boehmer 1998).

Answering the "When?" question with some degree of precision may ultimately prove to be the second most difficult of those examined here—"Why?" being the most difficult to answer scientifically. My own hunch is that predicting the precise day when fighting is likely to begin is forever beyond our powers of prognostication because of the influence of chance factors that I discuss later. For the same reason, I am dubious about our ability to predict the month or quarter-year in which fighting will begin, which leaves us with the year of onset as perhaps the most precise answer we can expect to achieve to the "When?" question. Even this level of precision will be difficult to achieve, I think, owing to the causal complexity of the genesis of fighting behavior. Before addressing this latter issue directly, let me briefly consider the "Where?" question.

WHERE?

With few exceptions (Houweling and Siccama 1988b), the spatial distribution of interstate fighting has not been a major focus of research. Indeed, until quite recently geographic factors played little direct role in analyses of fighting behavior.[6] This is unfortunate, I think, because geography certainly facilitates and constrains fighting behavior and probably does so in interaction with other factors like those discussed earlier. Hence, geography per se may not have a direct, independent effect on fighting, and its impact may be mostly reflected in its role in answering the "who-whom" question.

Nevertheless, the evidence for spatial contagion in fighting behavior is reasonably strong, and it appears that a fight in a particular region increases the likelihood that another fight will occur in that region (Bremer 1982; Faber, Houweling, and Siccama 1984). We do not know whether this is due to some direct spillover effect from one fight to the next or whether states in a region share a common political climate that encourages or discourages fighting behavior. One hypothesis that I have played with is that fights are like earthquakes that may or may not lead to a more stable configuration of potentially destructive forces. If the quake (fight) relieves pressure and does not destabilize other delicate balances in the region, then future quakes (fights) are less likely in the region. If, on the other hand, a quake (fight) does not relieve the underlying pressure that caused it and/or upsets other balances of force in the region, then quakes (fights) in that region will be more likely in the future. In the latter situation, we would expect to see regional epidemics of interstate violence not unlike those we have observed in the past (Hensel and Diehl 1994b).

WHY?

We come now to the big question: Why do states fight one another? This is by far the toughest and most important part of the central question being addressed. It very well may be that it is not possible to give a scientific answer to this question because of the impossibility of proving causality. Current philosophers of science are nearly unanimous in their view that causality is inherently a subjective framework that we impose on observations rather than an objective phenomenon that we can observe. From this, I conclude that the best we can hope for are plausible rather than "true" answers to the "why" question. I don't think we have any such answers yet that are fully satisfactory, but it may be useful to consider three types of answers—choice, destiny, and chance—that have been put forth.

Choice

The answer given to the "why" question in almost all journalistic (and many historical) accounts of interstate fighting is that two leaders (or groups of leaders) within two states decided that they would be better off fighting than not fighting. That is, through a process of "reasoned choice," decision makers concluded that it is in their best interests to fight. Often this type of answer looks a lot like armed robbery: state B has something that state A wants, state A demands that state B turn over the desired objects or else, state B refuses to do so, and a fight begins. There is something seductively simple about this type of answer to the "why" question. In a perverse way, it "humanizes" fighting since it makes decision makers the core of the answer and leads us to believe that, for good or evil, we are masters of our fate. It also facilitates dividing the world into good guys and bad guys, smart and stupid decision makers, risk-acceptant and risk-adverse actors, and so forth, and using such divisions to generate simple answers to complex questions. And, of course, rationality may be nothing more than a tautology; that is, by assuming that decision makers are rational, we inevitably are led to the conclusion that a fight occurs because decision makers believed that fighting was the best alternative available to them.

I think we need to resist the siren song of "choice" and be careful not to assign too much importance to it with reference to interstate fighting for several reasons. First, if such an answer rests on the accounts of the participants in a fight, then it is very likely that the answer will be biased by "reconstructed rationality." The need to justify actions ex post facto leads decision makers to rationalize their actions in terms of a clear cost/benefit calculation that may have been at the time, in fact, quite unclear and even (if we are to believe the views of psychologists who study how humans actually make decisions) secondary (White 1970). It may even be true that the least reliable source of an answer to the "why" question may be the decision makers involved because of the inherently biased nature of their recollections.

Second, if such an answer rests on the accounts of observers to a fight—be they journalists or historians—the same kind of bias is often present. The news media in particular seem to need to personify war, as is evidenced by their general treatment of the Gulf War. In that case, the Western media by and large followed the line that the war was due to the reckless/aggressive decisions of Saddam Hussein, and little attention was given to larger forces operating in the region.[7] The blame for this bias does not lie with the news media alone but rather with the public as well. They (or should I say "we"?) respond to the drama of "mano a mano" far more than they ("we"?) respond to the dry discussion of political and economic forces.

My third reason to doubt that choice can be the sole basis for a plausible answer to the "why" question is that while participants and observers may be aware of the immediate cause—what Aristotle called the "efficient" cause—of fighting, they may know little or nothing of the fundamental or "final" cause. I have long felt that one of the most interesting findings that emerged from the Stanford studies of World War I was that the decision makers involved saw themselves as being pushed by historical forces that left them no alternatives to war.[8] This leads directly to the second kind of answer to the "why" question: destiny.

Destiny

In contrast to the free will coloration of choice-based answers, answers that invoke destiny as a causal agent see deterministic forces at work, and these forces are large scale and slow moving rather than small scale and rapidly changing. Tolstoy invoked this kind of answer when he portrayed Napoleon as a small boy riding in a carriage with strings in his hands, believing that he thereby controlled the fate of Europe when, if fact, the reins of the horses pulling the carriage were in the hands of the unseen driver on top of the coach. Many of the explanations for fighting are of this type—power transition, imbalance of power, lateral pressure, hegemonic stability, polarity, imperialism, and so forth—in which pressures beyond the control of any decision maker impel them toward fighting.

Returning to my analogy that the interstate system is like a small, lawless town, I would point out that we know that poverty breeds crime. Not all poor people are criminals, of course, but economic conditions do have an observable effect on crime rates. A choice-based explanation for crime would maintain that criminals conduct a cost/benefit analysis and conclude that their expected gain from robbing the corner store is higher than the alternatives. Consequently, they undertake the robbery. But it is clear that the poor do not have the same options as the more wealthy, and therefore their range of choice is severely restricted by conditions over which they have little control. Their choices are much more limited and heavily conditioned by big forces that sweep through the community that render them expendable, unusable, and unnecessary to the functioning of the community. The result is that crime becomes a more attractive option because other options have been removed from the table by outside forces. I think we can see something like this also operating in the interstate system. For example, it has been argued that Japan was essentially "boxed in" by the United States prior to World War II, and, as a result, Japan had little choice but to attack the United States to escape its confinement. And there is evidence that the Kaiser held a similar view toward England prior to World War I. In short, I think before we enthusiastically embrace choice-based explanations for fighting, we should take into consideration how bigger forces impel and constrain decision makers and define their menu of choices.

Chance

Chance has two meanings. One refers to what might be called "pure randomness"—that is, events without causes. Most international relations scholars find it difficult to accept the notion that events can happen without causation because causal reasoning is the bedrock of explanation for them. But chaos theory suggests that randomness plays a role even in apparently very deterministic systems like sets of differential equations. It is not clear in my mind whether chaos theory directly challenges the notion of causation or whether it only sets limits on our ability to predict events due to the large impact that small disturbances can have. My sense is that the philosophical implications of chaos theory are still being sorted out. It may be that the interstate system is very chaotic, which would mean that our ability to predict behavior accurately is highly and inherently constrained.

The second meaning of *chance* is one with which I think most international relations scholars would be more comfortable—that is, "happenstance" or "coincidence." This occurs when two or more events or forces that are not causally related to one another accidentally align to produce an effect much larger than either could produce separately. My own theory of fighting is based on what I have called elsewhere the "concatenation of weak forces" (Bremer 1995b). By this I mean that fighting does not stem from any single, strong cause but rather from a combination of factors that by themselves are fairly harmless. But when mixed together in accordance with a specific recipe, they lead to interstate violence. The situation is actually more complicated than this because I think we need to recognize that several different recipes for fighting may be possible, involving different combinations of factors. As a consequence, I think it is vitally important that we conceive of fighting not as an event but rather a process, a process in which happenstance and coincidence may play a significant role.

To see how the latter may affect events, consider the outbreak of World War I. Most analysts would agree that the immediate cause of that war was the assassination of Archduke Ferdinand on 28 June 1914 in Sarajevo, and an examination of the events of that fateful day reveals many coincidences. On that day, several assassins sought opportunities to kill the archduke without success. The archduke, who had been greeted at the town hall, decided at the last minute to visit a military hospital on his way to a museum, which in turn required a change in the planned route of his motorcade. What happened next demonstrates how chance can affect events.

> The column of cars started to drive back along the Appel Quay, Grabež by the Kaiser bridge saw it coming but did nothing. For the seventh time within an hour the Archduke drove safely past a would-be assassin, and there were none left on the quay ahead. But fate then again took a hand and dealt Princip the ace of trumps. A hundred yards beyond the Kaiser bridge, for some reason which has never been explained, Gerde's car, instead of proceeding straight on, turned right into the Franz Joseph Strasse, and Loyka, Harrach's chauffeur, having been given no instructions to the contrary, followed it.
>
> Potioreck [who was riding with the Archduke] realised what had happened, turned round and told the chauffeur to get back on the Appel Quay. To do this Loyka had to pull up and change gear into reverse. He braked, and for a few seconds the car came to halt by the curb of the right-hand pavement in front of Schiller's delicatessen shop outside which Princip, unable to think of anything else to do, was still waiting in the hope of getting another chance of assassinating the Archduke. The car stopped within five feet of him. He raised his revolver, saw that Sophie was seated on the near side of it, and for a split second hesitated. But "a strange feeling" came over him and "greatly agitated," he fired two shots in quick succession. Since he fired without taking aim, "I had turned my head away," the odds against either of them doing any serious damage were long, but the first went through the right-hand door of the car and hit Sophie, and the second hit Franz Ferdinand in the neck. (Cassels 1984)

Reading this account certainly leaves one with the impression that coincidence—or, in this case, a simple mistake—gave Princip the opportunity to assassinate the archduke that he had been seeking all day without success. It has been argued that the assassination was only a trigger for the events that followed and that war was inevitable between Austria-Hungary and Serbia due to their sharply conflicting interests. If the assassination had not occurred, it is asserted that some other event would have precipitated the war, perhaps later but inevitably. But who can say whether a different triggering event, a day, a month, or a year later, would have led to the same chain of events that produced World War I?

Indeed, World War I is a wonderful example of how destiny, choice, and chance combine to produce war. The winds of nationalism were blowing through Europe, and they were shaking the foundations of the tottering house of Hapsburg. In retrospect it seems unlikely that the multinational empire that was Austria-Hungary could have survived under any circumstances, and it also seems improbable that the Austro-Hungarian leaders would have allowed their empire to disintegrate without a fight. This is an example of the big forces that destiny-based explanations for war invoke. But the element of choice was also present because the leaders of Austria-Hungary decided to resist those forces by sending the heir to their throne into a dangerous situation. Perhaps an equivalent action would be Britain sending Prince Charles to Belfast during the height of the violence in Northern Ireland to make a political statement. This would not be a prudent thing to do, but the Austrians chose this risky option nevertheless. And, as the quotation given earlier demonstrates, the immediate cause of the war was certainly influenced by chance. Our greatest challenge in answering the "why" question may be sorting out how choice, destiny, and chance interact to produce fights.

CONCLUSION

Having come to the end of my attempt to answer the question "Who fights whom, when, where, and why?" I must admit that this has not been a very successful endeavor. There is too much that we don't know yet, and some aspects of the recipe(s) for fighting may defy understanding and rigorous analysis. But the goal of our enterprise should not be "truth," for I believe that is unobtainable. Rather, we should seek the more modest objective of "uncertainty reduction," for if we can achieve that, we may find the recipe for "probable peace" in our little, lawless town of Interstate System.

NOTES

1. Enterline (1998) examined the relationship between domestic political instability and militarized conflict and found some evidence to indicate that the two are positively connected.

2. Throughout this chapter, I use *fighting* rather than *making war* to describe the behavior I seek to explain because this term embraces a wider range of uses of force that do not meet the Correlates of War definition of war.

3. This is the position taken by the local chapter of the National Rifle Association in Interstate System.

4. A cursory examination of wars between and among Huntington's (1996) civilizations conducted as a classroom exercise revealed that wars were not more frequent than expected between different civilizations once the effects of contiguity were removed.

5. The difference between polarity and power concentration is not always clear. To me, measuring polarity inevitably requires taking alliance structures into account, while measuring power concentration does not.

6. This neglect of geography is probably due to the frequent use of the systemic level of analysis where spatial factors play no role. These factors became truly relevant only after there was a shift from the systemic to dyadic level of analysis. On the importance of geography, see Starr (1991).

7. The same would appear to be true for the more recent fighting in Kosovo. In that situation Milosević is given full credit for the fighting, and other factors have been largely ignored.

8. It is interesting to note how the focus of the Stanford project shifted from the perceptions and choices of decision makers (e.g., Holsti, North, and Brody 1968) to the operation of large forces, or what I am calling "destiny" (e.g., Choucri and North 1975).

3

Escalation and War in the Twentieth Century
Findings from the International Crisis Behavior Project

Michael Brecher, Patrick James, and Jonathan Wilkenfeld

> I think it's kind of intriguing that everybody who was asked to con-
> tribute to [this volume] loves their variable; nobody was willing to
> stand up and say, "I give up my variable."
>
> —Dina A. Zinnes, Norman Thomas Lecture Series,
> Vanderbilt University, 16 March 1997

One of the great challenges for the scientific study of international conflict, crisis, and war is to decide among the many options for further testing. In particular,
what variables deserve pride of place in the increasingly sophisticated, multivariate research designs that are becoming standard in the field? Nowhere is the
choice more difficult than with respect to the escalation of crisis to war. The problem really is one of knowing too much and, therefore, too little. Many years of
data analysis on the correlates and potential causes of war have produced a wealth
of variables that, under the right circumstances, seem to play a role. Thus, the
amusing commentary from Zinnes highlights a fundamental question: What are
the areas of consensus and disagreement about the variables associated with crisis
escalation to war?

This chapter reviews and assesses research on the escalation of international
crisis in an attempt to answer the preceding question. The effort unfolds in four
stages. The first is an overview of the International Crisis Behavior (ICB) Project,
which is the only sustained enterprise on the subject of crisis escalation to war.
Second, the ICB Project's findings on crisis escalation to war are reviewed and
synthesized at four levels: (1) global or regional, (2) dyadic (i.e., pairs of crisis
actors), (3) monadic (i.e., individual crisis actors), and (4) interactive. The third
stage compares results from ICB research with those obtained by scholars using

37

the Correlates of War (COW) and Militarized Interstate Disputes (MID) data sets. Fourth, and finally, the state of common knowledge about crisis escalation is assessed and directions for future research are identified.

THE ICB PROJECT: PURPOSES AND EVOLUTION

Most frequent among hostile interactions in global politics during the twentieth century are those identified as *interstate military–security crises.* As late as the mid-1970s, however, little systematic knowledge could be identified about a range of important subjects: the myriad of crises in regions other than Europe; crises experienced by weak states; the precipitating causes of crises; crisis outcomes; and the consequences of crises for the power, status, behavior, and subsequent perceptions of participant states. Neither systematic work on protracted conflicts (i.e., enduring rivalries) nor a widely shared theory of crisis as yet existed.

Awareness of these limitations in our knowledge led to initiation of the ICB Project in 1975. Underlying the project are three assumptions: first, that the destabilizing effects of crises, as of conflicts and wars, are dangerous to global security; second, that understanding the causes, evolution, actor behavior, outcomes, and consequences of crises is possible by systematic investigation; and third, that knowledge can facilitate the effective management of crises so as to minimize their adverse effects on world order. While it would be impossible to cover all of ICB's activities over the past two decades, a few obvious priorities arise in setting the context for discussion of its contributions to the study of crisis escalation. Assumptions (already noted), objectives, definitions, methods, and the current state of the data set are introduced briefly in turn.

As a long-term, multinational effort to learn more about a pervasive phenomenon of world politics, the ICB Project features four specific objectives:

1. accumulation and dissemination of knowledge about interstate crises and protracted conflicts;
2. generation and testing of hypotheses about the effects of crisis-induced stress on coping and choice by decision makers;
3. discovery of patterns in key crisis dimensions—onset, actor behavior and crisis management, superpower activity, involvement by international organizations, and outcome; and
4. application of the lessons of history to the advancement of international peace and world order.

The ICB Project is both theory directed and policy-oriented. In the realm of theory, the data on crises facilitate the testing of hypotheses and thereby contribute to the framing of generalizations about world politics. Policy benefits also accrue from such a large-scale study: potentially improved crisis management, control over escalation, and reliable crisis anticipation. If the data support propositions regarding crises and state behavior, ICB will have created a reliable basis for projecting the profile of future crises. Moreover, an understanding of behavior under crisis-induced stress can assist in reducing the likelihood of a resort to violence in crisis management resulting from misperceptions of intentions. Thus, the ICB Project is a major enterprise within the scientific study of international politics.

To attain its specific objectives and more general goals, ICB undertook an inquiry into the sources, processes, and outcomes of all military–security crises since the end of World War I. Data collection included cases within and outside protracted conflicts, and across all continents, cultures, and political and economic systems in the contemporary era. ICB's methods are both qualitative and quantitative: in-depth studies of perceptions and decisions by a single state; and studies in breadth of the 412 international crises and 895 foreign policy crises spanning the period from the end of 1918 to the end of 1994.[1] The appendix to this chapter lists the ICB crisis cases that resulted in escalation to either serious clashes or full-scale war (thirty-three and thirty, respectively), along with the triggering action and year of initiation in each instance. After more than two decades of intensive effort, the time for a comprehensive review and codification of findings or "meta-analysis" seems just right.

Two conceptual and operational definitions of military–security crises, relevant to respective levels of analysis, continue to guide the ICB Project. At the system interaction level, two conditions define an international crisis: (1) a change in type and/or an increase in intensity of *disruptive*—that is, hostile verbal or physical *interactions* between two or more states, with a heightened probability of *military hostilities,* which in turn (2) destabilizes their relationship and *challenges* the *structure* of an international system—global, dominant, or subsystem. In terms of formal logic, these are *individually necessary and collectively sufficient* conditions. The likelihood that they will exist is illuminated by system, interactor, actor, and situational attributes (e.g., structure and level, conflict setting and capability, regime type and territory, trigger and violence). As such, these are *enabling* variables, the *most likely* conditions in which an international crisis will erupt, escalate, deescalate, or affect the adversaries and/or the system(s) of which they are members (Brecher 1993: 29–42).

Each international crisis begins with a disruptive act or event, a *breakpoint*, that creates a foreign policy crisis for one or more states. An international crisis ends with an act or event, an *exitpoint,* that denotes a qualitative reduction in conflictual activity. The ending of an international crisis coincides with the termination of the last active foreign policy crisis within its domain; that is, none of the crisis actors perceives that a crisis exists any longer.

A foreign policy crisis—that is, a crisis for an individual state—is a situation with three necessary and sufficient conditions deriving from a change in the state's internal or external environment. All three are perceptions held by the highest-level decision makers of the state actor concerned: a *threat to one or more basic values*, along with an awareness of *finite time for response* to the value threat, and a *heightened probability of involvement in military hostilities*. Thus, within the boundaries of an international crisis, one or more foreign policy crises will take place.

Foreign policy crisis, as a concept, concentrates on the perceptions and behavior of a single state.[2] Interaction among states, of course, also is explored, for crisis decisions are usually made in response to threatening physical and/or verbal acts by another state. The catalyst to a foreign policy crisis may be a destabilizing event in the international system. Nevertheless, the state remains the central object of inquiry into foreign policy crises: how its decision makers perceive change; how they choose in conditions of complexity and uncertainty and in the context of perceived escalating or deescalating threat, time pressure, and probability of war.

Initial planning for large-scale data collection began in 1975. Assembly of the ICB data sets for international and foreign policy crises proceeded in four stages.

- Stage 1: 1978–85—data collected for the 1929–79 period, which served as the basis for Brecher and Wilkenfeld (1988) and Wilkenfeld and Brecher (1988)
- Stage 2: 1986–88—data collected for the 1980–85 period, which, together with that from the first stage, served as the basis for Brecher and Wilkenfeld (1989)
- Stage 3: 1989–92—data collected for the 1918–28 and 1986–88 periods, which, together with those from the first two stages, served as the basis for Brecher (1993)
- Stage 4: 1993–95—data collected for the 1989–94 period, which, together with the preceding stages' data, served as the basis for Brecher and Wilkenfeld (1997b)

As work progressed, the range of subjects covered in ICB analysis increased significantly. During stages 1 and 2, the data analysis consisted primarily of identifying the basic characteristics of crises across the dimensions of onset, escalation, deescalation, and legacy. By stage 4, the subject matter had expanded to include superpower deterrence, ethnic conflict, democracy and peace, and a wide range of other contemporary flashpoints of debate.[3]

During stage 4, the project reopened many previously coded cases and added to the coding on the basis of new information that had come to light since the original coding. In the course of that process, it became clear that some earlier cases would need to be dropped from the data set, while still others would be combined and otherwise modified. Furthermore, several key variables, including gravity of threat and form of outcome, have been recoded for the entire seventy-six-year period because of serious shortcomings identified in their earlier formulations.[4] Finally, several new variables have been added to the data set, most notably those (1) assessing the ethnic content (if any) of a crisis and (2) distinguishing major power crisis activity from their activities as third parties. These additions reflect the concerns of the scholarly community in terms of both direct suggestions for an expanded range of variables and the project's desire to adapt as theoretical interests within the field continue to develop. Therefore, the current ICB data sets supersede all earlier releases for researchers interested in aspects of crises in the twentieth century.[5]

During stage 5, now in progress, data will be collected on interstate military–security crises for the period from 1995 to 2000. Moreover, serious consideration is being given to broadening the scope of the ICB Project to encompass two increasingly significant strands of international conflict: civil wars since the end of World War I that were catalyzed by ethnic drives, both secessionism and irredentism, and by nonethnic motives; and international economic crises, such as external runs on foreign exchange reserves, hyperinflation, and currency devaluation.

CRISIS ESCALATION: PROPOSITIONS AND TESTING FROM THE ICB PROJECT

While any means of organizing a wide range of data analysis must be arbitrary at some level, what follows is consistent with priorities of the field in general. The data analysis from ICB is presented in Tables 3.1, 3.2, 3.3, and 3.4, each of which corresponds to a plausible and easily recognized level of aggregation: (1) global and regional, (2) dyadic, (3) monadic, and (4) interactive.[6]

All of the tables are structured in the following way in attempting to explain crisis escalation to war. For a given proposition, the source, the proposition itself, an abbreviated rationale, measurement of the independent variable, and results from testing are listed. The source refers to the ICB publication in which the data analysis took place. Each proposition is stated in terms of implications for the likelihood of war. For example, the first entry in Table 3.1 refers to the international system, with a transitional period being hypothesized as having a higher probability of crisis escalation than a stable period. Constraints on space prevent more than an abbreviated rationale, but each study cited in the table contains a detailed explanation for the proposition that appears with it.[7] Finally, results from testing are assessed as either supported or not supported.[8] Unless otherwise noted, propositions in each table appear in chronological order.[9]

With respect to Table 3.1, system-level propositions are relatively few in number and receive mixed support. Crises are more likely to escalate to war in subsystems rather than the dominant system (i.e., under conditions of geographic proximity and regular interactions among its members), when the international system is polycentric (i.e., when there are two centers of military power [similar

Table 3.1 Crisis Escalation: Propositions and Testing at the Global and Regional Levels

Source	Proposition (where ">" means more of a disposition toward crisis escalation)	Abbreviated Rationale	Measurement of the Independent Variable (either by categories or continuous measurement)	Results from Testing[a]
James (1988)	International system: transitional > stable	System transformation creates greater potential for escalation	Stable (tightly bipolarity, 1948–58) and polycentrism (1963–), and transitional (1958–62)	Not supported
Brecher (1993)[b]	System level: subsystems > dominant system	Awareness among major powers of more serious systemwide consequences from violence in the dominant system	Hegemonial (unipolar), polarized (bipolar, multipolar), diffuse (polycentric)	Supported
Brecher (1993); Brecher and Wilkenfeld (1997b)	System structure: polycentrism > multipolarity > bipolarity	Lack of restraint on nonaligned states makes polycentrism most unstable; bipolarity produces more system management and is preferred to multipolarity	Hegemonial (unipolar), polarized (bipolar, multipolar), diffuse (polycentric)	Supported
Carment (1993)	Region: economically weak and dependent regions > others	Lack of caution due to systemwide dislike for status quo	Africa and Middle East versus other regions	Supported

[a] For all but Brecher (1993), the categories "supported" and "not supported" are used to assess the results. For that study, more nuanced categories are used because Brecher (1993) includes specific criteria for classification of results.

[b] Brecher (1993, 164), Brecher and Wilkenfeld (1997a, 1997b), and Carment and James (1997) focus on crisis escalation to severe violence, which includes serious clashes and full-scale war.

Table 3.2 Crisis Escalation: Propositions and Testing at the Dyadic Level

Source	Proposition (where ">" means more of a disposition toward crisis escalation)	Abbreviated Rationale	Measurement of the Independent Variable (either by categories or continuous measurement)	Results from Testing
James (1988)	Expected utility for initiator and defender: positive expected utility for initiator > absolute value of negative expected utility for defender	Lack of room for bargaining to avoid war	Magnitude of difference represents margin by which war is preferred to alternative bargain	Not supported
James (1988)[a]	Expected utility for initiator: positive > zero or negative	Expectation of gain from escalated conflict	Expected utility calculus, with capabilities and utility playing standard roles	Supported
James (1988)	Relative capabilities in the absence of intermediaries: initiator > defender	Stronger initiator in a better position to use violent means toward ends	Capabilities measured on the basis of national income	Supported
Brecher (1993)	Capabilities: discrepancy > equality in capabilities	Stronger actor expects goal achievement from use of violence	Dimensions are diplomatic, economic, and military	Not supported
Brecher (1993)	Regime type: authoritarian > democratic regime	Violence is the familiar choice for the military in power	Authoritarian versus democratic regime	Supported
Brecher (1993); Brecher and Wilkenfeld (1997b)	Conflict settings: protracted conflict > nonprotracted conflict	Extreme lack of trust and anticipation of violence within protracted conflicts	Protracted conflict (crisis occurs within a long series), nonprotracted conflict (crisis is isolated or one among many very small number)	Supported
Rioux (1996)	Enduring rivalry: higher number of past crises > lower number of past crises	Standard argument concerning enduring rivalries	Count of previous crises	Supported
Rioux (1997)	Enduring rivalry: present > absent	Greater disposition to violence based on past experiences	Standard measurement	Supported
Brecher (1993)	Geographic distance: contiguity > separation	Easier access and fear of preemption	Within versus outside of home region	Strongly supported
Ben Yehuda (1997)	Proximity: contiguous versus noncontiguous states	Contact creates greater potential for escalation	Border states	Supported
Brecher and Wilkenfeld (1997b)	Proximity: home territory versus other	Proximity to home territory increases disposition to violent means	Home territory versus other locations	Supported

[a] James (1988) relies on the Correlates of War Project's definition for interstate war. The study is based on a shorter series of ICB data, from 1948–75, due to the availability of data at the time.

Table 3.3 Crisis Escalation: Propositions and Testing at the Monadic Level

Source	Proposition (where ">" means more of a disposition toward crisis escalation)	Abbreviated Rationale	Measurement of the Independent Variable (either by categories or continuous measurement)	Results from Testing
James (1988)	For initiator: increase in latent conflict, controlling for positive bilateral expected utility > one or both conditions absent	Externalization of domestic conflict toward an interstate adversary	Latent conflict combines cost of living, unemployment; represents conflict "left over" for projection after controlling for government sanctions	Supported
James (1988)	For initiator: increase in manifest conflict, controlling for positive bilateral expected utility > one or both conditions absent	Externalization of domestic conflict toward an interstate adversary	Manifest conflict combines protest demonstrations, political strikes, armed attacks, and deaths from domestic violence	Supported
Brecher (1993); Carment (1993)	Age of state: new > older	Experience of violent struggle in independence phase	Date of independence before or after 1945	Supported
Rioux (1998)	Regime type of initiator: democratic > nondemocratic	Propensity to extreme reaction of democratic society when fully mobilized	Standard sources	Supported
Carment and James (1997)	Type of state: ethnic dominance and low political constraint > others	Autonomy and incentive for elite to pursue violence for goal achievement	Polity II and expert-generated coding of ethnic composition	Supported

Table 3.4 Crisis Escalation: Propositions and Testing at the Interactive Level

Source	Proposition (where ">" means more of a disposition toward crisis escalation)	Abbreviated Rationale	Measurement of the Independent Variable (either by categories or continuous measurement)	Results from Testing
Brecher (1993)	Number of participants: more > less	Expanding range of issues and disruptions	Number of states perceiving a foreign policy crisis: one or two versus three or more	Supported
James (1988)	Number of actors: multilateral > bilateral	Analogue to system-level argument in favor of bipolarity	Number of crisis actors	Supported
James (1988)	Balance of capabilities: initiator coalition is stronger than defender coalition > opposite ordering	Traditional balance of power	Capabilities measured on the basis of national income	Supported
Brecher (1993)	Heterogeneity of participants: more > less		Dimensions include military capability, political regime, economic development, and culture; division is no difference or one difference versus two or more differences between adversaries	Supported
Brecher and Wilkenfeld (1997b)	Regime type: higher proportion of nondemocracies > lower proportion of nondemocracies	Normative and structural explanations from democratic peace literature	Standard sources	Supported
Hewitt and Wilkenfeld (1997)	Regime type: proportion of nondemocratic > democratic states in each coalition	Normative and structural arguments from democratic peace literature	ICB coding product of proportion of democracies in each coalition and overall population of democracies as participants	Supported[a]
Brecher (1993)	Issues: more > less		Military, political, economic, or cultural; division is one issue versus two or more issues including military security	Supported

Table 3.4 Continued

Source	Proposition (where ">" means more of a disposition toward crisis escalation)	Abbreviated Rationale	Measurement of the Independent Variable (either by categories or continuous measurement)	Results from Testing
Carment (1993)	Ethnic conflict: ethnic > nonethnic	Affective motivation makes it more difficult to avoid extreme violence	Expert-generated coding of presence or absence of ethnicity as an issue	Supported
Carment (1993)	Ethnic conflict: irredentist > secessionist > anti-colonial > nonethnic conflict	Degree of affective motivation varies	Expert-generated coding of type of conflict	Supported
Carment and James (1995)	Role of ethnic conflict: irredentism > other issues	Affective motivation makes it more difficult to avoid extreme violence	Expert-generated coding of presence or absence of irredentist motive	Supported
Ben Yehuda (1997)	Territorial issue: territorial rivalry > nonterritorial rivalry	Territory is fundamental to survival	Rivalry that focuses primarily on territory versus other issues	Supported
Brecher and Wilkenfeld (1997a,b)	Ethnic conflict: ethnic > nonethnic	Affective motivation makes it more difficult to avoid extreme violence	Expert-generated coding of presence or absence of ethnicity as an issue	Supported[b]
Brecher (1993)	Major power activity: presence > absence	More basic value threats will be perceived by participants	Political, economic, or military aid or direct military intervention versus inactivity[c]	Supported
Brecher (1993)	Breakpoint/trigger: violent > nonviolent	Reciprocity	Violent versus others	Supported
Brecher (1993)	Response to triggering act: violent > nonviolent	Reciprocity	Violent versus others	Supported
Harvey (1995)	Threat to superpower: lower > higher	Superpower restraint in use of violence is elicited by high threat	Severity of threat based on geostrategic salience, heterogeneity of actors, and issue area[d]	Supported

[a] An alternative version of the hypothesis, which uses the sum of these components rather the product, is not supported.
[b] Brecher and Wilkenfeld (1997a), using shorter series of data, judge the proposition to be supported.
[c] The focus is on great powers from 1918–39 and superpowers from 1945–94.
[d] Harvey (1995) includes cases in which the superpowers are involved from 1948 to 1988.

to bipolar] and many centers of political decision [similar to multipolar]), and in economically weak regions. By contrast, the relative stability of the international system as a whole does not affect the likelihood of crisis escalation. Taken together, these results undoubtedly reflect the general shift in interstate conflict as a whole to the weaker, developing regions.

Four subsets of dyadic propositions, which appear in approximately chronological order, can be identified in Table 3.2. The first subset focuses on capabilities, the long-standing and conventional interest of research on conflict as a result of adherence to the realist paradigm. The results are mixed. One basic proposition from expected utility theory is supported, but a more specialized one is not. Finally, it is interesting to note that, in the context of the ongoing debate over preponderance versus parity, mixed results appear. In one study, neither discrepancy nor equality in capabilities is associated with crisis escalation; in the other, an advantage for the initiator of a crisis translates into greater likelihood of war.

One proposition pertains to regime type. Authoritarian dyads are found to be much more likely than democratic dyads to experience escalation to war.

Three propositions focus on long-term experiences in conflict as a contributor to crisis escalation. The related phenomena of enduring rivalry and protracted conflict are found to increase the likelihood of war.

Finally, three propositions deal with proximity of states in one form or another. The results clearly are favorable to the idea that proximity makes escalation to war more likely.

Overall, nine of the eleven dyadic propositions are supported. The larger number of propositions tested is consistent with the direction of the field as a whole in recent decades.[10]

Table 3.3, which summarizes the monadic propositions (i.e., those about actor characteristics), is interesting because it contains only five items, and all are supported. The two propositions about increasing internal conflict coupled with positive bilateral expected utility are confirmed. With respect to the age of a crisis actor, new states are found to be more prone to escalation than more established ones. The proposition about democracies, though supported, offers an interesting twist on the earlier dyadic result: A democracy will be *more* inclined to experience crisis escalation to war. This result, in fact, is consistent with the literature in general; while well disposed toward each other, democracies are more inclined to go all-out once a conflict with a nondemocratic adversary escalates. Finally, states with low political constraints and an ethnically dominant group also are prone to escalation.

These results are easy to synthesize: what can be said with confidence is that the characteristics and prior experiences of individual states clearly are relevant to crisis escalation.

Table 3.4, which reports on propositions at the interactor level (i.e., groupings beyond pairs of states), accounts for the greatest number among those tested at any level of aggregation. Propositions in this category refer to the characteristics of crises once they are in progress. The characteristics of the actors or issues involved, along with the actions taken by participants, are included.

Characteristics of the actors include their number and the distribution of traits among them. With respect to the number of actors, both a breakpoint and continuous effects seem to exist. The shift from two to three or more actors, as well as an increasing overall number, heightens the risk of war. The distribution of power makes escalation more likely when it favors the initiator's coalition. The more heterogeneous the set of actors in terms of culture and other traits, the higher the likelihood of war. Finally, the greater the proportion of nondemocracies among crisis actors, the more likely it becomes that escalation will occur.

Three different issue-related effects are apparent. One study reveals that the sheer number of issues contributes to the likelihood of war. Based on somewhat different approaches toward measurement, three studies that collectively test four propositions concur that the issue of ethnicity is linked to escalation. Finally, one study reports that territorial issues are associated with a greater likelihood of war.

With respect to actions, two propositions related to major powers are confirmed. One focuses on major power involvement and the other on threat experienced by a superpower. In each instance a clear connection is demonstrated with the greater likelihood of war. Two other propositions refer specifically to violence. Both violence triggering acts and responses are associated with crisis escalation.

When taken together, one thing stands out concerning the interactor propositions: all are confirmed by the data, some very strongly. The uniformly positive results may be explained in either of two ways. One is that ICB's selection of variables for more intensive study is well informed by experiences from the field as a whole. The other is that interactor variables may simply be the most important, by and large. Whatever the truth may be, it is clear that whether a crisis will escalate to war depends heavily on aspects arising after the stage of onset.

Tables 3.1–3.4 provide a very succinct summary of the results obtained from a vast amount of data analysis. What, then, can be said in more general terms about the ICB Project's analysis of crisis escalation to war? First, it is clear that the dyadic and interactive levels have received the most attention. Second, propositions from these levels, along with those cast at the monadic level, have received widespread confirmation. Third, propositions at the global and regional levels are few in number. Finally, crisis escalation clearly is a product of factors operating at multiple levels.

PROJECT-BASED RESEARCH AND CRISIS ESCALATION: ICB IN COMPARISON TO COW AND MID

When viewed in absolute terms, the ICB Project has tested and discovered support, often strong, for a wide range of propositions about crisis escalation to war.

The question of cumulation then arises: How does this data analysis compare with results obtained by project-based research that focuses more exclusively on the correlates of war?

While it is beyond the scope of this chapter to produce a review of the COW and MID analyses analogous to the one just performed for ICB, such a discussion is not essential. Fortunately, Stuart A. Bremer (chap. 2 herein) recently provided a very effective summary of research by COW and MID on the correlates of war that is sufficient for the task at hand.

Bremer's list of the most important variables in accounting for war permits the construction of Table 3.5, which compares the ICB Project's results with the areas of consensus from COW and MID. The table is organized in the following way. Bremer's list of factors that enjoy either strong or moderate support from the findings of COW and MID researchers are listed by level of aggregation, from global and regional through interactor. Running parallel to that exposition is a summary of results from ICB, divided into two subcategories. Findings that are either independent from or consistent with those of COW and MID at a given level of aggregation appear first. The findings from ICB that seem inconsistent with those of the other projects are listed second.

From the standpoint of the scientific study of international politics, the table's most immediate and impressive characteristic is the paucity of inconsistent findings in both absolute and relative terms. On only one occasion do the projects produce results that appear to contradict each other. COW and MID find overwhelming support for parity as a key variable, while ICB produces two different findings: (1) greater capabilities for the initiator relative to the defender (in the absence of intermediaries) are connected to crisis escalation, and (2) discrepancies in capabilities between adversaries (without, in this instance, role designations) show no such linkage.[11]

By contrast, ideological differences, rivalry, new states, major power involvement, and a confrontational style of bargaining all receive mutual support from the projects. This balance of findings in favor of consistency becomes even more encouraging when it is observed that different scholars conducted the research for each project with respect to all of the variables concerned.

Several variables identified by Bremer as very important have not as yet received attention from ICB, at least in the context of crisis escalation to war. Alliances, militarization, and level of development become potential priorities for the ICB Project in the future, because each seems to have some connection to war. The list of items pursued by ICB but not by COW or MID is much longer and reflects the wider range of variables in the data set, most notably with regard to the interactive level.[12]

CONCLUSION

This chapter has, inter alia, identified points of convergence and controversy for project-based research on crisis escalation to war. The primary focus has been on

Table 3.5   Crisis Escalation and War: A Companion of Findings from ICB with COW/MID

Level of Aggregation	COW/MID[a] Consensus as Identified by Bremer	Results from ICB	
		Consistent or Independent	Inconsistent
Global and regional		Polycentric system; weak regions	
Dyadic		Positive expected utility for initiator; capabilities favor initiator over target	
	Parity[b]		No connection for one of two studies; the other links a discrepancy favoring the initiator to crisis escalation
	Ideological differencies[b]	Authoritarian dyads	
	Rivalry[b]	Enduring rivalry; protracted conflict	
	Neighbors[b]	Proximity; home territory	
Monadic	Socially unconnected (e.g., alliance portfolios)	Internal conflict	
	New state[c]	Age of state	
		Democratic state; low constraint and dominant ethnic group	
	Well-armed state; less-developed state[d]	Three or more actors; greater number of actors; heterogeneity among actors; greater proportion of nondemocracies; number of issues; ethnicity; territory	
Interactive	Major power involvement[c]	Major power involvement	
		Threat experienced by superpower	
	Confrontational style[c]	Violent trigger; violent response	

[a] The summary of findings from COW/MID is based on Stuart A. Bremer's presentation at the Norman Thomas Lecture Series, 13 March 1997.
[b] Bremer assigns a subjective level of confidence of at least 80 percent to each of these factors.
[c] Bremer assigns a subjective level of confidence that ranges from 40 to 60 percent to these factors.
[d] This factor is consistent with the ICB system-level finding about regions.

the ICB Project in both absolute terms and relative to other large-scale efforts at explaining war. The basic conclusion in each area is a positive one. Across the global and regional, dyadic, monadic, and interactive levels of aggregation, ICB research identifies a wide range of important variables. To use the term introduced by Midlarsky (this volume, chap. 16), ICB appears to be well on the way to developing a "mature" theory of crises in world politics. Furthermore, in relative terms, ICB's findings are very consistent with the results produced by the COW and MID Projects. Thus, both the ICB Project and other scientific research on conflict, crisis, and war reinforce each other's findings on this essential aspect of world politics. This is crucial, as Vasquez observes (introduction to this volume), to fulfill the promise of the systematic study of international conflict, crisis, and war.

Some qualifications and embellishments are in order. First, escalation is just one of the major concerns of the ICB Project. The Unified Model of Crisis (Brecher 1993), tested in great detail by Brecher and Wilkenfeld (1997b), also seeks to explain many other aspects of this phenomenon, ranging from onset to legacy. A complementary strand of ICB research, in the form of seventeen comparative case studies, also yields significant generalizations, notably on how decision makers of states cope with foreign policy crises, including the use of violence (Brecher 1993).

The results of this recent large-scale effort have been very positive in each of the main areas of interest. A second point, offered as a qualification, is that Tables 3.1–3.4 report the findings from bivariate analysis based on ICB data. The project is working in stage 5 on multivariate analysis of crisis escalation and a range of other new and long-standing interests, which should produce a higher level of understanding than available in the past.

NOTES

1. For the most comprehensive ICB analysis of twentieth-century crises, see Brecher and Wilkenfeld (1997b).

2. The ICB case studies published thus far are Brecher (1979), Brecher with Geist (1980), Dawisha (1980), Shlaim (1983), Dowty (1984), Dawisha (1984), Jukes (1985), Hoffman (1990), and Anglin (1994).

3. Brecher and Wilkenfeld (1997b) and Brecher (1999) contain authoritative bibliographies of research based on the ICB data.

4. For example, the categories for Form of Outcome at the system (macro) level (i.e., FOROUT, in the terminology of the ICB Project), in the first three stages of coding, are as follows: Agreement, Tacit, Unilateral Act, and No Agreement/Other. However, in many cases, agreement turned out to be imposed rather than voluntary, and some agreements were formal (treaties), others semiformal (an exchange of letters), a distinction already incorporated in the actor (micro) level coding. To capture these important distinctions, two changes have been introduced: Agreement was split into Formal Agreement and Semiformal Agreement, and Imposed Agreement has been added. These changes, in turn, required the recoding of all 412 international crises in the ICB data set for FOROUT.

More far-reaching changes have been made in this variable at the actor level. The original categories of Form of Outcome (OUTFOR, in ICB terminology) were Formal Agreement, Semiformal Agreement, Tacit Agreement, Unilateral Act, and No Agreement/Other. To capture the many nuances in this variable, the five categories have been expanded to fifteen, as follows: Formal Agreement—Voluntary, Semiformal Agreement—Voluntary, Tacit Understanding, Unilateral—Self, Unilateral—Ally, Unilateral—Adversary, Compliance, Imposed-Imposer, Imposed-Imposee, Spillover, Other-GO Intervention, Other-Ally, Other-Internal or Nonstate Actor, Other-Miscellaneous, and Faded. This expansion of categories required the recoding of 895 actor-level cases in the data set.

   5. See Brecher and Wilkenfeld (1997b). Michael Brecher, Jonathan Wilkenfeld, and J. Joseph Hewitt have now produced a combined paperback/CD-ROM version of Brecher and Wilkenfeld (1997b) in which the data set and summaries are available in machine-readable form for further analysis. See Brecher and Wilkenfeld (2000).

   6. The nuances among these categories are as follows: (1) the global and regional levels correspond to the system level as defined by ICB; and (2) the dyadic level has become central in the field of conflict studies and therefore is granted a central place, so groupings beyond pairs of states are included under the interactor category in Table 3.4.

   7. Brecher and Wilkenfeld (1997b) provide a full explanation for the coding of ICB variables. Some of the propositions tested, however, require coding of variables beyond those included in ICB. For the most prominent hypotheses taken from the literature, references are made to standard measurements that are available elsewhere (e.g., from other chapters in this volume). In other instances, details can be obtained from the respective sources.

   8. This presentation of findings concentrates on the basic issue of confirmation (as judged by the respective authors) rather than nuances related to statistical significance. Since the ICB data contain a population rather than a sample of data, significance tests play at best an advisory role from the outset.

   9. Studies prior to 1988 are absent from the table for two reasons. One is that crisis escalation did not occupy a central place on the ICB Project's agenda during stages 1 and 2. The other is that the few studies from that era that focused on escalation to war are superseded by those with longer series of data from more recent years.

   10. For a more skeptical view of the long-term prospects of a dyadically oriented field of international relations, see James, Solberg, and Wolfson (1999).

   11. These results are reported, respectively, in James (1988) and Brecher (1993).

   12. The creation of the Behavioral Correlates of War (BCOW) data set should be noted as an effort to move in the direction of the analysis of interactions within the crisis setting. Leng (this volume, chap. 11) provides an excellent demonstration of the value of such research.

APPENDIX: CRISES THAT ESCALATED TO EITHER SERIOUS CLASHES OR FULL-SCALE WAR, WITH TRIGGERING ACTION AND YEAR OF INITIATION

Serious Clashes	Full-Scale War
Russian Civil War II, nonviolent military, 1918	Nagorny-Karabakh, internal challenge, 1991
Baltic Independence, internal challenge, 1918	Georgia/Abkhazia, political act, 1992
Teschen, political act, 1919	Hungarian War, political act, 1919
Bessarabia, political act, 1919	Third Afghan War, political act, 1919
Chinese Eastern Railway, nonviolent military, 1929	Cilician War, nonviolent military, 1919
Shanghai, political act, 1932	Vilna I, political act, 1920
Chankufeng, external change, 1938	Albanian Frontier, nonviolent military, 1921
Middle East Campaign, nonviolent military, 1941	Hijaz/Najd War, political act, 1924
French Forces/Syria, nonviolent military, 1945	Ethiopian War, political act, 1934
Pushtunistan I, nonviolent military, 1949	Spanish Civil War I, internal challenge, 1936
Hula Drainage, other nonviolent act, 1951	Invasion of Alliania, political act, 1939
Suez Canal, political act, 1951	Entry into World War II, political act, 1939
Burma Infiltration, nonviolent military, 1953	Finnish War, political act, 1939
Invasion of Laos I, nonviolent military, 1953	Invasion—Scandinavia, nonviolent military, 1940
Taiwan Straits I, political act, 1954	Pearl Harbor, political act, 1941
Hungarian Uprising, external change, 1956	Soviet Occupation—Eastern Europe, nonviolent military, 1944
Aborted Coup—Indonesia, nonviolent military, 1958	Indonesian Independence I, political act, 1945
Taiwan Straits II, nonviolent military, 1958	Greek Civil War II, internal challenge, 1946
Bizerta, political act, 1961	Palestinian Protest/Israeli Independence, external change, 1947
Algeria/Morocco Border, nonviolent military, 1963	Suez Nationalization-War, economic act, 1956
Cyprus I, political act, 1963	Six Day War, nonviolent military, 1967
Congo II, internal challenge, 1964	Invasion of Cambodia, political act, 1970
Che Guevera—Bolivia, internal challenge, 1967	Black September, political act, 1970
Libyan Plane, external change, 1973	Christmas Bombing, external change, 1972
Moroccan March, political act, 1975	October—Yom Kippur War, nonviolent military, 1973
East Timor, political act, 1975	Cyprus III, internal challenge, 1974
Rhodesia Settlement, internal challenge, 1979	Chad/Libya II, external change, 1978
Raid on Gafsa, internal challenge, 1980	Chad/Libya IV, political act, 1979
Burkina Faso/Mali Border, nonviolent military, 1985	Onset Iran/Iraq War, political act, 1980
Invasion of Panama, political act, 1989	Falklands/Malvinas, external challenge, 1982
Kashmir III—Nuclear, political act, 1990	Yugoslavia I—Croatia/Slovenia, internal challenge, 1991
	Yugoslavia II—Bosnia, political act, 1992

FACTORS THAT BRING ABOUT WAR

4

Territory
Theory and Evidence on Geography and Conflict

Paul R. Hensel

Most research on the sources of militarized conflict between nation-states has emphasized characteristics of the states themselves or of the larger interstate system, with little emphasis on the geographic context of relations between states. Vasquez (1998b), for example, finds that realist variables such as capabilities and alliances account for most variables and hypotheses used in quantitative research during the 1960s and early 1970s. The contents of this volume and such compilations as the *Handbook of War Studies* (Midlarsky 1989) indicate a substantial broadening of the research agenda since the 1970s, although a number of chapters continue to address capabilities or alliances and many of the additional chapters address such nongeographic topics as democracy, norms, and the historical context (in the form of interstate rivalries). The current chapter considers empirical research on geography and militarized conflict, to understand the role of geography as a context or source for conflict.

Diehl (1991) distinguishes between arguments treating geography as a "source of conflict," indicating that conflict occurs specifically because of geographic factors, and geography as a "facilitating condition for conflict." Vasquez (1995b) distinguishes geographic factors by the nature of the factor in question, identifying three general theoretical perspectives. The territoriality perspective—consistent with Diehl's "geography as a source of conflict"—suggests that geography is important primarily because states fight over territorial issues. The other two perspectives—associated more closely with Diehl's notion of a "facilitating condition for conflict"—suggest that geography is important primarily because it influences the ease with which states can reach each other militarily (the proximity perspective) or the frequency with which they interact with each other (the interaction perspective).

This chapter considers the theoretical arguments of these major explanations that have been suggested to link geography with interstate conflict processes. The empirical evidence on each explanation is examined, supplemented by several original analyses to help evaluate the explanations and resolve the empirical controversies among them. The chapter concludes by discussing some of the implications for current and future scholarly research on interstate conflict. As will be seen, the territoriality explanation of geography and conflict receives the strongest support, although important evidence indicates that proximity affects interstate conflict as well and there have been few direct tests of the interactions approach.

TERRITORIALITY

A common approach to studying interstate conflict begins with a disagreement between two or more states over some type of contentious issue(s). Depending on how the states attempt to settle these issues, they may or may not become involved in serious political conflict, and they may or may not escalate their disagreements to the threshold of militarized conflict or war. Under such a conception of conflict processes, the nature of the issues at stake between two states should influence both their bargaining strategies and the consequences of the bargaining process. In particular, issues that are seen by decision makers as being more "salient," or important, are expected to be more likely to lead to militarized conflict and more difficult to resolve to both sides' satisfaction (Mansbach and Vasquez 1981; Vasquez 1993, 1998b; Hensel 1999a).

Although many types of issues may be salient enough to lead to war, the territorial perspective suggests that territorial issues are especially salient and especially likely to lead to conflict and war (Vasquez 1993, 1995b, 1996; Hensel 1996b). Perhaps because of this salience, most recent empirical research on contentious issues has focused on disagreements over territory. Scholars have argued that territory is "conspicuous among the causes of war" (Hill 1945: 3), "perhaps the most important single cause of war between states in the last two or three centuries" (Luard 1970: 7), or "the source of conflict most likely to end in war" (Vasquez 1993: 124). Territory is often seen as highly salient for three reasons: its tangible contents or attributes, its intangible or psychological value, and its effects on a state's reputation.

In the most basic sense, territory can be viewed as important because of the tangible factors that it contains (Goertz and Diehl 1992b: chap. 1; Hensel 1996b; Newman 1999). Many territories have been the subject of dispute because they contained (or were thought to contain) valuable commodities or resources, such as strategic minerals, oil, fresh water, or fertile agricultural land. Certain territories are considered valuable because they provide access to the sea or to other commerce routes, particularly when they include deep water ports, warm water ports, or control over strategic waterways. Territory may also be seen as important for its population, particularly when it includes members of an ethnic or religious group that inhabits a neighboring state.

Another tangible benefit of territory is its contribution to a state's perceived power and security. Strategic territories such as the Golan Heights may allow for advance warning of an impending attack and may contribute to national defense, particularly to the extent that the territory in question contains defensible geographic features. Fearon (1995: 408) argues that territory with such strategic attributes can be an important source of war even for adversaries who would otherwise prefer a negotiated settlement, because the transfer of strategic territory can alter the two sides' relative bargaining positions. That is, control over the transferred territory may greatly increase the gaining side's chances for successful attack or defense in a future confrontation, which may make both sides reluctant to allow the peaceful transfer of such territory to an adversary.

Beyond its physical contents, territory can also be important to states for less tangible reasons (Goertz and Diehl 1992b: chap. 1; Hensel 1996b; Newman 1999). Territory is argued to lie at the heart of national identity and cohesion, with the very existence and autonomy of a state being rooted in its territory (e.g., Murphy 1990: 531). Many territories are seen as important for their perceived historical connections with a state or its citizens, particularly to the extent that the territory in question was the scene of significant events for a culture or religion. Examples include the Serbian attachment to Kosovo, considered the historical center of Serbian culture and identity, and the tendency for some Israelis to refer to the West Bank as "Judea and Samaria" (names that date back to Jewish rule over the area in biblical times). Similarly, Bowman (1946: 177) argued that there is a "profound psychological difference" between the transfer of territory and other types of interstate interactions or treaties, because of the strong personal feelings and group sentiments evoked by territory.

This intangible or psychological importance of territory may result in the creation of what Fearon (1995) terms "effectively indivisible issues." To Fearon, most disputed issues can be divided between two antagonists in such a way as to make peaceful compromise preferable to war for both sides. Although nearly all issues are divisible in the sense that they can be divided peacefully, perhaps through side payments or linkages with other issues, some issues may become effectively indivisible because of mechanisms such as domestic politics. Fearon (1995: 390) mentions the example of territory: "nineteenth- and twentieth-century leaders cannot divide up and trade territory in international negotiations as easily as could rulers in the seventeenth and eighteenth centuries, due in part to domestic political consequences of the rise of nationalism."[1] Toft (1997) makes a similar point regarding ethnic conflict within states, arguing that the members of a nation can develop an attachment to territory that becomes indivisible from their conception of self and nation, essentially preventing compromise over what is seen as a vital part of the national identity. In short, territory is often argued to have "a psychological importance for nations that is quite out of proportion to its intrinsic value, strategic or economic," and territorial disputes are seen as arousing sentiments of pride and honor more rapidly and more intensely than any other type of issue (Luard 1970: 7; see also Vasquez 1993).

In addition to its tangible and intangible value, territory can be important for reasons of reputation (Hensel 1996b). That is, if a leader gives in to an adversary on territorial issues despite the tangible and/or intangible importance of the territory, other adversaries might be encouraged to press their own demands on other issues. Evidence indicates, for example, that reputational considerations affected the British reaction to Argentina's invasion of the Falklands. Lebow (1985: 117–18) notes concerns by the British defense ministry and the *Economist* about the risks to British interests in Gibraltar, Belize, Guyana, Diego Garcia, Hong Kong, and Antarctica if Britain were to back down over the Falklands.

Schelling (1966: 118) makes a similar point about the importance of reputation in crisis behavior: "what is in dispute is usually not the issue of the moment, but everyone's expectations about how a participant will behave in the future. To yield may be to signal that one can be expected to yield." To Schelling (1966: 124), a country's reputation is one of the few things to be worth fighting for; even parts of the world that are not intrinsically worth the risk of war by themselves can be important because of the precedents that may be set for events in other parts of the world and at later times. Furthermore, Toft (1997) argues that state leaders may risk war to retain apparently "worthless" territories, out of the fear that acquiescence in one situation may lead to future challenges by other groups. Because of the high perceived salience of territory, then, states' actions over territorial issues may be more likely to produce reputational effects than actions over other types of issues.

The theoretical importance of territory has been used to suggest a series of implications for the study of interstate conflict. First, if territorial issues are more salient than most other issues because of their tangible, intangible, and/or reputational importance, then interaction over territory should be different from interaction over other issues. The literature on territorial disputes (e.g., Vasquez 1993, 1995b, 1996; Hensel 1996b) suggests that territorial issues should be more prone to militarized conflict behavior than most other issue types and confrontations over territory should be more escalatory than confrontations over other issues. As Brecher (1993: 153) argues, the more basic the values at stake in a crisis situation, "the higher the cost crisis actors are willing to incur to protect them, and the more extreme will be their crisis management (value-protecting) technique."

Similarly, territorial issues are argued to be more difficult to resolve than most other types of issues. Bowman (1946: 178), for example, noted that any territorial solution—no matter how fair it may seem—carries with it the risk of future attempts to regain lost territory. Arguments may always be raised in the future about past historical claims to the lost territory, especially in border zones of mixed ethnic or linguistic composition, and subsequent incidents may always be used to refocus attention on such historical claims. Bowman (1946: 180–81) further suggested that two or more states can often have irreconcilable claims to the same piece of territory, and that in some territorial disputes there may be no logical solution that both sides can find acceptable. Vasquez (1993) thus suggests that territorial issues can be very difficult to settle and that if two adversaries are unable to settle their territorial questions early in their relationship, the resulting dispute is likely to last for many years.

PROXIMITY AND INTERACTIONS

In contrast to the territorial explanation's focus on territory as a "source of conflict," the proximity and interaction perspectives focus attention on territory as a "facilitating condition for conflict" (Diehl 1991). These perspectives suggest that even if territory and borders "do not *cause* wars, they at least create *structure of risks and opportunities* in which conflictual behavior is apparently more likely to occur" (Starr and Most 1978: 444; italics in original). These two perspectives suggest that territory is primarily important to the extent that it contributes to proximity between two actors. Proximity between actors in turn influences force projection capabilities, threat perception, and interaction opportunities—each of which can affect the likelihood of interstate conflict and war.

PROXIMITY AND THE LOSS OF STRENGTH GRADIENT

The most basic argument on proximity as an explanation for conflict and war is that war can only occur between states that can reach each other militarily. Boulding's (1962) "loss of strength gradient" reflects this proximity perspective, arguing that the political and military strength of a state is greatest within its borders and declines as the state tries to project it farther beyond its borders. Knowing this, a state should be less likely to attempt to project its military strength farther from home, given the resulting reduction in capabilities.

Several scholars have drawn from Boulding's loss of strength gradient in studying interstate conflict. Gleditsch and Singer (1975) and Garnham (1976) consider the effect of proximity on war behavior, measuring proximity by the distance between two states' capitals. Bueno de Mesquita (1981: 83) also includes the effects of distance as a discount factor affecting a state's expected utility for conflict with a particular adversary, arguing that "the greater the distance between a nation's seat of power and the place where its power must be brought to bear in a war, the smaller the proportion of its total capabilities that it can expect to use." Although the effects of great distances can be offset somewhat by a high utility for military conflict with the other state or by a leader's propensity for accepting risks, a greater distance decreases the expected utility that a state has for conflict or war against a given opponent. Similarly, Lemke

(1995) attempts to identify pairs of states that can reach each other militarily, based on distance, the type of terrain between the states, and their technology levels. Lemke's data collection produces a set of cases "that might have had a war," excluding "dyads that have no prospect of fighting" because they "physically do not have the opportunity to fight" (Lemke 1995: 29).

The implication of such approaches is that two adversaries that cannot reach each other with sufficient military capability must be considered unlikely to become involved in militarized conflict, regardless of any other conditions that might be expected to influence conflict. Major powers are typically assumed to be able to project their military capabilities anywhere around the world, with the result that many applications of the proximity approach explicitly limit the effects of proximity to the remaining states in the interstate system. For so-called minor powers, though, states that are not considered sufficiently proximate are often excluded from analyses of conflict behavior or are at least expected to be very unlikely to start conflict over contentious issues, considerations of relative capabilities, or any other potential cause.

Proximity and Threat

The loss of strength gradient and its intellectual descendants focus on the obstacles posed by geographic distance for military force projection. A second argument based on proximity suggests that events closer to home are seen as more threatening than more distant events, and therefore more salient to policymakers. Starr and Most (1978), for example, argue that bordering states face greater uncertainty in their relations than more distant states, which can exacerbate the well-known security dilemma of world politics and lead to the outbreak of conflict. Similarly, Walt (1987: 23) suggests that states choose alliance partners based on the level of perceived threat from other countries and that "states that are nearby pose a greater threat than those that are far away."

Diehl (1985b, 1991) captures this threat perception element in suggesting that proximity affects states' willingness for conflict, as well as their opportunity. Events such as political instability or revolutions are thus more worrisome to policymakers when they occur in a neighboring state than when they occur in more distant states. Furthermore, states often define their national security perimeters based on proximity, as with the Soviet desire to keep Eastern Europe as a defensive perimeter after World War II. As Gochman (1990b: 1) suggests, "the immediacy of, as well as frequency of interaction with, neighboring entities are likely to foster the recognition and belief that proximate actors pose significant threats and opportunities with regard to self-interests." Gochman does not suggest that distant states never pose security threats, but he does argue that leaders will tend to pay closer attention to that which is near than that which is distant.

The threat dimension of proximity is expected to compound the effects of proximity that derive from military reachability. Nearby states are thus expected to be more likely than more distant states to engage in conflict because of their overlapping interests and perceived security threats, as well as because of their ease in projecting sufficient military capabilities against each other. It should be noted, of course, that it is extremely difficult to distinguish between these two expected effects of proximity, so most analysts do not attempt to make this distinction. Indeed, it can even be difficult to distinguish the territorial and proximity arguments, at least to the extent that most territorial claims involve proximate adversaries; contention over a shared border can be an important source of the conflicts of interest and security threats that are thought to characterize bordering states.

Interaction

The interaction perspective on territory and conflict suggests that territory is important primarily because it facilitates interaction between actors. From this perspective, states that are located near each other—particularly those that share a geographic border—will tend to interact more than states located farther apart. For example, Bolivia typically interacts much more frequently with Brazil than it does with Botswana or Bangladesh. The interaction perspective then suggests that greater interaction leads to a greater likelihood of conflict between states, much like Richardson's (1960b) observation that people are more likely to be killed by close family members (with whom they interact frequently) than by complete strangers.

EMPIRICAL PATTERNS

Recent research has tested propositions drawn from each of the three general theoretical perspectives. I now consider the empirical evidence that supports each perspective, beginning with general patterns before addressing more specific tests of the proximity, interactions, and territoriality perspectives. I then supplement this evidence with a series of original analyses and consider the relative support for all three perspectives.

Geography and the Frequency of Militarized Conflict

The contention that geography is related to militarized conflict and war is intuitively appealing and appears to fit with a quick reading of recent history. Many recent crises and wars seem to possess a territorial component of one type or another. Examples range from fighting among Croats, Serbs, and Muslims over land in the former Yugoslavia to conflicts over the Golan Heights, Kashmir, and the Falkland (Malvinas) Islands. Even crises and wars that lack a systematic territorial component frequently appear to involve neighbors. Systematic research on militarized conflict supports this preliminary impression about the importance of geography.

One important pattern relating geography to conflict concerns the frequency of conflict and war between neighboring states. The proximity approach suggests that the vast majority of all interstate conflict should occur between proximate neighbors, as does the interactions approach (at least to the extent that neighbors interact more frequently than more distant states). Although the occurrence of conflict between contiguous states does not necessarily indicate the presence of a territorial dispute, conflict between neighbors is also generally consistent with a territorial explanation for war. As Vasquez (1993: 134) notes, neighbors are more apt to have concerns about each other's territorial ambitions than are other pairs of states, so a clustering of conflict between neighbors would not be inconsistent with a territorial explanation.

Table 4.1 examines the contiguity of participants in militarized interstate disputes and interstate wars. Militarized interstate disputes are interactions between nation-states involving the explicit threat, display, or use of militarized force (Jones, Bremer, and Singer 1996); full-scale wars are militarized disputes that escalate to the point of sustained combat between regular armed forces and result in at least one thousand battle deaths. Over half of all militarized disputes between 1816 and 1992 and two-thirds of all full-scale interstate wars in this period began between at least two contiguous adversaries, where contiguity is measured by the existence of a direct land or river border between two states.[2] Importantly, these figures have not decreased over time, as improvements in communications or transportation technology have been bringing distant lands closer together. Over half of all militarized disputes and almost every full-scale war in the 1945–92 period began between at least one pair of contiguous adversaries, repre-

Table 4.1   Contiguity and Militarized Conflict

	1816–1945	1946–92	1816–1992
Militarized Interstate Disputes			
Dispute began between			
contiguous adversaries	346 (42.9%)	694 (56.6%)	1,040 (51.1%)
No contiguous adversaries	461	533	994
Total	807	1,227	2,034
Interstate Wars			
War began between			
contiguous adversaries	31 (56.4%)	22 (91.7%)	53 (67.1%)
No contiguous adversaries	24	2	26
Total	55	24	79

Sources: Correlates of War (COW) militarized interstate dispute date set (Jones et al. 1996); COW contiguity data set (Gochman 1991).

senting a noticeable increase from the previous period.[3] Contiguous states thus account for the majority of all interstate conflict, and this pattern actually appears to be strengthening over time.

Another important pattern is the frequency of territorial disagreements in world politics. Conflict between contiguous states may or may not indicate the presence of a territorial dispute, but disagreements over territory offer more direct evidence in support of a territorial explanation for conflict and war. Several recent studies have compiled information on the prevalence of territorial claims in the modern era. Kocs (1995) identifies forty-one territorial disputes between contiguous adversaries during the 1945–87 period, while Huth (1996b) identifies 129 territorial claims that were active between 1950 and 1990 (some of which involve noncontiguous adversaries). Focusing on a longer time period but a more limited geographic domain, Hensel (1999) finds competing claims to seventy-one distinct pieces of territory in the Western Hemisphere (North, Central, and South America and the Caribbean) between 1816 and 1996. It seems clear, then, that territorial disagreements have been common in the modern interstate system.

These dozens of territorial claims have produced a great deal of militarized conflict. Table 4.2 illustrates the frequency of territorial issues in the militarized disputes and wars examined in Table 4.1, as well as in an alternative list of wars compiled by Holsti (1991). Over one-fourth of all militarized disputes involve explicit contention over territorial issues, with the remainder involving such nonterritorial issues as the composition of governments or disagreements over specific governmental policies. Territorial issues are even more prominent in more severe forms of conflict, with over half of all wars in both the Correlates of War (COW) and Holsti lists involving explicit contention over territory.[4] This close

Table 4.2   Territorial Issues and Militarized Conflict

Militarized Interstate Disputes	*1816–1945*	*1946–92*	*1816–1992*
Dispute includes territorial issues	243 (30.1%)	340 (27.7%)	583 (28.7%)
No territorial issues	564	887	1,451
Total	807	1,227	2,034
Interstate Wars (COW)	*1816–1945*	*1946–92*	*1816–1992*
War includes territorial issues	29 (52.7%)	14 (58.3%)	43 (54.4%)
No territorial issues	26	10	36
Total	55	24	79
Interstate Wars (Holsti)	*1815–1941*	*1945–89*	*1815–1989*
War includes territorial issues	34 (55.7%)	26 (44.8%)	60 (50.4%)
No territorial issues	27	32	59
Total	61	58	119

Sources: COW militarized interstate dispute data set (Jones et al., 1996); Holsti (1991).

connection between territorial issues and conflict severity is supported by Kocs (1995), who finds that contiguous dyads with an unresolved territorial claim were more than forty times more likely than other dyads to go to war during the 1945–87 period.

Focusing on changing trends over time, Luard (1986) and Holsti (1991) suggest that—especially since 1945—territory is becoming less prominent as an issue leading to conflict or war. Table 4.2 reveals that the proportion of militarized disputes involving contention over territory has not changed significantly over time, with a barely perceptible decline from 30.1 percent of all disputes between 1816 and 1945 to 27.7 percent since 1945. Holsti's list of wars shows a noticeable decrease in territorial issues since 1945, from 56 percent to 45 percent, but the COW war list shows an increase from 53 percent to over 58 percent over this period.[5] Even where a decline has occurred, then, territory still accounts for nearly half of all wars in Holsti's list and almost as many militarized disputes as in earlier times. Territorial issues have thus been prominent as a source of interstate conflict and war, both over past centuries and in the post–World War II period.

Based on these first two tables, it appears that both the proximity/interactions and territoriality perspectives contribute to our understanding of conflict processes. Over half of all disputes begin between neighbors and over one-fourth involve territorial issues, while both contiguity and territory are involved in over half of all full-scale wars. These results tell us little directly about the interactions perspective, but given that perspective's close relationship to the proximity argument, these results are certainly consistent with the expectation that most conflict occurs between actors with frequent interaction.

It may be noted that more militarized disputes and wars in Tables 4.1 and 4.2 involve contiguous adversaries than involve territorial issues, which might be used to suggest that the proximity and/or interactions approaches are more useful than the territoriality perspective. The difference is much less for the most severe categories of conflict, though, as both contiguity and territory have been involved in over half of all full-scale interstate wars. Also, this difference is not especially surprising because of the range of possible issues that might lead to conflict. Both contiguous adversaries and states involved in an ongoing territorial claim can easily become involved in disputes over nonterritorial issues; Holsti (1991) lists over twenty specific issue types, only three of which are explicitly territorial in nature.

Tests of the Proximity and Interactions Perspectives

Several variants of the proximity and interactions perspectives are tested empirically in the academic literature. The simplest version suggests simply that the existence of a border matters—that is, that states sharing a common border are more conflictual than states lacking such a border. A more advanced version of this perspective treats the role of proximity as more continuous in nature than the simple dichotomy of whether two states are contiguous. This more advanced perspective focuses attention on such factors as the distance and terrain separating two states, in order to develop a more accurate indicator of the proximity between them.

As indicated by Table 4.1, the majority of interstate conflict has occurred between contiguous adversaries. Further evidence on the relationship between contiguity and the outbreak of conflict comes from Bremer (1992), who tests hypotheses on seven explanations for war. Of these seven explanations, contiguity produces the strongest effect, increasing the probability of war by over thirty-five times—more than such common explanations as alliances, major power status, and relative capabilities. After examining the available empirical evidence on "who fights whom, when, where, and why," Bremer (chap. 2 of this volume) concludes that most states that fight are neighbors. Bremer (1992) even goes so far as to recommend that contiguity should be included in almost all empirical studies of war, at least as a control variable.

Contiguity has also been shown to have strong effects on militarized dispute escalation. Diehl (1985b) finds that the probability of dispute escalation to full-scale war is much greater for dyads in which at least one of the states is contiguous to the site of the dispute. Only one of fifty-four noncontiguous dyads in his study escalated to war, compared to twelve of fifty contiguous dyads—and twelve of the thirteen wars in the study began in a site that was contiguous to one or both original adversaries. Similarly, Gochman (1990b) finds that the proportion of militarized disputes involving contiguous adversaries is greater for more escalatory dispute levels, and Senese (1996) finds that contiguous adversaries are more likely to escalate to the point of dispute-related fatalities. Studies of war diffusion offer evidence that contiguity is an important agent of war diffusion; states bordering one of the belligerents in an ongoing war are more likely to join the war than other states (Starr and Most 1978; Siverson and Starr 1990).

Several studies have also employed more precise measures of proximity than the simple dichotomy of whether two states share a common border. Diehl (1985b: 1208), for example, calls for a more precise indicator of proximity, because "it is probably inaccurate to aggregate all forms of noncontiguity together, implying that a site 100 miles away is as inaccessible as one ten or twenty times that far." Where such indicators have been employed, the results have been promising. Gleditsch and Singer (1975) and Garnham (1976), for example, find that states that fight wars tend to be closer to each other geographically than other states.

Similarly, Bueno de Mesquita (1981: 166) finds that greater distances preclude many states from initiating military conflict unless they have substantial capabilities. Major powers initiate 89 percent of the "long-distance wars" in Bueno de Mesquita's study, as compared to only 40 percent of the "neighborhood wars." Lemke (1995) also finds that "relevant" dyads in which both states can reach

each other militarily (based on distance, terrain, and technology) have been much more likely to become involved in militarized disputes or wars than other dyads in the same region.[6]

In short, numerous studies offer evidence that is consistent with the proximity and interactions explanations, although most of this evidence involves simple contiguity rather than more sophisticated measures of interaction or proximity. Contiguous states are more dispute- and war-prone than more distant states, and they are more likely to escalate their confrontations. Unfortunately, these existing tests have been unable to distinguish between the proximity and interaction perspectives. It is unclear whether contiguity (or total geographic distance) is important because it leads to greater interactions, because it offers greater opportunities for reaching an adversary militarily, or for some other reason; Bremer (chap. 2) suggests that the impact of proximity probably reflects both enhanced opportunities to fight and increased willingness to fight.

Despite some favorable evidence, though, there is reason to question the value of the proximity and interaction perspectives as primary explanations for militarized conflict. As Vasquez (1995b) notes, proximity is basically a constant; countries rarely move closer together or farther apart over time.[7] As a result, the proximity explanation faces difficulties in accounting for the outbreak of rare events such as conflict and war, since a constant independent variable cannot account for fluctuations in a dependent variable. Proximity may be a necessary condition for war, at least in the trivial sense that states must be able to reach each other before they can fight, but it does not seem to be a satisfactory cause war in and of itself.[8]

Also, the interaction-based perspective encounters difficulties in explaining why increased interactions should necessarily lead to greater conflict between states (Vasquez 1995b). A substantial literature by scholars such as Karl Deutsch suggests that greater levels of communication and transactions can contribute to cooperation and peace instead of war. Alternatively, states with greater levels of conflict and hostility would seem likely to reduce their interactions as their conflict levels increase, which would contribute to a weakening or reversal of the interactions–conflict linkage.

Another problem with both the proximity and interaction explanations involves their implications for temporal trends in conflict behavior. If the primary reason for a linkage between geography and conflict were simply that geography limits states' capacities to project their political and military strength abroad, then we would expect that these limitations would decrease with improvements in military and transportation technology. Similarly, we might expect that interactions between more distant states should increase with improving technology, as the states are better able to communicate, trade, and otherwise interact with each other than in previous eras. Yet (as noted earlier) time has not weakened the impact of contiguity on conflict. Even with the notable advances in transportation and military technology over the past several centuries, neighboring states still fight each other much more often than do more distant states. As Vasquez (1995b) notes, this continued importance of proximity despite technological advances raises serious doubts about the value of the proximity and interaction perspectives.[9]

Tests of the Territoriality Perspective

Several studies have identified substantial differences in conflict behavior over different types of issues. Militarized disputes involving territorial issues are much more likely than other disputes to lead to a militarized response by the target state (Hensel and Diehl 1994; Hensel 1996b). Senese (1996) finds that disputes over territorial issues typically produce a greater number of fatalities than disputes over other issues. Crises involving "vital issues" (issues of territory or national independence) typically reach higher levels of escalation than do crises over less salient issues (Gochman and Leng 1983). Similarly, militarized disputes over territorial issues are more likely to escalate to full-scale war (Hensel 1996b), even when controlling for the effects of dyadic power status, time period, and rivalry (Vasquez and Henehan 1999). These results indicate that decision makers are much more willing to risk dispute escalation to protect their interests on issues of high salience than when less salient issues are at stake. Territory thus appears to be seen by leaders as highly salient, justifying the risks of escalation to protect or advance one's interests much more than other types of issues. Even if threats over less salient issues can safely be ignored, the salience of territory seems to be great enough that a challenge over territorial issues is almost always met with a militarized response (with a corresponding increase in the probability of full-scale war).

Beyond dispute escalation, Hensel (1994, 1996a, 1996b) finds that confrontations over territorial issues are typically more likely to lead to recurrent conflict than confrontations over other issues. Regardless of the type of issues involved, over half of all militarized disputes are followed by another dispute between the same adversaries within fifteen years. Nonetheless, the issues at stake in a confrontation also make a substantial difference in the likelihood of recurrent conflict. When territorial issues are at stake, nearly three-fourths of all disputes are followed quickly by another dispute, and the statistical odds of a recurrent dispute are nearly twice as great for disputes involving territorial issues (Hensel 1996b). Furthermore, the next militarized dispute between the adversaries tends to happen sooner after a dispute over territorial issues than after a nonterritorial dispute, with territorial issues producing almost two years less "stability" before the outbreak of the next dispute than other types of issues. These effects on conflict recurrence and postdispute stability remain strong even after controlling for the outcome of the past confrontation; disputes over territorial issues are more likely to be followed by recurrent conflict than disputes over other issues, regardless of the dispute's outcome (Hensel 1996b).[10] Goertz and Diehl (1992b) also examine the conditions under which an exchange of territory between states is most likely to lead to recurrent conflict between the same adversaries. They find that future conflict is most likely when the territory is more valuable, particularly when the losing side is stronger than the gaining side militarily and when the exchanged territory involves homeland instead of colonial territory for the losing side.

Several recent studies have focused more explicitly on the dynamics of territorial claims, going well beyond the focus on militarized conflict that has characterized most research on territorial issues. Regarding the initial development of active territorial claims, Huth (1996b) finds that a border is more likely to be subjected to an active territorial claim when the territory in question has a strategic location, high economic value, or shared ethnic or linguistic groups along the border and less likely when a prior border agreement has been signed to settle the border. Focusing on the participants as well as geographic characteristics of the border itself, a claim is more likely to be raised when there is a prior unresolved dispute for the potential challenger state or a prior loss of territory by the challenger, and it is less likely to be raised when the challenger had previously gained territory.

Focusing on militarized conflict within territorial claims, Huth (1996b) finds that the level of conflict over an ongoing territorial claim is increased by a number of claim characteristics associated with issue salience. In particular, militarized conflict appears to be more likely in the presence of ties to a bordering minority, the presence of shared ethnic or linguistic groups along the border, a stalemate in negotiations, or an attempt by the target state to change the status quo (among other factors).[11] Similarly, Hensel (1999) finds that claim salience increases the likelihood of militarized conflict, along with a longer history of militarized conflict and of unsuccessful peaceful attempts to settle the underlying territorial claim.

The literature on territorial claims recognizes that military action is only one way to settle two states' contentious issues and has begun to study nonmilitary options as well. Hensel (1999), for example, finds that the likelihood of bilateral negotiations over a territorial claim is greatest when the claimed territory is highly salient and when past settlement attempts have been unsuccessful, although the likelihood decreases when the claim involves an island rather than mainland territory. Nonbinding third-party settlement attempts are most likely when the territory is highly salient, recent settlement attempts have been unsuccessful, and the two parties are fighting or have recently fought a full-scale war; they are less likely when a history of successful settlement attempts suggests that third-party assistance is not needed. Binding third-party arbitration or adjudication is somewhat less likely when the claimed territory is highly salient, consistent with the expectation that third parties are unlikely to be trusted on matters of vital national interest, and somewhat more likely when there is a longer history of recent militarized conflict over the territory. Similarly, Simmons (1999) finds that a history of unratified border treaties increases the likelihood of agreement on the submission of a claim to binding arbitration or adjudication.

Finally, several studies consider the ending of territorial claims. Nearly half of Huth's (1996b) territorial claims continued throughout the 1950–90 period of study, indicating that such disputes can be very difficult to resolve (whether or not they lead to militarized conflict). Huth (1996b) finds the prospects for peaceful resolution of territorial claims in a given year to be increased by the economic value of the territory under dispute and by a past defeat for the challenger (among other nonterritorial factors). Peaceful resolution appears to be less likely when the claimed territory has strategic value, bordering minority ties, or shared ethnic or linguistic groups along the border; when the target state attempts to change the status quo; and when there is a prior history of militarized conflict.

Recent research on the territorial perspective thus indicates that states contending over territorial issues appear to behave quite differently from states that have settled their territorial issues or that have never disagreed over territory. Table 4.2 indicates that territorial issues do not give rise to the majority of militarized confrontations between states. Yet research on conflict recurrence and on the dynamics of territorial claims suggests that disagreement over territory greatly increases the probability of militarized conflict at any given point in time, relative to states lacking territorial issues. Additionally, while as few as one-fourth of all confrontations involve territorial issues, these confrontations are much more likely to escalate to dangerous levels than the typical dispute over nonterritorial issues. While territory does not come close to accounting for all militarized conflict, then, contention over territory exerts a strong influence on interactions once conflict has begun.

Comparing the Perspectives

The evidence reviewed thus far has generally addressed the three theoretical perspectives separately. I now evaluate the comparative support for each perspective, drawing from several studies with analyses that address at least two of the three perspectives. After reviewing these results, I offer several original empirical analyses to clarify the value of each perspective and to increase our overall understanding of the role of territorial disputes in interstate conflict and war.

Gibler (1996: 77–78) classifies interstate alliances into several categories, including the territorial settlement treaty in which states "have either exchanged territory or have agreed to the status quo settlement of territory and have then cemented their new relationship with the signing of an alliance." Of the twenty-seven territorial settlement treaties since 1815, only four have been followed by future war involving an ally, which is much lower than the probability of war for other types of alliances. As Gibler (1996: 87) notes, this finding offers support for the territoriality perspective, because it involves a change in conflict levels that follows a change in the territorial issue with no corresponding change in levels of proximity or interactions.

Another relevant finding comes from Vasquez (1996a), who examines the escalation of disputes to war within enduring rivalries. In general, rivals go to war under two patterns: rivals that contend over territorial stakes tend to engage in dyadic wars, while rivals that contend over other stakes tend to join ongoing multilateral wars (or avoid war entirely). As Vasquez (1996a: 555–56) notes, these findings are consistent with the territorial perspective. Furthermore, to evaluate the likely response from the proximity perspective that these wars between rivals arose out of contiguity, Vasquez notes that each of these dyadic wars between rivals involves a dispute over territorial issues. Even if the rivals experienced high levels of interaction and high opportunities for conflict due to their contiguity, then, they were also contending over territorial issues—thereby supporting the territorial explanation.

Tables 4.3 through 4.6 offer further insight into the effects of territorial issues and contiguity through original empirical analyses. Table 4.3 illustrates the overlap between contiguity and territorial issues in militarized interstate disputes, breaking down each dispute into pairs of participants (dyads) to obtain the clearest illustration of conflict patterns in multiparty disputes that may involve many different adversaries.[12] Roughly half of the dyadic disputes in Table 4.3 (1,532 of 3,045 disputes, or 50.3 percent) involve neither contiguity nor territorial issues. Of the remaining cases, 495 (16.3 percent) involve both contiguity and territorial issues, 718 involve contiguous states contending over nonterritorial issues, and 300 involve territorial issues between noncontiguous states. Both contiguous and noncontiguous adversaries thus contend over territory, with two-fifths of all contiguous disputes (495 of 1,213, or 40.8 percent), and less than one-fifth of noncontiguous disputes (300 of 1,832, or 16.4 percent) involving territorial issues. While most militarized disputes over territory involve contiguous adversaries, then, a large number do not. Because there are numerous cases in which contiguity and issue type do not overlap, the militarized dispute data set allows for an especially useful comparison of the effects of territory and contiguity on conflict behavior.

Table 4.3   Contiguity and Territorial Issues in Militarized Disputes, 1816–1992

Contiguous Adversaries?	Nonterritorial Issues Only	Territorial Issues at Stake	Total
No	1,532	300 (16.4%)	1,832
Yes	718	495 (40.8%)	1,213
Total	2,250	795 (26.1%)	3,045

Sources: COW militarized interstate dispute data set (Jones et al. 1996); COW contiguity data set (Gochman 1991).

Table 4.4 examines the impact of both contiguity and territorial issues on dispute severity, measured by whether the dispute led to one or more dispute-related fatalities. The occurrence of fatalities represents an important threshold in interstate conflict, creating tangible losses from a dispute that are easily recognized by public opinion and that can limit a leader's flexibility in subsequent policy choices. Table 4.4 separates the militarized dispute data by the contiguity status of the disputants, to compare the effects of territorial issues in disputes between contiguous and noncontiguous adversaries.[13] The proximity and interactions explanations for war would suggest that the issue type in a given dispute should have little impact, with disputes between contiguous adversaries generally being much more severe than disputes between more distant adversaries. In contrast, the territoriality explanation would suggest that the issue type should have a great impact on escalation in both contiguous and noncontiguous disputes, with territorial issues producing greater escalation regardless of the proximity of the adversaries.

The results presented in Table 4.4 offer greater support for the territoriality perspective than for the proximity and interactions perspectives. Both contiguous and noncontiguous adversaries experience greater levels of escalation (i.e., a higher probability of fatalities in the dispute) when territorial issues are at stake than when only nonterritorial issues are at stake. Disputes between noncontiguous adversaries lead to fatalities about one-fourth of the time overall, including 52 percent of the time when territorial issues are at stake and only 24 percent of the time when nonterritorial issues are at stake. Similarly, disputes between contiguous adversaries lead to fatalities around one-third of the time overall, including 42 percent of all disputes over territorial issues and only 26 percent of all disputes over nonterritorial issues. In both analyses, contention over territorial

Table 4.4   Territorial Issues, Contiguity, and Dispute Fatalities, 1816–1992

Territorial Issues at Stake?	*No Fatalities*	*Fatalities in Dispute*	*Total*
Noncontiguous Adversaries			
No	1,088	343 (24.0%)	1,431
Yes	124	136 (52.3%)	260
Total	1,212	479 (28.4%)	1,691
$\chi^2 = 87.03$ (1 df, $p < .001$); odds ratio $= 3.48$			
Contiguous Adversaries			
No	452	161 (26.3%)	613
Yes	254	181 (41.6%)	435
Total	706	342 (32.6%)	1,048
$\chi^2 = 27.25$ (1 df, $p < .001$); odds ratio $= 2.00$			

Sources: COW militarized interstate dispute data set (Jones et al. 1996); COW contiguity data set (Gochman 1991).

issues significantly increases the likelihood of fatalities relative to contention over other types of issues ($p <.001$).[14] Regardless of the contiguity of the disputants, then, contention over territorial issues greatly increases the likelihood of dispute escalation to the level of fatalities.[15] Indeed, the impact of territorial issues appears to be even greater in noncontiguous disputes than in disputes between contiguous adversaries. Contention over territorial issues doubles the statistical odds of fatalities in disputes between contiguous adversaries (as indicated by the odds ratio of 2.00) and more than triples the statistical odds of fatalities in noncontiguous disputes (odds ratio = 3.48).[16] This finding is consistent with the results of Senese (1996), whose multivariate analyses reveal that contention over territorial issues appears to have a stronger effect on conflict severity than does contiguity.

Table 4.5 offers an additional perspective on the importance of territorial issues, by examining the conflict behavior of states involved in ongoing territorial claims. The earlier tables have examined the conflict behavior of all dyads in the interstate system that have been involved in militarized conflict over any issue. Table 4.5 allows us to examine whether the impact of territorial issues on conflict behavior is limited to disputes over territorial issues or whether two states' competition over territory spills over to other dimensions of their relationship. If states involved in territorial claims exhibit substantial differences in conflict behavior in disputes over territorial versus nonterritorial issues, then we can gain greater confidence in the territorial explanation. That is, regardless of any other characteristics or attributes that might be expected to affect conflict behavior (e.g., proximity or interactions between them), the issues at stake in a given confrontation would be found to change conflict behavior relative to other confrontations between the same adversaries. Alternatively, if there is little or no difference in conflict behavior between disputes over territorial and nonterritorial issues involving the same adversaries, then the results would be less straightforward. We might conclude from the territorial perspective that something about the territorial claim spills over to affect relations between the same states over different issues as well, if both territorial and nonterritorial disputes are much more severe than disputes between states not involved in a territorial claim. We might also

Table 4.5   Territorial Issues and Dispute Fatalities during Territorial Claims, 1950–90

Territorial Issues at Stake?	*No Fatalities*	*Fatalities in Dispute*	*Total*
No	183	62 (25.3%)	245
Yes	160	114 (41.6%)	274
Total	343	176 (33.9%)	519

$\chi^2 = 15.33$ (1 df, $p < .001$); odds ratio = 2.10

Sources: COW militarized interstate dispute data set (Jones et al. 1996); Huth (1996b).

conclude that some additional factor besides the specific issue(s) under dispute—perhaps proximity or interactions—shapes the conflict behavior of states, while the issues themselves make little difference.

Table 4.5 examines the dispute severity of all militarized disputes that occurred during territorial claims between 1950 and 1990, as identified by Huth (1996b). Slightly over half of these disputes (274 of 519, or 52.8 percent) involve territorial issues, while the remaining 245 remain limited to other issue types. As this table reveals, states involved in a territorial claim are much more likely to escalate to the level of fatalities in disputes over territorial issues than in disputes over nonterritorial issues ($p < .001$, odds ratio = 2.10). Closer analysis of the data (not presented in this table) reveals that disputes between states not involved in a territorial claim reach the level of fatalities about one-fourth of the time (26.2 percent) over the 1950–90 period covered by Huth's territorial claim data. This figure is statistically indistinguishable from the results in Table 4.4 for nonterritorial disputes, 24 to 26 percent of which reach the level of fatalities. Because there is no noticeable difference between these nonterritorial disputes and disputes between adversaries not involved in territorial claims, we have good reason to doubt that some additional factor accounts for the greater overall escalation of disputes within territorial claims.[17] If proximity, interactions, or some other factor accounted for the conflict behavior of states in a territorial claim, then we should expect that these same states would behave similarly in disputes over any issues, territorial or otherwise. The most important distinction between territorial claim dyads and other types of adversaries thus appears to lie in their contention over territorial issues.

A final analysis examines the ways that states involved in territorial claims attempt to manage or settle their claims, focusing on the salience of the territorial issues at stake. The discussion and analyses so far have emphasized militarized conflict and have treated all territorial issues as equally salient. Because the territorial perspective suggests that issue salience is an important influence on behavior, though, it would be desirable to examine salience in greater detail than is possible with a simple dichotomy between "territorial" and "other" issues. Additionally, most theoretical discussions of the territorial perspective (e.g., Vasquez 1993; Hensel 1999a) see militarized conflict as only one of the possible techniques available to states for managing or settling their issues. Table 4.6 examines the techniques that have been used to settle claims to territory in the Western Hemisphere from 1816 to 1992, using data drawn from the Issue Correlates of War (ICOW) project (Hensel 1999a). The options available to states include bilateral negotiations between the claimants, talks with no-binding third-party assistance (good offices, inquiry, conciliation, or mediation), submission of the claim to a binding third-party decision (arbitration or adjudication), and the unilateral initiation of militarized conflict.[18] Claim salience is determined by the characteristics of the claimed territory, focusing on four specific indicators: the presence of valuable resources and permanent population centers in the territory, as well as explicit ethnic or religious bases for the claim. For the purposes of Table 4.6, a given claim is considered to take on low salience when none of these four indicators is present, moderate salience when only one is present, and high salience when two or more are present.[19]

Table 4.6 indicates that bilateral negotiations have been the most common form of action taken over territorial claims, regardless of the salience of the particular claimed territory. Over half of all settlement attempts (51.8 percent) involve bilateral negotiations between the claimants, ranging from 45.9 percent of all settlement attempts for high-salience claims to 66.1 percent of all attempts for low-salience claims. Militarized conflict is the second most common type of settlement attempt, accounting for over one-fourth of all settlement attempts overall and ranging from 16.5 percent for low-salience claims to over one-third for high-salience claims. Nonbinding third-party settlement attempts are the next most common type, ranging from thirteen to nearly 20 percent of all attempts, and binding third-party settlement attempts account for less than 6 percent of all attempts in each category.

The results presented in Table 4.6 suggest several important conclusions about attempts to manage or settle territorial claims. First, despite the emphasis on militarized conflict in existing research on territorial issues in world politics, militarized conflict accounts for no more than one-third of all settlement attempts in any category of claim salience. Bilateral negotiations are more common than militarized disputes in each salience category, and the two types of third-party settlement attempts together are at least as frequent as militarized action for claims with low and moderate salience; it is only for high-salience claims that militarized conflict surpasses the two types of third-party action and approaches bilateral negotiations in frequency. The recent emphasis on militarized action over territorial issues, then, appears to overlook most actions that are taken to settle such issues.

Also, it seems clear that the salience of the specific territory at stake affects the actions that are taken to resolve a given claim. Militarized conflict over territorial issues is much more common in claims involving high-salience territory,

Table 4.6   Attempts to Settle Western Hemisphere Territorial Claims, 1816–1992

Salience of Claimed Territory	Bilaterial Negotiations	Third Party		Militarized Conflict
		Nonbinding	Binding	
Low salience	76 (66.1%)	15 (13.0%)	5 (4.3%)	19 (16.5%)
Moderate salience	184 (54.1%)	67 (19.7%)	20 (5.9%)	69 (20.3%)
High salience	191 (45.9%)	66 (15.9%)	11 (2.6%)	148 (35.6%)
Total	451 (51.8%)	148 (17.0%)	36 (4.1%)	236 (27.1%)

Sources: Issue Correlates of War (ICOW) territorial claims data set (Hensel 1999); COW militarized interstate dispute data set (Jones et al. 1996).

accounting for one-third of all settlement attempts as compared to one-sixth of all attempts involving low-salience territory. Bilateral negotiations account for a lower proportion of all settlement attempts in claims to high-salience territory, with 45.9 percent of all attempts as compared to 66.1 and 54.1 percent in claims to low- or moderate-salience claims. It should be noted that only sixteen of the seventy-one claims in the Western Hemisphere involve high-salience territory, while thirty-six involve moderate salience and nineteen involve territory of only low salience. When the number of claims of each type is considered, each type of settlement attempt is much more likely in high-salience claims, indicating that low-salience claims are likely to lead to little interaction of any type while higher-salience claims attract much greater attention. Based on the totals in Table 4.6, each of the sixteen high-salience claims has generated twelve rounds of bilateral negotiations, nine militarized disputes involving territorial issues, and almost five third-party settlement attempts (most of which involve nonbinding mechanisms).

Summary

After reviewing three prominent explanations for the territory–conflict relationship and examining the empirical evidence behind each one, the preceding review of recent research and the original analyses presented herein suggest that each explanation has some explanatory power. Contiguous adversaries are more conflict-prone than more distant states, for example, which helps support both the interactions and proximity explanations. A considerable body of recent evidence now supports the territorial explanation as well, with conflict over territorial issues tending to be more escalatory and more likely to lead to recurrent conflict, and with more salient territorial issues appearing to strengthen this effect.

To the extent that the evidence favors one explanation over the others, the territorial explanation appears to be strongest. In particular, as Hensel (1996b) notes and the present analysis confirms, the effects of territorial issues apply for both contiguous and noncontiguous adversaries, which suggests that territoriality is especially important. Thus, noncontiguous states that contend over territorial issues show much more escalatory conflict behavior than noncontiguous states that contend over nonterritorial issues, just as contiguous states are more escalatory when contending over territorial issues. Furthermore, even when analysis is restricted to states involved in active territorial claims, significant differences remain between individual confrontations over territorial and nonterritorial issues.

We should be careful not to conclude from this evidence that proximity and interactions have no impact on conflict behavior. There is too much empirical evidence from research by Bremer, Diehl, Lemke, and others to allow the outright rejection of either model. Additionally, Tables 4.1 and 4.2 indicate that contiguous adversaries account for much more militarized conflict than territorial claims, at least for lower-level forms of conflict. It appears that states that can reach each other militarily and that interact most often account for the majority of militarized conflict, although a good fraction of this conflict involves territorial issues. Furthermore, because there have never been more than several hundred pairs of adversaries contending over territorial issues and literally thousands of potential adversaries lack such issues (and some adversaries have already resolved their territorial issues), the likelihood of militarized conflict at any given point in time seems to be higher for states involved in a territorial claim than for other type of states. In short, the evidence appears stronger for the territorial explanation overall, particularly in studies that allow for direct comparison of the different explanations.

CONCLUSION

The empirical patterns and theoretical explanations considered in this chapter suggest a number of important conclusions about interstate conflict and implications for future research. Perhaps most important, there can be little doubt that geography affects interstate conflict behavior in systematic ways. A substantial body of empirical evidence, supported by this chapter's empirical analyses, finds a close relationship between conflict behavior and such geographic factors as contiguity and territorial issues.

I conclude with several suggestions for future research strategies to help resolve questions on the territorial and other explanations that remain unanswered (or that are only answered incompletely). Much of the research reviewed here has compared the expectations of one of the three general theoretical perspectives against the statistical null hypothesis of no systematic relationship among variables. Our understanding of the relationship between territorial disputes and conflict could be aided greatly by the direct comparison of hypotheses from one perspective with counterhypotheses from another perspective, rather than simply comparing each hypothesis with the statistical null hypothesis. Several possible strategies may be used to design such competitive tests.

One important area in which the expectations of the different perspectives diverge is the impact of changes in the territorial issues on conflict between adversaries. According to the proximity and interactions perspectives, changes in conflict behavior should result primarily from changes in the level of interactions between states or from changes in the ease with which the states can reach each other. According to the territoriality perspective, though, changes in the issues under contention—such as the resolution of part or all of a territorial claim—should be followed by changes in conflict behavior. Vasquez (1993: 147), for example, suggests that how and when two states attempt to deal with their territorial questions can have a "profound effect" on their subsequent relations, "determining the extent to which they will be basically hostile or friendly." Some evidence already suggests that changes in territorial issues produce changes in subsequent conflict behavior, as with Gibler's findings about territorial settlement treaties and Goertz and Diehl's findings about recurrent conflict after territorial changes. Vasquez (1993: 150–51), Huth (1996b: 189–92), Brams and Togman (1996), and Simmons (1999) offer additional suggestions about how territorial disputes might be resolved or managed, ranging from the deterritorialization of disputes to preventive diplomacy or intervention by external actors. Future research should examine the impact of changes in territorial issues; evidence that partial or total settlement of territorial claims reduces subsequent conflict propensities would support the territorial explanation over its proximity and interactions competitors.

Just as changes in territorial issues are only relevant to the territorial perspective as an influence on subsequent conflict behavior, other factors are only relevant to the proximity or interaction perspectives. The proximity perspective suggests that changes in the level of proximity of two states should produce changes in their conflict behavior. If one state gains territory that moves its borders closer to the other (through military conquest, the acquisition of colonies, or other means), then this perspective would suggest that the two states should be more conflict-prone than they had been previously. If one state loses territory that moves its borders farther from the other, this perspective would suggest that the two states should become less conflict-prone. Similarly, the interaction perspective suggests that changes in two states' interaction levels should produce corresponding changes in those states' conflict patterns. Existing research has not addressed these concerns directly. Future research is urged to develop systematic measures that can capture variations in the degree of proximity and the level of interactions between states. Once such indicators are developed and collected, scholars will be able to study the relationship between changing proximity or interactions and changing levels of interstate conflict. Evidence that is found to support these basic expectations would support the proximity or interaction perspective, respectively, rather than the territorial perspective.[20]

Distinguishing between the expectations of the territorial and proximity arguments is complicated by the high correlation between contiguity and territorial issues. For example, over 60 percent of the militarized disputes over territory in Table 4.3 (495 of 795) involve contiguous adversaries, suggesting that any apparent impact of territorial issues might be attributable at least in part to contiguity. To the extent that noncontiguous states engage in territorial disputes and that contiguous states engage in nonterritorial disputes, though, future research can address the competing theoretical perspectives more directly. The results of Tables 4.4 and 4.5 suggest that territorial issues produce more severe conflict behavior than other issues for both contiguous and more distant adversaries (implying that territory is a better predictor of conflict severity than contiguity) and that states involved in territorial claims are more conflictual in disputes over territorial issues than in those over other issues (implying that territory is a better predictor than interactions, since these states presumably engage in roughly similar interactions over time). Future research is urged to investigate such distinctions further, with an emphasis on cases that are consistent with only one of the competing approaches.

Future research could also benefit greatly from more precise conceptualization and measurement of issues than has typically been used in existing research. Much of the existing research on contentious issues has employed very limited conceptions of issues, often treating all territorial issues as comparable and testing whether "all territorial issues" lead to different forms of interaction than "all other issues." Realistically, though, great variation is likely both within and between issue categories. Even if "territorial" issues overall are more salient than "policy" issues, for example, there are undoubtedly some territorial issues with very low salience for decision makers and some policy issues with much higher salience. Several recent efforts have measured the salience of territorial issues by characteristics of the territory at stake, such as the area and population of the territory or the presence of valuable resources or ethnic minorities along the border area (Goertz and Diehl 1992b; Huth 1996b; Hensel 1999a). Indeed, Table 4.6 indicates that the salience of claimed territory exerts an important influence on the nature and frequency of attempts to manage or settle territorial claims. Future research on territorial issues should follow similar approaches, attempting to identify factors or characteristics that can help distinguish between more or less salient territorial issues. It would also be desirable to collect data on additional issues besides territory. The territorial explanation for conflict begins with the assumption that states manage different types of issues differently and that territory is a particularly salient and dangerous type of issue. The broader issues approach that is associated with this territorial explanation could be tested more effectively by collecting data on the scope and management of nonterritorial issues, to assess the extent to which territory is treated differently from other issues that are thought to be less salient.

A final suggestion involves the need to focus on the conditions under which states are likely to initiate overt militarized conflict, regardless of their territorial issues, proximity, or other interactions. Factors such as territorial claims and geographic proximity appear to remain largely constant from year to year, barring some infrequent type of change such as a resolution of issues or a change in borders. Yet despite this general consistency over time, most territorial claims do not lead to overt militarized conflict in most years, and most contiguous adversaries are not at war most of the time. Huth (1996b: 106), for example, finds that the territorial claims in his study remain limited to minimal or no diplomatic or political conflict in over half of the years examined. Moderate to high levels of diplomatic and political conflict occur in roughly one-third of the years in his study, while militarized confrontations occur in only 11 percent of the over three thousand years during which a territorial claim is active. Similarly, the nearly nine hundred (peaceful or militarized) settlement attempts in Table 4.6 are relatively rare events, averaging one attempt for each 5.5 years that a claim is active in the ICOW territorial claims data set. Additional factors would appear to be necessary to explain the year-to-year variations represented by such relatively rare events as escalating a claim to the level of militarized conflict or negotiating over a long-running claim.

Domestic political factors appear to offer an important part of the answer to these year-to-year variations in activity related to a relatively constant territorial claim. Huth (1996a, 1996b) finds strong results when considering the impact of domestic politics on territorial claims, with domestic factors being more important than many of the traditional realist factors in his models. Further research on the domestic political context would appear to be warranted, with an emphasis on domestic factors that change from year to year and might help capture more of the fluctuations in conflict behavior or negotiations. For example, social, political, and economic conditions within a country would appear to be relevant to leaders' decisions regarding foreign policy endeavors. Past research has found evidence that overall conflict behavior can be influenced by yearly fluctuations in economic growth (or stagnation), electoral politics, and domestic political conflict (e.g., Russett 1990). If such findings have been found to characterize overall conflict behavior against any foreign target, they may produce even stronger effects when considered against the background of a long-running territorial claim. For example, when the Argentine leadership in 1982 chose a foreign target to help rally domestic political support in a time of economic and political crisis, it does not seem accidental that the particular target chosen (the Malvinas/Falkland Islands) had been the subject of a territorial claim for well over a century.

In conclusion, recent research has examined a number of possible explanations for a possible linkage between geography and conflict. There can be little doubt that geographic factors affect relations between states, particularly with respect to the initiation and escalation of militarized conflict. Territorial claims appear to be a leading source of militarized conflict and war, increasing both the likelihood that militarized conflict will be initiated and the severity levels of the resulting confrontations, as well as influencing other forms of (bilateral and multilateral) interactions between states. Geographic proximity also accounts for over half of all militarized conflict in the last two centuries and appears to increase the likelihood of conflict severity. The impact of interactions has been more difficult to examine directly, because of the lack of appropriate data sets. To the extent that these factors have been tested comparatively, the territoriality approach has produced the strongest results, increasing conflict severity substantially even after controlling for the impact of contiguity or other measures of proximity. Future research on militarized conflict is encouraged to consider both proximity and the issues under contention, as well as to delve deeper into the interrelationship among these factors and their relative strengths and weaknesses.

NOTES

1. One could argue that generally concrete, tangible stakes such as territory might be more amenable to peaceful division and settlement than more symbolic stakes such as prestige or ideology. Yet the psychological importance of territory would seem to counter any potential advantages that might be gained from the concrete territorial object of dispute, by infusing the disputed territory with symbolic or transcendent qualities that make division more difficult (see Vasquez 1993: 77–78).

2. This table records the contiguity of the initial participants in each dispute or war, or those actors on each side that were involved from the day the dispute or war began. If all dispute or war participants are included, rather than just those who were involved from the very beginning, there is almost no change for militarized disputes, while up to 10 percent more wars involve contiguous adversaries. Table 4.1 focuses on the initial participants rather than all participants to avoid inflating the resulting figures by including dispute or war joiners, who may have entered the conflict much later for very different reasons than the initial participants (ranging from the spread of fighting across the border into neighboring states to the pursuit of political or financial gain, as with many Latin American states becoming involved in World War II or the Gulf War).

3. The two exceptions involve the Falkland/Malvinas War between Argentina and Great Britain and the Vietnam War, which is coded in the militarized dispute data set as beginning with an incident between North Vietnam and the United States (and soon spreading to involve many other countries, including contiguous South Vietnam). One may argue that Table 4.1 overstates the true relationship because an individual dispute or war may involve numerous participants, not all of whom are contiguous. When all participants are considered, a total of 40.5 percent of all dispute participants and 29.2 percent of all war participants share contiguous borders, indicating that many dispute/war joiners are major powers or other distant actors that do not share common borders with the initial participants.

4. As with Table 4.1, this table focuses on the issues at stake for the initial participants in each dispute or war. The Holsti results are produced by combining Holsti's issue types of "territory," "strategic territory," and "territory (boundary)"; Vasquez (1993) notes that adding territoriality-related issues to these explicitly territorial issues increases the proportion of wars involving territory to as high as 93 percent.

5. It is worth noting that Holsti's list of wars includes a number of cases that are not generally considered full-scale wars between nation-states. His 1945–89 list thus includes a number of internal conflicts, which would be coded as involving "national liberation/state creation," "maintain integrity of empire," or "state/nation survival" rather than territory. This list also includes a number of lower-level conflicts such as the 1983 U.S. invasion of Grenada and the 1983 U.S. involvement in Lebanon, which are technically militarized disputes rather than interstate wars. The apparent decline in territorial issues over this time period, then, may reflect the types of cases that are included in his list rather than a declining importance of territory as a source of war.

6. Lemke's original 1995 article deals with Latin America; more recent studies by the same author have produced similar results for Africa, the Middle East, and Asia.

7. Change in proximity is possible—albeit rare—with the acquisition or loss of territory due to military conquest or to the acquisition of colonies or foreign military bases.

For example, Ecuador and Brazil shared a border in the nineteenth century, although a series of diplomatic and military developments left Peruvian and Colombian territory between their current borders.

8. Similar charges could be leveled against the territorial perspective, on the grounds that territorial claims often last for many decades. Yet most territorial claims are eventually resolved, offering comparisons of interactions during and after the claim, and many claims also fluctuate over time as the adversaries resolve the ownership of portions of the claimed territory en route to a comprehensive final settlement.

9. This continued importance of contiguity may also be due to the composition of the interstate system. Most of the newly independent states since 1945 (the period during which the highest proportion of disputes and wars involved contiguous states) have been developing states, which typically lack the funding or technology to monitor and respond to events far beyond their own borders. Regardless of the overall state of communications and transportation technology, then, it is not surprising that such newly independent states continue to limit their conflictual interactions to nearby states. Such states are also likely to face substantial problems with unsettled borders, as their former colonial powers often established borders that are seen as illegitimate after independence or left borders undetermined. The increase in contiguous conflict since 1945 may reflect the influence of the territorial perspective as well as the proximity or interactions perspectives, then, although it is not clear that the proportion of conflict involving territorial issues has consistently increased since World War II.

10. These differences are most notable after decisive outcomes and stalemates, with much smaller effects after compromise outcomes—although the direction of the effect remains the same for all three outcome types, with territorial issues increasing the likelihood of recurrence.

11. Similar variables are found to increase the likelihood that a territorial claim will give rise to an enduring rivalry, including the strategic value of territory and the existence of ethnic minorities in the border area (Huth 1996a).

12. Version 2.10 of the COW dispute data set (Jones et al. 1996) is used, broken down dyadically following procedures described by Hensel (1996b).

13. The cases included in Tables 4.1 and 4.2 do not sum to 3,045 (the total number of cases in Table 4.3) because of missing data on dispute fatalities for some participants.

14. The χ^2 values and p values in Tables 4.4 and 4.5 measure the statistical significance of the relationship between an independent variable (contention over territorial issues) and a dependent variable (fatalities in a militarized dispute). Higher χ^2 values and lower p values indicate greater statistical significance, or a lower probability that the distribution of cases in the table could have been obtained by chance if the variables are actually statistically independent (Reynolds 1984).

15. Similar results are produced using alternative indicators of dispute escalation, including the likelihood of a militarized response by the target and the likelihood of escalation to full-scale war. In each case, the likelihood of escalation is much greater for territorial than nonterritorial issues regardless of the contiguity status of the adversaries.

16. The odds ratio is used to measure the substantive, rather than statistical, significance of a table. This number gives the ratio of the statistical odds of a value of the dependent variable (in this case the occurrence of fatalities in a dispute) given the value of the independent variable (Reynolds 1984). Odds ratio values of greater than 1.0 in Tables 4.4

and 4.5 indicate how much greater are the odds of fatalities in disputes that involve territorial issues than in nonterritorial disputes; a value of 2.0 indicates that the odds of fatalities are twice as great when territorial issues are at stake.

17. Roughly one-third of all disputes within territorial claims (176 of 519 of the cases in Table 4.5, or 34.0 percent) lead to fatalities, compared to 26.1 percent of disputes outside territorial claims over the 1950–90 period covered by Huth's data. This difference is statistically significant ($\chi^2 = 9.89$, 1 df, $p < .002$), and the statistical odds of fatalities are roughly one and one-half times as great for disputes occurring in the context of a territorial claim (odds ratio = 1.46).

18. All ICOW project codebooks, papers, and publicly released data sets are available on the World Wide Web at <http://www.icow.org>. Militarized conflict is identified as COW militarized disputes involving territorial issues, as reported in the earlier tables; all other settlement attempts are identified by the ICOW data set on attempted settlements of territorial claims in the Western Hemisphere.

19. Ethnic and religious bases have not been involved in any of the modern Western Hemisphere territorial claims used in this table, limiting the value of two of these indicators of claim salience. Virtually identical results are found using a preliminary version of the ICOW data on European territorial claims (some of which include explicit ethnic or religious dimensions), though, suggesting that this simple measure of claim salience appears to function quite well across different regions.

20. There is a risk that such findings could be contaminated by the influence of territorial issues. Changes in the level of proximity between two states also may result in the development of new territorial issues or the settlement of old territorial issues. Similarly, changes in the level of interactions between two states may result from the rise of new territorial issues or from changes in the level of proximity between them. Future studies must be careful to control for changes of this type.

5

Territory

Why Are Territorial Disputes between States a Central Cause of International Conflict?

Paul K. Huth

Territorial conflict has been a recu
rring feature of international politics for centuries. Recently, scholars have been conducting research on the theoretical and empirical relationships between territorial disputes and interstate military conflict. In this chapter, I review existing scholarship and develop the argument that territorial disputes are a central cause of interstate war, as claimed by some scholars (e.g., Vasquez 1993). I make three main arguments:

1. The results of empirical tests indicate a significant and strong relationship between the presence of a territorial dispute between states and the likelihood of militarized conflict and war.
2. A rational choice theoretical argument that draws on four explanatory variables can be developed to help us understand why territorial disputes are an important cause of armed conflict and war.
3. The testable implications of this theoretical argument provide a fruitful agenda for future research in which scholars examine the different causal pathways by which territorial disputes lead to international conflict.

This chapter is divided into the following sections. I first define what is meant by the term *territorial dispute* and discuss what other types of issues are often disputed between states. In the second section, I review the findings from a number of recent empirical studies that report a consistent relationship between territorial disputes and patterns of international conflict. I then turn to an analysis of theoretical arguments that might explain why territorial disputes escalate to armed conflict. I conclude by proposing an agenda for future research that focuses on developing and testing more specific hypotheses about the causal pathways by which territorial disputes escalate.

ISSUES IN DISPUTE BETWEEN STATES

What types of issues are often disputed by governments? To answer this question, I begin with the concept of a territorial dispute and then turn to other disputed issues. A territorial dispute exists when (1) two governments disagree over where their homeland or colonial borders should be fixed, or (2) one country contests the right of another to exercise any sovereign rights over some or all of its homeland or colonial territory. In either situation, both governments seek control of and sovereign rights over the same territory (Huth 1996b: chap. 2). Many territorial disputes center around conflicting claims to exactly where a border should be located. In other cases, however, the legitimacy of a border is severely questioned when one country seeks to incorporate some or all of the territory controlled by another state.[1] In Table 5.1 a summary list is provided of territorial disputes in the international system from 1919 to 1995.

What makes territory valuable to governments can include factors such as its natural resource endowment, the religious and ethnic composition of its population, or its military-strategic location. The reasons that two countries cannot agree on the exact location of a boundary or, more fundamentally, who has legitimate rights to sovereignty over territory can be quite diverse. In many disputes, the problem is rather technical and legally based as governments contest the interpretation and meaning of ambiguously written past treaties and historical documents that helped establish boundaries. In other cases, however, political conflicts stemming from deep-seated ideological and cultural differences can lead governments to seek control over territory to establish political dominance or to counter perceived political and security threats.

Throughout the remainder of this chapter, I will often make comparisons be-

Table 5.1 Territorial Disputes between States, 1919–95

		Time Period		
Region	*Number of Disputes*	*Pre-1945*	*Post-1945*	*Across Both Periods*
Europe	95	60	27	8
Middle and Near East	89	36	32	21
Africa	48	17	26	5
Asia	65	14	42	9
Americas	51	30	6	15
Total	348	157	133	58

tween territorial and other issues that are contested in international disputes; therefore, it is helpful to identify what those nonterritorial issues typically are. Drawing on the work of other scholars who have assembled data sets on international disputes, crises, and wars (e.g., Holsti 1991; Laurd 1986; Brecher and Wilkenfeld 1997b; Jones, Bremer, and Singer 1996; Sherman 1994), I would identify the following types of nonterritorial issues as often producing disputes and conflict between states:

1. Attempts by one country to destabilize politically another regime and remove its existing leadership from power. In such cases, conflicts have arisen due to differences in political ideology and/or the belief that a particular national leader poses a threat to the security of another country or its political leadership.
2. Economic conflicts relating to such issues as barriers to trade and the protection of home markets, the nationalization of foreign property and adequate levels of compensation, and compliance with bilateral and multilateral economic agreements.
3. Problems relating to cross-border movements of populations that governments find difficult to control or manage. One important set of cases revolves around large-scale refugee movements stemming from political and economic turmoil within neighboring states. A different set of issues arises over problems of illegal border crossings by citizens in one country who seek to evade existing immigration laws and establish illegal residence in another country.
4. Finally, efforts by one government to protect the rights of its citizens abroad and ensure their security when foreign governments are suspected of pursuing discriminatory policies or are unable to ensure basic law and order.

REVIEW OF EMPIRICAL STUDIES

The results of a number of recent historical and quantitative empirical studies converge on the conclusion that there is a strong correlation between territorial disputes and various types of international conflict behavior. In Figure 5.1, I summarize the main findings that indicate that territorial disputes are systematically related to the emergence and escalation of militarized confrontations between states. A variety of different types of historical evidence and data sets have been used to produce these consistent empirical results. I begin by summarizing findings that have been generated by scholars working with these multiple sources of empirical evidence.

Figure 5.1 Empirical Findings on the Relationship between Territorial Disputes and War

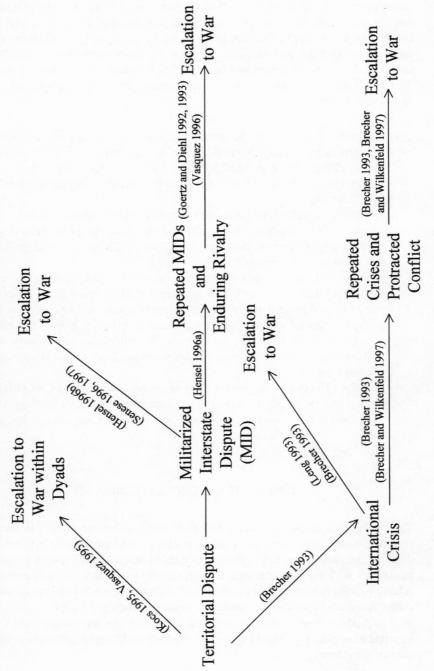

Comparative Historical Research on War and Issues at Stake

Two comparative historical studies by Holsti (1991) and Luard (1986) are particularly important because the authors have identified the issues over which states initiated wars since the inception of the modern state system in the seventeenth century. The historical evidence presented in Holsti (1991) supports the conclusion that territorial disputes have been the single most frequent issue related to the outbreak of war over the past four centuries. Holsti identifies a broad range of political and economic issues in addition to territorial conflicts in his study and he argues that multiple issues can be associated with the outbreak of an individual war. For example, Holsti (1991: 308) lists twenty-one issues other than territory that have been in dispute between states in a total of 177 wars from 1648 to 1989. Territorial issues, then, are not the only issue over which wars have been fought, but Holsti nevertheless presents strong evidence that territorial disputes, compared to other issues in dispute, are much more frequently associated with war. He (1991: 308) calculates that across five different historical periods, the percentages of wars involving territorial issues range from as high as 85 percent to no lower than 45 percent. Vasquez (1993: chap. 4) reexamines Holsti's classification of issue types and argues that he has actually understated the frequency of territorial issues; therefore, he combines some of the issue categories and concludes that territorial disputes are associated with somewhere between 80 and 90 percent of all wars (1993: 130).

Luard (1986) has also attempted to identify the issues over which states have fought wars and, like Holsti, considers a diverse set of issues such as religion, commerce and trade, national unification, ethnicity, and ideological struggles along with territorial conflicts. It is not possible to pinpoint the frequency of territorial issues as an issue related to war across historical periods since Luard does not present data on the issues at stake for each war in his survey of historical cases. Luard does argue, however, that no single issue predominates across all three periods (1648–1789, 1789–1917, 1917–83) that he examines. Nevertheless, in his discussion of cases for each historical period and from the list of cases presented in the appendix to the book, it seems that territorial claims come up again and again even when Luard argues that other issues (ethnicity and national unification) were in dispute. Thus, while Luard does not claim that territorial issues are the single most frequent issue associated with wars, his actual list of wars and his discussion of many cases indicates otherwise. I agree with Vasquez (1993: 131–32) that Luard clearly understates the frequency of territorial conflict, and I would argue that if one were to code carefully each war identified by Luard to determine whether territory was in dispute when a war was initiated, the conclusions drawn about the centrality of territorial disputes to the outbreak of war would be very similar to Holsti's. In conclusion, when wars are classified according to the issues in dispute, Holsti and Luard's historical analyses point to the same conclusion: territorial disputes have consistently been an issue that governments have been willing to go to war over.

Caution must be exercised, however, in drawing this conclusion from the research of Holsti and Luard due to one important limitation in the research design employed in their historical studies. In both cases, the scholars select only cases of wars for analysis, and therefore, while territorial disputes are correlated with the presence of war, we do not know whether the absence of war is also correlated with a relatively low frequency of territorial disputes between countries. As a result, data sets in which both war and no-war outcomes are included are necessary to examine before stronger conclusions can be drawn about the empirical relationship between territorial disputes and armed conflict.

The Militarized Interstate Dispute (MID) Data Set

This data set contains over two thousand cases of disputes between countries from 1816 to 1992 in which at least one state threatened or resorted to the use of military force but the actual outbreak of war is quite rare (Jones et al. 1996). Scholars have presented evidence from the MID data set that military escalation is more likely when territorial issues are at stake between states. Hensel (1996a) has reported that MIDs from 1816 to 1992 that involve territorial disputes are three times more likely to escalate to high levels, including war, compared to nonterritorial issues in dispute. He also notes that states that are the initial targets of militarized actions at the outset of a MID involving territory are more than three times likely to reciprocate with a military response. Thus, when state leaders are confronted with a military threat to territorial interests, they are unlikely to back away from a military confrontation. Senese (1997b) reports very similar findings to those of Hensel in his study of MID escalation to war. He finds that a territorial dispute increases the baseline probability of war by more than nine times. Senese (1996, 1997b) also examines patterns of fatality levels in MIDs, reporting that the likelihood and severity of fatalities is positively and strongly correlated with territorial issues.

Hensel (1996b: chap. 4), in his study of the evolution of enduring rivalries,[2] finds that the frequency of MIDs are much more likely if a territorial dispute exists between two countries. Other scholars, such as Goertz and Diehl (1992b, 1993), have presented strong evidence that enduring rivalries since the early nineteenth century have been much more likely to become involved in wars than nonenduring rivalries. Vasquez (1996a) has also argued that, while not all enduring rivalries escalate to war, the risks of war increase significantly if the rivals are entangled in a territorial dispute.

The Behavioral Correlates of War Data Set

Leng (1993) has constructed a data set of forty international crises from 1816 to 1980 that contains information on the diplomatic and military actions of the crisis participants. Using this data set, Leng (1993) has found strong evidence linking territorial disputes to war in his work on crisis bargaining and escalation. He reports that when states have vital or very salient security interests at stake (1993: chap. 3) the chances of escalation and war increase because states are more likely to adopt coercive bullying bargaining strategies and less likely to compromise. Vital or salient security interests in turn are defined by Leng to include disputes over control of national territory (1993: 48–49).

The International Crisis Behavior (ICB) Data Set

Brecher and Wilkenfeld (1993, 1997b) have compiled a data set on crises from 1919 to 1994 that contains over four hundred cases and includes a broad range of information on the behavior of the states involved and the attributes of each crisis. Rousseau and coauthors (1996) used the ICB data set and report that in crises from 1919 to 1988, territorial disputes are the most frequent issue at stake, comprising close to 50 percent of the cases. This finding is quite consistent with the earlier reported work of Hensel (1996b) on the greater likelihood of target states reciprocating the initial threat of force by challenger states in MIDs given a territorial dispute. In addition, the prevalence of territorial disputes in crises helps us understand why Holsti (1991) finds that so many wars involve territorial issues. Since most wars progress through stages of diplomatic conflict and then become crises that escalate militarily, it follows that if many crises center on territorial issues, then we would expect to find many wars that have escalated from crises to involve such issues as well.

Brecher and Wilkenfeld (1993, 1997b) do not directly test for the impact of territorial disputes on crisis behavior, but two findings in their work do provide support for the importance of territorial disputes. First, they identify protracted conflicts between states that produce multiple crises in their data set, and these protracted conflicts are more likely to escalate and involve armed violence than are nonprotracted conflicts. When their list of protracted conflicts is examined (Brecher 1993: 72; Brecher and Wilkenfeld 1997b: 821), it is very evident that a territorial dispute exists between states in many cases. This finding parallels the results from the MID data set that territorial disputes are highly correlated with enduring rivalries. Second, when military–security issues are at stake, crises are more likely to emerge and to escalate to high levels of violence (Brecher 1993: chap. 3), and the presence of a territorial dispute is coded as a military–security issue in the ICB data set.[3] Once again, these findings from the ICB data set on the correlation between territorial disputes and escalation and violence are very similar to the results generated by the MID data set on escalation to war and levels of fatalities.

Dyad Data Sets

Another type of data set used in empirical research on international conflict consists of pairs of states. Scholars examine the frequency of various forms of military conflict within these pairs of states over time. Kocs (1995) and Vasquez (1995b) both argue that even after taking into account geographic proximity between states, the presence of a territorial dispute between states is strongly correlated with the outbreak of war between states in a dyad. Kocs, for example, reports that war is forty times more likely among contiguous states if there is a territorial dispute within the dyad.

The range of consistent and convergent findings reported here indicates then that there is strong empirical evidence of a correlation between territorial disputes and the likelihood of militarized conflict and war between states. As presented in Figure 5.1, the presence of a territorial dispute is correlated with the escalation of MIDs, international crises, and enduring rivalries or protracted conflicts to war.

SHERFACS Data Set

The only possible exception to this pattern of consistent findings would be the results reported by Dixon (1996a) in his study of 688 international disputes from 1946 to 1984, using the SHERFACS data set (Sherman 1994). He reports that the presence of boundary or irredentist claims is not strongly related to higher levels of escalation across different phases of a dispute. Several important characteristics of the SHERFACS data set, however, lead me to the conclusion that it is very difficult to interpret the results of Dixon's study.

First, the coding scheme of SHERFACS does not specify what level of military force is used in a dispute. Instead, any use of force is classified as falling into a single phase or level of hostility for the dispute. As a result, no distinctions are made between minor or very limited uses of force and large-scale attacks associated with war. The findings of Hensel (1996b) and Senese (1997b), using the MID data set, report that escalation to war is more likely if territorial issues are in dispute, but Senese (1996) also finds that patterns of escalation short of war involving shows of force and limited uses of force do not differ significantly between territorial disputes and other issue types. As currently constructed, then, the SHERFACS data set does not directly address the question of whether territorial disputes are more likely to escalate to war compared to other issues.

Second, the SHERFACS data set divides up a single dispute into one of six possible phases according to the degree of military escalation. As a result, for any given dispute that does escalate to the phase or level of military force, the phase following the cessation of military conflict will necessarily be coded as a lower level of escalation. The result is that for any dispute involving military conflict, there will always be a negative correlation between the use of force in one phase and the level of subsequent escalation for the next phase following the termination of armed hostilities. Thus, even if territorial disputes are strongly and positively related to the outbreak of armed hostilities, they will also be strongly correlated with a subsequent deescalation phase. This pattern, then, of an upswing in escalation followed by some level of deescalation might very well produce a weak overall correlation between territorial disputes and escalation, as Dixon reports. If this is indeed how the data are coded in the Dixon study, then all of the phases immediately following the end of armed hostilities need to be removed from the data set before any valid tests can be conducted on the links between territorial disputes and patterns of escalation.

Third, a possible problem could be that the category of boundary and irredentist claims in the SHERFACS data set underreports the number of actual territorial disputes. Consequently, the correlation between territorial disputes and escalation could be weakened. In particular, the concern is that Dixon reports that ethnic/religious issues in dispute are positively related to escalation, but a number of territorial disputes arise because the territory is populated by ethnic and religious groups with ties to one country. For example, in my data set of 129 territorial disputes from 1950 to 1990, thirty cases (about 23 percent) involve conflicts in which an ethnic group is divided by existing borders and one government seeks to annex disputed territory populated by its ethnic conationals. In the SHERFACS data set, however, it is not clear whether the category of ethnic/religious issues in dispute overlaps with the category of territorial disputes. If they do not overlap, then the SHERFACS data set most likely is excluding from its set of territorial dispute conflicts with a high likelihood of escalation.

The overall conclusion, then, that I draw is that empirical work to date has produced a strong set of results. Of course, the number of empirical studies at this point is not that large so the degree of confidence one can have in drawing strong conclusions should be tempered. The only missing link in Figure 5.1 is that no empirical studies have tested and confirmed that the presence of a territorial dispute is highly correlated with the initiation of an MID. If such a test were conducted and supportive findings produced, we would then have a set of empirical findings that would establish that for each of the principal stages at which a dispute can escalate and eventually result in war, the presence of a territorial dispute strongly increases the risks of heightened conflict.

The final empirical finding to report is that while territorial disputes increase the risks of militarized conflict and war between states in a strong and consistent way, the fact remains that most territorial disputes do not involve militarized behavior or large-scale armed conflict. In my own research on 129 territorial disputes from 1950 to 1990 (Huth 1996a, 1996b), 50 percent of all such disputes did not involve any MIDs, less than 33 percent evolved into enduring rivalries, and war broke out in less than 20 percent of the disputes. As noted, I have extended my data set on territorial disputes to cover the period 1919–95, and there were 348 disputes during this time. In this larger data set, similar patterns of armed conflict are present. Thus, about 60 percent of the territorial disputes did not involve any MIDs, and war occurred in less than 20 percent of the disputes. Further evidence can be found in the MID data set that most territorial disputes do not escalate. For example, Hensel (1996b) reports that only about 7 percent of all MIDs involving territorial issues escalated to war. Finally, Goertz and

Diehl (1992a), in their study of over eight hundred territorial exchanges between states from 1816 to 1980, note that about 30 percent of all territorial transfers involved military conflict at some point in time. In conclusion, while scholars have produced strong evidence that territorial disputes compared to other issues are more likely to escalate to militarized conflict, it remains true that state leaders in most territorial disputes rely on diplomatic means to pursue their countries' interests and recognize the genuine risks of military conflict.

THEORETICAL EXPLANATIONS

What theoretical arguments can be advanced for drawing a causal connection between the presence of a territorial dispute and the increased likelihood of MIDs, crises, and war? If we refer to Figure 5.2, why would an international dispute over contested territory follow a trajectory that is more likely to result in outcomes such as 3a or 4a as opposed to 1a-1b, 4b-4c, or 2a-2b?

The prevailing argument advanced by scholars is that contested territory as a type of issue in dispute is particularly salient or important to national leaders and they are more willing, therefore, to risk armed conflict in pursuit of territorial claims. Thus, foreign policy leaders are less willing to make concessions over territorial issues and more resolved to use military force to achieve territorial goals compared to other issues that might be contested in a dispute (Hensel 1996a, 1996b; Vasquez 1993). I will argue that this line of argument by itself is insufficient and that a compelling explanation requires that additional factors be considered. Scholars are not incorrect in pointing toward issue saliency as important, but it is one part of a larger argument in which several features in combination make territorial disputes more likely to escalate to war.

Before exploring the logic of this argument in detail, I want to address what is often viewed as a counterargument to the proposition that territorial disputes are a distinctly important factor in explaining war (Vasquez 1995b). The opposing argument is that geographic proximity between states is more important than territorial disputes in explaining war. It is plausible to argue that because of proximity, state leaders are more likely to believe that military options are viable and potentially effective, thus resulting in a higher rate of military force being employed by contiguous states involved in a dispute. Numerous studies (e.g., Bremer 1992; Brecher 1993; Brecher and Wilkenfeld 1997b; Diehl 1985; Senese 1996) report strong positive correlations between proximity and various measures of dispute escalation and armed violence.

Nevertheless, this type of argument is unsatisfactory. Militarized conflict and war carry substantial risks, and I do not find it compelling to argue that the increased opportunity to use force is sufficient to explain why state leaders will resort to military means knowing the risks of such a course of action (see Siverson and Starr 1991). Recent findings from Senese (1997b) nicely illustrate this

Figure 5.2 Pathways to International Conflict Resolution and Escalation

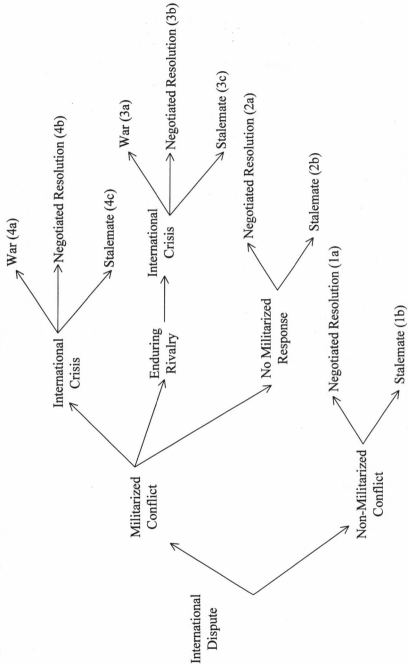

point. He reports that while proximity between states is correlated with a higher probability of escalation to war among MIDs, he also finds that the presence of a territorial dispute has a much stronger effect on the likelihood of war regardless of whether states in an MID are contiguous to one another (also see Hensel chap. 4 in this volume). The general point is that when we include in our tests variables that help explain why state leaders might be motivated and resolved to use force, we see that the empirical results are much stronger. A focus on the kinds of issues in dispute proves very helpful, then, in understanding the reasons that state leaders might risk military conflict.

Territorial disputes are undoubtedly correlated with geographic proximity between states. In my data set of 348 territorial disputes from 1919 to 1995, about 90 percent involve states whose homeland or colonial borders are contiguous. Instead of viewing proximity and territorial disputes as competing variables in empirical tests, it makes more sense to view a focus on territorial disputes as helping explicate more fully the theoretical importance of proximity as a causal factor leading to war. Proximity is related to militarized conflict and war not only because of the link to military capabilities and opportunities to use force but also because contiguous countries become involved in disputes over conflicting claims of sovereign rights to bordering territory. In this sense, then, I do not consider the variable of geographic proximity as challenging the theoretical utility of an approach that focuses on territorial disputes as a cause of war.

Why is it, then, that territorial disputes and questions of control over territory might significantly increase the risks of armed conflict and war? I would argue that four sets of reasons that, when taken together, explain why territorial disputes are more likely to result in military conflicts:

1. The high utility placed on controlling disputed territory
2. The greater capacity of foreign policy leaders to mobilize domestic support behind territorial claims
3. The appropriateness of military force as an instrument for achieving territorial goals
4. The propensity for leaders in authoritarian states to dispute territory

The combined effect of these four factors is to produce higher expected utilities for disputing and escalating territorial disputes compared to expected utilities for making concessions or accepting the status quo for challenger states (see Figure 5.3).

The Value of Territory

The first component of the argument centers on the multiple ways in which the control of contested territories would contribute to central foreign policy as well as domestic political goals of state leaders. The multidimensional benefits of se-

Figure 5.3 Expected Utility Calculations of State Leaders in Territorial Disputes

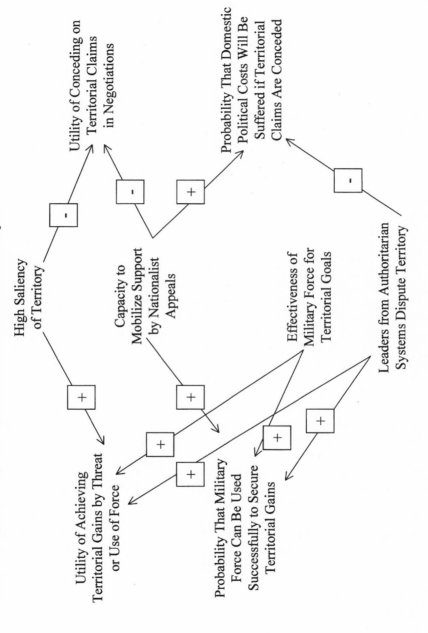

curing borders and controlling territory include military security, economic development and growth, and political goals such as national unification. Territorial
disputes often involve questions of access to and control over human and natural
resources that state leaders expect will contribute to the attainment of important
internal as well as external security goals. For example, natural resource deposits
within disputed territory hold the promise of generating considerable state reve-
nues through export sales. In other cases, control of bordering territory would
provide an effective defensive barrier to military attacks by ground forces from
a threatening country. Finally, the incorporation of neighboring territory could
unite an ethnic group within the borders of a single state that would better protect
that ethnic population from discrimination and violence by neighboring states.

Are territorial disputes, however, distinctive in that they typically include issues at stake that are highly valued by state leaders? In contrast, are other issues
such as economic disputes over trade policy or nationalization, attempts to overthrow neighboring governments, or efforts to combat terrorism against citizens
abroad less salient? I think the answers to these questions are not as clear as we
might think. I agree with the position that territorial issues are generally viewed
as quite salient, but whether territorial disputes are consistently more salient than
other issues at stake is more debatable.

For state leaders who feel threatened by the political and economic ideologies
of other regimes abroad, the goal of overthrowing such regimes could be very
salient. The concern that regimes abroad are trying to, or will have the effect of,
destablizing and possibly causing the removal of political leaders from power
cuts right to very core of issues that are of vital importance to state leaders. If we
believe that a fundamental goal of foreign policy leaders is to remain in power,
then threats to their political survival should produce a strong counterresponse
that could include a greater willingness to use military force. Put differently, as
an issue at stake, domestic security and tenure in office should be just as salient
as improving external security by the control of disputed strategic territory.

Another set of cases to consider are economic disputes, which are a common
source of conflict between governments. One could ask the question: Are economic disputes related to control of territory more conflict-prone than economic
disputes unrelated to territory? In either situation, I would argue that economic
issues are more positive-sum in nature and thus divisible and that in either case
politically powerful economic interests could pressure governments to pursue
certain economic policies. Furthermore, the economic outcomes associated with
any dispute settlement could translate into important political results for leaders
regardless of whether territory is at stake. Is there any reason to believe, then,
that the economic stakes in territorial disputes are consistently larger than the
stakes in nonterritorial based economic conflicts? I find it difficult to answer af-
firmatively.

Perhaps a stronger case for the higher saliency of territorial disputes can be
linked to disputes involving national unification and support for ethnic conation-

als in neighboring countries. Territorial disputes in these cases are often linked to larger goals of political self-determination, and self-determination has been a powerful political force since the nineteenth century. Other issues, be they economic or political-ideological rivalry, in contrast don't have that connection to questions of political self-determination. Of course, it still remains problematic to argue that territorial disputes linked to national unification and self-determination are more salient to state leaders than disputes in which leaders fear that their regime is threatened by political subversion from neighboring countries.

One possible implication would be that if the distribution of issues at stake in territorial disputes were clearly skewed toward issues of national unification, protection of ethnic nationals, or control of strategic territory, then that would help explain why territorial disputes were very likely to escalate. We don't have systematic data on the issues at stake in territorial disputes over an extended period of time, so it is not possible to draw firm conclusions on this question. In my study of 129 territorial disputes from 1950 to 1990 (Huth 1996b: 75–81), however, we find that strategic territory was at stake in twenty-five cases, national unification in thirty-six, and the protection of ethnic minorities in thirty. In total, about 71 percent of the territorial disputes (91 of 129) involved at least one of these three issues. There would seem to be some evidence, then, that territorial disputes tend to be over issues that are likely to have high saliency for state leaders.

Nevertheless, the weakness of the relative saliency argument centers on why territorial disputes would be more salient than disputes in which leaders sought to overthrow other regimes out of fear that those regimes were threats to their domestic political survival or their country's military security. Part of the answer may be due to problems of measurement in existing empirical tests that compare issue-types of territorial disputes and regime change. The MID data set contains a variable that codes whether a dispute centers on regime change (Jones et al. 1996), and scholars such as Hensel (1996a, 1996b) and Senese (1996, 1997b) have used the MID data set in their empirical analyses. A possible limitation of the MID coding scheme, however, is that it does not provide information on the country seeking to remove another regime regarding how much of a threat (internal or external security) the other regime posed to its leaders. I would suspect that if we pulled out those cases where high threats existed, then patterns of escalation for those regime change cases compared to territorial dispute cases might be quite similar.

In conclusion, the logical basis for arguing that territorial issues are generally more salient to leaders than other issues is open to question; therefore, I think that such an explanation is not sufficient to explain why territorial disputes seem to stand out as being strongly correlated with war. Instead, I would argue that the high saliency of territorial disputes is a necessary part of the explanation since saliency-type arguments establish that important issues are at stake in territorial disputes. If we understand that high stakes are involved in territorial disputes, then we would expect leaders to accept higher costs to obtain highly valued ends and also why it would be unattractive to leaders to avoid conflict by renouncing territorial claims or offering substantial concessions (see Figure 5.3). Thus, while the saliency of territorial disputes should be correlated with a higher utility for conflict and a lower utility for no conflict, it is possible to argue that other features of territorial disputes further skew expected utility calculations in favor of conflict and escalation.

Mobilization of Political Support

One such additional factor is that political leaders can draw on the language, themes, and symbols of nationalism to mobilize support for territorial claims. Compared to nonterritorial economic issues or conflicts of political ideology and regime change, I would argue that leaders can more effectively draw on popular and elite sentiments of patriotism and nationalism to justify support for territorial claims. The result is that we would expect foreign policy leaders in territorial disputes to be able to accomplish the following:

1. They should garner broader support with a unifying theme of nationalism that could enable the government to build a more durable domestic coalition in support of territorial claims. For example, by appealing to nationalism, state leaders may be able to avoid more divisive debates about whether the specific issues at stake in the territorial dispute only concern limited groups and interests in society. Similarly, by using nationalism to legitimatize claims to disputed territory, leaders may be able to convince political opponents to support the government even though they dislike government policies on other domestic and foreign policy issues. From the perspective of the domestic politics of building support for foreign policy goals, territorial disputes should provide a very favorable issue around which state leaders can mobilize and maintain support.

2. The converse of building support behind territorial claims is the ability of state leaders to be able to fight off domestic opponents who seek to challenge a government's policy. Once again, the government can use appeals to nationalism to disarm political opponents by equating opposition to territorial claims with unpatriotic behavior and by raising questions about the nationalist credentials of domestic opponents. If political opponents and aspiring leaders are generally rational and strategic, then we would expect them to criticize existing government policies when they believe the political prospects of successfully challenging the government are likely to be high and the political risks low. Opposition elites should be more cautious, then, in challenging a government over a territorial dispute, since they risk a credible threat of being attacked as unpatriotic. Furthermore, it is likely they would find considerable political support for the regime on the issue of the territorial dispute within the population and among other political elites. Given these unfavorable prospects facing opposition elites, the strategi-

cally sensible decision would be to avoid conflict on the issue of territorial claims and focus on more controversial policies being pursued by the government.

3. While nationalism can be used to mobilize domestic support and undercut political opponents, it also constrains the diplomatic options of state leaders, particularly their willingness to make territorial concessions. Having invoked nationalist principals to legitimize territorial claims, leaders open themselves up to charges of hypocrisy and deceit if they subsequently make substantial concessions to settle a territorial dispute. Thus, nationalist arguments once relied on to build support can also be used to discredit a government and its leadership. Put differently, the domestic political costs of accommodation in territorial disputes should be higher compared to most other foreign policy issues given that ruling elites are more likely to draw on nationalism to justify their policy position.

In sum, we should expect state leaders involved in territorial disputes to be more willing to accept the risks of military conflict in pursuit of territorial goals. A supportive domestic political context should exist for military action and incurring financial and military costs, since appeals to nationalism can be drawn on to convince citizens to accept such costs. If we refer to Figure 5.3, we find that territorial goals are not only highly valued, but the political prospects for using force to pursue such goals are favorable as well. Furthermore, in many territorial disputes we would expect state leaders to believe that they would be very likely to incur domestic political costs for making concessions in a territorial settlement. Thus, we see that by taking into account some aspects of the domestic political context of territorial disputes, the expected utility calculations of states are further skewed in favor of conflict over accommodation.

Utility of Military Option

The effectiveness of military force is quite high for territorial issues compared to nonterritorial issues. The occupation and taking of territory is what military organizations plan for and are trained to execute. As a result, the direct result of the successful use of military force in many armed conflicts is the ability to take control of territory. While the political utility of military force can be low for issues relating to the settlement of economic disputes over trade, refugee movements, or terrorist attacks, it is quite appropriate for the pursuit of territorial goals. The implication is that it is more likely that the military will advise political leaders in territorial disputes that armed force can be used successfully to achieve concrete military objectives and that the achievement of those military objectives will advance desired political-territorial goals.

This close link between military outcomes and political goals for territorial disputes is not as likely for disputes in which one government seeks to overthrow another. As I argued earlier, overthrowing hostile regimes may be a very salient goal for state leaders, particularly for weak or unstable regimes, but the ability of armies to use military force to ensure friendly neighboring regimes can be

quite elusive and costly. For example, military victories can force defeated leaders to flee from national capitals, but governments can function and still direct
military forces from more remote or protected regions of the country, or even
function in exile. Furthermore, when armies advance into national capitals and
the interior of countries to establish new governments, they often find themselves
vulnerable to guerilla warfare as they become committed to a longer-term military presence in support of weak governments. The new political leaders, which
have been selected by the foreign power, find it difficult to mobilize local support,
and thus the victorious army must remain to protect the regime from internal
opposition. Conversely, if a long-term military presence is rejected by the victorious side, then existing or new leaders in the defeated country are likely to have
strong domestic political incentives to oppose a conciliatory foreign policy
toward their enemy. In the first case, the military finds itself acting as an occupation force in a hostile political-military environment, whereas in the second case
military costs are reduced but political leverage over the policies of the defeated
regime have been weakened.

While it is true that the military defeat of another country increases the
chances of the defeated leaders being removed (Bueno de Mesquita, Siverson,
and Woller 1992; Bueno de Mesquita and Siverson 1995), it is less clear that
changes in leaders represent a change in regime ideology or basic policies. The
general point is that the large-scale use of military force to try to overthrow
threatening neighboring governments and replace them with new compliant leaders is a policy that military organizations are weary of pursuing. The reason for
this is that the invasion of territory and the establishment of a long-term military
presence risks provoking defiance and a political backlash against groups cooper-
ating with a foreign military power. A preferred policy for military leaders would
be to provide training, financial support, and weapons to domestic opponents of
a foreign regime with the hope that hostile regimes could be toppled by armed
insurgencies and coups carried out by these foreign groups. This strategy would
suggest, then, that even when state leaders attach considerable importance to
overthrowing regimes, we would not necessarily expect that large-scale military
force involving their own armed forces would be relied upon. This may help explain why disputes over regime change are not as likely to escalate to war as
territorial disputes, even though the issues at stake may be highly salient to state
leaders.

Authoritarian States as Challengers

The final argument is that territorial disputes are more likely to escalate to wars
because leaders from authoritarian governments are more likely to pursue
changes in the territorial status quo than leaders from democratic states, and leaders in authoritarian systems face fewer domestic constraints and risks in resorting
to the use of force. Thus, in territorial disputes we typically find leaders who are

more willing to gamble on the risky option of military force because they operate in a domestic political environment that makes it more difficult for political opponents to hold leaders accountable for failed or costly uses of force in pursuit of territorial claims.

The work of Randolph Siverson and Bruce Bueno de Mesquita (1996) is very useful in building the foundation for this argument. They argue that nondemocratic leaders should enter into interstate disputes concerning private goods more frequently than democratic leaders who should be predisposed to become involved in conflicts over issues with greater public goods characteristics. They argue that territorial disputes often involve private goods, while disputes over regime change are focused on public goods. Thus, authoritarian states should be involved in more territorial disputes, while democratic states should be involved in disputes over regime change, and their empirical results using the MID data set confirm this. In my data set of 129 territorial disputes from 1950 to 1990, challenger states are largely democratic in only about twenty cases, or about 16 percent (Huth 1996b: 136–37), which is consistent with the expectations of Bueno de Mesquita and Siverson. Furthermore, if my empirical test of territorial dispute initiation is reanalyzed by including a variable that codes whether a challenger state is democratic or not, we find that democratic challengers are less likely to initiate territorial disputes.[4] The argument that nondemocratic leaders are more capable of withstanding domestic opposition following military setbacks is confirmed by other studies by Bueno de Mesquita and Siverson (Bueno de Mesquita et al. 1992; Bueno de Mesquita and Siverson 1995). In their empirical analyses of regime duration and leadership survival after military defeats in war, they report that while all regimes and leaders are more politically vulnerable after defeat in war, the probabilities of regime change and leadership turnover are greater for democratic countries.

Two general implications for patterns of escalation in territorial disputes follow if we refer to Figure 5.3. First, the lower domestic risks associated with the use of force is positively related to a higher net utility for pursuing territorial claims, since fewer expected domestic costs have to be subtracted from expected gains. Second, authoritarian leaders may be more willing than democratic leaders to initiate the use of force in situations where the military prospects of success are more uncertain, since they face fewer domestic risks following the use of force. This does not imply that authoritarian leaders should consistently escalate the use of force in the face of an unfavorable military balance but only that they might be more risk-acceptant in situations where expected benefits are high but military options are more limited.

Problems of Commitment and Misrepresentation

While I have argued that several features of territorial disputes in combination skew expected utility calculations in favor of escalation, a different approach would shift the analysis to questions of strategic misrepresentation or problems of credible commitments to negotiated settlements as possible explanations. Fearon (1995) in particular has argued that problems of misrepresentation and the commitment to honor agreements are two powerful general explanations for why countries cannot resolve some disputes short of armed conflict and war.

Fearon does not focus on territorial disputes in his analysis, and he is not attempting to explain why territorial disputes might be more prone to war than other disputed issues. Instead, he is proposing a more general argument about why war arises, and I am interested in the question of whether his argument can help us understand why territorial disputes are more likely to escalate to war. If I apply the general logic of Fearon's argument to territorial disputes, I am not convinced for several reasons that they are particularly useful for answering the question we are addressing here.

First, is it logical to argue that state leaders in territorial disputes would be distinctly prone to strategic misrepresentation of their interests and military capabilities to maximize their chances of a favorable settlement? If strategic misrepresentation were unusually common in territorial disputes, that would help explain a higher incidence of crises and wars. A possible explanation for a very high rate of misrepresentation in territorial disputes would be that their high saliency causes leaders to use misrepresentation more frequently to achieve highly desired goals. Thus, high saliency of an issue in dispute would be correlated with a high rate of strategic misrepresentation. The problem, however, is, as I argued earlier, that I am not convinced that territorial disputes are consistently more salient than other issues that are often contested in international disputes. If several other issues are salient as well, then substantial differences in the frequency of misrepresentation would be unlikely when we compare territorial disputes to other issues. My concern with the Fearon-type argument is not that strategic misrepresentation would not hinder the peaceful settlements of territorial disputes but that such problems are probably not significantly more prevalent in territorial disputes compared to other issues.

Second, different pieces of empirical evidence suggest that commitment problems in territorial disputes are not distinctly acute. Put differently, do potential territorial settlement agreements often break down because the states involved have a very difficult time credibly committing to such agreements? Three sets of empirical findings raise questions about the explanatory power of such an argument:

1. The historical record since the early nineteenth century indicates that a clear majority of territorial agreements that were signed to delimit and demarcate borders have not been broken and subsequently rejected by states. For example, previously I have reported (Huth 1996b: 92) that 89 percent of territorial agreements signed between 1816 and 1990 were in force in 1995 with states complying with the terms of the agreement. Overall, the

record of state compliance with territorial dispute settlements does not seem obviously low and may even be high compared to other types of agreements—arms control, for example.

2. Gibler (1996; also see chap. 7 in this volume) reports that of the twenty-seven interstate alliances formed that were linked to territorial settlements from 1816 to 1980, in none of them did the states renege on the terms of the territorial settlement during the life of the alliance. While the empirical evidence reported in this chapter indicates that in practice state leaders often do honor territorial settlement agreements, it could nevertheless still be true that state leaders perceive or believe that other states are unreliable in abiding by the terms of agreements. If that were true, then problems of credible commitments could still hinder the settlement of territorial disputes.

3. The findings of Hensel (1996a) and Dixon (1996a) that territorial disputes are associated with higher rates of compromise and negotiated settlements, however, seem contrary to this last argument just presented. If leaders' perceptions are that other states will often renege on the terms of a territorial agreement, then we would not expect leaders in territorial disputes to conclude compromise agreements at relatively high rates compared to other types of issues that are disputed.

The finding that territorial disputes are more likely to result in negotiated agreements involving some degree of compromise may also not be consistent with some of the arguments I have previously discussed about the high saliency of territorial issues or the domestic political risks of making concessions over territorial claims. Before such a conclusion is warranted, however, we need to think more carefully about what we should expect to find. It might be argued, for example, that a higher rate of more formal negotiated agreements over territorial issues would not actually be that surprising. This may in fact reflect the saliency of territory and the desire of state leaders to get other countries to explicitly state their willingness to make concessions and accept particular definitions of boundary lines. Such formal documents and treaty texts can also be used by one country to put another state's bargaining reputation for reliability at risk if that country attempts to repudiate a prior agreement. In this context, formal agreements and written documents can serve as a basis of evidence to substantiate claims in the event that a dispute arises over the terms of an existing treaty. Furthermore, it may be that some form of negotiated agreement in territorial disputes is often reached only after armed conflict has occurred or in anticipation of violence. Thus, I have reported (Huth 1996b: chap. 6) that while challenger states are generally reluctant to make territorial concessions, following military defeats the likelihood of making concessions increases. This suggests that it may be important to understand the pattern of conflict that preceded the signing of an agreement in a territorial dispute. For example, it may be that Hensel and Dixon are picking up the fact that after armed hostilities occur, cease-fire agreements are often signed and that the terms of cease-fire agreements are coded as constituting some form of compromise even though no actual territorial settlement is reached. Finally, the Dixon and Hensel findings do not tell us how long it takes a territorial dispute compared to other disputed issues to reach a settlement. Thus, while it may be true that MIDs involving territorial disputes are more likely to end in some form of a negotiated compromise agreement, it may also still be true that it takes longer in general for territorial disputes to be settled by compromise or concessions than other issues. For example, in my study (Huth 1996b: 141, 144), I found that concessions were offered in only about 16 percent of the years that challenger states were involved in territorial disputes but that about 40 percent of all territorial disputes were resolved by concessions or compromise. Thus, it could be that the outcome of a negotiated settlement is more frequent for territorial disputes but that the time required to reach such a settlement is longer.

FUTURE RESEARCH

In this concluding section, I would like to outline an agenda for future research on territorial disputes by discussing a number of hypotheses that follow from the four central arguments presented in the previous section. If we start with the basic logic associated with each of these arguments, what types of diplomatic and military behavior would we expect to observe that would result in a higher likelihood of armed conflict and war? What are the causal pathways that would account for the generally strong and consistent empirical findings reported by scholars linking territorial disputes to conflict escalation? Some of the hypotheses I present will focus on comparisons between territorial disputes and other types of international disputes regarding conflict behavior, while other hypotheses are directed at explaining differences in conflict behavior only among territorial dispute cases. The hypotheses presented here are by no means exhaustive; instead, I offer examples of what kinds of hypotheses can be derived from the general arguments outlined in the previous section. My goal, then, is to suggest possible avenues for future theoretical and empirical work.

If territorial disputes are quite salient to state leaders, then a number of implications would seem to follow:

H1:   The period of time required before challenger states make concessions to settle a dispute should be greatest for those territorial disputes in which strategic issues are at stake or when they center on questions of political self-determination and national unification.

H2:   For those territorial disputes in which strategic issues are at stake or that center on questions of political self-determination and national unification, state leaders should be less likely to agree to various forms of third-party arbitration and adjudication.

H3: For those territorial disputes in which strategic issues are at stake or for those that center on questions of political self-determination and national unification, strategies of issue linkage and side payments should prove less effective in reaching a negotiated settlement.

H4: The propensity of democratic state leaders to accept compromise settlements to territorial disputes should be relatively low when strategic issues are at stake or when they center on questions of political self-determination and national unification.

Hypothesis 1 argues that the duration of territorial disputes should be a function of how salient the issues are at stake. We would expect state leaders to resist concessions on important issues for a longer period of time since they would prefer to avoid the domestic political risks of such a policy. The second hypothesis posits that the willingness of leaders to turn to more binding conflict resolution procedures should be inversely related to the saliency of issues in dispute. Hypothesis 3 argues that side payments and the strategy of offering to an adversary offsetting gains on nonterritorial issues in return for territorial concessions should not be highly effective. The reason is that securing gains on other issues may very well be viewed by the adversary as insufficient compensation for failing to achieve gains with regard to salient territorial goals. Given the high saliency of territorial issues, it should be more difficult to locate alternative issues that will be attractive enough to an adversary that its leaders can be induced to trade-off territorial losses with nonterritorial gains. Finally, Hypothesis 4 argues that while democratic institutions and norms should induce leaders to move toward negotiated settlements of disputes, we would still expect to find that democratic leaders would be least forthcoming in offering compromise solutions when salient issues are contested.

If we focus on the relatively high utility of using military force to achieve territorial goals, several additional hypotheses can be proposed:

H5: Compared to international disputes that center on efforts by one country to overthrow a neighboring regime, the use of force in territorial disputes should more frequently involve regular armed forces engaging in large-scale military operations. In contrast, for cases of attempted regime change, leaders should more frequently resort to the indirect use of force by supporting armed insurgencies and rebel attacks.

H6: Compared to other international disputes, territorial disputes should be characterized by a higher likelihood of arms races between states.

H7: Compared to other international disputes, changes in the status quo in territorial disputes should more frequently be due to the successful use or threat of military force by challenger states.

In Hypothesis 5, the argument is that while military means may be turned to frequently in both types of disputes, the critical difference will be that conventional military attacks will be more appropriate to seizing disputed territory than in attempting to overthrow foreign governments. Hypothesis 6 is premised on the logic that if conventional military operations are best suited to seizing or defending territory, then state leaders involved in a territorial dispute should have strong incentives to build up their military capabilities and to counter threats posed by an adversary's increasing military strength. Hypothesis 7 posits that since military force is well suited to seizing disputed territory, we would expect changes in the status quo to be accomplished by military actions more frequently in territorial disputes.

If territorial disputes are both highly salient to state leaders and leaders believe that military force is particularly effective for achieving territorial goals, then we might argue as follows:

H8: Compared to other international disputes, the pathway to compromise settlements in territorial disputes should be characterized by a high incidence of prior military conflicts and/or threats of force between states.

H9: Compared to other international disputes, territorial disputes should be characterized by a higher likelihood of state leaders resorting to militarized behavior in support of negotiations and diplomatic initiatives.

H10: Compared to other international disputes, territorial disputes should be characterized by a higher likelihood of state leaders resorting to militarized behavior following the failure of negotiations and diplomatic initiatives.

Each of these hypotheses is premised on the logic that (1) high saliency should help convince leaders that the risks of military conflict are worth accepting and (2) military threats and the use of force are often credible means by which to support diplomatic efforts.

The next set of hypotheses focuses on the ability of foreign policy leaders to mobilize political support behind territorial claims:

H11: Compared to other international disputes, domestic opposition groups and their leaders should less frequently challenge government policy in territorial disputes.

H12: Compared to other international disputes, when domestic opposition groups and leaders do challenge government policy in territorial disputes, their policies should be more hawkish than the regime's.

H13: Compared to other international disputes, governments should be more capable of maintaining elite and public support for territorial goals despite greater financial costs and military risks.

The common argument supporting Hypotheses 11 and 12 is that ruling elites can use nationalism to deter political opposition from challenging their policies in territorial disputes. As a result, if opposition groups are going to criticize the government's policies, they will most likely claim that the government's policies are not tough enough and are too accommodative. Hypothesis 13 proposes that state leaders can effectively use appeals to nationalism and patriotism to legitimize and sustain popular support for territorial claims even when the pursuit of such claims impose greater economic burdens and result in greater loss of life due to more frequent military conflicts. In contrast, for other disputes if economic and military costs are suffered, then support for regime policy should be less stable and more difficult to sustain.

The final set of hypotheses is derived from the argument that leaders from authoritarian regimes are more likely to be involved in territorial disputes:

H14: Among territorial dispute cases, leaders of authoritarian regimes should more frequently initiate MIDs and escalate them to large-scale armed conflicts than should democratic leaders.

H15: Among territorial disputes, those cases in which the military prospects of using force are most uncertain should be the cases in which the sharpest differences should exist between leaders of authoritarian and democratic regimes regarding the likelihood of initiating and escalating military conflicts.

H16: Among territorial disputes, leaders of authoritarian regimes should be more likely to engage in major reversals of policy in which unilateral concessions are made than should democratic leaders.

These final three hypotheses all draw on the argument that since authoritarian leaders are in a better position to suppress political opposition, they are more likely to pursue risky military and diplomatic policies. As a result, the domestic political risks of a military or diplomatic defeat should have less of a deterrent effect on the decisions of authoritarian leaders.

Collectively, these hypotheses provide an agenda for future research since existing empirical work has been concentrated on determining whether a relationship exists between territorial disputes and various outcomes associated with international conflict such as enduring rivalries, crisis escalation, and war. Scholars, however, have not tested for the more specific causal steps and processes that produce such international outcomes. These hypotheses and their supporting logic represent potentially new and more fully developed explanations for patterns of conflict among territorial disputes and other types of international disputes. Hopefully, these hypotheses will stimulate new empirical tests and encourage other scholars to refine existing arguments and develop new and more compelling theoretical explanations.

NOTES

This work draws on material presented in Paul Huth, "Territorial Disputes and International Conflict," in *Borderlands under Stress,* ed. Gerald Blake and Martin Pratt (London: Kluwer Law International, forthcoming).

1. It is important to recognize that my use of the term *territorial dispute* does not imply that a disagreement between governments over territory necessarily involves military conflict. In fact, of the 348 territorial disputes referred to in Table 5.1, more than 50 percent never involved any type of militarized dispute or conflict.

2. Enduring rivalries are defined by Hensel (1996b: chap. 1) to include a high frequency of MIDs over an extended period of time.

3. In this chapter, one of the hypotheses tested by Brecher is that multiple issues in a crisis should lead to a greater risk of crisis initiation, escalation, and violence. The results in reported in the tables, however, do not support this hypothesis but do support the hypothesis that military–security issues are correlated with patterns of crisis initiation and escalation.

4. Specifically, if the equation reported in my prior work (Huth 1996b: 72, Table 3) is reanalyzed by adding a variable that measures how democratic the challenger state is, the logit coefficient for this new variable is negative and significant ($b = -0.026$, t ratio $= -4.92$).

6

Alliances
The Street Gangs of World Politics—Their Origins, Management, and Consequences, 1816–1986

Zeev Maoz

Research on international alliances is one of the major branches of security studies, because alliances are one of the principal instruments for the management of national security. Alliances are used as a device for extending a nation's power beyond (or in substitution of) its internal resources. Thus, alliances are taken by national decision makers both as a means for ensuring peace through deterrence and as a vehicle for building of war-winning capability through the pooling of resources of two or more nations (Ward 1982). The literature on alliances can be divided into three related subsets, which differ in terms of the questions they attempt to address:

1. *The origins of alliances.* This subset deals with the factors that cause states to enter alliances. Because the entry into alliance involves some trade-offs— the most common of which is that between security and autonomy (Altfeld 1984)—the factors that affect such decisions serve as an important source for the understanding of how states deal with security problems in an anarchic world (Walt 1987).
2. *The management of alliances.* Once nations enter into alliances, they must decide whether, when, how, and in what ways they invoke the terms of the alliances. In addition, in some cases, alliances entail some maintenance costs, and the distribution of such costs over allies is also a matter of concern.
3. *The consequences of alliances.* Here the key questions concern the relations between alliances and war. In particular, studies are concerned with issues of whether alliances serve their purpose; that is, are alliances established as

a deterrent of war—indeed, as an instrument of deterrence? Do alliances increase or decrease the likelihood of war involvement of their members? Are states aligned with each other more, less, or as likely to fight each other than nonaligned states? What is the relationship between the alliance structure of the international system and its level of conflict and war?

Most studies dealing with international alliances focus on one aspect of the dynamics of alliances, but not on others. For example, studies looking at alliance initiation do not examine their consequences. Studies examining alliance maintenance and alliance reliability do not explicitly relate those factors to the origins of alliances. Research on the impact of alliances on conflict and war rarely combines this issue with the questions of alliance origins. However, in my view, it is impossible to divorce the consequences of alliances from the origins of the alliances. I believe that the lack of integration of these three aspects of alliance politics is probably one of the chief reasons for the state of knowledge on alliances in world politics, a topic to which I return in the concluding section. For now, however, I wish to examine some issues related to these three aspects of international alliances. I focus on three main questions:

1. What factors affect the formation of alliances? Why, and under what circumstances, would a state seek alliance partners? Why would two states form an alliance?
2. What factors affect the persistence of alliances? What are the conditions under which alliances continue to exist over time? What factors determine when an alliance would terminate?
3. What are some of the consequences of alliances? Specifically, how do alliances affect other types of national security behavior, particularly military allocations and conflict behavior?

Obviously, these questions constitute only a small subset of the issues concerning alliances in world politics. But they seem to be the most frequently studied and debated ones. Thus, a review of the state of the art in alliance politics must inevitably deal with these questions.

This chapter is organized as follows. First, I discuss the theoretical and empirical literature dealing with alliance formation. I examine the general arguments about the conditions and factors that determine when and why states form alliances. Next I discuss some of the factors that affect alliance duration. Questions about the operation of alliances and the maintenance costs (e.g., Olson and Zeckhauser 1966) are discussed but not examined empirically here.[1] I then examine some of the consequences of alliances, in particular the effect of alliances on military allocations and on international conflict.

In each of the cases, I attempt to address the question of whether different types of states exhibit different alliance-related behaviors. In those sections, I bring to bear new empirical evidence. Finally, I discuss the various controversies in this literature and suggest some directions for future research aimed at resolving some or all of them.

ALLIANCE FORMATION

An *alliance* is a formal agreement between or among states stipulating a manner of consultation or joint action in a number of prespecified contingencies (Maoz 1990: 193). As noted, an alliance is seen as a strategy for expanding a state's power beyond its resource limits. However, joining an alliance results in some degree of autonomy loss because the alliance treaty specifies circumstances in which the focal state is required to use, or prohibited from using, its own power that are not under the direct control of the state. The stronger the commitment made by a state, the more autonomy loss is involved (Altfeld 1984).

The standard classification of formal alliances is that of Singer and Small (1966), consisting of defense pacts, nonaggression treaties, and ententes. *Defense pacts* are formal treaties in which each state vows to defend its allies in the event of the attack on one of them. *Nonaggression treaties* commit the parties against attacking each other. *Ententes* involve a policy of consultation on matters of mutual concern. Obviously, defense pacts involve more security and more autonomy loss than nonaggression treaties, and nonaggression treaties entail more security and more autonomy loss than ententes (Maoz 1997b).[2]

Alliance formation is seen as a major item in the repertoire of nations' strategic responses to security-related challenges in an anarchic world. However, being one item in this menu, it may not always the most preferred one. Indeed, if a state can meet these challenges through the use of its own internal capabilities, for example, through allocation of human and material resources to defense, then it may prefer that option to the formation of international alliances. This makes the state more self-sufficient in terms of the provision of security to its people. It also ensures a greater degree of autonomy over when and how to deploy and use these resources. Thus, from some perspectives, a hypothesized trade-off exists between a state's relative security, as measured by military capabilities, and its inclination to form or join international alliances. The safer a state feels when comparing its capabilities to the capabilities of a strategic reference group, the less inclined it is to enter alliances (Maoz 1997b).

However, this logic may apply differently in different political systems. For example, in democracies, alliances may be preferred—under certain domestic circumstances—to internal military allocations as a strategy of security management. Because the public does not like paying for defense out of its own pockets or sacrificing its time and life for serving in the armed forces, political leaders may opt for alliances because these entail less direct internal cost.

Walt (1987) examines the literature on the origins of alliances—more specifically, the explanations of alliance formations that are firmly grounded in the realist and neorealist tradition. He explores two competing conceptions of alliances: balance of power and balance of threats. He rejects the notion that alliances are formed in a *bandwagoning* fashion—that is, states joining existing coalitions to enjoy the spoils of the coalition either in terms of added security or in terms of the spoils of wars waged by these coalitions. His empirical research of alliances in the Middle East leads him to conclude that alliances are formed not to balance capabilities but rather as a device for countering threats (cf. Sorokin 1994).

Maoz (1997b) offered a model of national alliance formation that combines both internal and external determinants of alliances. In addition, the model offers a specific distinction between the effects of strategic factors and the effects of political factors on the extent and type of nations' alliance commitments. This study examined alliance formation as part of a more complex causal model of strategic behavior in which states' choices of response to environmental and internal challenges include military allocation and conflict initiation in addition to alliance formation. Here I replicate that analysis focusing exclusively on alliance formation. The principal factors incorporated in the model as potential determinants of alliance choices of states include the following:[3]

STRATEGIC FACTORS

1. *The number of states making up the focal state's politically relevant international environment (PRIE).* The larger that number, the more alliances is the focal state expected to seek.
2. *The ratio of the military capability of the focal state to the overall military capabilities of states making up its PRIE.* The higher that ratio, the less threatened is the focal state likely to feel, thus the fewer alliance commitments is it expected to seek. (This corresponds to the balance-of-capabilities notion of alliance formation; Walt 1987).
3. *The number of alliance commitments of states composing one's PRIE, which exclude the focal state.* The more alliances are formed in the state's *PRIE*, the more insecure the focal state is likely to feel, hence the more it would seek to enhance its security, inter alia, through alliance formation of its own. (This may correspond to both the balance of capability and to the balance of threats notion).
4. *The level of conflict in the focal state's PRIE (not involving the focal state).* The more conflict in the PRIE, the more unstable the system, hence the more likely is the focal state to seek security through alliance. (This appears to correspond to the balance-of-threat notion.)
5. *The number of conflicts directed at the focal state.* The more conflict is directed toward the focal state, the more threatened it is likely to feel, hence the more alliances it would seek. (This clearly reflects a balance-of-threat motivation for alliance formation.)

POLITICAL FACTORS[4]

1. *Regime score.* Democracies, as noted earlier, may have a stronger incentive to achieve security through alliances. This is so principally due to domestic reasons; alliance-based security is seen as a substitute to security based on internal resources. Autocracies seek security more through reliance on their own resources, because these resources serve both internal (i.e., regime support) and external functions.

2. *Regime persistence.* States that have undergone major political changes feel increasingly insecure in the initial postrevolutionary period (Maoz 1989, 1996); thus, the more likely they are to seek alliances. States with durable political systems, on the other hand, feel, ceteris paribus, less threatened by their surrounding international environment and thus are more concerned with autonomy than with security through alliance.

3. *Revolutionary change in the state's PRIE.* The more revolutionary political changes in the states making up one's PRIE, the less secure the focal state feels, thus the more likely it is to seek security through alliance formation. (This may correspond to notions of balance of threats, especially given Walt's [1996] later notions on revolutions and war.)

4. *Level of democratization in the state's PRIE.* The more democratic one's PRIE, the less threatened it would feel, thus the less likely it is to seek security through alliances.

STRUCTURAL INTERSTATE DIFFERENCES

1. *The alliance behavior of democracies is different from that of nondemocracies.* Democracies regard alliances as primarily defensive or deterrent instruments of policy. On the other hand, autocracies use alliances as offensive as well as defensive instruments. These functions of alliances may account for the differences in the effects of various factors on the incentives to form alliances.

2. *The alliance behavior of major powers differs significantly from that of minor powers.* The incentives and calculations of alliances by major powers are similar to those of democratic states, while the incentives and calculations of alliance formation of major powers are similar to those of nondemocratic states.

The nation-level analysis of alliance formation focuses on the number of alliances of a state and their type as the principal dependent variable. This analysis examines the kinds and number of allies that a state seeks as a function of strategic and political inputs. This analysis is a pooled time-series analysis of volumes and types of national alliance commitments over time.[5]

Table 6.1 provides the results of the analysis of the nation-level alliance formation hypotheses.This table suggests several things about the factors that account

Table 6.1 Determinants of Weighted National Alliance Commitments, 1816–1986, and Cross-Sectional Time-Series Regression with Panel-Corrected Standard Errors

Independent Variable	All States	Democracies	Nondemocracies	Major/ Regional Power	Minor Powers
Number of states in PRIE	0.059** (0.005)	0.095** (0.009)	0.050** (0.005)	0.070** (0.015)	0.063** (0.010)
Capability ratio, state-to-PRIE	3.811* (1.668)	3.291 (2.347)	3.382** (1.175)	− 1.571 (4.684)	− 3.630** (1.254)
Proportion of alliance commitments in PRIE	0.113** (0.027)	0.284** (0.041)	0.129** (0.028)	1.296+ (0.797)	0.104** (0.016)
Proportion of conflicts in PRIE	− 0.122** (0.028)	− 0.093+ (0.051)	− 0.124** (0.031)	− 0.923** (0.372)	− 0.096** (0.017)
Number of MIDs directed at focal state	− 0.104** (0.030)	0.117 (0.076)	− 0.172** (0.031)	− 0.140 (0.135)	− 0.100* (0.022)
Proportion of revolutionary changes in PRIE	0.537** (0.187)	0.087 (0.454)	0.728** (0.206)	3.254 (2.459)	0.409** (0.114)
Proportion of democracies in PRIE	0.493** (0.198)	1.257** (0.386)	0.537** (0.217)	0.324 (3.043)	0.489** (0.119)
Regime score of state	0.002* (0.001)	0.009* (0.004)	− 0.001 (0.001)	0.006 (0.007)	0.001 (0.001)
Persistence of regime	0.001 (0.002)	− 0.013** (0.003)	− 0.008** (0.002)	− 0.001 (0.009)	− 0.001 (0.001)
R^2	0.460	0.100	0.350	0.038	0.064
N	7,867	2,564	5,296	929	6,946
Number of states	148	72	124	9	146

Note: Democratic/nondemocratic breakdown at regime = 0.

+ $.05 \leq p < .10$.

* $.01 \leq p < .05$.

** $p < .01$.

for alliance formation and alliance initiation. These results can be summarized by the following points.

1. The size of a state's strategic reference group has a consistently positive effect on alliance commitments. The more states that make up one's strategic reference group, the larger the number of alliance commitments of the focal state, and the more likely the state is to initiate new alliances. This seems intuitive, as the problems of national security tend to mount with the number of states that form one's strategic reference group.
2. The proportion of democracies in the PRIE of a state has a consistently positive impact on its propensity to form alliances. While the findings of this variable are identical for both democracies and nondemocracies, I suggest that two different factors are at work here. For nondemocracies, a high

proportion of democracies indicates a growing level of threat, and thus the tendency to address these threats via alliance formation increases. For democracies, just the opposite happens. A high proportion of democracies in their PRIE creates an opportunity to deal with security problems outside the democratic network (Maoz 2000) through alliance formation. However, it is important to note that this is a speculation. The findings neither prove nor disprove this claim.

The relations of the other variables to the dependent variables exhibit some important variations across strata:

1. In the general population, in the case of both alliance commitments and alliance initiation, the higher the capability ratio of the focal state to its PRIE, the more alliance commitments it tends to have. For democracies, the effect of capability ratios on alliance formation is not statistically significant. The same holds for the effect of capability ratios on the alignment pattern of major powers. For the minor power subpopulation, this effect is negative and significant. This runs against previous findings about a possible alliance–capability trade-off (Maoz 1997b). However, the explanation for that is primarily methodological. Military capabilities here are treated as exogenous variables. In fact, they are endogenous and tend to exhibit a negative nonrecursive relationship with alliances.

2. The alliance commitments of other states in one's strategic reference group have a significantly positive effect on the weighted number of alliance commitments of the focal state. This suggests that the focal state tends to respond to alliance formation in its strategic environment by similar behavior.

3. The rate of conflicts in states' politically relevant international environment (PRIE),[6] which do not involve them, had a generally negative effect on the number and types of alliance commitments of states.

4. The average number of conflicts directed at the focal state in the previous three-year period had a generally negative impact on the weighted number of alliance commitments of the state. I discuss the reasons for that later.

5. The proportion of revolutionary political changes in the state's PRIE had a positive effect on the magnitude of alliance commitments in the general population, for nondemocracies, and for minor powers. However, the alliance formation process of democracies and major powers does not appear to be sensitive to revolutionary changes in these states' PRIEs.

6. The regime score of a state had a significant positive effect on the magnitude of alliance commitments of states in the general population and on the alignment patterns of democracies.

Clearly, some of these findings go against conventional wisdom and against previous findings regarding national alliance portfolios. To account for them, it is important to realize that the study of national alliance behavior, while useful, is somewhat limited. It takes two to tango in alliance politics. A major link missing from the analysis of alliance behavior of nations is the analysis of the factors making up alliances at the dyadic level. While we may have some reasonable grasp on the factors affecting individual states' alliance formation patterns, the real question concerns the calculus of "who aligns with whom." In dealing with this question, we must examine the "push-and-pull" syndrome of alliances at the dyadic level.

The "push" factor of alliance formation is expressed in a set of national calculations for seeking alliances as a device of furthering or preserving national security goals. These calculations may include factors considered earlier in this chapter or other factors not considered here, but they refer to questions regarding the conditions and factors pushing states to form alliances. These also include the security–autonomy dilemma (Morrow 1991); substitution effects (Most and Siverson 1987; Morrow 1993; Gartzke and Simon 1998), and other kinds of alliance-seeking behavior as expressions of affinity. These factors may determine the effort that a state puts into alliance formation diplomacy. They may not be good predictors of the success of such diplomacy.

In fact, it is quite conceivable that some of the factors that drive a given state to seek security through alliances are the very same factors that render other states reluctant to form an alliance with it. This is the "pull" factor in the alliance process. For example, a state that lives in a dangerous, politically and strategically unstable international environment may be pushed to seek security through aligning with members outside its strategic region. However, external powers may be reluctant to align with it precisely because such a state is a prime candidate for alliance paradoxes and is likely to get them involved in conflicts which are not their own.

The push-and-pull factors may work the other way around as well. A factor or characteristic of a state that makes it reluctant to enter alliance may be the very same factor or characteristic that renders it a desirable alliance partner. For example, democracies are considered to be reliable alliance partners because—by virtue of their domestic norms of consistency and adherence to contractual obligations—they are more likely to fulfill their treaty obligations. Thus, democracies may be reluctant to enter into alliances for fear that they would be dragged into unwanted conflict. But this image of reliability may render democracies more desirable alliance partners than nondemocracies.

To get a better sense of the push-and-pull syndrome in dyadic settings, it is important to examine the "who allies with whom" question. But this question is only part of the issue, because the question of when two states decide to become allies is of no less importance, given that some attributes of the dyad or of its members change over time. To answer these questions, an analysis of alliance formation was performed on a population of politically relevant dyad-years ($N = 67, 117$), over the period from 1816 to 1986.[7] The dependent variable here is the initiation of an alliance between two politically relevant dyads (*ALLYINIT*). This variable is coded 1 for any given dyad year that represented the first year of a dyadic alliance and 0 otherwise (thus, all subsequent years for which this alliance persisted are censored).[8]

Several variables were examined as potential predictors of alliance initiation, alliance persistence, and alliance termination. These include several categories of variables: (1) the strategic structure of the dyad members' politically relevant international environments (PRIEs); (2) the political structure of dyad members' PRIEs; (3) the strategic characteristic of dyad members; (4) the political characteristics of dyad members; (5) the past relationship between members of the dyad. Table 6.2 provides the results of the various factors. The variables included in the analysis of dyadic alliance initiation along with the results obtained for these variables are discussed next.

STRATEGIC CHARACTERISTICS OF DYAD MEMBERS' PRIES

1. *Number of states in each member's PRIE.* The more states that make up the politically relevant international environment of each state, the more likely is such a state to seek an alliance, because the more likely is each state to feel insecure. The minimum number of states in the PRIE was used. Thus, if state A had five members in its PRIE and state B had seven members in its own PRIE, then the former number was used. This variable generally has a positive effect on the probability of dyadic alliance initiation. The one exception is the case of dyadic alliance initiation between democracies where this relationship is not statistically significant.

2. *Average number of disputes in PRIE not involving dyad members.* The number of militarized interstate disputes that have been taking place in members' environment, but that do not directly involve the states in question, reflects the degree of strategic turbulence in members' PRIE. This may represent a level of uncertainty or threat that is not as immediate as in the case of disputes directly involving dyad members. Nonetheless, this is also a potential for high environmental risk assessment and thus an incentive to form or maintain an alliance. This variable does not have a significant impact on the probability of dyadic alliance initiation.

3. *Average number of alliance commitments in PRIE.* When many states in the *PRIE* of members form alliance commitments that exclude the focal states, the latter tends to feel increasingly threatened and thus prone to form alliances. This variable exhibited a significant positive effect on alliance initiation in the general population, for nondemocratic dyads and for dyads involving only minor powers. Jointly democratic dyads and dyads involving at least one major power were not significantly affected by the extent of alliance commitments of members of the focal states' PRIEs.

POLITICAL CHARACTERISTICS OF DYAD MEMBERS' PRIES

1. *Number of revolutionary political changes in PRIE.* Rapid and extensive political changes in states' composing one's PRIE are expected to increase

Table 6.2 Factors Affecting the Initiation of Dyadic Alliance Commitments: Weibull Event-History Analysis, Politically Relevant Dyads, 1816–1992

Independent Variable	All Politically Relevant Dyads	Jointly Democratic Dyads	Nonjointly Democratic Dyads	At Least One Major Power	Minor-Minor Dyads
Minimum number of states in PRIE	0.020** (0.004)	0.007 (0.008)	0.031** (0.005)	0.012** (0.005)	0.193** (0.055)
Proportion of MIDs in PRIE not involving dyad	0.038 (0.053)	0.081 (0.105)	0.017 (0.064)	0.021 (0.067)	−0.010 (0.105)
Proportion of alliance commitments in PRIE	0.052** (0.012)	0.023 (0.026)	0.072** (0.016)	0.013 (0.019)	0.144** (0.024)
Proportion of revolutionary political changes in PRIE	0.658** (0.180)	0.166 (0.347)	1.289** (0.245)	0.625** (0.121)	3.094** (1.017)
Minimum average regime score in PRIE	0.003 (0.003)	0.008 (0.009)	0.002 (0.004)	0.003 (0.005)	−0.022** (0.006)
Minimum capability ratio, state-to-PRIE	7.284** (1.551)	6.338 (4.056)	7.171** (1.693)	9.005** (1.588)	−154.731** (29.920)
Minimum number of MID involvements of members of dyad	−1.177 (1.070)	−1.082 (2.420)	−1.056 (1.203)	0.618 (1.166)	−6.122* (2.988)
Minimum number of alliance commitments of dyad members	−0.068** (0.011)	−0.009 (0.013)	−0.147** (0.020)	−0.038** (0.010)	−0.589** (0.063)
Revolutionary change of a member of dyads within last four years	0.596** (0.115)	1.434** (2.232)	0.387** (0.130)	0.477* (0.151)	0.832** (0.191)
Minimum regime score	−0.001 (0.001)	0.029** (0.008)	−0.003+ (0.002)	0.003 (0.002)	−0.004+ (0.002)
Cumulative past disputes between dyad members	0.030* (0.014)	0.024 (0.033)	0.034* (0.016)	0.010 (0.018)	0.057+ (0.030)
Capability ratio: strongest to weakest	0.001* (0.000)	−0.000 (0.000)	0.001** (0.000)	0.000 (0.000)	−0.052** (0.012)
Pseudo-R^2	0.078	0.158	0.111	0.080	0.268
N	56,071	13,633	42,438	41,584	14,487
Number of valid dyads	1,242	598	1,073	870	438
Number dyadic alliance initiations	335	76	259	197	138

+ $.05 \leq p < .10$.
* $.01 \leq p < .05$.
** $p < .01$.

a state's threat as well as its opportunity perceptions. Hence, such changes are expected to form incentives for either defensive or offensive alliances. This hypothesis was generally supported by the data analysis on dyadic alliance initiation. Again, the only exception to this rule is the case of jointly democratic dyads.

2. *Average regime score of states in PRIE.* Increased democratization in states' PRIE is expected to reduce threat perceptions and thus diminish the tendency to form or maintain alliances. This variable had no apparent effect on the probability of alliance initiation, except in cases involving at least one major power.

STRATEGIC CHARACTERISTICS OF DYAD MEMBERS

1. *Capability ratio of state-to-PRIE.* The expectation here is that the more powerful a state is compared to its PRIE, the less inclined it is to seek security through alliance. The minimum score over the two states was used. Here the results contradict the hypothesis. Both in the general population and in the case of nondemocratic dyads or dyads with at least one major power, the higher the minimal ratio of military capabilities of the states relative to their PRIEs, the more likely they are to form an alliance. Only in the case of dyads involving strictly minor powers is there a statistically significant negative association between capability and alliance initiation.

2. *Average number of dispute involvements of the focal state.* Here, too, the minimum number of dispute involvements of dyad members in the past three years indicates the extent of security problems these states experienced in the near past; thus, this variable suggests a positive incentive to seek security through alliance. Using the minimum number of dispute involvements within the dyad implies that the state with the fewest security concerns forms the weakest link in the chain of alliance formation incentives and thus determines whether an alliance is to be formed. This was not confirmed by the data analysis. No significant relationship was found between dyad members' exposure to outside dispute and their probability of joining each other in an alliance.

3. *Number of alliance commitments of members.* The more alliance commitments each member of the dyad already has, the less likely it is to seek an additional alliance, because prior alliances may have already alleviated whatever security concerns it seeks to address via alliance formation. Here, too, the minimum of the weighted number of alliance commitments for both members was used. This hypothesis was generally supported—with the exception of jointly democratic dyads—by the data analysis.

POLITICAL CHARACTERISTICS OF DYAD MEMBERS

1. *Revolutionary political change in preceding four-year period.* If one of the members in the dyad experienced a revolutionary political change over the

preceding period, it would have an incentive to form alliances to boost both its security and its legitimacy. This is the push factor. However, the other member of the dyad may be more reluctant to form an alliance than when the focal state was relatively stable. Political change—especially when it is revolutionary in nature—may deter potential alliance partners due to generally higher perceptions of threat from the member and due to fear of changing political orientation of the new regime (Maoz 1996). It appears that the push factor in this case is more powerful than the pull factor, because the existence of a revolutionary political change within a dyad has a consistent positive effect on the probability of alliance initiation.

The interpretation of this result is more complex than it would appear at first blush. The nature of the political change is a major factor in this context, and the result relating political change to the probability of alliance initiation should be interpreted with caution. In one case, however, is this result meaningful and fairly interpretable: jointly democratic dyads. In this case, the existence of a regime change implies that one or both members of the dyads changed from nondemocracies to democracies. Thus, this means a political change took place in the preceding four-year period that rendered the particular dyad, at the point of time where an alliance was initiated, a jointly democratic dyad. This implies that the change of a state into a democracy increases the probability of aligning with another state that has been or has recently become a democracy as well. This finding relates to the next proposition.

2. *Minimum regime score of members of the dyad.* If democracies tend to flock together in strategic alliances, then the higher the minimum regime score of a dyad, the more likely they are to form an alliance, and the longer their alliances are likely to persist.[9] This variable does not appear to affect the probability of dyadic alliance initiation in the general population of dyads, but it has a statistically significant effect on the probability of alliance initiation between democratic states. It appears from this result that democracies do indeed tend to flock together. But this does not apply to mixed dyads or to nondemocratic ones. On the contrary, in these cases, the higher the minimum regime score of the dyad (meaning that one of these states tends to be anocratic in nature), the less likely an alliance is to be formed.

RELATIONS BETWEEN MEMBERS OF DYAD

1. *Cumulative number of past disputes between members of the dyad.* A high number of past disputes between members of the dyad typically indicates a bad relationship; thus, the likelihood of alliance formation in a dyad that had experienced considerable conflict is relatively low. Likewise, if an alliance is formed, a history of rivalry typically suggests that it would be short-lived. Surprisingly, the number of past disputes between dyad members

seems to *positively* affect the probability of alliance formation in the general population as well as in nondemocratic dyads and in dyads composed only of minor powers.

This is a finding begging for explanation, but—upon reflection—it does appear to represent a historical reality of flexibility in alliance formation processes. Such was the case in both nineteenth-century Europe and postwar Europe where states that had fought each other a great many times found themselves in the same alliance (e.g., France, Great Britain, with Germany; Turkey with Greece; the Balkan states that became members of the Warsaw Pact, etc.)

2. *Capability ratio within the dyad.* Typically, it is assumed that states form alliances with similar states in terms of capability. Specifically, powerful states may be reluctant to form alliances with weak powers because the latter are more likely to become a strategic burden than a strategic asset (Maoz 1990: chap. 7; Snyder 1984). While weak states may have a strong incentive to ally with stronger states, they also must consider the fact that their loss of autonomy in such asymmetrical alliances is higher than for symmetrical ones.

This factor does not seem consistently to relate to the probability of alliance initiation. In the general population there is a positive relationship between the dyadic capability ratio and the probability of alliance initiation. The same applies to alliance initiation between nonjointly democratic states. In both cases, the finding runs contrary to the hypothesis stated here. However, in cases of dyads involving strictly minor powers, the effect of dyadic power ratios on alliance initiation is negative.

Two comments must be made about the breakdown of the general population of politically relevant dyads into distinct subpopulations. First, jointly democratic dyads appear to be more affected by political calculations and by regime affinities in their alliance formation behavior than nonjointly democratic dyads. The latter types of dyads (which include both mixed dyads and dyads involving nondemocratic states on both sides) appear to be guided primarily by strategic considerations, both considerations related to the nature of their strategic environment and their own military and strategic attributes.

Second, alliance behavior in cases involving at least one major power entails more strategic considerations than in cases of dyads wherein both states are minor powers. Both points suggest that there are significant differences between types of dyads in terms of their regime structure and power status.

The results of the analyses on alliance initiation at the nation and dyadic levels reveal considerable cross-level consistency but also some cross-level differences. These differences may be due to the fact that at the dyadic level we consider only politically relevant dyads, whereas at the individual level we consider all nation-years. However, there may be more to the story.

The "who aligns with whom" issue is not always consistent with the question of what drives states to seek security or to accomplish foreign policy goals through alliances.

ALLIANCE DURATION

Once two states enter into an alliance, what determines how long it will persist? Alliances are supposed to have strategic goals that can be used to balance against power, balance against threats, or provide states with offensive opportunities that they did not have by their own. However, given that alliances are said to limit states' autonomy, the conventional wisdom is that once they finished serving their purpose, they become a strategic burden rather than an asset (Bennett 1997b: 851–52).

The literature that focuses on alliance duration (e.g., Bennett 1997b; Gaubatz 1996; Gartzke and Simon 1998) typically examines the same variables as those presumed to affect alliance formation. The underlying logic is that the factors that account for decisions to initiate alliances are operative in decisions to terminate them. I follow this practice here. It does not make sense to examine the alliance duration issue in a nation-level context because a state may exit one alliance and enter another one. The relevant level of analysis for this issue is the dyadic level.

For the dyadic level, the key question is what affects the termination of an alliance bond between two states. Thus, the proper estimation method is event-history analysis, in which alliance termination (or in the case of nation-level analyses, net reduction in alliance commitments) is considered as a "failure" event. However, the population under examination is not all dyads or all states but rather only those dyads that had an ongoing alliance, and only for the duration of that alliance. For individual states, we ignore states that have been completely nonaligned. Table 6.3 provides the dyadic level test of alliance termination.

Before going on to an analysis of alliance termination at the dyadic level, a caveat is in order. As can be seen at the bottom of Table 6.3, the number of dyadic alliance terminations for jointly democratic and minor power alliances is generally very small. The principal reason for that is that most of the democratic-democratic alliances in the postwar era were right censored, having not ended in 1986. The same applies to minor-minor alliance commitments (wherein the alliance commitment structure between minor power members of the Warsaw Pact were still valid in 1986, though ending five years later). This makes the democratic-nondemocratic breakdown in the case of alliance termination somewhat tenuous. Thus, the breakdowns for democratic-nondemocratic and major-minor alliance dyads should be taken as highly tentative. An updating of the alliance data through 1991 may alleviate the problem with the major-minor breakdowns, but not with the democratic-nondemocratic ones.

Table 6.3   Factors Affecting Dyadic Alliance Termination: Weibull Event-History Analysis of Politically Relevant Dyads, 1816–1986

Independent Variable	All Politically Relevant Dyads	Jointly Democratic Dyads	Nonjointly Democratic Dyads	At Least One Major Power	Minor-Minor Dyads
Minimum number of states in PRIE	−0.020** (0.007)	−0.011 (0.014)	−0.018** (0.009)	−0.018** (0.007)	−0.467** (0.102)
Proportion of MIDs in PRIE not involving dyad	0.168** (0.047)	0.045 (0.148)	0.192** (0.051)	0.211** (0.065)	0.102 (0.093)
Proportion of alliance commitments in PRIE	−0.309** (0.035)	−0.292** (0.083)	−0.344** (0.042)	−0.322** (0.049)	−0.395** (0.057)
Proportion of revolutionary political changes in PRIE	1.307** (0.303)	0.742 (0.635)	1.635** (0.427)	1.560** (0.361)	−0.081 (1.767)
Minimum average regime score in PRIE	−0.031** (0.005)	−0.062** (0.021)	−0.029** (0.006)	−0.046** (0.007)	0.013 (0.011)
Minimum capability ratio, state to PRIE	8.605** (1.914)	4.856 (10.731)	8.166** (2.101)	8.882** (2.032)	−18.047 (41.716)
Minimum number of MID involvements of members of dyad	0.096 (1.170)	6.008* (2.584)	−1.279 (1.365)	−0.973 (1.676)	3.701+ (2.082)
Minimum number of alliance commitments of dyad members	0.044** (0.011)	−0.002 (0.020)	0.066** (0.014)	0.042** (0.013)	0.321** (0.079)
Revolutionary change of a member of dyads within last four years	0.605** (0.159)	−0.113 (0.414)	0.744** (0.177)	0.568** (0.180)	1.251** (0.435)
Minimum regime score	−0.004* (0.002)	0.039* (0.021)	−0.002 (0.002)	−0.004 (0.002)	−0.002 (0.005)
Cumulative past disputes between dyad members	−0.076** (0.021)	−0.248* (0.111)	−0.084** (0.022)	−0.075** (0.023)	0.025 (0.054)
Capability ratio: strongest to weakest	0.004+ (0.002)	−0.001 (0.003)	−0.006* (0.003)	−0.004+ (0.002)	−0.008 (0.034)
Pseudo-R^2	0.458	0.353	0.515	0.535	0.454
N	20,004	6,136	13,868	11,419	8,885
Number of valid dyads	330	134	279	163	173
Number of dyadic alliance terminations	181	32	149	139	42

+ $.05 \leq p < .10$.
* $.01 \leq p < .05$.
** $p < .01$.

Having said this, the results of the dyadic analysis can be summarized by the following points.

1. The number of states in the PRIE of the dyad members has a negative impact on the probability of alliance termination (i.e., the more states in the allies' PRIE, the longer an alliance is likely to persist). This is true in

all cases except in alliances between democracies. Thus, the more potential security concerns dyad members have, the more likely they are to
maintain their alliance commitment.

2. The proportion of environmental disputes—that is, disputes in members'
   strategic environment, but not directly involving dyad members—seems
   to have a positive effect on alliance termination. Again, this is true in the
   general case and for nonjointly democratic dyads and dyads involving at
   least one major or regional power. This suggests that the pull factor gets
   to work when the environmental uncertainty level decreases, because one
   state observing growing instability in the PRIE of the other state becomes
   reluctant to continue its commitment, lest it gets involved in conflicts that
   are not in its interests.[10]

3. The proportion of alliance commitments of states in dyad members'
   PRIEs has a negative impact on the probability of alliance termination.
   This is the case in the general population as well as in the various breakdowns of the population. The more alliance commitments are formed by
   the potential rivals of dyad members, the more likely dyad members are
   to maintain their alliance commitments over time.

4. Domestic political instability in members' PRIE, measured by the proportion of states in their respective PRIEs undergoing political change, has a
   positive effect on alliance termination. The same push logic that operated
   in the decisions to form alliances apparently operates in the maintenance
   of alliance ties. Environmental political instability creates potential threats
   to dyad members. Thus, the maintenance of alliance commitments is one
   of the instruments they use not only to ward off strategic threats but also to
   deflect threats emanating from domestic political instability (Maoz 1996:
   157–62; 1989).

5. The level of democratization in the PRIE of dyad members has a generally
   negative effect on the probability of alliance termination. The more democratic the PRIE, the less likely alliance commitments were to end, for reasons that are fundamentally different for jointly democratic dyads than for
   mixed or nondemocratic ones. In the former subpopulation, an increasingly democratic PRIE creates incentives to maintain an alliance because
   it reduces the risk of members invoking alliances in war against other
   members of the PRIE, thus minimizing the likelihood of alliance paradoxes. In the case of nondemocratic dyads, a growing level of democratization represents a higher threat; thus, alliances in this case serve a security purpose.

6. The capability ratio between a given state and its PRIE has a positive impact on the probability of alliance termination. The capability–alliance
   trade-off, though not obvious in the case of alliance initiation, appears to
   be present quite prominently in terms of alliance maintenance. The better
   off members of the dyad are in terms of their power relative to their PRIE,

the less threatened they tend to feel and hence the more likely they are to require alliances to increase security. This applies to all cases except to democratic-democratic and minor-minor alliance dyads.

7. The extent of militarized interstate dispute (MID) involvement of dyad members does not appear to have a significant impact on the probability of alliance termination except in the case of alliances between democracies and between minor powers, and these are unreliable breakdowns. It seems that, in practice, the fact that one or both allies are involved in disputes does not have an impact on the duration of alliances. This result warrants further refinement and exploration, for reasons discussed later.

8. The more alliance commitments of members of the dyad, outside the alliance between them, the more likely their alliance is to terminate. This makes sense because if both states seek other partners, the need for each other diminishes.

9. Revolutionary change in one or both of the dyad members has a significant positive impact on alliance termination. Just as environmental political instability invokes the pull factor and serves to shorten the lives of an alliance, domestic instability of members of the dyad renders the other one skeptical of the willingness, ability, and commitment of the changing state to reliable alliance partnership. Moreover, revolutionary change makes the changing state more likely to engage in international conflict (Maoz 1996; Walt 1996), thus making the other member of the dyad more wary of continued commitment.

10. The regime score of the dyad members has a negative effect on alliance termination in the general case, but no significant effect in other cases. This may be due in part to the bias in right censoring of the NATO and Warsaw Pact states, which make up a considerable portion of dyadic alliance memberships. Yet, this does call into question the issue raised by Gaubatz (1996) and corroborated by Reed (1997) and Bennett (1997b) that alliances between democracies last longer than alliances between mixed dyads or between nondemocratic states.

11. The most surprising finding of this study, in the case of both alliance initiation and alliance termination, is that states with high numbers of past disputes appear to have a higher probability to maintain their alliance commitments with one another than states with shorter alliance spans. This result calls for explanation.

12. The capability ratio in the dyad appears to have inconsistent effects on alliance termination. In the general population, there appears to be a weak negative impact of capability ratios on alliance termination: the more equal the capabilities of dyad members, the less likely their alliance is to end. However, in the case of nonjointly democratic dyads and dyads in which at least one member is a major or regional power, the effect is posi-

tive. That is, for these subpopulations, the larger the capability disparity, the more likely the alliance is to terminate.

How does this analysis compare with other empirical studies of alliance duration?[11] Not surprisingly, the answer to this question is mixed. On a number of issues, the results of the present analysis corroborate previous investigations. Perhaps most significant is the fact that democracies do indeed tend to flock together (Siverson and Starr 1994), and their alliances tend to last longer (Bennett 1997b; Gaubatz 1996; Reed 1997). In addition, strategic factors, such as the degree of threat, the extent of alliance commitments in members' PRIEs, and capability ratios, also exhibit similar relationship to alliance duration as in some of these studies, though the measurement of these variables here is quite different from that of other studies.

In contrast to those of Bennett (1997b), my findings indicate that revolutionary political change in one or both states making up a dyad tends to shorten the life of their alliance. Likewise, the findings suggesting that a bellicose history of the members of a dyad in fact *increases* alliance duration prospects have to be investigated in more detail.

THE IMPLICATIONS OF ALLIANCES:
ALLIANCE AND INTERNATIONAL CONFLICT

One of the most studied aspects of alliance politics, and one of the most controversial issues, concerns the question of the relationship between alliance and warfare. Different studies suggest different results. Also, the results of certain studies show that this relationship, to the extent that it exists, is far from robust. Oren (1990: 213–14), Vasquez (1993: 312–14), and Kegley and Raymond (1994: 187–98) note that the relationship between alliances and conflict is complex at best and uncertain in most cases.

Alliances have been shown to be both positively and negatively related to war (Singer and Small 1968; Oren 1990). Levy (1983) argues that most alliances among major powers are followed by war participation. Alliances were also shown to be positively and negatively related to war expansion (Levy 1983; Siverson and King 1979, 1980; Kegley and Raymond 1994). Negative relationships were found between alliances and war in the nineteenth century, and positive relationships were established for the twentieth century.

Bueno de Mesquita (1981) found that allies are more likely to fight one another than nonaligned states. However, more exhaustive dyadic analyses of the factors affecting the probability of conflict and war among dyads (Bremer 1992, 1993b; Maoz and Russett 1993; Maoz 1996: chap. 4) show a consistently negative relationship between alliance and conflict, in general, and between alliances and escalation, in particular.[12] It is difficult to say that we have approached a better understanding of the relationship between alliances and conflict.

Part of the difficulty to assess the nature and kind of relationship between alliances and war is based on fundamental differences among studies in terms of the unit of analysis, type of baseline population used, breakdown of the entire population into temporal or substantive subsamples, measurement of alliances, and bivariate versus multivariate model specifications. In this morass of scientific findings, it is difficult to generate coherent conclusions.

Smith (1995) notes that this confusion is due to the lack of formal specification of the kind of incentives for would-be aggressors or would-be targets that alliance tends to create. He offers a refined formal model of this issue, but the model creates so many propositions that it turns out to be of limited empirical value. In Bueno de Mesquita's (1981b) expected utility model of conflict, alliances play an important role in determining war and peace issues. However, it does not actually stipulate the conditions relating alliance to war on an aggregate level beyond his general observation about war between allies.

A more refined theory of alliance and war seems to rest, first and foremost, on a national decision-related level. Given that a state joins an alliance, it makes sense to ask whether and under what conditions this fact tends to affect its war initiation or war participation decisions (Altfeld and Bueno de Mesquita 1979). The decision to ally rests in part on a long-term outlook of what a state can or cannot do within a given alliance framework (Altfeld 1984; Snyder 1984; Maoz 1990: chap. 7; Morrow 1991; Smith 1995). Thus, any explanation of the relationship between alliances and war must be related to an explanation of alliance formation: The same factors that account for the formation of alliances may be active in determining how alliances may be related to war.

If a state forms an alliance to be able to wage a war that it could not have waged without an alliance, then even if other members of the alliance join in for the purpose of war prevention, alliances may be related to both the initiation and the expansion of war. The focal state may start a war because it believes its allies would either help in the fighting or deter third parties from aiding its opponent. Other members of the alliance may face a credibility problem if they do not join the war at the request of the initiator and may thus be drawn in despite their will (Maoz 1990: chap. 7).

Even if an alliance is formed solely for defensive purposes, there is no guarantee that opponents of the alliance members would interpret it as such. A security dilemma may be formed not only in the context of states seeking security through military allocations. It may also be formed and strengthened by the aggregation of alliances. Likewise, an offensive alliance may have unintended stabilizing implications. Once a pair of states joins an alliance for the purpose of pooling capabilities to attack an opponent successfully, they may cause that opponent to align with another state, thus balancing the excessive power of the first two members.

The findings reported later in this chapter offer another cut at this issue. As done in previous sections of this study, I focus at the relationship between alliance and war at the nation level and the dyadic level. In addition, since this question was examined extensively at the aggregate systemic level, I expand the analysis to this level as well. Table 6.4 provides the results for the nation level of analysis, using the same control variables as in previous sections.

Space constraints prohibit extensive discussion of the relationship between the various control variables, on the one hand, and the dispute-/war-dependent variables, on the other.[13] I restrict the discussion to the effect of alliance involvement on conflict behavior of nations. The most important observation about this linkage is that the whole is not related to its parts. Specifically, the relationship between alliance commitments and dispute or war involvement of states depends on the regime-type breakdown. *The alliance commitments of nondemocratic states have a negative impact on their dispute and war involvement. The more and more significant types of alliance commitments a nondemocratic state has, the less likely it is to get involved in militarized interstate disputes and in war.* On the other hand, *the alliance commitments of democratic states have a positive impact on their dispute and war involvement: the more alliances a democratic state has, the more likely it is to get involved in militarized interstate disputes and in war.* This finding suggests that the ally paradox is likely to operate on democratic states but not on nondemocratic states. Whereas alliances tend to provide a significant measure of security to nondemocratic states and thus reduce the likelihood of their involvement in conflict and war, democracies tend to be drawn in to the very same problems that alliances were supposed to prevent.

This is an extremely significant finding because it entails a number of important implications. First, if it is the case that alliances serve different functions for different states, then a fundamental paradox emerges. It is typically assumed that the role of alliances for democratic states is defensive or deterrent in nature, whereas for nondemocratic states, alliances have a more proactive—sometime offensive—function. If that is the case, then alliances for both types of states tend to have consequences that are diametrically opposed to those intended. In fact, for nondemocratic states, alliances seem to have a deterrent effect. They reduce the need to resolve security problems through the threat, display, or use of force. On the other hand, for democracies, alliances tend to increase the inclination to get involved in disputes and in wars.

Another issue that the analysis on alliance and war reveals for the national level of analysis is that, as expected, the proportion of allies in states' PRIEs has a consistently deterrent impact in terms of their propensity to engage in conflict and war.

We can now turn to explore the relationship between alliance and conflict at the dyadic level. This is given in Table 6.5, which again uses the customary control variables for this level.

Here the relationship is clear and consistent. Alliance commitment has a

Table 6.4 The Conflict Implications of Alliance Involvement: Nation-Level Relationships between Alliances and Conflict, 1816–1986

Independent Variable	Dispute Involvement			War Involvement		
	All States	Democracies	Nondemocracies	All States	Democracies	Nondemocracies
Number of states in PRIE	0.005* (0.002)	−0.00 (0.002)	0.006+ (0.004)	−0.002 (0.003)	−0.017** (0.005)	0.005 (0.005)
Capability ratio, state to PRIE	0.984* (0.485)	0.898** (0.393)	0.308 (1.141)	0.382 (0.856)	−0.242 (1.192)	−0.890 (1.350)
Proportion of alliance commitments in PRIE	−0.054* (0.026)	−0.018 (0.032)	−0.051 (0.035)	−0.099 (0.061)	−0.058 (0.065)	−0.014+ (0.008)
Proportion of conflicts in PRIE	0.213** (0.044)	0.264** (0.049)	0.191** (0.060)	0.479** (0.062)	−0.027+ (0.015)	0.086** (0.031)
Number of MIDs directed at focal state	0.535** (0.069)	0.628** (0.105)	0.522** (0.083)	0.278** (0.096)	−0.105* (0.044)	0.196* (0.097)
Proportion of revolutionary changes in PRIE	1.072* (0.487)	0.806 (0.675)	1.434* (0.676)	1.091 (1.096)	−0.151 (0.197)	0.182 (0.125)
Proportion of democracies in PRIE	−0.687* (0.384)	−1.992** (0.353)	0.076 (0.417)	−1.963** (0.780)	−0.430** (0.124)	−0.094 (0.131)
Regime score of state	−0.001 (0.001)	−0.002 (0.004)	−0.002 (0.003)	−0.005* (0.002)	−0.001 (0.001)	0.001 (0.001)
Persistence of regime	0.000 (0.001)	−0.001 (0.002)	−0.001 (0.002)	0.004 (0.003)	0.003* (0.001)	0.001+ (0.001)
Minor/regional/major power status	0.536** (0.111)	0.435** (0.122)	0.647** (0.135)	1.194** (0.284)	1.631+ (0.939)	0.681** (0.191)
Weighted Number of Alliance Commitments of State	−0.019 (0.018)	−0.003 (0.011)	−0.003 (0.043)	−0.060 (0.059)	0.008** (0.003)	−0.019* (0.009)
Wald Chi-Square	759.88**	1,510.58**	848.54**	255.92**		
N	8,790	2,999	5,783	8,790	2,574	5,312
Number of states	153	78	127	153	72	124

+ .05 ≤ p < .10.
* .01 ≤ p < .05.
** p < .01.

Table 6.5 Effects of Alliance Commitments on Dyadic Dispute/War Involvement: Cross-Sectional Time-Series Probit Regression, Politically Relevant Dyads, 1816–1986

Independent Variable	Dispute Occurrence			Dispute Escalation		
	All States	Democracies	Nondemocracies	All States	Democracies	Nondemocracies
Contiguity level	0.121**	0.093**	0.119**	0.212**	NC	0.122**
	(0.011)	(0.022)	(0.025)	(0.035)		(0.054)
Capability ratio	−0.001**	−0.001*	−0.001*	−0.004**	NC	−0.024**
	(0.000)	(0.000)	(0.000)	(0.001)		(0.008)
Minimum regime score	−0.002**	−0.006**	−0.003**	−0.003*	NC	−0.003**
	(0.000)	(0.001)	(0.001)	(0.001)		(0.001)
Cumulative number of past disputes in dyad	0.070**	0.076**	0.057**	0.021**	NC	0.020**
	(0.002)	(0.005)	(0.005)	(0.006)		(0.003)
Revolutionary change in dyad	0.019	−0.047	0.005	0.150*	NC	−0.133+
	(0.021)	(0.037)	(0.033)	(0.066)		(0.073)
Dyad status	0.010	0.038	−0.016	0.102**	NC	0.016**
	(0.015)	(0.032)	(0.031)	(0.048)		(0.005)
Minimum proportion alliance commitments in PRIE	−0.001**	−0.002**	−0.001	−0.005**	NC	−0.002**
	(0.000)	(0.000)	(0.001)	(0.001)		(0.001)
Alliance commitment?	−0.319**	−0.406**	−0.269**	−0.347**	NC	−0.402**
	(0.031)	(0.075)	(0.057)	(0.113)		(0.121)
Pseudo-R^2	0.096	0.113	0.091	0.065		0.110
N	55,955	17,633	48,495	55,868		48,495
Number of dyads	1,223	560	402	1,120		1,063

Note: NC = no convergence (no wars).
+ .05 ≤ p < .10.
* .01 ≤ p < .05.
** p < .01.

significant and consistently pacifying effect on conflict outbreak, conflict occurrence, and conflict escalation, irrespective of specific breakdown. This corroborates numerous other studies that examined this relationship either in the context of other hypotheses (e.g., Maoz, and Russett 1993; Russett and Oneal 1997) or as a specific hypothesis (e.g., Bremer 1992).

The effect of the degree of alignment in dyad members' PRIEs on their propensity to start or escalate militarized interstate disputes was less explored in the literature in the past. Here the findings suggest that—by and large—high levels of environmental alignment have a generally pacifying effect on the focal dyad, probably for fear that conflict with the member of the dyad might provoke others to join in.

We now turn to examine the effect of alliances on systemic conflict in a manner that extends the basic theoretical argument about the defensive and offensive functions of alliances. To do that, I discuss the concept of *alliance networks* (Maoz 2001). An alliance network describes a situation wherein three or more members of a strategically interdependent community of states are bound together by alliance ties. Presumably, if alliance ties affect common interests of states (Maoz 1997a; Farber and Gowa 1995, 1997), then in an environment that is otherwise conflict-prone, multiple alliance ties may have a pacifying effect. States that are strategically interdependent and thus display high a priori probability of conflict and that enter alliance networks should reduce the level of conflict not only within the network but in their general environment as well. This also follows from the seemingly pacifying effects of environmental alliances on conflict propensity that was observed at the national and dyadic levels of analysis.

Maoz (2001) operationalized an alliance network by examining the proportion of states in regional subsystems that are (1) politically relevant to each other and (2) bound together by alliance ties. In addition to alliance networks, and in accordance with previous analyses focusing on the effects of regime structures on international conflict, I consider democratic networks as well. A democratic network is a set of three or more states that (1) are politically relevant to each other and (2) have democratic regimes. Table 6.6 provides the results of this analysis.

The contents of this table seem to suggest that both alliance networks and democratic networks have a pacifying regional effect. As the states making up a region are increasingly linked to one another in alliance ties, the level of conflict in the region—defined in terms of the number of militarized disputes and wars in the region—seems to decline.

This is true for the entire 1816–1986 period and for the twentieth century, but not for the nineteenth century. In the latter case, the relationship between alliance networks and militarized disputes and war is positive. When the dependent variable is the proportion of disputes that escalated to war in a given year, the significant negative association between alliance networks and wars is maintained again only for the twentieth century. This brings back the old intercentury puzzle

Table 6.6   The Effect of Alliance Networks and of Democratic Networks on Regional and Global Levels of Conflict, 1816–1986

Dependent Variable	Independent Variable	Parameter Estimates (SE)		
		Entire Period	19th Century	20th Century
Number of Disputes[+]	Proportion of dyads in democratic networks	−2.227** (0.861)	−4.089** (1.809)	−2.924** (0.507)
	Proportion of dyads in alliance networks	−0.461** (0.136)	2.810** (0.984)	−0.726** (0.177)
		$\chi^2 = 20.64$	$\chi^2 = 10.28**$	$\chi^2 = 39.22**$
		$N = 797$	$N = 308$	$N = 489$
		Regions = 6	Regions = 5	Regions = 6
Number of wars[+]	Proportion of dyads in democratic networks	−3.278** (1.121)	−3.646 (3.926)	−4.096** (1.015)
	Proportion of dyads in alliance networks	−1.989** (0.463)	4.477** (1.356)	−3.062** (0.537)
		$\chi^2 = 54.62**$	$\chi^2 = 685.14$	$\chi^2 = 39.75$
		$N = 797$	$N = 308$	$N = 489$
		Regions = 6	Regions = 5	Regions = 6
Proportion of wars[++]	Proportion of dyads in democratic networks	−0.217** (0.032)	−0.204 (0.175)	−0.2556** (0.075)
	Proportion of dyads in alliance networks	−0.123** (0.011)	0.171 (0.117)	−0.149** (0.028)
		$\chi^2 = 133.08**$	$\chi^2 = 4.10$	$\chi^2 = 31.86**$
		$N = 797$	$N = 308$	$N = 489$
		Regions = 6	Regions = 5	Regions = 6

Source: Maoz (2001).

    [+] Cross-sectional time series Poisson regression.

    [++] Cross-sectional time series regression with panel-corrected standard errors and correction for autocorrelation and heteroskedacticity.

(Singer and Small 1968), which seems to have disappeared in Oren's (1990) analysis on the systemic relationship between alliances and war. However, the analysis in Table 6.6 is predicated on a notion that regional patterns mediate between dyadic and systemic levels of analysis (Maoz 1996, 2001). To examine the relationship, consider Table 6.7, which focuses on the linkage between alliances and international conflict in the global system.

Here the results are generally consistent with the regional findings. The proportion of states in the system that are part of alliance networks is *negatively associated with the frequency of disputes and war in the system.* As in the regional analyses, democratic networks have a consistently pacifying effect on the system as a whole. Here, too, the intercentury puzzle is evident. Alliance net-

Table 6.7   General Systemic Analysis of Democratic and Alliance Networks and Conflict Levels, 1816–1986—Autoregressive Poisson Analysis

Dependent Variable	Independent Variable	Parameter Estimate (SE)		
		Entire Period	*19th Century*	*20th Century*
Number of disputes	Proportion of democratic networks	−2.272** (0.779)	−4.630[+] (2.497)	−5.046** (0.819)
	Proportion of alliance networks	−0.001** (0.000)	0.014* (0.076)	−0.001** (0.000)
	Year[a]	0.032** (0.002)	0.028** (0.006)	0.029** (0.004)
	Rho1	0.626** (0.077)	0.031 (0.115)	0.865** (0.106)
	Rho2	0.086 (0.077)	0.102 (0.120)	−0.099 (0.106)
		$N = 165$	$N = 79$	$N = 86$
		$R^2 = 0.792$	$R^2 = 0.246$	$R^2 = 0.764$
Number of wars	Proportion of democratic networks	−12.380** (2.046)	−1.231 (7.954)	−12.305** (2.086)
	Proportion of alliance networks	−0.003** (0.001)	0.056** (0.018)	−0.004** (0.001)
	Year	0.050** (0.006)	0.048** (0.014)	−0.057** (0.011)
	Rho1	0.565** (0.079)	0.155 (0.124)	0.782** (0.107)
	Rho2	0.071 (0.079)	0.456* (0.209)	−0.040 (0.105)
Number of years		$N = 165$	$N = 79$	$N = 86$
		$R^2 = 0.514$	$R^2 = 0.213$	$R^2 = 0.638$

[a] This variable *YEAR* is simply the calendaric value of the year. It was added to control for the changes in the number of disputes over time, principally due to the growth in the size of the interstate system (Maoz 1996: chap. 3).

[+] $.05 \leq p < .10$.
* $.01 \leq p < .05$.
** $p < .01$.

works seemed to have a positive effect on conflict and war in the nineteenth century and a pacifying effect on conflict and war in the twentieth century.

CONCLUSION

Alliances are a central item on the national security menu of states. Strategic considerations clearly play an important role in the extent to which states enter alliances, in the choice of specific alliance partners, and in the persistence of existence alliance ties. This effect was demonstrated by numerous previous investigations as well as by the present study. What was less known given past research but seems to emerge very clearly in the present study is that alliance formation, alliance persistence, and the strategic implications of alliances seem to be related to seemingly nonstrategic—especially domestic political—factors. In particular, political change and regime structures seem to have a very important impact on alliance formation and alliance persistence.

Moreover, the effects of alliances on war and conflict seem to differ dramatically across different political systems, and these differences seem to defy strictly realist logic. Not only do democracies behave differently from nondemocracies, but the effect of alliance on the conflict behavior of democracies is at odds with conventional wisdom.

Two additional implications need to be discussed here. First, there are clear connections between different aspects of alliance behavior. These connections are not straightforward. I have suggested that to consider the implications of alliances—in particular, their effect on conflict and war behavior—we need to take into account the factors that go into the decisions to form new alliances and to maintain existing ones. For a number of key factors, the linkage between variables that affect alliance formation, alliance maintenance, and the consequences of alliance participation is fairly linear and thus logically straightforward. For example, the number of states in the politically relevant environment of a given state (or a given dyad) represents the extent of potential risk. The same can be said about the proportion of a state's PRIE that are aligned. Both factors presumably serve as an impetus to form alliances and to maintain them, and both factors explain why a given state may be more likely to get involved in conflict behavior.

However, for other factors, the relationship is not straightforward, and in some cases it can be even seen as paradoxical. For example, the number of disputes in a state's PRIE did not have the same effect on alliance formation and alliance persistence.

Second, alliance behavior is not consistent across specific subgroups. The democratic/nondemocratic breakdown appears to be a potent divider of the entire population, more so than the minor/major power divider. Both the origins and the implications of alliances display a great variability across regime types.

These two findings are of major significance for a number of reasons. First, substantively, different political systems have different calculations regarding alliance formation and alliance behavior. This is an important qualification about the extent to which general patterns exist in strategic interactions, in general, and in interactions involving international alignments, in particular. Second, these findings have important implications for the realists-versus-others debate in world politics (e.g., Vasquez 1997a; Waltz 1997; Walt 1997). It appears that not all political systems behave alike, and the key determinant of those differences is a domestic characteristic—regime structure—not an international one—geopolitical status (major or minor power). However, it must be noted that in many respects there are considerable similarities between the behavior of democracies and those of major powers, and between the behavior of nondemocracies and minor powers in terms of alliance formation, alliance persistence, and the implications and consequences of alliances.

In terms of the questions that guide this volume, the following tentative conclusions can be stated:

1. *Are alliances correlates of war?* The general answer to this question is an unequivocal yes. This answer emerges from numerous studies on the subject dealing with different levels of analysis, time periods, and measures of alliances and of conflict and war. The study of alliances and war is an important subject of investigation not only from a theoretical point of view but also from a policy relevant perspective. Alliances can be formed and terminated by national decisions. How and under what conditions alliances increase or decrease the probability of conflict at various levels of analysis are issues that can have important impact on national and international policy.

2. *Can a pattern be documented?* The answer at this point is negative. There are too many discrepancies, too many inconsistencies, and far too many nuanced relationships to be able to identify a coherent pattern. At this point, we must admit that the study of alliances and war has yet to produce consistent and scientifically meaningful findings. What may strike one as most important of the findings I have discussed here is the cross-regime-type differences and the seeming relationship between regime-related and status-related breakdowns.

3. *Are there alternative explanations in the literature?* One of the most important reasons for the confusion regarding the relationship between alliances and war is the multiplicity of explanations. Another feature of this confusion relates to the fact that no satisfactory formal model of alliances and war goes across levels of analysis. Different theoretical models tend to produce different measures of alliance and different results. There is an urgent need for a more comprehensive and more systematic model of alliances, not as a separate variable but as an element in the national security calculus of states, dyads, regions, and international systems.

4. *How do we deal with these problems?* Following are some suggestions for progress in this field.
    a. *Develop a multilevel model of alliances.* This model has to start, in my view, from an attempt to account for the determinants of alliance formation at the national level and proceed from there to the dyadic level. It must also deal with questions regarding the size of alliances. This aspect of the model needs to focus on the factors that push some states to seek alliances, as well as to select specific alliance partners. A model of this sort that stays strictly at the monadic level of analysis may be insufficient.

b. *Explore multiple implications of alliances.* Alliances, as we have seen, have both intended and unintended consequences. Thus, such a model must account for the implications and consequences of alliance behavior. Likewise, alliances leave an impact on states that are part of them as well as on states that are excluded. We have focused here on one of the most important consequences of alliances—that is, the relationship between alliances and conflict. However, other issues concerning alliances—for example, how and to what extent they tend to shape the economic and diplomatic relations among members—also need to be addressed.

c. *Deal with the reciprocal effects of alliances and international systems.* Most accounts of alliance politics at the system level focus on how system structures shape the type and the duration of alliances. However, we need to be aware that there is a possibility that the causal arrow goes the other way as well. In other words, decisions to make or unmake alliances can reshape the structure of the system as well. Thus, the nature of the relationship between alliances and the structure of the international or regional system must be derived from below, not to be restricted to a macrosystemic or balance-of-power explanation of the operation of global politics (Maoz 1995).

METHODOLOGICAL APPENDIX

This appendix spells out the research design of all statistical analyses conducted in this study. Requests for data should be directed to the author.

Spatial and Temporal Domain

The temporal domain includes the 1816–1986 period. The upper bound of this domain is due to availability of data on alliances (discussed later). The spatial domain depends on the unit of analysis used in each analysis. In particular, the following units of analysis are employed here:

1. *Nation-year.* For the individual state level, I use all the independent system members, each state over its entire history of statehood. In some analyses, states with fewer than ten years of independence are omitted because of problems of estimation of autocorrelation structures. Alternatively, states are omitted because they lack data on some key variables used in the analyses. Out of the 177 independent system members make up 10,346 observations. In the individual nation-year analyses, valid data were available for only 7,899 nation-years across 148 states.[14]

2. *Dyad-years.* For this analysis I use the set of politically relevant dyads over

the 1816–1986 period. The reason for using this list is that of convenience, as the size of estimation matrices for the entire population of dyads from 1816 to 1986 (a total of over 459,000 dyad-years) is too large to estimate. This has some implications for the findings because dyadic alliance relationships between states that are not politically relevant to each other are not included. This is partially rectified in the next unit of analysis.

3. *Regional systemic analysis.* All dyad-years corresponding to a given region are aggregated over the states in the region. Units of analysis here are region-years, with the following regions identified: Western Hemisphere, Europe (including Russia/Soviet Union and Turkey/Ottoman Empire), Africa, Middle East and North Africa (including Turkey/Ottoman Empire), Asia (including Russia/Soviet Union), and an extraregional category that applies to all other nation-years.

Data Sources

Data on alliance commitments are derived from the Correlates of War (COW) project alliance data set. The quality of the data set and its coverage is high up to 1986, but subsequent versions that cover later periods are still not entirely clean. One of the implications is that some alliances in analyses of alliance duration are right censored, although they have been formally terminated. (A key example is the Warsaw Pact.)

Data on dispute and war behavior are based on the COW new militarized interstate dispute data set (Jones, Bremer, and Singer 1996).

Data on military capabilities are based on the COW military capability data set.

Data on political attributes of states (regime, political change) are based on the POLITY III data set (Jaggers and Gurr 1995).

Measurement of Variables

Table 6.A1 provides information about the variables used in this study and their empirical measures.

Table 6.A1 Variables, Definitions, Measures, and Sources

Variable	Measure	Sources and Comments
Dependent Variables		
Nation Level		
Weighted number of alliance commitments of the state	*WGHALLY*: sum of all alliance commitments of a state weighted by type of alliance and (major/minor power) status of alliance partner.	Maoz (1997b); period covered, 1816–1990

Table 6.A1 Continued

Variable	Measure	Sources and Comments
Dispute/war involvement	$DISPUTE \equiv$ number of dispute involvements per year; $WAR \equiv$ number of war involvements per year	Maoz (1996, 1997b, 1997c)
Dyadic Level		
Alliance initiation	$0 =$ No alliance commitment of any type; $1 =$ first year of alliance commitment	Similar analyses conducted on defense pacts only (years in which alliance commitment was in place were censored)
Alliance termination	$0 =$ alliance commitment in place; $1 =$ first year of no alliance	Analyses performed only on dyad-years with existing alliance commitments
Dyadic conflict	$0 =$ no MID; $1 =$ MID	Analyses conducted for both MID outbreaks (only first year of MID coded as 1) and for MID occurrence (all years of MID coded as 1)
Dyadic conflict escalation	$0 =$ MID but no war; $1 =$ war	
Regional/Systemic Level		
Proportion of dyads in alliance	Proportion of all dyads in the system that have alliance commitments	Maoz (2001)
Proportion of alliance networks	Proportion of all politically relevant dyads in a regional system that have alliance commitments	Maoz (2001)
Magnitude of disputes/wars	Number of MIDs/wars in the global/regional system	Maoz (1996, 2001)
Independent/Control Variables Nation Level		
Number of states in PRIE	Number of states in the politically relevant international environment (PRIE) of the state	Maoz (1997b, 2001)

Regime score	Modified Maoz-Russett regime score: $MODREG \equiv (REG + 100)/2$. Maoz-Russett regime score defined as $REG \equiv (DEMOC - AUTOC) \times CONCEN$	Maoz and Russett (1993) and Jaggres and Gurr (1995); adjusted to allow for positive values across the scale
Regime persistence	$PERSIST \equiv$ number of years current regime.	Maoz and Russett (1993); lagged values of $MODREG$ and $PERSIST$ also used
Revolutionary regime change	Change from one $REGTYPE$ to another. $REGCHG \equiv 0$: no change, 1: regime change	Maoz (1996; 1997a); period covered, 1816–1992
Political change in PRIE	$ENVCHG$: number of regime changes in PRIE over the previous four-year period divided by the number of states in the PRIE	Maoz (1996, 1997b); period covered, 1816–1992
Proportion of democracies in PRIE	$PRDEMPRE$: proportion of states in PRIE that are democratic	Maoz (1996; 1997b); period covered, 1816–1992
Capability ratio state/ PRIE	$AVCPRAT$: three-year moving average of the ratio of the state's military capabilities to the sum of military capabilities over all states making up its PRIE	Maoz (1997b); source for data: COW (1996); period covered, 1816–1992
Environmental conflict	$ENVDIS$: sum of all dispute involvements of states in one's PRIE not involving the focal state divided by the number of states in the PRIE	Maoz (1997b); period covered, 1816–1992
Disputes directed at the focal state	$AVGTARG$: three-year moving-average of the number of disputes in which the focal state was a primary target.	Maoz (1997b, 1997c)

Table 6.A1   Continued

Variable	Measure	Sources and Comments
Weighted alliances in PRIE	*ALLYPRIE:* number of alliance commitments of states in PRIE, excluding alliances with the focal state, weighted by type and partner's status, and divided by the number of states in the PRIE	Maoz (1997b); period covered, 1816–1992
Dyadic Variables[a]		
Capability ratio	Ratio of strongest member capabilities to weakest member capabilities	Maoz and Russett (1993)
Cumulative number of past disputes	*CUMDIS* cumulative number of past disputes divided by number of years of dyad	
Regional/Systemic Factors		
Proportion of states in democratic networks	Proportion of states in the regional/global system that are both politically relevant to each other and jointly democratic	Maoz (2000)
Proportion of states in alliance networks	Proportion of states in the regional/global system that are both politically relevant to each other and share a direct alliance	Maoz (2000)

[a]All dyadic variables that reflect minima of individual attributes are discussed earlier. This section examines specific dyadic attributes.

Research Methods

Three principal research methods are used here. First, for the national-level analyses, I conducted a TSCS procedure with panel-corrected standard errors (Beck and Katz 1995). This allows me to estimate national alliance formation patterns, controlling for both panel-specific autocorrelation and heteroskedasticity. In the national-level analyses, all independent, right-hand variables in the equations are averaged over the preceding three years. Thus, the equation estimated in the national-level analysis is given by:

$$
\begin{aligned}
WGHALLY_{it} = \; &\alpha_{it}\, NOPRIE_{I(t-3\,\to\,t-1)} + AVCPRAT_{I(t-3\,\to\,t-1)} + \\
&PRALYPRE_{I(t-3\,\to\,t-1)} + ENVDIS_{I(t-3\,\to\,t-1)} + \\
&AVGTARG_{I(t-3\,\to\,t-1)} + ENVCHG_{I(t-3\,\to\,t-1)} + \\
&ALLYPRIE_{I(t-3\,\to\,t-1)} + PRDEMPRE_{I(t-3\,\to\,t-1)} + \\
&REGIME_{I(t-3\,\to\,t-1)} + PERSIST_{I(t-3\,\to\,t-1)} + \varepsilon_{it}
\end{aligned}
$$

The analysis on initiation and termination of alliances is conducted via Weibull event-history analysis in which the dependent variable is the natural log proportion of dyadic alliances initiated/terminated in a given year ($\ln[p/\{1-p\}]$, where p is the proportion of dyads forming/terminating an alliance at a given year). Here, too, the independent, right-hand variables in the equations are averaged over the preceding three years.

The analyses relating alliances to MIDs/wars are similar in structure to the national and dyadic analysis of alliance formation. In the national case, I performed CSTS analysis with autocorrelation and heteroskedacticity controls. For the dyadic analysis, a similar analysis was performed. However, since the dependent variable in this case was a binary (dispute/no dispute or war/no war) variable, the distribution family used was the binomial distribution, and the link function was the logit function.[15]

Finally, for the regional and systemic analyses, I specify the type of estimation procedures used in the footnotes of the table. A more elaborate discussion of these equations is given in Maoz (2000).

NOTES

1. For a good review of the literature on these issues, see Sandler (1993).

2. This classification was criticized on the grounds that it is overly formalistic and does not include major alliances and other patron/client relations that were not formalized in alliance treaties. Nor does this classification include treaties of friendship that sometimes entail more commitments than ententes but rely on a general mode of cooperation that is more fundamental than the other categories (see Walt 1987; Sorokin 1997).

3. The reasons for these expected relationships are explained in detail in Maoz (1997b).

4. It is important to note that political realists do not consider most of these factors instrumental in alliance formation processes.

5. Panel-corrected standard errors are used. Within-state autocorrelation structures are assumed; see Beck and Katz (1995). While the number of panels—in the case of the entire population—approaches that of the number of time periods, this is not considered to be a problem given that time periods exceed twenty for virtually all cases (Beck, personal correspondence).

6. For a definition and discussion of this concept and its implications, see Maoz (1996, 1997b).

7. The analysis of politically relevant dyads is somewhat problematic in that it misses quite a few alliances between nonpolitically relevant states. In fact, politically relevant dyads capture only 375 of 1,078 dyadic alliance formations (or 34.8 percent) and only 10,856 of 35,493 allied dyad-years over the 1816–1986 period (30.6 percent). The reason for limiting this analysis for politically relevant dyads concerns the difficulty for computing the various independent variables for the entire dyad-year population (over 428,000 dyads). This measure differs from that of Gartzke and Simon (1998) in that it looks at alliance initiation only, not at the change of alliance status in a dyad, which includes both initiation and termination. The latter aspect of alliances is discussed separately later.

8. A dyad may have more than one alliance initiation over its history. The Weibull estimates of initiation allow for reentry.

9. Note that the minimum regime score of a dyad is not a simple linear continuum going from autocracy to democracy but rather a curvilinear function, the middle part of which represents anocracies, or unstable regimes. Because of this characteristic of this variable, the democratic/nondemocratic breakdown of the entire population is of special significance.

10. It must be noted that in the case of politically relevant dyads, there appears to be a considerable overlap between the PRIEs of both dyad members. However, this is not generally true for dyads involving at least one major or regional power. Analyses were performed on a more refined status breakdown (i.e., minor-minor, minor-regional, minor-major, regional-regional, regional-major, major-major). The results were generally similar to the breakdowns reported here.

11. Note that despite the fact that I discuss the term *alliance termination* while other studies deal with *alliance duration*, substantively the two variables are identical. Since the "failure" event in the event-history analysis is the end of an alliance and the entry date is the alliance formation year, then it does not really matter how the failure event is termed conceptually.

12. Bremer (1992) argues that the finding that allies are more likely to fight each other than nonaligned states is true for bivariate analyses of alliances and conflict. However, this relationship is reversed in multivariate analyses. Replication of this argument (Maoz and Russett 1993; Maoz 1996) corroborates this statement.

13. An extensive discussion of these factors' relationship to disputes and war is given in Maoz (1997b).

14. Most of the missing cases are due to lack of military capability data.

15. *Stata 6 Reference Manual,* vol. 4: 338–48.

7

Alliances
Why Some Cause War and Why Others Cause Peace

Douglas M. Gibler

$\mathbf{A}$re alliances a factor that increases the probability of war? This question is still open to debate despite over thirty years of systematic, empirical investigation into the alliance/war question. For example, Jack Levy (1981: 581), in one of the most definitive investigations into the relationship between alliances and war, concludes that, "for the period as a whole and also for each of the last five centuries, the evidence clearly contradicts the hypothesis that alliance formation is generally associated with high levels of war. To the contrary, it is more often associated with peace, particularly in the nineteenth and twentieth centuries." Levy argues this point despite the presentation of his own findings indicating that alliances were much more likely to be followed by war than by peace in four of the last five centuries (the nineteenth century produced the anomalous results).

Levy's (1981) contention is based on evidence showing that most wars are not preceded by alliances. This evidence seems to support logical contentions that discard the alliance/war findings as spurious to the processes of war. Since Levy's original study, however, empirical studies have begun to accumulate that show alliance formation is much more likely to generate war than peace. The growth of this evidence has led Vasquez (1993: 168), in a recent synthesis of the Correlates of War (COW) findings, to argue "alliances do not prevent war" and to contend that alliances "appear to be associated with war, particularly when an alliance is made with a major state." According to Vasquez, Levy's finding that nineteenth-century alliances were peaceful is only an indication that the war-prone effects of alliances can be stripped away; it does not discount the fact that most alliances, in all but one of the last five centuries, are more likely to be followed by war than by peace.

Even after Vasquez's strong conclusions, the answer to the alliance/war question apparently remains open. For example, Smith (1995: 405–6) contends that, "despite numerous studies of the empirical relationship between alliance formation and the occurrence of war, there are few robust findings. The evidence is often contradictory and generally inconclusive." However fruitful Smith's overall argument is in the sense of reexamining the logic behind alliance formation and war, this statement misses the empirical truth that we know quite a bit about what to expect when an alliance is formed. Instead of discarding years of alliance research, our goal should be to accumulate and synthesize this research in a productive manner. By underscoring the logic of what leads alliances to either war or peace, Smith (1995) is highlighting the correct path and is echoing the efforts of past scholars who called for reconceptualization of the alliance variable (Bueno de Mesquita and Singer 1973; Ward 1982; Vasquez 1993: 171). However, that path should be followed to its logical end by explaining the empirical patterns that have linked some alliances with war and still other alliances with peace.

This chapter presents an effort toward that end, toward synthesis of the alliance/war findings. After summarizing the theoretical arguments behind alliances causing either war or peace, the chapter follows with a presentation of the major empirical findings related to the alliance/war question. The second half of the chapter describes the theoretical and empirical support behind a new typology of alliances. This typology is shown to be capable of interpreting the types of signals that alliances send, which, in turn, aids in distinguishing between the war-prone and the peaceful alliances.

THE THEORETICAL FOUNDATIONS OF THE ALLIANCE/WAR RELATIONSHIP

Alliance theory originally developed as an extension of balance of power theory; alliances were formed to make sure that the capabilities of major state coalitions remained relatively equal. Equality of power was believed to promote peace because no sane leader would risk a war if they had a 50 percent chance of losing; war comes with preponderance, when a state has an easier chance of winning. At the state level, each nation has the choice to either arm itself or to pursue a policy of alliances when confronted with the prospect of a possible threat (Most and Siverson 1987; Walt 1987; Waltz 1979). If a nation chooses to arm, it risks an endless spiral of increasing armaments that could result in an arms race. According to balance-of-power theory, choosing alliances allows states to respond more quickly and with more precision to increased threats from other states. Diplomats and statesmen are able to use alliance networks to properly balance the capabilities of opposing nations that would maintain peace in the international system. Alliances, in this framework, function only to serve the balance of power.

Alliance commitments are also said to reduce the level of uncertainty in the system and minimize the likelihood of war that may result due to misperception and miscalculation (Singer, Bremer, and Stuckey 1972: 23). These commitments can also reduce the chances of catastrophic shifts in the systemic balance of power (Osgood 1967: 86). Some balance-of-power theorists claim that alliances are also necessary to avoid the most dangerous wars. A belligerent world power, seeking domination of the system, would likely restrain itself when confronted with an alliance system poised against it. Alliances, then, are an indispensable means of maintaining equilibrium in the system (Gulick 1955: 61–62).

Alliances are also thought to preserve peace in other ways. Major states may use alliances to constrain revisionist alliance partners, or an alliance can preserve peace by enhancing the prestige of a failing power whose collapse could be destabilizing to the international system (Liska 1962: 31–32; 37–40). Many neorealists argue that these alliances become meaningless in periods of bipolarity since the major state has enough capabilities to ignore the belligerent policies of its weaker allies (Waltz 1979: 169). Nevertheless, even intense periods of bipolarity have seen the growth of intricate alliance systems.

Waltz's observation that the major state must have enough power to ignore the policies of its allies was a response to anecdotal evidence that weaker allies tended to bring major state allies into expanded wars—an observation that has since been confirmed by more systematic investigations (Siverson and King 1979, 1980; Yamamoto and Bremer 1980).

That minor states bring major states into war is only one hypothesis linking alliances to war in the traditional literature, however. Traditional arguments linking alliances to war are as numerous and varied as those associating alliances with peace. For example, a state seeking alliances to show resolve could be interpreted by another state as attempting a strategy of encirclement. The targeted state would naturally respond by seeking counteralliances (Kaplan 1957: 24; Wright 1965: 774). Although such alliance partners may have been hard to find prior to the signing of the initial alliance, the developing cleavages could make other states more likely to become involved (Ray 1995: 375). The polarized system or region could also simply clarify the situation and make it easier for the aggressor to determine its odds of winning. As Bueno de Mesquita (1981: 151) notes, "The reduction of uncertainty brought about by such information may be all that is needed to facilitate an aggressor's desire to attack another state."

Balance-of-power theory can also support the existence of large, systemwide wars against potential dominance caused by alliance formation. In the example given earlier, the revisionist state is seeking dominance of the system but is confronted with an alliance against it. Instead of being rebuffed by this alliance, the revisionist state continues its policies and fights the war.[1] As Levy (1989b: 230) notes, a number of general wars over the past five centuries appear to fit this proposition. These include the "wars against Philip of Spain in the late sixteenth century, against Louis XIV in the late seventeenth century, against revolutionary and Napoleonic France a century later, and against Germany twice in this century" (1989b: 230–31).

As is obvious from these debates, no clear understanding of the relationship between alliance formation and war has ever been developed. Alliances in the traditional literature have been revered as sources of peace when acting as balancing agents and reviled as sources of war when the same alliance system breaks down. Based mostly on logic and historical anecdote and often mired in post hoc balance-of-power explanations, the traditional literature has not produced a convincing, consistent, theoretical explanation of the relationship between alliances and war. Not until the investigatory process turned empirical did researchers begin to start a process of cumulation that has provided many of the answers to the alliance/war puzzle.

THE EMPIRICAL FINDINGS ON ALLIANCES AND WAR

One of the first empirical tests of the alliance/war relationship was Singer and Small's (1966) examination of the behavior of major states. They found that states ranking high on alliance activity also rank high on war engagement, initiation, and battle deaths. This study provided the first systematic evidence that alliances were associated with war, which contradicted the traditional, realist balance of power literature. Following this work, Wallace (1973) and Bueno de Mesquita (1975, 1978) examined the effects polarization has had on war onset. Wallace found that very high or very low levels of polarity in the system produced war. Refining the indicators of polarity, Bueno de Mesquita showed that the "tightness" of an alliance system is not necessarily related to war onset. However, he found that increases in the tightness of alliances are correlated with war. Discrete alliances, on the other hand, are not associated with war.[2]

Levy (1981) reformulated the questions about alliance formation and war and, with a limited extension of the Correlates of War data, found that, with the exception of those in the nineteenth century, most alliances are followed by war. More significantly, a relationship between power and alliance formation was found, since all "Great Power" alliances in the sixteenth, seventeenth, and twentieth centuries were followed by war within five years (Levy 1981: 597–98, Table 7).

Alliances between major states may also be linked to increased probabilities of war in a second and less obvious way, according to Vasquez (1993: 163–64). Schroeder (1976) has discussed how major, "predatory" states may sign nonaggression pacts to remove potential adversaries before attacking smaller states. Moul (1988b: 34–35) shows that there is an increased likelihood for unequal states to go to war in the presence of a nonaggression pact with another state. These "pacts of restraint," or *pacta de contrahendo,* limit the expansion of war but promote hostilities between unequals.

The studies by Moul (1988b) and Schroeder (1976) are important indicators that alliances can, in some instances, be used as methods of limiting the expansion of war. However, in most cases alliances have been shown to be an important link in the spread of war once it begins. For example, Siverson and King (1979,

1980) have shown that participation in a multilateral war is often determined by alliance ties. The presence of alliances contributes to expanded wars as smaller states bring their major state allies into their wars. A similar analysis links alliances to the types of wars fought. Vasquez (1997) has shown that wars among noncontiguous, rival states almost always happen in the presence of an alliance. The original territorial issue that begins a conflict will drag noncontiguous allies into an expanded war; the implication is that, had the alliance not existed, the war was much more likely to remain bilateral.

Alliances may also have some unanticipated effects regarding which side states choose to fight on in a coming war. A small literature exists on the probability of "friends" becoming "foes." Expected utility theory notes that it is sometimes rational for allied states to end up in war with each other rather than against a common foe (Bueno de Mesquita 1981). Most arguments start between friends or acquaintances, and it follows that alliances may increase the probability of war between states. Ray (1990), however, has noted that this probability is quite small and depends on both the definition of war and the definition of alliance (in both cases, dyadic or multilateral). Bremer (1992) has seemingly ended this controversy by controlling for the proximity of the allies. Noting that allies are more likely to fight each other than unallied states, Bremer also finds that the addition of contiguity into a multivariate analysis eliminates the relationship between alliance ties and war. Although the logic of opportunity is consistent with Bueno de Mesquita's argument, Bremer's findings suggest that allies are becoming "foes" not because of their alliances but because they are neighbors. Allies that are not neighbors are not likely to go to war with each other. Bremer (1992) did find, however, that allies that were highly militarized had an increased chance of fighting each other. This suggests that Bremer may have statistically isolated the cases in which alliances promoted war between signatories.

Despite these results, the dangers of alliance formation should be noted. Research has shown that alliances increase rather than decrease the chances of war against nonallied states, and even Bremer's research has shown that alliances can increase the chances of war even against allies in certain situations. Both of these findings run counter to realist prescriptions advocating the quickly formed alliance, and both underscore the dangerous potential that alliances may have for naive policymakers.

The findings presented here that show that alliances are often associated with war have been tempered, however, by the inability to explain a large number of "anomalous," peaceful alliances. Nineteenth-century alliances, for example, are much more likely to be followed by peace than by war. Maoz (chap. 6 in this volume) and Levy (1981), among others, have clearly shown that many alliances are not followed by war. The presence of these peaceful alliances makes it difficult to come to any definitive conclusions on alliances as a correlate of war.

My argument in this chapter is that these alliance/war "inconsistencies" present important clues to understanding the multifaceted relationship among alliances, war, and peace. Inconsistent results persist because early empirical investigations concentrated their "brush-clearing" exercises on alliances in the aggregate rather than differentiating among the types of alliances being formed. Without a clear understanding of alliances as a multifaceted behavior, early research often found weak or inconsistent intercentury results. Trusting balance of power theory to explain alliance formation often led researchers to miss large groups of alliances that were not responses to either power or threat. To produce consistent findings linking alliances with war, peace, or even both, alliance research would have to reexamine the concept of alliance and what states were actually doing when they agreed to form one. The next section shows how reconceptualization of the alliance variable can make sense of the disparate findings produced thus far and also provide a guide for future research into the alliance/war question.

TWO TYPES OF ALLIANCE SIGNALS

How concerned states interpret an alliance will depend on the type of signal the alliance sends. Jervis (1970) has argued that states transmit two types of images, those that can be manipulated and those that cannot be manipulated. Within this context, the terms of alliances, their tenure, and how alliance commitments are broadcast to the world are all signals that can be controlled by the allied states. The alliance signals that cannot be manipulated are derived from the characteristics of the states that enter an alliance, and it is these signals that concerned states monitor closely. I contend that who forms an alliance is more closely watched than what agreement the alliance conveys. In an obvious example of this logic, it would matter more that Hitler and Stalin agree to divide Europe rather than, say, Ecuador and Peru during the same time period. Also, since most empirical analyses of commitment types (the signals that can be manipulated) have been unable to link specific types to changes in the war-proneness of states (see Bremer 1992: Table 1; Singer and Small 1966: Tables 8 and 9; Levy 1981), it seems appropriate for researchers to turn attention to the signals derived from the types of states in alliance (the signals that cannot be manipulated).[3]

Security Alliance Cues

This section outlines the variables that have been demonstrated to affect the war-proneness of alliances (Gibler 1997b). It is believed that these variables are some of the major indicators that concerned states monitor most closely when alliances are formed.

Status (Major or Minor)

One of the principle findings in the alliance literature thus far has been the discovery of the relationship between the status of the signatories and the onset of war. Singer and Small (1966: 130), for example, find strong associations between alliances and war when major states are present. Levy's (1981) analysis of "Great Power" wars and alliances provides more evidence linking status and war since he finds that the Great Power alliances are more likely than other types of alliances to be followed by war. These alliance findings are consistent with a number of studies that show major states are more likely to be war-prone. For example, Bremer (1980) shows that as state power increases, so does the likelihood of a state becoming involved in a war. This relationship also holds for involvement in militarized interstate disputes (Eberwein 1982; Gochman and Maoz 1984: 606–9).

These findings suggest that alliances involving major states may be more war-prone simply because major states are more war-prone. However, Vasquez (1993: 158–62) goes further than this, arguing that major states are socialized by a realist construction of reality and thereby learn to handle certain situations through the use of power politics practices, including alliance making. Not only, then, are major states more prone to get involved in wars and alliances than minor states, but once they have formed an alliance, their probability of going to war increases further. It could be inferred from this that minor states, outside the European, power politics culture, are less likely to involve themselves in these practices and are more cautious in their dealings with other states. Since their capabilities are also substantially less than the major states, minor state alliances would be viewed within the system as less threatening and as a probable attempt to avoid a future war.

Based on the findings discussed earlier, it can be inferred that, ceteris paribus, alliances formed solely by major states are more war-prone than the alliances formed by major and minor states. These latter alliances are, in turn, also more war-prone than alliances made solely by minor states.

Success in War

In conjunction with status, one of the factors that is most important in determining the bellicose effects of an alliance is the rate of success in the previous war the alliance signatories experienced. Political actors try to avoid previous mistakes and try to repeat policies that have succeeded (for elaboration, see Mansbach and Vasquez 1981: 263–73; Vasquez 1976). States that have failed in war are less likely to repeat actions that may lead to war once again, and since alliances are often associated with war, states are less likely to form alliances. The successful states do not show such hesitancy toward alliance formation, and their very success leads them to seek such alliances.

Empirical evidence supports the success-in-war logic. Singer and Small (1974: Tables 2 and 3), for example, show that states that have won wars in the past are more likely to get involved in wars in the future, and states that lose wars are less likely to get involved in future wars. More recently, Nevin (1996) has shown that war initiation is often dependent on a state's previous success in war. Using Levy's (1983) extension of the COW data set to 1495, Nevin finds that, as states experience more success in war, their probability of initiating another war increases; as states suffer losses, this proclivity to initiate decreases. Similarly, previous successes and losses influence the time span between initiations. Repeated wins lead to initiation much sooner than repeated losses.

Reiter's (1996) research suggests that the tendency to pursue previous successful strategies also applies to strategies of alliance formation. Examining the minor states in the system between 1921 and 1967, Reiter finds that minor states will pursue alliance strategies congruent with successes in previous world wars. Minor states will change alliance strategies if they suffered losses in previous world wars. Reiter's findings show that the alliance behavior of states is affected by their previous experiences in war.

Satisfaction

Theoretically related to success in war is the satisfaction level of the states in an alliance. While success in war captures how willing a state is to repeat past experiences, the satisfaction level of an alliance measures the willingness of alliance members to alter the status quo. For many years, historians and a few political scientists have argued that the satisfaction of a state greatly influences its actions (see especially Organski 1958 for this argument). It is posited that states satisfied with the status quo have little incentive to change it. States that are dissatisfied with the status quo are more likely to take steps to alter current distributions of power and/or wealth, even through the use of violence or war. Therefore, it can be inferred that alliances made by dissatisfied states are the alliances most likely to be formed to alter the status quo. Alliances formed by satisfied states are attempts to maintain the status quo.

Democracy

The proposition that democracies behave differently than other regime types is not new to political science; Levy (1989) has argued that the fact that democracies do not fight each other is the closest thing we have to a law. Nevertheless, until recently, hypotheses derived from the democratic peace proposition have not been directed to the alliance/war literature. Siverson and Emmons (1991) were the first to point out that democracies treat alliances differently than other states. They found that democracies tend to ally with each other much more frequently than with other types of states; democracies also tend to ally with each other more than other regime types ally with like regimes. However, these findings have recently been called into question (see Simon and Gartzke 1996; Thompson and Tucker 1997), and, even if empirically true, they still do not address the potential linkages between democratic alliances and war or peace.

Maoz (chap. 6 in this volume) has recently begun to research the effects of alliance formation by democracies on the prevalence of war in the system, region, and dyad. Summarizing his preliminary analysis, he finds that democracies behave differently from other states and are more similar to major states in their alliance choices. He also observes that the war-proneness of a democracy *increases* as it involves itself in more alliances, but nondemocracies *decrease* their war-proneness with alliance involvement. These results suggest that democracy may be an important variable affecting the war-proneness of states in alliance.

An Exception to the Security Alliance: The Territorial Settlement Treaties

One commitment type that does seem to affect the war-proneness of states is the territorial settlement treaty (Gibler 1996, 1997a, 1997b). According to the territorial explanation of war, the principal factor that escalates a dispute to the point of war is the presence of a territorial issue that actors try to resolve through the use of power politics (Vasquez 1993: 123–52). Recent evidence indicates that contiguity is highly correlated with an increased probability of war for a rival (Diehl 1985a, 1985b; Bremer 1992) and that most wars between rivals begin with territorial issues (Holsti 1991: 307–11). However, not all contiguous states experience hostilities, and not all territorial issues end in military conflict. The difference between the territorial disputes that end in war and those that do not can be found in the different methods used to resolve the issue. States that pursue power politics measures—targeting alliances, arms races, and so forth—in response to a territorial dispute are likely to generate hostility and countermeasures by their rival. However, if states pursue a strategy of conflict resolution and mediation that attempts to find a legitimate compromise or settlement of the issue, peace can be maintained for a prolonged period of time (Vasquez 1995b, 1993: chap. 4).

The territorial explanation of war places great emphasis on how territorial issues are handled by states. Nevertheless, most tests of this thesis have concentrated on the war-producing effects of territorial issues (Vasquez 1996; Kocs 1995; Hensel 1994; Goertz and Diehl 1992b; Holsti 1991) and, with the possible exception of Kocs (1995), have ignored the possible pacifying effects of *settling* territorial issues. It has been demonstrated that states may attempt to resolve some of their territorial disputes through the use of alliances (Gibler 1996, 1997a, 1997b). Instead of conforming to realist expectations that alliances serve to balance power between states or in the system, these treaty commitments are methods of diplomacy that states use to formalize the terms of territorial settlement. They are often followed by formal alliance commitments cementing the new understanding between states.

Like most of the research on territorial issues, the research on alliances has been dominated by attempts to link the independent variable to war rather than to peace. This emphasis has led many scholars to eschew the significant minority of alliance cases that are actually quite peaceful. Even though an extensive body of evidence has been accumulated showing that alliances are more often followed by war than by peace (Levy 1981; Singer and Small 1966) and that alliances are associated with the expansion of war (Siverson and King 1979, 1980; Siverson and Starr 1990), the territorial settlement treaties are likely to be peaceful because they remove the dangerous issue of territory from the agenda of states.

Measuring the Effects of Alliance Cues

To assess the empirical validity of the theoretical expectations presented here, the characteristics believed to represent the most intense signals of conflict or cooperation in alliance were analyzed over a two hundred–year historical period using the Correlates of War formal alliance data set.[4] For this analysis, an alliance is considered to be war-prone if it is followed by a war of any type within five years after the date of inception, excluding the first three months immediately following inception. Controls were also established to ensure that the war was related to the alliance that preceded it (Gibler 1997b). The five-year time period has been generally accepted (Singer and Small 1966; 1968; Levy 1981), although there has been experimentation with different temporal ranges (Ostrom and Hoole 1978).[5]

Tables 7.1 and 7.2 present conditional probabilities that assess the individual effects of each of the alliance cues. The conditional probability table reports the actual and expected war counts for both alliance types, followed by the total number of that alliance type. The expected war counts are the number of wars that would be expected given the total number of alliances of that type (i.e., the more alliances of a particular type, the more likely it is that wars would follow at least some of these alliances). Wide variation between expected and actual wars is a good first clue that a variable may potentially be important. The conditional probability of war for the alliance type is reported as P(war) in the fourth column; this is the actual probability that an alliance having this characteristic is followed by war.

In a method similar to Bremer's (1992: 325–27, Table 1), this table also calculates a difference-of-proportions test that measures the statistical likelihood of obtaining the given conditional probability. It compares the conditional probability of war by alliance type to the unconditional probability of war. The unconditional probability of war is also the base probability of war for all alliances. Positive Z scores for the difference of proportions test indicate more wars were observed than were expected; negative Z scores indicate fewer wars were observed than were expected. The pr(Z) value reflects the statistical significance of the Z score; $p < .05$ (less than a 5 percent chance that the value would occur randomly) is generally accepted as an appropriate level of significance in social science.

Table 7.1 Conditional Probabilities of War Involving an Ally—Territorial Settlement Treaties, 1815–1980

Alliance Characteristic	1815–1980 War Counts		N	Z	pr(Z)
	Actual	*Expected*			
Territorial Settlement Treaties					
Territorial settlement	1	(7.97)	27	−2.94**	0.0016
No territorial settlement	56	(49.03)	166	1.19	0.1170
Average alliance[a]	57	(57.00)	193	P(war) = 0.2953	

Source: Adapted from Gibler (1977, Table 5.1a).

**p < .01.

[a] P(war) for the average alliance constitutes the base probability of war for all alliances during that time period.

Table 7.2 Conditional Probabilities of War Involving an Ally by Alliance Type, 1815–1980

Alliance Characteristic	1815–1980 War Counts Actual	Expected	N	Z	pr(Z)	1815–1899 War Counts Actual	Expected	N	Z	pr(Z)	1900–1980 War Counts Actual	Expected	N	Z	pr(Z)
Successful/Unsuccessful															
Both successful	23	(15.36)	52	0.36*	0.0132	7	(4.23)	11	1.72*	0.0427	16	(11.18)	41	1.69*	0.0455
Mixed	23	(30.42)	103	−4.00**	0.0013	5	(8.08)	21	−1.38	0.0838	18	(22.36)	82	−1.08	0.1401
Both unsuccessful	11	(11.22)	38	−1.60	0.2033	3	(2.69)	7	0.24	0.4052	8	(8.45)	31	−0.18	0.4286
Status															
Major-major states	25	(14.47)	49	1.31**	0.0047	7	(8.85)	23	−0.79	0.2148	18	(7.09)	26	4.80**	0.0000
Major-minor states	24	(23.33)	79	−2.06	0.4960	6	(4.62)	12	0.82	0.2061	18	(18.27)	67	−0.07	0.4721
Minor-minor states	8	(19.20)	65	−4.82**	0.0000	2	(1.54)	4	0.47	0.3192	6	(16.64)	61	−3.06**	0.0011
Dispute-based measure															
Both satisfied	24	(28.94)	98	−1.09	0.1379	12	(12.31)	32	−0.11	0.4562	12	(18.00)	66	−1.66*	0.0485
Mixed	19	(21.85)	74	−0.73	0.2327	3	(2.69)	7	0.24	0.4052	16	(18.27)	67	−0.62	0.2676
Both dissatisfied	14	(6.20)	21	3.73**	0.0001	0	0.00	0	n/a	n/a	14	(7.16)	21	4.05**	0.0000
Tau B measure															
Both satisfied	18	(25.10)	85	−1.69*	0.0455	2	(5.77)	15	−2.00*	0.0228	16	(19.09)	70	−0.83	0.2033
Mixed	13	(12.11)	41	0.31	0.3783	2	(2.31)	6	−0.26	0.3974	11	(9.55)	35	0.55	0.2912
Both dissatisfied	26	(19.79)	67	1.66*	0.0485	11	(6.92)	18	1.98*	0.0239	15	(13.36)	49	0.52	0.3015
Democracy															
Both undemocratic	38	(35.74)	121	0.45	0.3264	13	(10.77)	28	0.87	0.1922	25	(25.36)	93	−0.08	0.4681
Mixed	16	(17.13)	58	−0.33	0.3707	2	(4.23)	11	−1.38	0.0838	14	(12.82)	47	0.39	0.3483
Both democratic	3	(4.13)	14	−0.66	0.2546	0	0.00	0	n/a	n/a	3	(3.90)	14	−0.49	0.3121
Average alliance[a]	57	(57.00)	193	P(war) =	0.2953	15	(15.00)	39	P(war) =	0.3846	42	(42.00)	154	P(war) =	0.2727

Source: Adapted from Gibler (1997b, Table 5.1).

*$p < .05$.

**$p < .01$.

[a] P(war) for the average alliance constitutes the base probability of war for all alliances during that time period.

Territorial Settlement Treaties

Only one of the twenty-seven territorial settlements was followed by a war involving an ally within five years after formation, according to Table 7.1. This is an average rate of 3.7 percent versus an average war-rate of 39 percent for all other alliances. The very low Z scores for territorial settlement treaties reflect the pacific nature of these alliance types. In both the nineteenth and twentieth centuries, far fewer war onsets followed these alliances than were statistically expected. Slightly more wars than were expected followed nonterritorial settlement alliances in both centuries. However, neither of these scores was significant. It is of equal theoretical interest to note that the probability of war increases only marginally for alliances that do not attempt to resolve territorial disputes. The implication here is that resolving territorial issues decreases the chances of war for an alliance, but the probability of war for alliances that do not settle territorial issues are determined by other factors. As has been demonstrated elsewhere, the results for the territorial settlement treaties are robust and consistent (Gibler 1996, 1997a). Their pacific nature cannot be attributed to the presence of any other state-based variables.

Security Alliances, 1815–99

The post-Napoleonic nineteenth-century results are presented in the second column of Table 7.2. This part of the nineteenth century has been described as the formative years for the traditional balance-of-power system. Beginning with the early congress system, and culminating with the rise of Bismarck in the 1870s, this century witnessed a drastic change in alliance politics. An elaborate alliance system was developed to control revisionist states and to balance the power between potential belligerents. The flexible, ad hoc alliances, so important in the traditional literature (Morgenthau 1967), seemed to be prevalent. However, it is equally apparent that these alliances did more than balance power. Similar to the territorial settlement treaties and the Congress of Vienna system, alliance politics tried to include all states in a system of governance and control the types of war fought. For example, major state alliances are not war-prone during this century. Thirty percent are followed by war (seven of twenty-three). Half of the mixed status and minor alliances are followed by war (six of twelve). All of these results produce probabilities that are not significant at a .05 level, however.

No alliances were made by states that had lost a dispute with the most powerful state (the dispute-based satisfaction measure). The probability that this type of alliance distribution would happen by chance is quite small (out of thirty-nine total alliances). Alliances made by states whose alliance portfolios were similar to Great Britain's were also peaceful. Only two of fifteen were followed by war (13 percent, $p = .02$), and those three alliances were the only alliances formed. It seems that the major powers were adept at including all states, even potential belligerents, in alliance systems.

Despite the attempts at universalism during this century, some alliances were followed by war, and these alliances were of a very specific type. First, alliances made by successful states were war-prone. Seven of eleven were followed by war (64 percent, $p < .05$). The presence of an unsuccessful state in an alliance decreased the probability of war to 28 percent (eight of twenty-eight). The mixed-status alliance was also war-prone. Half of these alliances (six of twelve, not significant) were followed by war. States whose alliances policies diverged greatly from the status quo (measured by the tau B score of alliance portfolios) were quite war-prone.[6] Sixty-one percent of these alliances (eleven of eighteen, $p = .04$) were followed by war.

These results seem consistent with the types of wars that were fought during this century. The nineteenth century was a period of colonialism for the major powers. Africa, East Asia, and, to some extent, the Americas were all contested regions. It is possible, then, that some alliances were used as a method of preparing for predatory wars. States at odds with the status quo distributions of territory and power (as evidenced by alliance portfolio agreement) were likely to form alliances to seek change. Russian and Austro-Hungarian predation in the Balkans are probably the best examples of this.

Instead of using alliances as a method of preparing for war, alliances became a method of diplomacy used to avoid war, but this was not the realist prescribed system of power checking power. Instead, the early nineteenth century witnessed the development of a managed system of governance. Major states, acting in concert, developed an alliance system dedicated to developing consensus on certain issues; for example, the previous chapter noted several territorial issues settled by these alliances. The dissatisfaction measured by the tau B scores is probably capturing the alliances and wars made by states during the transition between particularist periods, from 1849 to 1870, when these attempts at incorporation faltered (see Wallensteen 1984).[7] Prussia's state-building alliances and wars account for much of the relationship, but also present are the separate alliances between France and Sardinia and France and Russia.

The differences, then, between the nineteenth century and centuries prior is that nineteenth-century alliances were not perceived to be threatening to the status quo. Instead, they were concerned with peripheral regions and dedicated to colonial or imperial interests. Eventually, however, alliance politics began to change once more. With the decline of Bismarck, the intricate system of managed alliances began to break apart, and its remnants have often been credited with the expansion of the Balkan crises into the First World War. The last section of Table 7.2 examines whether, in aggregate, a sea change was witnessed in alliance politics at the turn of the century.

Security Alliances, 1900–80

The twentieth-century alliances produce some results that are consistent with previous periods. For example, the status of the alliance members once again affects the war-proneness of an alliance. Alliances made by major states are followed by wars involving one ally almost 70 percent of the time (eighteen of twenty-six). Alliances formed by minor powers only experience war six times even though sixty-one alliances were formed by these states. Mixed status alliances have a probability of war similar to that of the base probability for all alliances (26 percent vs. 27 percent, respectively).

Dissatisfaction, measured in two separate ways, is also an important factor in determining the likelihood that an alliance will be followed by war. Alliances made by states that had lost their last dispute with the most powerful state in the system (the dispute-based measure) were followed by war fourteen of twenty-one times (67 percent, $p < .05$). Alliances made by states satisfied with the status quo were followed by war only twelve of sixty-six times (18 percent, $p < .01$). There is more than a 300 percent drop in the likelihood of war between these two alliance types.

Prior to the twentieth century, no alliances were formed solely by democracies; in the twentieth century this number is fourteen, and only three of these were followed by war. Even though these results are not significant at a .05 level (due to the relatively small number of this alliance type), it is interesting to note the types of wars in which the three war-prone alliances become involved. All three of these alliances are followed by complex, multilateral wars, and all three of these are Great Power wars: two were followed by World War II, and one was followed by the Korean War. If one accepts Vasquez's (1993: chap. 7, 1996) distinction between the types of wars—the fact that dyadic wars are different and involve different paths to war than multilateral wars—then these results are consistent with the democratic peace proposition. It is my contention that the results for these democratic alliances are due chiefly to the contagion effects of alliances. If the types of war are controlled, these alliances are strongly peaceful for dyadic wars and mildly peaceful for all wars.[8] Despite these arguments, however, the relative paucity of purely democratic alliances and the generally mixed nature of results for these alliances limit the usefulness of this measure as a predictor of alliance war-proneness.[9]

A TYPOLOGY OF ALLIANCES

The alliance signals analyzed in the last section offer important information about how states interpret newly formed alliances and also form the empirical support for a new typology of alliance formation (Gibler 1997b: chap. 5). This typology follows the logic outlined earlier and divides alliances into two basic types: the territorial settlement treaty and the security alliance. It further divides the security alliances into three separate categories according to their probable level of threat. Table 7.3 presents the predicted and actual effects of each alliance type.

Table 7.3 The Overall Relationship between Alliances and War (Predicted and Actual)

Type of Alliance	Anticipated Reaction	Predicted Result	Actual Result		
			Wars	N	Rate
All alliances (regardless of type)	Unknown	Unknown	57	193	0.2953
Territorial settlement treaty	Decreased armament levels Decreased involvement in crises Decreased involvement in alliances	Peace	1	27	0.0370
Security alliances					
Low-bellicosity alliances (bellicosity score: 1–3)	None	No effect/peace	6	40	0.1500
Medium-bellicosity alliances (bellicosity score: 4–9)	Uncertain	Situation-dependent	31	91	0.3407
High-bellicosity alliances (bellicosity score: 12–27)	Increased armament levels Increased involvement in crises Increased involvement in alliances	War	19	35	0.5429

Source: Adapted from Gibler (1997b, Table 6.1).

The territorial settlement treaties are listed first. The theoretical expectations for these alliances are that they will produce decreased armament levels, less crisis involvement, and fewer counteralliances and are most likely to be followed by peace. The results show that only one alliance of twenty-seven was followed by war within five years. The percentage rate of 3.7 percent is dramatically less than the base probability for all alliances (29.4 percent), a difference that is also statistically significant ($Z = -2.99$, $p < .01$). Although the theoretical expectations regarding armament levels, crises, and counteralliances are not tested, the empirical confirmation of the predicted result supports the logic behind the territorial explanation of war (Vasquez 1993).

Security alliances are divided into three groups and ranked according to their likely "bellicosity." Each of the three measures tested in the previous section can have three values—absent, mixed, or present—and since there are three measures—success in war, satisfaction, and status—there are a total of twenty-seven possible combinations of factors for an alliance. To develop a bellicosity score, the alliances were rated according to the presence or absence of the three variables, and then the entire distribution of alliances was divided into three parts: low-, medium-, and high-bellicosity alliances. Low-bellicosity alliances generally have at least two of the dangerous factors absent, and high-bellicosity alliances have at least two of these factors present. Mixed-bellicosity alliances, as the term implies, tend to have a mixed presence of these factors.

The security alliances are divided into three groups. The results for the least war-prone group are given first. These alliances are expected to have little impact on the security concerns of other states because the states forming these alliances have neither the opportunity nor the willingness to change the status quo (Siverson and Starr 1990). Although peace is predicted to follow these alliance types, it is a different form of peace than the one that follows the territorial settlement treaties. The territorial settlement treaties are attempts at conflict resolution and, if successful, are likely to result in decreased hostility levels between states. The peaceful security alliances are not attempts at conflict resolution, but they are not provocative attempts to change the status quo either. Therefore, the predicted result of these alliances is better described as "no effect." The results in Table 7.3 confirm these expectations. Of forty low-bellicosity alliances, only six were followed by war within five years after alliances formation. Only 15 percent of these alliances are followed by war compared to a base probability close to 39 percent for all alliances ($p < .01$).

The mixed-purpose alliances, as the label describes, are alliances formed by different types of states for different reasons. A satisfied state may seek an alliance with a dissatisfied state to pacify it, or a major state may seek control over a minor state (Schroeder 1976). The predicted reaction to these alliances by other states is uncertain and is dependent on contextual situations, such as the presence of rivalry, repeated crises, or continuing arms races. If the alliances are formed during times of hostility, then the chances of war obviously increase. Conversely, during times of low hostility levels, the alliances are likely to produce an increased sensitivity in other states but are unlikely to generate the processes that would lead to war. Of ninety-two alliances, over one-third (thirty-one) are followed by war within five years. The 4-percent increase in the likelihood of war over alliances in aggregate is significant at the .05 level.

The alliances meant to build war-winning coalitions are highly provocative attempts to influence and eventually change the status quo. They are likely to promote increased armament levels, crises, and an increase in counteralliances. Their predicted result is war. Of thirty-five high-bellicosity alliances formed between 1815 and 1980, over half were followed by war within five years. These alliances are almost twice as likely to generate war as a result than alliances in general (*p* < .01) and are probably attempts to build war-winning coalitions.

CONCLUSION

The results summarized here show that we know a lot more about alliances than we originally thought. Reconceptualization of the alliance variable has shown that Vasquez (1993) was correct in his assertion that alliances are associated with war and that Levy (1981) was correct in emphasizing the importance of the many "anomalous," peaceful alliances. After disaggregating alliances into various smaller groups based on type, theories can be constructed that assess the variegated effects of alliance formation. The peaceful alliances can be separated from other alliances to examine their ability to manage conflict. The war-prone alliances can be isolated from the larger set of general alliances so as to better assess the processes that led their alliance members to war. Finally, the remaining group of mixed-purpose alliances can be studied in further detail to delineate the types of situations in which these alliances are likely to generate war. All of these results point to the fact that alliance type should guide the conduct of future research and may have important implications for foreign policy (see Gibler 1997b for this argument).

In the end, it has been demonstrated that alliances have the power to remove dangerous issues from the agendas of states, making war much less likely. But many dangerous alliances also have the unique ability of creating insecurity and conflict in targeted states that, in turn, spurs the processes that lead to war. The question that began this chapter still remains: Are alliances a factor that increases the probability of war? The answer has been shown to be complex but not elusive; after controlling for alliance type, alliances made by dissatisfied major states that have been previously successful in war are a factor in the onset of war.

NOTES

1. The revisionist fights for a number of reasons (even if its capabilities do not match those of the coalition against it): the adversaries show a lack of resolve, the revisionist

state is risk-acceptant, and/or perhaps the revisionist believes a surprise attack could swing the balance of power in its favor.

2. Bueno de Mesquita has discounted these findings as a potential levels of analysis fallacy; that is, one or two states could be driving the systemic polarization results even though the remaining states in the system are moving away from polarization. Nevertheless, the polarization studies seem to provide evidence that intense polarization is a necessary systemic condition for large magnitude wars (Vasquez 1993: 248–58). Although polarization is not necessarily associated with the war-proneness of single alliances, alliances formed during periods of intense polarization do have an increased chance of being followed by large magnitude wars. This interpretation is consistent with the findings of Siverson and King (1979) and Sabrosky (1985) on war expansion as well as Organski and Kugler's (1980: 49–56) analysis of world wars.

3. This dichotomy does not mean to suggest that alliances cannot serve other purposes as well. For example, alliance formation may provide domestic political benefits (Barnett and Levy 1991), or alliances may also serve as methods of controlling the foreign policies of other states (Schroeder 1976). However, I believe that these purposes are often missed by other states when the alliance signal is interpreted. Since ancillary purposes are often mixed with security purposes, the level of threat to other states is still dependent on the types of states involved in the alliance.

4. For empirical tests using an extended data set of alliances, 1648 to 1815, see Gibler (1999b, 1997b).

5. The independent variables were measured as follows: Status was defined according to Correlates of War definitions of major and minor status (Small and Singer 1972; Gibler 1999a). Success in war was based on Correlates of War definitions of war winners. Two separate indicators were used to measure the impact of satisfaction: (1) the traditional tau B alliance portfolio measure (Lemke and Reed 1997) and (2) a dispute-based measure that assesses the level of past conflict with the most powerful state in the system (Maoz and Mor 1995). Polity III measures were used for definitions of democracy. A complete discussion of reliability and validity is included in Gibler (1997b: chap. 2).

6. The tau B score is calculated using alliance portfolios prior to the alliance in question to avoid circularity.

7. Wallensteen identified two basic types of historical periods in which the policies of the major states differed dramatically. Universalist periods are "understood to be concerted efforts among major powers to organize relations between themselves to work out acceptable rules of behavior. . . . Particularist policies, in contrast, are understood to be policies which emphasize the special interest of a given power, even at the price of disrupting existing organizations or power relationship" (1984: 243). Wallensteen found particularist periods associated with much more conflict than universalist periods.

8. An alternative explanation of these results is less charitable to the democratic peace proposition. It could be argued that contagion does not bring democracies into the larger wars, but instead, the large wars are composed of democracies fighting revisionist states. Democracies do not fight each other because they collectively control the system. When that system is challenged by revisionist states, then larger wars result.

9. It should be noted that multivariate results using these same indicators produce significant results for the democracy variable. The differences between the bivariate and multivariate results may also explain why these findings diverge from those of Maoz (chap. 6

of this volume). However, even his multivariate findings (Table 6.4) show that the regime score of the state in alliance is not related to war- or dispute-proneness. All other variables produce consistent and robust results at the multivariate level, confirming the bivariate relationships presented here (Gibler 1997b: chap. 5; Gibler and Vasquez 1998).

8

Military Buildups

Arming and War

Susan G. Sample

$\mathbf{D}$o arms races cause wars? For a variety of reasons, one of the most elusive pieces of this war puzzle has been the role that military buildups play in the occurrence of war. It is a question intricately bound up with foreign policy choices that countries make each day in an effort to enhance their security. As such, the empirical question of the impact of arming for security has also been wrapped up in direct political controversy between those convinced that arming will cause war and those convinced that *not* arming will cause war. The social-scientific literature has been slow in finding an authoritative answer to this question due to controversies over how to structure a test properly, a debate that has often seemed to overshadow the real questions at its heart: do arms races cause wars; and what impact, if any, do military buildups really have on a nation's security?

The political controversy stems from a real theoretical disagreement. There are, in fact, two mutually exclusive theoretical arguments about how arming affects the relationship between states. The first, what we refer to as the *para bellum* argument, derives from the ancient Latin creed: "If you desire peace, you must prepare for war." In this formulation, preparing for war has the seemingly nonintuitive effect of staving off conflict. This is the argument of deterrence; if a country prepares for war, it is able to make any potential attacker believe that the costs of an attack will be too high to make the act of aggression worthwhile. The policy implication of this view is that armaments programs may be pursued because they serve the double purpose of decreasing the likelihood of war, while simultaneously making it easier to fight any war that cannot be deterred or otherwise avoided. It is a clear, logical argument based on the assumption that policymakers rationally calculate the costs and benefits of all actions as they relate to the national interest of a country.

In complete contrast to this theoretical argument, the lesson derived from

World War I was that the arms buildups prior to the war had significantly contributed to its occurrence. Mutual arming, the argument goes, leads to a situation in which both countries may plausibly believe that the other intends threatening or aggressive behavior. With no supranational arbitrator of their disputes, countries depend on their own arms to give them security. However, by creating the impression of threat (and the capability of threat), arming increases the chance that war will occur, while ensuring that any war that does happen will be extremely costly for everyone involved.

Addressing the question of whether arms buildups lead to war is more complex than it first appears. Controversies over conceptualization (How exactly should we conceptualize an "arms race"?), research design, and measurement (How do we know an arms race when we see it?) have taken on a life of their own in the literature. The methodological controversies have served to stunt the theoretical growth of the literature on arms races. There has been a notable lack of evolution in our attempts to develop a strong explanation (in light of what we *do* know) for why arms increases might lead to wars that would not occur in their absence (Diehl and Crescenzi 1998).

Another important issue that must be addressed if we are to discern the probable outcome of arms programs is the role now played by nuclear weapons. The advent of nuclear weapons added a whole new dimension to the controversy, scholarly and political. The enormous cost attendant with a nuclear exchange added a great sense of urgency to the question. Did the advent of nuclear weapons fundamentally alter the nature of interstate relations, as some argue, making war between the major states rationally incredible as long as the weapons existed? Or, alternatively, did nuclear weapons mean that the spiral of threat and hostility that states initiated with an arms race could now have utterly devastating results for all the world?

This chapter considers what we know from tests previously conducted on these issues and reformulates some questions to give a more nuanced estimation of the effect of military buildups on international security. The conclusions of this study suggest that, like many political questions, the answer is far more complex than either side of the political debate would prefer. In the end, I offer what I intend to be a stronger and more consistent theoretical argument to explain what might at first appear to be theoretically contradictory empirical findings. Those findings are a positive and significant empirical relationship between mutual military buildups and war occurrence that may have changed substantially in the face of the nuclear threat.

I argue that to explain what otherwise seems contradictory, we should focus our attention on the norms, or rules of behavior, in the international system for dealing with conflict. An exploration of the nature, growth, and change in the norms states employ to determine what constitutes appropriate behavior in the context of their relationships with other states is critical to our analysis. Understanding these norms will make it possible to explain why states tend to react to military buildups with policies that tend to escalate the violence, while at the same time explaining more of the observed behavior of major states during the Cold War than either deterrence theory or its opposite. In this chapter, I outline the dimensions of the conflict over the role of arms buildups in the empirical literature, then address three major questions that help assess what, empirically, the relationships really are, before weaving the empirical findings into the larger theoretical argument.

THE CONTROVERSY IN THE LITERATURE

A large part of the controversy in the empirical literature on the effects of arming stems from the work of Michael Wallace. His initial study (Wallace 1979) found an extraordinarily strong relationship between countries rapidly arming and disputes between them escalating to war. Of ninety-nine total dyadic disputes between 1816 and 1965, twenty-eight occurred while both countries were rapidly building up their weapons, and twenty-three of those escalated to war. Only three disputes in the group became wars in the absence of arms buildups. The conclusion was a strong statement that arms races led to wars.

This observation did not stand unchallenged. The findings of this initial study were criticized on several grounds, but the focal points of the criticism were the set of disputes Wallace used and his index for determining when an arms race was occurring. The primary concern regarding the dispute set was that the findings might be the result of dividing the multilateral World Wars into bilateral dyads, perhaps artificially increasing the number of disputes characterized by both arms buildups and war outcomes. Several research notes by Wallace and others explored this possibility, and it was discovered that the strength of the findings could be affected by manipulating the dispute set, though the direction of the relationship remained the same (Wallace 1980; Weede 1980; Altfeld 1983).

Several possible problems with the index were also explored. While Wallace intended to capture intense mutual military buildups, it seemed that the index might be capturing intense *unilateral* buildups and/or war preparations themselves (Altfeld 1983). In either case, they might be associated with war occurrence, but the theoretical link offered by Wallace between arming and war would obviously not be a valid explanation for the finding.

Diehl (1983, 1985) stepped into the continuing controversy with an independent test of the military buildup–war connection. He used a new measure of military buildups and avoided many of Wallace's problems with the dispute set by including only disputes occurring within rivalries. Those studies only found a weak relationship between arming and dispute escalation. Despite its contribution, Diehl's study did not fully resolve the controversy because he used both a new dispute set and a new means of measuring arms buildups. It was therefore impossible to determine which change led to the findings that differed so much from Wallace's. Diehl cast substantial doubt on Wallace's findings but could not really banish them.

The real problem with the research for a number of years was an apparent assumption that the various criticisms of Wallace's study could not, in fact, be tested to determine their validity. But they could be. Holding the measure of military buildups constant while testing with different dispute sets allows us to determine what impact the exact dispute set has on the statistical findings. Holding the dispute set constant while testing with different measures of arming allows us to determine what effect that measure has on the statistical findings. Thus, it was possible to resolve the debate over the nature of the bivariate relationship between arms buildups and dispute escalation (Sample 1996, 1997). As it turned out, the changes in dispute set and arming measure did make slight statistical differences, but none that actually altered the conclusions.[1] While the uncovered relationship never appeared as strong as Wallace concluded, there is a significant positive link between arming and dispute escalation in complete bivariate testing.

MISSING PIECES OF THE PUZZLE

While resolving that controversy over the bivariate relationship was an important step forward in our understanding of the relationship between arms buildups and national security (or insecurity), it doesn't answer all of our questions. Three other pieces to this particular puzzle were not addressed originally, and they needed to be for us to determine what we really know and advance our understanding of these relationships. The first is a question of research design. While we have some evidence that military buildups increase the chance of a dispute escalating to war, we don't know whether they contribute to the *occurrence* of disputes in the first place. As it turns out, this question is far more important theoretically than it might first appear.

The second question is the obvious issue of whether this bivariate relationship holds up under multivariate scrutiny. Perhaps it is not the military buildup that increased the chance of war at all but rather some other variable or variables entirely. The early tests were rather primitive in that sense.

The last question is that of the impact of nuclear weapons in the state system after World War II. If nuclear weapons have qualitatively altered the relations between countries that possess them, we have to consider what that means for our overall understanding, not only of arming but of the dynamics of international relations more generally. Has the behavior of the major states changed, and if so, is it due primarily to a change in the structure of the international system, or the result of an effective evolution of the norms the states employ in their interactions?

WHAT EFFECT DO MILITARY BUILDUPS HAVE ON
THE OCCURRENCE OF DISPUTES?

The question of whether military buildups encourage disputes in the first instance is an important, though neglected, question. The original research design to address the impact of military buildups on dispute escalation has been criticized on the grounds that by including the militarized dispute as an intervening variable, the actual question of cause and effect between arming and war gets hopelessly offtrack. Houweling and Siccama (1981) argue that Wallace's original study, because it looked at the outcome of militarized disputes rather than the results of arms races per se, could not be assured that it was finding a causal relationship rather than just an association. For instance, both arms buildups and war could be the result of ongoing enduring rivalries, making the statistical relationship spurious (Diehl and Crescenzi 1998; Goertz and Diehl 1993).

Houweling and Siccama (1981) assert that by including the militarized dispute as an intervening variable, the results can only be considered a conjunction of the effect of military buildups and the dispute. This is, of course, entirely true. However, by beginning with a set of militarized disputes, the disputes themselves are a constant in the formulation. Any variation in the outcome must be the result of the independent variable—the military buildup—rather than the constant. There is a statistically significant correlation between military buildups and war, given the occurrence of a militarized dispute. The correlation between militarized disputes and war certainly exists; it is determined by the fact that war is defined as a militarized dispute that reaches a certain intensity.

Theoretically, the criticisms are more telling. This is so primarily because the research design does not purport to begin with all arms races and seek instances of wars but rather takes the shortcut of starting with disputes. Although this is entirely adequate for determining whether a relationship exists between military buildups and dispute escalation to war, this formulation (due to the inclusion of disputes as an intervening variable) is not a compelling way to test whether military buildups lead to war. It might logically be inferred that disputants should be deterred from escalating to war when both countries have rapidly built up their militaries in preparation. However, it is significant that the research design eliminates the possibility that there would have been more militarized disputes (and possibly wars) if the arming had not happened as it did. The logic of deterrence would certainly suggest that a country might be deterred from challenging the status quo (initiating a dispute) if its potential opponent were rapidly increasing its military capability. The flip side of this, of course, is that there is also no way of knowing whether the rapid military buildups led to disputes that would not have otherwise occurred.

It is possible that arms buildups coincident with militarized disputes *are* more likely to escalate than disputes in which neither party is arming rapidly, while at the same time, arming has the general tendency of deterring disputes from occurring. This division of outcomes from arming might be the result of a self-selection bias into the phase of a militarized dispute. In other words, for a country to get into a militarized dispute, overcoming the deterrent effect of the other's arms buildup, it must really be willing to settle the conflict by force if necessary. Such disputes would naturally be more likely to escalate than disputes in which the initiator did not have to overcome the deterrent barrier of the other's buildup (Fearon 1994).

Because of this possibility, the relationship between arming and dispute occurrence is often considered the critical missing element in the arming-to-war equation. If arming leads to disputes, the finding would contradict the tenets of deterrence theory: military buildups could not be counted on to discourage either the occurrence of disputes or their escalation. A positive relationship between arming and dispute escalation suggests that deterrence may somehow be faulty, but it does so in an indirect way. It does not directly address the possibility of different outcomes of arming when considered independent of the intervention of an already hostile relationship (as shown by the occurrence of militarized disputes). If deterrence works, then arming should not be associated with the occurrence of disputes, even if it might be related to the escalation of disputes once that barrier is broken.

One way of determining how arming affects the chance of conflict is to take dyad-years as the unit of analysis and discern whether arming affects the likelihood of a dispute occurring between any given pair of states. The test in this case is a fairly simple one and a first cut at trying to pin down what relationship exists between arming and dispute occurrence. The unit of analysis is the dyad-year from 1816 to 1993 among the major states in the system. This yielded 2,444 dyad-years for which it was possible to calculate a measure of mutual military buildup (eliminating a number of cases following immediately on the heels of a major war). There was at least one dispute in 198 of those dyad-years.

The test was conducted twice, using the same two measures of a military buildup used to resolve the initial controversy.[2] The findings suggest that there does appear to be some slight positive relationship between mutual military buildups and the chance that countries will be involved in militarized disputes. In bivariate logit analysis, the relationship was statistically significant using one measure of arming, but not so over the whole Correlates of War (COW) period using the other.[3] Tables 8.1 and 8.2 show the proportion of dyad-years in which there was a dispute, given by whether the countries involved were rapidly arming in that year or not.

If we look at the likelihood of a dispute occurring in a given dyad-year, we see a clear difference between mutually arming dyads and the others. We see a militarized dispute occurring in 15 or 16 percent (depending on the specific arms measure used) of the dyad-years characterized by a mutual military buildup. This is nearly twice the proportion of dispute occurrence in a given dyad-year than

Table 8.1 The Relationship between Dispute Occurrence and Military Buildup—Diehl's Index

In a Given Dyad-Year	Neither Arming	One Arming	Both Arming	Total
No dispute	1,217	797	232	2,246
Dispute	79	75	44	198
Total	1,296	872	276	2,444
Proportion of dispute-years to total dyad-years	6%	8.6%	16%	8.1%

$\chi^2 = 30.1$ $p < .01$
phi $= .11$ $p < .01$

when neither country, or only one country, was arming. Although the relationship is not extremely strong, it is worth investigating, because it is not the negative correlation we would expect if arming discouraged dispute occurrence.

While the argument has been made that arming could have two different effects depending on timing and selection bias (stemming the occurrence of disputes, but aggravating those that do occur), the evidence herein suggests that this in not the case. This is not an altogether surprising finding when we consider the evidence that conflicts between rapidly arming states are far more likely to escalate than other militarized disputes. If disputes characterized by mutual military buildups have a much higher probability of escalation than disputes between non-arming states, it does seem unlikely that predispute arming would lead to deterrence, despite the apparent logic of such an argument. Evidence regarding the "missing link" in this first instance, then, supports the notion that rapid military buildups increase both the chance that states would engage in a dispute and also the chance that disputes happening in that context would be particularly likely to escalate all the way to war.

Table 8.2 The Relationship between Dispute Occurrence and Military Buildup—Horn's Measure

In a Given Dyad-Year	Neither Arming	One Arming	Both Arming	Total
No dispute	1,574	575	97	2,246
Dispute	142	39	17	198
Total	1,716	614	114	2,444
Proportion of dispute-years to total dyad-years	8.3%	6.3%	15%	8.1%

$\chi^2 = 9.7$ $p < .01$
phi $= .06$ $p < .01$

IS THE BIVARIATE CORRELATION JUST AN ARTIFACT OF THE RELATIONSHIP OF OTHER VARIABLES?

The second big question we must address to understand the role military buildups play in dispute escalation is whether the bivariate relationship is robust in multivariate testing. Obviously, if other factors are significantly related to both military buildups and the likelihood of dispute escalation, then the link between arming and escalation may be an artifact of one or more of those relationships.

A number of factors could plausibly be leading to both military buildups and dispute escalation. The statistical impact of this in bivariate tests would be to suggest that there is a relationship (perhaps implying a causal relationship) between arms buildups and war but that in reality that correlation is only a reflection of others. To determine whether this is true, my analysis considers the impact of several other variables. The impact of the power balance between the states is considered, as well as the speed and nature of change within that power balance, the defense burden of each state, whether the states possess nuclear weapons, and the salience of the issue at stake.[4] In each case, we have a viable alternative that might be related to escalation and military buildups in such a way as to create an illusory impression that the dynamic process of a buildup is somehow unique in its particular impact on the likelihood of further conflict. The variables represent other explanations for whether and how disputes escalate that are based on profoundly different theoretical underpinnings than the thesis regarding arms buildups.

Traditionally, our analyses of war have concentrated on power: How is power distributed between states? How are changes in that distribution likely to impact the relationship between states? The theoretical underpinnings of these queries are grounded in the idea that states must seek power in an anarchical international environment and that they are rational in that pursuit. However, disagreement persists in the literature over the exact nature of the relationship. Traditional realists argue that war is least likely when states are roughly equal in power because both will rationally avoid the consequences of the possible loss to an adversary as capable as they. They argue that war is likely when one state is much more powerful than another because that state can rationally expect victory in any conflict.

The argument of the power transition thesis is precisely the opposite. War, it is argued, is unlikely when one state holds enormous power because the state can exert its dominance over a weak opponent in more efficient ways. When two states have equal power, they can each rationally assume they have a good chance of winning a war. If the prize to be won is the ability to determine the rules of the international system, states have a powerful incentive to attempt to defeat anyone who has a real capacity to challenge their status. A most dangerous time occurs when one state approaches and passes another in power (Organski 1958; Organski and Kugler 1980).

In both theories, the key to understanding how wars come about lies in understanding power and the dynamics of power. While it is obvious that both cannot be correct, it is equally obvious that these arguments must be addressed if we are to understand whether or how military buildups impact state interaction. If mutual military buildups do significantly alter the political dynamics of disputes, it is possible that the power distribution or changes in it would not be highly significant once arming patterns are taken into account. Independent of the power distribution between states, a militarized dispute between two rapidly arming countries may suggest to one or both states that their buildup, perhaps intended to prevent or deter conflict, has failed, and any further display of resolve short of war is likely to be unsuccessful. Alternatively, arms buildups may only represent a shift in the balance of power that is fundamentally more significant to the relationship than the military buildup itself. It could easily be that military buildups are a mere symptom of the overarching struggle over power in the international system. Any statistical relationship between military buildups and war would only be reflective of that larger relationship.

The study includes three power-based variables. The first variable determines whether two states are equal in power at the time of the dispute. The second variable considers whether the states have experienced a power transition in the last decade (one state has passed the other in relative power).[5] And the third looks at whether one state has been *rapidly* closing the gap with the other over the course of the last decade.[6] Although they cannot be used to make general conclusions, bivariate tests can provide a valuable "snapshot" as we begin to investigate relationships. The bivariate conditional probabilities of dispute escalation have been calculated for all three and placed in comparison with the conditional probability of a dispute escalating in the context of a military buildup (see Table 8.3).[7]

Table 8.3　Bivariate Conditional Probabilities of Escalation of Major State Disputes and Military Buildups Compared to Power-Based Variables

	Number of Dyadic Disputes	*Number of Dyads Escalating*	*P(esc)*	*Z score*	*P(Z)*
All major state dyadic disputes	257	31	0.12	NA	NA
Mutual military buildups	29	12 (3.5)	0.41	4.8	<0.01
Equality	85	11 (10.2)	0.13	0.2	0.41
Rapid approach	78	11 (9.4)	0.14	0.5	0.31
Transition	34	7 (4.1)	0.21	1.6	0.05

The numbers in parentheses indicate the predicted number of escalating disputes if the variable had no significant impact on the likelihood of escalation. The number above it in the second column is the number of dyads with that characteristic that actually escalated. In Table 8.3, we see that the unconditional probability of a dispute escalating to war across 257 dyadic major state disputes is about 12 percent. The probability of a dispute escalating in the context of a military buildup for the period was about 41 percent, which is significantly different from the unconditional probability.

However, the only one of the three power-based variables that appears to show a direct relationship with dispute escalation in this bivariate analysis is the occurrence of a transition in power in the preceding decade, which is significant at the .05 level. If we were to stop at bivariate analysis, we must conclude that some support exists for the power transition thesis. The other variables are not significant at all, even in a bivariate testing. This suggests that when we include them in a multivariate model, the only variable likely to affect the statistical relationship between military buildups and dispute escalation might be a preceding power transition.

Another factor we must consider in determining the real role of military buildups is the level of militarization, or defense burden, of each state. This is important because it gets to the issue of dynamism. The argument that military buildups increase the chance of war assumes that there is something to the *action* of the buildup that creates the change. Taking a measure of the defense burden is a related, but different, concept. The defense burden is the portion of resources a state dedicates to the military. A high defense burden might be unsustainable over long periods, lending a sense of urgency to any conflict, thus enhancing the chance of war without the increase being theoretically related to the immediate rate of change of military expenditures. On the other hand, imagine the scenario when two countries with abundant resources are not spending a large portion of their resources on the military, but they've just begun to rapidly increase their expenditures from year to year. That is a situation in which the defense burden is low, but a rapid military buildup is going on. The escalation of disputes like this would suggest that it is not the proportion of resources dedicated to the military that is problematic but the rapid increase and its impact on decision making. By considering the impact of both military buildups and the states' defense burdens, we can begin to determine whether the increased chance of escalation is related to one or the other (or perhaps both).

Table 8.4 indicates the unconditional probability of a dispute escalating when one or both states at the time of the disputes have a high proportion of their resources dedicated to the military. As it turns out, the defense burden does appear to be highly correlated with the chance of dispute escalation. We would predict that nine or ten disputes would escalate, but twenty do, a significant difference. Multivariate analysis will allow us to see whether our measure of a mutual military buildup is really only representing cases in which the countries have high

Table 8.4   Bivariate Conditional Probability of Escalation of Major State Disputes if One or Both States Have a High Defense Burden

	Number of Dyadic Disputes	Number of Dyads Escalating	P(esc)	Z score	P(Z)
All major state dyadic disputes	257	31	0.12	NA	NA
Defense burden	81	20	0.25	3.6	<0.01
		(9.7)			

defense burdens. This would indicate once again that the relationship we see between military buildups and escalation is an artifact of another variable related in some way to both.

While the impact of nuclear weapons on the dynamics between states will be considered in some depth further on, it is important to begin to address them in this context. Proponents of nuclear deterrence argue that a buildup of nuclear weapons should profoundly decrease the chance that disputes will escalate. The interplay between arms buildups and nuclear weapons, when we consider the period of the Cold War, seems undeniable. When we look at the bivariate conditional probability that a dispute will escalate when at least one of the states involved in the dispute had nuclear weapons, we see that the chance of such a dispute escalating is far below the unconditional probability of escalation.

Does Table 8.5 suggest that nuclear weapons *have* fundamentally altered the nature of relations between states? It certainly must be considered. The table also highlights the importance of discovering how these relationships hold up in multivariate analysis, since the impact of possessing nuclear weapons seems to be acting in one direction, while arms buildups seem to be acting in the other.

The last variable considered here is the relationship between the issue under contention in a given dispute and the likelihood that dispute will escalate. Specifically, the study looks at the issue of territory. In general, the importance of issues as causes of escalation has been ignored in our studies of war because of the dominance of power-based explanations. It has been assumed that any given

Table 8.5   Bivariate Conditional Probability of Escalation of Major State Disputes if One or Both States Possess Nuclear Weapons

	Number of Dyadic Disputes	Number of Dyads Escalating	P(esc)	Z score	P(Z)
All major state dyadic disputes	257	31	0.12	NA	NA
Nuclear	114	1	0.01	3.6	<0.01
		(13.7)			

issue was not, in fact, the cause of conflict, just the trigger of the moment. The implication of this assumption is that the disputes over different issues should have the same probability of escalation. A number of studies (Diehl 1992; Holsti 1991; Mansbach and Vasquez 1981; Vasquez 1993, 1995b; Gochman and Leng 1983; Leng 1993) have suggested that this is not the case. In Table 8.6, we see that disputes over territory have about a 22 percent chance of escalating, nearly twice the unconditional rate of escalation. This study focuses on the issue of territory because it may be a particularly salient issue: and long-standing conflicts over a particularly salient issue may lead to both arms buildups and escalation.

It is obvious from the results of the bivariate tests that multivariate testing is mandatory to discover to what extent these relationships might be artifacts of the bivariate analysis. The multivariate test used in this survey employs logistic regression to test the relationships.[8] Each of the independent variables is coded dichotomously: arming, the issue of territory, rapid approaches, power parity, transition, possession of nuclear weapons, and high defense burdens are coded as 1, otherwise 0.[9]

The equation estimated in the analysis is:

$$\log W_i = a + b_1(\text{MutualMilitaryBuildup}_i) + b_2(\text{Issue}_{i)} + b_3(\text{RapidApp}_i) + b_4(\text{Parity}_i) + b_5(\text{Transition}_i) + b_6(\text{DefenseBurden}_i) + b_7(\text{Nuclear}_i),$$

where W_i is the conditional log odds of a dispute escalating to war given the influence of the variables in the model. The model has been estimated using all major state dispute dyads and employing Horn's measure of arms buildups.

As Tables 8.7 makes clear, the relationship between preceding mutual military buildups and the escalation of disputes to war is positive and significant.[10] A dispute that occurs during a mutual military buildup is more than twice as likely to escalate than disputes that occur in the absence of military buildups, once the effects of other variables are considered. The findings here suggest that it is the dynamic aspect of the mutual military buildup that somehow affects the outcome of the dispute, rather than the more static or structural factors. The only one of the other variables that remains highly significant in multivariate testing is the possession of nuclear weapons.

Table 8.6 Bivariate Conditional Probability of Escalation of Major State Disputes if the Dispute Is over the Issue of Territory

	Number of Dyadic Disputes	Number of Dyads Escalating	P(esc)	Z score	P(Z)
All major state dyadic disputes	257	31	0.12	NA	NA
Issue	54	12	0.22	2.3	0.01
		(6.5)			

Table 8.7   Logit Model: Escalation to War, 1816–1993, All Major State Dispute Dyads

Factor	B	SE	Wald	p	R	Exp(B)
Mutual Military Buildup	1.1088	0.5249	4.463	0.0346	0.1141	3.0308
Rapid Approach	−0.8905	0.7190	1.534	0.2155	0.0000	0.4104
Equality	0.5234	0.5621	0.867	0.3518	0.0000	1.6877
Transition	0.7720	0.7676	1.012	0.3145	0.0000	2.1642
Defense Burden	0.9127	0.4922	3.439	0.0637	0.0872	2.4911
Nuclear	−1.6652	0.6527	6.5091	0.0107	−0.1544	0.1892
Territorial Issue	0.7877	0.4864	2.623	0.1054	0.0574	2.1984
Constant	−2.4258	0.4149	34.18	0.0000		
Log-likelihood	189.24					
Model log-likelihood	150.43					
Model χ^2	38.80; df 7; $p < .0001$					

Table 8.8 calculates the predicted probability of a dispute escalating to war given the parameter estimates from the logistic regression. When all variables were set at zero, the probability of a dispute escalating between the major states in the COW period from 1816 to 1993 was 0.08. When both states were arming, but all other conditions were absent from the dyadic dispute, the probability of escalation to war leaps to 21 percent. When at least one country has a high defense burden, the odds of escalation are increased from the base probability of 8 percent to 18 percent. Presumably at least one country has realized that its capacity to maintain current levels of spending may begin to diminish, making it necessary either to come to a political détente or to precipitate a war while it perceives

Table 8.8   Probabilities of Escalation to War, 1816–1993, Based on the Estimated Coefficients in Table 8.7

	Probability of Escalation
1. Baseline: all independent variables at zero	0.08
2. Mutual Military Buildup; all others at zero	0.21
3. High Defense Burden; all others at zero	0.18
4. Military Buildup and Defense Burden; all others at zero	0.40
5. Dispute over Issue of Territory; all others at zero	0.16
6. Military Buildup, Defense Burden, Territorial Dispute; others at zero	0.59
7. Military Buildup, Defense Burden, Territorial Dispute, Parity, Transition, Rapid Approach; Nuclear at zero	0.69
8. Nuclear; all others at zero	0.02
9. Military Buildup and Nuclear; others at zero	0.05
10. All variables at 1	0.25

that it still has a chance of winning. While the variable measuring the defense burden is not highly significant in the multivariate model, there does appear to be some relationship. In the same vein, the issue of territory may have some positive impact on the likelihood of escalation, but the measured variable is not statistically significant in this model.

The parameter estimates for the power-related variables were not significant.[11] Bivariate logit models were run for each variable as well, and in that analysis a power transition was positively related to the likelihood of escalation at the 0.10 level of significance, but that relationship vanishes in the multivariate model. When other, specifically political variables are controlled for, the power distribution, and changes in it, cease to be significant indicators of war potential in particular disputes.

Much more important to the chance of two disputing nations going to war are the particular foreign policy choices taken in the preceding few years, specifically the decision to vastly increase military capabilities. However, the parameter estimates for both parity and transition are in the direction proposed by power transition theory, and the probability of a war outcome does increase to its highest level when they are included. The probability of a dispute escalating to war given a mutual military buildup, a high defense burden, and a territorial dispute as the base of the conflict is 0.59. If the states are also at parity after a rapid approach and have recently experienced a transition, the chance of escalation to war increases to 0.69.

ARMING AND WAR: THE THEORETICAL CONNECTION

As previously mentioned, the research on the impact of arming has been greatly hampered by the failure to develop a strong theoretical argument connecting arms policies with war occurrence. Richardson (1960: 307) argued that at the root of unstable arming between states was the security dilemma: each country justified its own military expenditure by comparing it to that of potential rivals. For Richardson, the true tragedy of the security dilemma was that war came about because of mutual fear, not design. Two countries might be arming for their own security in an anarchic international environment, but each would assume that the arming of the other country was meant as a threat, thus making war the result of a series of miscalculations. Although this explanation of war, and the view of mutual military buildups, is symmetrical in terms of cause and effect—an action–reaction cycle of arms growth that explodes in hostility and fear—it has proven empirically inadequate. A hostile spiral model requires interactive, accelerating arms growth between the parties, and those behaviors are rare indeed. A better explanation must be more theoretically complex to account for what we do know about the arming of nations.

The evidence here suggests that rapid military buildups do increase the likelihood of war and that military buildups are positively related to the occurrence of a militarized dispute between two countries. Within the context of militarized disputes, a mutual military buildup significantly increases the chance that the dispute will escalate to war, suggesting perhaps that the buildup itself affects the nature of the dispute or leads the countries involved to choose a path of increasing escalation in a crisis.

The key to understanding how arming affects the dynamics of interstate relations is in the junction between objective threat, the effects of subjective cognitive interpretations of events by policymakers, and, significantly, the impact created by the political norms associated with realism, the traditionally dominant theory of international politics. The political norms of realism prescribe certain foreign policy choices in the face of threats to security, both real and potential. These prescriptions are based on assumptions about international politics that include the pervasiveness and inevitability of conflict. One of the policies promoted to counter existing and potential security threats is the increase of a country's armaments.

The contribution that cognitive psychology can make to an understanding of decision-making behavior is important to an overall understanding as well. The potential threats to security, more than the sure ones, are the driving force behind the choice of policies and the overall orientation toward international politics that is characteristic of realism. In cases in which information is limited, cognitive psychology tells us, it is not unusual to employ shortcuts for defining situations and drawing conclusions about necessary and appropriate action in those contexts (Khong 1992: chap. 2; Jervis 1976). Realism has served the apparently functional purpose of providing decision makers of major states with a default cognitive framework for international politics since the Treaty of Westphalia in 1648—a framework that both defines the nature of politics and provides behavioral norms for acting within that political structure (Vasquez 1983, 1993).

Cognitive psychological approaches emphasize misperception in international politics, but they cannot satisfactorily explain why the balance of uncertainly so often tips in favor of conflict. Nevertheless, an analysis of the interplay between patterns of cognitive understanding and the political norms offered by realism goes a long way toward explaining why military buildups increase the likelihood of war.

When faced with direct security threats, realism prescribes that states augment their power through increasing arms (and solidifying alliances). These behaviors serve double purposes. Realism suggests that displays of resolve and capability will deter aggression, so arms and allies should help avoid unwanted conflict escalation. If that fails, however, they are useful tools for fighting a war. It is important to remember that realist policy prescriptions are meant to keep the peace by balancing a relationship so that no actor feels that violence would be a low-cost, rational option to achieving their objectives.

Despite their intentions, the choices associated with realist norms and practices may increase the chance that war will be the outcome of militarized disputes, and the evidence herein suggests that arming increases the chance that disputes will occur in the first place. The assumption of the pervasiveness of conflict in the foreign policy culture may lend itself to the promotion of conflict, and this effect can be reinforced and redoubled by the patterns of cognitive (mis)perception evident in individual behavior. When faced with situations in which the motives of another actor can only be assumed, individuals (including policymakers in their official capacity) tend to assume that observed behavior is the product of coordination, not accident. They tend to perceive an overall high level of centralization and planning on the part of the other that may or may not exist. They assume that their own motivations must be clear to the opponent and, significantly, tend to believe that they play a central role in the policies of others (Jervis 1976: 62). Each of these elements can contribute to the overall level of risk in a dispute in which both countries have been arming. Policymakers often act in ways consistent with the norms related to realist theory, but the outcomes of those choices are more consistent with the psychological arguments regarding escalation (Leng 1993).

Mutual military buildups taking place before and during the occurrence of a militarized dispute are interpreted as current military threats, but it may be that the threat issues from hostility that goes back over the several years of the buildup. If countries tend to assume that they play a central role in the policy of others during (if not before) a militarized dispute, they are highly likely to assume that they were the target of the other's arms buildup from the beginning. This may or may not be misperception on their part, but it will serve to increase the level of danger in the current situation. This is all the more likely when we consider that disputes themselves are somewhat more likely to occur when countries are arming. The association between arming and dispute occurrence implies that countries may indeed worry about the arms policies of others before a dispute occurs.

A state that initiates the militarized dispute has presumably come to the conclusion that the target, despite its own military buildup, will either back down or that it will be unable to provide a serious threat to the initiator in the event of war. The target state, on the other hand, is faced with a challenger who has been building up its military and has now initiated a dispute, showing a seemingly clear willingness to fight while simultaneously not being deterred from initiating the conflict by the target's own military buildup. While realism suggests that a clear show of resolve is the best means of avoiding a major confrontation, a country that has already been actively building up its military is likely to believe that it has shown resolve and that it has not been sufficient to prevent aggression. It now appears that the country's security is seriously jeopardized by the threat and animosity displayed by the other (it may be or seem that the initiator intends to initiate a war), and the chance that violence will be deemed a necessary response under the circumstances is increased.

Unlike disputes in which neither party has been arming at high rates, there is little chance that this dispute will be interpreted as the product of momentary conflict, or an opportunistic testing of the waters. War may seem to be the likely outcome of the relationship, whether in this dispute or a subsequent one. Even if the issue at stake would not normally be considered critical, it may now take on symbolic value in the view that to surrender on this issue puts the continued security of the country at serious risk, given an opponent that (apparently) has been planning aggression for some time. Indeed, the tenets of realism are reinforced in the minds of decision makers: they increased their arms to increase their security; the dispute proves that their security was in jeopardy and that building up the country's arms was necessary. The next step in the realist prescription is to make one's resolve clearer and to fight, if necessary.

In the absence of a mutual military buildup, the complex dynamics of the relationship are altered, and certainly those of the dispute are different. Disputes are somewhat less likely, and when they do occur, the perception of their meaning is different. There is not the same impetus for each state to interpret the dispute as the outcome of a coordinated policy and arming process aimed at them over the period of several years or a possible failure of deterrence. There does not appear to be the same increase in the hostility level resulting from those interpretations, nor does the target presume a heightened and deliberate threat resulting from the failure of their own increased military to prevent militarized conflict. Disputes that do not begin with a declaration of war are thus less likely to escalate to it in the absence of a mutual military buildup. These findings strongly suggest that the rules of behavior that are dominant in the international system are clearly related to the likelihood of war in that system.

HAVE NUCLEAR WEAPONS FUNDAMENTALLY CHANGED INTERNATIONAL POLITICS?

Thus far, we have addressed two related questions regarding the role of arms buildups in war: whether arming increases the likelihood of militarized disputes between states, and whether they increase the chance that such a dispute will escalate to war. The third pillar of this research must be an evaluation of the impact that nuclear weapons have had on these dynamics in the post–World War II era. Have major state politics fundamentally altered, as some argue, so that the existence of nuclear weapons acts as a shield against war; or are states playing an always dangerous game with now unfathomably deadly weapons? To what extent can a consideration of norms in the international system (or rules of acceptable behavior) contribute to a more complete understanding of the observed behavior of the major states, particularly the superpowers, during the Cold War?

The dramatic explosion of nuclear weapons into international politics gave birth to two competing views of the weapons, theoretically grounded in the long-standing arguments about the consequence of military buildups. First, there was the argument that arms races increased the chance of war; therefore, a nuclear arms race could easily lead to nuclear war. The obvious policy implication of this view was to advocate disarmament, as quickly as possible. Second, there was the argument of nuclear deterrence, which was the basis of policy for the nuclear states throughout the Cold War.

In a very early discussion of the meaning of nuclear weapons in international politics, Brodie (1946) argued that nuclear weapons fundamentally altered the nature of war and politics. The dangers inherent in allowing conflict to escalate in the nuclear era meant that war, quite simply, could no longer be viewed, as it had traditionally been, as a "continuation of politics by other means," as Clausewitz (1962) had put it.

The frightfully efficient capacity to destroy cities and countries without the necessity of meeting their armies on the battlefield led many to conclude that war as humankind had known it must be at an end. Any country with a secure second-strike capacity, able to cause massive damage in retaliation for a first attack against it, could not rationally be challenged or threatened or attacked. Any country with nuclear capacity facing a nonnuclear opponent could be secure because it possessed the unquestionably more devastating arsenal. Nuclear weapons give to their possessor the capacity to inflict such costs on the opponent that no potential benefits to challenging them would be worth the risk of reprisal. Nuclear weapons could be used to avoid war among the major states and perhaps limit it elsewhere.

This is the heart of classical nuclear deterrence theory, the premises of which have provided an acceptable explanation of the unprecedented lack of major state war in the half-century following World War II for most national leaders and many international relations scholars. They point to the fact that the two primary nuclear antagonists in the postwar era, the United States and the Soviet Union, never went to war, despite clear and repeated disputes over a period of some years. And China and the Soviet Union, despite long-running hostility and border clashes, also avoided escalating their conflicts to all-out war.

These facts make it clear that any discussion of arming and its effect on war must explicitly consider the effect brought by nuclear weapons in the international system. To address that issue, this part of the study focuses on two questions. The first is the extent to which the postwar period really is different from the prewar period, and the second looks at the causes for the lack of war between major states following World War II. Is that peace best explained by the existence of nuclear weapons, or is it attributable to other causes?

Regular forces of the major countries have only faced each other in war once, during the Korean War, in the last fifty years. Despite the considerable costs of the Cold War, this lack of a major state war has lasted for a longer period than the post-Napoleonic peace that was stifled on the slopes of the Crimea. If deterrence theory attributes the relative peace to the effect of nuclear weapons, some maintain that other explanations for the postwar order are possible. For example, Mueller (1993) suggests that after two utterly devastating wars in the course of thirty years, those states capable of initiating a third were in no rush to do so, no matter what their conflicts might be.

There are numerous reasons for evaluating the merits of these arguments. Theoretically, a clearer understanding of which best explains the empirical record of major state relations over the last fifty years will tell us a great deal about our continued search for factors associated with increased or decreased chances of war. The implication of nuclear deterrence is that other factors, such as arms buildups increasing the chance of war and mutual democracy decreasing the chance of war, become more or less irrelevant in the presence of a nuclear deterrent. Understanding what role nuclear weapons truly play, then, may offer us a great deal of insight regarding the impact of nuclear proliferation on international security in the long term.

To preface my conclusion, the results here indicate that nuclear weapons have played a substantial role in decreasing the likelihood of war among the major states in the last fifty years. However, the picture is not that simple: nuclear deterrence does not appear to be a *sufficient* explanation for the actual behavior of states during the period. Rather, the lack of major state war must be attributed to a combination of two things: the deterrent effect created by the nuclear threat and the growth of rules and norms of behavior between the nuclear rivals of the Cold War era. These rules of behavior evolved out of a shift in the power structure, but the change in the power structure cannot alone explain the real interaction of states in this period. It is less than clear whether newer nuclear rivals would have, or take the time to develop, a modus vivendi that functions as that of the United States and the Soviet Union did. If they do not, there is no guarantee that they would avoid war in the face of critical challenges to their real or perceived interests, even given the possession of nuclear weapons by their rival.

MAJOR STATE PEACE AND THE POSTWAR ERA

Our first question is whether the postwar period is really that different once we consider other variables. We can answer that question by dividing the whole Correlates of War period of 1816–1993, using 1945 as a break point. This allows us to examine the way the relationships might change from before World War II to after. In Table 8.9, it is evident from the statistical analysis that the pattern of dispute escalation has altered significantly in the postwar era. The relationships we saw over the whole era really reflect the 1816–1945 period. It is clear that military buildups in the period from 1816 until World War II are positively associated with the escalation of disputes to war: arming at unusually high rates did nothing to deter the occurrence or the escalation of disputes between countries. It is worth noting, too, that while the relationship between territorial disputes and

Table 8.9 Logit Model: Comparing the Patterns of Escalation to War by Era

Factor	B	SE	Wald	p	R	Exp(B)
Mutual Military Buildup:						
1816–1993	1.1088	0.5249	4.463	.0346	0.1141	3.0308
1816–1945	1.1831	0.5659	4.372	.0365	0.1301	3.2646
1945–93	13.713	599.6	0.0005	.9818	0.0000	9.0×10^5
Rapid Approach:						
1816–1993	−0.8905	0.7190	1.534	.2155	0.0000	0.4104
1816–1945	−0.9526	0.7924	1.445	.2293	0.0000	0.3857
1945–93	−6.63	89.66	0.0055	.9411	0.0000	0.0013
Equality:						
1816–1993	0.5234	0.5621	0.867	.3518	0.0000	1.6877
1816–1945	0.9404	0.6236	2.274	.1316	0.0442	2.5609
1945–93	0.5974	1.644	0.1321	.7163	0.0000	1.8173
Transition:						
1816–1993	0.7720	0.7676	1.012	.3145	0.0000	2.1642
1816–1945	−0.0796	0.8631	.0085	.9265	0.0000	0.9234
1945–93	8.104	89.66	.0082	.9280	0.0000	3,308.6
Defense Burden:						
1816–1993	0.9127	0.4922	3.439	.0637	0.0872	2.4911
1816–1945	0.4536	0.5525	.6741	.4116	0.0000	1.5740
1945–93	015.48	130.3	.0141	.9055	0.0000	5.3×10^6
Nuclear:						
1816–1993	−1.6652	0.6527	6.5091	.0107	−0.1544	0.1892
1816–1945						
1945–93	−0.9297	879.8	0.0000	.9992	0.0000	0.3947
Territorial Issue:						
1816–1993	0.7877	0.4864	2.623	.1054	0.0574	2.1984
1816–1945	01.332	0.5280	6.363	.0117	0.1765	3.7882
1945–93	−9.595	229.7	0.0017	.9667	0.0000	0.0001
Constant:						
1816–1993	−2.4258	0.4149	34.1818	.0000		
1816–1945	−2.3061	0.4207	30.0465	.0000		
1945–93	−16.926	870.1	0.0004	.9845		

1816–1993		1816–1945		1945–93	
Log-likelihood	189.24	Log-likelihood	140.11	Log-likelihood	27.90
Model log-like	150.43	Model log-like	123.43	Model log-like	9.97
Model χ^2	38.80	Model χ^2	16.68	Model χ^2	17.94
df 7	$p < .0001$	df 6	$p = .01$	df 7	$p = .01$

escalation is not significant over the whole period, it is highly significant before World War II.[12]

The evidence of the Cold War period paints an entirely different picture. All the relationships that are significant before the war fail utterly in the era after World War II. Disputes occurring during that period, even when the major countries were arming heavily, did not escalate. Highly contentious disputes over territory did not escalate. The answer to our first question, of whether the postwar period was really that different, must be a resounding yes.

The one variable in the analysis that changes from the earlier period to the later is the existence of nuclear weapons in the arsenals of first the United States, then eventually the other major states as well. It is vital to point out at this time that this statistical test does *not* directly test the results of possessing nuclear weapons. In fact, virtually every dispute after World War II occurs when at least one of the disputants has nuclear weapons. In other words, the variable isn't varying much. In reality, all the statistical test can tell us at this point is that the major states in the international system behave very differently after 1945 than they did before. And while the statistical findings cannot offer us any sort of definitive answer about nuclear weapons themselves, it certainly makes it clear that we really need to consider how we answer this question of the cause of the long postwar peace.

The first, obvious explanation for this era of peace (or, perhaps more appropriately, lack of war) in major state rivalries *is* the power of nuclear weapons. Even though this statistical analysis cannot make the fine distinctions we would like regarding nuclear weapons versus other possible causes of the long peace, we certainly cannot ignore their import. Classical nuclear deterrence theory predicts that nuclear states will not risk war once they have achieved levels of power capable of mutual destruction. The potential for mutually assured destruction (MAD) has been credited with bringing about a long-lasting period during which war among the major states was irrational, therefore impossible (Intriligator and Brito 1989).

Several possibilities in addition to nuclear deterrence have been put forth as explanations for the half-century absence of a major state war, however. Mueller (1993) argues that even in the absence of nuclear weapons, the likelihood that the superpowers would go to war after World War II was very small. He gives several reasons for this. Given two devastating world wars in thirty years, he maintains, the major states could easily have been restrained by their fear of a dispute escalating to a third total war, nuclear or not. After the war, the only countries really in a position to start a third world war would have been the Soviet Union and the United States, and they were essentially content with a status quo that favored their interests.

Despite its logical appeal, Mueller's argument that nuclear weapons were "essentially irrelevant" is not entirely convincing. Each of the given reasons for the postwar peace has its own empirical flaws. If the superpowers were restrained by their belief in the possibility of escalation to another total war on the scale of

World Wars I and II, American behavior in the face of the North Korean attack on South Korea is inexplicable. Leaders in the United States believed that the Korean crisis was a Soviet-inspired venture and that it was meant to distract Western attention from the real attack anticipated in Europe. Despite this, American leaders did not hesitate to get involved militarily, thus, in their own calculations, risking a third major war in forty years (Spanier 1980; Truman 1956). In addition, the Soviet Union and the United States may have been relatively content with the status quo, but that does little to explain the unprecedented numbers of militarized disputes they engaged in over the course of the Cold War. And though the chance of war would not have been high during the Cold War anyway if the conflicts were over low-salience issues, this study shows that the issues in contention during the Cold War were not substantially different from those before the war. There were many territorial disputes between the superpowers, but the escalatory propensity observed before World War II vanishes after the war.

Singer (1991) also puts forth a perhaps exhaustive list of possible explanations for the postwar peace among the major states. The list includes Mueller's reasons but also displacement of wars away from the center system to the periphery, cultural changes against war, the increase in communications technology, and the character of the international system in the Cold War period.

Keeping in mind the possibility that war might have been avoided because of a combination of all these factors, the results of this study suggest that it is impossible to ignore the effect of nuclear weapons. The strong escalatory effects of arming and of territorial disputes are both swamped in the postwar era, and nuclear weapons must be part of the explanation for the findings. But what part do they play? Classical nuclear deterrence theory argues that the overwhelming force given states by the possession of nuclear weapons means that they cannot be challenged by nonnuclear states, or compelled to behave against their own interests, or attacked by nuclear states. Fortunately, there has been no use of nuclear weapons in war since World War II, so deterrence is difficult to test. It is possible, however, to test deterrence theory indirectly by considering how well the logical implications of the theory have held up empirically (Kugler 1984).

For deterrence to have worked perfectly, we have to assume that there would have been a war without the existence of nuclear weapons. This assumption has two components. First, if either the United States or the Soviet Union intended to attack the other but did not because of the threat of nuclear weapons, then deterrence worked. Because there is no compelling evidence that such attacks were ever seriously considered, we cannot conclude that deterrence worked in this way (Vasquez 1991). However, general deterrence of a direct attack is not really the question addressed in this study. Once a militarized dispute has occurred, a certain threshold has been crossed, and it is a failure of general deterrence. The question apropos to this study is whether nuclear weapons deterred the escalation of militarized disputes to war after that line had been crossed. Examination of the data suggests that the answer, tentatively, should be yes.

This answer is tentative because it would be premature to presume that the dynamics of warfare have clearly and permanently altered. As a solitary explanation for the postwar peace, deterrence is not sufficient, especially when the results of miscalculation are contemplated. Too many empirical incongruities must be skirted or ignored for deterrence to be accepted. It is worth noting, in fact, that while the explanations Mueller offers for the lack of a major state war do not really conform to many of the events we observe, none of those events can easily be explained by deterrence theory, either.

Classical deterrence theory simply does not hold up to a careful examination of the behavior of states in the nuclear era. Although Gaddis (1987) offers some evidence suggesting that U.S. policymakers feared Soviet nuclear retaliation, this does not translate into systematic evidence wholly supporting deterrence in practice. In policy, the superpowers, particularly the United States, showed little inherent caution or fear of escalation during the Cold War; nuclear weapons were often used as a means of policy coercion (George and Smoke 1974). China chose to intervene in the Korean War against the United States despite the nuclear threat. That the one war between two states in the post–World War II era was initiated despite a clear chance of nuclear counterattack fatally undermines deterrence theory.

Huth and Russett (1984) found that possession of nuclear weapons was not greatly associated with cases of successful deterrence. Also, in his study of behavior in extreme crises, Kugler (1984) discovered that not only did nonnuclear countries feel capable of challenging nuclear states, but they often got what they wanted when they did so. Paul (1995) argues that this behavior was evident because the nonnuclear powers were aware that the nuclear powers would not violate the "taboo" against the use of the weapons. Although this may provide an explanation for later behavior, it hardly explains China's willingness to engage the United States less than a decade after World War II. In any case, a taboo against the use of nuclear weapons is a (perhaps valid) normative, rather than power-based explanation, at odds with deterrence theory. The possession of nuclear weapons clearly did not stop either the occurrence of militarized disputes or their escalation to violence short of war among the major states (Kugler 1984; Organski and Kugler 1980; Vasquez 1991). None of this behavior should have been evident if nuclear deterrence worked as the theory argued. Nuclear weapons do have a deterrent effect, but nuclear deterrence is a myth.

To explain the nonescalation of disputes over the period of the Cold War, any explanation including the deterrent effect of nuclear weapons must be coupled with the development of a modus vivendi in the superpower relationship. The failure of any disputes between the major states to escalate to war after Korea can probably be attributed to a number of fortunate factors. But chief among these was the development of a set of rules to govern behavior among the nuclear countries to accompany the actual deterrent effect of their nuclear arsenals (Kremenyuk 1994; Midlarsky 1994). The development of this set of rules and norms for doing business contributed significantly to the peaceful outcome of the Cold War. In terms of interaction, the Cold War cannot be considered a pure game of either prisoner's dilemma or chicken because the Soviet Union and the United States could communicate and negotiate, and "the game" was repeated over and over. Under those circumstances, the development of cooperative relations is not impossible (Russett 1983; Axelrod 1984).

These rules for behaving, or modus vivendi, although not granting ideal circumstances to either party, were not intolerable for either the United States or the Soviet Union. They maintained their spheres of influence while allowing some shift in structure: the European alliances were set in stone, while other alliances were more flexible. The scope of allowed activity within those spheres of influence was extremely broad; the Soviet Union was free to crush dissidents in Eastern Europe, and the United States was free to interfere with incipient socialist states in the Western Hemisphere (Organski and Kugler 1980). The pace of militarized disputes between the superpowers did not fall off substantially, but their intensity did (Kugler 1984: 479). A threat to use force was progressively less and less plausible over time: militarized disputes became a ritualized way of publicizing positions and testing resolve.

The effect that nuclear weapons had (and have) was to raise the threshold of provocation between states (Lebow 1985). The calculus of potential costs and benefits of a war are changed with the possession of nuclear weapons, and the enormous cost of escalation to war does decrease the likelihood that national leaders will choose to escalate. Disputes that might once have been resolved with war were not resolved that way during the Cold War. Although the basic calculus is the same for this argument and classical deterrence theory, there is a fundamental difference. Deterrence theory predicts 100 percent success given reasonable leaders: neither war, nor disputes. In doing so, it fails to explain a great deal of international behavior over the last fifty years. On the other hand, the argument that nuclear weapons increase the threshold of provocation explains the decrease in the likelihood that war will occur without making it an impossible choice in the face of sufficient provocation.

The implications of this development for the preservation of nuclear peace over time are mixed. In the early years of their rivalry, the United States and the Soviet Union went to the brink of war over Berlin and Cuba. Although they had deep symbolic significance, neither was the home territory of the participants. Would a more direct confrontation over vital issues have led to a different outcome at the beginning stages of the Cold War, before their relationship became normally ritualized? The relationship between the Soviet Union and China bespeaks a similar course. The casualties resulting from the 1969 Damaksky Island skirmishes show that those two countries came close to war when their conflicts began to generate militarized disputes. That they did refrain from outright war suggests that the threshold of provocation has most certainly been raised and that peace may be preserved between nuclear states *if* they can survive the game long enough to create norms for their interaction. And those norms are more complex than behavior based on an assessment of relative power. Rivals may develop norms for conflict short of war when the costs of escalation are so enormous, but the nuclear rivalries between the United States and the Soviet Union, and the Soviet Union and China, show that this takes time. The fact that they came so close probably indicates that the outcome owed something to luck as well. Countries have initiated wars when they knew that the probable costs of doing so far outweighed the probable benefits (Vasquez 1991: 215). That uncertain period of massive destructive capabilities and highly salient rivalry, if not tempered by the establishment of clear rules of engagement, could be an explosively dangerous combination; we cannot be certain that all rivals will develop a new normative context for their interaction.

The relationship between Pakistan and India indicates that in a direct confrontation over critical issues, the risk of war, even with the threat of nuclear escalation, may be very high. The issue of Kashmir became so heated in 1990 that forces in both countries were on full alert (Chari 1995); in a controversial article, the *New Yorker* reported that this included readying nuclear weapons in both countries (Hersh 1993). A year after the 1998 nuclear tests by both countries, they were engaging once more in border clashes in Kashmir, not, it appears, overly concerned with the threat of escalation. Imagine two nations (such as Iran and Iraq) fighting a total war for several years: if one were on the verge of victory, and the other possessed nuclear weapons and did not believe that it could realistically appeal to the international community to be saved, nuclear escalation is not a far-fetched notion. Such circumstances are exceedingly rare, but that does not mean the results could not be devastating.

The road by which the United States and the Soviet Union traveled to arrive at a relatively stable relationship by the end of the Cold War was a hazardous one. It is not determined that other national leaders would react the same way when faced with a dispute as extreme as the Cuban Missile Crisis, and volatility may be reintroduced into the international relationship when a country experiences massive domestic upheaval. Certainly, warfare within the former Soviet Union since the end of the Cold War suggests that it is the breakdown of the political rules rather than the threat of overwhelming force that has led to conflicts.

While nuclear deterrence theory cannot provide a full and adequate explanation for the observed behavior of nuclear and nonnuclear states in the Cold War era, it is equally clear that nuclear weapons have not been irrelevant to the long postwar peace. They serve the function of raising the threshold of provocation at which states will determine that the benefits of war outweigh the costs, allowing us to explain the apparent deterrent effect while also explaining why nuclear states continued to engage in disputes with each other. War did not alter entirely from being "politics by other means" to being impossible. During the Cold War, disputes occurred at an unprecedented pace and stopped just short of war on several occasions. Both nuclear and nonnuclear countries continued to challenge nuclear opponents, a fact incongruent with deterrence theory. However, a large number of disputes with none escalating also indicates that the Soviet Union and the United States at least developed rules and norms in their rivalry. These rules allowed a reasonably certain international structure, while incorporating enough flexibility to encourage prudent behavior in the face of militarized disputes over low-salience issues.

Both elements of the postwar peace, the norms of engagement and the lifting of the threshold of provocation, are necessary to explain the long-term relationship. If nuclear rivals fail to develop rules delineating acceptable and predictable behavior between them, their relations are more likely to be governed by the patterns of escalation that prevailed in prenuclear crises. And it should not be forgotten that the majority of rivalries remain nonnuclear, leaving those countries in the position of following well-worn paths toward war if they do not consciously avert their course.

CONCLUSION

The purpose of this volume is to examine what we know about war by focusing first on a number of proposed correlates of war, then considering how these relationships fit together in a larger theoretical explanation for war. I contend that this chapter can contribute successfully to both elements of the overall research project. The empirical findings here show us that the choice to engage in military buildups is positively associated with the occurrence of militarized disputes and with the escalation of disputes to war before World War II. After the war, something quite different is going on: the relationships have changed in the postwar or nuclear era. Neither military buildups nor territorial disputes are any longer associated with escalation.

The theoretical explanation usually offered by those who argue the dangers of arms races revolve around the idea of a hostile spiral: states progressively see more and more threat from their arming rival, whether it is intended or not, and, in objective terms, overreact irrationally in the face of the perceived threat. The theoretical explanation offered by those claiming that arming is not dangerous but is, in fact, necessary, is that states behave rationally in the face of threat. Obviously, both arguments cannot be right. The behavior of states is clearly more complex than either side would suggest. The thread that brings this tapestry together, that allows us to find commonality in what seem to be incompatible findings, is the role that norms play in dealing with conflict.

To understand this, it is necessary to begin with what the findings tell us about the nature of war, the international system, and the role of policymaking in (re) creating that international system. Traditional international relations theory explained war in terms of power and shifts in power. In other words, war essentially results from factors largely beyond the control of policymakers. While they can alter their arms and alliance policies, real power is more intrinsic than that and virtually impossible to fundamentally change over the short run. The distribution of power is part of the structure in which states operate.

The crucial element of the arms-to-war argument offered in this chapter is the impact of specific arms policies within the context of the political norms accepted by national policymakers. If we venture beyond the belief that war is determined by structural factors outside human control, it is impossible to underestimate the importance of political norms for handling conflict. That does not mean that the accepted norms in the international system at a given time will necessarily create peace—that depends on the norms. It is evident, for instance, from this and other studies that the norms for dealing with territorial disputes promote the use of violence to resolve conflicts.

More generally, realism provides a set of norms intended to create security in an insecure international environment. The evidence indicates that while realism may advise certain policies as a means of avoiding war, they can in fact increase the occurrence of the wars they are intended to avert. Rapidly building up arms, like tightening alliances, is meant to project decisiveness and so deter, but the policies do not appear to succeed in their task. When decision makers accept the political assumptions of realism, they anticipate threat and perceive the only proper reaction to be the use of force. This set of norms does not successfully deter war, no matter what its goal.

Despite the dominance of this tradition in the political culture of international relations, it has not been unchallenged, even in the modern era. Wallensteen (1981, 1984), for example, finds that some periods, like the immediate post-Napoleonic era in Europe, have had fairly clear established guidelines for behavior, and in those times, the major states have been far less likely to use war as a means of resolving conflicts. In addition, if war is indeed less likely among democracies than in other contexts, it would also appear to indirectly confirm the importance of norms in international politics. Democracies may resolve their conflicts peacefully because there is an interplay between their belief that democracies do not fight and the policy choices that they make to bring about a peaceful resolution. Equally, countries whose decision makers believe in the inevitability of war are more likely to choose policies that increase the likelihood of war.

The evidence after World War II directs us along a path that is not so dissimilar as it might first appear. It is impossible to say that nuclear weapons had no deterrent effect for the superpowers, but a comprehensive view of the evidence suggests that the superpowers developed norms for handling their interactions with each other, which is critical to understanding the outcome of their relationship. The chance of war between the superpowers was not constant over the course of the Cold War; the disputes in the early years came close to war more than once, culminating in the Cuban Missile Crisis. After that, tensions were never again so high as they were in the 1950s and beginning of the 1960s. This was due partially to the rational fear generated by going to the brink of nuclear war and partially

to the fact that the superpowers immediately set themselves on a course of vigor-
ous policy interaction (including the quick negotiation of the first test ban treaty)
meant to make such an event far less likely in the future. The new rules for interacting, though not ending the rivalry, certainly changed how it was played out.

   This study points to several related questions worthy of further consideration.
I have emphasized the fact that the rules and norms within the superpower relationship were unique to that rivalry. It is possible, however, that the relationship
and its place in history over the last half century have contributed to the development of a larger norm against the use of nuclear weapons as a tool of mass destruction. To what extent have these states (and the reaction of other states to
them) created an international norm regarding the acceptability of using nuclear
weapons, thus changing the international context in which other nuclear rivals
(e.g., India and Pakistan) now operate? Between the world wars, the international
system developed a norm against the use of chemical weapons in war, and that
norm proved highly resilient during the six years of total war in World War II.
We must seriously consider the possibility that the international system, as
complex as it is, is to a large extent what we make of it through our own policy
choices.

   Another element of this research we might want to explore is the issue of minor
state interactions and interactions between major and minor states. The study here
focuses on relations among major states, concluding that the norms these states
have for dealing with conflict are highly important determinants of what we observe in the system. Do minor states exhibit similar or different behavior? How
do major and minor states relate? The implication of a normative argument would
be that context matters, that we can't implicitly assume that all types of states
will act the same. That is an empirical question that needs to be addressed for
several reasons related to this study. First, it will allow us to determine whether
the original relationship between military buildups and conflictual issues holds
up across minor states. Second, it allows us to assess the post–World War II peace
with some more nuanced distinctions (there will be more variation in that nuclear
variable). Finally, it will allow us to address the question of whether different
types of states really do have different norms or contexts in which they interact.

   What explains both these patterns is the norms that they reflect. War is the
consequence of a series of policy choices that states make, and the policies chosen are governed by norms that prevail in the international system at a given time.
The major states learned a new pattern of behavior during the Cold War that cannot be entirely attributed to the power of nuclear weapons. Before that, they em-
braced norms that told them to build up their militaries for security in an uncertain environment, and they apparently failed to deliver on that security. Most of
the international system is made up of nonnuclear states that may still operate in
that environment. The important role that our rules for governing conflict play
gives us both cause for hope and reason for caution—caution because we know
that behavioral norms do not have to promote peace, hope because it shows us

that the international structure does not foreordain war: it is possible to make choices and develop norms that create peace.

NOTES

1. It is clear from that study that the vast difference between the findings of Diehl and those of Wallace are the result of Wallace's index. Since Wallace's index has not been replicated, his findings are interesting but cannot be accepted on their face because of that. The article continues to be important more for the other criticisms of it, which are likely to be of interest in any test of arming phenomenon.

2. Both of these measures are based on military expenditures made by the countries in each year. The use of expenditure data has been criticized on several fronts. There is the fear that the data are not sufficiently reliable to justify making such nuanced conclusions. Diehl and Crescenzi (1998) suggest using stockpiles or military personnel as a basis for determining when a buildup is ongoing. This does not mean military expenditures as a measure of arming behavior should be abandoned. As a reflection of affective hostility or amity, a critical component in determining both arms policies and the effect of those arms policies, changes in expenditures in a given year do reflect policy choices quite well (Sample 1996, 1998a). However, other measures and data should be considered to the extent that they can provide an equal or more valid general measure over the same spatial-temporal frame and perhaps can be more reliable. My concern is that virtually any data source is going to be imperfect; therefore, abandoning one for another would be a mistake. I would advocate following the same strategy regarding this question as I followed to resolve the initial debate over Wallace's work: develop or make use of at least two other measures of military buildups and test what specific results they lead to. Such a test is beyond the scope of this chapter, but it would unquestionably be worthwhile to determine to what extent we can trust the Correlates of War expenditure data and its validity as a measure of military buildup.

3. The results of the bivariate logit analysis of the relationship between arming and dispute occurrence is shown in the following tables, one employing Diehl's measure and one using Horn's:

Variable	B	SE	Wald	df	p	R	exp (B)
Military buildup	0.5119	0.1008	25.8019	1	.0000	0.1316	1.6685
Diehl constant	−2.7806	0.1096	644.1680	1	.0000		

Variable	B	SE	Wald	df	p	R	exp (B)
Military buildup	0.0802	0.1279	0.3939	1	.5303	0.0000	1.0835
Horn constant	−2.4571	0.077	784.9702	1	.0000		

The fact that Horn's measure better divides the disputes that escalate from those that do not, whereas Diehl's index of arming is more closely associated with dispute occurrence, is not particularly surprising. Horn's measure of arming behavior is more conservative than Diehl's, and the difference is commensurate with the likelihood of dispute escalation. This means that Horn's measure finds far fewer cases of mutual buildups among the disputes or by dyad-year. Diehl's measure, which finds that more of the disputes themselves are characterized by mutual military buildups (though it does not distinguish so well the likelihood of war escalation) is therefore necessarily going to find a closer relationship between arming and dispute occurrence. However, that finding itself is contingent on their being a relationship between arming and dispute occurrence: if arming and dispute occurrence were not related, then each measure would likely find many instances in which two countries were both rapidly arming but had no dispute in a given year. The relationships reveal that this is not the case: Diehl's measure shows a relationship between arming and dispute occurrence, whereas Horn's fails to, not because it finds an overwhelming number of cases of arming where there was no dispute but rather because it only finds arming during a relatively small minority of the disputes themselves.

4. A complete discussion of each variable and its measurement can be found in Sample (1998b).

5. This variable has been empirically investigated in several studies, including Hensel and McLaughlin (1996) and Lemke (1993, 1996).

6. Wayman (1996) argues that the speed with which a gap between two states is being closed can have a significant impact on the security concerns that the change generates in the states.

7. This and all subsequent analyses in this chapter make use of Horn's measure of a military buildup. Compared to Diehl's, the measure is somewhat more conservative; however, these tests were all conducted originally using both measures. Small differences exist, but they do not alter the substantive conclusions of the study.

8. The following section follows the analysis in Sample (1998b).

9. The military buildup measure used in this analysis is Horn's. The issue codings were taken from the Militarized Interstate Dispute data. The measures of power were based on the Correlates of War capabilities data, a commonly used measure that correlates highly with the gross national product (GNP) (another good measure, but one for which adequate data do not extend over the entire 1816–1993 time period). Each of the military, economic, and demographic indicators were weighted equally. Pairs of countries were compared on the basis on their average holdings of these factors of national power. If the weaker country of the two had holdings that equaled at least 80 percent of the holdings of the stronger, they were considered to be at parity. A rapid approach is said to have occurred when the gap between the holdings of two countries closed by at least 40 percent in the preceding ten years, and a transition occurred in the preceding decade when their power positions were reversed. The measure for defense burden is adapted from that used by Diehl (1985). Because of fluctuating availability of data and macrotrends in military expenditure patterns, the COW period is broken into four periods: 1816–60, 1816–1914, 1919–39, and 1945–93. Although the ratio of defense spending to GNP would be the preferred way of measuring the defense burden, the lack of adequate GNP data for this study prevents the use of the measure. Rather, I looked at military expenditures as a function of available economic resources (represented by the economic indicators of the Corre-

lates of War capabilities data). For the three periods after 1860, I regressed all the major states' annual military expenditures on their coal/steel production and energy consumption separately. The actual annual economic indicators from the capabilities data were then fed back into the resulting equation to determine an estimate for predicted expenditures in that year. The two ratios of actual to predicted military expenditures were averaged. If the result was more than one standard deviation from the mean for that country, then the state was said to have a high defense burden in that year. At the last step, countries were only compared to their own typical spending pattern, rather than the spending pattern of major states in general. In each historical period, one country provided such an outlier in the data that its spending would swamp all others (Prussia, the Soviet Union, and China) so that no other country would ever be determined to have a high defense burden. Before 1860, adequate economic data are unavailable, so I regressed military personnel on total population, otherwise calculating the defense burden in the same manner. Military personnel as a function of total population is a good measure of defense burden in this historical period, since this is the era of mass mobilization in the wake of the Napoleonic wars. Each dispute dyad is then coded on the basis of whether at least one of the disputants had a high defense burden in that year.

10. Despite what may appear to be fine theoretical distinctions between some variables, in no case did the partial correlations between the measures of any independent variables approach a customary 0.7 cutoff point for problems with multicollinearity (none exceeded 0.5). Moreover, the standard errors do not appear to be particularly high, as one should expect in cases in which collinearity is an issue.

11. Models testing interaction effects of these variables did not alter the findings.

12. In fact, if we consider the actual number of disputes that occurred over territorial issues before and after the war, we find that there were twenty-two such disputes after the war, none of which escalated. Before the war, twelve of thirty-two escalated. This finding is interesting in the context of deterrence theory. It suggests that we certainly cannot make the argument that war between the major states was absent simply because they never contested over salient issues; in fact, the issues over which they contested were not substantially different from those before, but the outcomes were.

9

Rivalries
The Conflict Process

Gary Goertz and Paul F. Diehl

$\mathbf{T}$he traditional international conflict literature, or what we have labeled as the "causes of war" approach (Goertz and Diehl 1995a; Diehl and Goertz 2000), has assumed that conflicts are essentially independent of one another across space and time (the clear exception has been the work on conflict diffusion; see Most, Starr, and Siverson 1989; Siverson and Starr 1991). A typical study in that genre selects a set of crises or militarized disputes and then seeks to predict whether those conflicts will escalate to war by reference to national, dyadic, or systemic attributes at the time or immediately preceding the opportunity for escalation. In contrast, a concern with rivalries, and to slightly lesser extent with recurring conflict, presumes that conflicts are not independent but are actually related to each other over time and space. This suggests that our understanding of conflict and its potential for escalation to war is a function not merely of the attributes of the protagonists or the prevailing international system but also of the dynamics and interactions of the protagonists' rivalry relationship.

In this chapter, we first explore the extant empirical evidence on the impact of rivalry process (and related studies of recurring conflict) on interstate conflict and the prospects for war. In effect, we look to ascertain whether previous empirical studies indicate that conflict events can indeed be considered independent of one another. We then outline the two competing views of rivalry and recurring conflict that seek to explain these patterns: the "punctuated equilibrium" and the "evolutionary" models, respectively. Finally, we review the evidence for these competing approaches and discuss a range of factors thought to affect rivalry processes.

THE INTERCONNECTION OF CONFLICT OVER SPACE AND TIME

The contention that conflicts are related over space and time seems logically plausible and indeed consistent with our impressions of long-standing conflicts such as those between India and Pakistan as well as between Israel and her neighbors. Yet, there has not necessarily been a substantial amount of research that seeks to confirm the dependence of conflict over space and time. Generally, that research has taken place within the rivalry framework of analysis (Goertz and Diehl 1995a; Diehl and Goertz 2000) or more broadly under the rubric of recurring conflict at various levels of analysis. The latter has been a sporadic topic for international conflict research over the past several decades. Rivalries and their dynamics, however, have only recently been the subject of analyses; even early work on rivalries used them only as case selection devices and not a subject of inquiry themselves.[1]

Rivalry Conflict

The concept of a rivalry inherently assumes that conflicts are related over space and time. Nevertheless, it must be demonstrated that conflicts within rivalries are not independent of one another. At a general level, we argue (Goertz and Diehl 1992a; Diehl and Goertz 2000) that enduring rivalries, as opposed to lesser rivalries we label as isolated or protorivalries, are inherently more dangerous. Effectively, we are stating that the context of the rivalry (in terms of its length and level of competitiveness) will influence the dynamics of the individual conflict interactions. Unlike other studies cited later, the assumption here is not that one specific conflict affects another conflict, but there is a general interrelationship of conflict events brought about by the rivalry context. To test this, we look at the conflict propensity of different rivalry types. If rivalry contexts do not matter, and conflicts are largely the product of contemporaneous independent factors, then there should be no difference in conflict behaviors across rivalry contexts.

A series of results (Diehl and Goertz 2000) indicate that rivalry context has a significant impact on conflict behavior. The first analysis looks at the percentage of militarized interstate nonwar disputes that occur within different rivalries. Table 9.1 provides the distribution of disputes for each category of rivalry.[2]

We first note that less than 26 percent of militarized disputes are of the isolated

Table 9.1   Rivalry Context and the Freqency of Militarized Disputes, 1816–1992

Rivalry Type	Number of Rivalries	Dispute Frequency
Isolated	880 (75.5%)	525 (25.8%)
Proto	223 (19.1%)	705 (34.7%)
Enduring	63 (5.4%)	804 (39.5%)
6–13 disputes	36 (3.1%)	222 (10.9%)
>13 disputes	27 (2.4%)	582 (28.6%)
All	1,166 (100%)	2,034 (100%)

variety; this suggests that assumptions of independence in traditional conflict studies may be badly misplaced.[3] Almost 40 percent of militarized disputes occur within the context of enduring rivalries. Thus, only a small percentage of all conflictual dyads (5.4 percent), and an even smaller percentage of all possible dyads, accounts for a disproportionate amount of international conflict. The results are even more dramatic with respect to the most intense of enduring rivalries. Almost 30 percent of all disputes are generated by less than 2.5 percent of the rivalries, or twenty-seven dyads. Militarized disputes are used to define rivalries, and therefore one might expect greater dispute propensity in that context; yet, even given that dispute frequency is used to define rivalries, it is stunning that more than twice as many disputes as expected occur in enduring rivalries than in isolation.[4] The vast majority of disputes (almost three-fourths) take place in some rivalry context, be it proto- or enduring.

In contrast, the results with respect to the severity of those disputes are less dramatic.[5] The relative severity of disputes does not increase as we move along the rivalry continuum. There is a greater propensity for the most severe event, full-scale war, in enduring rivalries. But every dispute in enduring rivalries is not more severe than every dispute in other rivalry contexts. Rather, enduring rivalries usually include disputes of a variety of severities. Indeed, the average severity of a dispute may be misleading for enduring rivalries, because it is unlikely that war erupts frequently in repeated disputes within the same rivalry. In rivalries with greater than thirteen disputes, three or four wars is a large number, but with so many disputes, the average level of severity is reduced by the other, lower-level disputes.

A more useful comparison of the relative severity level is the occurrence of war in the rivalry; this can indicate how frequently the most severe level of conflict is reached in a rivalry. Tables 9.2 and 9.3 provide clear evidence that enduring rivalries have a greater propensity for war than other categories of international conflict. Table 9.2 uses war as the unit of analysis, and thus each war is counted only once. Table 9.3 uses rivalry as the unit of analysis; hence, multilateral wars may

Table 9.2   Rivalry Context and the Frequency of Interstate War, 1816–1992

Rivalry Type	Number of Rivalries	War Frequency
Isolated	880 (75.5%)	14 (17.7%)
Proto	223 (19.1%)	26 (32.9%)
Enduring	63 (5.4%)	39 (49.4%)
6–13 disputes	36 (3.1%)	10 (12.7%)
>13 disputes	27 (2.4%)	29 (36.7%)
All	1,166 (100%)	79 (100%)

Note: Unit of analysis = war.

Table 9.3   Rivalry Context and the Probability of at Least One War, 1816–1992

Rivalry Type	Probability of War (N with War)
Isolated	0.16 (139)
Proto	0.32 (71)
Enduring	0.59 (37)
6–13 disputes	0.56 (20)
>13 disputes	0.63 (17)
All	0.21 (247)

Note: Unit of analysis = rivalry.

be counted more than once. Only 17.7 percent of wars occur in isolation, whereas almost half (49.4 percent) take place in enduring rivalries. In addition, a dispute in an enduring rivalry is almost twice as likely to end in war than one in isolation.

Another test is to treat the rivalry as a unit of analysis to see whether at least one war occurs at some point in the rivalry. As Table 9.3 reveals, the propensity for war grows dramatically as one moves from isolated conflict to the most severe enduring rivalries (almost four times as great in enduring rivalries as in the lowest rivalry category). In enduring rivalries, the chances are better than 59 percent that the two states will go to war at some point in their competition. These findings show that not only is the propensity of a single dispute ending in war greater, but so is the chance of war sometime in the relationship as the rivalry becomes longer and more serious.

Hensel (1998a) largely confirms these findings, even though he defines rivalry context somewhat differently.[6] He finds that enduring rivalries account for a disproportionate fraction of interstate interactions according to six different aspects of interstate conflict: peaceful and violent territorial changes, militarized disputes, low-level and violent international crises, and full-fledged wars.

Based on these results, there is a clear tendency for the rivalry context to influence the conflict behavior of states and their propensity for war. The only argument against conflict interdependence in rivalries is made by Gartzke and Simon (1999), who claim that the distribution of enduring rivalries across a continuum of dispute frequency is similar to that predicted by a random events model. In effect, they are arguing that repeated militarized disputes might easily occur by chance. Nevertheless, their analysis only looks at enduring rivalries and does not consider lesser rivalries as well, a more valid test; indeed, Cioffi-Revilla's (1998) results indicate that looking only at enduring rivalries can produce misleading results and incorrect conclusions. Their argument also ignores that conflict patterns, described earlier, do not occur randomly. For example, there is a pattern of greater hostility and war likelihood in more enduring rivalries (a random events model would predict no difference in conflict patterns across different kinds of rivalries). More direct empirical evidence for the nonindependence of disputes is found in the literature on recurring conflict.

Recurring Conflict

Another series of works focuses not on rivalry contexts as a whole but generally on the impact that one conflict has on subsequent conflict, representing perhaps a slice of the rivalry context. The part of the work on recurring conflict that concerns us is at the dyadic level of analysis (i.e., repeated conflict between the same pairs of states) rather than repeated conflict involvement at the national level (i.e., a single state "addicted to conflict"; see, e.g., Stoll 1984) or the system level (i.e., the tendency for conflicts to cluster in time within a system; e.g., Houweling and Siccama 1985). Dyadic recurring conflict most closely parallels what we signify as rivalries between the same pair of states, although usually the concern with recurring conflict has been with one-time, short-term recurrence rather than with repeated conflict over a long time period, which is characteristic of enduring rivalries.

The phenomenon of dyadic recurring conflict is hardly rare. Maoz (1984) reports that 76 percent of disputes are followed by another dispute between the same states. These findings are mirrored in several other studies that find a link between previous conflict and the likelihood of future conflict between the same states (Richardson 1960b; Anderson and McKeown 1987). A history of previous disputes between the same states is a good predictor of future conflict (Diehl, Reifschneider, and Hensel 1996), but this begs the question somewhat of why that conflict is likely.

The consequences of recurring conflict appear fairly clear: recurring conflict between the same set of states appears to increase the chance of conflict escalation and war. Leng (1983) found that states adopted more coercive bargaining strategies in successive confrontations with the same opponent, with war almost always the result after three disputes. Brecher (1984) notes similarly that protracted conflicts are more violent with a greater risk of war than nonrecurring conflict. Huth (1988) suggests that the use of "bully" or "conciliation" strategies in a past confrontation lessens the probability that future deterrence attempts will be successful.[7]

The literature on recurring conflict indicates that repeated violence between the same pairs of states is more common than might be expected and with dangerous consequences. Together with the findings on rivalry context, it is clear that conflicts between the same pairs of states are related over time; there is little work on spatial interconnectedness over time (see Kirby and Ward 1987). Delineating those patterns and accounting for them, however, is subject to considerably more uncertainty.

COMPETING VIEWS ON RIVALRY PROCESSES
AND RECURRING CONFLICT

Although substantial evidence indicates that conflicts are not independent of one another and rivalry context makes a difference, there is disagreement over the dynamics of rivalries and what elements of the rivalry context are responsible for those processes. The two primary views of the rivalry context are the "punctuated equilibrium model" and the "evolutionary" model.

The Punctuated Equilibrium Model

The punctuated equilibrium model has its origins in evolutionary biology (Eldredge and Gould 1972); more recently it has been applied to public policy formation in the United States (Baumgartner and Jones 1993). The biological application of this model suggests that the development of species is a very slow process, characterized by long periods of stability with little or no change and interrupted by brief periods of rapid change. The application of the punctuated equilibrium model to rivalries similarly suggests that enduring rivalries, once established, are relatively stable phenomena over time, continuing for decades until they are dislodged by sudden environmental shocks (Diehl and Goertz 2000).

The punctuated equilibrium model of rivalry depends centrally on the concept of a "basic rivalry level," or BRL (Goertz and Diehl 1998). Azar (1972) proposed that each pair of countries has a "normal relations range," or an average level of hostile or cooperative interaction, around which their relations vary; we reformulate this as a BRL around which relations fluctuate. Periods of conflict and détente are seen as essentially "random" variations around this basic level; there is no secular trend toward more conflictual or more peaceful relations. In statistical terms, the difference between the severity of any given confrontation and the overall dyadic BRL is a random variable that is independent of past disputes and wars and remains constant from one dispute to the next (i.e., the standard assumptions one makes about error terms in linear models). Simply put, the punctuated equilibrium model anticipates that conflict patterns within rivalries will "lock in" quickly at the outset of the rivalry relationship and remain that way throughout the rivalry.

According to the punctuated equilibrium model, rivalries primarily begin because of the influence of structural or exogenous factors, including domestic factors such as regime change. We identify (Goertz and Diehl 1995b; Diehl and Goertz 2000) political shocks as an important source of rivalry, noting that shocks represent dramatic changes in the interstate system that can fundamentally alter the processes, relationships, and expectations driving interactions between states. Political shocks thus set the stage for rapid change in interstate relationships, perhaps leading to the outbreak of new rivalries or the termination of ongoing rivalries. Additional factors not specified by the model that generate rivalry might include characteristics of the international system (e.g., polarity), the dyad (e.g., joint democracy, geographic proximity, or relative power distribution between two adversaries), or individual nation-states (e.g., wealth).

Once a rivalry has begun, the punctuated equilibrium model suggests that relations between the rivals are characterized by great stability in conflict behavior, with no secular trend of increasing or decreasing conflict levels during the rivalry. This is not to suggest that all conflict within a rivalry is exactly the same over time. Indeed, this model expects some variation in severity and duration across different disputes, occasionally including large deviations (full-scale interstate wars) from the basic rivalry level. We do not list specific factors that are thought to account for any observed variation in conflict severity levels, although we argue that there is no systematic impact from past confrontations or interactions (beyond the impact of the BRL, which itself is determined exogenously) and that the strongest influences are likely to be structural or exogenous. Finally, although the punctuated equilibrium model does not predict that all enduring rivalries are more severe than all lesser conflicts, its proponents (Diehl and Goertz 2000) do suggest that, on average, enduring rivalries will be the most severe form of interstate conflict.

The Evolutionary Model

In contrast to the sudden change and then protracted stability of the punctuated equilibrium model, Hensel (1996) offers an evolutionary model of rivalry development. The evolutionary model does not assume that structural conditions determine the development of rivalries. Rather, the evolutionary approach to rivalry argues that rivalries change over time in response to interactions between the rival states, meaning that conflict patterns within rivalry are likely to vary systematically over the rivalry process. Whereas the punctuated equilibrium model assumes that enduring rivalries exhibit a distinct conflict pattern from the outset that is inherently more dangerous than isolated or protorivalries, the evolutionary approach suggests that the distinctions among what have been called "isolated," "proto-," and "enduring" rivalries (Diehl and Goertz 2000) are not immediately evident. Instead, potential rivalries are assumed to pass through different "phases," each with its characteristics and conflict patterns. Events and interactions within each phase influence the outbreak and severity level of subsequent confrontations and help determine whether a given conflictual relationship will advance to the next phase (perhaps eventually reaching enduring rivalry).

Past research using this evolutionary model (e.g., Hensel 1996, 1998a) identifies three general phases in the evolution of rivalries. In the early phase of rivalry, relations between two states are guided by little or no history of past conflict, and there may be little expectation of future interactions to guide their strategies. Hensel argues that conflict in this phase is likely to be less severe, to involve less coercive bargaining, and to be less likely to be followed by future confrontations than conflict in other rivalry phases. The intermediate phase—coming after two adversaries have engaged in several confrontations but before they can meaningfully be described as true enduring rivals—is a transition phase in which both the push of the past (the lengthening history of past conflict) and the pull of the future (the expectation of continued future conflict) begin to have an important impact on conflict behavior. The advanced phase of rivalry is characterized by substantial threat perception and competition between the rivals, corresponding to the time when two adversaries have reached the level of "enduring rivalry," as we have described it. Conflict in the advanced phase is expected to be even more severe than in the earlier phases because of the accumulation of hostility and grievances from the past and expectations about the future; and conflict occurring in this phase is seen as likely to be followed by recurrent conflict shortly afterward.

According to the evolutionary model, rivalries begin because of the way states handle any contentious issues between them (see also Hensel 1998b, 1998c, 1999). As two adversaries begin to use militarized means rather than peaceful techniques to settle their issues—whether they be highly salient issues such as territory or less salient issues such as economic policies—they create an atmosphere of distrust and hostility that can culminate in rivalry. Hensel (1996, 1998a) describes two distinct types of evolutionary factors that help account for movement between the different phases of rivalry. The first is a general expectation that, ceteris paribus, relations between two adversaries will become more conflictual as two adversaries accumulate a longer history of militarized conflict. Each confrontation between two adversaries is likely to lead to a general deterioration in relations as the result of increased feelings of hostility, distrust, or enmity, as well as any death or losses that may have resulted. As a result, each successive confrontation between the same adversaries is seen as pushing them closer to the recognition of long-term rivalry and its implications.

Beyond this general effect, the second type of evolutionary factor involves the specific effects of past interactions, such as the outcomes and severity levels of past confrontations. For example, a confrontation that ends in a stalemate is likely to increase distrust and hostility between two adversaries without resolving any of their disputed issues to either side's satisfaction, while a confrontation ending in a negotiated compromise may produce the opposite effect.[8] In short, between the specific and general effects, the evolutionary approach sees rivalry developing out of earlier interactions between two adversaries. In each case, the impact of these evolutionary factors is likely to be greater when the past conflict activates the domestic political scene on each side by attracting the attention and interest of important domestic actors in government, the political opposition, and the mass public. An activated political scene can help prolong rivalry by rewarding aggressive behavior by leaders and by punishing conciliatory actions toward the rival (Hensel 1998b, 1998c).

Maoz and Mor (1999) have developed their own evolutionary model of enduring rivalries, which is related to the work of Hensel but also draws on some of the insights from the punctuated equilibrium approach. They regard the strategic interaction of the rivals as key to defining rivalry evolution. A number of factors influence the enduring rivalry process. As rivals interact, each state learns about its opponent and the opponent's preferences and behavior. The interaction also produces an outcome, which may alter the status quo and therefore the preferences of the rivals involved (e.g., a formerly satisfied state may suddenly be dissatisfied after losing a dispute). Offering a middle ground between Hensel's evolutionary model and our punctuated equilibrium model, Maoz and Mor argue that stability in enduring rivalries may set in very quickly or this process may take an extended period of time. Once preferences and perceptions stabilize, rivalries are likely to end, according to Maoz and Mor. As with other evolutionary models, the emphasis of their approach is on strategic interaction and not on the structural conditions that may influence rivalry processes.

A Comparison of the Two Models

Both the punctuated equilibrium and evolutionary models postulate that the rivalry context affects the likelihood and severity of future conflicts between two states. They also agree that enduring rivalries—*once established*—are relatively stable phenomena, requiring environmental shocks or favorable domestic and international conditions to end these protracted conflictual relationships. The biggest disagreement between the two models lies in how and when rivalries become established in the first place. Whereas the punctuated equilibrium model suggests that enduring rivalries are established quickly because of structural and issue factors, the evolutionary model suggests that rivalries may take longer to develop their distinctive patterns of behavior, with the exact speed of development depending on how two prospective rival states interact with each other along the way.

Specifically, the punctuated equilibrium and evolutionary models diverge on a number of expectations. To begin, the punctuated equilibrium model argues that enduring rivalry conflict patterns are evident from the outset of that conflict, and thus it is appropriate to identify such rivalries in a post hoc fashion. In contrast, the evolutionary model argues that enduring rivalries are indistinguishable from their lesser rivalry counterparts in the early stages of the competition, only developing distinctive patterns of behavior with the passage of time and the accumulation of a history of conflict. Only the evolutionary model would expect to see changes in conflict severity over time, while the punctuated equilibrium model would generally expect to see consistency from the first confrontation through the final confrontation in a given rivalry.

The second set of differences, a corollary of the first, concerns the outbreak of full-scale war. Looking at wars allows us to test whether the expected relationships are present for all levels of conflict severity—including minor incidents as well as the bloodiest wars—or merely after some critical threshold. Under the evolutionary approach, wars—the most severe forms of interstate conflict—are expected to be more common in later stages of enduring rivalries, after two adversaries have built up a legacy of hostility and distrust in previous confrontations.[9] The punctuated equilibrium model, in contrast, expects a more random distribution of wars over the course of an enduring rivalry, with war-fighting rivalries simply reflecting a higher basic rivalry level from the beginning of their relationship than other adversaries that never reach full-scale war.

Third is the proposition that there is no difference in the severity of conflicts in the early phase of enduring rivalries and lesser conflicts (i.e., isolated and protorivalries). The evolutionary model anticipates that these initial conflicts help determine whether two adversaries will eventually become enduring rivals or whether they will be able to end their conflict short of such an outcome. As a result, the initial conflicts should appear largely the same, regardless of whether the disputes repeat into an enduring rivalry or never reoccur between the same states. The punctuated equilibrium model predicts that early enduring rivalry conflicts will, on average, be more severe than lesser order conflicts, because the sources of the ultimate "basic rivalry level" are already in place.

The fourth and final set of propositions involves the sources of militarized dispute severity. The punctuated equilibrium model suggests that conflict behavior is influenced primarily by the external determinants of a given rivalry's BRL and that these influences should be roughly constant from the beginning of a rivalry until its conclusion. Unfortunately, the punctuated equilibrium model is largely silent on what those factors might be. The evolutionary model argues that interactions in the early stages of a potential rivalry will help determine which relationships will eventually develop into enduring rivalries and which will avoid such development. As a result, the evolutionary model puts much more emphasis on past interactions as a source of conflict behavior and much less emphasis on external factors such as political shocks. Finally, the evolutionary model would predict greater variation in the conflict patterns during rivalries than would the punctuated equilibrium approach; the latter would expect such variation to be around the level specified by each rivalry's BRL.

AN EXAMINATION OF THE EMPIRICAL EVIDENCE

The extant evidence indicates that rivalry context is an important influence on conflict dynamics, but there is some disagreement over the general patterns of conflict within rivalries, indicated by the two models described in this chapter. In this section, we first consider what empirical studies say about the validity of the two approaches. Furthermore, somewhat independent of either model, we also look at the various influences (endogenous, exogenous, or structural) that might be said to affect rivalry dynamics and context.[10]

General Patterns

Although neither model has received much direct empirical attention in the recent rivalry literature, some empirical evidence supports the punctuated equilibrium model and its underlying basic rivalry level concept. We explore (Goertz and Diehl 1998; Diehl and Goertz 2000) whether the early development of enduring rivalries follows the predictions of the basic rivalry level concept, the so-called volcano model (a pattern of rising hostility culminating in war and the end of the rivalry), or several other patterns.[11] We find only a relatively small number of rivalries showing increasing or convex trends over time, which fits the volcano model and is most consistent with a gradual evolutionary process because of the expectation that the effects of rivalry take time to develop. Yet the null hypothesis model of no secular trend is the dominant pattern (about two-thirds of the cases), which is consistent with the predictions of the punctuated equilibrium model because of the expectation that the effects of rivalry center almost immediately around two adversaries' basic rivalry level.

We also note (Goertz and Diehl 1998; Diehl and Goertz 2000) that the basic rivalry level appears to "lock in" at the outset of the rivalry and does not "fade out" at the end. That is, the basic rivalry level is established early in the rivalry relationship and is not easily disrupted throughout the life of the rivalry. In examining the first three and last three disputes in the rivalry sequence, we do not find a trend toward either escalation at the outset or deescalation at the conclusion of the rivalry. Also consistent with the notion that rivalry patterns are stable over time and require dramatic shocks to interrupt this stability, we report (Goertz and Diehl 1995) that that political shocks at the systemic or nation-state level are virtual necessary conditions to start or end a rivalry. Eighty-seven percent of all rivalries begin within ten years of a political shock of some type, and 92 percent of all uncensored rivalries end within ten years of a shock. The occurrence of a shock is also found to increase both the probability that an enduring rivalry will begin in the next decade and the probability that an ongoing rivalry will end in the next decade.[12]

Similarly, Levy and Ali (1998) report the importance of political shocks on the stability of rivalry relationships. The Thirty Years' War in Germany is cited as a shock that profoundly altered Dutch relationships with both current and potential rivals in the seventeenth century. The death of Frederick Henry also brought a lull to the Dutch-Spanish competition and set in motion events that led to increased competition with the British. In effect, an exogenous and an endogenous shock had the effect (along with other factors) of ending one militarized rivalry and beginning another. This is consistent with the punctuated equilibrium model's notion of rivalry stability that is only likely to be disrupted by abrupt environmental change.

Other findings offer mixed support for the punctuated equilibrium model, the quick lock-in of the basic rivalry level, and lack of a fade-out pattern. In their game-theoretical analysis of four Middle East rivalries, Maoz and Mor (1996) find that the enduring rivalries exhibit acute conflict at the outset, with a constant motivation to extend the conflict from the beginning; this suggests that conflicts do not "evolve" into enduring rivalries but may exhibit severe rivalry characteristics from their origins. For Cioffi-Revilla (1998), stability is defined as the probability of rivalry continuation into the future. In his analysis, a hazard rate for termination is used to indicate whether rivalries show an increasing or decreasing tendency to end, with the latter signifying a stable relationship. His results indicate three phases of rivalry stability: initial stability, maturation, and termination. In the initial phase, Cioffi-Revilla discovers that rivalries were very stable and therefore not prone to end in their early phases. The maturation or midlife period shows that rivalries become mildly unstable, with an increasing hazard rate for termination; perhaps this indicates that many rivalries never go beyond the protorivalry stage, and enduring rivalries are special cases that seem to run against the tide. In the termination phase, within the latter stage of rivalries (when the advanced stage of enduring rivalry is reached), they have a strong propensity to end (this is consistent with the findings of Bennett 1998).

Somewhat less empirical evidence directly examines the evolutionary model, although much of it is supportive. Hensel (1996) finds that as a pair of adversaries engages in more frequent militarized conflict and thus moves along toward enduring rivalry, their relationship tends to become more conflictual, particularly in terms of an ever-increasing likelihood of repeated conflict. Vasquez (1998) also reports a pattern of rising conflict in recurrent disputes during the U.S.-Japan rivalry that led to World War II. In seeking to account for conflict patterns within a rivalry, Hensel (1996) still finds that rivalry context is an important factor, even controlling for a host of other influences (e.g., contentious issues or capability shifts). He also shows the influence of past interactions on rivalry behavior in noting that the likelihood of a recurrence of conflict in a rivalry was reduced when the dispute ended in a decisive or compromise outcome.

Other follow-up studies by Hensel also generally, although not universally, support the evolutionary model. Hensel (1998a) finds that the likelihood of conflict recurrence increases dramatically as one moved into the later rivalry phase; the likelihood of recurring conflict doubles in the intermediate rivalry phase and quintupled in the most advanced or enduring rivalry phase. Using events data, Hensel (1997) finds that later phases of a rivalry exhibit more intense conflictual (and, interestingly enough, more cooperative as well)[13] interactions; this helps establish that previous findings based exclusively on militarized disputes are not unique to that phenomenon or to the militarized dispute data set. Hensel and McLaughlin (1996) also find that a history of past disputes is associated with greater conflict in a rivalry. Yet, contrary to the evolutionary view, they also find that war is more likely *earlier* in a rivalry. Also casting some doubt on the evolutionary approach are Maoz and Mor (1998), who find that the games of "Deadlock" and "Bully" are the most common in young rivalries, suggesting that the early stages of enduring rivalries are marked by hostility on both sides with few attempts (at least successful ones) at conciliation, cooperation, and conflict resolution.

Maoz and Mor (1999) find general confirmation of their evolutionary model in both case studies and large *N* analyses. Learning and preference change were generally strong associated with rivalry dynamics. Maoz and Mor provide a model that is capable of accounting for the emergence, evolution, and termination of rivalries. Despite the strong support for their model, the authors acknowledge that they cannot account for sudden changes in rivalry stability, which they attribute to unspecified exogenous factors. Of course, such sudden shifts are consistent with the political shock effects noted in the punctuated equilibrium model.

Overall, there is some empirical support for both the punctuated equilibrium and evolutionary models, largely from studies conducted by proponents of each approach. A handful of studies by other scholars offer mixed conclusions on the validity of each approach. None of these studies directly tests competing propositions of the two models. Two recent conference papers (Hensel and Sowers 1998; Stinnett and Diehl 1998) attempt to model the development of enduring rivalries. Each looks at the impact of structural and behavioral factors, roughly corresponding to the punctuated equilibrium and evolutionary models, respectively, on the onset of rivalry. The findings of each study reveal that both structural (e.g., power distribution) and behavioral (e.g., dispute outcomes) factors influence the development of enduring rivalries. Nevertheless, such studies do not provide tests of the two models against one another. This is similar to many studies of the democratic peace in which normative and institutional explanations are each found to have some validity. Rarely are the two explanations tested against each other using competing propositions.

Endogenous Factors

Part of what constitutes a rivalry context is what happens within that rivalry. The interactions of the rivals establish a past, or history, that can influence future conflict interactions. A primary focus of rivalry and recurring conflict studies has been on how the outcomes of one dispute affect the conflict dynamics in subsequent disputes. This is reflected in McGinnis and Williams (1989), who modeled the U.S.-Soviet rivalry over time with appropriate consideration for how past actions affected contemporary and future decisions; even though the model was only for the superpower dyad, its applicability to other rivalries appears reasonable.

Empirically, studies of recurring conflict indicate that it may be that decisive outcomes or imposed settlements in previous disputes dampen the tendency for conflicts to reoccur, suggesting that stalemated outcomes may have the opposite effect (Maoz 1984). Hensel (1994) had similar findings but further added that the prospects for future disputes were also influenced by shifts in military capability between the states; for example, he reports that stalemates and compromises were often followed quickly by new disputes initiated by the stronger state, which was declining in relative capabilities. Anderson and McKeown (1987) also speak of the victor in a previous dispute initiating another conflict to reestablish victory. We found (Goertz and Diehl 1992b) that recurring conflict after a territorial change was most likely when that change was formalized by a treaty and was considered very important to the losing side; territorial changes were more stable when the losing side was relatively weak and the gaining side regarded the territory as important.

Studies that specifically look at rivalries produce similar results. Wayman and Jones (1991) consider the impact of previous disputes on subsequent disputes in a rivalry; they find that certain outcomes (e.g., capitulation) of those disputes are more likely to produce frequent future disputes or disputes that are more violent (after stalemates). Similarly, Hensel (1996) reports that decisive or compromise outcomes to disputes lessen the likelihood of future rivalry confrontations.

Beyond simple analyses of outcome effects on the next dispute, Maoz and Mor (1998, 1999) attempt to identify patterns of learning from rivalry interaction. They define learning as a reevaluation of prior beliefs that is triggered by a discrepancy between expectations and experience. A key finding from their study is that there cannot be a fixed game assumption in trying to model the processes of enduring rivalries. The preferences and perceptions of the players shift over the course of the rivalry. Thus, iterative game analyses that use Prisoners' Dilemma or Chicken (common in deterrence analyses) to try to understand state bargaining behavior are unlikely to produce coherent results. Different game structures and preferences occur throughout the rivalry, and one must be able to understand the process of preference and structural change to model the interactions accurately. Nevertheless, Maoz and Mor indicate that learning cannot really account for the game transformations that occur over the course of a rivalry. The appearance of exogenous and endogenous shocks are again associated with this transformation. Here, the authors point to significant shifts in capability (consistent with Hensel 1996, as noted earlier) and leadership change in the rival states as important factors conditioning game transformations (see also Goertz and Diehl 1995b). Thompson (1995) also emphasizes preference change at the end of rivalry.

Maoz and Mor do find, however, that some adaptive learning does occur within rivalries, but their model is often incorrect in predicting the behavior of the rivals. They cite perceptual shifts about what game is thought to be in play and incomplete information about the process by scholars as possibly responsible for this discrepancy. In any case, there appears to be less learning and its subsequent impact than one might expect, although such processes are often hard to identify and assess (see Levy 1994b). Nevertheless, Larson (1999) argues that the United States and the Soviet Union learned conflict management and how to avoid war based on their behaviors during successive crises.

Although it is widely assumed that endogenous factors condition the rivalry context, the evidence for a strong, systematic effect is thus far limited. This is largely because few scholars have investigated these factors empirically but also because the results thus far are weak and disappointing.

Exogenous Influences

A second component of rivalry context is the degree to which rivalries are interconnected with other conflicts and rivalries; this is one of the few areas where the spatial interrelationships of conflicts are explored. Several formal models assume such an interconnection. Muncaster and Zinnes (1993) create a model for an N number of states that is capable of tracking the evolution of rivalries, including how those rivalries influence the relations (and potential rivalries) of other states in the system. A dispute involving two states not only influences their future relations but also impacts all other dyadic relations in the system. Also in the formal modeling tradition, McGinnis (1990) offers a model of regional rivalries that identifies optimum points for aid, arms, and alignments in those rivalries; this again provides for exogenous conflicts to influence the dynamics of rivalries.

A number of empirical case studies confirm the significance of third-party conflict to the dynamics of rivalries. Ingram (1999) notes that the British-Russian rivalry was influenced by these states' relations with Asian client states. Schroeder (1999) boldly states that the Franco-Austrian rivalry was kept from being resolved by its interconnection with other ongoing European rivalries. Similarly, Vasquez (1998) attributes, in part, the Japanese attack on the United States and United Kingdom in the 1940s to escalation to war of other rivalries in Europe. According to Levy and Ali (1998), the end of the Dutch revolt against Spain led to the conditions that permitted Dutch economic expansion and the initiation of the rivalry with England in the seventeenth century. States sometimes have limited carrying capacities in the number of rivalries to which they can devote attention and resources. Huth (1996b) makes a similar point with respect to territorial conflicts; the presence of additional conflicts increases the likelihood of peaceful resolution of extant territorial disputes. Yet the Anglo-Dutch rivalry was also linked with the Anglo-French rivalry. England's undeclared war against France resulted in the seizure of Dutch ships that were trading with France, analogous to the contagion model noted by Siverson and Starr (1991) in which a given conflict spills over to encompass neighboring countries. The intersection of these two rivalries had the effect of escalating the competition between the Dutch and the British, who had previously managed their disputes without resort to war.

Kinsella (1994a, 1994b, 1995) examined the dynamics of some rivalries in the Middle East with special attention given to how the superpower rivalry influenced these minor power rivalries. There is a pattern of action-reaction to superpower arms transfers to that region. He finds that Soviet arms transfers exacerbated rivalry conflicts in several cases, whereas U.S. arms supplies to Israel had no strong positive or negative effects. He also notes that U.S. arms transfer policy may have actually dampened conflict in the Iran–Iraq rivalry. It is clear from Kinsella's studies that the superpower rivalry affected the dynamics of the minor power rivalries in the Middle East, although the reverse was not generally true. We further confirm (Goertz and Diehl 1997) that rivalries are closely linked, which has a clear impact on their conflict levels. The conflict levels of linked rivalries were higher than those of unlinked rivalries, but generally only for minor power rivalries. This is largely because major power rivalries had an exacerbating effect on lower-order conflict, but the reverse was not true; we did not have enough cases of major-major rivalries to evaluate statistically their impact on each other. The volatility of some linked enduring rivalries was also greater, but the results were not as robust. Their findings were largely the same for the frequency of war as they were for the conflict level. A cross-temporal analysis of rivalries that had prelinked, linked, and delinked periods showed little variation in their basic conflict level, but war was more common during linkage and less so in the other two periods, especially in the prelinked periods. Bennett's (1996) analysis of rivalry termination also indicated that some rivalries end when the rivals begin to have common external security threats; in effect, the advent of new rivalries with negative links to extant rivalries causes the latter to end. This is consistent with our notion (Goertz and Diehl 1995b) of political shocks being the impetus for the end of rivalries: the end of a major power rivalry (e.g., the Cold War) may have been a sufficient shock to the international system so as to terminate other rivalries linked to that global competition.

Although rivalry context seems to be influenced by interconnections with other rivalries, there is apparently less direct impact from other exogenous influences. Specifically, external attempts to mitigate rivalry or recurring conflict are largely ineffective, at least in the short term; this is largely consistent with the BRL argument that conflict patterns are not easily disrupted and then only as a consequence of dramatic political shocks. A study of international mediation attempts in rivalries (Bercovitch and Diehl 1997) found that the basic rivalry levels appear largely unchanged by mediation efforts (except for a modest effect on waiting times for the next dispute), at least in the short term. Furthermore, the presence or absence of those efforts does not appear to have any impact on significant deviations from those levels—namely, the occurrence of war. Bercovitch and Regan (1994) also discover that conflict management attempts are considerably less successful in enduring rivalries than in lesser conflicts.[14] In addition, United Nations intervention in a crisis has not been found to have a significant impact on whether two disputants will clash again in the near future (Diehl, Reifschneider, and Hensel 1996).

There is clear evidence that conflict events are linked with other contemporaneous disputes and crises, and the severity and likelihood of war are partly a function of this aspect of rivalry context. Thus far, however, there is little indication that external attempts to mitigate conflict influence the rivalry context.

Structural Factors

A final set of factors that seem to influence rivalry dynamics and the prospects for recurring conflict are structural factors. These largely focus on the issues under dispute, characteristics of the rivals, system attributes, or other traditional correlates of war. It is not entirely clear from past research whether these elements interact with aspects of the rivalry context or whether they are better accommodated under the traditional cross-sectional, "causes of war" research approach.

As with the conflict studies literature in general, structural influences on rivalries are varied. Most prominently, however, are territorial issues. In a case study of the Pacific Theater of World War II, Vasquez (1998a) cites the importance of territorial issues as a basis for enduring rivalries. A broader study of conditions for war in rivalries by the same author (Vasquez 1996a) also indicates that unresolved territorial issues are key predictors of escalation to war. Thompson (1999) makes a similar argument in noting that the Anglo-American rivalry did not experience war, in part, because any territory in dispute between the British and the Americans was judged not to be worth fighting over. Rule (1999) further notes that the competition over territory (along with ideology) was an important element in the origins of the France–Spain rivalry of the late fifteenth century. Although a large number of ongoing claims have been made over territory, not all of these have resulted in militarized disputes or the development of long-standing rivalries. Huth (1996a) looks at the role of territorial claims since 1950 in the origins of enduring rivalries. He uses a modified realist model, which includes both domestic and international political factors, to explain how states become involved in enduring rivalries over territory. Importantly, he notes that the relative strength of the challenger does not have much of an effect and that states also do not frequently challenge allies or extant treaty commitments by resort to militarized action. Rather, domestic concerns, especially ethnic and linguistic ties between one's own population and those living in the disputed territory, are significantly associated with the recurrence of militarized conflict. Hensel (1996) finds that rivalries with a prominent territorial component and those that experience a capability shift among the rivals are more likely to have recurring conflict and have that conflict recur sooner.

According to limited current research, some aspects of the international system were important for the onset of war in rivalries, but generally they were not central. Another trend uncovered by Cioffi-Revilla (1998) is that bipolar systems produce more unstable rivalries than multipolar ones. The balance of power at the system level is a classic neorealist factor, but Levy and Ali (1998) note that this made little difference in the rivalry development or war between the British and the Dutch. Nevertheless, Vasquez (1998a) cites another systemic variable largely ignored by realism and its variants: international rules and norms. He notes that the breakdown of the Washington Conference structure, which sought to control military competition (especially in weaponry) between the major powers after World War I, removed the rules and norms necessary to "manage" the competition between the leading Pacific states. In this way, limiting the anarchy of the international system can have a mitigating effect on rivalry competition, and while perhaps international norms and rules may not be enough to prevent or end rivalries, they might assist in restraining the most severe manifestations of rivalries. A similar argument is made by Larson (1999) in her assessment of why the superpower rivalry managed to avoid war.

Other conventional factors thought to be associated with war also receive a mixed assessment from current studies. The power distribution is often a centerpiece of models of international conflict, although scholars disagree considerably over whether parity or preponderance is the most dangerous condition. Geller (1998) finds no general relationship between the capability distribution and the identity of the initiator of wars in major power rivalries. Nevertheless, he points out that *unstable* capability distributions are substantively associated with the occurrence of war, although he is quick to acknowledge that they approach a necessary, but not a sufficient, condition for conflict escalation in the rivalry.

Another conventional factor thought to be associated with war is alliances. Vasquez (1998a) argues that the alliance structure in the Pacific did not prevent war, suggesting there was little deterrent effect. Despite this general pattern, Vasquez does link alliances with the march toward war in the Pacific. He argues, "Once a major state aligns with a weak state . . . this can increase the probability of war because when weak allies are led by hard-liners they will not support compromises that avoid war. Therefore . . . [alliances] put a constraint on conciliatory acts" (Vasquez 1998a: 216). This conception of alliances and war is quite different than the traditional capability aggregation view of alliances and conflict. Instead, it suggests that we consider how alliances affect bargaining and how the alliance variable interacts with other concerns, here domestic political processes.

Domestic political processes again were found to be critical in the dynamics of enduring rivalries. Vasquez (1998a) notes that domestic hard-liners pushed for war in Japan, preventing that country from making more conciliatory gestures and accepting some peace offers short of war. Levy and Ali (1998) also note strong domestic pressures in England for hard-line policies and external actions. Perhaps this is why the English adopted a hard-line bargaining strategy that prevented effective conflict management. In contrast, Thompson (1999) argues that domestic political pressures in Britain actually encouraged deescalation and lessened the chances for war in its relations with the United States.

The "democratic peace" has also been the subject of analysis vis-à-vis war in rivalries. Modelski (1999) claims that the rivalry between Portugal and Venice several hundred years ago was more benign than other rivalries because of its "democratic lineage" and that democratic rivalries are more peaceful and more likely to be resolved "on their merits" rather than by military force. Thompson (1999) also cites mutual democracy as a pacifying condition in the Anglo-American rivalry. The presence of a democratic dyad also apparently has a dampening effect on conflict recurrence in the rivalry (Hensel 1996).

Another study (Hensel, Goertz, and Diehl 2000) found that the democratic peace effect extends to rivalries, with joint democratic status making participation in rivalries unlikely (and foreclosing participation in the most severe of rivalries) and conflict levels lower. Only 62 (of 1,166) rivalries over the period 1816–1992 involved states that were both democratic throughout the entire rivalry. These rivalries were generally short term with few disputes and therefore never developed into enduring rivalries. Twenty-three rivalries involved states whose regimes moved toward or away from democratic status during the course of the rivalry. Militarized disputes were generally much less likely during periods of joint democracy as compared to other periods; the exception is that regime-change dyads that evolved into enduring rivalries continued with their patterns of disputatious behavior regardless of the regime types of the rivals. Among rivalries that are transformed to joint democratic status, however, the conflict level tends to be lower when there is a democratic dyad, and the rivalry almost always ends shortly thereafter. Consistent with these findings, Bennett (1997) finds that joint democracy helps end a rivalry, although the process of democratization seems to have little impact on rivalry duration.

CONCLUSION

The study of rivalries and recurring conflict has received considerably less scholarly attention than other subjects (e.g., capability distributions, alliances) in the study of war, and many unanswered questions remain. Although our preference would be to address those questions within the framework provided under the rivalry approach to war and peace, several research items deserve priority whatever the approach adopted.

The first item on any research agenda should be to settle the controversy occasioned by the punctuated equilibrium versus evolutionary models debate on rivalry dynamics. One test would be to analyze conflict patterns within the population of enduring rivalries. The hypothesis to be tested could be that conflict in early stages of enduring rivalries is less severe than in later stages. A corollary proposition is that there is no significant difference in conflict severity in enduring rivalry early stages and comparable phases in lesser rivalries. The evolutionary model is consistent with each of these hypotheses, and the punctuated equilibrium model would predict the opposite: more severe conflict in enduring rivalries than other rivalries and severity relatively consistent over the life of rivalries.

Another concern is with the maintenance of rivalries. Cioffi-Revilla (1998) and Bennett (1998) indicate that rivalries are unstable in their later phases, suggesting that some process sets in to reverse the effects of rivalry maintenance factors. Yet according to conventional definitions of enduring rivalries, they can last forty years or more. Some factors are at work that seem to mitigate the unstable tendencies of rivalries, or there may be "stress" that appears only later, allowing some rivalries to persist well into the future. A valuable line of research would be to identify the conditions that make rivalries persist and conflict to recur repeatedly in the rivalry. Results from Maoz and Mor (1999) indicate that a focus on preference change and perceptions of the opponent may be a promising first line of inquiry.

The priority of other items for the research agenda depends, in part, on resolving the punctuated equilibrium versus evolutionary debate. If the punctuated equilibrium model is more accurate, greater attention might be devoted to identifying further the structural factors that account for higher BRLs and therefore the greater likelihood of war in some rivalries. A research agenda occasioned by the evolutionary model would necessarily focus more on the maturation process of rivalries and on the thus far disappointing results with respect to learning. Greater attention would need to be paid to how some rivalries apparently are able to manage their conflicts (even as they endure) without war, whereas others repeatedly escalate to war.

NOTES

This chapter contains material reprinted from Paul F. Diehl and Gary Goertz, *War and Peace in International Rivalry* (Ann Arbor: The University of Michigan Press, 2000). Reprinted with permission. This research was supported, in part, by National Science Foundation grant #SES-9309840.

1. Of course, work has been done on prolonged competitions between states. Yet this work on rivalries has not carried the rivalry moniker and has primarily been confined to the analysis of a single prolonged competition between two or more states; most prominently have been those concerned with the United States–Soviet Union rivalry and the Arab-Israeli conflict. These are primarily descriptive studies that, although insightful on individual events, do not offer much in the way of a theoretical understanding of how rivalries evolve; there is not much concern with process, as the analysis tends to be static. Furthermore, they offer little in the way of generalizations that extend beyond the single case at hand. Except as excellent sources on the history of individual rivalries, we largely ignore this segment of the literature.

2. *Enduring rivalries* are defined as those rivalries with at least six militarized disputes between the same pair of states and lasting at least twenty years. *Isolated rivalries* are one- and two-dispute rivalries. *Protorivalries* consist of those remaining rivalries not satisfying the definitional requirements of the other two categories.

3. Because of multiple participants, a dispute or war can be part of more than one rivalry. In this instance, it was considered part of the most severe rivalry. This seems reasonable in that many of the disputes and wars stem from multilateral competitions such as World War II and fall into isolated rivalries such as those between distant states on the Allied side and Germany or Japan. Furthermore, the original dyads prompting such multi-

lateral wars are almost always part of proto- and enduring rivalries, whereas those pairs that join the conflict later are more likely to be part of isolated rivalries. To include all the dyads from multilateral wars in this analysis would have the latter drive the results and do so in a misleading fashion.

4. The expected percentage of disputes for each rivalry category is calculated by reference to the minimum number of disputes necessary for each rivalry category and the actual number of rivalries in each category.

5. This analysis includes all disputes, including all combinations from multilateral wars. Unlike the analysis of wars provided earlier, there is a different severity score of each dyad, and the inclusion of multilateral wars does not necessarily distort or drive the results. See Diehl and Goertz (2000) for the full results.

6. Hensel defines rivalry according to phases, and therefore a rivalry does not become enduring until it reaches a certain threshold. In contrast, we define enduring rivalries in a post hoc fashion with even early conflict considered part of the enduring rivalry if that rivalry ultimately lasts a prescribed period of time.

7. It may be the past interactions, and less the strategies themselves, that account for this success (see Goertz 1995).

8. It should be noted that the specific and general effects of rivalry may exert opposite influences on future relations between two rivals. That is, while the general effect due to a long history of past conflict may lead to increased hostility between two rivals, a negotiated compromise outcome may help decrease hostility, and an especially severe confrontation—while perhaps increasing hostility—may lead to actions meant to manage or settle the rivalry.

9. This is true for the Hensel conception of evolution but may not be for Maoz and Mor.

10. There is a substantial literature on definitional issues (e.g., Thompson 1995) that uses enduring rivalries as a case selection device (e.g., Geller 1993). We largely ignore this literature except as it rarely addresses the question of rivalry context or its dynamics.

11. These two studies were conducted on slightly different populations of enduring rivalries and used somewhat different indicators of conflict severity (conflict duration is also discussed in Goertz and Diehl 1998). Nevertheless, the results were quite similar across the two studies.

12. It should be noted that Bennett (1998) finds that the effect of shocks on rivalry termination may depend heavily on the specific measurement used.

13. Separate analyses of cooperative and conflictual forms of interaction reveal that enduring rivals engage in more intense activities of each type than other adversaries, indicating that rivals' interactions often include many attempts to limit or manage their conflict as well as the more prominent militarized confrontations. Further aggregated analysis reveals that on balance, relationships between rivals are more conflictual than those between nonrival adversaries.

14. Nevertheless, they find that when conflict management is successful in enduring rivalries, it tends to exhibit a more durable positive effect in the rivalry relationship than comparable successful initiatives in other contexts.

10

Rivalries
Recurrent Disputes and Explaining War

Frank Whelon Wayman

The scientific goal of my research on war—which is explanation of why wars occur—involves the closely related tasks of predicting the onset of war from some set of independent variables and providing some broader theory, or logical reason, that explains why these variables produce or are associated with war. How successful have we been in completing these twin tasks? John Norton Moore (1995), in taking stock of our field, recently rated as our four biggest accomplishments (1) the initiation of scientific work by Quincy Wright, (2) the insight attributed to Kenneth Waltz (1959) that levels of analysis mattered, (3) the Correlates of War (COW) Project that brought to fruition Wright's efforts at creating an empirical database for the field, and (4) the first counterintuitive, powerful finding, by R. J. Rummel, that democracies don't fight each other.

A more empirical stock-taking of our progress, by Bremer (1992), finds that several variables we have long been assembling and investigating do indeed predict well to the onset of war. More precisely, when included in a multivariate regression model, each predicts a two- to fivefold increase in the probability of war between a pair of states, indicating reasonably strong predictive power for each of the variables and no single dominant explanation of war. For instance, Bremer's study of the democratic factor so dear to Moore reveals that it is only of average predictive power among the seven independent variables. One's glow at finding several important predictor variables may eventually dim when it sinks in that, although each predictor is valuable, no single explanation or even succinct explanation stands out. Worse, the most powerful predictive and explanatory variable is one obvious to a schoolchild: geographic contiguity of two states makes war between them more likely than if they are not adjacent to each other. Well, contiguity is indeed "predictive" in that being contiguous provides a 5.4-fold increase in the probability of war, and it is indeed "explanatory" in the sense that there are at least two plausible reasons that it would lead to war. Contiguity provides opportunity to attack and may also provide motive in the form of a border dispute. Also, I do concede it would be valuable to know whether the opportunity or the motive matters more, so demonstrating the role of contiguity is a progressive step that makes it possible to move on to a subsequent investigation.

Nonetheless, doesn't this example shows the shallowness of such prediction and such "explanation"? Who wouldn't have expected that nations next to each other are more likely to fight each other than nations far away? The explanatory variable in this case (contiguity) is both trivial in the sense of being obvious rather than surprising and trivial in the sense that no scientific or normative theory or any important policy prescriptions hinge on whether this predictor variable works.

As for the lesser variables in Bremer's analysis, we have a number of nonobvious (and for that reason interesting) contributions: war is more likely between a pair of states when at least one is economically advanced, at least one is a major power, at least one is nondemocratic, and neither one is overwhelmingly preponderant over the other. (There are also effects of their being allied with each other, but these two effects work in opposite directions and appear to fluctuate greatly with the specification of the model.) My conclusion from Bremer's article is that it provides an important synthesis of how much we have collectively accomplished in thirty years by identifying and measuring the variables Bremer selected.

But I find that even such a creative and admirable summary as Bremer's study leaves us far short of the theoretical integration we would need to convince ourselves that we had really explained war. Instead, we have three and a half decades now of studies, almost all of which (being more narrow in focus than Bremer's) show the slight importance of one or two variables as predictors of war. Is it any wonder that we are under assault from antiscientific critics who argue that we have little cohesiveness to show for our efforts? And even scientific skeptics abound. When David Singer began the COW Project thirty-four years ago, Anatol Rapoport, then his colleague at the Mental Health Research Institute of the University of Michigan, said to him in effect, "Surely you boys don't expect to explain war. The best you're going to be able to do is debunk the explanations people usually offer." If, a third of a century after Rapoport spoke, we have something more to celebrate, I would suggest that our glass of celebratory champagne is at most half full.

This somewhat disconcerting state of affairs led many scholars to heed the call of Bremer and Cusack and meet in 1991 in a conference dedicated to integrating the explanations of war (Bremer and Cusack 1995). The rallying cry of that conference, and point of departure of the resulting book, was a statement from Dina Zinnes. She said that while, through hundreds of empirical studies, we were attaining additive cumulation in studying the onset of war, we were far from attaining the more important integrative cumulation (Zinnes 1976). Today it remains true that the marginal utility of one more theoretically isolated empirical study, when we have so many, is likely to be less than the marginal utility of an empirically informed synthesis that shows how the mosaic of empirical work can be put together to provide a coherent perspective on the causes of war or factors that lead to war.

In this context, supplanting long-standing predictor variables such as polarity with newer predictor variables such as joint democracy, international trade volume, recurrent disputatiousness, and rivalry runs the risk of creating a field with "additive cumulation" of more and more unrelated predictor variables. And, if the future is like the past, these will each explain some of the variance in war, but none will in themselves provide a synthesis or dominant answer.

In particular, study of rivalry and recurrent disputes, the focus of this chapter, threatens to be at best one more atoll in our unconnected archipelago of "islands of theory" (Snyder and Diesing 1977). I have been reluctant to devote my efforts to the "ordinary science" of merely establishing firm footing on just another emerging island in the archipelago. Hence, our task in studying repeated disputes and rivalry needs to be showing how recurrent disputes and rivalry and other variables are likely to fit into the big picture of explaining war. The approach I am going to take toward that task follows methodologically in the footsteps of Bremer (1995b), Vasquez (1995a), and Wayman (1995) in the last three chapters of the Bremer and Cusack book on *The Process of War* and substantively in the tradition established by Vasquez (1993) in his book on the process of war and wars of rivalry.

INTEGRATIVE CUMULATION IN THE STUDY OF WAR

Integration of our scholarship, or, in other words, the development of "a coherent explanation of the onset of war" (Vasquez 1995a), takes four forms (Wayman 1995). In the first of these, the methodological approach, we discover which research designs, measures, and techniques have yielded the most reliable and valid findings, so that we can focus on the most valid studies and give less attention to distractions of the many less valid analyses (e.g., Wayman and Singer 1990). But in itself this approach is most useful for identifying good techniques for future use and identifying the best extant studies for others to synthesize.

Second, research findings can be grouped into more or less mutually exclusive and exhaustive categories. An ambitious example, the levels of analysis approach, pioneered by Waltz (1959) and Singer (1961), has become probably the most widespread way of summarizing what we know (Cashman 1993; Geller and Singer 1998). The basic problem with this approach to synthesis is that it usually is used to summarize literature and conduct analyses at each level of analysis—usually the individual, role, organizational, state, societal, dyadic, and international systemic; no way of integrating the findings from level to level is decisively brought to play (Wayman 1995). Also, the findings having been grouped by the level of analysis or aggregation, which is not a theoretical category in either the normative or empirical sense, are not categorized in a manner particularly conducive to theoretical synthesis. Bremer (chap. 2), in the thought-provoking chapter to this book, provides a fresh and helpful alternative to levels of analysis groupings by a new categorization scheme, in which he places research findings into who-whom, when, where, and why categories.

Process models of integration of findings (Vasquez 1987; Bremer 1995b) are a third and more ambitious approach. They trace war as the outcome of a process from emergence of conflicts of interest, to outbreak of militarized disputes, to escalation of the disputes, to onset of war, to spread of war, to consequences of violence for future wars. Fourth, several scholars have attempted theoretical integration, which is the most ambitious and can include process theories (e.g., Vasquez 1987, 1993) but also expected utility and game theory (Bueno de Mesquita 1981; Bueno de Mesquita and Lalman 1992), political realism (Cusack and Stoll 1990; Wayman and Diehl 1994), and handbooks encompassing a variety of prominent theoretical foci (Midlarsky 1989, 2000a).

This chapter provides a view of repeated disputes and rivalry through the lens of my own theoretical synthesis (Wayman, forthcoming), which is not intended to be idiosyncratic but rather is designed to be broad enough that we can all use it to see the forest and not just the trees. To paraphrase Paul Diehl, I don't think any one synthesis will be "The Theory of World Politics." That works only with simpler systems such as planetary motion and Newton's theory of gravity. Rather, in studying the onset of war, syntheses are useful in a way analogous to maps. One map of Colorado may emphasize the roads, another the elevations, another the national park system, another the ski facilities. The fact that we need several maps to plan a trip to Colorado doesn't mean the maps are false; likewise, the fact that we will need many theoretical perspectives to make sense of the onset of war doesn't mean that the theories are false, only that each theory must be parsimonious and hence highlight different aspects of the whole picture.

The synthetic approach I have taken contrasts political realism with three alternative frameworks, or alternative types of maps. The purpose of this scheme of contrasting frameworks is to better identify the limits of realism, which has been the dominant approach for centuries in international relations and to see how much validity is possessed by the various alternatives to it. Realism, as defined in Wayman and Diehl (1994: 9) consists of ten core propositions, plus an eleventh central principle about the eternal validity of the first ten: (1) states are the key actors; (2) the state system is anarchic; (3) states are unitary and pursue state interests, not the interests of subnational groups; (4) states are rational and are not constrained by ethics other than self-interest; (5) states aim to survive, to maintain their own territorial integrity, and to enhance and maintain their own power; (6) states focus on military security; (7) national material capabilities, leadership, and unity create power, and other power centers are threats and must be monitored, especially when revisionist (i.e., willing to use force to overturn the status quo); (8) the state should (and does) strengthen its capability relative to other states; (9) the state should (and does) form alliances to balance power when its own power is insufficient; and (10) the state should (and does) resolve crises to further enhance its power over outcomes. Realism, in short, provides an approach to international relations and war that emphasizes power and strategy and (in its final principle, number 11) does claim to present uniform principles that are valid for all states across all time (and space). For example, citing the realist par excellence, Hans Morgenthau, J. David Singer (1961) describes Morgenthau's focus on the international system, saying it "inevitably requires that we postulate a high degree of uniformity in the foreign policy codes of our national actors" (81). Alternatively, realists can shift down from the systemic level of analysis to the other "external" source of foreign policy, the dyadic level of analysis, and postulate such causes of war as power transitions (Organski 1958; Kugler and Lemke 1996). Again, at this dyadic level of analysis, as with Morgenthau at the systemic, the emphasis remains on how foreign policy of a state is set by its power position relative to other powers, and not determined by domestic forces or by ideological and economic differences among states and the societies they govern.

For this reason, I call the opposite of the realist framework the "issues and actors" framework—namely, a framework that emphasizes that different state (and nonstate) actors interact differently, depending on the position they hold on the different issue dimensions that define the global issue space in which the actors reside. Examples of hypotheses in this issues and actors framework would be claims that joint democracy ensures peace, that trading partners will be less likely to fight each other because they have a common interest in peace, and that war is becoming obsolete because of the growing ethical sense that it is morally wrong.

Both the realist framework and the issues and actors framework are macro in orientation, focusing primarily on variables out of the control of most government officials. These macroelements largely beyond human manipulation include the polarity of the system, whether a power transition is under way, whether a nation and its potential adversary are both stable democracies, and the strength of norms against use of nuclear weapons, norms against wanton combat deaths, and even emerging norms against war itself. These macroframeworks, starting with the most ancient, Thucydides' "growth of Athenian power and the fear this caused in Sparta," are often the underlying causes of war that need to be contrasted with more immediate causes that are addressed at the microlevel of analysis, where time frames are shorter and the scope of variables less sweeping.

At the microlevel, I contrast the rational deterrence framework, derived from realism (Wayman and Diehl 1994), with an antirealist "crisis behavior framework" that emphasizes the psychological and sociological processes such as misperception, bias, and reaction to enemies in politics.

The resulting analysis (see Table 10.1) is built around what Aron (1967) called "antinomies," which are contradictions or inconsistencies between two apparently reasonable principles or laws (from Greek *nomos,* law). Aron contrasted such opposites as realism and idealism in his study of peace and war; from our perspective, his study is lacking in the guidance from the subsequent three decades of behavior/empirical research. The two "antinomies" I have selected are the dialectical relations, first, of realism and deterrence, which share a focus on power and strategy, versus their challengers, which emphasize the positions of actors on issues; and, second, of macro- versus microprocesses. My aim in presenting this fourfold typology, like the aim of Bremer and Cusack (1995) in their process model of war, is to have a model broad enough to include most work in the field, clear and parsimonious enough (with just two contrasts) to be easily understood, yet capable of providing a sense of where past work has been leading and where future work may profitably go. While full explanation of interstate war will require all four frameworks, it remains important to see balance among them and the role each plays in the overall architecture of the process leading to war. The end result is intended to be a summary of our field that provides a sense of the relation of empirical work to the major theories, paradigms, and policy dilemmas posed by our international relations colleagues.

RIVALRIES AND THE PROCESS LEADING TO WAR

Vasquez (1987), following the trail laid by what might be dubbed "real-centric" empirical work, has described the steps to war as involving the rise of security issues, the formation of alliances, arms races, and crisis escalation. While the

Table 10.1   Four Paradigms for Explaining War

	Psychological Action–Reaction Patterns Based on Issue Positions and (Mis)Perception[a]	*Power, Strategy, and Rational Choice*[b]
Scale: Macro	Issues and actors paradigm (e.g., democratic peace; rivalries)	Realist paradigm (e.g., Waltz 1959)
Scale: Micro	Crisis behavior paradigm (e.g., Allison 1971)	Rational deterrence paradigm (e.g., Huth 1988; finding that short-term balance of forces affects deterrence success)

[a] Generally dovish policy implications.
[b] Generally hawkish policy implications.

scholars around the COW Project often opposed realism (e.g., Wallace 1982), they tested realpolitik-inspired hypotheses to, in the words from Rapoport's and Singer's conversation, debunk the conventional (and often realist) wisdom on the subject. We shall see in a few pages, however, a major limit to this work. That limit is that these realpolitik-inspired investigations begin well along into the funnel of causation on war, when security issues have already arisen and nations are forming alliances to protect themselves from threats. At this limited stage in our progress toward explaining war, to look at it from the point of view of my research on the realpolitik framework, I feel I have established important scientific evidence for several claims. A multipolar concentration of power in the system sets the stage for big (e.g., world) wars, and increasing bipolarization of alliance blocs is followed shortly by the outbreak of war (Wayman 1984). Power transitions, or even rapid approaches toward power transition, between major powers that are antagonistic, double the probability of a war breaking out in the next decade (Wayman 1996). Alliances themselves have a more ambiguous role, seeming to have little net effect on the probability of war in the next decade, with their pacifying and war-inducing features canceling each other out: alliances may deter war (as long as they don't create an overly bipolarized situation) but also help it spread if it starts (Wayman 1990).

Continuing beyond my work and further along "this funnel of causation," or along what Vasquez calls the "steps to war," we come step-by-step to the brink of destruction. Vasquez's (1987) next step is that arms races and the conflict spiral they induce may further contribute to the impetus toward war, though it is controversial whether arms races help cause war (Wallace 1982) or not (Diehl 1983) or whether certain types of arms races cause war (Morrow 1989). The final step in Vasquez's journey, in any event, is the escalation of conflict to war. This brings us to the immediate causes of war, as we have left macrosociological forces and moved to the microlevel of choices of individuals in crisis settings (Brecher and James 1988).

Crisis escalation involves a trade-off between victory and peace, in that showing more resolve in crises leads to victory (Maoz 1983), but states that learn that lesson and escalate to higher levels in subsequent crises with the same enemy usually find themselves in war (Leng 1983). In the deterrence literature, we learn how rationality and reason and judicious use of power can maintain peace and security. Huth (1988: 73, 80–81) finds that allies who extend their deterrence commitments to threatened protégés can deter attack by a potential revisionist if the defender establishes superiority in the immediate- and short-term balance of forces, responds to probes with tit-for-tat military moves and firm but flexible bargaining, and has behaved with similar skill, rather than being too conciliatory or intransigent, in prior encounters with the same adversary. But, on the other hand, voices advancing the fourth, or crisis behavior framework, emphasize that many human biases and bureaucracies get in the way of peace: a variety of misperceptions and organizational biases can lead to war (Allison 1971; Janis 1982; Levy 1983, 1986).

In short, this process explanation of war is primarily based on realism, deterrence, and crisis behavior analysis. Missing from this account, because it has been the least studied by empirical scholars, is the issues and actors framework. This leaves realism dominant among the macroapproaches to the study of war, with almost all the scholars, even if they disagree with realism normatively, testing realpolitik hypotheses when working at the macrolevel. Yet logic alone tells us this is profoundly problematic. Niou, Ordeshook, and Rose (1989), when they formalize the realist balance of power model, are able to create a logically consistent balance-of-power model, but it seems necessarily to entail bizarre behavior. On the other hand, the prize-winning study by Morgan (1994) shows that a formal treatment that includes the position of actors on issues can account for international bargaining and war with considerable face validity. Moreover, Vasquez (1987) points out a major gap in the realist view of the process leading to war when he says:

> The beginnings of wars can be traced to those situations in which some leaders believe that their state's security is threatened and start to take measures to protect themselves. Contrary to realist assertions, however, not all actors, particularly states, are always engaged in a struggle for power. It seems more accurate to assume that security issues and the power-politics behavior associated with them only occur at certain stages in inter-state relationships and predominate only in certain periods of history. (118)

This gap in realist theory is filled by alternative theoretical frameworks, such as idealism, which emphasizes how free societies now commonly dubbed democracies may not fight each other, or neofunctionalism, which emphasizes how economic integration may also foster peace, thus detouring states off the path to war long before the first step even analyzed by realism. There are two complementary bodies of evidence for demonstrating the exact strength of these antirealist propositions. The two are captured in the subtitle "zones of peace, zones of turmoil" in the Singer and Wildavsky (1993, 1996) interpretation of the post–Cold War world, but those phrases have little-recognized but very long-standing historical relevance, going back not to the fall of the Soviet empire in 1989 but to the earliest COW militarized dispute data in 1816. Propositions about the interdemocratic peace have demonstrated that zones of peace have emerged in such places as U.S.–Canada, the Nordic area, and, more recently, the European Union. But this process dates basically to the early twentieth century because until about a century ago, the United States was the only major power in which a majority of adults or adult males could vote. A deeper demonstration of the validity of Vasquez's point comes from the COW MIDs data set, which allows us to identify recurrent disputes between pairs of nations in "zones of turmoil," from which most wars spring.

Beginning in the early 1980s, Diehl and I and others around the COW Project saw that it was possible to chain the recurrent MIDs between a pair of countries into groupings that we called "rivalries." Wayman 1982 and Diehl 1983 were the first to report results. Initially I thought of the main purpose of this as simply the creation of a third variable, or what Goertz and Diehl (1996) call a "case selection device," so that I could compare the effect of power transitions on war between rivals with the effect of power transitions on war between nonrivals (Wayman 1982). To ensure a large number of cases in each of these two categories, the barrier to a relationship being classified as a rivalry was kept low. Later, an effort was made to identify more persistent and intense, so-called enduring rivalries, which were fewer in number and more likely to generate war and high-level militarized disputes (Wayman and Jones 1991). Both these rivalries and enduring rivalries lists demonstrated that there were "zones of turmoil" that accounted for the bulk of the MIDs and wars. This was an important research finding because it documented the error of the realist claim that insecurity was pervasive throughout the international system and documented the accuracy of Vasquez's observation that conflict is isolated to limited areas. The discovery of the rivalries and discovery of the interdemocratic peace by Rummel and others about the same time were two sides of the same coin. The coin's story is that war's destruction is mostly on one side of the coin (the face of rivalry) and somewhat penetrated into the interior of the coin, but not at all on the side of joint democracy. Contrary to what realism had indicated, warfare is not evenly distributed.

The model that emerged from my initial investigation into rivalry, focusing on its role in the relationship of power transitions to war, can be summarized as follows (Wayman 1989, forthcoming; see Figure 10.1): Power shifts (i.e., power transitions and rapid approaches) do double the risk of war, as Organski's (1958) work suggested; furthermore, power shifts between a pair of states increase the likelihood those states will have repeated disputes and develop a militarized rivalry. Such rivalry increases the risk of war directly and (in an interaction effect) also increases the risk that a power shift will lead to war. In another interaction

Figure 10.1 Power Shifts, Rivalry, and War: A Causal Model with Interaction Effects

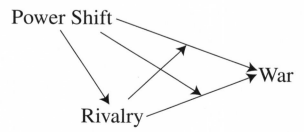

effect, power shifts increase the probability of a rivalry going to war. In short, the development of rivalry intensifies the security problems that realism analyzes so well, so the more rivalry, the more pertinent the realist model of international relations.

Why, then, do some pairs of states have rivalries and others don't? I address this problem elsewhere (Wayman and Jones 1991; Wayman 1993, forthcoming), with an emphasis not on the static comparison of rival dyads to nonrival dyads (from Wayman 1996) but rather on three process or dynamic questions:

1. Why do rivalries start? (Hensel, Goertz, and Diehl 1996; Huth 1996b)
2. How do we account for the fluctuating intensity of rivalries in the years between their onset and termination? (Goertz and Diehl 1997; Hensel 1996)
3. Why do rivalries end? (Bercovitch and Diehl 1997; Bercovitch and Regan 1994)

The rivalries I have worked with in examining the three questions are the enduring rivalries (Wayman and Jones 1991). This set of enduring rivals is created with the aim of providing a relatively short list of long-term rivals whose persistence in conflict allows for examination of fluctuation in their conflict over time. The operational definition (Wayman and Jones 1991) is that a dyad qualifies as an enduring rivalry when three conditions are met:

1. *Severity.* There must exist at least five reciprocated militarized disputes involving the same two states, such that each of these disputes lasts a minimum of thirty days. (Incidentally, the Cuban Missile Crisis does qualify easily, as the events embedded in it continued beyond the famous "thirteen days.") Disputes that last for more than one full year are counted for definitional purposes as one reciprocated dispute for each year of duration. In case of multiparty confrontations, a particular dyad is recorded as meeting the Wayman–Jones threshold if there is evidence that those two states directly confronted each other for at least thirty consecutive days.
2. *Durability.* There must be at least twenty-five years between the outbreak of the first dispute and the termination of the last dispute. Enduring rivalries end after the conclusion of the last dispute if (1) the territorial domain and issues in question have been mutually settled without further disputes for a period of ten years, or (2) one side scores a decisive military victory coupled with an imposed settlement and there are no further disputes for a period of twenty-five years, or (3) no further militarized disputes occur over a twenty-five-year span.
3. *Continuity.* When the gap between any two militarized disputes exceeds ten years, an enduring rivalry will be allowed to continue only if the territorial domain and issues remain unresolved and there is at least one militarized dispute within a period of twenty-five years.

Table 10.2 presents twenty-eight examples of enduring rivalries of various lengths.

Identification of the factors that lead to rivalry, those that increase or decrease the intensity of ongoing rivalry, and those that end rivalry is important to explaining war because without rivalry much of the realpolitik explanatory apparatus for war is irrelevant, and fewer wars (other than imperial and colonial and civil wars) will occur. Of course, war can still happen without the several years of rivalry reflected in repeated disputatiousness, but the psychological aspects of rivalry

Table 10.2   Enduring Rivalries, 1816–1986 (by the above tripartite definition)

Rivalry	*Duration*
Major Powers (Seven Enduring Rivalries):	
U.K.–France	Pre-1816–1840
Italy–Austria/Hungary	1843–1918 (Italy a major after 1860)
France–Germany	1850–1945
USSR–Japan	1895–1945
USSR–China	1898–1986 (ongoing; China a major after 1950)
United States–USSR	1946–1986 (ongoing as of 1986)
United States–China	1949–1974 (China a major after 1950)
Major-Minor (Six Enduring Rivalries):	
U.K.–United States	Pre-1816–1861
USSR–Turkey	pre-1816–1918
USA–Mexico	1836–1921 (USA a major after 1898)
Japan–China	1874–1945
Italy–Turkey	1880–1926
China–India	1950–1986 (ongoing)
Minor Powers (Fifteen Enduring Rivalries):	
Greece–Turkey	1829–1922, 1958–1986 (ongoing)
Chile–Argentina	1843–1902, 1952–1984
United States–Spain	1850–1898
Bolivia–Chile	1857–1920
Ecuador–Peru	1858–1986 (ongoing)
Peru–Chile	1872–1921
Bolivia–Paraguay	1887–1938
Iran–Iraq	1934–1986 (ongoing)
India–Pakistan	1947–1986 (ongoing)
Egypt–Israel	1948–1979
Syria–Israel	1948–1986 (ongoing)
Afghanistan–Pakistan	1949–1986 (ongoing)
North Korea–South Korea	1949–1986 (ongoing)
Thailand–Cambodia	1954–1986 (ongoing)
Somalia–Ethiopia	1960–1986 (ongoing)

can be taking hold below the threshold we measure with repeated disputes. Particularly important in Vasquez's funnel of causation, or steps to war, is the origin of rivalry, in which nations develop the conflicts of interest that make it seem worth it to confront each other at the brink in crises and try to back the other side down.

ORIGINS OF RIVALRY

Geographic contiguity, which creates a persistent opportunity for attack and the possibility of territorial dispute, is one factor common to most rivalries (Goertz and Diehl 1992b; Bremer 1992; Vasquez 1993; Huth 1996b). More than that, conflicting claims to sovereignty, stemming from the principles of legitimacy of the conflicting parties, underlie many of these struggles.

At least a third of the twenty-eight enduring rival dyads are born feuding. Three cases date from the time of creation of both sides: India–Pakistan, 1947–86; Syria–Israel, 1948–79; and North Korea–South Korea, 1949–86. All three cases involve a common land boundary—and overlapping claims to territory. In one case (North Korea–South Korea), the two states each claimed to represent the same Korean people, thus denying the right of the other to exist. In another case (India–Pakistan), one side (Pakistan) claimed to represent their own people (South Asian Moslems) living in the other side's territory. In the third case (Syria–Israel), one side (Syria) had territorial ambitions over the other along with ideological reasons to deny the other's right to exist.

More often, one side had existed as a sovereign state for a long time, but the rivalry dates from the birth of the other (Maoz 1989). These cases include France–Germany, 1850–1945; Greece–Turkey, 1828–1922, 1958–86; Egypt–Israel, 1948–79; Thailand–Cambodia, 1954–86; Afghanistan–Pakistan, 1949–86; and Ethiopia–Somalia, 1960–86. All these involve a common land boundary, with five of the six (all but Israel–Egypt, separated by desert) entailing "bleeding borders," in which dominant ethnic groups on one side also live as a minority on the other side of any conceivable state boundary. Even in the Israeli-Egyptian case, many Palestinian Arabs live in each country, particularly in the border area (Gaza Strip), and they play a major role in polarizing the rivalry.

Two South American cases, while harder to classify, display similar patterns. Ecuador versus Peru basically fits the born feuding concept, as does the case of Chile versus Bolivia. Ecuador, which became a state in 1830, was recognized as independent by 1835 but did not become a member of the Russett–Singer–Small interstate system until it was more fully recognized in 1854. Hence, the enduring rivalry is dated from the first dispute in 1858. Ecuador and Peru had already had disputes before Ecuador's official entry into the Russett–Singer–Small system. The origin of this enduring rivalry is the breakup of Great Colombia in 1830, when Ecuador did not get secured access to the Amazon because parts of Great Colombia federated with Peru.

Likewise, the Chile versus Bolivia rivalry erupts with the breakup of the Peruvian-Bolivian federation in 1839. The two cases of Chile versus Peru and Chile versus Bolivia are linked by a frequent alignment of Bolivia and Peru against Chile, in several disputes as well as in the War of the Pacific. In this sense, they resemble the twentieth-century rivalries of Israel versus Egypt and Israel versus Syria. A further parallel can be drawn between the United Arab Republic of Egypt and Syria, and the federation of Bolivia and Peru. But the former broke apart on its own, while the latter was deliberately destroyed by a Chilean invasion. Chile and Bolivia clash over territory, eventually wrested from Bolivia, which had provided Bolivia's only access to the sea. These clashes all go back to the Spanish pull-out and territorial claims based on the doctrine of *uti possidetis,* according to which a belligerent is entitled to territory actually occupied and controlled by it.

Later, Bolivia seeks an alternative outlet to the sea, via rivers flowing to the Atlantic. Consequently, Bolivia and Paraguay begin to clash over the Chaco Boreal, a previously unsettled territory. Thus, the rivalry of Bolivia and Paraguay develops much like the Himalayan rivalry of China and India, which followed the Chinese consolidation of power in western Tibet. A similar expansion of interests into remote territories occurs in southern Patagonia, setting off the enduring rivalry between Argentina and Chile in the 1870s. Meanwhile, Chile's gains in the War of the Pacific left it in control of Tacna and Arica and thus in direct territorial contact with Peru for the first time. Several disputes follow over this territory, formerly owned by Peru. These four cases all seem to involve "lateral pressure" (Choucri and North 1989), in which clashes occur because of expanding and then overlapping spheres of interest.

TERMINATION OF ENDURING RIVALRIES

A more difficult topic, also of vital importance, is why enduring rivalries end. The first problem is that most don't. Of the twenty-eight enduring rivalries, twelve were not over when our data set ended in 1986. Enduring rivalries are so persistent that there is a very small sample ($N = 16$) available to those who wish to study their termination. Despite the small N, some patterns are clear.

Of the thirteen enduring rivalries involving a major power, ten have ended, while of the fifteen involving minor powers, only six have ended. This difference is statistically significant at the .05 level. (The difference would become even more pronounced if, updating our data set from 1986 to the present, one were to classify the Soviet-American major-major rivalry as terminated.)

Of course, since many of the minor-minor rivalries are so recent in origin, it remains to be seen whether this pattern is mostly an artifact of the relatively short span of time between their birth—at the end of European colonialism—and the present day. As enduring rivals are born feuding, so enduring rivalries often end with death of one of the parties. No fewer than three (France–Germany, Russia–Japan, and China–Japan) ended with the unconditional surrender and political destruction of the Axis regimes in World War II. Another, Italy versus Austria–Hungary, ended with the destruction of the latter in World War I.

In the four decades from World War II until Gorbachev and the end of the Cold War, we saw the end of only one enduring rivalry, that in a cascade of military and diplomatic events beginning with the Sadat's limited-aims Yom Kippur war of 1973 and ending in the intense diplomatic efforts led by President Carter at Camp David. More recently, it appears that the U.S.-Soviet enduring rivalry of the Cold War is itself over, following the transformation of Soviet goals during the Gorbachev era of perestroika and glastnost from 1985 to 1990. But as the contemporary cases of Israel–Egypt and U.S.–USSR suggest, termination of such rivalries can be a tenuous thing. Historically, we can see that enduring rivalries, like volcanoes, may seem extinct when they are only dormant. For example, Russia–Japan had a flare-up of very minor militarized disputes in the 1980s, with the Soviets being the initiators of the border violations (showing planes, showing ships). Both Chile versus Bolivia and Chile versus Peru flared-up, with one minor case each, in the late 1970s, after a gap of over a half-century.

This ambiguity about when an enduring rivalry is over makes analysis difficult. While it sure seems over in the four aforementioned cases of termination in the total defeat of one of the parties, in the other twelve cases, one can never be sure. Chile and Argentina had a peaceful interlude of thirty-six years, Greece and Turkey, of fifty years, before their rivalries restarted. There are isolated militarized disputes after the termination of several of the terminated rivalries. In one of the more dramatic, Russia, after a twenty-eight-year interlude, resumed pressuring Turkey in 1946, only to be dissuaded by an American show of force foreshadowing the Cold War (Blechman and Kaplan 1978). Thus, deciding whether a rivalry is over is a bit like deciding whether a volcano is extinct. Any conclusions, or analyses based on them, must be treated with caution.

FLUCTUATION OF CONFLICT DURING ENDURING RIVALRIES

If becoming mature consists of learning to find alternatives to war as a way of settling disagreements, then our rivals show little sign of maturity. Excluding the three rivalries that started before 1816, there remain twenty-five rivalries whose full history can be traced from their inception through their silver anniversary. These rivalries escalated to war eighteen times (even more times if one traces them beyond that anniversary). Five of those wars occurred in the first five years of rivalry, three in the second five years, three in the third five years, four in the fourth five years, and three in the last five years. Hence, there is no upward or downward trend in the tendency to escalate to war. And there are more than enough wars to justify scholarship on how these enduring rivalries escalate to such deadly levels. (These figures are on interstate wars as compiled by Small and Singer [1982].)

In such studies, one would examine the escalation and deescalation of conflict over the history of one, some, or all enduring rivalries and attempt to predict that escalation and deescalation with independent variables. This can be modeled in discrete or continuous time (Coleman 1964). One can use calendar time (e.g., years) as the time variable, as in standard time-series analysis, or each unit of time can be the onset of the next dispute in the rivalry (scaling time in an ordinal fashion, as in panel studies and this chapter).

Leng (1983, 1988) hypothesized that a loss in the previous dyadic encounter would lead decision makers to shift to a more coercive strategy in the next dispute; however, a win in the previous dispute would encourage decision makers to repeat the successful strategy. Following the realpolitik tradition, this view suggests that militarized confrontations between states are dominated by considerations of power politics and hence, prescribes bargaining strategies that demonstrate military power and resolve. Systematic empirical work on escalation in recurrent militarized disputes has demonstrated that past conflicts do indeed affect present behavior. Maoz (1983), Leng (1983), and Huth (1988) all found a relationship between the outcome in a previous dispute and the behavior exhibited in a subsequent encounter. The winners attribute their victory to effective strategy and hence tend to repeat past behavior; the losers change their strategy in favor of using higher levels of hostility in an attempt to restore their damaged reputation. Further support can be found in work relating influence strategies and outcome (Leng and Wheeler, 1979; Leng 1980, 1983) and behavioral models of escalation (Maoz 1983). As for what affects the decision to initiate another dispute, Maoz (1984) found that victorious outcomes and imposed settlements produce longer gaps before the next dispute between the same nations.

CONCLUSION

The role of recurrent disputes and rivalry in explaining the onset of war would thus seem to involve several elements:

1. Recurrent disputatiousness is a measurable variable tapping an underlying dimension of rivalry, including first conflict over issues, then behavior such as arms races and disputes, and hardening attitudes of "enemies in politics" (Mansbach and Vasquez 1981; Wayman 1984b, 1989; Vasquez 1993).
2. Recurrent disputatiousness is caused by such disparate factors as economic

and ideological conflicts of interest (not readily measured yet by our field) and realist and more readily measured items such as power transitions.

3. Rivalry implies a struggle between equals or at least "wanna-be" equals and hence is more likely to arise in power parity or near-parity rather than overwhelming preponderance (and this could best be tested with comparative measures of material capability, perhaps adjusted for loss-of-strength gradient if the geographic locus of the rivalry is near one state but far from the other). Some rivalries, like Taiwan–China, may involve power disparity at the moment but date back to a time of parity and/or anticipate a time when the weaker may ultimately prove stronger.

4. Recurrent disputatiousness and rivalry will explain some variance in war on their own, because they tap (currently) unmeasured variables such as hostility and distrust between the rivals. This effect can be measured both directly and as a interaction term with other variables such as power shifts. For the same or similar reasons, recurrent dispute patterns will predict to future disputes (e.g., Wayman and Jones 1991).

5. Disputatiousness and rivalry also have a role to play as control variables.

6. Inclusion of rivalry as a variable will highlight the importance of nonrealist elements in the macrolevel explanation of war.

To test these claims, we need simply to continue the work by the outstanding types of scholars already investigating these questions, such as Diehl, Goertz, Hensel, Huth, and Jones. Appropriate relations to be tested, including the many listed in this chapter, would include in my mind as a high priority all the linkages identified by Mansbach and Vasquez (1981) and Vasquez (1993) in their writings on the spread of conflict from issues over such concrete matters as territory to actor issues such as whether the other side can be trusted or needs to be eliminated. The net result of such investigations should be a better balance of macrotheories, putting the realist and nonrealist explanations of war more in their proper balance.

11

Escalation
Crisis Behavior and War

Russell J. Leng

Interstate wars typically are preceded by militarized crises—that is, disputes that escalate to the point where force is threatened, and the threat is resisted, before one of the parties attacks the other. What causes states to become embroiled in such dangerous situations has been the subject of preceding chapters. This chapter focuses on the most immediate cause of war: the behavior of states in escalating militarized crises.

TWO COMPETING PERSPECTIVES

If it is true that behavior begets behavior in interstate disputes, then the pattern of escalating hostility would be a direct predictor of the likelihood of a militarized crisis ending in war. That, in fact, is the perspective taken in most studies of escalation and aggression by behavioral and social psychologists (Rubin, Pruitt, and Kim 1994; Berkowitz 1992; Osgood 1965; Rapoport 1960), as well as a number of political scientists (Jervis 1976; Holsti 1989). Moreover, beginning with the Stanford study of the 1914 crisis (North, Holsti, and Brody 1964), there has been growing empirical evidence to indicate that *certain patterns* of interstate crisis escalation are highly associated with war (see Leng 1993).

A competing perspective views crisis escalation as a manageable process of communication and bargaining, in which each party gains a better understanding of the resolve of the other as the crisis escalates. That is the view held by students of international conflict working within the classical realist tradition (Snyder and Diesing 1977; Kahn 1965). Certainly, there is evidence of crises that rapidly escalated to high magnitudes of hostility without ending in war, and some studies challenge the notion that the pressures generated by crises reduce the rationality of national decision makers (Oneal 1988; Brecher 1993).

Classical Realists and Conflict Strategists

Classical realists, such as Morgenthau (1946, 1960), do not deny the role played by emotion and misperception in conflicts among nations, yet their policy prescriptions are based on the assumption of competition with a calculating, rational adversary.[1] Realists do not argue that states always behave rationally but that the expectation of rational behavior leads to the most effective bargaining strategies. The difference between the expected behavior of states and the actual effects of cognitive errors and emotional arousal on state policymakers in militarized crises is analogous to that between the carefully calculated military strategies mapped out by generals on the eve of combat and the chaotic fighting that actually takes place on the battlefield. In neither instance is fully rational behavior expected, but its assumption, it is argued, offers the best basis on which to design an effective course of action. In fact, the manipulative bargaining strategies of conflict strategists, such as Kahn (1965) and Schelling (1960, 1966), who work within the realist tradition, can be seen as an extension of the theory of war to militarized crises. As Schelling (1960: 4) put it, "The advantage of cultivating the area of 'strategy' for theoretical development is not that, of all possible approaches, it is the one that evidently stays closest to the truth, but that the assumption of rational behavior is a practical one." Just as strategies of war are concerned with the application of force, the conflict strategists are concerned with "the exploitation of potential force"—that is, the successful use of coercion (Schelling 1960: 5).

Conflict strategists view crisis bargaining as a competition in risk taking in which the each side attempts to demonstrate a greater willingness to accept the costs and risks of war to achieve its objectives. The escalation of the crisis is seen as a communication process. Each side employs coercive tactics to discover the resistance point of the other, while signaling its own resolve. As the crisis escalates, each party gains a better understanding of the intentions and motivation of the other through the influence attempts employed by the other side, as well as through the other's responses to the party's own influence attempts (see Snyder and Diesing 1977). An analogy may be drawn to the ritualistic fights of animals, say, two stags competing over a female in mating season. The demonstration of resolve and displays of strength serve the purpose of clarifying the balance in motivation and capability without crossing the threshold to full-scale violence (see Archer and Huntingford 1994).

Conflict strategists place a high premium on demonstrating resolve—that is, a willingness to risk war to achieve one's objectives. The risk of being misperceived as weak is presumed to be greater than the risk that war will result from a misperception of aggressive intentions. War still can occur through misperception but as the consequence of a failure to accurately perceive the comparative war-fighting capabilities and motivation of the two sides, as opposed to a misperception of intentions. Blainey (1973: 122) puts the assumption of rationality in its starkest terms when he describes the onset of war as a failure of "measurement"—that is, of at least one party's failure to properly assess the comparative resolve and war-fighting capabilities of the two sides. The assumption of rationality on the part of the adversaries implies that the escalation will not spiral out of control and that the boundary between coercive bargaining and war will be clear to both sides.

The Psychological Perspective

Whereas realists view conflict as the inescapable expression of an essentially competitive interstate system, the psychological perspective views conflict as a pathology, a problem that has arisen in the relationship between states. For realists, the goal of crisis bargaining is to win; for those viewing crises from a psychological perspective, the goal is to find a means of moderating and, ultimately, resolving the dispute.

When crisis escalation is viewed from this perspective, it becomes both a symptom and a cause of an increasingly contentious relationship between states. The psychological perspective focuses on the two-way interaction of cognitive limitations and emotional arousal as the intensity of the crisis escalates (see Rubin, Pruitt, and Kim 1994: chaps. 5–7; Holsti 1989; Leng 1993: chap. 1). Much of the research on escalation by social psychologists focuses on the role played by anger (Baron 1977; Berkowitz 1992, 1994), or "psychological reactance" to threats (Brehm 1966; Worchal 1974) in escalating hostility.[2] These theorists argue that the escalating hostility exacerbates national leaders' emotional reactions to the coercive actions of the other side, while their cognitive performance is weakened by the stresses produced by the increasing risk of war. As the crisis escalates, the relationship between the adversary states worsens—coercion begets coercion—and the danger of misperception, miscalculation, or emotionally driven behavior increases. The escalation of hostility becomes self-generating as the parties become "locked in" to tit-for-tat exchanges of increasingly coercive behavior. There is a growing risk that one of the parties will assume prematurely that the threshold between coercive bargaining and war has been crossed.

From the realist perspective, the crisis structure ultimately determines the crisis outcome. The role of escalation is to provide the participants with more accurate estimates of their comparative interests and capabilities. The psychological perspective, on the other hand, argues that the escalating hostility *changes* the crisis structure; by raising the reputational stakes for each side, it weakens their capacity to make rational judgments and decisions.

The predictions of competing perspectives with regard to the relationship between the crisis structure, escalation, and war are illustrated in Figure 11.1.

In an empirical study (Leng 1993: chap. 4) of forty militarized crises occurring

Figure 11.1   Structure, Escalation, and War: Realist and Psychological Models

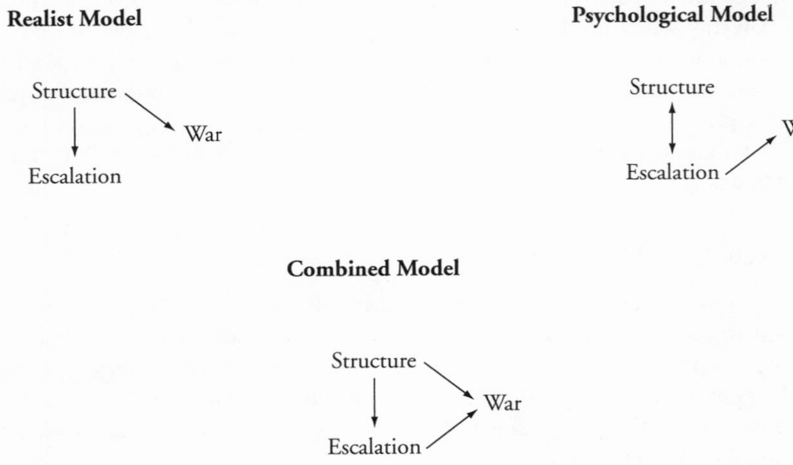

Realist Model   **Psychological Model**

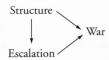

Combined Model

between 1816 and 1980, I found that the behavior of the participant states was relatively consistent with the *prescriptions* of classical realism but that the *consequences* of that behavior often were more consistent with the psychological perspective. But before discussing those findings, along with findings from a closer look at specific crises, it is necessary to consider the special case of nuclear crises.

Nuclear crises (i.e., those crises in which both sides possess nuclear weapons) represent a special case because of the destructive potential of the weapons.[3] If the bargaining during a crisis in which there is a risk of escalation to conventional war resembles a Prisoner's Dilemma game, that during a nuclear crisis more closely resembles a game of Chicken.[4] In a conventional militarized crisis, war may be preferred to surrendering to the demands of the other side; in a nuclear crisis, war is a catastrophe for both sides. Those working within the realist tradition see this as a good thing, because the crisis, rather than war, serves as the ultima ratio in conflicts among nuclear states (Snyder and Diesing 1977: 453–54). Some have even seen it as an argument for nuclear proliferation (Waltz 1981).

But awareness of the catastrophic consequences of a nuclear war also could have the ironic effect of raising each side's "tolerance level"—its willingness to accept attempts at coercion before responding with force. Snyder and Diesing (1977: 453–57) have argued that the mutual desire to avoid nuclear war leads each side to perceive the other as having a greater tolerance for bullying, thereby *encouraging* higher escalation. Because the unacceptability of war has the effect of making the crisis the ultima ratio; it becomes more important to policymakers concerned with their state's reputation for resolve to demonstrate a willingness to run risks and to hold their ground in the face of bullying in such crises. Geller (1990) has found evidence that nuclear crises have been more likely to escalate to a higher *magnitude* of hostility than conventional crises, despite the fact that none of the nuclear crises that have occurred since World War II has ended in war.

If the stress generated by an escalating crisis exacerbates the emotional arousal and cognitive limitations of policymakers, as those representing the psychological perspective argue, then the higher magnitude of coercive bargaining associated with a nuclear crisis, coupled with the stress created by the potentially catastrophic consequences, would add to the risk of the crisis escalating out of control. Returning to the analogy to a game of Chicken, in which each party is intent on demonstrating superior resolve, only the imminent threat of nuclear war would cause either to swerve from the course of escalating coercion. Was war avoided in the four nuclear crises between the United States and Soviet Union because they were able to maintain rational control over the escalation of coercion throughout the crises? Or was it because they became aware that they were rushing to the brink of nuclear war and veered away at the last moment?

The discussion that follows considers that question along with the broader issue of the comparative validity of the realist and psychological perspectives on escalation. The reported findings are drawn primarily from my previous work on crisis behavior along with recent findings from a closer look at some particular crisis. But before discussing those findings, it is important to clarify what is meant by escalation and how it is measured.

Describing Escalation

The Escalation Process

"Escalation" has been part of the discourse on interstate conflict since the 1960s to refer to a *process of rising hostility* in an evolving dispute.[5] The analogy to a moving escalator emphasizes the dynamics of the process, as opposed to a static condition.[6] The differences between the realist and psychological views of escalation are based largely on the effects of that process, not just the magnitude of hostility reached at the peak of the crisis.

When we consider the escalation occurring within a particular crisis, there are variables of interest. The first is the escalation exhibited in the actions of each of the participants. The second is the dyadic relationship between the escalating actions of the two sides. To what degree are the two sides locked into a pattern of reciprocating coercive actions and reactions?

There are three dimensions to the escalation (or deescalation) of hostility by each participant: rate, magnitude, and intensity. The *rate* of escalation describes the rapidity with which coercive behavior increases over the course of the crisis or time interval of interest. *Magnitude* of hostility refers to the magnitude of coercive action at a given observation point. *Intensity* of escalation refers to the mean magnitude of escalation over the course of the crisis or within a time interval of interest.

None of these measures sufficiently describes escalation on its own; each complements the others. Rate of escalation provides the best predictor of the risk of events running out of control, but the perception of risk also is related to the magnitude of hostility. Magnitude of hostility provides an indicator of how close the actions of the parties have come to the threshold of war, but it is important to know the rate at which the crisis escalated to that point and to know whether the magnitude of escalation remained at a high level of intensity or represented simply a spike in an otherwise relatively low magnitude of hostility over the course of the crisis. Intensity of escalation provides an indicator of the magnitude of hostility over the course of the crisis or within a specified time interval, but, as with all mean measures, it tells us nothing about variation in escalation/deescalation.

Reciprocity

A necessary component of any description of the escalatory process is some measure of the relationship between the patterns of escalation for the contending parties. The symmetrical conflict spiral of Rapoport's (1960) "Fight" escalates upward with the two sides locked in to responding in kind, but at a higher magnitude, to each other's increasingly coercive actions. On the other hand, there are crises in which one party leads the way throughout, with the other responding at a lower magnitude of coercion. This pattern has been described as an "aggressor–defender" model of escalation by Rubin et al. (1994: 73–74). The two patterns might yield comparable overall escalation scores, but they differ in the degree of reciprocity exhibited in the exchanges of the two sides.

Two attributes of the degree of reciprocity are of interest in describing the escalatory process. *Distance* refers to the difference in the magnitude of hostility directed by each side at the other as the crisis evolves. *Direction* refers to the degree of congruity in the direction in which each party is moving from one observation point to the next—that is, toward more contentious or more cooperative behavior. A high distance score would mean that one side exhibited considerably more conflictual (or cooperative) behavior than the other over the course of the crisis; a low distance score would mean that the two sides generally responded to each other's actions in kind and magnitude. The direction indicator tells us whether the parties became more contentious or cooperative *at the same time* or whether they tended to move in different directions, so that, as one side was increasing its hostility, the other was turning to more accommodative tactics.[7] A high degree of reciprocity would require that the hostility exhibited by the two parties be of roughly the same magnitude at each time interval and that the parties move toward greater or lesser hostility at the same time. In a Fight, for example, the distance between the hostility scores of the two sides would remain small throughout the escalatory process, and both parties would be moving in the same direction at the same time.

Operational Indicators

The author's research on crisis behavior has employed events data from the Behavioral Correlates of War (BCOW) data set, which contains data on the actions taken by participant states in a sample of forty crises occurring between 1816 and 1980. These data have been drawn from accounts in newspapers, diplomatic histories, government documents, and memoirs, and then coded according to the BCOW typology of actions (see Leng and Singer 1988 for a description). Times series of the actions of key participants within each of the crises have been generated by classifying and weighting actions according to the degree of hostility or cooperation associated with the action type and then aggregating the weighted actions of each party to obtain daily hostility scores (see Leng 1993: 37–38). The aggregate daily hostility scores are the basis for the three escalation and two reciprocity measures described earlier. The operational procedures for obtaining each measure have been described in an earlier work (Leng 1993: chap. 4). Composite indicators of escalation and reciprocity are obtained by standardizing and summing the scores for each of the indicators within the sample.

Models of Escalation

By making a dichotomous distinction between high and low composite measures of escalation and reciprocity, it is possible to distinguish among four models of escalation: *Fight, Resistance, Standoff,* and *Put-Down*.[8] The classification of particular crises as one or another of the four types is determined by comparisons of the statistical scores for each of the escalation indicators within a larger sample of militarized crises. The best way to illustrate the patterns for each of the four types, however, is through the visual pictures provided by time series of the escalatory process. In the discussion that follows, the time series from four prominent historical cases are used to illustrate each of the types.

Crises in which there is both high escalation and high reciprocity exhibit a pattern of symmetrically increasing coercive behavior akin to Rapoport's (1960) description of a Fight, in which the two parties become locked in to reciprocated escalating coercive actions. An illustration of a Fight appears in Figure 11.2, which depicts the time series for the final month of the crisis preceding the Six Day War between Israel and its Arab neighbors in 1967.

A Fight represents the prototypical model of escalation feeding upon itself in an upward spiral of increasingly coercive actions and reactions as envisioned by

Figure 11.2   Fight: Six Day War Crisis, 1967

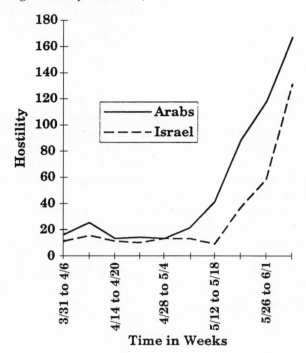

the psychological perspective. Within the sample of forty crises I analyzed, six of the eight crises categorized as Fights ended in war (Leng 1993: 85–89).

The second type, Resistance, exhibits high escalation but low reciprocity. These typically are crises in which one party leads in escalating the crisis with a coercive "bullying" influence strategy, while the other responds in kind. Typically, the party leading in the escalation of hostility moves to increasingly more coercive influence attempts until the other yields, or the crisis escalates to war. Of the thirteen cases in the sample that fit the Resistance model, seven ended in war and five ended with one side yielding to the demands of the other (Leng 1993: 85–89).[9] The Cuban Missile Crisis of 1962, which is depicted in Figure 11.3, illustrates the type.

A Standoff occurs when there is high reciprocity in the interactions of the two sides but relatively low escalation. These are crises that appear to be effectively managed. Typically, the crisis escalates early but then levels off and either ends in a stalemate or deescalates until the parties reach a compromise settlement. Standoffs most often occur between adversaries of relatively even capabilities and motivation, with neither side willing to run the risk of escalating the crisis to

Figure 11.3   Resistance: Cuban Missile Crisis, 1962

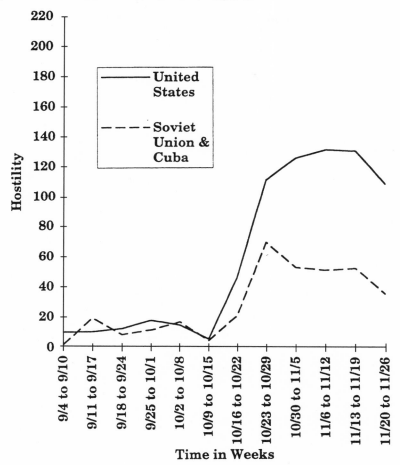

a high magnitude, or to submit to the other. There were twelve Standoffs in the sample; eight ended in compromises, and one ended in a stalemate (Leng 1993: 86). The Soviet-American "Alert" crisis that occurred during the 1973 Arab-Israeli war, which appears in Figure 11.4, is an example of the type.

The last escalation model is a Put-Down, a crisis in which the composite scores for both escalation and reciprocity are relatively low. One side employs coercive tactics, but the other responds with a more accommodative mix of behavior, so that the crisis does not reach a high level of escalation. We would expect Put-Downs to be disputes in which a more powerful state is able to bully its adversary into submission. That is true of four of the seven cases of Put-

Figure 11.4   Standoff: Alert Crisis, 1973

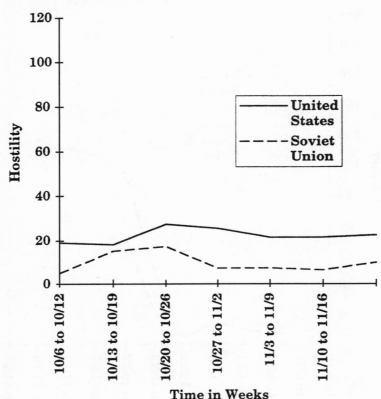

Time in Weeks

Downs in the sample (Leng 1993: 86). These outcomes are consistent with findings indicating that a *significant* power preponderance diminishes the magnitude
of escalation and the likelihood of war in militarized disputes (Bremer 1992)
and militarized crises (Leng 1993: chap. 3). But three of the seven instances of
Put-Downs in the sample ended in war.[10] It appears that the pattern associated
with a Put-Down also occurs when the more aggressive and powerful party de-
cides, early in the crisis, to achieve its objectives through war, rather than to rely
on coercive bargaining.[11]

    The escalation pattern of a typical Put-Down is illustrated in Figure 11.5 by
the 1938 Anschluss crisis between Germany and Austria.

Escalation and War

In the sample of forty crises I considered, 62 percent of the crises with high escalation scores ended in war compared to just 21 percent of those crises with low

Figure 11.5   Put-Down: Anschluss Crisis, 1938

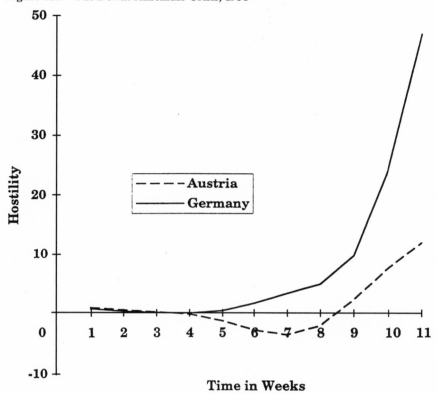

escalation scores (Leng 1993: 86). The findings support the view that escalation provides a useful predictor of the likelihood of a crisis ending in war. Moreover, 75 percent of Fights, which represent the classic pattern of two sides locked into a pattern of spiraling escalation, ended in war. Those results are consistent with the psychological perspective, which argues that high escalation promotes emotional arousal and cognitive limitations that increase the likelihood that crises will end in war.

But the same study found a positive association between the crisis structure and escalation that is consistent with the realist perspective. Seventy percent of the crises in which vital issues—territorial integrity or political independence—were at stake for both sides, and each side was optimistic regarding its war-fighting capabilities, escalated to higher levels (Leng 1993: 96–97).[12] Some evidence of a positive association between the presence of vital issues at stake and the use of physical threats of force has also been found (Gochman and Leng 1983). That crises are more likely to escalate to higher levels when each side is optimistic about its chances in a military showdown is consistent with a number of studies indicating that a *significant* power imbalance diminishes the likelihood of escalation in disputes (see Gochman 1993: 59).[13]

The latter findings suggest that there is a rational foundation, consistent with the realist tradition, to the escalation of militarized crises. Policymakers are more likely to resort to more coercive influence techniques and more likely to respond in kind to attempts at coercion when the stakes are higher and when they are more confident of their war-fighting capabilities. But there also is a psychological explanation for the tendency for disputes between equals to be more likely to escalate to higher levels, which, interestingly, is not inconsistent with classical realism. The role of national pride and a concern for a state's reputation has long been recognized by classical realists (Aron 1966; Morgenthau 1960) and contemporary scholars working within the realist tradition (Snyder and Diesing 1977). Working from that perspective, it can be argued that there is an equity norm among states. It is acceptable for weaker powers to submit prudently to the threats of stronger states, but maintenance of a state's prestige requires that it not submit to coercion from relative equals. Some evidence to support the working of an equity norm has been found in the responses of states to coercive inducements from adversaries of varying military capabilities (Leng 1980; Gochman and Leng 1983).

Within the sample I studied, when the scores for crisis structure and crisis escalation were in agreement in predicting whether the crisis would end in war, they were correct 92 percent of the time. That finding suggests that there is some truth to *both* the realist and psychological models of crisis escalation. The findings suggest that the crisis structure plays a significant role in determining the degree of crisis escalation. It also is clear that high escalation is positively associated with the onset of war. What is not clear from these findings is whether high escalation plays a causal role in the onset of war, as the psychological model suggests, or whether the escalation is simply a symptom of the structure of the crisis, which may be the key determining element in *both* the escalation of the crisis and the onset of war.[14]

Bargaining and Influence Strategies

Another way of approaching the question of the relationship among the crisis structure, escalation, and war is through an examination of bargaining by the states—that is, the influence strategies employed by the participants. One of the implications of the bargaining prescriptions of conflict strategists, with their strong emphasis on demonstrating superior resolve, is that the escalation and outcome of a crisis can be controlled through aggressive manipulative bargaining. Some evidence to support this view appears in research by Maoz (1983) of 164 militarized disputes. Maoz found that the party that was the first to threaten force and exhibited the highest magnitude of coercive military actions was the party most likely to prevail. My research on militarized crises is consistent with Maoz's findings in cases of crises ending in peaceful, one-sided outcomes, but it also indicates a positive association between the uses of escalating coercive tactics and war (Leng 1993: chap. 5). States employing escalating coercive bullying influence strategies found themselves in crises that escalated to war two-thirds of the time. On the other hand, states employing firm but flexible reciprocating influence strategies, which began by demonstrating firmness in the face of threats without escalating the magnitude of coercion, and then reciprocated both coercive and accommodative inducements, avoided war and achieved either diplomatic victories or compromise settlements two-thirds of the time (Leng 1993: chaps. 7, 8).[15] The relative effectiveness of this firm but flexible approach also has been found in instances of extended deterrence (Huth 1988). The success of reciprocating strategies suggests a middle ground in crisis bargaining that recognizes the validity of the both the realist commandment to demonstrate firmness in the face of coercion and the psychological perspective's implied admonition to avoid signaling unintended aggressive intentions.

Summary

Based on the aggregate studies described here, it is not possible to draw definitive conclusions regarding the causal relationship between escalation and war and, consequently, the relative validity of the realist and psychological perspectives on crisis escalation. The findings do indicate that high escalation is positively associated with war outcomes, but so are the crisis structure and the bargaining strategies used by the crisis participants. Variations in the crisis structure are strongly associated with whether the crisis escalates, which raises the issue of whether the crisis escalation influences the crisis outcome or is merely a symptomatic effect of the crisis structure. The findings on the relationship between the crisis structure and war are consistent with the realist view that wars occur when both sides are confident of their prospects in war. Conversely, the findings on the escalation of the crisis and the association of escalating coercive influence strategies with escalation and war are consistent with the psychological perspective. Perhaps the best clue to the relative validity of the two perspectives on crisis escalation lies in the findings indicating the effectiveness of reciprocating influence strategies, which combine the realist admonition to demonstrate resolve with the psychological perspective's emphasis on avoiding actions that would be interpreted as aggressive, while remaining open to mutually accommodative moves. Those findings suggest that both perspectives have some validity.

Another way of approaching the issue is by supplementing the aggregate findings with examinations of the behavior of the participants in some individual crises. The remainder of this chapter is devoted to a consideration of the two high-escalation crises depicted in Figures 11.3 and 11.4: the pre–Six Day War crisis of 1967 and the Cuban Missile Crisis of 1962.

CRISIS BARGAINING AND ESCALATION

The Six Day War and Cuban Missile crises offer a direct comparison between a conventional crisis that is said to have escalated out of control and a purportedly well-managed nuclear crisis. In fact, the authors of the pre–World War I study that introduced the notion of a crisis spiraling out of control found a contrasting model of a well-managed crisis in their subsequent study of the Cuban Missile Crisis (Holsti, Brody, and North 1969). Policymakers and scholars shared a similar view, even if they disagreed over whether it was the Kennedy administration's display of resolve or its care in communicating its intentions and its concern with avoiding allowing the escalation to run out of control that led to the avoidance of war (see Jarosz and Nye 1993: 175–78). The crisis preceding the Six Day War, on the other hand, appears to be a classic case of a conflict spiral, in which one coercive act led to another and "all concerned over-reacted outrageously" until the crisis escalated to war (Yost 1968: 319). A recent study (Leng 2000) that takes a closer look at the behavior of the participants over the course of the Soviet-American and Egyptian-Israeli rivalries shows that both views are oversimplifications. The descriptions of the Six Day War and Cuban Missile crises, which follow, are drawn from that study.

Six Day War Crisis

The early phase of the Six Day War crisis consisted primarily of Arab cross-border raids and Israeli retaliations. The crisis escalated suddenly, and rapidly, in mid-May when Egyptian forces displaced the United Nations Emergency Force (UNEF) that had patrolled the Sinai since the Suez War of 1956. After Egypt proceeded to occupy all of the Sinai and to institute a blockade of the Straits of Tiran, which cut off Israeli access to the Red Sea, Israel launched a preemptive attack on Egypt. Figure 11.6 depicts the evolution of the crisis, beginning with the signing of a mutual defense pact aimed at Israel by Egypt and Syria on 4 November 1966.[16]

The most dramatic feature of the time series of Arab-Israeli interactions depicted in Figure 11.6 is the rapid escalation of hostility in May 1967 (Figure 11.2). The increase in coercive action is led by the Arabs, with Israel responding in kind and magnitude. In its final phase, the crisis preceding the Six Day War closely approximates the conflict spiral of a Fight. But it also is clear from Figure 11.6 that the Arabs are leading in escalating the level of coercion, albeit with Israel responding in kind. The time series of Arab and Israel actions preceding the final phase depicts an intriguing pattern of the two sides alternating in moving to more accommodative or coercive behavior, although they appear to be fairly in sync with regard to the overall magnitude of hostility. Until May, when Israel issued sterner warnings with regard to retaliation against Syria for encouraging terrorist activities, there is a clear pattern of tit-for-tat in Arab guerrilla raids and

Figure 11.6   Six Day War Crisis, 1967 (Israel vs. Arabs)

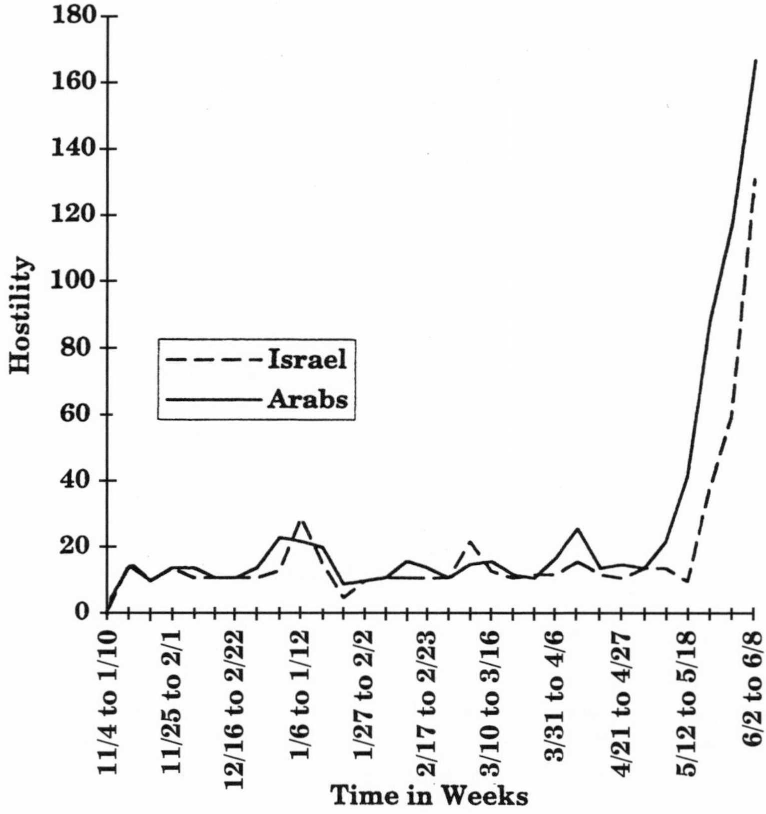

Israeli retaliations. Most of that activity, however, was occurring on Israel's borders with Syria, Jordan, and Lebanon, not with Egypt.

Now compare Figure 11.6 with the pattern of escalation between just Israel and Egypt, which is depicted in Figure 11.7. As this figure illustrates, there was little interaction between Israel and Egypt prior to the movement of Egyptian forces into the Sinai in mid-May. Until then, the emerging crisis was primarily between Israel and Syria. In fact, from the late summer of 1966 to the sudden escalation of the crisis in May 1967, the Egyptian-Israeli border was the quietest it had been since the Suez War. Nasser's fateful move into the Sinai in 1967 was prompted by concern over an imminent Israeli attack on Syria, with which Egypt had a mutual defense pact. But Nasser was misinformed; no such attack was planned.[17] The critical Egyptian-Israeli confrontation began with a misperception. Nasser had come under increasing criticism for Egypt's failure to come to the aid of Syria and Jordan in response to Israeli retaliatory raids. The move of

Figure 11.7   Six Day War Crisis, 1967 (Egypt–Israel)

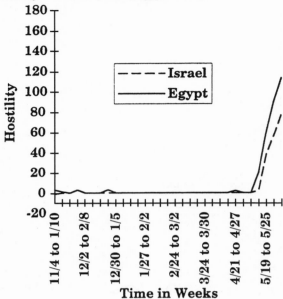

Egyptian forces into the Sinai was initially intended as a show of force to deter a potential Israeli attack on Syria and to bolster Nasser's prestige at home and among other Arab leaders (see El-Gamasy 1993: 22; Mor 1993: 127). The action, however, had the effect of transforming the dispute into a rapidly escalating Egyptian-Israeli crisis. After 12 May, Egyptian-Israeli interactions account for 70 percent of the *intensity* of the escalation of the crisis.[18]

It is clear from Figure 11.7 that Egypt was leading in escalating the crisis, with Israel responding in kind to the escalating hostility. There is considerable reciprocity in the *direction* of the mix of conflictive and cooperative actions by the two parties, but there also is a notable *distance* between the magnitudes of hostility exhibited by the two sides.[19] Throughout this period, Nasser was openly talking about preparing for war.

Nasser had not expected the UNEF troops to evacuate all of the Sinai. Provided that the UNEF forces remained in Gaza and Sharm-el-Sheikh (the high ground overlooking the Strait of Tiran), Nasser expected Israel to accept the Egyptian show of force in the Sinai. In fact, as Figure 11.7 indicates, the initial Israeli reaction (12–18 May) to the Egyptian move was quite mild. It was only after UN Secretary-General U Thant ordered UNEF forces to depart the Sinai on 18 May and Nasser moved Egyptian forces to Sharm-el-Sheikh three days later that Israel responded in kind to Egypt's escalatory moves. When he made the critical decision to occupy Sharm-el-Sheikh and blockade the strait, Nasser is said to have told his senior advisers that the probability of war had shifted from 50 percent to 100 percent (Sadat, quoted in El-Gamasy 1993: 27). After solidifying his position, Nasser indicated a willingness to consider a diplomatic solution to the crisis and placed Egyptian forces in defensive positions in the Sinai. By then it was too late.

Israel pursued a two-pronged, reciprocating strategy: respond in kind to Nasser's preparations for war and seek a diplomatic solution through American intervention. When Nasser closed the strait on 22 May, a "national unity" cabinet was formed, which added more hawkish advisers to the Eshkol government. When Foreign Minister Eban of Israel returned from Washington empty-handed on 4 June, the Arab states surrounding Israel were accelerating their preparations for war, and Soviet arms were flowing into Egypt at an increasing rate. It appeared to Israeli leaders that war was unavoidable. Aware of the unacceptable costs of a long war, and remembering the dramatic success of their surprise invasion of Sinai in 1956, the Israeli cabinet decided to launch a preemptive attack. The escalatory process did not lead to a better understanding of the structure of the crisis but to misperceptions by each of the other's intentions.

Three elements to the escalation of the Six Day War crisis are especially significant to the issue of the rationality of the escalatory process and its likely effect on the crisis outcome. The first is the role played by misperception. The Egyptian-Israeli escalation began with Nasser's misperception of Israeli intentions toward Syria. It was exacerbated by Nasser's misjudgment of the UN reaction to his demand to move troops into the Sinai, which led to pressure for Egyptian forces to fill the vacuum left by the departing UNEF troops. Finally, the Israeli perception of the high probability of an Egyptian attack contributed to the decision to preempt.[20]

The second element is the effect of the escalating crisis itself on the Egyptian and Israeli misperceptions. Nasser's willingness to accept the questionable reports of Israeli preparations to attack Syria, and his consequent decision to move Egyptian forces into the Sinai in a show of force, were encouraged by the growing political pressure to take action arising from his failures to respond to Israeli retaliatory raids against Syria and Jordan earlier in the crisis. His decision to occupy all of the Sinai was prompted by the power vacuum created by his attempted show of force; his decision to blockade the strait followed from the public pressures, both at home and among other Arab leaders, that had been generated by the escalating crisis. And as Nasser was propelled into increasingly coercive behavior by the momentum of the escalating crisis, Israel became convinced, again wrongly, that Nasser was preparing to attack.

The third element is the absence of any direct communication between Israel and Egypt. Nasser's subsequent defense of his perception that Israel was planning to attack Syria was based on his reading of ambiguous public statements by Israeli leaders, as well as information from third parties. Israeli policymakers were forced to judge Nasser's intentions from his aggressive public statements and military preparations. Israel had not planned to launch a major attack on Syria, and Nasser did not intend to attack Israel, but both sides issued statements and undertook military actions designed to demonstrate their resolve in the face of perceived threats from the other. Those statements contributed to the other party's misperception of its adversary's intentions.

Cuban Missile Crisis

The time series of weekly hostility scores in Figure 11.3 depicts the rapid escalation of the Cuban Missile Crisis during the crucial thirteen days from 16 October, when the discovery of the surface-to-surface missile sites were reported to Kennedy, to 28 October, when the Soviets agreed to remove the missiles. The most striking feature of the pattern in Figure 11.3 is the high *rate* of escalation depicted in the steep upward slope in the magnitude of predominantly coercive actions between 16 and 28 October. In fact, the rate of escalation for the Cuban Missile Crisis not only is the highest of the four American-Soviet crises but also ranks higher than any nonwar crisis in the random sample of forty crises.

The pattern of high escalation and relatively low reciprocity depicted in Figure 11.3 is consistent with the Resistance model of escalation. One party leads the escalation by employing an escalating coercive bullying bargaining strategy, and the other side responds in a tit-for-tat manner. In this case, the coercive moves by the United States led the escalatory process throughout the crisis, with the Soviets reacting at a lower level of hostility. The outcome, an American diplomatic victory, is consistent with the realist view that, in a dispute between relatively evenly matched adversaries, the side showing superior resolve will prevail. A more complex picture emerges, however, when the escalation of hostility during the crucial two weeks following the discovery of the missiles by the United States is examined on a daily basis. Figure 11.8 presents the time series for daily hostility scores.

Prior to Kennedy's "quarantine speech" of 22 October, the Soviets did not know that the United States had discovered the missile sites.[21] Consequently, during the first week of the crisis, there was virtually no movement in the magnitude of Soviet-Cuban expressions of hostility, while that of the United States begins to escalate rapidly on 22 October. On the following day, 23 October, there is a dramatic escalation in the Soviet-Cuban hostility scores, but the pattern of Soviet hostility becomes more erratic after that, while the magnitude of American hostility continues to escalate rapidly. From the time series in Figure 11.8 it is clear that the Soviets are not responding in a consistent manner but employing something more akin to a "trial-and-error" influence strategy (Leng 1993: 142–43). The erratic pattern exhibits the inconsistency among the actions taken by the Soviets and the Cubans. On the 24th, for example, Khrushchev placed Soviet forces on alert and threatened to sink any American ships that attempted to enforce the

Figure 11.8 Cuban Missile Crisis, 1962 (daily scores)

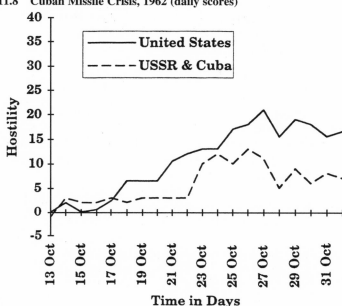

blockade, but Deputy Prime Minister Mikoyan ordered Soviet ships approaching the blockade to slow down or reverse course. By the afternoon of the 25th, over a dozen Soviet ships had done so. The U.S. hostility scores reach a peak on the 27th, the day when Robert Kennedy presented the United States' carrot-and-stick ultimatum to Soviet ambassador Dobrynin, but those for the Soviets drop slightly, despite the Cuban downing of the American U-2 and Khrushchev's increase in demands over the previous day's proposal. The Soviet and Cuban scores for negative actions are higher for 26 October than the 27th; the dip in the hostility scores reflects the more explicit accommodative proposals made by Khrushchev in his second proposal.[22]

More than one explanation is possible for the inconsistencies in the Soviet bargaining following Kennedy's speech. Mikoyan's action suggests disagreements over strategy within the presidium. Based on earlier experiences with Kennedy—the Vienna Summit of 1961 and the Berlin Wall crisis—Khrushchev may have believed initially that the American president could be bullied into softening his position but then became uncertain in the face of Kennedy's strong stand. But there also was an emotional component to Khrushchev's behavior. According to his former speech writer and adviser on Eastern European affairs, Khrushchev "had sharp political skills, but was very emotional . . . a risky man" (Burlatsky, quoted in Blight and Welch 1989: 234–35). It may well be that Khrushchev's initial reaction to Kennedy's 22 October speech reflected his anger at having his carefully laid stratagem discovered prematurely, at Kennedy's belligerent rhetoric, and at the U.S. military challenge.[23] There is no doubt that Khrushchev's rambling message of 26 October grew out of a palpable fear of the escalation running out of control.

The time series of American actions in Figures 11.3 and 11.8 are consistent with an escalating coercive bullying influence strategy. The strategy was carefully applied, with considerable effort devoted to clear communication, but the U.S. actions had an emotional element as well. Kennedy's speech on 22 October was notable not only for the initiation of the blockade of Cuba and the accompanying U.S. shows of force but also for the bellicosity of his rhetoric. As his brother later told Dobrynin (1995: 80), the president was particularly upset at having been deliberately deceived by Khrushchev. In his internationally televised speech, Kennedy described Khrushchev's attempted fait accompli as a "clandestine, reckless, and provocative threat to world peace" comparable to Hitler's aggression in the 1930s. Kennedy went on to appeal publicly to the "captive people" of Cuba to rise against the "puppets and agents of an international conspiracy." Then, when Robert Kennedy delivered the carrot-and-stick threat, which he insisted was *not* an ultimatum, to Dobrynin on 27 October, he stressed that the president was under increasing pressure to bomb the missile installations, an action that the president feared would trigger a "chain reaction" that would be impossible to reverse. Dobrynin's report to the Kremlin that evening emphasized Robert Kennedy's agitated emotional state and his fear of events running out of control (Dobrynin 1995: 80).[24]

Thus, it appears that the emotional reactions of the leaders on both sides—Kennedy's outrage at Khrushchev's attempted deception and Khrushchev's outrage at being discovered, at being publicly compared to Hitler and challenged militarily—contributed to the rapid rate of escalation. The escalation, in turn, led to fear, on both sides, of events running out of control and escalating to nuclear war. Khrushchev's fears are apparent in his message of 26 October; Kennedy's surface in his brother's meeting with Khrushchev on the next day. In what is often cited as the quintessential example of skillful American crisis diplomacy, emotional arousal contributed to the rapid escalation of the crisis, and the rate and intensity of escalation contributed to bringing about its resolution.

There is no evidence that either of the parties was encouraged to use more coercive bargaining tactics because of a perception that there would be a higher "provocation threshold" in a nuclear crisis; rather, each side became increasingly alarmed at the rate with which the crisis was escalating. The Cuban Missile Crisis is less a case of carefully controlled escalation than of the leaders of the two superpowers pulling back in horror from a crisis that threatened to spiral out of control.

Summary

The Cuban Missile Crisis demonstrates the role that emotional arousal can play in an escalating crisis; the Six Day War crisis demonstrates the consequences of misperceptions by national leaders attempting to interpret the intentions of their adversary in an escalating crisis. One could argue that, nevertheless, the structure of the crisis ultimately determined the outcome in both cases. The superpowers were restrained from going to war because of their relative capabilities and their mutual recognition of the costs and risks of war. Israel decided to launch a pre-emptive attack on Egypt because Israeli policymakers believed, based on previous experience, that they could win at a relatively low cost if they struck first. Both the United States and the Soviet Union recognized that military hostilities could lead to a catastrophic nuclear war; once the crisis escalated to the point where each had a good understanding of the balance in motivation, which favored the United States, a settlement was reached. That is what the realist perspective tells us. What the psychological perspective tells us is that, had the leaders of both sides acted in an entirely rational manner, neither crisis would have escalated to the point where the leaders had to confront those decisions at the brink of war. In the Cuban Missile Crisis, the escalation was not as easily managed as the realist perspective would lead us to assume. It came dangerously close to running out of control. In the Six Day War, the adversary's intentions were misperceived by both sides.

CONCLUSION

Two sets of conclusions are to be drawn from this study—one, substantive; the other, methodological. Any consideration of the substantive conclusions must begin with the caveat that the research reported in this chapter deals solely with the most proximate causes of war: the escalation of prewar crises and the behavior of the participant states. Why states become embroiled in such dangerous situations in the first place has been the subject of preceding chapters.

The chapter began by posing two competing views of crisis escalation, the realist and psychological perspectives. The extant empirical research on crisis escalation and war indicates that realists are correct in stressing the important role played by the crisis structure (the comparative interests at stake and the perceived comparative war-fighting capabilities of the contending states) in predicting the escalation of the crisis and the likelihood of war. The empirical research also indicates that there is a positive association between high escalation and war, which is consistent with the psychological perspective. What the extant aggregate studies do not tell us is whether the association between escalation and war reflects the emotional and cognitive effects of escalation hypothesized by the psychological perspective, or whether it is an artifact of the influence of the crisis structure on both escalation and war. To gain a more complete perspective on the relationship among these variables, we took a closer look at two well-known post–World War II crises: the Cuban Missile Crisis and the pre–Six Day War crisis. The examination of those two crises indicated that nonrational factors— cognitive errors in the Six Day case and emotional reactions in the Cuban one— played a significant role in fueling the escalation and that the escalation of the crisis affected the crisis outcome. One would not want to overgeneralize from two cases, but it can be said that these two cases indicate that it would be unwise to ignore the potential nonrational effects of escalation in influencing the outcomes of militarized crises. In sum, based on the available evidence, the most plausible model in Figure 11.1 is the "Combined Model," which indicates a two-way interaction between the crisis structure and crisis escalation and between both the crisis structure and crisis escalation with the crisis outcome.

This chapter leads to two methodological conclusions. The first is that any examination of dispute escalation that does not consider its dynamic character is incomplete. It was the *rate* and *intensity* of the escalation that appeared to generate the nonrational responses of national leaders in both the Cuban and Six Day crises. The second methodological conclusion is that neither aggregate data studies nor case studies alone will enable us to answer the most interesting questions regarding the relationship between crisis escalation and war. The dangers of generalizing from a few case studies are well known to students of quantitative international politics. But the findings from large aggregate data studies are likely to be based on descriptions that are too coarse to yield reliable insights into the relationships of greatest interest. On the other hand, there is no good reason that the two methodological approaches, like the realist and psychological perspectives on crisis behavior, should not complement each other.

NOTES

1. Morgenthau (1946: 192–93) sees humans as driven by an innate lust for power, which overcomes rational restraint; moreover, he emphasizes the near impossibility of states making reliable judgments of comparable capabilities. Nevertheless, the realist prescription for policymakers is to act according to a rational calculation of power and interest.

2. A more complete discussion appears in Leng (1993: chap. 1).

3. I have not included a separate category for crises between nuclear and nonnuclear powers because there is no evidence that the possession of nuclear weapons by just one side exerts either an escalatory or inhibiting effect on the nonnuclear state (see Geller 1990).

4. It should be noted that this assertion is not a consensus view among game theorists. See, for example, the different views regarding which of the two games more accurately depicts the dynamics of the Cuban Missile Crisis in Brams (1985) and Zagare (1987).

5. I do not know who was the first to coin the term. It is not used by Rapoport (1960) in his 1960 book, but it had become common parlance by the time Kahn published *On Escalation* in 1965.

6. Kahn (1965) and Snyder and Diesing (1977) occasionally use the mixed metaphor of the "ladder of escalation" to demarcate discrete levels in the escalatory process, but the accepted image is of a continuous upward movement of increasingly coercive actions.

7. Fuller descriptions of the construction of the operational indicators and the summary measure of reciprocity appear in Leng (1993: 70–72).

8. The high-low distinction is based on whether the composite measure falls above or below the median for the sample of forty crises in Leng (1993).

9. The one exception, the Cyprus crisis of 1963–64, ended in a stalemate, due largely to major power intervention through the United Nations.

10. A useful survey of recent findings regarding the relationship between systemic and national attributes and the escalation of disputes to war appears in Gochman (1993).

11. The three Put-Downs with war outcomes in the sample were the Russo-Turkish War of 1976–77, the Chaco War of 1931–32, and the Manchurian War of 1931. All are cases in which the more aggressive party attacked its adversary early in the crisis.

12. When borderline cases were removed from the structural measures, the proportion of correct predictions was 81 percent (Leng 1993: 97).

13. For an intriguing exception, see Siverson and Tennefoss (1984).

14. There were too few cases in the sample in which the predictions based on the crisis structure and the degree of escalation diverged to draw any conclusions as to whether either condition was a sufficient predictor of the outbreak of war or whether both were necessary conditions. Based on the few cases in which the predictions of the two variables did diverge, the crisis structure was the better predictor of the onset of war (see Leng 1993).

15. A state employing a reciprocating or firm but flexible strategy (1) demonstrates firmness in the face of threats by responding in kind but (2) avoids escalatory actions that might be construed as reflecting aggressive intentions; (3) responds in kind to accommodative moves; and, (4) after having demonstrated firmness, (5) indicates a willingness to engage in reciprocated cooperative moves (Leng 1993: chap. 8). The last two characteristics distinguish reciprocating strategies from the game theoretic version of tit-for-tat, which begins with a cooperative move and then follows a strict tit-for-tat strategy (Axelrod 1984).

16. The parties on the Arab side whose actions are included in Figure 11.6 are Egypt, Syria, Jordan, and guerrillas associated with one or another branch of the Palestine Liberation Organization.

17. The question of just why Nasser believed that Israel was preparing for an attack swirls around who said what and to whom, when. The best Egyptian account is that of El-Gamasy (1993).

18. Calculation of escalation scores for interactions between Egypt and Israel, as compared to interactions between Israel and other Arab participants in the crisis in the period between 12 May and 6 June, indicate that Egyptian-Israeli actions account for 68 percent of the rate of escalation, 64 percent of the magnitude, and 70 percent of the intensity of escalation.

19. The composite reciprocity score for the crisis actually falls very close to the median

point in the larger sample—that is, on the borderline between the Fight and Resistance models of escalation.

20. I say "contributed to" because it could be argued that the change in the balance of power in the region created by the Egyptian control of Sharm-el-Sheikh and the blockade of the strait necessitated a military response on the part of Israel.

21. In fact, in the week between the discovery of the missiles by the Americans and Kennedy's speech, the Soviets continued to deny the presence of the missiles to American leaders who, for their, part did not reveal their knowledge of the Soviet deception.

22. American policymakers at the time, and analysts since, have viewed the first of Khrushchev's messages as more accommodative, partly because of its emotional content indicating Khrushchev's concern with the risks of nuclear war and partly because its lack of specificity demanded less of the United States, in particular the exchange of Turkish for Cuban missiles. But the more sober statement on the 27th is notable for the absence of the bombastic threats that appear in the earlier communication.

23. Once the missiles were fully operational and capable of self-protection against an American air strike, Khrushchev planned to announce their presence publicly at the opening of the United Nations session in November.

24. How the United States would have reacted if the Soviets had not accepted the American demand for the removal of the missiles in return for removing their own missiles in Turkey and pledging not to invade Cuba had not been decided (see McNamara in Blight and Welch 1989: 262).

12

Material Capabilities
Power and International Conflict

Daniel S. Geller

In an international system characterized by anarchy, military force is frequently brought to bear as the ultimate arbiter in deciding conflicts of interest. Even when not directly employed in war, force is often threatened for coercive effect. As a result, explanations of patterns of war and peace usually grant a primary position to the power of states and to their relational balances.

This chapter will discuss a body of quantitative empirical evidence regarding material capabilities and war at three analytic levels: the state, dyad, and international system. As this analysis will demonstrate, systematically derived quantitative evidence has led to the identification of power-related patterns of war at all three levels of analysis, and theoretical mechanisms have been developed to explain these empirical regularities. In short, the scientific study of the relationship between material capabilities and international conflict has produced an impressive domain of cumulative knowledge in world politics.

STATE-LEVEL PATTERNS OF POWER AND CONFLICT

The relevance of the power base of a state as a determinant of its involvement in international conflict is a principal component of realist thought. Whether conceptualized as military capabilities alone or as a broader set of military, economic, and demographic capabilities, the power base of a state has long been considered to be an important factor shaping foreign behavior. While many theories of international conflict and war focus on dyadic- or systemic-level capability distributions, there remains a substantial body of literature dealing with state-level capabilities.

Power Status

There are strong a priori reasons to expect that extant patterns in the onset (occurrence/initiation)[1] of war and the seriousness (magnitude/duration/severity)[2] of war may be quite dissimilar for major powers and minor powers. For example, major powers may be more likely to engage in war because the hierarchy of which they are a part is structured and restructured primarily through the use of violence. Major powers tend to define their interests more broadly than do minor powers, and the pursuit of those interests may bring them more frequently into violent conflict with other states. Moreover, given the fact that major powers possess greater military capabilities than do minor powers, it is reasonable to assume that their wars will tend to be more destructive than those of minor powers.

The earliest cross-national quantitative research on capabilities and conflict attempted to isolate possible differences in behavior between strong and weak states. Hence, the power status of nations was postulated to be a factor influencing conflict patterns. For example, Wright (1964) reports a positive correlation between state capabilities and belligerency. However, in a subsequent study, Rummel (1968), using the Dimensionality of Nations (DON) database for seventy-seven nations from 1955 to 1957, finds no substantive relationship between national capabilities and foreign conflict. In contradistinction to Rummel, Weede (1970)—also employing the DON data (for a longer time period of 1955–60) and using different operations in measure construction—reports that state capability is positively related to verbal foreign conflict.

Two definitive studies on the subject of power status and war are by Small and Singer (1970, 1982). Using the original (1816–1965) and expanded (1816–1980) Correlates of War (COW) databases, Small and Singer demonstrate that major powers are much more likely to engage in wars than are minor powers. Köhler (1975) examines the war behavior of fifteen "imperial leaders" at different stages of leadership (COW database) to answer the question of whether dominant nations become less war-prone after the loss of hegemony, and he concludes that once-dominant states become more peaceful following the loss of their leadership status. Bremer (1980), also using COW data, contributes to the evidence on power status and conflict by reporting that nations that rank high on a composite index of national capability (CINC) are involved in a greater number of wars and initiate wars with greater frequency than do lower-ranked states. He notes that nations with greater aggregate capabilities also tend to suffer from more severe wars (i.e., battle-death totals). Eberwein (1982), in a replication of Bremer's (1980) study, adds the finding that more powerful nations tend to use military force more frequently and that power status alone accounts for over 60 percent of the variance in "joining" ongoing militarized interstate disputes. Lastly, a study using the COW database on wars and battle deaths for the participants (Geller 1988) reports that major powers are more likely to fight severe wars (more than fifteen thousand battle deaths) and less likely to fight moderate wars (between one thousand and fifteen thousand battle deaths) than are minor powers, whereas they are equally likely to engage in small wars (fewer than one thousand battle deaths).

Militarization

Studies dealing with the relationship between the level of militarization of a state and its foreign conflict behavior have also produced consistent findings. For example, Feierabend and Feierabend (1969) report a positive correlation between militarization and foreign conflict for the subset of highly developed states. Similarly, Weede (1970), using the DON database for the period from 1955 to 1960 and defining "militarization" by the twin ratios of military personnel to total population and defense expenditures to gross national product (GNP), notes a positive association between militarization and both verbal and violent foreign conflict behavior. Kemp (1977), using COW and Stockholm International Peace Research Institute (SIPRI) data for the years between 1925 and 1939, also reports positive and significant links between state-level arms expenditures and international violence.

Power Cycle

Power cycle theory (i.e., Doran 1983, 1989, 1991, 1995; Doran and Parsons 1980) holds that certain critical points in a major power's cycle of increasing and decreasing capabilities (relative to the major power system's capability pool)[3] are associated probabilistically with both its initiation and involvement in war. The thesis maintains that major powers move through a general, cyclical pattern (i.e., power cycle) of capability growth, maturation, and decline. The pattern itself is a function of differential rates of development among the set of major powers. These differences result from variations in resource distribution, political development, and industrialization.

The power cycle thesis asserts that a state's foreign policy is shaped by its position on this capability cycle. According to Doran and Parsons (1980: 947, 949), "As a nation gains in power relative to others, its capacity to exercise leadership grows; as it falls behind, the capacity to influence international politics wanes. . . . As the cycle evolves and the role changes, significant adjustments are required of the government and the society." Collectively, the evolution of the power cycles of the principal states defines the hierarchy of the international system (Doran 1983: 427).

Doran identifies four critical points on the cycle: the two inflection points occurring on either side of the cycle and the lower and upper turning points. These four points on the evolutionary curve of a state's relative capabilities—termed "critical points"—are important because they represent a disjuncture between a state's interests or aspirations and its actual capabilities. Due to the shift in direction or rate of capability growth, the state's leaders must reevaluate their relative position, capability base, and foreign policy objectives. Doran (1985: 294) maintains that the foreign policy stakes at these critical points are enormous—involving status, security, and power—and are therefore more likely to lead to war involvement. It should be noted that power cycle theory measures time in decades, and critical points are not considered to be instantaneous transformations. Similarly, the perceptions of leaders as their states approach critical points may change in a gradual fashion. However, abrupt overreaction to the points is considered more probable. Doran and Parsons (1980: 951–52) suggest that the critical points most likely to produce the imprudent use of force or the encumbrance of unyielding foreign policy positions are the two inflection points (where the tangents reverse direction). In short, power cycle theory holds that major power war results from a government's inability to adjust to shifts in its capacity to exercise power and influence. The critical points on the power cycle are especially likely to produce overreaction, misperception, and the aggressive use of force in foreign policy.

For the initial study (Doran and Parsons 1980), capabilities are measured by an index composed of five material indicators, with the population inclusive of all major powers for the years between 1816 and 1975. War data are drawn from the COW database. Doran and Parsons conclude that a major power's point on the power cycle is an important determinant of the probabilities of both its initiation and involvement in war, as well as affecting the characteristics of the wars in which it engages. Subsequent studies by Doran (1989, 1991) reinforce and elaborate the previous results, indicating that 90 percent of major powers passing through a critical point on the power cycle engage in war.[4]

Summary

At the analytical level of the state, national capabilities—whether measured in terms of military capabilities alone or a combination of military, economic, and demographic variables—reveal strong and consistent linkages to foreign conflict. Most notable are the distinctions among nations in power status and war behavior. Power status has shown a positive relationship to the frequency of war, the initiation of war, and the severity of war. The level of a state's militarization also reveals a positive association with violent foreign conflict. Lastly, critical points on a major state's power cycle are strongly associated with both war initiation and war involvement. In sum, at the analytical level of the state, power—defined in terms of material capabilities—reveals strong and consistent positive linkages to the probabilities of a nation's war initiation, war involvement, and severity of war engagements.

DYADIC-LEVEL PATTERNS OF POWER AND CONFLICT

Quantitative empirical research has demonstrated a close and consistent relationship between certain dyadic capability balances and general patterns of international conflict. Recent research has also shown that the distribution of material capabilities among status quo challengers and defenders affects the likelihood of war in rivalries as well as the probable identity of the war initiator. The following sections examine the extant evidence in these areas.

Capability Balances

The relationship between capability distributions and war is a recurring theme in the literature on international relations.[5] Balance of power, long cycle, power transition, hegemonic decline, and world economy theories all focus on the distribution of capabilities and shifts in these distributions as a principal factor associated with interstate conflict. At the level of the dyad, static (stable) and dynamic (unstable) capability balances can be analyzed in terms of static parity and preponderance, or dynamic shifts and transitions.

An extensive body of work in international politics involves the connection between static capability balances and war. At the dyadic level of analysis, two opposing theoretical positions have been articulated: "balance of power" and "power preponderance." Balance of power theory maintains that an approximately equal distribution of capabilities *reduces* the likelihood of war. This thesis rests on the logic that victory becomes problematic under a condition of relative parity and that the resulting uncertainty enhances deterrence and discourages aggression. A capability imbalance (i.e., preponderance) will tend to support aggression and weaken deterrence by increasing the probability for the successful use of force by the stronger state (e.g., Wright 1964; Waltz 1979).

This argument is rejected by the power preponderance theorists. Their thesis holds that the probability of war *increases* under a condition of relative parity. The logic of this position is that the likelihood of war is greatest when *both* sides see a prospect for victory, and that this condition is met when parity characterizes the balance. With the alternative capability distribution—preponderance—the weaker cannot afford to fight, and the stronger usually does not have to in order to achieve its goals (e.g., Blainey 1973).[6]

An important corollary to the basic preponderance logic is offered by the power transition theorists, who maintain that dynamic as well as static capability distributions are related to war. For example, Organski (1958), Organski and Kugler (1980), Gilpin (1981), Modelski (1983), and Thompson (1988) all focus on shifting capability distributions as a principal factor in the wars that shape the hierarchy of the international system. The general thesis suggests that great power wars are the result of unstable capability balances: the erosion of a dominant nation's relative capability advantage as a consequence of a challenger's rising power trajectory increases the probability of conflict. This argument appears in the configuration of power transition (Organski), hegemonic decline (Gilpin), and long cycle (Modelski) theories. All of these formulations focus on a mechanism for war in the operation of dynamic capability distributions that lead away from preponderance and toward equality.

The basic arguments of Organski, Gilpin, and Modelski have been supplemented through studies by Levy (1987) on preventive war, Wayman (1996) on power shifts, and Gochman (1990) on rapid capability convergence and divergence. Dynamic capability balances can be divided into two categories: shifts (capability convergence or divergence) or transitions (a reversal of relative capability position). At the level of the dyad, factors internal to nations that lead to changes in capability balances include those associated with development (e.g., industrialization, urbanization, technological advance, resource reallocation) and those associated with decay (e.g., decreasing investment, lower productivity, corruption). These processes influence the differential capability growth rates between rising and declining nations and result in capability shifts and transitions. Levy (1987) and Wayman (1996) provide explanations as to why dyadic capability shifts and transitions may lead to conflict. The basic rationale, however, rests on the possibility of furthering national interests or of a perception of threat to national interests that may be created by closure or transition in relative capabilities.

Most theories of international conflict initiation and strategic interaction are based on assumptions of rationality. Typically, these explanations also incorporate decision-maker estimates of the relative capability balance between antagonists. Indeed, many studies demonstrating an empirical connection between war initiation and subsequent victory interpret the association as evidence reinforcing the rationality assumption: war initiators calculated the capability differentials and expected to win (e.g., Singer 1972; Bueno de Mesquita 1978, 1981b; Small and Singer 1982; Wang and Ray 1994). For example, if weaker states initiate wars against stronger states, it should be under conditions of relative parity (where contextual battlefield factors or first-strike advantages might seem to provide a decisive edge) or in response to a shift or transition (where capability closure [shift] or loss of position [transition] provide either a new military option resulting from convergence or increasing pressure to strike preemptively before further loss of position is sustained). In sum, these arguments suggest that static and dynamic capability differentials may evidence not only empirical association with the *occurrence* of war but with the *identity* of the war initiator as well.

Preponderance and War

Balance of power theory (e.g., Claude 1962; Wright 1964; Waltz 1979) posits that the likelihood of war increases among disputants if one side possesses preponderant capabilities. Moreover, it is suggested (implicitly or explicitly) that the more powerful state will be the war initiator. At least partial evidence in support of the initiation hypothesis is found in Bueno de Mesquita (1980), who reports that initiators of interstate wars (COW data 1816–1974) are approximately twice as likely to be stronger than their targets. Although Bueno de Mesquita notes that expected utility theory produces even more impressive results than a simple comparison of capabilities, he records that the capability balance results are statistically significant. Siverson and Tennefoss (1984) also provide evidence in support of the basic hypothesis. Using data for the years 1815 through 1965, they examine both the initiation and escalation of international conflicts. Their dyadic-level findings suggest support for balance of power theory: few disputes among major powers (presumably equal in capabilities) escalate to mutual military action, whereas a much higher proportion of conflicts initiated by major powers against minor powers escalated to reciprocated military action. However, they also note that approximately 19 percent of the total conflicts involved minor power initiation against stronger states and that over 25 percent of these escalated to the mutual use of force.

Equality and War

A greater number of empirical research studies provide evidence supportive of the parity-leads-to-war hypothesis. An early study by Mihalka (1976), using COW data for the years between 1816 and 1970, indicates that the probability of a confrontation escalating to the level of military violence was significantly lower when the capability differentials between the disputants was high. More evidence supportive of the parity and war hypothesis is provided in a study by Garnham (1976b). Comparing "lethal" with "nonlethal" dyads for 1969 to 1973, Garnham reports that relative parity is associated with violence irrespective of whether power is measured by a composite capability index or by separate indicators. Weede (1976), employing COW and SIPRI data on contiguous Asian dyads for 1950 to 1969, concludes that war was much less frequent under a condition of overwhelming preponderance than in its absence. Mandel (1980) examines interstate border disputes for the years between 1945 and 1974 with Managing Interstate Conflict (MIC) data and reaches a conclusion consistent with those of Mihalka, Garnham, and Weede: violent border disputes were more likely to occur under a condition of relative parity in capabilities. Moul (1988a), focusing on patterns of dispute escalation among the European great powers (COW database 1816–1939), reports that over 50 percent of the disputes under a condition of relative parity escalated to war, as opposed to a less than 3 percent escalation rate under an unequal distribution of capabilities. Kim (1991) also examines great power wars (COW database 1816–1975) and reports that the probability of war for major power dyads whose capabilities were equal is more than double the probability for dyads whose capabilities were unequal. The difference between the two distributions is statistically significant.

In an expanded analysis, Kim (1996) examines the interaction of dyadic capability balances, status quo orientation, and alliance relationships among great powers for the period from the Peace of Westphalia in 1648 to 1975. His findings indicate that basic equality in capabilities between satisfied great powers and dissatisfied challengers increases the probability of the onset of war. In the most comprehensive study to date, Bremer (1992) analyzes all dyads in the interstate system present in the COW database (202,778 nondirectional dyad-years) for the period between 1816 and 1965. Relative capability was determined by CINC (composite index of national capability) scores using the COW material capabilities data set. Bremer concludes that war is about 33 percent more likely in dyads with small or medium differences in relative capabilities than in dyads with large capability differentials. Lastly, a study (Geller 1993) examines dispute-to-dispute war probabilities for a set of twenty-nine enduring dyadic rivalries (COW database 1816–1986) inclusive of 456 militarized conflicts. This subset of all interstate dyads is the most violence-prone group of nation-pairs in the interstate system and is responsible for almost 40 percent of all militarized disputes which occur during the period under examination. The conclusion is that static parity (measured by military capability) is roughly twice as likely to be associated with war in these dyads as is static preponderance.

Shift/Transition and War

The corollary to the basic parity and war hypothesis involves dynamic capability shifts and transitions as a source of conflict (e.g., Organski 1958; Gilpin 1981; Modelski 1983; Wallerstein 1984). Organski and Kugler (1980) provide evidence in support of Organski's original power transition theory based on an analysis of dynamic capability balances among selected nations from 1860 to 1975. They report that differential capability growth rates (measured by GNP) that produce transitions in relative position within "contender" dyads are associated with war. In a more comprehensive study, Anderson and McKeown (1987) examine seventy-seven wars (COW database 1816–1980) in terms of capability balances and report that an unstable military balance is associated with war. Houweling and Siccama (1988) reanalyze the Organski and Kugler power transition test using a more extensive set of nations (all major powers) and a composite indicator of national capabilities (instead of GNP). They conclude that differential growth rates that result in capability transitions are strongly associated with the occurrence of dyadic-level major power war. Another study (Geller 1998) examines the military balances among a set of dyadic major power rivalries for the period between 1816 and 1986 (COW database) that culminate in ten wars. Eight of these war-dyads had capability balances that could be estimated over time, and all eight dyads possessed unstable military balances in the years preceding their wars. These distributions suggest that an unstable military balance among great power rivals approximates a necessary (although not sufficient) condition for the occurrence of war in this population.

The rate of capability convergence has been postulated in some studies (e.g., Levy 1987: 97–98; Schampel 1993: 397–99) as a key factor in the occurrence of war. Rapid approaches (Wayman 1996) and rapid convergence/divergence

(Gochman 1990) have been posited as exacerbating the conflict potential in rival dyads. It is argued that a rapid shift in relative capabilities provides little time for peaceful adjustment and may increase both the sense of threat and opportunity. Alternatively, a gradual change in relative capabilities allows more time for non-violent adjustment to the shifting power balance. The evidence on the salience of rate of change is mixed: Schampel (1993: 405) and Gochman (1990: 154–55) report results indicating substantive effects for rapid approaches on the probability of war, whereas Kim (1992: 171) and Kim and Morrow (1992: 917) report the absence of any statistically discernible association between war occurrence and the rate of capability change among major power rivals.

Focusing on conflict initiation in militarized disputes, Huth, Bennett, and Gelpi (1992) report significant effects for capability transitions on dispute initiation patterns (COW database) among a set of eighteen great power rivalries from 1816 to 1975. The findings indicate that the presence of a capability "transition" (defined as a military expenditure growth-rate differential of 10 percent or more) has a significant impact on the initiation of militarized conflict among great power rivals. In a similar study, Huth and Russett (1993) analyze dispute initiation patterns (COW database) for ten nondirectional enduring rivalries that appear in the post-1945 period. The study reports the substantively important effects of shifts in the military balance on the probability of militarized dispute initiation. Another analysis (Geller 1992b) focuses on the relationship between capability differentials and dispute/war initiation among the set of strongest nations for the period between 1816 and 1976 (COW database). The population consists of a restricted group of great power "contenders" with inclusion based on the possession of 10 percent or more of the capability pool available to the larger set of all major powers. The study examines thirteen war dyads and seventy-one subwar dispute dyads and reports that a shifting capability balance within contender pairs is substantively associated with patterns of militarized dispute initiation.

In an analysis (Geller 1993) of differences within dynamic balances for twenty-nine enduring rivalries (COW database 1816–1986), it is noted that capability shifts—and particularly shifts toward parity—are associated with higher probabilities of war than are actual transitions in relative capabilities. These results are consistent for both composite capability and military capability indices. Lastly, Wayman (1996) analyzes a set of major power rivalries (COW database) and compares their capability and war patterns with nonrival dyads. He reports that the statistical association between capability shifts and war is stronger among rival states than for nonrivals and that a capability shift within a rival dyad approximately doubles its probability of war—from 14 percent to 31 percent.

Summary

The review of quantitative empirical research on the relationship between dyadic-level capability balances and conflict has focused on patterns of dispute/war initiation and dispute/war occurrence for populations of all interstate dyads, major power dyads, and enduring dyadic rivalries. The analysis indicates a growing and cumulative body of evidence pointing to the salience of both static and dynamic capability balances for the occurrence and initiation of militarized disputes and warfare. Specifically, conditions of approximate parity and shifts toward parity are consistently and significantly associated with conflict and war irrespective of population. Although broadly based composite measures of relative capability evidence these relationships, recent research is beginning to suggest the greater importance of narrowly defined military capabilities.

Status Quo Orientation and Conflict

One of the principal insights provided by Organski's (1958) original thesis on power transition involves the interaction of capability distributions and status quo orientation (Vasquez 1996b: 35–36). Specifically, it has been argued that whether the status quo challenger or defender has the advantage in relative capabilities could have important effects on the probability of war. For example, a status quo defender with a relative capability advantage over a challenger may have no incentive to attempt to use that superiority and be satisfied with a posture of deterrence, whereas a status quo challenger possessing a capability advantage over a defender may have a strong incentive to attempt to exploit its superiority through war. Even states committed to defending the status quo may experience pressure for the initiation of preventive war if the balance of capabilities appears to be shifting in favor of the opponent and future war is anticipated (e.g., Levy 1987; Powell 1996). Thus, the interaction of capability distributions and status quo orientation may influence not only the *occurrence* of war but also the identity of the war *initiator*.

Status Quo Orientation, Relative Capabilities, and War

Early work in this area may be found in Organski's (1958: 330–33) power transition theory, which focuses on the distinction between the dominant nation satisfied with the status quo and a dissatisfied challenger. He argues that as the capability trajectories of these states converge, war becomes increasingly probable. Rummel (1979: 264) also hypothesizes that an actual or growing weakness of the party favoring the status quo compared to the anti–status quo party will be positively correlated with violence. Status inconsistency producing dissatisfaction with the status quo is offered by Anderson and McKeown (1987) as a possible explanation for conflict. They suggest that a discrepancy between national aspirations and national achievements may lead governments to attempt to alter their external environments and that the extant balance of dyadic capabilities may then influence patterns of war initiation. The status-inconsistency theories of war by Galtung (1964), Wallace (1971), and Midlarsky (1975) present similar arguments. Maoz (1982: 203) also notes that crisis initiation is likely to be tied to national dissatisfaction and a commitment to revise the status quo, particularly when this is coupled with a rapid capability growth rate relative to that of an opponent.

Ray's (1995: 195–96) comparative case study of the Fashoda Crisis and the Spanish-American War suggests that the distribution of capabilities between status quo challengers and defenders may have had a critical impact on the outcomes of these two confrontations. Specifically, Ray argues that war was avoided in the Fashoda Crisis due to British (status quo defender) military superiority over France; whereas in the Spanish-American confrontation of 1898, the United States (status quo challenger) possessed military superiority over Spain and therefore that crisis ended in war. The reasoning that war initiation is likely when the balance of military capabilities favors the status quo challenger rather than the defender is also found in Huth, Bennett, and Gelpi (1992: 489).

However, Maoz (1982: 74–75) advances the logical chain by noting that defenders of the status quo may also have incentives for the initiation of conflict and that it is reasonable to expect that under certain dynamic capability balances, war initiation by status quo defenders should be likely. Gilpin (1981: 191, 201) and Levy (1987: 83–84) explore the reasons why capability convergence may lead to defender-initiated wars, arguing that a declining advantage relative to the increasing capabilities of a faster-growing challenger creates a strong incentive to initiate war before that diminishing advantage disappears. In sum, there is a sound theoretical basis for expecting patterns of both war occurrence and war initiation to be influenced by the power balance between status quo challengers and defenders.

Analysis of the interactive effects of capabilities and status quo orientation on the *occurrence* of war is found in studies by Werner and Kugler (1996) and Lemke and Werner (1996). Werner and Kugler (1996) examine power balances and the rate of military expenditures between a small set of major powers (i.e., "contenders") for the period between 1816 and 1980, with an interest in postdicting the Franco-Prussian War and World Wars I and II. Werner and Kugler (1996: 200) report, "No military buildups escalated to war except those that occurred under conditions of relative equality and when the challenging country was increasing its rate of growth of military expenditures at a faster rate than the dominant country." In short, parity in capabilities coupled with an advantage in the rate of military growth for the status quo challenger is associated with the occurrence of contender wars.

Lemke and Werner (1996) expand the previous analysis by including four minor power "local hierarchies" in South America (1860–1980) as well as the hierarchy of major power contenders (1820–1980) in their database. As in the Werner and Kugler (1996) study, Lemke and Werner hypothesize that the interaction of relative capabilities and status quo orientation will affect the occurrence of war. Their analysis indicates that a condition of power parity in which the status quo challenger is exceeding the rate of military expenditures by the status quo defender is strongly associated with the occurrence of war. This relationship holds for dyads composed of both major power contenders and for the set of minor power South American dyads as well.

Huth, Gelpi, and Bennett (1993: 617–18) report findings for a set of nine major powers (COW database 1816–1984) in "extended and direct immediate deterrence encounters" that suggest the salience of the conventional military balance between challengers and defenders for probabilities of conflict escalation. They conclude that a shift in the military balance "from a three-to-one defender advantage to a three-to-one challenger advantage increases the probability of escalation by approximately 33%." In other words, a conventional military power transition providing the challenger with a substantial advantage is associated with dispute escalation.

With regard to the question of status quo orientation, capabilities, and the identity of the war *initiator,* less extant evidence is available. Anderson and McKeown (1987) analyze seventy-seven wars (COW database 1816–1980) in terms of capability balances and the degree to which belligerents' "aspirations diverge from actual or expected achievements" (status quo orientation). Their model also allows for preemptive war initiated by a status quo defender. The basic hypothesis is that dissatisfied nations examine the power balance and initiate war when the military ratio is favorable. The findings of Anderson and McKeown (1987: 19) indicate that an unstable military balance is associated with war initiation by both challengers and defenders of the status quo.

Another study (Geller 1999) examines the question of the identity of the war initiator as it relates to both military balances and status quo orientation for a set of twenty nation-dyads that formed long-term rivalries from 1816 to 1986 (COW database). The study analyzes the forty-three wars that occurred between these "enduring rivals" and concludes that status quo challengers are the most probable war initiators and are equally likely to initiate wars whether they are superior or inferior in capabilities to their rivals,[7] whereas status quo defenders initiate wars almost solely under unstable military balances.

Summary

Based on the results of a number of recent studies, patterns of conflict escalation, war occurrence, and war initiation appear to be affected by the distribution of military capabilities between status quo defenders and challengers. Specifically, convergent findings have been presented indicating that an unstable military balance favoring the status quo challenger over the status quo defender is associated with both the escalation of conflict and the occurrence of war. The results reported by Anderson and McKeown (1987), Huth et al. (1993), Werner and Kugler (1996), and Lemke and Werner (1996) support this conclusion.

Regarding the identity of the war initiator, two implications of the findings by

Anderson and McKeown (1987) and Geller (1999) bear heavily on explanations of war decisions. First, the finding that the patterns of war initiation emerge only when relative capabilities are measured by military criteria rather than by a more broadly based composite index of power suggests that decisions to initiate war tend to focus on those factors that will have an immediate bearing on military success. Advantages or disadvantages in relative industrial or demographic strength may appear less relevant in such circumstances than existing military capabilities. A second implication of these results involves the initiation of preemptive or preventive war by status quo defenders. Almost every case of defender-initiated war for a set of rivals occurred under an unstable military balance (Geller 1999). This pattern suggests that stable military balances of either preponderance or parity are generally interpreted by status quo defenders as supportive of deterrence, whereas unstable balances producing capability shifts or transitions are deemed dangerous enough to provoke preemptive military action.

SYSTEM-LEVEL PATTERNS OF POWER AND CONFLICT

The literature of international politics is rife with discussions on the effects of the "polarity" of the international system on war. Unfortunately, due to the ambiguity of the concept of polarity and the multiple ways in which it can be operationalized, confusion rather than clarity has characterized the debate. The essence of this problem involves the question of whether the polarity of the international system is determined by the number of major states or by the number of distinct clusters of states emerging from the configuration of alliances. For example, should a system with five major states that have coalesced into two opposing alliances be categorized as multipolar or bipolar? For the purposes of classifying data-based studies in this area, the following terminology will be used: the *polarity* of the international system is determined by the number of major actors. Possible configurations include *unipolarity* (one dominant state), *bipolarity* (two major states of approximately equal capabilities), and *multipolarity* (three or more major states of approximately equal capabilities).

Opposing theoretical schools have developed regarding the war effects of the number of major actors. For example, some analysts argue that unipolar systems should be the least war-prone of the various system structures (e.g., Organski 1958; Gilpin 1981; Modelski 1983; Wallerstein 1984; Thompson 1988), while others maintain that characteristic should inhere in bipolar systems (e.g., Waltz 1979) or in multipolar structures (e.g., Morgenthau 1967).[8] Explanations regarding the effects of polarity on war range from the "stable order" imposed by the dominant state in a unipolar system (e.g., Organski 1958; Modelski 1972; Gilpin 1981), to "balanced power" in a bipolar configuration (e.g., Waltz 1979), to "flexibility in alignment" in multipolar systems (e.g., Deutsch and Singer 1964; Morgenthau 1967). Data-based evidence, however, is mixed.

Polarity

Mansfield (1988) examines international wars from 1495 to 1980 and reports that the mean number of wars initiated per year was higher during eras when a "hegemonic" state dominated the system (unipolarity) than during eras when hegemony was absent. However, both Thompson (1986) and Spiezio (1990) report opposite results for unipolarity and war. Thompson's analysis covers a period similar to Mansfield's (1494–1983 [COW database and Modelski and Thompson database]) and specifies categories of bipolarity, multipolarity, and near-unipolarity, in addition to unipolarity. Thompson's evidence suggests that warfare was least likely to occur when the system was unipolar or near-unipolar; he also reports that bipolar and multipolar systems were equally war-prone. Spiezio's study covers the more limited temporal period of 1815 to 1939 (COW data) in terms of the rising and falling relative economic/military capability base of Great Britain. He reports that the relative size of Britain's capability base was negatively and significantly associated with the frequency of war in the international system and concludes that his findings support the unipolar thesis that conflict is inversely related to the capability advantage of the hegemonic state.

Brecher, James, and Wilkenfeld (1990) and Wayman (1984) examine the effects of polarity in terms of international crises and war magnitude (i.e., total nation-months of war). The Brecher et al. analysis covers the temporal span of 1929 to 1985 (International Crisis Behavior [ICB] database) for international crises using system categories of bipolarity and multipolarity. They report that the mean number of international crises per year was higher for the bipolar period (1945–62) than for the multipolar era (1929–39). However, based on an analysis of major power crisis involvement, they conclude that bipolarity is a more "stable" structure than multipolarity. Wayman (1984) examines the dependent variable of major power war magnitude for bipolar and multipolar periods over the years 1815–1965 (COW database). He reports that periods characterized by "power multipolarity" were much more likely to evidence high levels of war magnitude than were periods of "power bipolarity." These differences were statistically significant.

Hopf (1991) and Levy (1984) examine the frequency, magnitude, and severity of wars using polarity (Hopf) and "system size" (Levy) as predictors. Hopf's database includes warfare in the European subsystem for the restricted temporal period of 1495 to 1559. The system is classified as multipolar for the years 1495 to 1520 and as bipolar for the years 1521 to 1559. Hopf reports that the amount of warfare during these two periods was essentially equivalent. He states that polarity has little relationship to patterns of war for the historical period under examination. However, Midlarsky (1993) questions Hopf's conclusions, arguing, instead, that the relationship between polarity and war is contingent on the scarcity of desired international resources.[9] Levy (1984) explores a possible linear association between the number of great powers (system size) and war for the extended temporal span of 1495 to 1975. His findings coincide with those of Hopf. He reports that the frequency, magnitude, and severity of war in the international system are unrelated to the number of major powers in the system.

The cumulative findings in the area of polarity and warfare are mixed. Aside from the evidence of Thompson (1986) and Spiezio (1990) on a relationship between the presence of an hegemonic state (unipolarity) and lower frequencies of warfare, other findings indicate higher numbers of crises during bipolar periods (Brecher, James, and Wilkenfeld 1990) but lower war magnitudes (Wayman 1984) than with multipolar systems. The study with the longest time line and the most extensive set of war variables (Levy 1984) indicates the lack of a substantive linear relationship between the number of great powers and the frequency, magnitude, or severity of warfare.

Hierarchy

The results of data-based studies on polarity and warfare indicate no definitive pattern regarding unipolar, bipolar, and multipolar configurations and the occurrence of war. The only polar structure that appears to influence conflict probability is unipolarity. At least part of the difficulty in identifying a stable pattern may result from an interaction effect between factors at multiple analytic levels, as the onset (occurrence/initiation) of major power warfare is determined less by the number of major powers than by the static or dynamic capability distributions among the strongest states themselves. Every international system possesses a hierarchy based on relative capabilities, and the extent of the capability differential between the leading state and potential challengers matters. If the hierarchy is clear, with the leading state in possession of a substantial capability advantage over its nearest potential rival, then the probability of action to rearrange the hierarchical order is likely to be low. However, if the capability advantage of the leading state is small or is eroding, other states may choose to attempt to alter the hierarchy. The challenges may be directed against the leading state or lesser states within an increasingly unstable international order. This logic is found in the works of Organski (1958), Gilpin (1981), Modelski (1983), Wallerstein (1984), and Thompson (1988). Other studies (Doran 1989, 1991, 1995; Geller 1992a, 1996; Houweling and Siccama 1993) have presented empirical analyses of these complex cross-level dynamics and indicate that capability-based changes in the hierarchical arrangement of major powers are associated statistically with the onset of great power warfare.

In sum, shifts in system-level power structure appear to have an interactive effect with dyadic capability distributions in the onset of both major power and global (or systemic) wars. As the international system moves from a high concentration of resources in the leading state toward multipolarity (power diffusion), lower-order conflict among the set of major states becomes increasingly probable, due to the weakening of the principal defender of the hierarchy. Movement toward power parity within secondary nation-dyads may trigger violent interactions that—though not related to system leadership—are still of considerable consequence. This suggests that the erosion of the system-level power structure links lower-order wars among major powers to system-shaping global wars. In this way, power distributions at both the systemic and dyadic levels of analysis interact synergistically to produce war among the set of major powers.[10] The clarity and stability of the hierarchy rather than the number of major powers is the critical factor affecting the onset of global wars (Geller and Singer 1998).

Capability Concentration

The distribution of capabilities is an element that is intrinsic to war decisions. However, as Singer, Bremer, and Stuckey (1972) argue, some explanations of war emphasize "uncertainty" (e.g., misjudgment, misperception, faulty expectations, etc.), whereas other explanations emphasize "certainty" (e.g., clarity, order, and predictability). They suggest that the concentration of capabilities among major powers heavily influences the level of decision-maker certainty or uncertainty—capability concentration enhances certainty, whereas deconcentration reduces it—and that a capability concentration index[11] may therefore be used to test war explanations based on the level of decision-making certainty or uncertainty. Using six variables reflecting three dimensions of national capabilities (military, demographic, and economic) for the set of major powers from 1820 to 1965 (COW database), Singer et al. regress three measures of capability concentration against the variable of major power nation-months at war. The results indicate a negligible (nonsignificant) association between the concentration of capabilities and "magnitude" (nation-months) of war for the entire period between 1820 and 1965.

Bueno de Mesquita (1981a) replicates the Singer et al. analysis with a simple alteration: he measures war occurrence (a dichotomous event—either present or absent) instead of war magnitude (total nation-months) over five-year periods (COW database). His results are congruent with theirs—the concentration of capabilities is statistically unrelated to the occurrence of major power war over the period between 1820 and 1965. Bueno de Mesquita and Lalman (1988) also examine a more extensive set of system-level attributes ("tightness" and "polarity") along with capability concentration ("balance") for major powers between 1815 and 1965 and report, once again, that system-level capability concentration is unrelated to the occurrence of major power war.

Summary

The empirical findings regarding capability concentration and major power war indicate the absence of a substantive relationship. One reason for these results may be found in the construction of the concentration index—a measure of *ag-*

gregate system-level concentration or dispersion. If major power wars are based on estimates of capabilities, then the *relative* capabilities of *specific* opponents may be of greater consequence than the aggregate concentration/dispersion of power throughout the system. The clarity or ambiguity of the system-level major power hierarchy takes on more meaning when relative capabilities of antagonists are measured (e.g., Houweling and Siccama 1993; Weede 1994; Geller 1996).

The results of studies on polarity and war fail to produce definitive findings. However, an empirical pattern indicating a cross-level dynamic affecting the onset of both major power and global (or systemic) wars has been noted. Multiple empirical studies have identified an interaction effect—between the rising/declining capabilities of the leading state in the international hierarchy relative to those of potential challengers and shifting dyadic-level capability balances among lesser major powers—as a factor influencing the onset of wars among this set of states. This suggests that the erosion of the system-level power structure links lower-order wars among major powers to system-shaping global wars.[12] In this way, power distributions at both the systemic and dyadic levels of analysis interact synergistically to produce war among the set of major powers. The clarity and stability of the hierarchy rather than the number of major powers are the critical factors determining the onset of global war.

CONCLUSION

Wars are contests of power. They may develop over any of a large number of issues such as territory, security, wealth, or ethnicity. However, the presence or absence of certain factors increases the probability of the onset and seriousness of such events (Geller and Singer 1998). One such factor—material capability—determines the capacity of actors to decide contested issues by force. Obviously, other power-related factors may impinge on this relationship. For example, the use of force may be affected by alliances or proximity—where the addition of third-party capabilities or a loss-of-strength gradient may be applicable. Other mediating factors may act as dampers to conflict escalation (Vasquez 1993, 1998b), as with the availability of institutions for nonviolent conflict resolution or where the presence of democratic governments in opposing states creates a normative expectation for peaceful settlement.

With regard to material capabilities, state-level factors of power status and position on the power cycle evidence consistent associations with the onset of war. Power status is also associated positively with the severity of war engagements. At the analytical level of the dyad, relative parity in capabilities and shifts toward parity present consistent empirical associations with the onset of both militarized conflict and war. In the case of rival dyads, convergent evidence indicates that an unstable military balance favoring the status quo challenger over the status quo defender is related to the escalation of conflict and to the occurrence of war; it is also strongly related to the initiation of preventive or preemptive war by the status quo defender. At the level of the international system, the presence of an unstable hierarchy among the major powers increases the probability of global war. In short, power and conflict possess an intrinsic and scientifically demonstrable relationship at multiple levels of analysis in the patterns of international politics.

NOTES

1. The Correlates of War (COW) Project defines an international war as a military conflict waged between national entities, at least one of which is a state, and that results in at least one thousand battle deaths of military personnel. Unless otherwise noted, the following definitions apply to these terms:

War occurrence—a dichotomous variable indicating either the presence or absence of war for the unit of observation

War initiation—the war initiator is the state that started the actual fighting or first seized territory or property interests of another state

2. Unless otherwise noted, the following definitions apply to these terms:

War magnitude—the sum of all participating nations' separate months of active involvement in each war

War duration—the length in months from the inception of the war to its termination

War severity—total battle deaths of military personnel in each war

3. Doran and Parsons (1980: 948, 954) identify critical points in a state's power cycle based on a state's share of the total resource pool available to all major powers at a given point in time. However, as Houweling and Siccama (1991: 643) note, "A critical point on a nation's capability trajectory is an absolute property of the nation concerned." Critical points, therefore, are classified as state-level predictors of warfare.

4. For an application of power cycle theory to subwar crisis involvement, see James and Hebron (1997).

5. Holsti (1991: 158, 171–72) discusses changes in the conceptions of power over time and how, from the mid–nineteenth century on, power calculations increasingly concentrated on relative military capabilities.

6. Wagner (1994), in a formal mathematical analysis, notes that each of these contradictory propositions (i.e., war is less likely if power is distributed equally/war is less likely if power is distributed unequally) is derivable from a plausible set of premises.

7. This finding is consistent with Paul's (1994: 173) analysis of six cases of asymmetrical war initiations by weaker states. He notes that militarily inferior states may use force to reduce uncertainty, alter an unacceptable status quo, or gain sympathy from other parties. Paul concludes that a significant capability advantage may be insufficient "to deter an adversary who is highly motivated to change the status quo." The conclusion also is reinforced by the findings of Huth (1996: 85) as reported in his analysis of relative military strength between challengers and targets engaged in territorial disputes (1950–90; 129 dispute cases). Specifically, Huth notes that "the balance of conventional military forces

between challenger and target *did not* have a powerful effect on the decisions of the challenger to dispute territory."

8. Midlarsky (1988: 44–78) examines both mathematically and historically the multiple issues inherent in these opposing positions.

9. Midlarsky (1993) maintains that if such resources are abundant in the international system, then the occurrence of war in bipolar and multipolar systems should be essentially equivalent. However, under conditions of resource scarcity, a multipolar structure should be more war-prone. See also Midlarsky (1988: 44–78; 1989).

10. See Thompson (1983a, 1983b), Doran (1983, 1989, 1991, 1995), Geller (1992a, 1996), Geller and Singer (1998), Houweling and Siccama (1993), and Weede (1994) for discussions of cross-level dynamics.

11. The concentration of capabilities in the system and the polarity (the number of major states) of the system are different measures of the systemic distribution of power. A standard index of capability concentration devised by Ray and Singer (1973) is

$$CON_t = \sqrt{\frac{\sum_{i=1}^{N_t} (S_{it})^2 - 1/N_t}{1 - 1/N_t}}$$

where

S_{it} = the proportion of the aggregate capabilities possessed by the major powers that major power i controls in year t;

N_t = the number of major powers in the system in year t.

This is a statistical measure that takes on values from 0 to 1 and reflects the aggregate inequality of capabilities as distributed among all major powers in the system. It is not directly related to the number of major powers in the system. See Mansfield (1994: 72–75) for a discussion of this statistic.

12. For multilevel explanations of the onset and seriousness of global wars, see Vasquez (1993: 225–62) and Geller and Singer (1998: 156–90).

FACTORS THAT PROMOTE PEACE

PART III

FACTORS THAT PROMOTE PEACE

13

International Norms

Normative Orders and Peace

Gregory A. Raymond

> An inclination toward restraints and prohibitions in war is perceptible
> among enough of our species earlier civilizations . . . for the historian
> of humankind to regard it as essentially a normal aspiration, more or
> less as old as war itself.
>
> —Geoffrey Best (1994: 15)

In a squat, mud-brick building, which once served as a government archive in the capital city of Amarna,[1] archeologists have found nearly four hundred cuneiform tablets describing the diplomatic relations between pharaonic Egypt and its neighbors. Unparalleled in their historical detail, these tablets reveal that by the fourteenth century B.C.E., states throughout the Near East had adopted an elaborate code of international norms known by the Akkadian term *parsu* (Cohen 1996: 246). According to this code, the so-called Great Kings of Egypt, Hatti, Mittani, Babylonia, and Assyria were members of an extended family: they possessed rights and duties based on rank, they followed elaborate protocol when interacting, and they held common expectations about what constituted proper behavior. Like brothers, the Great Kings occasionally quarreled, though their rivalries were tempered by norms that reduced the probability such conflicts would escalate to fratricidal violence.

For peace researchers, several things are noteworthy about this code of conduct. First, it provided a medium for discourse: when the Great Kings spoke, they used the idiom of prevailing norms to articulate their positions. Second, the code held sway among states that possessed different languages, religions, and political traditions. Third, many rules within the code sought to restrain when and how states used military force. Finally, its injunctions were generally followed, even without a central authority to enforce compliance. In short, the archeological evidence from Amarna suggests that international norms influenced state behavior by communicating shared understandings about the scope of a state's entitlements, the extent of its obligations, and the range of its jurisdiction.

Based on research into other multistate systems, it appears that international life as described on the Amarna tablets was not unique to the ancient Near East. All independent political entities with regular intercourse have developed conventions defining appropriate behavior for certain situations, including the resort to war (see Ginther 1995; Tieya 1991; Singh 1989; Pavithran 1965; Viswanatha 1925; Walker, 1899; Nys 1894; and Leech 1877). Whether these conventions took the form of tacit understandings, informal assurances, or written agreements, they guided state behavior by delineating when using deadly force was legitimate, how it should be used, and against whom it could be applied. As Bull (1977: 179) has summarized the historical record, "In any actual hostilities to which we can give the name 'war,' norms or rules, whether legal or otherwise, invariably play a part."

The specific role played by international norms is a matter of some controversy. For every Fluellen who believes that the rules of warfare are staunch injunctions, there seems to be someone willing to flout them. Are norms ex ante sources of behavior? Or, are they merely post hoc rationalizations of self-interest? I will make a case for the importance of international norms in the study of war, arguing they have explanatory power that is irreducible to the optimizing behavior of sovereign, egoistic actors.

What follows is an attempt to synthesize and integrate the findings from data-based analyses of the impact of norms on the occurrence of war. I begin by addressing the concept of "norm" and showing how individual norms are connected in an overarching pattern or normative order. These preliminaries are important due to the semantic confusion surrounding the concept. In the past, notes Ewald (1991: 140), the word *norm* led a "quiet, unremarkable existence, whereas today, along with its panoply of derivations and associated terms, it has become one of the most used and abused terms of our contemporary vocabulary, whether we speak colloquially or as social scientists."[2] Scholars disagree on how international norms should be defined, whether they can be measured, and which classification schemes are the most fruitful (Raymond 1997). Before declaring whether international norms are a correlate of war, I shall delineate my conceptual approach, which treats norms as standards of behavior, not merely as standard behaviors.

After describing the nature of norms and normative orders, I move on to analyze evidence on the relationship between different types of orders and the incidence of militarized interstate conflict. Although international norms recently have received considerable attention from constructivists and neoliberal institutionalists, many of those who today trumpet the importance of these ideational phenomena overlook earlier empirical work on the role of norms in world politics. Their neglect is like that of the art critic who discusses the articulation of plastic space in paintings by Frank Stella without making reference to the previous work of Caravaggio. Based on the proposition that positivist epistemology and behavioral methodology are essential for the social-scientific study of ideational phenomena, I trace those patterns involving international norms that have been associated empirically with movement back and forth between peace and war.

Finally, in the last section of the chapter, I conclude by taking stock of how far we have come in the study of international norms and then propose new avenues for cross-level research.

NORMS AND NORMATIVE ORDERS

In a speech delivered on 25 July 1988, Soviet foreign minister Eduard Shevardnadze told an audience of government officials, "We should not pretend, Comrades, that norms and notions of what is proper, of what is called civilized conduct in the world community do not concern us. If you want to be accepted in it you must observe them" (cited in Marantz 1995: 200). International norms, as Shevardnadze's comments suggest, are social phenomena with deontological content. They entail a collective evaluation of what ought to be done, a collective expectation as to what will be done, and particular reactions to compliant versus noncompliant behavior. Communicated through a rich lexicon of legal symbols and reinforced by diplomatic ritual, international norms are more than modal regularities; they are intersubjectively shared understandings that oblige national leaders to act in a certain way. Conformity with a norm's instructions elicits approval from nearly all other relevant states; deviance, disapproval. Moreover, these voices of praise and protest encourage conformity by influencing an actor's affective image of itself and its reputation among others.

Norms, in other words, express who we are. They are buttressed by feelings of shame, embarrassment, guilt, and the like, especially when one's identity is at stake. As suggested by recent neurological research, these powerful emotions are central to decision making, eliminating some options and highlighting others. Effective social behavior, including the observation of norms, appears to be heavily influenced by somatic markers, biasing devices generated by emotions that "predict" the outcomes of certain scenarios (Damasio 1994; also see Devlin 1997). When a negative marker is associated with an anticipated future outcome, it acts like an alarm that warns against behaving in a certain way; but when a positive marker is connected, it functions like a guide.[3] If, as these findings imply, people acting under the sway of norms are influenced by such markers, then emotions are not just physiological reactions to external stimuli that color one's outlook. They are feelings about determinate objects that structure how we experience the world and are as integral to purposive-actor explanations of behavior as are the concepts of instrumental rationality and self-interest.

International norms do not exist in isolation. They fit together in a complex mosaic to form a normative order. Because of uneven growth among norms within different arenas of state activity, the pattern of interlocking norms that develops over time lacks symmetry and elegance. Normative orders grow by accretion. Rules that regulate behavior arise incrementally to deal with new situations,[4] and they are predicated upon the prior existence of constitutive rules that define what counts as a certain practice. In basketball, for example, rules regarding goal tending, lane violations, and the three-point line emerged bit by bit in response to new generations of taller front court players, and they had meaning only in the context of antecedent rules defining what counted as a field goal.

Normative orders also vary along several dimensions. They differ regarding (1) the amount of discrepancy between the order's professed principles and its applied rules, (2) the degree to which members of the state system have internalized those rules, and (3) whether the rules complement or contradict one another. Variations along these three dimensions affect the strength of a normative order. Those orders with high levels of normative consistency, consensus, and congruence have a greater probability of influencing international outcomes than those ranking lower on these dimensions.

To identify the attributes that strengthen a normative order is not to specify whether such an order will dampen or kindle the flames of war. For an answer to this question, we need to look beyond consistency, consensus, and congruence and examine the substantive content of a given order. At the core of every normative order is a set of norms that defines its axiology, or value orientation. Some orders are highly permissive insofar as they give national leaders considerable latitude to do whatever they believe must be done to protect the state and advance its position relative to competitors. Other orders are more restrictive, giving leaders far less leeway to engage in unbridled self-help. Since each type of normative order has been promoted by different theorists as conducive to peace, let us compare the nature of permissive versus restrictive orders before turning to the empirical evidence on which type reduces the prospects for armed combat.

Permissive Normative Orders

Embedded within the axiology of permissive orders is a distinction between private morality, which guides the behavior of common people in their everyday lives, and reason of state, which governs the conduct of leaders who are responsible for their nation's security. Although some people have argued that a nation's "foreign policy actions should be derived from the same standards of ethics, honesty, and morality which are characteristic of the individual citizens of the nation" (Jimmy Carter as cited in Garrett 1996: 9),[5] those who champion the doctrine of reason of state insist that the "moral obligations of governments are not the same as those of the individual" (Kennan 1991: 60).[6] Government leaders "do what they have to do in order to protect . . . the physical security of their citizens" (Gray 1993: 9). According to Machiavelli (1950: 64), this requires them to imitate the lion as well as the fox. Whereas the former uses strength and courage to frighten potential aggressors, the latter relies on guile and deception to outwit them. Although the devious stratagems of the fox may seem loathsome in the light of private morality, reason of state warrants their use if they enhance state security.

Evidence of an implicit understanding of reason of state can be found throughout antiquity, scattered among the commentaries of such prominent Greeks and Romans as Thucydides and Sextus Julius Frontinus (Pouncey 1980: 35, n. 184; Dawson 1996: 157). Explicit theorizing about reason of state did not begin until the sixteenth century, however. Over the next two centuries, the doctrine became so influential that even its critics conceded, "All writers on the science of policy are agreed . . . that all governments must frequently infringe the rules of justice to support themselves; that truth must give way to dissimulation; honesty to convenience; and humanity to reigning interest" (Burke, 1899: 29).[7]

Reason of state enjoys a prominent place within permissive normative orders as a device for defending violations of reigning state practice. Those who violate international norms generally mount one of three types of defense: challenging the factual basis of a charge ("We did not do X."), denying that the action in question falls under an accepted definition of wrongful behavior ("What we did was not really X."), or justifying the action by referring to certain qualities of the situation ("We did X, but there were extenuating circumstances."). The last of these defenses has four variants. First, appeals to *force majeure* purport that an irresistible force makes someone physically incapable of complying with an obligation. Second, appeals to *duress* claim an obligation was violated due to the use or threat of coercion by another state. Third, appeals to *fortuitous events* declare that an unforeseen incident made it impossible to know one was acting in breach of an obligation. Finally, appeals to *necessity* challenge the wrongfulness of an act on the basis that it was the only means of safeguarding an essential interest against a grave and imminent peril.[8]

In permissive normative orders, defenses based on necessity draw upon the central tenet of reason of state: given the coarse realities of international anarchy, national leaders must disregard the moral scruples that apply to ordinary people and act in terms of interest defined as power. Typical expressions of the argument from necessity take the form "Circumstances required that I do X." Since courts have held that "necessity may excuse the non-observation of international obligations" (Judge Dionisio Anzilotti as cited in Cheng 1987: 71), examples of the argument abound in modern diplomatic history. James Carter, defending the American seizure of fourteen Canadian schooners, appealed to necessity in his oral argument before the arbitration tribunal in the *Behring Fur Seal* case of 1893; Viscount Kilmuir used the concept when justifying the British military operation against Egypt in 1956; and Chaim Herzog drew upon its practice when defending Israel's 1976 armed rescue of hostages in Uganda (Collins and Rogoff 1990: 88–89, 92).

Effective policy, these statesmen would agree, hinges on complying with strategic necessities. On the other hand, the fate of Duke Hsiang of Sung illustrates what happens when they are ignored. In 638 B.C.E., the duke refused to attack an army from the rival state of Ch'u while it was crossing the Hung River, even though his forces were outnumbered and would probably be vanquished if their adversaries made it to the other side. Believing that such an attack would be immoral, the duke waited until the army from Ch'u had forded the river. By not recognizing the strategic imperatives of the situation, he is said to be responsible for the terrible defeat suffered by Sung.

The tale of Duke Hsiang demonstrates that strategic necessities force leaders to choose between problematic alternatives. Like Hektor, who tells his wife Andromache at a brief meeting on the walls of Troy that he must return to battle, many leaders face a conflict between what they see as necessary and what they believe would be desirable. Yet those who subscribe to the doctrine of reason of state insist that they must heed the former, even if their behavior violates moral norms. "It is possible," according to Mackie (1977: 159), "for a means which is itself bad to be outweighed . . . by a sufficiently good end." "To know with despair that the political act is inevitably evil," adds Morgenthau (1946: 203), "and to act nonetheless, is moral courage."[9]

One form of strategic necessity accentuated by permissive normative orders concerns the use of war as an instrument of foreign policy. While some wars may involve choice, others are said to be beyond anyone's control. Abraham Lincoln exemplified this view during his second inaugural when he depicted the American Civil War as something that "came of itself, the personified process overriding personal agents" (Wills 1999: 64). From this perspective, political leaders are frail beings "caught in a tide of events" (Elfstrom 1990: 49).[10] Sometimes they have no latitude when deciding whether to wage war. Survival may necessitate taking up arms, and occasionally it may require launching a preemptive attack. As Sukra asserts in the *Nitisara*, self-preservation can compel a leader to undertake a treacherous war (*Kuta Yudha*), in which ordinary restraints on initiating hostilities do not apply (Chacko 1958: 132, 140).[11] "War is just to whom it is necessary," the Roman historian Titus Livy once remarked, "and arms are pious when there is no hope but in arms" (cited in Chanteur 1992: 39).

A second strategic necessity can be found in attempts to justify extraordinary acts committed in violation of existing rules of warfare. Appeals to the exigencies of military necessity assert that extreme danger overrides conventional prohibitions on who can employ deadly force, how it should be used, and against whom it may be applied. "We must make war as we must," Secretary of State for War Lord Kitchener of Britain once proclaimed, "not as we should like" (cited in Howard 1991: 31). His sentiments were echoed a few decades later by Lord

Whitelaw, a member of the British government during the Falklands War. Explaining why the submarine HMS *Conqueror* sank the *General Belgrano* when the Argentinean cruiser was outside the Maritime Exclusion Zone, he professed, "we had to take the opportunity we had" (cited in Coates 1997: 213). Similar attitudes have been voiced by political leaders to rationalize other forms of military of action. For example, necessity was invoked in 1854 by the United States to defend the bombardment of Greytown, Nicaragua; it was used by Great Britain to justify mining the North Sea during World War I; and it was employed by Germany to excuse the devastation of the Somme region during the retreat of 1917. As expressed in the aphorism *Kriegsraison geht vor Kriegsmanier* (necessity in war overrules the manner of warfare), any acts of violence are acceptable if they are required for victory. To quote Colonel Lowell P. Weicker, the American architect of Operation Shatter, a plan to bomb German cities during World War II to break civilian morale, "you cannot always use the Marquis of Queensberry's rules" (cited in McElroy 1992: 156).[12]

Finally, a third strategic necessity involves the ability to extricate oneself from burdensome commitments. As expressed by the norm *rebus sic stantibus* (as matters stand), national leaders can terminate treaty agreements unilaterally if a fundamental change occurs in the circumstances that existed at the signing of the agreement. Advocates of permissive normative orders believe that widespread acceptance of such an elastic conception of promissory obligations contributes to international peace in several ways. First, by promoting fluid coalitions, it increases uncertainty and allegedly breeds caution. Second, by supporting alignments that shift from one issue to the next, it creates overlapping pursuits among states. Finally, by encouraging leaders to disavow onerous agreements and keep their options open, it allows them to avoid being entrapped by others.

In sum, reason of state enjoins political leaders to defend their country's primary interests, those that cannot be compromised and that must be upheld at any cost. Within permissive normative orders, strategic necessities allow them to waive the moral prohibitions that otherwise constrain human behavior. As agents of the state, whose survival comes before all else, they are "realizing historical necessity"[13] and cannot be judged by the same standards that apply in private life. Like Hoerderer in Jean-Paul Sartre's play *Dirty Hands*, they may have to plunge themselves up to the elbows in blood.

Restrictive Normative Orders

In contrast to a permissive normative order, restrictive orders consist of norms that neither give decision makers untrammeled discretion nor license their appeals to the exigencies of necessity. Strict criteria exist on when to wage war and how to fight.[14] Concomitant with these limitations is support for amicable procedures of conflict resolution, including adjudication, arbitration, and mediation. Expediency, in other words, cannot be used as a defense for attacking others or for violating a standing code of military conduct.[15]

An early statement of this position can be seen in Cicero's praise of the Athenians for rejecting Themistocles' proposal to launch a surprise attack against the Spartan fleet at Gytheum following the Persian Wars (Cicero 1991: 118). The "laws of the Hellenes" (*nomima Hellēnōn*) made Athenian restraint obligatory, even if it meant forgoing the opportunity to weaken a rival. These same laws called on states to arbitrate their disputes, as can be seen in treaties like the one between Hierapytna and Prianosos carved on a large marble slab during the early third century B.C.E. The arbitration clauses in these treaties were reinforced by oral teachings. For instance, Inachus, the mythical king of Argos, was said to have been assisted by the river gods Cephisus and Asterion in arbitrating a disagreement between Poseidon and Hera. Drawing upon many examples of this sort, Isocrates (1929: 19) insisted that the restrictive laws of the Hellenes were important: "you will all impute extreme folly and madness to those who think that injustice is advantageous." In making this assertion, he reflected a moral theme expressed in the *Ilioupersis* and the *Nostoi* about how one should conduct warfare. The former epic delineated the sacrileges committed by the Greeks during the sack of Troy; the latter described the hardships they suffered because of their ruthless behavior.

Beyond communicating how disputes ought to be resolved, restrictive normative orders also stipulate how promissory obligations should be interpreted. *Pacta sunt servanda*, the "groundnorm"of restrictive orders (Kelsen 1952), holds that commitments are binding. Like the *Nibelungentreue* given by Kaiser Wilhelm II to Austria-Hungary on the eve of World War I, they are irrevocable pledges that must be honored even during trying times. In contrast to permissive normative orders, which elevate necessity to a virtue, restrictive orders appeal to duty and fidelity. Respect for the sanctity of agreements, it is believed, builds a reputation for reliability, inspires international collaboration, and nurtures a sense of the common good. Disregarding one's word causes both friend and foe alike to distrust the most solemn oath.

Finally, restrictive orders contain norms that limit the geographic scope of competition. Rules governing jurisdiction over airspace, maritime zones, and territory diffuse potential conflict by coordinating national expectations around simple, unambiguous, and prominent lines of demarcation. Rules regarding neutrality, nonalignment, buffer zones, and spheres of influence also reduce friction by removing certain regions from military contention (Raymond 1997). Because these kinds of limitations help keep explosive issues off the political agenda, they allow states to respond to disagreements with multilateral, accommodative strategies (Vasquez 1993: 278).

To sum up, a restrictive normative order exists when states agree to limitations on the use of force, the prerogative to cancel agreements at will, and the geostrategic boundaries of their competition. Unlike permissive orders, which give national leaders the liberty to follow Kanika's (1964: 262) advice in the *Mahābhā-rata* and "ceaselessly watch for the flaws of their foes and take advantage of them," restrictive orders seek to foster a climate of trust. Yet many people insist that permissive orders offers a better guarantee of peace than restrictive orders because they lubricate the balance-of-power process with rules that allow leaders to adapt to changing circumstances and exploit emerging opportunities. Given the disagreement over this assertion, let us examine the empirical evidence on the pacifying effects of each type of normative order.

THE CONTRIBUTION OF NORMATIVE ORDERS TO PEACE

The transition from peace to war may be thought of as a multistage process, in which chance, various contextual factors, and the sequence of choices made by the interacting parties affect the aggregate outcome. More than one combination of these ingredients may lead to war, and different combinations may lead to different types of wars (Bremer 1993). Two stages in this process are (1) the transition from nonviolent conflicts of interest to disputes involving the threat, display, or use of military force and (2) the transition from militarized disputes to war. Though limited, the empirical evidence to date suggests that the international norms associated with strong, restrictive orders are a contextual factor that reduces the probability of escalation during both stages.

From Conflicts of Interest to Militarized Disputes

Although conflicts of interest are common in world politics, most dissipate before either side resorts to military force. One reason that this may occur is because prevailing norms bestow an aura of legitimacy on certain actions, with the result that those in opposition seldom entertain the idea of using force to thwart those actions. The norm of decolonization, for instance, had a significant impact in the aftermath of World War II on limiting military conflict when previously dependent territories received their independence. Relinquishing territorial possessions was not always in the military or economic interest of the metropole, yet norms endorsing national self-determination have been shown to exert a strong influence over whether a peaceful transition would ensue, even when it was not in the self-interest of the colonial power (Goertz and Diehl 1994).

Another reason for many conflicts of interest to dissolve before anyone wields violent, heavy-handed tactics lies in the use of amicable modes of redress. Two types of procedural norms are conducive to resolving conflicts of interest. The first are actor-universal. Their injunctions pertain to everyone and derive from opinions about proper action that are modal among members of the state system. An example would be the Convention Respecting the Limitation of the Employment of Force for the Recovery of Contract Debts, which was adopted at the

Hague Conference of 1907 to oblige states to use arbitration rather than armed force as a means of redressing economic grievances. Whenever wounded sensibilities and aroused national passions threaten to transform conflicts of interest into confrontations, actor-universal norms of procedure like those embodied in the 1907 Hague Conference offer disputants a template for working out their disagreement. By facilitating amicable third-party intercession, they slow the tempo of events, provide an opportunity to unravel the layers of misperception that frequently envelop such conflicts, and allow the adversaries to escape contests of resolve without humiliation.[16] Simply put, these kinds of norms recast conflicts of interest as problems to be solved, not bouts to be won. They channel quarreling parties in a conciliatory direction by framing contentious issues in terms of rights, obligations, and accountability (Rothman 1981: 330).

Data-based research on actor-universal rules of procedure shows that increases in normative support for pacific third-party settlement techniques leads to more states using arbitration to resolve their disagreements and an upswing in the importance of those issues being arbitrated (Raymond 1980: 72–73). Furthermore, the greater the support for procedures like arbitration, adjudication, and mediation, the less unilateral acts of coercive self-help are accepted as legitimate by members of the state system (Kegley and Raymond 1981: 181). Support for these amicable settlement procedures tends to be strongest when there is a stable rank order of states, relative parity exists among the major powers, and changes in the distribution of military capabilities among these powers are modest (Raymond and Kegley 1985: 47).

The second type of procedural norm associated with resolving conflicts of interest is partner-specific. Rather than being universally held, these norms apply to a subset of the population of states (Cohen 1980: 130–31). Most norms governing these interactions only concern limited aspects of the overall relationship that generate discord. They are war averting rather than peace building. As ongoing exchanges become more complex, however, new partner-specific norms may evolve to perform functions beyond managing quarrels and diluting defensive noncooperation (Barkun 1970: 22–24). These norms may arise through protracted bilateral give and take or through the activities of third-party intermediaries (Princen 1992: 29; Mandell and Tomlin 1991: 54; Sanders 1986). To the extent that such norms assist states in working together toward some superordinate goal, they help build a reservoir of mutual confidence that facilitates logrolling, nonspecific compensation, and other integrative approaches to reconciling seemingly incompatible interests. However, as Bueno de Mesquita and Lalman (1992: 122) note, a "conciliatory norm that favors negotiation over the use of force appears to diminish in its effectiveness if there is uncertainty about a rival's likelihood of following the norm."

Recent empirical studies of the virtual absence of war among constitutionally secure democracies highlights the role played by these partner-specific norms of procedure. Based on tolerance and a respect for the rights of opponents, democratic political cultures shun lethal force for settling disagreements.[17] Politics is seen as a non-zero-sum game, so that the policymaking process contains a spirit of give-and-take. Compromise, the use of persuasion rather than coercion, and a reliance on legal procedures to resolve rival claims are the primary means of dealing with conflict. Everyone is believed to lose if politics degenerates into violence.

According to this literature, conflict resolution practices used at home are also employed when dealing with international disputes. Leaders socialized within democratic political cultures share a common outlook. Viewing international politics as an extension of domestic politics, they externalize their norms of regulated competition. Disputes with kindred governments rarely escalate to war because each side accepts the other's legitimacy and expects their counterparts to rely on peaceful means of conflict resolution (Dixon 1996b, 1994). What is more, they often act on this expectation by allowing third-party intermediaries to play a judicial role in ameliorating festering issues (Raymond 1996, 1994). In contrast, belligerents are less likely to grant third-party intermediaries the authority to render a binding judgment whenever the dispute involves one or more nondemocracies. Lacking shared democratic norms and the trust in law such norms encourage, autocratic leaders are predisposed to restrict any third party to functioning as a go-between rather than as an umpire. By so doing, they defend what they believe is their right to be the final judges of whether a transgression has been committed and how it ought to be redressed. Limiting the power of a third-party intermediary eliminates the dilemma of being obliged to adhere to a verdict that might injure perceived national interests.

Although democracies conduct their foreign policies according to pacific norms of conflict resolution, they are not reticent to use force against illiberal adversaries who have a history of resorting to intimidation. Reliance on a conditionally cooperative strategy fades when an opponent consistently chooses a non-cooperative strategy (Axelrod 1986). While partner-specific norms facilitate mutual accommodation among fellow democracies, those perceived as despots are expected to use the very bullying tactics that characterize their domestic political processes (Russett 1993: 33). Closed polities lack what Checkel (1999: 87; 1997) calls a "cultural match" between their domestic values and many of the procedural norms in restrictive international orders.

From Militarized Disputes to Interstate Wars

Once a disputant employs coercive measures, can international norms prevent matters from spiraling toward armed hostilities? Do norms speak too softly to be heard amid the bedlam of arms? Although we are faced with a dearth of systematic, empirical research on these questions, the evidence that does exist underscores the pacifying effects of certain international norms.

Militarized disputes may evolve in various ways: some are settled; others fester for generations without resolution; still others escalate to war. The results from several studies suggest escalation is less likely when unilateral, opportunistic behavior is encapsulated within a cocoon of norms that establish mechanisms for refereeing controversies and upholding agreements. During times of flux, when an ascendant state seeking to revise the political status quo is on the verge of matching or possibly surpassing its rivals in military capability, violations of these mechanisms can trigger a violent response. Consider, for example, the events leading to the Franco-Prussian War of 1870–71. Prussian efforts to place Prince Leopold von Hohenzollern-Sigmaringen on the vacant Spanish throne after an insurrection had driven Queen Isabella II into exile "violated an international norm forbidding Great Powers from placing members of their reigning houses on a foreign throne without the prior consent of all other Great Powers" (Welch 1993: 89). Coming on the heels of friction over the status of Luxembourg and the more general issue of compensation for Napoleon III's neutrality during the Seven Weeks' War, the violation aroused Gallic indignation, which combined with clumsy French diplomacy and Bismarck's duplicity to bring Paris and Berlin to blows.

Prussia's violation of a norm that had been established at the 1815 Congress of Vienna and confirmed during regime changes in Greece (1831), Belgium (1848), and Tuscany (1859) aggravated Franco-Prussian relations at an unstable juncture. The distribution of power between these neighboring rivals was undergoing a rapid shift, with upstart Prussia challenging France's longstanding position as the dominant military power on the European continent. Wallensteen's (1984) work reveals that the probability of war increases when great powers fail to maintain standards and strategies to handle troublesome issues, especially those involving territorial questions. Other researchers report similar findings. At the close of periods of extreme instability, great powers pay considerable attention to designing security regimes. Critical to the success of such regimes are the criteria for explicating the conditions under which forcible actions short of war are seen as legitimate. While a consensus among the great powers on a set of restrictive criteria may not speak to freedom, justice, or self-determination for other members of the state system, it does lower the likelihood that militarized disputes will escalate to war (Kegley and Raymond 1986). The greater the normative support for wide latitude in the use of retorsion, reprisals, and other nonamicable modes of dispute settlement, the greater the incidence of warfare. Conversely, normative support for good offices, conciliation, and other amicable procedures lowers the odds of war (Kegley and Raymond 1981: 180).

Conventions for dealing with dangerous disputes rest on the assumption that promises will be kept. Unless commitments are considered binding by the parties to an agreement, their impact will be marginal. All international exchanges are influenced by beliefs about credibility, reliability, and the willingness of the opposing side to abide by promissory obligations. The results from one recent study of promissory obligations indicates that when the climate of normative opinion embraces *pacta sunt servanda* as an actor-universal norm, serious disputes decline, the percentage of major powers involved in them decreases, and fewer escalate to war (Kegley and Raymond 1990: 252–54). Not only is war less likely when international norms uphold the sanctity of commitments, but should it occur, the magnitude, severity, and intensity of the fighting tend to be lower in the restrictive environment of binding agreements. Contrary to what proponents of permissive normative orders claim, the norm *rebus sic stantibus* breeds a culture of mistrust. In such an opaque world, colored by suspicion over who is in league with whom, *lex talionis* is the court of first resort.

Similar results have been reported for partner-specific norms. Gelpi (1997) has found that bilateral security norms established in dispute settlements affected the behavior of states in subsequent militarized encounters by providing referents which fostered a reputation for trustworthiness. Those who reneged on the terms of a settlement generally recognized coercive responses by the defending state as legitimate punishment for their infraction and not the prelude to aggressive demands for further concessions. Normative referents thus altered the interpretation given to defender actions. Cooperation between states representing security risks to each other was stabilized because the challenger became less intransigent in its bid to overturn the status quo and more willing to return to the previous focal point solution.

CONCLUSION

In a speech delivered to Pentagon employees on 15 August 1990, President George Bush sought to place the recent Iraqi invasion of Kuwait within a larger normative framework. "Might does not make right," he declared. The "cause of justice" is served by "an international order—a common code . . . that promotes cooperation in place of conflict. This order is imperfect; we know that. But without it, peace and freedom are impossible. The rule of law gives way to the law of the jungle."[18]

As I have argued throughout this chapter, not all normative orders mitigate the most pernicious aspects of an anarchic state system. Permissive orders, whose axiologies ennoble the perceived necessities of reason of state, are a correlate of war. Throughout history, they have been associated with the ruthless pursuit of advantage. Bards and playwrights, those insightful observers of the human condition, have long told us that the lure of expediency is difficult to resist. Even in the age of chivalry, when minstrels sang of honor in combat, medieval prohibitions against killing a knight's horse occasionally were violated so infantry could defeat cavalry (Röling 1975: 140). Sadly, in a world where prevailing norms acquiesce to expediency, life takes on the capricious nature of a "perpetual and restless desire of power after power that ceaseth only in death" (Hobbes 1946: 49).

By way of contrast, restrictive normative orders that possess high levels of consistency, consensus, and congruence tend to lower the probability that (1) conflicts of interest will escalate to militarized disputes and (2) militarized disputes subsequently will escalate to interstate wars. Recognizing that foreign policy choices are not leashed to what Melville (1979: 218) called "the straight warp of necessity," the norms of restrictive orders offer political leaders principles and procedures for defusing confrontations and containing human costs when conflict resolution fails.

Strong restrictive orders promote reciprocal cooperative exchanges, which reinforce the injunction that states should not injure those who have helped them.[19] During an iterated chain of contacts, consistently returning good for good inspires trust. Leaders gradually establish a reputation for being trustworthy by responding in kind to positive acts, complying with international agreements, and foregoing opportunities for unilateral gain that would injure others.[20] Within an atmosphere of trust, what begins as a sequence of straightforward transactions on a single issue often grows into deeper, more diffuse exchanges across several issue areas. Conversely, in permissive normative orders, which suffer from a dearth of trust, leaders harbor suspicions about others and avoid placing themselves at the mercy of their peers unless they can identify common interests, verify commitments are being fulfilled, and retaliate in a manner that makes betrayal unprofitable.[21]

While evidence regarding the tendency of restrictive normative orders to promote reciprocity-based trust is compelling, many questions remain unanswered. Within such orders, how do discrete nodes of partner-specific norms that have developed around mutually trustful dyads affect actor-universal norms at the systemic level of analysis? Is their relationship influenced by the type of dyad? Does the interaction have the same impact on compulsory ("Thou shall do X.") and prohibitive ("Thou shall not do X.") norms? These are just some of the intriguing questions that beckon researchers to begin thinking about norms as nested phenomena infused with important though not widely understood cross-level effects.

In summary, a small but growing body of reproducible evidence suggests that international norms are factors exogenous to any given state that mediate when and how national leaders use their capacity to act. The normative climate of opinion at different points in time frames state behavior and therein shapes the meaning ascribed to it by the performing agent, as well as by external observers. The web of expectations created by the actor-universal norms in a strong, restrictive order add predictability to world politics by providing leaders with inference warrants from which they can make judgments about appropriate behavior in different situations. Yet as significant as actor-universal norms may be, what we have learned during the past decade about relations among democratic polities indicates that the role of partner-specific norms in peace building deserves greater attention in our future research.

One line of investigation with far-reaching policy implications would be to explore the possibility that the spread of these norms may be stimulated by a demonstration effect (Starr 1991). As the proportion of democracies in the world passes a certain threshold, norms of nonviolent conflict resolution may cascade throughout the state system. A critical mass of democratic states, argue Maoz and Russett (1993: 637), might make it possible to construct a restrictive normative order from the bottom up: if enough countries become stable democracies, the standards of permissive behavior that developed when the state system was populated by autocracies could undergo dramatic change. Major democratic states would function as norm entrepreneurs, using their resources, expertise, and moral stature to persuade others that the old order should be replaced by more restrictive norms. Once a sufficient number of states agree, more might follow suit, which would result in a greater percentage of the system's membership embracing the new norms, therein triggering yet another round of adoptions, and so on. Assuming the diffusion pattern follows a step-function model of contagion, when emerging norms spread, they would do so slowly at first, then rapidly, and then slowly again. As Finnemore and Sikkink (1998: 895) suggest, different "logics of action" may come into play at each stage in this process.

Regardless of whether the current wave of democratization will yield the critical mass needed to initiate such a vast systemic transformation, recent findings on the democratic peace present a major challenge to those theorists who are interested in norm formation and decay: How can we unravel the linkages between partner-specific and actor-universal norms. The factors that encourage the rise of the former most likely differ from those that cause them to evolve into the latter. What domestic and international conditions breed norms that curb the use of force between the members of a particular identity group? How do they propagate outside of that group? Researchers have identified some key pieces in this cross-level puzzle; nevertheless, work remains to be done on assembling them into a dynamic model from which we can deduce fresh, nonobvious propositions for further testing. It is a task that returns us to our roots as peace researchers, for, as Nie (1991: 17) reminds us, "moving back and forth between the generation of new data and the reanalysis of existing observation played off against prevailing or proposed models is really what the scientific enterprise is all about."

NOTES

1. Located on the east bank of the Nile approximately 160 miles south of modern Cairo, Amarna was constructed by Amenhotep IV (later known as Akhenaten) to replace Thebes as Egypt's capital. The royal court was returned to Thebes after his death.

2. This predicament is part of a larger definitional morass. Norms regarding acceptable state behavior often are viewed as part of an international political culture. What this means depends on one's notion of culture. Decades ago, 165 definitions were identified for the term, and definitions have proliferated over the intervening years as the expression "political culture" has grown in popularity (Kroeber and Kluckholn 1952; Moore 1952).

For assessments of the problems for theory building arising from the many meanings attributed to political culture, see Lehman (1982) and Pateman (1971). Examples of recent efforts to use culture in international relations theory include Chay (1990), Eriksen and Neumann (1993), Hudson (1997), Lapid and Kratochwil (1996), and the special issue in volume 22 of *Millennium* (1993).

3. One of the most stricking tales of shame buttressing identity norms is the Sophoclean portrayal of Ajax's suicide following his slaughter of a flock of sheep and cattle, which he mistook for the Greek military leaders who had denied him Achilles' armor. The identity that led him to conclude he could not continue to live was bound up in a code of conduct that valued *kleos*, what others said about a warrior. See Williams (1993: 72–74).

4. Occasionally a surge of rule making may occur within a single issue-area. For example, a congress was hosted by Prince Tsai K'ung of Chou in 651 B.C.E. at K'uei-ch'iu that established rules on how Chinese states should treat each other after natural disasters. Similar gatherings were later held in Sung (580 B.C.E.) and Chêng (562 B.C.E.). See Iriye (1968: 33, 45).

5. Almost five centuries earlier, Desiderius Erasmus (1997: 19) made a similar argument: "If you cannot defend your kingdom without violating justice . . . then abdicate." Another example can be found in the *Great Law of Peace*, an elaborate code of behavior handed down orally for centuries among the Mohawk, Oneida, Onondaga, Cayuga, and Seneca nations within the Iroquois Confederacy.

6. Kennan's argument that statecraft is not fit for evaluation in the same terms as daily life has roots in Renaissance political discourse. "The justice, virtue, and probity of the sovereign proceed quite otherwise than those of individuals," wrote Pierre Charron almost four hundred years ago. "They have larger and freer scope on account of the great, weighty, and dangerous charge they bear"(cited in Donaldson, 1988: 213).

7. For reviews of the vast literature on reason of state, see Church (1972) and Meinecke (1965).

8. For an extended discussion of arguments from necessity, see Raymond (1998/99, 1999).

9. Paradoxically, onlookers often revere those whose actions allegedly were unavoidable. For example, de Callières (1963: 43), author of the first systematic treatise on negotiation, admired Monseigneur d'Ossat for being "firm as a rock when necessity demands."

10. Recently, the Vietnam War has been interpreted by one writer as a war driven by the tide of geostrategic necessities. See Lind (1999: 284).

11. In a similar vein, von Pufendorf (1749: 200) argued that "no other obligation ought to outweigh . . . [one's] own safety."

12. For examples of legal treatises that support the permissive norms of military necessity, see Lueder (1898) and Rivier (1896). Military strategists such as Bissing, Blüme, Disfurth, Goltz, Hindenburg, and Moltke also condoned military necessity (Garner 1920).

13. This phrase was used by the activist Lev Kopolev to justify brutal acts perpetrated by the Stalinist regime in the Soviet Union (cited in Moynahan 1994: 119).

14. Among the guidelines that typify restrictive orders are just cause (acting in self-defense), right intentions (fighting to achieve peace rather than out of hatred of the enemy), immediacy (facing imminent danger), last resort (all other means of conflict resolution have been tried), discrimination (respect for noncombatant immunity), proportionality (the good achieved must outweigh the harm done), and responsibility (the decision

must be made by a competent authority who is subject to judicial review). The British were cognizant of these guidelines when they defended their 1807 bombardment of Copenhagen by claiming that the danger they faced "was certain, urgent and extreme." Similarly, in the *Caroline* incident of 1837, Secretary of State Daniel Webster defended U.S. actions by characterizing the situation as "instant, overwhelming, leaving no choice of means and no moment for deliberation" (Taoka, 1978: 39).

15. See *The Trial of Alfred Felix Alwyn Krupp von Bohlen und Halbach and Eleven Others* (Law Reports of Trials of War Criminals, 10, 1949), 139.

16. Sometimes rules regulate the sequence of certain settlement procedures, with deliberate pauses built into the progression. For a presentation of different sequences that have been crafted to aid in settling interstate disputes, see Habicht (1931: 985).

17. The number of empirical studies on the relationship between democracy and war has grown rapidly over the past decade. For a summary and interpretation of the findings presented in these works, see Chan (1997).

18. United States Department of State, *Current Policy No. 1293* (Washington, D.C.: Bureau of Public Affairs, 1990). Of course, George Bush has not been the only national leader to employ legal rhetoric to justify his foreign policy actions. As any hard-boiled realist will attest, denouncing the improprieties of others is often accompanied by a posture of legal self-permissiveness. An example can be seen in Ronald Reagan, who once vowed "when the rules of international behavior are violated, our policy will be one of swift and effective retribution." Cited in the *New York Times,* 3 February 1981, p. A13. Disturbed by the case Nicaragua brought against the United States on 9 April 1984, Reagan subsequently withdrew U.S. acceptance of compulsory jurisdiction under the Optional Clause of the Statute of the International Court of Justice (Article 36[2]). In so doing, the United States abjured what Kim (1997) calls "normative power"—that is, the ability to champion and legitimize a restrictive code of international conduct.

19. For a summary of research findings from the enormous body of literature on reciprocity, see Patchen (1998).

20. Trust is a complex, multidimensional concept. When trusting someone, we believe (1) what they say is true, (2) they have concern for our welfare and are moved by the knowledge that we are counting on them, (3) they possess the capability to follow through on their pledges, and (4) there is consistency between their words and deeds. The stronger our beliefs along each of these dimensions, the greater our overall trust. To put it in more technical terms, trust can be conceptualized as a point on a distribution of expectations that represents the level of *subjective* probability with which we assess that the other party will perform a particular act. The probability score can range from a value of 1.00 (complete trust) to 0.00 (complete distrust), and it is the product of our evaluation of the other party's credibility, goodwill, competence, and reliability. Thus, trusting is a matter of degree, and the magnitude of trust required for political leaders to accept different kinds of international agreements varies. The greater the potential injury arising from an act of betrayal, the higher a leader's subjective probability score must be to reach a significant agreement with another state. See Jones (1996: 14), Mishra (1996: 264–69), and Gambetta (1988: 218).

21. Of course, trust cannot eradicate conflict. The temptation to behave opportunistically can arise, even with full trust, when the anticipated time horizon of a relationship is short (Hwang and Burgers 1999). Sometimes trust can encourage inflexible aspirations and contentious tactics. A trusted state with a history of accommodation may be expected to give in to the demands of others whenever its position does not seem firm (Pruitt and Rubin 1986: 38).

14

Democracy

On the Level(s), Does Democracy Correlate with Peace?

James Lee Ray

One thing that "we know about war" with unusual, or even unparalleled, confidence is that it almost never involves two democratic states in conflicts against each other. Over a decade ago, even before most of the recent flurry of "well over 100 theoretical and empirical papers" (Thompson and Tucker 1997: 428) on the democratic peace proposition appeared in print, Levy (1988: 662) declared that "the absence of war between democracies comes as close as anything we have to an empirical law in international relations." After the evidence on that point had been augmented considerably, Levy (1994: 325) asserted even more confidently that "the idea that democracies almost never go to war with each other is now commonplace. The skeptics are in retreat and the proposition has acquired a nearly law-like status." At about the same time, U.S. deputy assistant secretary of defense Joseph Kruzel (1994: 180) observed that "the notion that democracies do not go to war with each other . . . has had a substantial impact on policy."[1] In short, "the notion that democracies rarely wage wars against one another has gained remarkable acceptance in scholarly and policy circles" (Solingen 1996b: 139).

This chapter will address the question of whether democracy correlates with peace or, in more general terms, whether there is a correlation between regime type and international conflict. It will focus particularly on the more interesting question of whether there is a nonspurious relationship between democracy and peace on the national, dyadic, or systemic level of analysis. The term *level of analysis* refers to the unit of analysis, or the social entity (e.g., single states, pairs of states, or the entire international system) about which a given study offers descriptions, explanations, or predictions. A "nonspurious" relationship is one that is not evidently brought about by some prior third factor that accounts for the variation in both regime type and conflict (Simon 1969: 162). There is little doubt, for example, that pairs of states having alliance ties with *each other* are more likely than states without such alliance ties to get into interstate wars with *each other.* In other words, there is for pairs of states in the international system a correlation between the presence of alliance ties and the subsequent probability of wars between the states in those pairs (Bueno de Mesquita 1981; Ray 1990; Bremer 1992; Maoz and Russett 1992).[2] However, Maoz and Russett (1992), Bremer (1992), and Oneal, Oneal, Maoz, and Russett (1996) all report that if contiguity is controlled for, the positive correlation between alliance ties that states have with each other and the probability that they will get into interstate wars with each other disappears. In fact, it becomes a significant *negative* correlation.[3] In my view, this makes the positive correlation between alliance ties between states and probability of war between those states fundamentally uninteresting, even though there is a rather elaborate theoretical basis for it (Bueno de Mesquita 1981). A substantial amount of empirical evidence suggests that states that form alliances with one another, and those that fight wars against each other tend to be geographically proximate to each other. So, there is no persuasive basis for concluding that alliances between the same states cause them to go to war with each other, even though within pairs of states the presence of alliance ties and the probability of interstate wars are associated with each other in a "significant" way.

THE RELATIONSHIP BETWEEN DEMOCRACY AND PEACE: THE NATIONAL LEVEL OF ANALYSIS

Everybody knows that while democratic states do not fight interstate wars against each other, democratic states are as war-prone as states in general. Maoz and Russett (1993: 624) assert categorically that "there is something in the internal makeup of democratic states that prevents them from fighting one another *despite the fact that they are not less conflict prone than nondemocracies"* (emphasis in the original). One can find equally categorical statements, by Gleditsch (1992: 369–70), Starr (1992: 43), and Bueno de Mesquita and Lalman (1992: 148), among many others.

But everybody may be wrong. In fact, "the nearly unanimous consensus in the literature on the democratic peace proposition that democracies, though unlikely to fight each other, are in general as conflict and war prone as undemocratic states rests on rather shaky empirical ground" (Ray 1995: 20). A series of studies from the 1960s and 1970s (East and Gregg 1967; Salmore and Hermann 1969; Zinnes and Wilkenfeld 1971; East and Hermann 1974; this generation of evidence is nicely summarized in Sullivan 1976), a book by Geller (1985), as well as evidence presented by Maoz and Abdolali (1989), Morgan and Schwebach (1992), Bueno de Mesquita and Lalman (1992), and Bremer (1992) all suggest that democratic states are less conflict-prone than autocratic states, period, and not just in their relationships with each other.

Substantial more recent evidence reinforces that conclusion. Siverson (1995) reports that "wars initiated by democratic leaders are significantly less lethal than wars initiated by non-democratic leaders." Reanalyzing data used by Weede (1984) to come to a different conclusion, Benoit (1996: 654) argues that analytical techniques more appropriate to the data at hand will reveal that "democracies were significantly less likely, on average, to be involved in international wars during the 1960s and 1970s than less free states." Rousseau, Gelpi, Reiter, and Huth (1996b: 527) conclude that "democracies are less likely to initiate crises with all other types of states." Huth (1996b: 187) asserts that his findings do not support the "conventional wisdom that democratic states are only more pacific in their political and military relations with other democracies." Instead, his findings suggest that "increasing levels of democracy reduce escalation and promote peaceful conflict resolution consistently, regardless of who the adversary was in a territorial dispute." Gleditsch and Hegre (1997: 10) report that "during the Cold War, democracies participated significantly *less frequently* in war than nondemocracies"; further, that "at least in the modern era, democracies would appear to *initiate* violence rarely," that "the seven most violent interstate wars in the entire COW period . . . were all initiated by nondemocracies"; and, finally, that "if democracies participate at all, they tend to be on the reactive side, at least in the major wars" (13). And Enterline (1998c: 804) provides evidence that "independent of the political composition of their neighborhoods, new democratic regimes [as opposed to new autocratic regimes] are less likely to initiate disputes against neighboring states."[4] So, when Rummel (1995, 1997) argues that "Democracies *Are* Less Warlike Than Other Regimes," he no longer stands in isolation as he did for so many years after he first made this argument (Rummel 1979).

Furthermore, it should be said in favor of this evidence regarding a national-level correlation between regime type and international conflict that it supports theoretical notions making it possible to integrate it within whole sets of related propositions. That democracies are less war-prone, period, and not just in their relationships with each other, for example is one of thirty-three interrelated propositions about the causes of international conflict (and twenty-one additional propositions regarding the phasing, ending, and description of international conflict) arising out of "intentional humanism," the theoretical framework developed in Rummel's *Understanding Conflict and War.*[5] In a specific form involving the number of deaths they experience in wars they initiate, this national-level correlation between regime type and international conflict also can be integrated into a growing list of propositions arising from a theoretical framework currently being developed by Bueno de Mesquita et al. (Bueno de Mesquita and Siverson 1996, 1997; Bueno de Mesquita, Morrow, Siverson, and Smith 1999). This framework, to be discussed in more detail in a later section, focuses on the impact of the size of the body of people selecting the government within a regime (the "selector-ate"), as well as the size of the winning coalitions that emerge (the "win set").[6]

However, the current status of our knowledge about the national-level relation-ship between regime type and conflict makes it appropriate (and perhaps some-what sobering) to acknowledge that the consensus regarding it is distinctly less firm than that regarding the dyadic-level relationship to be discussed later. One reason for this is that it is easy to think of lots of exceptions to any alleged rule to the effect that democratic states are more peaceful or less conflict-prone than autocratic states. Democratic states clearly can be aggressive, as has been the United States, for example, in taking over much of the North American continent and as were British and French imperialists. The evidence regarding this proposi-tion is less clear-cut than that regarding the absence of interstate wars between democratic states, for example. One reason for this is that the proposition "Dem-ocratic states are less conflict prone than autocratic states," and many apparently equivalent propositions, are upon inspection quite ambiguous. Assume away all the problems having to do with defining and measuring "democracy." That leaves a wide variety of plausible meanings of "less conflict-prone." That phrase can refer to the frequency of disputes, or crises, or wars (interstate, international, and/or "extrasystemic"). It can refer to disputes, crises, or wars (of the several different types) that democratic states initiate, or those in which they are the tar-get, or those in which they join, or all three. "Less conflict-prone" may also al-lude to the degree of violence associated with the disputes, crises, or wars they initiate, or are the targets of initiators, or join. Once one takes into account all the permutations of types of conflicts (disputes, crises, or wars), roles (initiator, target, joiner), and frequency versus degree or intensity of conflict, prudence sug-gests that one recognize immediately that in fact a whole range of propositions is at issue here. Furthermore, it is quite apparent that the evidence regarding each of the propositions falling within that range is inconsistent.

Confusion traceable to these different interpretations of the phrase *less con-flict-prone* or *less war-prone* has plagued discussion of the proposition in ques-tion right from the beginning. Rummel (1983) made a claim regarding the rela-tive conflict-proneness of democratic states, period (rather than only in their relationships with each other), which was contested by Chan (1984) and Weede (1984). Rummel (1983) himself focused *primarily* on relative degrees of violence in the conflicts involving democratic states, while Chan (1984) and Weede (1984) focused exclusively on the frequencies of conflict.[7] Rummel has complained ever since (with some justification, I believe) that neither Chan nor Weede really ad-dressed the national-level proposition he had in mind. What is clear to me, at least, is that blanket statements to the effect that "democratic states are just as conflict- (or war-) prone as states in general" are not supported by the evidence. This is not to say that it is compellingly clear, to repeat, that democratic states are less conflict- (or war-) prone, period, than autocratic states. But it is quite clear that there is some substantial evidence in favor of the proposition that democratic states are less conflict- (or war-) prone, using definitions and measures of conflict-proneness that are plausible intuitively, and, furthermore, that this national-level proposition can be supported theoretically.

However, very little evidence exists regarding the crucial question of whether the national-level correlation between regime type and conflict-proneness might be a spurious one. Perhaps advocates of this proposition have been faced with such an overwhelming consensus that they are wrong that they have focused almost exclusively on establishing the simple existence of a systematic relationship between democracy and peace on the national level of analysis. They have not, at any rate, devoted much effort to an examination of the impact of possibly confounding variables. It could be, for example, that wealthy regimes tend to be democratic, and at peace, so that the two are related only by virtue of their common origins in wealth or economic development. But I would concur with Gleditsch and Hegre (1997), who conclude their review of research on the national-level relationship between regime type and conflict-proneness with the observation that "few if any studies control for third variables in a convincing manner."[8]

Probably the most effective, and best publicized, published attack on the democratic peace proposition is that by Mansfield and Snyder (1995a, 1995b). The quantitatively oriented tribe of international politics specialists may owe a debt of gratitude to the authors of this work (1995b), because I suspect it contains the first quantitative analysis ever to appear in the prominent journal *Foreign Affairs*. It is also noteworthy, perhaps, that this particular article does not launch a frontal attack on the democratic peace proposition in its dyadic form. Mansfield and Snyder offer no argument against the idea that stable, democratic regimes have not and are not likely to fight international wars against each other. Their claim (pertaining to the national level of analysis) is rather that states *in transition* to democracy are particularly war-prone. To some extent, this argument simply reinforces the idea espoused by Doyle (1986) as well as Russett (1993), for example, that only stable democracy is likely to have an important or dependable pacifying effect (and, they both insist, only on the dyadic level of analysis). But the thesis of Mansfield and Snyder (1995a, 1995b) goes well beyond that point. They insist that not only does new or emerging democracy fail to exert a pacifying effect; in their view, newly emerging democracy is positively dangerous, making states involved in such transitions more war-prone than either stable autocracies or stable democracies.

Mansfield and Snyder make a strong argument and defend it ably (Mansfield and Snyder 1996). Nevertheless, I suspect on general principle that it is no more likely that the proposition "Democratizing states are more war-prone, period," can be dependably or consistently supported in all its possible permutations than can the proposition asserting that "Democratic states are just as war- (or conflict-) prone as autocratic states, period," for all the reasons already discussed. The arguments and evidence provided by Enterline (1996, 1998b, 1998c), as well as Thompson and Tucker (1997) increase my confidence in that assertion. Moreover, as Weede (1996, 182) points out, even assuming that democracy does have an important pacifying effect, "it does not follow that new democracies invariably reduce the risk of war. . . . Imagine an autocracy surrounded only by autocracies. If such a country became democratic, this should not at all reduce the risk of war. . . . The general point is that some geopolitical configurations should reduce and others might enhance the peace benefits of democratization." Weede's argument here is certainly plausible. The impact of democratization may well depend on whether it increases the political similarity or the political distance between itself and those states with which it interacts most intensely, which for many states will be those in its geographic proximity. In other words, it is not the democratization itself that has the most important direct effect on a state's conflict-proneness but rather its political distance from its neighbors, or the difference between the degree of democracy it has achieved, and the degree to which its neighbors are democratic. Oneal and Russett (1997: abstract) provide systematic empirical evidence covering the years from 1950 to 1985 that supports their conclusion that "states undergoing a process of democratization are more likely to experience conflict only if they have autocratic neighbors." Additional evidence to support this conclusion can also be found in Oneal and Ray (1997), Bremer (1996), Maoz (2001), as well as Gleditsch and Hegre (1997).

THE RELATIONSHIP BETWEEN DEMOCRACY AND PEACE: THE DYADIC LEVEL OF ANALYSIS

Everybody knows that democratic states, although they are as war-prone as other states in general, never fight wars against each other and, furthermore, that this perfect dyadic level correlation between regime type and conflict is not spurious (i.e., brought about by some prior third factor that produces both the democracy and the peace). Bremer (1993b: 246), having conducted a thorough examination of the possibility that the dyadic-level relationship between democracy and peace is spurious, concludes that

> there may still exist some conflict-reducing variable which is being deprived of its proper credit because its explanatory power is being falsely credited to democracy. My conclusion, based on results reported here, is that this is unlikely, and our time would be better spent on deeper analyses of the relationship between democracy and conflict than on searching further for the phantom factor masquerading as democracy.

Similarly, Gleditsch and Hegre (1997: 291) conclude that "even if the relationship is 'very strong' rather than perfect, the search for single third variables seems unpromising."

Is it possible that everybody is wrong about this correlation, too, both about its existence on the bivariate level and in the confident conclusion that it is not spurious? Ray (1995) argues that the two most important sources of doubt about the existence of a simple bivariate correlation between democracy and peace stem from the statistical rarity of democracies and wars, as well as the difficulty of defining democracy. Estimations of the number of wars among democratic states must rely on thresholds such as "7" on the Polity III democracy scale (Jaggers and Gurr 1995). That scale is sufficiently complex that neither 7 nor any other threshold has any clear, intuitive, or theoretically significant meaning. The proposition that there is a significant relationship between regime type and international conflict is most vulnerable to criticism that wars and democracies have been so rare historically that it is not possible to be very confident about the "significance" of whatever correlation may be found between democracy and peace on the dyadic level of analysis, even if that correlation is perfect. The interdependence of the observations compounds this problem.[9]

A good beginning is made in the effort to establish that the correlation between regime type and conflict is not spurious in Maoz and Russett (1992). Potentially confounding variables are entered into analyses one at a time, rather than all together simultaneously, making it much easier to discern what their individual effects might be on the relationship between regime type and conflict.

Nevertheless, Maoz and Russett (1992) do report that a control for political stability does eliminate the relationship between democracy and peace. "Stable states are far less likely to fight one another than expected, regardless of their regime type. This suggests that political stability, rather than or in addition to regime type, may account for the low rate of disputes among democracies." One might assume that subsequent to this discovery, Maoz and Russett could be expected to investigate further whether political stability accounts entirely for the relationship between democracy and peace. But neither Maoz and Russett (1993), nor Oneal et al. (1996), Oneal and Russett (1997), Oneal and Ray (1997), and Russett, Oneal and Davis (1998), include political stability as a control variable in analyses also including democracy as an explanatory factor. So we cannot tell from these analyses whether democracy would remain as a "significant" predictor of conflict in the face of a control for political stability.

This is not to suggest that there is some kind of conspiracy to hide the fact that the correlation between democracy and peace is a spurious one. In the first place, in a chapter written with Maoz that in many respects is identical to an article coauthored with Maoz (i.e., Maoz and Russett 1993), Russett (with Maoz 1993: 87) does present an analysis that includes political stability as a control variable, while retaining joint democracy as a predictor variable. In this analysis, joint democracy continues to have a "significant" relationship to conflict involvement.

In fact, it is unlikely that political stability, on logical and theoretical grounds, is actually a viable candidate for the role of confounding variable. Maoz and Russett (1992) do not argue that political stability leads to democracy and peace and that therefore the correlation between democracy and peace is spurious. Rather, they argue that "democracies are far more stable than anocracies or autocracies" (Maoz and Russett 1992; see also Gurr 1974). This suggests that political stability is a variable that intervenes in the process leading from democracy to peace, rather than a confounding variable that leads to both democracy and peace. This would mean in turn that the relationship between democracy and peace is indirect, rather than spurious.

In their follow-up study, Maoz and Russett (1993) include a table entitled "Effects of Joint Democracy and Potentially Confounding Factors on Conflict Involvement and Escalation." The factors included in that table, in addition to joint democracy, are wealth, growth, alliances, contiguity, and capability ratios (but not political stability). Wealth and economic growth might plausibly lead to democracy, as well as peace, so they are legitimate candidates for confounding variables. However, democracy may also lead to wealth and growth, in which case those two factors are again intervening as opposed to confounding variables. (For at least partially contradictory recent research results on this question, see Burkhart and Lewis-Beck 1994; Londegran and Poole 1996; Przeworski and Limongi 1997.) On balance, it is fair to wonder whether wealth or growth are potential candidates for confounding factors with respect to the relationship between democracy and peace.

But are alliance ties potentially a confounding factor in the sense that they bring about both democracy and peace? Does being allied make two states more likely to be democratic, as well as more likely to have peaceful relationships? It seems more likely that being democratic makes two states more likely to be allied (see Siverson and Emmons 1991; Simon and Gartzke 1996; Thompson and Tucker 1997). So, like political stability, alliance ties seem a more likely candidate for an intervening rather than a confounding factor with respect to the relationship between democracy and peace. According to King, Keohane, and Verba (1994: 173), *"we should not control for an explanatory variable that is in part a consequence of our key explanatory variable"* (emphasis in the original). They advise against this because an intervening variable will, if controlled for, as will a confounding variable, eliminate the relationship of major interest, but with very different consequences for conclusions about that relationship. If a potentially confounding variable is controlled for, and the major relationship of interest is eliminated, then the conclusion should be that the original relationship of interest is spurious and relatively uninteresting. If a potentially intervening variable is controlled for and the relationship of major interest disappears, then the warranted conclusion is that we have a better understanding of the relationship of major interest. That is, we have some more detailed idea about the causal process leading from the explanatory factor to the outcome in which we are interested.

The final two potentially confounding factors included for analysis by Maoz and Russett (1993) are contiguity and capability ratios. Neither of these two are theoretically plausible in the role of potential confounding variable with respect to the relationship between democracy and peace among pairs of states. Does being contiguous make two states more likely to be jointly democratic? It may be the case that one state next to a democratic state is more likely to be democratic, but that is a different matter. In other words, two propositions are at issue here that appear to be similar but are in fact quite different. One proposition is that any state next to a democratic state is more likely to be democratic itself. Since democracy may have a tendency to diffuse from one state to its geographic neighbors (Starr 1991), this proposition is plausible. The second proposition is that two states next to each other are more likely to be jointly democratic. Why any two states that are next to each other might be more likely to be jointly democratic than pairs of states that are not contiguous is not at all clear, at least to me.[10] And it is the second proposition implied by Maoz and Russett's categorization of contiguity as a factor that might confound the relationship between democracy and peace. Similarly, there would seem to be no plausible basis for an expectation that the ratio of the capabilities of pairs of states will have an impact on their regime type or the likelihood that they will be jointly democratic.

So, in Maoz and Russett's list of potentially confounding variables, there are two that might be confounding (except to the extent that they are also products of democracy), one that is more likely to be intervening, and two that are more plausibly categorized as irrelevant to the question of whether the relationship between democracy and peace is spurious, because they are almost certainly not related to regime type at all. Putting all these factors together in the same model for analysis might, because of the statistical (even if not causal or theoretically plausible) correlations among them, produce confusing results.

Potential confusion could be increased by Oneal et al. (1995: 18), who include interdependence in the form of trading relationships as another control variable but exclude wealth on the grounds that wealth never proves significant when trade is in their equation. The introduction of trade as a control variable has a tendency to eliminate the significance of the relationship between democracy and peace. (This impact is reduced in Oneal and Ray 1997, with a different measure of joint democracy and the introduction of "political distance," or differences in degrees of democracy or autocracy, as an explanatory factor.) But is trade a plausible candidate for a confounding factor? Is it not rather a potentially intervening variable? Bliss and Russett (1998) show that joint democracy does seem to encourage higher levels of international trade. And since we know that trade is affected by alliance ties (Gowa and Mansfield 1993; Gowa 1994), what is the impact of introducing these interrelated factors, both of which may intervene in the process leading from democracy to peace?

Admittedly, most of these questions are of a type that would lead us to suspect that the analysts in question have come to an unwarranted conclusion that the relationship between democracy and peace is spurious. That is, the analyses in question do seem to have been structured in such a way as to make it more likely to come to produce erroneous, negative conclusions regarding the potentially pacifying impact of democracy, rather than to foster overly optimistic conclu-

Chapter 14

sions about that impact. Moreover, as we have already noted, in the view of some, there is no point in being concerned that a relationship that is so close to being "perfect" might be spurious (Gleditsch and Hegre 1997).

However, the relationship between joint democracy in pairs of states and peace between them is a *long* way from being perfect. In fact, it is such a modest relationship according to conventional ways of evaluating such things that it is something of a minor miracle that it has yet to be swallowed up entirely by the sea of control variables into which it is typically submerged. Consider Tables 14.1, 14.2, and 14.3, which show in bivariate tabular form the basic relationship between democracy and peace as it emerges from the data relied on in three important works focusing on that relationship: Bremer (1992), Russett (1993), and Russett (1995). The relationships shown in all three cases are "perfect" in the sense that joint democracy is shown to be a sufficient condition for peace to prevail in every single case. This is reflected in Yule's Q coefficients, which are 1.0. (Yule's Q will always be 1.0 if any one cell in such a table $= 0$.) However, the phi coefficients (equivalent to Pearson's r for 2×2 tables) are only 0.01, 0.01, and 0.07, respectively. Like most of the analytical techniques that have been applied to data regarding this relationship, the phi coefficient also reflects the number of observations for which joint democracy is absent and war does *not* break out.

A one-way or asymmetrical measure of association such as Yule's Q is arguably more appropriate for ascertaining the validity of the democratic peace proposition. No advocate of the proposition has ever suggested that joint democracy is *necessary* to bring about peace between states. In light of the fact that 99 percent of pairs of states in the world are at peace roughly 99 percent of the time whether or not they are jointly democratic, it would obviously be foolish to offer such a proposition. It is more plausible to assert that joint democracy is *sufficient* to ensure peace between pairs of states, and the analyses in Tables 14.1–14.3 suggest that, in fact, in recent history, there are no exceptions to that rule. Yet I believe that the majority of analyses evaluating the validity of the democratic peace proposition (or the relative predictive power of joint democracy versus other explanatory factors) have counted all observations in which joint democracy is ab-

Table 14.1 Relationship between Regime Type and Interstate War for Pairs of States, 1816–1965 (annual observations)

War Initiated?	Jointly Democratic	Not Jointly Democratic
No	21,644	177,844
Yes	0[a]	85

$\chi^2 = 10.34, p < .01$; phi $= 0.01$; Yule's $Q = 1.0$; $N = 199, 573$.

Source: Based on data from Bremer (1992: 326).

[a] Bremer does report one war between democracies, between France and Thailand at a time when France was controlled by the Vichy regime. He acknowledges that this is an anomaly produced by his coding procedures.

Table 14.2 Relationship between Regime Type and Interstate War for Pairs of States, 1946–86 (annual observations)

War Initiated?	Jointly Democratic	Not Jointly Democratic
No	3,878	25,171
Yes	0	32

$\chi^2 = 4.93, p < .05$; phi $= 0.01$; Yule's $Q = 1.0$; $N = 29,081$.

Source: Based on data from Russett (1993: 21).

sent but in which peace nevertheless prevails as evidence tending to discredit the democratic peace proposition.[11] This may be an issue to keep in mind if and when it is claimed that the dyadic-level relationship between democracy and peace is spurious.

What should be said of the quality of the theory supporting this dyadic-level relationship between democracy and peace? A widespread opinion asserts that the absence of war between democratic states is merely an empirical observation with no basis in a well-developed or convincing theoretical explanation. But Rummel's (1977, 1979) *Understanding Conflict and War* devotes three whole volumes to the development of an epistemological and theoretical basis for the democratic peace proposition, finally presented in the fourth volume (see Ray 1998.) A formal model from which the democratic peace proposition can be derived is presented in *War and Reason* by Bueno de Mesquita and Lalman (1992). In *Grasping the Democratic Peace*, Russett (1993) develops a cultural or normative explanation of the democratic peace idea into a set of nine specific, interrelated propositions. These focus on the impact of norms about conflict resolution that will be developed in bargaining about international conflicts and how these will affect interactions between democratic states. Russett also provides a detailed exposition of a structural/institutional model that focuses on the impact of checks and balances present in most democracies, as well as the effects of decentralized power and the need for public support on bargaining among democratic states.

Solingen (1996a: 81–84) provides an informative summary of theoretical work

Table 14.3 Relationship between Regime Type and Interstate War for Pairs of States, 1946–86 (regime dyads)

War Initiated?	Jointly Democratic	Not Jointly Democratic
No	169	1,045
Yes	0	37

$\chi^2 = 5.96, p < .02$; phi $= 0.07$; Yule's $Q = 1.0$; $N = 1,251$.

Source: Based on data from Russett (1995: 174).

regarding the democratic peace proposition, highlighting five main themes. She points out that in theory, democracy has pacifying effects on relationships between democratic states because of their domestic legitimacy and accountability, their institutional checks and balances, the transparency of their political processes, and the resulting lower costs of "regime" creation, the relative ease democratic states have in making credible commitments, and, finally, the relatively sensitivity within democratic polities to human and material costs of war.

Some recent research (e.g., Oneal and Russett 1997; Russett, Oneal, and Davis 1998) focuses theoretical attention on the importance of trading ties and mutual memberships in international organizations on relationships among democratic states.[12] A formal model developed by Bueno de Mesquita, Morrow, Siverson, and Smith (1999) regarding the connections between internal domestic politics and foreign policies as well as international relationships begins with the fundamental assumption that the highest priority of political leaders is to stay in power. This model highlights the impact of the size of the winning coalition in democracies compared to that in the typical autocracy. Democratic leaders must satisfy relatively large winning coalitions (or "win sets"). They cannot command a sufficiently large pool of resources to satisfy their win sets with private goods or individual payoffs. General policy successes, or failures, are relatively important to democratic leaders. Autocratic leaders, in contrast, can retain power, even in the wake of significant policy failures, such as a loss in an international war, by paying off members of their relatively small win sets, or governing coalitions, with tax breaks, receipts from official corruption, or economic and political rewards. This makes democratic leaders more cautious about launching wars they might lose.

In addition, democratic states are particularly formidable opponents in international wars (Lake 1992; Stam 1996). Furthermore, democratic leaders are in fact more likely to lose power in the wake of a lost war than are autocratic leaders (Bueno de Mesquita and Siverson 1995). In short, democratic states avoid wars against each other for reasons based ultimately on the desire of their elected leaders to keep themselves in power. This is not, it is important to note, because public opinion is so unerringly opposed to bellicose policies. Public opinion in democracies is obviously not pacifically inclined on a consistent basis.[13] What is important, rather, is that democratic leaders can accurately anticipate that public opinion will react negatively to a lost war and that they will be hard-pressed to maintain themselves in power after such a policy failure.

In building their model on a basic assumption that "political leaders in democracies, autocracies, military juntas, monarchies, and any other form of government all are motivated by the same universal interest: they desire to remain in office" (Bueno de Mesquita et al. 1999), these authors reinforce arguments made by Rummel (1977: 109, 149) and Ray (1995: 39–40). Furthermore, this assumption is arguably more fundamental and general than the standard realist or neorealist assumption that states seek power or security (Morgenthau 1967; Waltz 1979). While conceding that state leaders are likely to be motivated in important

part by the goals of power and security, the emphasis on their even more fundamental desire to stay in power "provides theoretical purchase on the extent to
which political leaders involved in international interactions must play a 'two-
level game' " (Ray 1999: 24).[14] In other words, current theoretical work on the
relationship between democratic peace can take into account the impact of domestic political considerations on foreign policies and international politics in an
axiomatic, theoretically coherent fashion. The correlation between democracy
and peace on the dyadic level of analysis is not "an empirical regularity in search
of a theory." On the contrary, current research focusing on that dyadic level relationship relies on an emerging theoretical framework that may prove capable of
incorporating the strengths of the currently predominant realist or neorealist research program, and moving beyond it (Ray 1999).

THE RELATIONSHIP BETWEEN DEMOCRACY AND PEACE:
THE SYSTEM LEVEL OF ANALYSIS

Until very recently, little attention has been paid to the relationship between the
distribution of regime types in the international system and the amount of conflict
in that system. Maoz and Abdolali (1989: 29) did report that "the proportion of
democracies in the system positively affects the number of disputes begun and
underway." Gleditsch and Hegre (1997: 284) offer a possible explanation of this
relationship. "Given the conventional wisdom—that democracies hardly ever
fight each other, but overall participate in war as much as other countries—it
follows logically that the probability of war in a politically mixed dyad must be
higher than the probability of war between two nondemocracies and that the relationship between peace and democracy at the system level must be bell-shaped
(i.e., parabolic)." They also argue that the frequency of war in the system should
peak at that point in which the proportion of democratic states in the system
reaches 50 percent, "at which point half the dyads are mixed; hence any further
democratization must replace a mixed dyad with a pure dyad of one sort or another" (Gleditsch and Hegre 1997: 20). In other words, if mixed dyads are the
most conflict-prone, and adding democracies to the system increases the proportion of mixed dyads to the system, then up to a point the addition of democracies
can be expected to increase the amount of conflict in the system. This would
account, perhaps, for the positive correlation between the proportion of democracies in the system and the number of disputes. Gleditsch and Hegre (1997) also
provide preliminary evidence suggesting that there is a curvilinear relationship
between the proportion of democracies and the amount of conflict in the system,
traceable to the impact of the proportion of democracies on the proportion of
mixed dyads in the system.

But, of course, the relationship between the proportion of democracies in the
system and the proportion of mixed dyads in the system is a mathematical as

opposed to a causal or empirical relationship. That is, the proportion of jointly democratic dyads and the proportion of mixed dyads are arithmetically, rather than causally connected to each other. Jervis (1997: 34) points out that "we cannot understand systems by summing up the characteristics of the parts or the bilateral relations between pairs of them." A corollary of such an argument is that if the system's operation *can* be predicted by a simple summation of characteristics or behavior of its constituent parts, then systemic-level influences are apparently not important, and system-level analyses will under those circumstances add nothing to our knowledge of the behavior or processes in question that cannot be acquired by simple, straightforward arithmetic calculations.

If system-level analyses regarding the relationship between the distribution of regime types and the incidence of conflict in the system are going to add to our knowledge of conflict processes, the theoretical arguments about system-level processes that support them will need to stipulate that the relationships in question are more than just simple summations or extrapolations of relationships on lower levels of analysis. The accompanying system-level analyses will also need to be structured in such a way as to demonstrate that the relationships revealed are not simply the arithmetic function of processes self-contained and entirely accounted for by factors and processes pertaining to lower levels of analysis.

System-level analyses of the relationship between the distribution of regime types in the system such as those by McLaughlin (1996), Senese (1997), Gleditsch and Hegre (1997), and Crescenzi and Enterline (1999) all focus on general, undifferentiated measures of the levels of conflict in the system.[15] For Gleditsch and Hegre (1997: 304), for example, the dependent variable is "the fraction of country years at war to all country years." Crescenzi and Enterline (1999) attempt to account for variation in the percentage of states in the system engaged in war annually. Analyses like these lump together interstate conflicts or wars initiated by democratic *and* autocratic states against similar *or* polar opposite regimes, as well as wars involving third parties targeted by other states of the same or different regime type. They also fail to discriminate between those "joiners" that became involved of their own initiative and those that joined ongoing wars entirely against their preferences (e.g., when Belgium "joined" both world wars). In short, analyses that focus on total, undifferentiated amounts of conflict in the international system are "opaque" in the sense that they obscure entirely answers to the crucial question of who did what to whom. The results of such analyses are difficult at best to interpret in a logically coherent or theoretically meaningful way, especially if the hypotheses in question emphasize fundamental differences between the behavior of democratic and autocratic states.

It is simply not possible, in other words, to infer in a logical or convincing way the existence of a relationship between the distribution of regime types and the incidence of conflict in the system solely from estimates regarding the relative war proneness of mixed dyads. Obviously, changes in the proportions of mixed dyads in the international system will necessarily coincide with changes also in the proportions of jointly democratic and jointly autocratic dyads. Just as obviously, a theory addressing the relationship between the distribution of regime types and the incidence of conflict in the international system would need to deal with the possible impacts of those changes.[16] Perhaps, for example, as democracies become increasingly predominant in the international system, they will provoke augmented hostility from the increasingly outnumbered autocratic states. Perhaps, also, the increasing predominance by democracies will produce increased confidence, assertiveness, or even aggression by them against autocratic states. At the same time, relationships among democracies could become more conflict-prone, as the unifying impact of numerous, powerful, antagonistic autocratic states diminishes. Then, too, the amount of conflict in the system might be affected by the tendency of the increasingly common democratic states to join ongoing wars in support of each other (Raknerud and Hegre 1997), thus increasing the volatility of any wars that do occur. Additionally, the increasingly besieged, outnumbered autocratic states might be encouraged to engage in less conflict and more cooperation among themselves.

Any attempt to make predictions about the impact of changes in the distribution of regime types on levels of conflict in the system would need to take into account the fact that several of these impacts are contradictory and offsetting. Theories aimed at such predictions should take these potentially countervailing effects into account and offer fairly precise estimates regarding their relative strengths. Then, too, states are extremely different in size and importance, so that equal proportions of states in the system being democratic can have drastically different implications for the proportion of the world's resources that are under the control of democratic states.[17] An appreciation of all these complexities should make one skeptical about attempts to interpret the results of any analyses that totally obscure who does what to whom by focusing simply on total amounts of conflict in the system. It may well be necessary to carry out a *series* of analyses regarding the relationship between the distribution of regime types in the system and the amount of conflict within it, with each analysis structured in such a way as to enable analysts and interpreters of the results to discern who is doing what to whom as the distribution of regime types in the system changes.

CONCLUSION

The recent, sustained interest in the democratic peace proposition has evoked parallel curiosity about the relationship between democracy and peace as it might pertain to other than the dyadic level of analysis. It has been repeatedly asserted that although democratic states never or rarely fight wars against each other, they are just as conflict- and war-prone in general as autocratic states. The validity of that national-level proposition is dubious, partly because it is vague. Certainly some recent research has uncovered substantial evidence supporting various versions of the proposition that democratic states are less conflict- or war-prone than states in general, and not just in their relationships with each other. However, there is also substantial evidence that democratic states can be not only war-prone but warlike and quite aggressive in their relationships with autocratic states. In addition, at least some of the empirical tendency for democratic states to be less conflict-prone might be a kind of reflection of the dyadic level relationship between democracy and peace. To the extent that democratic states are less conflict-prone in general than autocratic states merely because of their more pacific relationships with each other, the national-level pattern is of less theoretical interest.

There has been until recently little disagreement regarding the validity of the proposition that democratic states have unusually peaceful relationships with each other. Even with the recent appearance of some dissenters, one answer to the question of what we know about war that is unusually clear, and supported by unusually unambiguous evidence, is that democratic states are unlikely to fight interstate wars against each other. There is also substantial evidence that this dyadic-level relationship between democracy and peace is not spurious. That is, as far as we can tell at this point, there is no third, prior factor that brings about the correlation between democracy and peace in such a way as to make that correlation nothing more than some statistical artifact. Nevertheless, not all of the attempts to evaluate the impact of possibly confounding variables on the relationship between democracy and peace have produced results that are entirely clear in their implications. In addition, some analytical techniques relied on to evaluate the democratic peace proposition fail to take into account its clear implication that joint democracy is sufficient but not necessary to bring about peace in relationships within pairs of states.

Whether or not there are important relationships between the distribution of regime types and the incidence of conflict in the international system remains to be seen. It might seem obvious that if democratic pairs of states are peaceful in their relationships with each other, then increases in the proportion of democratic states in the system will make it more peaceful. However, such a conclusion overlooks what might be countervailing tendencies that could come into play as the proportion of democracies in the system increases. If the system is dominated by autocratic states, adding democracies to it will increase the proportion of mixed pairs within the system and therefore might increase the incidence of conflict and war. In addition, changes in the distribution of regime types in the system might have impacts on relationships among democratic states, between democratic and autocratic states, and among autocratic states, that cannot be anticipated simply by extrapolating from relationships on lower levels of analysis. If we can assume that increases in the proportion of democratic states in the system will not alter conflict propensities among democratic states, we can safely conclude that a universally democratic system will be free of international war. Conclusions beyond that about the impact of changes in the distribution of regime types in the international system may well be unwarranted.

NOTES

1. In Kruzel's (1994: 49) view, "there are very few propositions in international relations that can be articulated this clearly and simply, but when you have one, you can really cut through the clutter of the bureaucratic process and make an impact."

2. Maoz and Russett (1992: 260), for example, report that "we find a positive relationship between alliances and conflict involvement. Allies are far more likely than expected to engage in conflict with one another, and this relationship holds across regime categories." Admittedly, this finding focuses on conflict involvement rather than involvement in international war, but Bremer (1992) reports a positive correlation between alliance ties and war involvement for pairs of states from 1816 to 1965b.

3. Barbieri (1996) reports that with contiguity controlled for, there is no correlation between alliance ties and the probability of war within pairs of states from 1870 to 1938.

4. Since this tendency is "independent of the political composition of their neighborhoods," this means that it is a pattern that applies to democratic states generally, and not just in their relationships with each other.

5. The specific proposition in question is "the more libertarian a state, the less it tends to be involved in violence" (Rummel 1979: 292; see also Ray 1982).

6. It might also be added here that this national-level correlation is a problem for the theoretical framework developed in Bueno de Mesquita and Lalman (1992), as well as the cultural version of the democratic peace proposition offered by Maoz and Russett (1993) and Russett (1993), to the extent that these frameworks imply that democratic states are just as war-prone in general as other kinds of states.

7. "Although Rummel's . . . hypothesis refers to an ordinal or interval data relationship, I will dichotomize both my independent and dependent variables" (Chan 1984: 621). "Rummel . . . relied for the most part on a foreign conflict intensity scale. . . . I shall focus on war only" (Weede 1984: 654). By this Weede means he used a simple dichotomous, two-category measure of war involvement, equal to 0 for observations where no war occurred and 1 for those observations in which a war did occur.

8. The exception to the rule they mention is Schjolset (1996). It is also possible that a national-level correlation between democracy and peace is brought about mostly as a kind of reflection of the tendency of democratic states to have peaceful relationships with each other. In other words, perhaps democratic states do become involved in less conflict than autocratic states simply because they face a smaller pool of potential antagonists than autocratic states, each of whom tend to get involved in conflicts with democratic as well as autocratic counterparts.

9. Significant progress has been made in dealing with some of the more technical aspects of this problem. See Raknerud and Hegre (1997) and Beck, Katz, and Tucker (1998).

10. The two propositions pertain to different units, or levels of analysis. The first proposition pertains to individual states, whose regime type is predicted to be determined to some extent by the character of regimes next to them. The second proposition pertains to pairs of states.

11. Most and Starr (1989: 57) argue that in evaluating an hypothesis such as Bueno de Mesquita's (1981) that positive expected utility is necessary (but not sufficient) for war initiation to take place, the cases in which positive expected utility occurs but no war initiation takes place are irrelevant. An analogous argument would assert that the large number

of cases in which joint democracy is absent but peace nevertheless prevails is similarly irrelevant to an evaluation of the democratic peace proposition.

12. Contrasting evidence regarding the relationship between trade and peace can be found in Barbieri (1996a, forthcoming). The debate on this relationship continues in Barbieri and Schneider (1999) and Oneal and Russett (1999).

13. In addition, a pacifistic public opinion may make a state more rather than less war-prone (Bueno de Mesquita and Lalman 1990).

14. "When national leaders must win ratification . . . from their constituents for an international agreement, their negotiating behavior reflects the simultaneous imperatives of both a domestic political game and an international game" (Putnam 1988: abstract).

15. In some analyses, Maoz (2001) also uses general measures, such as the number of disputes taking place in the system on an annual basis.

16. To their credit, Gleditsch and Hegre (1997) are aware of this problem. They stipulate that their conclusions about the impact of changes in the proportion of mixed dyads in the system are based on the assumption that the probabilities of war among democracies, and among autocracies, remain constant.

17. If, for example, 98 percent of the states in the world are democratic, but the only two percent of autocratic states left are China and India, the system might still be extremely war-prone.

PART IV

LESSONS AND CONCLUSIONS

15

Reflections on the Scientific Study of War

Jack S. Levy

The chapters in this volume demonstrate what has become increasingly clear to most of those engaged in the systematic study of international conflict: we have made significant progress in the analysis of the causes of war and the conditions of peace over the last two decades, as a result of improved theoretical frameworks, research designs, and statistical techniques. At the same time, there have been important changes in the empirical world that we want to explain, and these changes have also affected the study of war and peace.

My aim in this brief chapter is to identify some of the more notable developments in the scientific study of war. I emphasize the movement away from a preoccupation with the great powers, the shift from the systemic level to more emphasis on dyadic-level interactions and on societal-level explanatory variables, and the increasing complexity of our theories of international conflict.[1]

One trend concerns the empirical domain of our investigations. As a field, we have shifted from a long-standing concentration on the great powers to more attention to conflicts among and within smaller states in the world system. This shift is the result of the end of the Cold War and of the bipolar rivalry that dominated much strategic thinking during the last four decades, the collapse of the Soviet Union and the Soviet empire, and the proliferation of interstate wars between smaller states in the system and especially civil wars within them (Holsti 1996).

Many of these conflicts are ethnonational conflicts or "identity wars" that are fought between communal groups rather than between states and that often cut across state boundaries. Although for years the analysis of ethnonational conflicts tended to be descriptive and idiographic, in the last few years scholars working in this area have become more systematic and rigorous in terms of data analysis and formalization (Gurr 1993; Licklider 1995; Holsti 1996; Carment and James 1997; Fearon and Laitin 1996). This change has been facilitated by the development of new databases that include communal groups and other nonterritorial actors as well as states (Wallensteen and Solenberg 1998; Marshall 1999; Wayman, Sarkees, and Singer 1997), in recognition that conventional conceptualizations of warfare need to be modified.

Another significant trend has been the shift away from the systemic level in the analysis of war. This takes two forms. One is a greater interest in explaining dyadic-level behavior as opposed to systemic-level patterns.[2] The other is a greater interest in societal-level variables in the explanation of state foreign policies and dyadic-level interactions.

A number of reasons explain this growing interest in dyadic-level behavior. Scholars have come to realize that some of the key causal arguments that had previously been associated with conventional systemic-level models are better specified at the dyadic level. Many of the causal arguments invoked in support of both the power parity hypothesis and the power preponderance hypothesis, for example, are essentially dyadic in nature, though these hypotheses are often confounded with systemic-level balance of power and power transition theories (Levy 1989b: 232). Similarly, although hypotheses on the relationship between economic interdependence and war are sometimes formulated at the systemic level (Mansfield 1994), many of the theoretical arguments that are advanced in support of these hypotheses refer to commercial or financial interdependence between two particular adversaries and the presumed negative impact of war on the benefits from economic interdependence. Thus, many hypotheses on economic interdependence and war are better specified at the dyadic level (Barbieri 1996a; Oneal and Russett 1997), and we should recognize that dyadic-level causal linkages cannot be automatically applied to the systemic level.

Another consideration behind the shift to the dyadic level is the increasing influence of bargaining models in the international relations field as a whole, for these analytical frameworks emphasize the fact that war is inherently a dyadic phenomenon (Morgan 1994; Fearon 1995; Leng, chap. 11 of this volume). In addition, the Cold War and the Soviet-American rivalry that defined it helped generate questions about the origins, evolution, and termination of enduring rivalries in international politics (Diehl 1998; Thompson 1999; Goertz and Diehl, chap. 9 of this volume; Wayman, chap. 10 in this volume).

Interest in dyadic-level behavior derives also from the fact that systematic empirical research has generated much stronger findings at the dyadic level than at the monadic or systemic level. The democratic peace is the most obvious example. Whatever the relationship between democracy and peace at the monadic or systemic level, it cannot match the nearly law-like relationship at the dyadic level (Russett 1993; Ray 1995; Ray, chap. 14 in this volume). Another illustration is the dyadic relationship between territory and war, which is also quite strong (Vasquez 1993; Diehl 1998; Huth 1996b, chap. 5 in this volume).[3] Finally, while debate goes on about the form of the relationship between the distribution of military capabilities and war at the systemic level, there is a growing consensus that at the dyadic level an equality of capabilities is significantly more likely to lead to war than is a preponderance of power (Kugler and Lemke 1996).

It would be premature to abandon the systemic level entirely, however, because the weak findings of some systemic theories may derive from the fact that those theories have not been properly specified. In particular, scholars tend to posit a single international system and neglect the role of regional subsystems that operate within the international system and that interact with it (and with each other) in important but relatively unexplored ways. The failure to distinguish between the global system and the European subsystem is particularly serious (Levy 1998:148–49). When Rasler and Thompson (1994) analyze trends in the distribution of capabilities at each of these levels, for example, they find that an increasing concentration of military power at the regional level often contributes to large-scale regional wars, but these regional wars escalate to global wars only under conditions of a deconcentration of naval power and economic wealth at the global level.

Similarly, it would be useful to explore interaction effects between dyadic relationships and the systemic context within which they occur. Geller (1993, chap. 12 in this volume) finds that dyadic power transitions are correlated with war under conditions of decreasing systemic concentration but not under conditions of increasing systemic concentration, where no dyadic transition war has occurred. These are powerful results, and they suggest that the investigation of the interactive dynamics of global and regional systems is an important question for further research.

There has also been a significant shift to societal-level explanatory variables, including regime type (democratic or authoritarian), the political security of governing elites, public opinion, and other characteristics of society. Before the late 1980s, scholars studying international conflict devoted less attention to the societal level than to any other level of analysis, but that situation has completely reversed itself, as some of the most exciting new work in the field is now being conducted at the societal level. We can trace this shift to growing frustration with the inability of structural systemic models to explain enough of the variance in war and peace (either in the system as a whole or in dyadic relationships between states); to the decline of systemic imperatives arising from the bipolar Cold War structure; to the increasing salience of smaller, politically unstable states and ethnonational movements in the post–Cold War world; to the impressive explanatory power of democratic regime type and particularly of joint democracy; to the availability of good quantitative data on key societal variables (Gurr 1989); and to recent developments in the discipline that emphasize the impact of domestic political institutions on policy choices and outcomes.

Another distinct trend that has emerged in the literature is an increasing recognition of the complexity of the question of the causes of war and various attempts to model various aspects of that complexity. To begin with, guided by the levels-of-analysis framework (Waltz 1959; Singer 1962), scholars have devoted a disproportionate amount of time over the last three decades to the question of which level of analysis provides the most powerful explanations of the causes of war and of international behavior more generally.[4] The debate has shifted, however, and we now find more and more efforts to integrate variables from different levels of analysis into a single model. Many statistical models of international conflict now include domestic as well as structural-systemic variables. Game-theoretic models, which a decade ago were applied almost exclusively to problems of strategic interaction between states, now incorporate domestic structures and processes as well.

Despite this shift toward multilevel theories, most of the models in the quantitative-empirical literature (whether they consist of explanatory variables from a single level or several levels) have been additive in nature and do not incorporate true interaction effects.[5] This is gradually beginning to change, however, and scholars are slowly beginning to incorporate interactive effects into their models. This is either done directly by including an interaction term in the model or indirectly by estimating a model separately for different values of a third variable. It is increasingly common, for example, for researchers to conduct separate analyses of war for contiguous and noncontiguous states, to incorporate the interaction effects between contiguity and alliances (Siverson and Starr 1991), trade (Oneal and Russett 1997), and a variety of other variables. These models are still in the minority, however, and simpler additive relationships are still the norm. In the conclusion I return to the importance of building interaction effects into our models of war.

Applications of game-theoretic models have also become more sophisticated and more complex.[6] Prisoner's Dilemma and related 2 × 2 games were useful for the analysis of simple strategic situations (Rapoport and Guyer 1966; Snyder and Diesing 1977), but the move to extensive form games, particularly those involving incomplete information, marked a significant theoretical advance. These games better reflect empirical reality because they model conflict as a sequence of choices by actors that typically lack complete information about the preferences and intentions of their adversaries. This significantly expands the range of theoretical questions open to investigation.

The treatment of war in terms of a sequence of choices, which has long been common in the qualitative literature on decision making, represents an increasingly dynamic conceptualization of war that is also reflected in much of the recent quantitative empirical literature. Early studies in the correlates-of-war tradition looked for simple empirical associations between systemic structures and the frequency and severity of war, reflecting rather static balance of power propositions.[7] This research tradition has evolved in a way that now conceptualizes international conflict as a process or series of steps (Vasquez 1993) that lead from background conditions to the occurrence and evolution of militarized disputes to the outbreak and evolution of international war, and war in turn affects background conditions (Bremer 1995b).

The increasing complexity of theories of war and peace is also manifested in the greater attention to the possibility of reciprocal causation and other forms of "endogeneity," in which the values of the explanatory variables are determined, at least in part, by the dependent variable (King, Keohane, and Verba 1994). Scholars have increasingly come to recognize that previous attempts to model actors' responses to exogenous events, institutions, and other external shocks neglected the possibility that those events or institutions were themselves the endogenous result of conscious strategic behavior.[8] That is, the causal arrow leading from the independent explanatory variable to the dependent variable may be reversed.

Studies of the democratic peace, for example, look not only at the impact of democracy (or joint democracy) on war and peace but also at the extent to which peace creates the conditions under which democracy is able to flourish (Thompson 1996). Similarly, while scholars have investigated the liberal hypothesis that trade promotes peace (Oneal and Russett 1997), it is also clear that peace often creates the conditions favorable to trade, and it will ultimately be necessary to incorporate both of these effects into a single model (Reuveny and Kang 1996).[9]

There are numerous other examples of endogeneity problems and attempts to deal with them. Although many empirical studies of deterrence conclude that the impact of military power differentials on crisis bargaining outcomes is somewhat limited, these studies, which use the existence of a prior threat as a criterion for case selection,[10] ignore the fact that such power considerations may have determined whether an actor chose to make the initial threat to begin with. The finding by Huth and Russett (1984) that extended deterrence is significantly more likely to fail if the protégé has a preexisting alliance with a major power defender is explained by the fact that the aggressor will only initiate the prior threat if it is highly motivated and willing to defy the anticipated deterrence threat by the protégé's great power defender (Levy 1989a: 117–20). If the challenger is weak, it will not make the initial threat, and this "nonevent" will not appear in the sample of cases to be analyzed. Thus, examining cases in which an initial threat has been made involves a biased sample of cases. This "selection effect" is generated by the fact that the occurrence or nonoccurrence of the initial threat is endogenous to the balance of power and interests.

Although some earlier studies identified endogeneity problems and their related selection effects in particular studies, they failed to provide ways of dealing with the problem. More recently, rational choice models have sensitized researchers to endogeneity problems[11] and have begun to model the strategic dynamics involved, and in the process they have generated important and sometimes counterintuitive predictions. Fearon's (1994) signaling game model of immediate deterrence, for example, shows that ex ante measures of the balance of interests based on alliance ties or geographic contiguity between a target and its defender are associated with the failure of immediate deterrent threats, because the challenger has already incorporated these considerations into its calculations.[12]

Similarly, one explanation for the common finding that states frequently do not honor their alliance commitments after their ally is attacked focuses on the conditions under which military attacks occur in the first place. A challenger is more likely to attack when it expects that the target's ally is unlikely to intervene than when it expects intervention. If we look at the relative frequency with which allies come to the aid of their friends, we would fail to count those cases in which attacks do not occur because of the challenger's anticipation of intervention, and this would lead to a biased sample and erroneous causal inferences (Smith 1995).

Another significant shift in the study of war is toward the construction of multi-method research designs, either in a single study or in a broader research program. Two decades ago there were relatively few studies that combined decision or game-theoretic models with statistical tests, but this is the norm today.[13] We also find many examples of scholars combining case studies with statistical analyses (Huth 1988).

Though many regard game theory and case studies as noncomplementary methods, this significantly underestimates their respective synergistic effects. Case studies can be a useful means of illustrating the dynamics specified in game-theoretic models (Bueno de Mesquita and Lalman 1992: chap. 7; Brams 1994) and of suggesting how those models might be refined. They can also be used to assess the preferences that are treated exogenously in many models. Finally, game-theoretic concepts can provide a useful guide for case study explanations of individual episodes. The research program on "analytic narratives" (Bates et al. 1998), for example, is a methodologically self-conscious effort by scholars in several fields to combine rational choice theory with case study methods. Both "hard" and "soft" rational choice models have been used in attempts to explain the causes of particular wars (Bueno de Mesquita and Lalman 1992: chap. 7; Levy 1990/91).

One example of the utility of a research program that combines large-N statistical studies, case studies and (increasingly) game-theoretic models by numerous scholars is the study of the interdemocratic peace. Quantitative studies have been indispensable in demonstrating the basic descriptive-level finding that democratic states rarely if ever fight each other. They have also been essential in determining that this finding cannot be traced entirely to the effects of wealth, geography, alliances, or other possible confounding variables and that the finding reflects something about joint democracy itself (Russett 1993; Ray 1995, chap. 14 in this volume).

Qualitative studies have been useful in exploring the hypothesized anomalies in the democratic peace proposition; in examining the extent to which decision makers perceived their adversaries as democracies (which is a testable implication of many theoretical formulations of the democratic peace); in attempting to assess whether the peaceful resolution of crises between democratic states in individual cases was due to the democratic character of their regimes or to other factors; and in exploring in individual cases the plausibility of alternative explanations of the democratic peace phenomenon (Brown et al. 1996; Elman 1997).

Even those who accept the lawlike character of the democratic peace proposition, however, concede that we have no fully satisfactory theoretical explanation for it. Scholars have recently begun to construct game-theoretic models in an attempt to provide a more rigorous model of the complex strategic interactions of states with their adversaries and with their own domestic publics (Schultz 1998). Although we still lack a fully satisfactory theory of the democratic peace, many scholars will agree that the cumulative results of the aforementioned efforts have been far more convincing than those produced by any single method (Ray, chap. 14 in this volume).[14]

CONCLUSION

In my emphasis on scholars' growing recognition of the complexity of the social world and on their attempts to model it, I have noted the recent effort in the quantitative empirical literature to move from purely additive models to the incorporation of interaction effects. It is interesting to note that this trend has a parallel in the literature on the comparative method. Some have begun to emphasize the importance of "multiple conjunctural causality" (Ragin 1987), in which outcomes are the product of the intersection of several distinct conditions and in which the impact of one condition is contingent upon the presence of another condition.

Moreover, a given outcome can occur through several alternative causal paths,[15] and variables important or even necessary in one sequence may have no impact in another (Levy 1989b: 296; Vasquez 1993; Braumoeller 1999). It is conceivable, for example, that an outcome may arise from several different causal sequences, each of which consists of a set of variables that is jointly sufficient for the outcome but not jointly necessary. Moreover, there may be an individually necessary condition nested within each set of jointly sufficient conditions, so war cannot occur through one particular causal path unless a particular condition is present. The presence of a particular factor may have little impact on war in the vast majority of circumstances but have a decisive effect when certain combinations of other variables push nations to the brink of war. As a result, the processes leading to war can be highly context-dependent and nonlinear (Beck, King, and Zeng 1999).

To the extent that this kind of complexity exists in the social world, it poses a challenge for those engaged in the systematic study of war. It is difficult for conventional statistical methods to deal with such interactive, context-dependent, and nonlinear relationships, given the assumptions of linearity and normality in those models. Moreover, the standard practice of adding variables to capture these interaction effects may not always be practical. The number of variables needed to capture complex interaction effects quickly becomes large, consumes degrees of freedom, inflates standard errors, and makes it harder to achieve statistical significance. The loss of degrees of freedom is particularly critical because war is a relatively rare event.[16]

International relations scholars are just beginning to grapple with the problem of how to systematically analyze phenomena that arise from highly nonlinear, interactive, and contingent processes. Case study researchers tend to deal with these problems as they arise in individual cases, but they face the problem of how to generalize their findings to other cases and to validate those generalizations empirically. More quantitatively oriented scholars have recently begun to develop methods for dealing with such problems (Ragin 1987; Beck et al. 1999; Braumoeller 1999), and the further refinement of these methods is an important task for future researchers.

NOTES

I thank Jonathan DiCicco and William Mabe, Jr., for helpful comments on an earlier version of this chapter.

1. This study builds on Levy (1998).

2. For example, the distribution of power in the international system is a systemic-level variable, whereas the distribution of power between two particular states is a dyadic-level variable.

3. Bremer (1992) shows that the probability of war is thirty-five times higher for contiguous dyads than for noncontiguous dyads for the 1816–1965 period, and Vasquez (1996a) shows a strong tendency for wars involving contiguous states to be dyadic but for wars involving noncontiguous states to be multilateral.

4. That is, do the causes of war derive primarily from systemic-level power distributions, alliance patterns, or related variables; from national-level societal characteristics or governmental structures or processes; or from individual-level belief systems, personalities, or emotional states?

5. An additive relationship is represented by the sum of two or more variables, each of which can have an impact independently of the presence of other variables. Interaction effects are represented by the product of two or more variables, and the impact of each variable depends on the value of the other.

6. We should not forget that little more than a decade ago some of the most influential rational choice modeling in the international relations field was based on expected-utility models (Bueno de Mesquita 1981). The shift to game-theoretic models (Bueno de Mesquita and Lalman 1992) represented a major paradigm shift.

7. Early examples of more dynamic approaches to the study of international conflict include models of arms races (Richardson 1960), power transitions (Organski 1958; Kugler and Lemke 1986; see also DiCicco and Levy 1999), and lateral pressure (Choucri and North 1975). More recent work that emphasizes the dynamics of conflict processes at the systemic or dyadic levels includes theories of long cycles (Thompson 1988) and enduring rivalries (Diehl 1998; Thompson 1999; Goertz and Diehl, chap. 9 in this volume).

8. An "exogenous" variable is one that is taken as given and is not caused by other variables in the model. An "endogenous" variable is one that is explained by other variables in the model.

9. Realists and Marxists dissent from the view that trade promotes peace (Barbieri 1996), and some evidence indicates that trade sometimes continues between adversaries during wartime, contrary to common applications of both liberal and realist theories (Barbieri and Levy 1999).

10. If the defender issues a deterrent threat in response to this initial challenge, and if the challenger then fails to implement its threat, it is assumed that deterrence is successful. Without an initial threat, however, it would not be clear whether the absence of an attack was due to the success of deterrence or to the fact that the challenger had no intentions of attacking in the first place.

11. Research on "system effects" (Jervis 1997) has made a similar contribution.

12. Ex ante measures refer to information that existed before a crisis begins.

13. Scholars have recently questioned whether the assumptions of standard statistical models are technically compatible with the game-theoretic models they are used to test, and these scholars have been developing new methods that better capture the strategic dimensions of conflict behavior that are emphasized in game-theoretic models (Signorino 1999; Smith 1998).

14. Another research program in which scholars have combined quantitative, qualitative, and formal modeling methods in effective ways is the diversionary theory of war (Russett 1990; Morgan and Bickers 1992; Levy and Vakili 1992; Richards et al. 1993).

15. Systems theorists call this "equifinality."

16. A "degrees of freedom" problem arises when a model has too few parameters relative to the number of data points.

16

Mature Theories, Second-Order Properties, and Other Matters

Manus I. Midlarsky

International relations research currently is rich in theoretical lacunae. Among the subjects composing the field are capability and power transitions, the democratic peace, crisis escalation, rivalries of various sorts, territorial disputes, alliances, military buildups, cultural or identity conflicts, and norms. This is a full menu of current research emphases in the field; it demonstrates the breadth of coverage of contemporary international relations as a discipline.

The current abundance of theory-driven research contrasts strongly with the much earlier reputation for solely empirically based research in much of the systematic IR research community, including the Correlates of War (COW) Project. The rational choice approach appears to have emerged as a strong swing of the pendulum in the theoretical direction, almost two decades ago. And one cannot help but be pleasantly surprised that the role of theory in COW-based research has now assumed a much greater prominence. This is a major sign of progress for the collection of scholars represented in this volume, or perhaps any such group that has begun to find its intellectual moorings in certain theoretical approaches. This is perhaps a necessary pathway for any research program to follow, after its earlier immersion in the real-world data.

To distinguish among existing theories of international conflict, I would like to introduce the concept of maturity. Mature theories are those whose core properties already have received considerable empirical validation. By *theory,* I do not mean assumptions about a virtual state of societal nature as in realism or rational choice. The realist, for the most part, assumes a virtual Hobbesian state of international society with limited agreed-upon constraints (e.g., alliances), while the rational choice scholar assumes that the dictates of rationality underlie virtually all aspects of conflict decision making. Although these approaches can give rise to genuine theories as in balance of power theory (Morgenthau and Thompson

329

1985) or variants of game theory (Bueno de Mesquita and Lalman 1992), in themselves they are not to be counted as theories. By *theory* here, I mean an explicit set (one or more) of hypothesized relationships between societal variables within a particular domain of inquiry—in this case, conflict behavior.

In my view, only two theoretical foci already have demonstrated certain properties of maturity that hopefully will accrue to other theories as well. These theories are the power transition[1] and the democratic peace,[2] the latter probably emphasized in the field now more than any other. I have selected these two because their degrees of empirical validation and a consequent maturity already demonstrate what I call second-order theoretical properties. These are properties of the theory that are investigated seriously only after an extensive empirical validation of the theory's core properties. And although other theories may be approaching this threshold, it strikes me that only these two have crossed it.

How do we know whether one or another theory is an appropriate candidate? There are markers or signals that suggest themselves. For example, when Bremer (chap. 2 in this volume) asks for the meaning of a status quo power and how we signify operationally the presence of such a power, this question immediately suggests that more basic properties of the power transition have already passed empirical muster. Geller (in chap. 12), comprehensively reviewing the empirically based literature, indicates precisely that conclusion. Power parity and the power transition tend to be associated with war, while hegemony is associated with peace. Only after acceptance of the core properties of the theory can we begin to explore what I call second-order properties that are intrinsically less salient. The specification of an approximate equality in capability between contending powers and a closing gap between them are inherently more salient properties of the theory than the precise characteristics of the status quo power. In other words, we concern ourselves with these precise characteristics as a secondary matter only after our primary theoretical concerns have been satisfied empirically.

Our second theory is that of the democratic peace. Here the indicators of second-order concern are the extent to which democracies fight more or less than nondemocracies or the degree of dispute involvement by democracies with each other. Note that neither of these questions raises the core issue of war between democracies. That is treated pretty much as a closed issue, at least for the contemporary period. Here, too, the questions asked now are not the same as the core question that initially motivated the research program: namely, do democracies wage war against each other? Second-order issues concerning the extent to which democracies in themselves are war-prone against *anyone*, or their dispute- (not war-) proneness against other democracies, are currently being debated. Whatever the outcomes of these debates, they do not reflect on the core issues of this research program.[3] There are other potential theoretical candidates for this status, but they generally are not brought forward in the same fashion.

Another marker or signal of this second-order status is the apparent acceptance or at least publicity of a theory within the public domain. Although this criterion certainly is not the best indicator of a theory's acceptability (witness, e.g., the initial acceptance of the so-called domino theory by Robert McNamara at the start of the Vietnam War), nevertheless it does suggest at least a minimal level of consensus among international relations scholars that then filters out of the academic community or, alternatively, a degree of persuasibility and face validity of the theory. Here, the democratic peace appears to have come to the attention of policymakers, as evidenced by reports in weekly news magazines such as *The Economist*. Indeed, a major argument used against NATO's expansion centered on the democratic peace, for in this view, it is far more important to ensure that stable democracy is embedded in Russia than it is to expand the NATO alliance eastward.

Under the precepts of democratic peace theory, a stable democratic Russia would be a stronger guarantee of peace in Eastern Europe than would a moderate enlargement of NATO. A successful democratization of Russia would yield the largest Eastern European democracy to join in the democratic peace with other Eastern European countries such as Poland, already on the way to a fairly stable democracy. Thus, NATO's expansion, to the extent that it stokes nationalistic fires in Russia thereby impeding democratic development, could have precisely the opposite consequence from that intended. Instead of peace based on the widespread diffusion of democracy in Eastern Europe, there would exist one large new potentially unstable democratic or only quasi-democratic power that could nurture its resentment at NATO's expansion into warlike behavior against neighboring countries.

It can even be argued that NATO's potential expansion to the Russian border risks alienating Russia to the point of alliance with China. Such an alliance would be beneficial both to Russia, threatened by an encroaching NATO,[4] and to China, perhaps poised at the brink of a power transition with the United States, including all of the potential hostilities and instabilities associated with such a transition. A solution to this security dilemma for the United States is to bring Russia directly into NATO, even if that decision incurs substantial monetary costs (Russett and Stam 1998).

In addition to public awareness of the democratic peace, there is some evidence for decision makers' awareness of the power transition and perhaps status inconsistency theory[5] in recent relations between the United States and China. Despite the fairly widespread assumption that business interests have heavily influenced the relatively benign China policy of the Clinton administration, it is likely that security concerns also have contributed heavily. Given the size and rapid economic growth of China, it could hardly have been otherwise. And in an effort to smooth the more dangerous aspects of a potential power transition as well as to placate the status concerns of a China newly emergent as a competing great power, the Clinton administration may have opted for the minimally contentious policies of recent years.

Certain aspects of the power transition may pertain to culture, as in the civilizational conflict idea put forward by Huntington (1996). Specifically, was it cultural commonality that made the power transition between the United States and Great Britain a peaceful event, and is it cultural difference that might make such a transition between the United States and China more conflict-prone? Even Russia, with its nonseparation of church and state, is a potential candidate for a future culture clash with the West, at least according to Huntington. The elevation of Russian Orthodoxy to essentially protected status relative to other Christian denominations in Russia and the consequent widespread protests in the West (Witte and Bourdeaux 1999) may be a case in point. Certainly, Russian behavior in Kosovo, especially in the preemptive seizure of the Pristina airport shortly after the Serb capitulation, does not augur well for future cooperation with the West. At that time, Prime Minister Sergei Stepashin's warning to the United States not to assume the role of a global police officer (Broder 1999) was consistent with this worsening of relations, although the current president, Vladimir Putin, apparently has been seeking better relations. The matter of culture and its close relative, identity,[6] clearly is on the agenda of international relations research both in the issues dealt with here and beyond. However, in the case of Islam, cultural or identity differences are not likely to lead to civilizational conflict with the West (Midlarsky 1998).

It is surely no accident that the two theories selected here for mature status, the power transition and the democratic peace, are based principally on the dyad, and the dyad is the unit of analysis of a vast majority of the newer studies in international relations. The end of the Cold War and its bipolar systemic configuration likely augmented this dyadic emphasis. An emphasis on systemic concerns clearly has been abandoned in favor of the dyad. Yet to fully understand the import of the power transition, it may be necessary to invoke the hierarchy of states in a systemic sense, for as Bremer (in chap. 2) observes, the higher the state is positioned in the hierarchy of states, the more important is the capability shift. This is but one of the interconnections between theory and methodology or, more important, evidence of the necessity to use several levels or units of analysis simultaneously to maximize explanatory power.

The choice of a unit of observation is an idea whose importance has been emphasized by Ray (chap. 14 in this volume), as well as in the research of Goertz and Diehl (chap. 9) and Hensel (chap. 4) on interstate rivalries. An intriguing question concerns the relationship of such rivalries to the rational choice approach. Can that framework begin to explain enduring rivalries, or do we require other perspectives that go beyond the expected utility calculations of the actors? The learned hostility or cooperation between two groups or nations may require a different framework of analysis than that provided by rational choice. Simultaneous equation models for the analysis of disparate but theoretically linked variables such as alliances and wars (Huth, chap. 5 in this volume), may be very useful in distinguishing between competing explanations. Endogenous and exogenous variables can be combined in the same model. Maoz's observation (in chap. 6) that the origins of alliances cannot be divorced from their war consequences is important here.

The interpretation of findings is important and often is context dependent. According to Vasquez (1993), territory provides a salient context, both real and symbolic, within which many conflict processes occur. How border and territorial disputes are managed becomes critical to the escalating or defusing of such conflicts. More specifically, a complete research program would examine how peaceful dyads manage such disputes in comparison with war-prone dyads. This discussion raises the issue of proximal and distal, or remote causation. Wayman (chap. 10 in this volume) suggests the funnel of causality as a means of determining levels of causation.

In addition to traversing a wide range of important issues, an extraordinarily pleasing aspect of the current state of systematic international relations research is its generation of surprising findings. In the sense of the equivalence of surprise with information, this research is extremely informative. For example, in his treatment of the covariance of conflict and cooperation, Hensel (chap. 4) finds disputes between noncontiguous states over territory to be more conflictual than disputes between contiguous states. Here, territory itself is found to be more important than contiguity. Or, given the literature on the democratic peace, it is surprising that Brecher, James, and Wilkenfeld (chap. 3) find that disputes originating within democracies tend to escalate more readily than disputes originating within nondemocracies.

Important theoretical perspectives on crisis behavior are juxtaposed by Leng (chap. 11) in comparing realist (i.e., structural) and psychological (i.e., perceptual) approaches. Crisis escalation here can be interpreted as a communication process, hence the escalation can be managed. Raymond's (chap. 13) treatment of norms, including problems of measurement, is laden with research potential, signifying here the return of this subject to centrality within the international relations research agenda. This full menu of international relations research concerns also, appropriately, gives rise to a large number of research questions that very likely will be examined systematically in the foreseeable future. In this fashion, additional theories hopefully will exhibit the quality of maturity, and the field will continue to progress rapidly as it has during the past several decades.

NOTES

1. There is now a considerable literature on the power transition. For an earlier review, see Kugler and Organski (1989); a later review is found in Kugler and Lemke (2000).

2. Two extensive reviews of the now vast literature on the democratic peace are Chan (1997) and Russett and Starr (2000).

3. Another indicator here is the extension of the theory well beyond its original "demo-

cratic" core. Russett and Starr (2000), for example, have pushed the boundaries of the theory well into what they call a Kantian liberal peace, one that is founded on postulates broader than the political condition of democracy alone.

4. As George Kennan puts it (Ullman 1999: 4):

I have never seen the evidence that the recent NATO enlargement (that brought the Poles, the Czechs, and the Hungarians into the alliance) was necessary or desirable. We are now being pressed by some advocates of expansion to admit the Baltic countries. I think this would be highly unfortunate. I agree that NATO, as we now know it, has no intention of attacking Russia. But NATO remains, in concept and in much of its substance, a military alliance. If there is any country at all against which it is conceived as being directed, that is Russia. And that surely is the way the Poles and others in that part of the world perceive it.

5. On the matter of status inconsistency, see, for example, Midlarsky (1975).
6. The impact of identity on international conflict is treated in Midlarsky (1999, 2000).

17

What Do We Know about War?

John A. Vasquez

As we enter a new millennium, the identification of the factors that bring about war is still high on the human agenda. The chapters in this book summarize the current state of scientific knowledge about the role of territory, alliance making, arms races, interstate rivalry, crisis escalation, and the distribution of power in bringing about war. In addition, two of the chapters look at the democratic peace and the role of norms in reducing the incidence of war. This is not to say that other factors, such as economic variables, play no role (see Bremer, chap. 2); it is only to say that we have emphasized those factors about which we think we know the most in terms of current scientific research.

It must be emphasized that scientific knowledge is always a work in progress. What is "known" today may be overturned tomorrow. This is particularly true in young sciences, such as political science and international relations, in which the data and research are limited and there are a variety of competing explanations. Nevertheless, many think the body of research conducted in the last thirty-five years or so has provided evidence that certain factors are more related to the onset of war and the promotion of peace than others. Although this research has not produced the kind of knowledge found in the physical sciences, it should not be concluded, as perennial skeptics would, that we know nothing. We have learned some things about the onset of war. In some areas, our knowledge may even be more precise than in the physical sciences—for example, we can do better in predicting war than seismologists do in predicting earthquakes. Their predictions typically state that a major earthquake can be expected in a certain area of the Earth's crust (which has certain characteristics) within the next fifty years. Some of the research reported in this book does better and predicts that pairs of states that have certain characteristics will have a high probability of going to war within five years and that others will have a very low probability. The knowledge in this book, while probabilistic and highly tentative, is not without utility. This does not mean that we do not still have a long way to go before we reach the level of knowledge in the mature physical sciences, but neither does it mean that we know no more than Thucydides or other ancients who studied war (see Midlarsky, chap. 16).

With these caveats in mind, the remainder of this chapter will turn first to what we know about the factors that increase the probability of war. Next, the much more limited research on what we think we know about the factors that promote peace will be reviewed. In each instance, not only will the main findings be summarized, but the major questions that need to be answered to deepen our knowledge further will be noted. Lastly, some of the important lessons we have learned about *how* to study war will be delineated. In many ways, these latter lessons may be the most important, especially for scholars and students from other disciplines who study the etiology of war.

FACTORS PROMOTING WAR

The first thing to keep in mind is that most of the research reported in this book is confined to interstate war (i.e., warfare between formally recognized states). While some of this research goes back to 1495, most of it deals with the post-Napoleonic system after 1815. What have we learned about these wars and the factors that bring them about?

Territorial Disputes

If we look at the militarized disputes that give rise to these wars, as many of the authors in this book have, we find that states who have territorial disputes have a higher probability of going to war than would be expected by chance. Hensel (1996a: Table 2) finds that territorial disputes in the Militarized Interstate Dispute (MID) data are about three times more likely to escalate to war than nonterritorial disputes (see also Hensel, chap. 4 in this volume). Vasquez and Henehan (1999) examine this relationship in more detail by breaking the nonterritorial category into its component parts: policy, regime, and other. When this is done, they find that for those states that engage in territorial disputes, the probability of war is 0.091, whereas those engaged in policy disputes have a probability of going to war of 0.033, and regime disputes a probability of 0.078. The overall (base) probability of war in this sample is 0.058, which means that policy disputes are less likely to go to war than would be expected by chance, while territorial disputes are more likely to go to war than expected by chance. Regime disputes go to war just about what would be expected by chance.[1] Lastly, Ben Yehuda-Agid (1997), using data on crises from the International Crisis Behavior (ICB) Project (see Brecher, James, and Wilkenfeld, chap. 3), finds that crises that focus on territorial issues are much more likely to escalate to war than crises focusing on nonterritorial issues. Taken as a whole, these three sets of findings mean, all other factors being equal, that states that resort to some form of force to settle territorial questions are more apt to go to war than other states.

Hensel (1996a, chap. 4 in this volume) provides some clues as to why territorial disputes are so war-prone. He finds that when states are faced with territorial disputes, they are more likely to respond to these challenges in a militarized manner, rather than in a nonmilitarized fashion or ignoring the action altogether. Likewise, Mitchell and Prins (1999: 174, n.13) find that territorial disputes are more apt to be reciprocated than nonterritorial disputes. Hensel (1996a) also finds that territorial disputes once initiated also have a high probability of recurring. Both of his findings indicate that states often find territorial disputes of high salience and are willing to risk increased escalation to support their stand. Ultimately, this seems to end in states being more willing to spill blood on these disputes than would be expected by chance. Senese (1996) provides some evidence that states are more willing to incur fatalities over territorial disputes as opposed to other types of disputes. Likewise, Hensel (chap. 4) finds that territorial disputes are more likely to produce fatalities than nonterritorial disputes.

While territorial disputes increase the probability of war breaking out, they do not make war inevitable; indeed, the mere presence of a militarized dispute over territory is not sufficient to make any given territorial dispute escalate to war. The overwhelming majority of individual territorial disputes do not escalate to war, although if these repeat, the probability of war can increase dramatically. It is important to understand that although states that militarize their territorial disagreements increase the probability that they will go to war, that this, in and of itself, is far from sufficient to bring about war. Most militarized confrontations over territorial questions will not escalate to war, but this is, in part, a function of the fact that most militarized confrontations do not escalate to war. Of the 2,034 militarized disputes from 1816 to 1992, only 102 escalated to war, and of these, several escalate within the context of an ongoing war (especially World War I and World War II). Much of the recent research of the Correlates of War Project has centered on trying to identify those factors that distinguish the 102 disputes that escalate to war from the 1932 disputes that do not. Since one of the key factors that distinguishes the war-prone disputes is that they are over territorial questions, it can be concluded that territorial disputes increase the probability that war will break out but are not a sufficient condition for war. Nevertheless, as will be seen later, if these disputes recur and escalate in intensity over time, then the probability of war can increase dramatically.

If we return to Bremer's (chap. 2) opening question of "who" fights wars, then one of the new things we learn from the recent research reported herein is that states that have territorial disputes are also likely to come to war. How does this finding relate to Bremer's (1992, chap. 2) proposition that wars are much more likely to occur between neighbors? Contrary to the contiguity or proximity explanation that explains neighbors' fighting because they have the opportunity to have more interactions and hence more wars, the territorial explanation maintains that any set of states (whether or not they are neighbors) will have a greater probability of going to war if they are disputing territorial claims through the threat or use of force. This suggests that neighbors become involved in war usually because they are fighting over territorial disputes.

Hensel's analysis (chap. 4) provides evidence to show that both contiguous and noncontiguous states have disputes with fatalities, if territory is at stake. Senese (1997b) goes a bit further and finds that the probability of war for contiguous and noncontiguous states that have territorial disputes is always higher than the probability of war for contiguous or noncontiguous states that are contending over nonterritorial disputes. In other words, when territorial disputes are present, the probability of war or of having fatal disputes goes up whether or not states are neighbors. In fact, Senese (1997b) finds that noncontiguous states with territorial disputes have a higher probability of going to war than contiguous states with territorial disputes.

Both Hensel (chap. 4) and Senese (1997b) analyze individual disputes; Vasquez (forthcoming) tests the same two propositions by examining whether pairs of states whose relations are dominated by territorial disputes are more apt to have a war (regardless of whether they are contiguous) than states whose relations are dominated by regime or policy disputes. His analysis provides additional evidence in support of the territorial explanation over the contiguity or proximity explanation. Huth (chap. 5) raises questions about the theoretical adequacy of the contiguity explanation and tries to incorporate proximity in terms of loss-of-strength gradient considerations and their effect on territorial disagreements.

In light of these findings, it should come as no surprise that wars that are fought are frequently over territorial disputes. Of the ninety-seven wars that had an explicit claim in the dispute that escalated to war, fifty-three (54.6 percent) are associated with territorial disputes in the MID data, even though territorial disputes constitute only 28.6 percent of the 2,034 disputes that occur during 1816–1992. Wars can be fought over other questions, of course, even when these disputes as a class have a low probability of going to war. Policy disputes account for 32 percent (thirty-one of ninety-seven) of the wars. These disputes, however, may go to war not because they have a high probability of escalating (in fact, their probability of going to war is less than would be expected by chance) but simply because they occur so frequently—policy disputes constitute 46.3 percent of the disputes that occur during 1816–1992.[2] Only 9.3 percent (nine) of the wars are over regime questions, and the remaining four wars are classified being over "other" questions. Recent research using the MID data set has made it possible to give an answer to the question Diehl posed in 1992: "What are they fighting over?"

Although over half the interstate wars fought since 1815 have arisen out of territorial disputes, many individual territorial disputes end without going to war

(Hensel, chap. 4; see also Simmons 1997). This raises the question of whether some kinds of territorial issues are more prone to escalation and war than others. Here, Huth's analysis (1996a 1996b, chap. 5) is very relevant. Huth defines territorial disputes broadly to include not just militarized disputes but any claim to territory whether or not it gives rise to the threat or use of force. He has collected and analyzed data on all such territorial claims between states from 1950 to 1990. These data permit an examination of whether certain types of territorial claims are more apt to be militarized and more apt to go to war. The extension of his data back to 1919 (which is reported in chap. 5) shows that about 60 percent of the territorial claims never give rise to MIDs or to war. An analysis of claims after 1950 shows that ethnic issues (including ties to bordering minorities and attempts to unify divided nations) are most prone to militarization and to war (Huth 1996b: Table 9, 109); disagreements over strategic territory come next. Disagreements stemming from the economic value of the land are the least likely to be militarized and most likely to be settled.

Given these findings, what do we think we know at this point? First, states that are involved in territorial disputes have a higher probability of going to war than would be expected by chance and have a higher probability of war than states involved in nonterritorial disputes. Second, although the presence of territorial disputes increases the probability of war, this is far from a sufficient condition of war. Most individual disputes do not escalate to war. Third, since both neighbors and noncontiguous states that contend over territorial disputes are more apt to go to war than neighbors and noncontiguous states that contend over nonterritorial disputes, territory rather than contiguity seems to be the more important underlying factor associated with war, although this conclusion must remain more tentative than the other two, pending further research. Fourth, the territorial disputes that go to war may share certain characteristics (e.g., disagreements over ethnic questions as opposed to economic disagreement) that distinguish them from the territorial disputes that are peacefully resolved, but precisely what these characteristics are still needs to be rigorously documented. Fifth, territorial disputes may have a higher probability of going to war because they recur and fester.

These five conclusions embody a set of "statistical facts" and patterns that need to be explained. Scholars have differed in how to explain them, which is why different scholars have contributed chapters on this topic. Both Hensel (chap. 4) and Huth (chap. 5) give different explanations for these findings, and Vasquez (1993, 1995b) provides yet a third. While this is not the place for an appraisal of these theoretical explanations, suffice it to say here that theory construction in light of documented patterns and informed by empirical research is what Singer (1980: xvi–xvii) had in mind when he started the Correlates of War Project (see also Geller and Singer 1998). He eschewed highly deductive theories that assumed patterns, often on the basis of anecdotal evidence, and insisted that adequate explanation would only emerge once we as a field had a better sense of what factors are associated with war (Singer, chap. 1). This does not mean that there are no preexisting theoretical hunches or even propositions to guide data collection and testing (Singer 1979). Explanation, however, means explaining why things occur and this usually entails explaining patterns. Even Waltz (1979: 5, 6, 9) maintains this. The research on territory has documented certain patterns. Competing explanations of these patterns should lead to more detailed knowledge and to the uncovering of more patterns as testable differences between the various explanations are delineated.

What are some of the queries that theoretically informed research in the future needs to answer to produce more cumulative knowledge about the role of territory in bringing about war? One has already been mentioned—namely, a clear delineation of what distinguishes the territorial disputes that go to war from those that do not. There are three obvious places to search for these characteristics: the substantive nature of the territorial issue (e.g., ethnic vs. border question), the process by which states contend over the issue (e.g., use or nonuse of certain foreign policy practices such as the resort to power politics or certain bargaining strategies (see Leng, chap. 11), and the structure within which contentions occur, including both the international structure and the domestic political environment of states. Second, and related to the first query, is what distinguishes territorial issues that are peacefully resolved from those that fester and/or stalemate but do not go to war. Third, one wants to know what the impact is of successfully and decisively settling territorial disputes (either through war or some peaceful process) on the subsequent relations of states. Does the resolution of border and other territorial issues produce an era of peace between the disputants, as the limited evidence suggests (Vasquez 1993; Kocs 1995), or does it merely lead to other issues in a constant struggle for power as realists, such as Morgenthau (1960: 38), maintain? Fourth, why do states raise territorial issues in the first place, how do disagreements over territory become MIDs, and what impact do these two processes have on whether such territorial disputes escalate to war?[3] While there are other propositions specific to differing explanations about the role of territory that would establish the relative merits of one explanation over another (see Vasquez 1993: 310–11; 1995b), answering these queries would enhance the knowledge base about the role territory plays in the onset of war.

Alliances and Military Buildups

The role of alliances and military buildups, including arms races, has long been an area of inquiry not only among those who take a scientific approach (see Singer and Small 1966; Choucri and North 1975; Levy 1981; Richardson 1960a; Singer 1979; Wallace 1972) but also within international relations generally (see Morgenthau 1948; Gulick 1955; Huntington 1958). Theoretically, much of the discussion on these two factors has been centered on realism and its critics. Realists have generally seen alliances and military buildups as practices that can avoid war, if they balance capability. Critics, going back at least to Woodrow Wilson, have seen alliances and arms races as part of a power politics syndrome of behavior that encourages war. The more sophisticated of these critics often rely on analyses of the security dilemma to explain how and why alliances and military buildups can increase the probability of war.

Much of the disagreement between these two approaches is empirical, and, as such, one would think that it could be easily resolved. The collection of replicable evidence has helped promote a more empirically oriented discussion of the competing approaches, although the findings are still far from definitive, as both Maoz (chap. 6) and Gibler (chap. 7) make clear.[4]

Early research saw alliance formation somewhat associated with war involvement. Singer and Small (1966) found that states that rank high on alliance making also rank high on the amount of war they have. Levy (1981) found that in the sixteenth, seventeenth, eighteenth, and twentieth centuries, alliances involving at least one major state tend to be followed by war within five years. These findings are contrary to the classic realist notion that alliances can balance power and thereby reduce the probability of war. Whether this is because the alliances in question failed to balance or whether having balanced, war occurred anyway, cannot be determined without additional research. Levy (1981) also finds that many wars in his sample occur without a preceding alliance, which indicates that alliances are not a necessary condition of war.

For the nineteenth century, Levy (1981) finds that alliances involving a major state were not followed by war as frequently as in other centuries. Singer and Small (1968), as well as others (Singer, Bremer, and Stuckey 1972), have also found differences between the nineteenth and twentieth centuries. These findings reveal a different pattern from those of the other four centuries. All of this has made finding patterns difficult (see Maoz, chap. 6), although a strong argument can be made on the basis of this early evidence that, with the exception of the nineteenth century, alliances involving major states are much more frequently followed by war than by peace (see Vasquez 1993: 158–77).

Maoz (chap. 6) provides new research to try to answer some of these questions in a more definitive manner. His main finding is that alliances seem to operate differently and have different effects depending on whether they are made by democratic or nondemocratic states or by major or minor states. In addition, the politically relevant environment needs to be taken into account. Maoz concludes that, at this point, no definitive conclusion on the general relationship between alliance formation and war can be made, except that this relationship will vary depending on the regime type and status of the states involved. Both of these new findings are consistent with what we know about major and democratic states—namely, that major states have a greater proclivity to enter wars (Bremer 1980, chap. 2) and that democratic states do not fight each other (see Ray, chap. 4).

Maoz's analysis (chap. 6) basically finds that sometimes alliances are associated with war and sometimes they are not. Gibler (chap. 7) starts with this premise and then proceeds to develop a typology of alliances that will uncover which of the alliances are dangerous and which are followed by peace. He finds that alliances that consist of a coalition of states that are major (as opposed to minor states), that have been successful in their last war, and that are dissatisfied with the status quo are more apt to be involved in war within five years after signing an alliance. This is true for any one characteristic or any combination. For example, alliances made by states that have been successful in their last war are more likely to be followed by war than those that have been unsuccessful. Likewise, alliances made exclusively of states dissatisfied with the status quo are more apt to be followed by war than alliances composed of solely satisfied states. As with Maoz, he also finds alliances made of major states are more war-prone than minor state alliances (see Gibler 1997b, chap. 7; see also Gibler and Vasquez 1998). Gibler (chap. 7) combines these three characteristics to develop a measure of the status, success, and satisfaction of an alliance and uses that to predict the war-proneness of alliances fairly successfully.

Gibler (1997b, chap. 7) employs a signaling rationale to explain these effects. Alliances that bring together a coalition of states that are dissatisfied, that are major states, and that have been successful in their last war are going to be seen as threatening by a possible target. This is because they have a reason for going to war (since they are dissatisfied with the status quo, they are powerful and involved) and they have learned from their success in their last war that armed force is a way of attaining foreign policy goals. Conversely, alliances that are made by states that are satisfied, that have been unsuccessful in their last war, or that are minor states will not be seen as threatening and are not apt to lead to a cycle of interactions that increase hostility.

It is important to emphasize that the time lag of five years or so means that alliances in and of themselves do not immediately bring about war.[5] This five-year period may simply mean that there is a time lag before the threatening effect of alliances is converted into a war action, but more likely it suggests that some other factor(s) in the interlude between the signing of the alliance and the outbreak of war accounts for the decision to go to war. Gibler (chap. 7), as well as Vasquez (1993), argue that making an alliance increases threat perception and hostility and thereby increases the probability of war. Gibler's main contribution is to clearly document and theoretically explain which alliances are apt to be seen as threatening and therefore increase the probability of war and those that are not and therefore are followed by peace.

In addition to this typology, Gibler (1996, 1997b) finds that there is a unique type of alliance that settles territorial questions and is rarely followed by war. These alliances are not directed toward an outside party that might be threatened by the alliance but constitute a resolution of outstanding territorial disagreements among the signatories that is then sealed by an alliance. The fact that such alliances are not followed by war supports the territorial explanation of war (Vasquez 1993: chap. 4), which maintains that once territorial disputes are settled between states the probability of war drops dramatically. Rather than posing a threat to any third state, these alliances eliminate the underlying source of threat. By identifying the territorial settlement treaty as one type of alliance and developing a typology of security alliances, Gibler (1997b, chap. 7) has increased our knowledge of when and why most alliances, outside the nineteenth century are followed by war and when and why some, particularly those in the early nineteenth century, are followed by peace.

In light of Maoz (chap. 6), Gibler (chap. 7), and the research they review, what do we think we know about alliances and war? First, from the early research (Small and Singer 1966; Levy 1981), we know that, except for the nineteenth century, alliances involving major states tend to be followed by war within five years. Second, there appear to be different types of alliances—those that have been followed by war and those that have not, with the former being most frequent, except in the nineteenth century. Third, alliances that settle territorial questions are rarely followed by war. Fourth, alliances that consist of major states that are dissatisfied and/or have been successful in their last war have a higher probability of being followed by war within five years than would be expected by chance. Conversely, alliances that have been made by minor states that are satisfied and/or have been unsuccessful in their last war have a lower probability of being followed by war within five years than would be expected by chance. Fifth, the making of an alliance does not lead immediately to war in many cases, but only results in war after a period of time. Sixth, most wars involving major states have not been preceded by the formation of an alliance, therefore alliances are not a necessary condition of war. Seventh, there is little evidence across centuries to support the realist claim that alliances prevent war between two or more parties by balancing power, although more rigorous research will need to be conducted on this question before any definite conclusion can be reached.

These and other findings in the literature suggest a number of unanswered questions that should guide future research. First, in light of Maoz's analysis (chap. 6), it must be asked: How do alliances composed of democratic states differ in their impact on the probability of war (and militarized disputes) compared to alliances composed of nondemocratic states? Second, what accounts for the reduced probability of war in the nineteenth century compared to the sixteenth through eighteenth and twentieth centuries? Is it the type of alliance, a systemic effect, or some other factor? Third, to what extent can system characteristics, including norms and attempts to manage the system by major states or regional powers, strip war-prone alliances of their bellicose effects? Fourth, do alliances followed by war fail to prevent war because as realists would suggest they (1) fail to balance power and/or (2) fail to make a credible commitment that leads potential opponents to doubt that the alliance is reliable (see Smith 1995, 1996)? Fifth, what factors occur within five years after the signing of an alliance that can either increase or reduce the probability of war? Sixth, what effects do alliances that score high on status, success, and dissatisfaction (compared to those that score low) have on increased armament levels between disputants, repeated MIDs, and the making of counteralliances (Gibler, chap. 7)? Seventh, what effect does making an alliance have on the domestic political environment of the signatories and possible targets, particularly the balance between hard-liners and accommodationists? Eighth, does the causal sequence of wars that break out without a preceding alliance differ in a theoretically significant manner from the causal sequence of wars that are preceded by an alliance? What does this tell us about the causal impact of alliances?

As with the literature on alliances, the literature on arms races and military buildups has been a division between realist critics—who see arms races as promoting war and dangerous—and realists—who see arms racing as not inherently leading to war and military buildups, but as possibly preventing war in certain circumstances. Early research on this question, especially by Richardson (1960a), seemed to make progress, as did theoretical work and preliminary empirical research that looked at military buildups in the context of other variables (Choucri and North 1975). As Sample (chap. 8) relates, however, much of this research has become bogged down in a debate over measurement and research design questions. Sample's data analysis (1997, 1998b, chap. 8) has, in many ways, broken this deadlock. She constructs a number of tests to assess the debate between Wallace (1979, 1982) and Diehl (1983) (see also Weede 1980). She finds that while numerous disputes do not escalate to war in the presence of an ongoing arms race or mutual military buildup, as Diehl finds, a large number of them are followed within five years by subsequent disputes between the same parties that *do* escalate to war. This means that the relationship between arms races and dispute escalation is questionable primarily if one insists that the effect must be immediate and the subsequent MIDs between two parties are treated as independent.

As with the research on alliances, the effect of this variable, then, seems to require some intervening step to war, although it is probably fair to say that arms racing is often chronologically closer to the decision to go to war than alliance formation. Thus, Sample's research (1997, chap. 8) suggests that the presence of an ongoing arms race frequently has a more immediate effect on escalation to war than the signing of an alliance. In this sense, the probability of going to war after having a dispute in the context of an arms race is higher than the probability of going to war after the signing of an alliance, although such a conclusion must be tested in light of Gibler's (chap. 7) typology of alliances.

Sample (chap. 8: Table 8.8) also examines under what circumstances the probability of dispute escalation to war in the presence of arms races increases or decreases. The predicted probability of escalation to war with just an ongoing mutual military buildup is 0.21. If this buildup leads to a high "defense burden," then the predicted probability increases to 0.40. If, in addition, the states are engaged in a territorial dispute, then the predicted probability increases to 0.59. If, in addition to these three factors, the military buildup has produced a "rapid approach" (where one side is closing in on the capability of the other) and no nuclear weapons are present; then the predicted probability goes up to 0.69 (see Werner and Kugler 1996 for a related finding on capability shifts). These findings are very interesting and help outline the various steps to war (Vasquez 1993) and what factors in combination might increase the probability of war in the context of militarized disputes, although they do not tell us anything about causal sequences per se. Nevertheless, they illustrate the potential importance of examining what Ragin (1987) calls "multiple conjunctural causality" (Levy, chap. 15) (i.e., in which the impact of one variable is contingent on several others).

Sample's (1998b, chap. 8) other major finding is that the presence of nuclear weapons has a dramatic effect on the arms race/dispute escalation relationship. She finds that the presence of nuclear weapons greatly reduces the likelihood that escalation will occur; thus, the overall predicted probability of war for mutual military buildups and escalation is 0.21, but in the presence of nuclear weapons the predicted probability drops to 0.05 (Sample, chap. 8: Table 8.8). Similarly, territorial disputes are not associated with dispute escalation after 1945. As she states in her conclusion, whether this finding is due to nuclear weapons raising the provocation threshold, the impact of deterrence, or the presence of norms is something that must await further research. Only with that research will it become clear whether the system of world politics has been fundamentally changed by nuclear weapons—that is, whether nuclear weapons (as opposed to norms related to successful U.S.-Soviet management of their rivalry) have eliminated the risk of war that arms races presented to disputants from 1816 to 1945.

Several conclusions can be made about arms races and war in light of the debate between Wallace (1979 1982) and Diehl (1983) and the recent research of Sample (1997, 1998b, chap. 8). First, there is a statistically significant relationship between the presence of an ongoing arms race and the outbreak of a dispute that will escalate to war, if a five-year window of opportunity is examined. Second, this probability of war breaking out during a militarized dispute in the presence of an arms race can greatly increase in the presence of certain other factors—such as a high defense burden, territorial disputes, and a rapid approach in capability. Conversely, the presence of nuclear weapons greatly mutes the probability of war brought about by these factors. Third, arms races are most strongly related to the outbreak of war in the context of militarized disputes. There has not been much research on the effect of arms races directly (i.e., without MIDs as an intervening variable) on the outbreak of war. What little there has been (Morrow 1989; Smith 1980) is consistent with the finding that arms races (in some form) significantly increase the probability of war.

Although progress has resumed in this area of inquiry, many unanswered questions still remain. First, we need to know just how much of a direct connection there is between the presence of arms races and the onset of war. The research centered around the debate between Wallace and Diehl, including Sample's (1997), is based on a research design that first identifies the presence of an MID and *then* sees whether there is an ongoing arms race and a war. To test the proposition on the direct effects of arms racing requires the identification of pairs of states that are arms racing and then seeing if they go to war (see Diehl and Crescenzi 1998). Such a test has been hampered by the lack of data on arms racing and measurement problems (see Smith 1980). Nevertheless, both Sample (1998a) and Diehl and Crescenzi (1998) recognize that this is the way to proceed.

Second, the existing research has been limited to the use of military expenditure data as a way of measuring arms races. There is a pressing need to identify and collect other indicators on military buildups—such as instituting conscription, extending the time of military service, increasing the number reserves, purchasing new types of weapons, increasing stockpile of weapons or certain kinds of weapons. Such indicators may also be useful in identifying arms races in the nineteenth century, which with present measures, appears not to have many arms races. Third, data on arms racing between minor states need to be collected and analyzed to see whether this relationship is confined only to major states (as Wallace [1979] argued) or is more generalizable. Fourth, research needs to be conducted on how arms races are linked to other factors thought to be associated with the outbreak of war. Specifically, one would want to know how arms races are related to alliance formation and alliance tightening, what impact military buildups and arms races have on the occurrence and recurrence of MIDs, and whether arms races are more apt to develop due to some kinds of disputes (e.g., territorial disputes) than other kinds of disputes. Fifth, are there factors other than the presence of nuclear weapons that reduce the probability that arms races promote dispute escalation to war? What role do norms (and other management practices, such as arms control agreements) play in either reducing the probability that arms races will make disputes escalate or the probability that arms races will even emerge between disputing states? Sixth, what effect does arms racing have on the domestic political environment, particularly the balance between hard-liners and accommodationists? Seventh, are there any theoretically significant differences between the way wars preceded by arms races break out and the way wars without preceding arms races break out?

Rivalry and Recurring Disputes

We have already seen from the review of territorial disputes, alliances, and arms racing that one of the reasons the probability of war (and any correlation) is so low is that it frequently takes more than one dispute for war to break out. We saw with alliances and with arms racing that using a five-year window of opportunity—in which any one dispute that escalates to war will count in favor of the hypothesis—will uncover a stronger relationship. As Bremer (chap. 2) puts it, states that go to war have "a history of fighting one another."

Leng (1983) was one of the first to show that for many dyads their first dispute does not escalate to war but that frequently repeated disputes will escalate to war. He studied MIDs that exhibited certain characteristics that he feels make an MID a crisis.[6] To treat each MID as independent, as many studies have done, is to underestimate the impact of a factor, like alliance making or arms racing, as well as to fail to incorporate within research designs the idea that the onset of war is a process that comes out of the interaction of states taken over time.

Leng (1983) believed that when crises recurred between the same disputants that the behavior and outcome in one crisis had an impact on the next one, because decision makers learned from their previous bargaining behavior (see Leng, chap. 11). In his early analysis, he uncovered two important patterns: (1) while war did not always occur during the first crisis, it usually did by the third crisis, and (2) the reason this happened is that states (both the previous winner and loser) escalated their interactions as they moved from one crisis to the next. Likewise, there are findings in the ICB project that dyads that have a number of crises are more apt to have a greater disposition to employ violence and a greater likelihood that a crisis will escalate to war (Brecher et al., chap. 3: Table 3.2).

Leng's analysis set the stage for distinguishing dyads in terms of whether they had recurring disputes. Wayman (chap. 10) and Goertz and Diehl (chap. 9) were among the first to see the importance of adjusting research designs to take account of interstate rivalry. Wayman (1982, 1996), as well as Diehl (1985a), initially used rivals to identify dyads that posed threats to each other. In Wayman's case, only such rivals were seen as being particularly sensitive to power transitions; in Diehl's case, rivals were used to help identify the target of military buildups. From these initial uses as a control variable, rivalry began to be studied in its own right with various lists and definitions being constructed (Goertz and Diehl 1992a, 1993; Wayman and Jones 1991).

Rivalries became an important subject of study for both theoretical and methodological reasons. Up until this time, most scholars had compared and quantitatively analyzed individual disputes and crises without controlling for the particular states involved. It makes sense theoretically that one should study relations between states over time, rather than disputes one at a time, since it is probably the underlying relations between the states that are governing the onset of disputes and what happens within them (see Wayman, chap. 10). Methodologically, scholars began to realize that MIDs were not statistically independent, and to analyze them this way, as they had been doing, was underestimating relationships (see Goertz and Diehl, chap. 9).

While the study of interstate rivalries is still fairly recent, there are some important findings. First, interstate conflict in the form of MIDs is not evenly or randomly distributed across pairs of states in the international system but clustered within certain dyads. Goertz and Diehl (chap. 9) find that 2.5 percent of the dyads (27 of 1,166) have almost 30 percent of all the MIDs from 1816 to 1992 (see also Goertz and Diehl 1992a; Diehl and Goertz 2000).[7] Second, and more important, it has been found that states that are rivals have a greater propensity to go to war. Wayman (1996) found this to be explicitly the case in his study of power transitions. Goertz and Diehl (1992a, chap. 9) find that 49.4 percent of the wars that occur from 1816 to 1992 arise from enduring rivalries. Likewise, Thompson (2000) finds in his analysis of principal rivalries that about three-fourths of all wars are linked to rivalries.

The study of interstate rivalry is important not only for its findings but for its theoretical insights about how to study war. Because disputes and wars are clustered by dyads, this suggests that scholars should compare pairs of states and specifically their *relations* to understand why these disputes and wars occur. From this perspective, the comparison should be between dyads that are rivals and those that are not, or between rivals or dyads that go to war and those that do not, rather than comparing individual disputes regardless of the dyads that were promulgating them.[8]

In addition, the very concept of rivalry theoretically predisposes one to see war as coming out of an interactive process rather than suddenly appearing as a reaction to the appearance of a set number of variables. This makes the study of the onset of war less confined to static, if not mechanistic, models (see Leng, chap. 11). It encourages longitudinal analysis and a greater interest in historical cases (see Thompson 1995; 1999), as well as learning (see Maoz and Mor, forthcoming) and evolutionary models (Leng 1983; Hensel 1996a; Goertz and Diehl, chap. 9).

These insights, though promising, are just beginning to produce research results. Thus, what we know about interstate rivalry and recurring disputes is fairly limited. Nevertheless, important bits of knowledge need to be taken into account in any explanation of war. First, most interstate wars and disputes since 1815 are associated with a comparatively few number of dyads, and these can be seen as rivals. Interstate rivals produce a disproportionate share of conflict and violence in the system. Second, the probability of war among states involved in an enduring rivalry is comparatively high—0.59, which means that they are almost four times as likely to have a war than states that have only one or two disputes (Goertz and Diehl, chap. 9: Table 9.3). This suggests that recurring conflict, what causes it and the effects it produces, are key factors to study for understanding the onset of war. Third, disputes between states are not independent; dyads that have only one or two disputes (what Goertz and Diehl in chap. 9 call "isolated conflict") have a different behavior profile from states that have recurring disputes (see Brecher et al., chap. 3). Fourth, as disputes recur they seem to have an impact on each other (exactly what that impact is, however, needs further research, but it is thought to produce an increase in hostility, threat perception, and some form of escalation, all of which increases the probability of war).

What is it about rivalry that produces recurring disputes and a tendency to go to war? This is a main topic for further research, but some tentative findings suggest some queries worth pursuing. First, we would want to know what distinguishes states that never have a dispute from those that do and, more important, what distinguishes states with one or two disputes from those that have a long-term rivalry? Maoz (1984), as reported by Goertz and Diehl (chap. 9), finds in an analysis of an early MID data set that 76 percent of the disputes in his sample recur at least once. What makes disputes recur? Hensel (1996a) finds that territorial disputes are more apt to recur than other types of disputes. This suggests that it would be useful to examine the issues over which dyads and rivals contend to see what impact that has, if any, on their relations. Second, what are the origins of rivalry? Realists would suggest that their origin lies in power struggles; indeed, in realism rivalry is simply another word for power struggle. Those who adhere to the territorial explanation of war would see the origin, at least of modern rivalries, as more limited and confined to disputes over borders and tracts of land (Vasquez 1993: 141). Wayman (chap. 10) provides some evidence for the latter in his review of rivalries among minor states, which he sees as growing out of territorial disputes. Huth (1996a) finds that some kinds of territorial disputes— namely, those associated with ethnic questions—are more likely to give rise to these (territorial) rivalries. Rasler and Thompson (1998) argue that while territorial issues are the source of many rivalries, the more important rivalries for the history of the global political system are struggles over global leadership, which they regard as a "positional" issue (see Thompson 1995).

Third, what processes make rivals go to war? Does hostility evolve within a rivalry, increasing escalation across crises, as Leng (1983) found in his small sample? What is the impact of one dispute on the next, both in terms of the foreign policy of states and the domestic reaction to that policy within each state (e.g., on the balance of hard-liners and accommodationists)? Do states learn from their previous disputes to behave differently in their subsequent disputes? Are there certain foreign policy practices that distinguish dyads that are rivals from those that are not and that distinguish dyads that go to war from those that do not? Fourth, how should change within enduring rivalries be modeled? Should it be seen in terms of an evolutionary model (Hensel 1996b), a punctuated equilibrium model (Goertz and Diehl, chap. 9), or some other form (see also Goertz and Diehl 1995b)?

Fifth, how do rivalries end, and why do they last as long as they do? Here Bennett's (1996, 1997a) work has provided important research and data. Rather than simply using a certain number of years without an MID, as Wayman (chap. 10) and Goertz and Diehl (chap. 9) do, he argues that a rivalry ends when the underlying issue the parties are contending over is resolved. Using this definition, Bennett has produced a set of termination dates that are more historically informed than we have previously had. Such dates are particularly important for using duration models to analyze rivalries—a technique that can provide useful information (see Cioffi-Revilla's 1998 analysis). Sixth, can rivalries be managed to reduce the probability of war or its severity, if it breaks out? Here what quantitative research exists suggests that conflict resolution techniques may have limited utility (see Bercovitch and Diehl 1997; Goertz and Diehl, chap. 9). Nevertheless, there are some hopeful findings. Gibler (1997a) finds that states that settle their territorial disputes have a longer period of time between disputes and less intense disputes under certain conditions. A number of case studies, especially those on the Arab-Israeli rivalry and Soviet-American rivalry (see Maoz and Mor, forthcoming; Larson 1999) also suggest that rivalries can be managed and peacefully terminated.

Crisis Escalation

Many of the process explanations of war see the last step in the onset of war as the appearance of a crisis that escalates to war (see Wallace 1972; Vasquez 1993). The work on rivalry and recurrent disputes is consistent with this view and helps explain the dynamic that leads to that "ultimate" crisis. Nevertheless, this research raises the question of what, in particular, about this "last" crisis increases the probability of its escalating to war. The work on crisis escalation by Leng (1993, chap. 11) and the work of the ICB Project (Brecher 1993; Brecher and Wilkenfeld 1997b; and Brecher et al., chap. 3) provide some findings and insights on this question.[9]

Leng's (1983, 1993) work has concentrated primarily on examining the effects of crisis bargaining on escalation to war—are certain bargaining strategies more associated with the outbreak of war than others? To answer this question, Leng has been guided by two different theoretical approaches: a realist perspective and a psychological perspective. His findings are based on a collection of data that details the actions each side takes toward the other. Because these data are very time-consuming to collect, his research is based on a random sample of forty crises. While his research is not definitive, some interesting patterns emerge.

Overall, he finds that bargaining strategies that are escalatory (i.e., increase the level of hostile behavior) have a greater probability of going to war. Of the crises that have a high escalation score, 62 percent end in war as opposed to 21 percent with low escalation (Leng 1993: 86; Leng, chap. 11). To better capture the dynamic of bargaining, Leng classifies his crises into four types: Fight, Resistance, Standoff, and Put-down. One type, which has high escalation and follows a model of what Leng calls a Fight, has a bargaining dynamic in which the two sides become locked into a pattern of spiraling escalation (Leng, chap. 11). Among the crises he identifies as having this Fight pattern, 75 percent end in war. Leng also finds that 70 percent of the crises that escalate to a higher level arise over territorial issues or questions of political independence and are characterized by each side being positive about its relative capability. This implies that both the issues at stake and the relative power of states are important determinants of the strategy employed and the level of escalation states are willing to tolerate.[10]

As well as these overall patterns, Leng (chap. 11) is able to distinguish specific influence strategies in terms of their effects on the probability of war or a nonwar settlement. He finds that a strategy he labels as bullying usually results in a crisis escalating to war two-thirds of the time. Conversely, a reciprocating influence strategy avoids war and results in either a victory or compromise settlement two-thirds of the time (Leng, chap. 11; 1993: chaps. 7–8, see also Leng and Wheeler 1979). These findings are not inconsistent with case research by Snyder and Diesing (1977), who look at the game-theoretic structure of a crisis to distinguish which will end in war.[11] When Leng (chap. 11) uses both structural factors (type of issue and capability distribution) and escalation dynamics (level and type of influence strategy), he is able to predict accurately whether the crises in his sample end in war 92 percent of the time.

The ICB Project has concentrated on collecting and analyzing data on international crises that have occurred since the end of World War I. The findings that are most relevant to the question of bargaining are those dealing with protracted conflict and the crisis management techniques employed. Brecher and Wilkenfeld (1997b) find that protracted conflict, which is operationalized in terms of repeated crises between the same parties, has a greater probability of going to war than nonprotracted conflict (Brecher et al., chap. 3). Crises that recur are also more apt to be violent in some form, with the violence likely to be central to the strategies employed by parties and likely to be severe and involve some increase in the gravity of threat that is posed.[12] Brecher (1993) suggests that one of the reasons for this is that protracted conflict produces an extreme lack of trust and an expectation that violence will be used. All this suggests, as with Leng (chap. 11), that protracted conflict is associated with certain kinds of strategies, especially those in which violence is used as the central management technique.

James (1988) (cited in Brecher et al., chap. 3) also finds that when the initiator has a greater capability, the likelihood of crisis escalation to war is higher. He takes greater capability as an indicator that the initiator has a positive expected utility of gain from the use of escalatory bargaining. This is consistent with Leng's (chap. 11) finding that "fights" and the use of a "bullying" strategy increase the likelihood of war (see also Bremer, chap. 2). Similarly, when a crisis is initiated by a violent trigger, there is a higher probability of escalation to war (James and Wilkenfeld 1984; see also Gochman and Leng 1983). Brecher (1993) also finds that when there is a violent response to the triggering act, crisis escalation is more likely.

On the basis of these findings, the characteristics of crises that seem to distinguish those that escalate to war from those that do not are the nature of the initial trigger (whether or not it is violent), the gravity of threat posed, and the technique used to manage the crisis (i.e., the extent to which violence is present and central to the strategies being employed).

Two other characteristics that encourage crisis escalation are the number of actors and issues involved in a single crisis. Both James (1988) and Brecher (1993) find that the more participants involved, the more likely escalation to war is; this is particularly true when major states intervene in a crisis. A similar pattern was found in an early Correlates of War project study of serious disputes in the twentieth century, in which Cusack and Eberwein (1982) found that multiparty disputes have a much higher probability of going to war than two-party disputes (see also Vasquez 1993: 190–93).

Brecher (1993) argues that such crises are more difficult to settle because they involve multiple issues. Mansbach and Vasquez (1981) argue that when issues are linked (especially in the context of what would today be called a rivalry), then settlement becomes more difficult because actors are reluctant to settle one issue unless all are settled (see Vasquez 1983b for some evidence). Compromising on one issue in the face of several, especially if the issues most salient to one's allies are not being settled, is the bargaining equivalent of signing a separate peace during wartime. Brecher (1993) provides evidence for this proposition; he finds that crises with more than one issue are not only less likely to be resolved but are more prone to escalation.[13]

Not only the number of issues but their content matters; in other words, what states fight over, has a impact on whether a crisis is likely to escalate to war. Members of the ICB Project find that crises over territory are more likely to escalate to war than those not involving territorial questions (Ben Yehuda-Agid 1997) and that the closer the crisis to the home territory of a state, the greater the disposition to use violence (Brecher and Wilkenfeld 1997b). Likewise, ethnic questions, especially if they recur, are likely to be violent and to escalate to war (Brecher and Wilkenfeld 1997b: 791–92, 802; see also Huth 1996b). However, it must be pointed out that in the ICB data set, 60 percent of the ethnic crises involved explicit territorial threats, so ethnic issues should not be seen as necessarily a separate issue. Carment (1993) and Carment and James (1995) provide evidence that ethnic issues that involve irredentist (or even successionist) claims are the most war-prone (all cited in Brecher, chap. 3).

The ICB Project also finds that certain kinds of actors seem to have a greater proclivity to violence, although this may be simply because they are more apt to be revisionist actors or more threatened. Two types are worth mention. The first are new states. Brecher (1993) and Carment (1993) find that states that have become independent since 1945 and have experienced a violent struggle related to independence are more apt to have crises that escalate to war. This is very similar to a finding by Maoz (1989) for the entire post-1815 period that new states that enter the system through revolution or some other form of struggle are more apt to experience wars (see also Wallensteen 1981; Maoz 1996).

The second type of actors apt to use violent strategies are authoritarian states. Brecher (1993) hypothesizes that for the military the use of violence is a familiar choice; therefore, states in which the military is in power are more apt to employ violent strategies in a crisis. He finds this to be the case when authoritarian regimes are compared with democratic regimes. Brecher and Wilkenfeld (1997b: 811–14) also find that the more democracies that are involved in a crisis, the less likely that violence is central and the less severe the violence is. However, if violence becomes central, then the gravity of threat and whether the crisis was initially triggered by violence becomes more important than the number of democracies (see Senese 1996). This, of course, is another way of saying that at this stage of escalation the number of democracies in a crisis has no impact (unless, of course, they are all democracies, since we know that democracies do not fight each other in this data sample).

A number of these findings are consistent with what has been found using the MID data set (see Brecher chap. 3, Table 3.5) even though the ICB data set is a distinct (albeit overlapping) sample: Both data sets reveal a pattern of recurring disputes and crises increasing the probability of war, especially if the actors become locked into an enduring rivalry or protracted conflict. This increased probability toward war is most likely a result of increasing escalation in the strategies that are employed. Even when it is not, crises and disputes that have a confrontational style centered around violent strategies are more likely to escalate. Crises and disputes involving territorial disputes are likely both to recur and to escalate to war compared to nonterritorial crises and disputes. Multiparty crises and disputes have a greater probability of escalating to war, especially when major states intervene in a crisis. Crises and disputes associated with new states that entered the system through some form of violence are more apt to go to war. Crises and disputes consisting primarily of democratic states are less likely to escalate to war.

What do these findings tell us about crisis escalation and the characteristics of crises that lead to war? First, the bargaining strategy between parties has a big impact on the probability of war. No one crisis or dispute, regardless of the type of issue or actor, need inevitability escalate to war. Whether it does depends very much on the level of violence and the strategy(ies) used by the actors in initiating the dispute and responding to each other. Disputes that involve escalating strategies are more apt to go to war, all other factors being equal. Second, as disputes recur they are more apt to have a pattern of increasing escalation. Third, multiparty disputes are more apt to escalate to war. Fourth, territorial disputes that recur are more apt to escalate to war. Fifth, crises involving certain types of actors—for example, new revolutionary states or primarily democratic states—have very different probabilities of going to war.

What do the findings suggest in terms of further research? First, while we know that growing escalation within a crisis and across crises increases the probability of war, we need more detailed knowledge about what specific kinds of strategies are employed and what pattern of interactions emerges that increases or decreases the probability of war. Second, we need to know the impact of crisis bargaining on the domestic politics of each side and how domestic political forces affect crisis bargaining (see Bueno de Mesquita and Lalman 1992). Related to this we need to know how the impact of a crisis outcome on the domestic political environment of a disputant affects behavior in *subsequent* crises. Third, are crises over territorial issues more prone to escalatory bargaining and, if so, when are disputants apt to resort to such strategies? Fourth, do multi-issue crises have a greater probability of escalating to war, and how are such crises related to multiparty crises? Fifth, among rivals how do the later crises or disputes that go to war differ from the earlier ones that do not (see Hensel 1998c for some preliminary findings)? Sixth, do all crises that escalate to war exhibit the kind of hostile spiral associated with the 1914 crisis, or do some exhibit a more controlled and perhaps planned pattern? Seventh, what nonrational factors are exhibited in crises bargaining, are these associated with increases in escalation, and are some crises more affected by these factors than others? Eighth, what types of actors specifically increase or decrease the probability of crisis escalation to war, and why do they have these effects? Ninth, how do system norms—especially those related to the transfer of territory, the resolution of disputes, and the limiting of contagion effects (e.g., by limiting intervention into ongoing crises)—reduce the probability of war among crises with characteristics that research has found to be prone to war?[14]

Capability Distributions

The relationship between power and the onset of war has been one of the most discussed and studied topics within the field. Most of the theoretical work on this topic has been informed by realist analysis in its various forms and a great deal of it has been widely contested, not only by critics of realism but by various theoretical perspectives within the realist paradigm, broadly defined. The findings have been varied and at times inconsistent but have provided a more complex and detailed picture of the role capability plays in the onset of war.

Among those who maintain that capability plays an essential and important role in the onset of war are those who hold the classic realist position that a balance of power is important in preventing an attack and the adherents of the power transition approach, who argue that the most likely time for war to break out is as contending major states approach parity (Organski 1958; Organski and Kugler 1980). A variety of other theoretical work around this question (such as that of Doran and Parsons 1980, Thompson 1988, and others) is reviewed in detail by Geller (chap. 12).

The most important result to come out of the extensive research on this question is that when dissatisfied major states are compared with defenders of the status quo, it appears that relative parity or balance is associated with the outbreak of war, while overwhelming preponderance is not. Organski and Kugler (1980) provide evidence to show that a power transition is a necessary condition for the biggest wars in the system. Kim's (1991, 1992) extensive tests of this proposition, however, raise serious questions about the generalizability of this finding when power transition and power balance variables are compared with other variables.

Studies that focus on the difference between dyads that are relativity equal and those that have a wide disparity of capability tend to support the hypothesis that parity is more associated with war and disparity with peaceful settlement. Bremer

(1992, chap. 2) finds that dyads that have only small or medium differences in capability are 33 percent more likely to go to war (reported in Geller, chap. 12; see also his discussion of Siverson and Tennefoss 1984 and of Moul 1988a). Geller (1993) finds, among enduring rivalries, that states relatively equal in military capability are much more likely to have wars than those where one side has a preponderance. Similarly, Huth (1996b: Table 10, 115) finds that when there is very large discrepancy in military capability, there is a lower probability that a state will escalate its territorial disagreements to the point that it resorts to the use of force; whereas when the balance of military forces is more equal such escalation is common. To attain this muting effect, however, the balance of military forces has to go from a three-to-one advantage to a nine-to-one advantage.

The most consistent evidence in favor of the power transition and related power parity thesis is that of Wayman (1996), who finds for rivals that there is a relationship among war and power transition, parity, and rapid approach. As Geller (chap. 12) reports, Wayman (1996) finds that a power transition within rival dyads increases the probability of war from 14 percent to 31 percent. In fact, war is most likely when there is a rapid approach toward power parity between rivals.

Two things need to be kept in mind about this research. First, the findings are strongest—indeed, only seem to hold—when the satisfaction of states is taken into account. Comparing all states regardless of whether they are dissatisfied with each other tends to produce a random relationship between power transition or parity and the onset of war. It is necessary to introduce this political variable, which is why Wayman's (1996) analysis of rivals seems to produce the strongest results. Second, whether it is the specific distribution of capability, the phenomenon of catching and overtaking, or the rapidity of the approach that is key is still an open question. All we really know is that among major states dyadic parity in capability seems to increase the probability of war, if the states are rivals or one is challenging the other. The strongest findings, then, occur at the dyadic level, rather than the system level, which has been generally true in conflict research (Vasquez 1998b: 194–95, 204; Levy, chap. 15).

Early research at the system level—for example, Singer, Bremer and Stuckey (1972), who examined the concentration of systemic capability—found that parity is associated with lower amounts of war (as measured by nations months of war) in the nineteenth century (after 1815), but higher amounts in the twentieth century (until 1965). This intercentury difference led to discussion as to whether the two centuries were different (as Singer, Bremer, and Stuckey argued) or whether the findings really indicated that for the entire 1816–1965 period the relationship between systemic capability concentration and war was random. Geller (chap. 12) takes the latter position, which is consistent with Bueno de Mesquita (1981a), who eliminated the intercentury difference by changing the dependent variable from the magnitude of war to war/no war.

Nevertheless, there may be some system-level effect if one examines the impact of systemic changes in capability on dyadic relations. Geller (1992b) was among the first to do this (see also Thompson 1992). He finds that shifts in the distribution of capability at the systemic level can interact with dyadic power shifts to increase the probability of war. Specifically, he finds that when a power transition at the dyadic level occurs in conjunction with a decreasing concentration of capability at the system level, war is more likely. Although this association is low, it is statistically significant and provides some support for both long cycle theory (Modelski and Thompson 1989; Thompson 1988) as well as the power transition thesis. From this and the preceding tests, it can be concluded that dyadic shifts in capability among rival states or those dissatisfied with each other are relevant to understanding the onset of war and that this relevance is enhanced if there is a concomitant shift in capability at the systemic level (see Levy, chap. 15). Such findings reinforce Geller's (chap. 12) conclusion that an unclear and unstable hierarchy is a more critical factor than the actual number of actors in the system (see also Geller and Singer 1998).

There has been considerable testing on the effect of polarity on the frequency of war. Much of this research has produced inconsistent findings, leading Geller (chap. 12) to conclude that these studies have failed to produce definitive findings. It is certainly the case that neither bipolarity nor multipolarity seems to be more peaceful. In this sense, war can occur in either, and if one means by stability the absence of war or severe conflict, then one is not more stable than the other. A study by Bueno de Mesquita (1999) on Waltz (1979) finds that the recent bipolar era was not any more "stable" than previous multipolar eras in terms of the number of wars and disputes that occurred.

Nevertheless, findings suggest that the two different types of systems may produce different types of wars. Wayman (1984a) finds that the most severe wars (in terms of battle deaths) and high magnitude (in terms of nation-months of war) occur in periods of multipolar distributions of capability and that wars of lower magnitude occur in bipolar periods (see also Levy 1985 for a similar conclusion). Bueno de Mesquita (1978) finds that an increase in the number of poles in the system is associated with longer wars among major states. Since Levy and Morgan (1984) find that when wars are frequent, they tend not to be severe, this suggests, in light of Wayman's findings, that multipolar distributions of capability are characterized by infrequent but severe wars, whereas bipolar periods are characterized by frequent but not very severe wars.

When bipolarity and multipolarity are defined in terms of alliance polarization, Wayman (1984) finds the opposite—a bipolarization of states into a two-bloc system is associated with an increase in the severity and scope of wars. Similarly, Bueno de Mesquita (1978: 259–60) finds that it is not the polarity of power that is important but whether alliances tighten blocs within the system. He finds that 80 percent of the wars involving more than two states occur in periods of rising tightness and no large wars occur in periods of declining tightness. Likewise, for the world war–dominated twentieth century, he finds that 84 percent of the wars begin after a period of alliance tightening; whereas 89 percent of the periods of declining tightness are followed by peace.[15] Both of these studies suggest that alliances are a contagion mechanism that makes wars spread (see also Siverson and King 1979; Siverson and Starr 1991). Specifically, alliances that reduce multipolar systems of capability into two polarized blocs seem to be associated with world wars (see Vasquez 1993: chap. 7). All of these findings suggest that the distribution of capability, particularly as it is affected by alliance aggregation of capability, is more associated with the type of wars that are fought than with the presence or absence of war.

More successful than the system work on polarity has been the work on status inconsistency. This early work (e.g., Wallace 1972; Midlarsky 1975) sees the difference between the capability of a state and its recognized status as making a state dissatisfied and hence prone to change the status quo, if necessary, by initiating militarized disputes and wars. Early studies provided some interesting findings on the role of status inconsistency, but for some unknown reason, this line of research has not been pursued. When it has, it has been looked at in the context of power transition. Wallensteen (1981), for example, finds that a power transition between two major states increases the number of militarized confrontations between them but is not associated with the onset of war.

One clear finding on capability is that the strongest states in the system are the most war-prone (Geller, chap. 12). Bremer (1980) has clearly demonstrated that major states are the most war-prone and the most likely to initiate wars (see also Bremer, chap. 2). Indeed, he finds that even among the strongest states that the stronger a state is the more wars it is apt to experience. Likewise, Small and Singer (1982) show that a relatively small number of states account for most of the wars that have been fought since 1815, and these are the major states.

The finding that the strong resort more frequently to the use of force is not a surprise to either realists or their critics. A number of findings on the dyadic level show that strong states that have an advantage, particularly in terms of military capability are more apt to initiate disputes and wars (Geller, chap. 12). The most extensive evidence in this regard is provided by Bueno de Mesquita (1981) who finds a positive expected utility (which requires greater capability) as a necessary condition (defined in probabilistic terms) for dispute and war initiation (see also Bueno de Mesquita and Lalman 1992). Huth, Gelphi, and Bennett (1993), as reported in Geller (chap. 12), find that in deterrence encounters, a shift in the military balance in favor of the challenger increases the probability of escalation. Similarly, Huth (1996b: 115–56) finds that among states that have territorial disagreements, those that have a three-to-one military advantage tend not to compromise and instead "often adopt a firm negotiating position." States that are relatively equal are more apt to escalate their territorial disagreements, while states that have an overwhelming military advantage to begin with see no need to do so (Huth 1996b: 114–15; see also Mandel 1980, cited in Geller, chap. 12).

These findings suggest that overwhelming preponderance does not lead to war but that advantages that are significant among relative equals do increase conflict.

Indeed, the findings on rapid approach and relative equality suggest that states with fundamental disagreements consciously try to increase their capability and thereby become entangled in a struggle for power. If during that struggle they sense they have an advantage, they *may* try to exploit it and gain a further advantage by initiating first. Such a hypothesis would help explain the many findings that show that approaches toward parity (or unstable balances of power) increase the onset of war (see Geller, chap. 12).

Anderson and McKeown (1987) find that unstable military balances are related to war initiation. Likewise, Geller (1999) finds unstable military balances associated with war initiation.[16] It is important to note, as Geller (chap. 12) does, that in these studies it is only imbalances in military capability—as opposed to the more long-term economic or demographic capabilities—that have this effect on war initiation. Obviously, one of the things that makes for unstable military balances are attempts by one side or both to increase their military capability. Werner and Kugler (1996) and Lemeke and Werner (1996) show (for, respectively, major states and South American dyads) that military buildups among relative equals (where the dissatisfied state was growing faster than the status quo state) leads to a greater likelihood of escalation to war (see Geller, chap. 12). These findings, of course, are consistent with the findings on arms races and war.

While such findings support the realist focus on power, they also support nonrealist psychological explanations that emphasize the role of perceptions and security dilemmas that see such attempts to increase capability as leading actors down the realist road to war (see Vasquez 1993; Lebow 1981). From the latter perspective, unstable balances are a product of following the foreign policy practices of power politics, which are seen as increasing the probability of war rather than reducing it.

In this regard, it is interesting to note that for highly salient issues, dissatisfied states are not "deterred" from attacking stronger states unless there is close to a nine-to-one military advantage, and even then weaker states or weaker coalitions have been known to attack, hoping that other advantages, such as a surprise attack, would give them a chance. Huth (1996b: 87), for example, finds "many examples of very weak states disputing the borders of their powerful neighbors." Geller (1999, chap. 12) finds that among enduring rivals, dissatisfied challengers have an equal probability of initiating war, regardless of whether they are stronger or weaker than their rivals. Dissatisfied states may prefer to wait to attack when they have a greater capability but do not feel compelled to wait for such an advantage. In other words, they failed to be "deterred" by greater capability the way realists would expect. Likewise, Zinnes, North, and Koch (1961) argue that Germany and Austria–Hungary initiated World War I, even though they were weaker than the entente, and Doran and Parsons (1980: 956–57) show that Germany was weaker than others and in decline yet still initiated World War II (see also Midlarsky 1988: 146–47). Likewise, Japan was much weaker than the United States in 1941, when it attacked Pearl Harbor. T. V. Paul (1994) identifies this as one of six important cases of weak states initiating war against stronger opponents in which the weak states were not "deterred" (see Geller, chap. 12: n. 7). If dissatisfied weak states are not prevented from attacking stronger states, then it should not be too surprising that dissatisfied states are more willing to jump the gun, if a balance is seen as unstable.

In light of this research, what have we learned about the role of capability in the onset of war? First, major states are much more likely to become involved in wars than minor states and account for most of the interstate wars since 1815. Second, the static distribution of power at the system level does not seem to have much impact on whether the system is at peace or war. Specifically, there does not seem to be much difference between bipolarity or multipolarity in terms of the onset of war, but there may be some association between these systems and the type of war they encourage (although this needs further research). The clarity and stability of the system-level hierarchy seem to be more important factors in the onset of war than either the polarity or the number of major states in the system. Third, dyads consisting of a dissatisfied state, on one side, and a defender of the status quo, on the other, that are relatively equal and experience shifts in military capability are more apt to go to war than dyads consisting of states where there is a great disparity of military capability. The former is the condition that Geller (chap. 12) identifies as an unstable military balance; it reflects a dynamic change rather than simply a static condition, and a number of studies seem to find it associated with the onset of war between states that have preexisting disputes. Fourth, dissatisfied states that have a military advantage are more apt to initiate disputes and wars than dissatisfied states that are weaker than their opponents, but often dissatisfied states will initiate disputes and war irrespective of the capability balance in the dyad. Why they do this requires further research. Fifth, differences in capability seem only important in bringing about war for states that have severe disagreements (e.g., dissatisfied states vs. satisfied states or rivals) and not for all states in general. Sixth, differences in military capability and shifts in them seem the most relevant indicator for predicting the onset of war rather than differences in economic or demographic capability, although economic capability may be more important for predicting who will win a war (see Rosen 1972; Wayman, Singer, and Goertz 1983; Kennedy 1987; Vasquez 1997b). Seventh, status inconsistency, usually brought about by secular increases in economic and demographic capability, makes states dissatisfied with the status quo and hence more likely to initiate disputes and wars.

Despite the extensive studies conducted on the role of power in the onset of war, there are still things we would like to know. First, what is more important for bringing about a war between two states—a power transition, a rapid approach, or any uncertainty associated with a shift in one of the indicators of capability? Second, is a power transition, rapid approach, or shift in capability a necessary condition of the onset of war, a sufficient condition, or just a factor that increases the probability of war without being necessary or sufficient? Third, do weaker states that initiate disputes and wars against stronger opponents have long-lasting territorial disputes and/or a domestic political environment dominated by hard-liners? Fourth, how are capability shifts related to other factors that increase the probability of war, in particular, alliance formation, arms races, and repeated disputes?

FACTORS PROMOTING PEACE

The most fundamental thing we know about peace is that it actually occurs in the international system; indeed, it is much more common than one would expect from reading realist international relations theory. Morgenthau (1948, 1960: 38), the classic twentieth-century realist, asserted, "All history shows that nations active in international politics are continuously preparing for, actively involved in, or recovering from organized violence in the form of war." Waltz (1979: 121), Morgenthau's neorealist successor, maintained that such a pattern is due to the fact that the international system is anarchic and that such a system produces not only war but "balance-of-power politics." Given this realist emphasis, it is not unreasonable to expect war to be the modal condition and peace to be primarily a respite between wars in which states recover and prepare for the next war. In other words, there is no true peace but simply an absence of "actual fighting" without a reduction in "the known disposition" to war, as Hobbes (1651: Part I, chap. 13) put it.

It is difficult to measure disposition to war, and there has been no systematic test of this Hobbesian argument. Nevertheless, statistically, existing data on war and militarized disputes show that periods of actual fighting among recognized states during the post-Napoleonic period have been relatively rare, despite the fact that war is nowhere near being abolished. As Geller and Singer (1998: 1) point out, 150 states never experience even one war in this period; an additional 49 have only one or two wars. In fact, few states have three or more wars, and a handful of states account for a great deal of the interstate warfare since 1815: France, Britain, Germany, Italy, Russia, Greece, Egypt, and Turkey. To this list one would probably add in the post-1945 period Israel, India, Pakistan, and the United States.

If one looks at the number of dyads in the system or pairs of neighbors that could go to war, then war is even rarer, since there are several thousand such dyads but only a little over a hundred wars since 1815. Small and Singer's (1982: 59–60) data record only 67 interstate wars and 51 other wars from 1816 to 1980 involving at least one recognized nation-state, which is a total of 118 wars (see Vasquez 1998b: 208–9). Geller and Singer (1998:1) conclude that the possibility for war far exceeds its actualization given that there were about 400 pairs of states (nondirectional dyads) in 1816 and 18,000 at the end of the twentieth century, and forty bordering states in 1816 and 317 in 1993.

Another way of making the same point is to examine the number of militarized disputes since 1815 and compare that to the number that escalate to war. There are 2,034 militarized disputes, but only 102 escalate to war, and some of these escalate to the same war, because they involve disputes that lead the participants to join an ongoing war, as happens several times during the two world wars.

Given this relative paucity of wars in terms of the possibility for war, it is unlikely that all states involved in international politics are in some condition of preparing for, or recovering from, war when they are not actually at war. While it is possible that the states with two or more wars are just recovering, this does not seem to be the case with countries and dyads that have not experienced any wars or even those that do not experience war for long stretches of time. This is especially true for certain regional peace systems that have long been known to political scientists—such as the Nordic peace system and parts of Latin America (see, e.g., Choucri 1972). More recently, there has been much discussion about "zones of peace" among certain sets of countries (Kacowicz 1995; Singer and Wildavsky 1996), such as the West European peace going on since 1945, which do not fit the realist description of international politics at all (see Vasquez 1998b: 211).

Peace research has even shown that among the most war-prone states in the system (i.e., major states), it is possible to have periods of peace. Wallensteen (1984) establishes that there are certain periods in the post-Napoleonic era that have no wars among major states and that reduce the number of militarized confrontations among these states by half. Peace, then, does exist. The question is what promotes it for individual countries, among certain pairs of states, and the entire major-state system during certain periods of time.

Wallensteen's (1984) early research provides some clues. He found periods of peace among major states by assuming that when major states attempt to establish "rules of the game," they are more likely to be able to resolve their disputes without using force; whereas, when there are no such rules they have to rely on their own unilateral acts. After he demarcated periods according to whether major states followed universalist policies (according to some rules of the game) as opposed to particularist policies, he found that the former had no wars between major states.

Although this measure is subject to criticism because it is based on the coding of historians' judgments, it points to an important insight; namely, that norms have an impact on the probability of war. Raymond (chap. 13) discusses this hypothesis and reviews the arguments and evidence in favor of it. Even before Wallensteen (1984), there was research with more rigorous measures in support of the hypothesis. Kegley and Raymond (1982, 1990) find that when states accept the more restrictive *pacta sunt servanda* tradition of international law that sees alliance treaties as binding as opposed to the more permissive *rebus sic stantibus* tradition, wars and the occurrence of militarized disputes, especially among major states, are less likely. In addition, Kegley and Raymond (1990) find that if wars do occur, they are less severe and less likely to spread. Raymond (chap. 13) finds that when the normative system supports the use of third-party settlement procedures, more states use arbitration and unilateral acts of coercion (which Wallensteen 1984 finds associated with war) are seen as less legitimate (see Raymond 1980; Kegley and Raymond 1981, 1986). This is similar to Simmons's (1999) finding that the mere presence of arbitration treaties between Latin American states increases their willingness to settle boundary disputes. All of this research suggests that the presence of norms and procedures for the settlement of disputes reduces the incidence of war by permitting states to settle their disputes without having to resort to unilateral acts of coercion.[17]

Raymond (chap. 13) argues that it is not necessary to construct a systemic or regional restrictive normative order to reduce violent conflict; it is also possible for a pair of states to generate their own "partner-specific" norms to reduce the likelihood of war between them. We know that it is possible to moderate and manage even intense rivalries, like the Soviet-American Cold War rivalry, if both sides are able to evolve certain rules of the game and procedures for crisis management (see George et al. 1983; Mansbach and Vasquez 1981: chaps. 10–11). Indeed, such partner-specific norms can so evolve through practice and negotiation that both sides can even be successful in crisis prevention, as the United States and USSR were during détente. More generalizable evidence for this hypothesis is provided by Gelpi (1997), who finds that bilateral norms that are established in dispute settlement have an impact on the behavior of these actors in their subsequent disputes (reported in Raymond, chap. 13).

What Raymond (chap. 13) has in mind, however, is the ability of democratic states to avoid war with each other. This democratic peace, he believes, is a result, in part, of these states' sharing norms about how to deal with conflict and disputes with each other. Even when disputes emerge, democratic states are more apt than other pairs of states to resort to conflict resolution techniques, as Dixon (1994) shows (see also Raymond 1994, 1996). This finding fits Raymond's (chap. 13) overall claim that the emergence of restrictive normative orders reduces the probability of war.

The democratic peace has attracted a great deal of attention. Ray (chap. 14: 299), who reviews some of this research, says, "One thing that 'we know about war' with unusual, or even unparalleled, confidence is that it almost never involves two democratic states in conflict against each other." A great deal of research has found that democratic states do not fight each other in interstate wars (Levy 1988: 662). The earliest scholar to test this hypothesis explicitly was Babst (1964), but until recent research, his analysis was ignored. It was only with Rummel (1983) that the hypothesis was tested in a manner and stated in a theoretical fashion that made it visible to the field of international relations, even though one can find the relationship in Small and Singer (1976) and in Rummel's (1979) earlier work. This visibility was increased through Doyle's (1986) theoretical analysis. Nevertheless, it was not until the work of Maoz and Abdolali (1989),

Maoz and Russett (1993), and Russett (1993) that the claim that democratic dyads never fight each other became accepted by a number of important scholars.

This acceptance became more widespread as Ray (1995) was able to dismiss a number of possible counterexamples and as other research began to show that pairs of democratic states not only did not fight each other but were also less likely to have militarized disputes (Bremer 1993b) and more likely to use conflict resolution to try to settle what militarized disputes they had (see Dixon 1994). Researchers also found that democratic dyads in ancient systems were not likely to fight each other (Russett and Antholis 1992; Wert 1998). The democratic peace research agenda was extended as researchers found that democratic states are also more likely to win wars and more likely to align together (Lake 1992; Siverson and Emmons 1991).

Despite this success, several researchers have challenged the findings, mostly questioning whether certain states can be dismissed as nondemocratic and whether other cases do not constitute wars between democratic states (see Elman 1997; Gowa 1999). The statistical analyses and research designs have also been challenged (see Spiro 1994 and Russett's 1995 response). Ray (chap. 14: 305) states that the statistical rarity of democracies and war makes one hesitant "to be very confident about the 'significance' of whatever correlation may be found between democracy and peace at the dyadic level," although clearly he thinks the evidence supports the proposition.

Mansfield and Snyder (1995a, 1995b), as Ray (chap. 14) notes, provide a different challenge. They maintain that as new states adopt a democratic form of government, they may, for a variety of reasons, become more rather than less war-prone. Enterline (1996) and Thompson and Tucker (1997), however, question their analysis. Nevertheless, the age and stability of democracies point to an important reason for the democratic peace and a hypothesis as to why it might be spurious—namely, that stable states (of which mature democratic dyads are only one subset) do not fight each other (Ray, chap. 14). An early study by Maoz and Russett (1992) found evidence supporting this hypothesis, and critics of the democratic peace would do well to pursue this line of inquiry further.

Theoretical rationales for the democratic peace were deepened, as Ray (chap. 14) notes, when Bueno de Mesquita and Lalman (1992) provided a formal model from which the hypothesis "Democracies don't fight one another" could be derived and as Bueno de Mesquita et al. (1999) developed a rational choice framework that looks at how differing "selectorates" and "win sets" of regimes affect their calculations about war. Meanwhile, Russett and Oneal have begun systematically testing the other two pillars of liberalism—namely, that economic interdependence (including trade) and international organization reduce conflict and war (see Oneal and Russett 1997a; Russett, Oneal, and Davis 1998). Barbieri (1996a, forthcoming) challenges the findings on trade and war, however (see also Barbieri and Levy 1999).

Ray (chap. 14) explores whether the dyadic relationship between democracy and peace can also be extended to the national (monadic) and system level—that is, whether democratic states are generally more peaceful than other types of states and whether one can expect the system to become more peaceful as the number of democratic states grows. Ray (chap. 14) is not too sanguine about the last proposition, but he does provide some evidence, as well as a theoretical argument to support the claim that democracies are in fact less war-prone in general and hence truly pacific.

This is basically the Wilsonian version of the democratic peace. Some have argued that such a version of the democratic peace places insufficient weight on democratic bellicosity and is prone to misperception driven by ideological bias (see Vasquez 1998b: 356–58). While it may be true that democratic states do not fight interstate wars with one another, some democratic states, and specifically the United States, have used covert operations to overthrow duly elected governments when they have not liked the outcome of an election or have interfered with an election to ensure an outcome consonant with their interests rather than with the will of the selectorate. For example, the United States interfered in elections in France in 1948, in Italy in 1948 and 1972, and Chile in 1964 and again in 1970, as well as toppling popular leaders, like Mossadegh in Iran (1953) and Arbenz in Guatemala (1953) (see Prados 1996: 33, 323, 315–16, 92–98, 98–106, respectively). Forsythe (1992) provides a systematic test that supports the hypothesis that democracies do fight each other through the use of covert actions.

The proposition that democracies are inherently peaceful also disregards the particular aversion (and at times intolerance) democracies have against countries that are different from them (see Vasquez 1998b: 354–55). It also underestimates the extent to which democracies might be peaceful because they are defenders of the status quo and satisfied states, while many of the nondemocratic states that fight wars are dissatisfied revisionist states. The Wilsonian version of the democratic peace also would seem to predict that the public within a democracy should be pacific, but often they are subject to war fevers and actively push their leaders toward wars that may have been avoidable, as in the Spanish-American War and the Crimean War (see Small 1980 and Richardson 1994, respectively). Several researchers grant that while democratic publics may be sensitive to casualties once wars start, they can be quite bellicose prior to a war (see Ray, chap. 14). Before too much weight can be placed on the statistical evidence that democracies are generally peaceful regardless of their opponent, the preceding questions will need to be addressed.

Nevertheless, the proposition that democratic dyads do not fight wars has been a major breakthrough in quantitative peace research. It has spurred an active research agenda that has produced new findings and oriented the field to study things that it has not previously researched. A particularly fruitful line of inquiry is to ask *why* democratic states do not fight each other. Mitchell and Prins (1999), for example, find that democracies typically do not have territorial disputes, which other research has shown to be particularly war-prone. Hensel (1995) finds that when democratic dyads do have territorial disputes, these often recur and escalate more than their other types of disputes, although never to war from 1815 to 1992, depending on how one measures democracy.

What can be concluded about peace up to this point? First, peace is possible and has occurred in the modern global system, even among the very war-prone major states. Many individual states have never experienced an interstate war since 1815, and most dyads in the system (including politically relevant dyads) have not had a war. Second, despite the criticism and the possible statistical fragility of the finding, it does seem that democratic states rarely fight interstate wars with one another. Third, what limited evidence there is suggests that norms and attempts to establish rules of the game in the global system attenuate the outbreak of war among major states and reduce the number and maybe the intensity of militarized disputes.

This is not much knowledge, but then again considerably less research has been done on peace than on war. Nonetheless, these findings do suggest two fruitful strategies to increase our knowledge. The first is to try to identify the characteristics (or correlates) of peaceful eras, and the second is to try to identify the characteristics of zones of peace. Here, the early work of Doran (1971) and the very recent work of Kegley and Raymond (1999) provide an important insight to guide the way (see also Doran 1991). Each of these books suggests that peace does not simply happen but must be built (see Vasquez 1993: chap. 8; 1995). They each examine the peace systems that were constructed after the major cataclysmic wars of Western history to evaluate how well they were built. This provides clues as to what distinguishes the peace systems that are fairly durable and successful from those that are not. It also suggests that peace is learned through the pain of war and the domestic reaction to that pain (Vasquez 1993: 289; 1997b: 673–78). Peace is most likely when such war weariness results in a traumatic reaction to the experience of war (see Richardson 1960b; Mueller 1989; but see also Levy 1986).

One reason for durable peace may have to do with the ability of the peace system to handle and resolve issues, a topic that is the focus of Randle's (1987) final book. Vasquez (1993: chap. 4, 1995) has argued that neighbors who are able to resolve their territorial disagreements permanently will be able to establish peaceful relations. Kocs (1995) provides evidence to support that claim, as does Gibler (1996). It may be that part of the reason democracies do not fight each other is that many settled their borders with each other before they became democracies, and it may also be the case that states that have territorial disputes and wars have more difficulty becoming stable and mature democracies (see Midlarsky 1995; Thompson 1996; cf. Mousseau and Shi 1999). Examining the issues states contest during peaceful eras and in zones of peace (and comparing them to issues states contest in periods of war and zones of turmoil—see Wayman, chap. 10) will provide us some important answers about what impact issues, and specifically territorial issues, have on peace and war.[18]

The work on norms suggests that how issues are handled and, more important, the informal institutions and practices that exist for states to settle their disputes distinguish the peaceful periods from those of war. Early peace research suggests that the mere presence of intergovernmental organizations (IGOs) reduces the use of unilateral acts like power politics. Wallace (1972) for example identifies a path to peace that is distinguished from a path to war, primarily by the fact that the former is characterized by the presence of IGOs and the latter by alliances and arms races. Looking at the global institutional context and how it changes over time provides another fruitful area for future research.

These areas of research—norms, the democratic peace, the characteristics of peace, and the role of international organizations—provide a starting point. This is an important foundation because when we know little about a subject, there are so many questions that we do not know where to begin. In addition, the preceding review suggests that the following questions would be worth researching.

First, are peaceful eras or dyads less likely to have territorial disputes or more likely to have norms or procedures that can settle these sorts of disputes without resorting to the unilateral practices of power politics? What kinds of practices (e.g., collective problem solving, third-party mediation) are negatively correlated with power politics? Second, are peaceful systems the result of the types of issues on the agenda or the absence of power politics or both? Third, to what extent are peaceful eras and dyads associated with the absence of threatening alliances and arms races? Fourth, what specific kinds of norms are associated with peaceful systems? Are norms over certain issues (e.g., the transfer of territory) more essential to keeping the peace than others? Fifth, do norms that keep the peace have specific characteristics; for example, are more precise rules associated with peace than ambiguous rules or those that have loopholes? Sixth, what characteristics of peace systems created after a major war make them durable and less likely to decay? Seventh, what role do IGOs (and other formal institutions) play in the establishment and maintaining of peace? What makes them effective? Eighth, is there an economic foundation to peace (open markets vs. autarkic empires; expanding global economy vs. depression; economic interdependence; trade; lack of scarcity), and, if so, what is it? Ninth, is peace associated with learning that war is not worth its costs? Lastly, to what extent do the factors outlined in the above questions help explain why democracies do not fight each other?

CONCLUSION: "ISLANDS OF FINDINGS"

Fifty years ago, Harold Guetzkow (1950: 421) said, "[T]he surest and quickest way to world peace is an indirect one—the patient construction over the years of a basic theory of international relations. From this theory may come new and unthought-of solutions to end wars and to guide international relations on a peaceful course." Guetzkow had thought it would be possible to construct "islands of theory" about different aspects of international behavior that could then be integrated into a basic theory. We are still very far away from even constructing islands of theory about the processes that lead to war, but this book has shown that we have identified what might be called "islands of findings," which can then be explained by existing or new theories.

What are these islands of findings that have been delineated? Eight can be derived from this book:

1. Territorial disputes increase the probability of war, especially as they recur, but they are not a sufficient condition for war.
2. Certain types of alliances are followed by war (within five years). Other alliances are not, but these tend to be alliances that either settle territorial questions between the signatories and/or do not pose a great threat to third parties, rather than alliances made to prevent war through increasing capability.
3. Disputes occurring in the presence of an ongoing arms race increase the probability of escalation to war in the next five years, if nuclear weapons are absent.
4. Disputes that recur between the same parties increase the probability of war between them. Hence, "enduring" rivalries are associated with a higher incidence of war.
5. Crises that exhibit a bargaining pattern of increasing escalation either within a dispute or across a series of crises are likely to end in war.
6. The strongest states in the system are the most war-prone. Rival states that experience a rapid change in their relative military capability that approaches parity have an increased probability of going to war.
7. When major states work out rules of the game and other norms to restrict their unilateral acts, there appears to be a great reduction in their tendency to go to war with each other.
8. Democratic states, particularly in the post-1945 era (where we have most of the evidence), do not go to war with each other.

Are these correlates of war? Some, like those on recurring disputes and crisis bargaining, might be. More conservatively, they are better seen as factors that increase either the probability of interstate war or the probability of peace. One of the lessons of the scientific study of peace and war is that the onset of war is so complex that a simple list of correlates may mask the role of important variables that, while not sufficient for war, may play a critical role in increasing the probability of war. In fact, it may be that only when several factors that increase the probability of war combine that the conditions are sufficiently ripe for war to break out, although we are far from knowing whether war follows this sort of process. Likewise, it may be that the causal sequences that precede wars may vary, which would mean that there are different paths to war and hence different types of war. All of this means that while some factors may appear to be correlates, we should be hesitant to drop variables that do not appear to be correlates without first carefully examining whether they increase the probability of war, even if they are not sufficient to bring about war. One way to do this is to follow Bremer's (chap. 2) framework of trying to delineate who fights whom, when, where, and why (and I would add over what).

While the eight-point list of findings does not exhaust all that we know about war or even what has been reported in this chapter, it does encompass the kernels of knowledge that can be derived from the topics that have been the focus of this book. Each is a core of knowledge around which islands of findings can be built. These islands of findings themselves must be explained by midrange theories, which Guetzkow called islands of theory, which then must be integrated into an overall explanation of war.

Explanations for these islands of findings may differ, as has been seen in those chapters in which authors have ventured to interpret the findings they have reviewed. The main purpose of this book has not been to appraise the various explanations or "theories" of war within the field but to identify a core of knowledge that any adequate theory of peace and war must explain. The islands of findings delineated in this chapter provide such a core and serve as a challenge to international relations theorists. They show that the scientific search for the sources of war and of peace has produced important and nonobvious findings and remains the best hope for uncovering the underlying forces that bring about war.

NOTES

My thanks to Daniel Geller, Marie Henehan, James Lee Ray, and J. David Singer for comments. They, however, should not be seen as necessarily agreeing with the interpretations given here.

1. In other words, there is no statistically significant difference between the conditional probability of war for regime disputes and the overall base probability. The differences for the conditional probabilities of the other two types of disputes and the base probability are statistically significant at <0.001.

2. Of course, it may be the case that the policy disputes that go to war have some common characteristic that distinguishes them from the policy disputes that do not go to war.

3. This fourth query is a more theoretically informed way of addressing the question of selection bias within the existing MID data set. In others words, it would be interesting to know whether territorial issues, even before they have been militarized, have a greater probability of going to war than claims over other issues. One way of getting at that question in the absence of a full data set of all issue disagreements between states is to compare states that do not have any territorial claims but do have some level of conflict (as indicated by event data or historical sources) with those that do have territorial claims against each other.

4. This review does not focus on the question of the effect of a mutual alliance on the probability that the signatories will fight each other but simply looks at the probability that war will follow the signing of an alliance. Bueno de Mesquita (1981b, 1982) finds that states that are allied with each other have a greater probability of going to war with each other. This finding was retested by Ray (1990) and also confirmed, although the relationship was found to be weaker than that in the original analysis. Bremer (1992) finds that much of the relationship is a function of contiguity (see Ray, chap. 14), although whether controlling for contiguity is theoretically relevant is a subject of debate.

5. Ostrom and Hoole (1978) find for the post-Napoleonic period that a three-year period is the one in which most wars occur after an alliance has been signed. Thereafter, until the twelfth year, alliances are not likely to be followed by war. By the thirteenth year of an alliance, the relationship between alliance formation and war is random.

6. It should be noted that many MIDs are not reciprocated either because they are ignored by their intended target or there was no clear target and no one responded.

7. Their sample is confined to all pairs of states that have at least one MID to begin with.

8. In this sense, the recent emphasis on analyzing disputes by dyad-years is a step backward because what is being compared are individual disputes; "true" dyads; that is, the relations (consisting of all MIDs) between two given states are not being compared. Obviously, dyad-years are even less statistically independent observations than disputes.

9. The early work on crisis, which is quite extensive, is not reviewed here. This work includes the 1914 studies on hostile spirals, the work by Hermann (1969, 1972) on the impact of crises on foreign policy decision making, and the work by McClelland (1972) on how crises increase the frequency of interactions and involve a sharp break from the previous pattern of conflict and cooperation. The work most relevant to crisis bargaining is that of the 1914 studies, which finds for that case: (1) in the presence of hostility, states express hostility (Zinnes, Zinnes, and McClure 1972), (2) perceptions of hostility lead to violence, (3) both sides tend to exaggerate threats and think the other side is being more hostile than it actually is (Holsti, North, and Brody 1968), and (4) both sides see the other as having more options than themselves (Holsti 1972). All of these factors led to a hostile spiral in 1914 that got out of control and resulted in war.

10. Leng (chap. 11) argues in light of his findings on capability that when both sides are confident in their ability to win, war is more likely (see also James 1988; Brecher et al., chap. 3: Table 3.2). Leng interprets this as consistent with the realist perspective, and it is, but it should also be noted that the psychological perspective sees overconfidence in one's capability as one of several images that precede war (see White 1970).

11. For a formal theory that provides a spatial analysis of the various factors that affect bargaining and the probability of war versus negotiated settlement, see Morgan (1994), who specifies the role that capability, resolve, cross-issue trade-offs, and third parties might play and illustrates these processes in six cases.

12. It should be noted, however, that some of these results are based on including intrawar crises (see Brecher and Wilkenfeld 1997b: 832–33).

13. It should be noted that linking issues into one grand issue of "us versus them" is not the same as bringing in previously "unlinked" issues that can then be used for the purpose of trading (i.e., "you give me this and I will give you that"). Such cross-issue bargaining can be very useful in crises, as Morgan (1994) and conflict resolution theorists (e.g., Pruitt and Rubin 1986) argue (see also Mansbach and Vasquez 1981).

14. For additional research questions on crisis escalation to war, see Brecher and Wilkenfeld (1997b), Brecher (1999), and Vasquez (1993: 316–18).

15. Further discussion of how the complicated findings on polarity and alliances may be related to the onset of world war can be found in Vasquez (1993: 248–62).

16. See also Geller (1992b), who finds a shifting balance associated with dispute initiation among the strongest states in the system.

17. This finding is consistent with the early research of Wallace (1972), who found intergovernmental organizations negatively related to arms races and hence the escalation of disputes to war.

18. In preliminary research, Vasquez (forthcoming) finds that in Wallensteen's (1984) universalist peaceful periods, there are fewer territorial disputes than in his particularist war-prone periods, and what territorial disputes there are have a lower probability of going to war. Likewise, in these periods fewer arms races exist.

References

Aiken, Henry D., ed. 1948. *Hume's Moral and Political Philosophy.* New York: Hafner.

Alker, Hayward R. 1988. "Emancipatory Empiricism: Toward a Renewal of Empirical Peace Research." Pp. 219–41 in *Peace Research Achievements and Challenges,* ed. Peter Wallensteen. Boulder, Colo.: Westview.

———. 1996. *Rediscoveries and Reformulations.* Cambridge: Cambridge University Press.

Allcock, John, Guy Arnold, Alan Day, D. S. Lewis, Lorimer Poultney, Roland Rance, and D. J. Sagar. 1992. *Border and Territorial Disputes.* 3d ed. London: Longman.

Allison, Graham. 1971. *Essence of Decision: Explaining the Cuban Missile Crisis.* Boston: Little, Brown.

Altfeld, Michael. 1983. "Arms Races? And Escalation? A Comment on Wallace." *International Studies Quarterly* 27: 225–31.

———. 1984. "The Decision to Ally: A Model and a Test." *Western Political Quarterly* 37: 523–44.

Altfeld, Michael, and Bruce Bueno de Mesquita. 1979. "Choosing Sides in War." *International Studies Quarterly* 23: 87–112.

Anderson, Paul A., and Timothy J. McKeown. 1987. "Changing Aspirations, Limited Attention, and War." *World Politics* 40: 1–29.

Anglin, Douglas G. 1994. *Zambian Crisis Behaviour: Confronting Rhodesia's Unilateral Declaration of Independence, 1965–1966.* Montreal: McGill-Queen's University Press.

Archer, John, and Felicity Huntingford. 1994. "Game Theory Models and the Escalation of Animal Fights." Pp. 3–32 in *The Dynamics of Aggression: Biological and Social Processes in Dyads and Groups,* ed. M. Potegal and J. F. Knutson. Hillsdale, N.J.: Erlbaum.

Aron, Raymond. 1969. *Peace and War: A Theory of International Relations.* New York: Doubleday.

Axelrod, Robert. 1984. *The Evolution of Cooperation.* New York: Basic Books.

———. 1986. "An Evolutionary Approach to Norms." *American Political Science Review* 80: 1095–111.

Azar, Edward. 1972. "Conflict Escalation and Conflict Reduction in an International Crisis: Suez, 1956." *Journal of Conflict Resolution* 16: 183–201.

Azevedo, Jane. 1997. *Mapping Reality: An Evolutionary Realist Methodology for the Natural and Social Sciences.* Albany: State University of New York Press.

Babst, Dean V. 1964. "Elective Governments—A Force for Peace." *Wisconsin Sociologist*

3, no. 1: 9–14; Reprint, pp. 381–85 in *Classics of International Relations,* ed. J. Vasquez, 3d ed. Upper Saddle River, N.J.: Prentice Hall.

Ballis, William. 1937. *The Legal Position of War.* The Hague: Martinus Nijhoff.

Barbieri, Katherine. 1996a. "Economic Interdependence: A Path to Peace or a Source of Interstate Conflict?" *Journal of Peace Research* 33: 29–49.

———. 1996b. "Interdependence and the Characteristics of Conflict, 1870–1992." Paper presented at the annual meeting of the American Political Science Association, San Francisco.

———. Forthcoming. *Trade and Conflict: Assessing the Impact of Interdependence on Militarized Conflict.* Ann Arbor: University of Michigan Press.

Barbieri, Katherine, and Jack S. Levy. 1999. "Sleeping with the Enemy: The Impact of War on Trade." *Journal of Peace Research* 36: 463–79.

Barbieri, Katherine, and Gerald Schneider. 1999. "Globalization and Peace: Assessing New Directions in the Study of Trade and Conflict." *Journal of Peace Research* 36: 387–404.

Barkun, Michael. 1970. "International Law From a Functional Perspective." *Georgia Journal of International and Comparative Law* 1: 22–24.

Barnett, Michael, and Jack Levy 1991. "Domestic Sources of Alliances and Alignments." *International Organization* 45: 369–96.

Baron, Robert A. 1977. *Human Aggression.* New York: Plenum.

Bates, Robert H., Avner Greif, Margaret Levi, Jean-Laurent Rosenthal, and Barry R. Weingast. 1998. *Analytic Narratives.* Princeton, N.J.: Princeton University Press.

Baumgartner, Frank R., and Bryan D. Jones. 1993. *Agendas and Instability in American Politics.* Chicago: University of Chicago Press.

Beck, Nathaniel, and Jonathan N. Katz. 1995. "What to Do and Not to Do with Time-Series Cross-Section Data." *American Political Science Review* 89: 634–47.

Beck, Nathaniel, Gary King, and Langche Zeng. 1999. "Improving Quantitative Studies of International Conflict: A Conjecture." *American Political Science Review* 94: 21–35.

Beck, Nathaniel, Jonathan Katz, and Richard Tucker. 1998. "Taking Time Seriously: Time-Series–Cross-Section Analysis with a Binary Dependent Variable." *American Journal of Political Science* 42: 1260–88.

Bennett, D. Scott. 1996. "Security, Bargaining, and the End of Interstate Rivalry." *International Studies Quarterly* 40: 157–83.

———. 1997a. "Democracy, Regime Change, and Rivalry Termination." *International Interactions* 22: 369–97.

———. 1997b. "Testing Alternative Models of Alliance Duration, 1816–1984." *American Journal of Political Science* 41: 846–78.

———. 1998. "Integrating and Testing Models of Rivalry." *American Journal of Political Science* 42: 1200–32.

Benoit, Kenneth. 1996. "Democracies Really Are More Pacific (in General): Reexamining Regime Type and War Involvement." *Journal of Conflict Resolution* 40: 636–58.

Ben Yehuda-Agid, Hemda. 1997. "Territoriality, Crisis and War: An Examination of Theory and 20th Century Evidence." Paper presented at the annual meeting of the International Studies Association, Toronto, Canada.

Bercovitch, Jacob, and Paul F. Diehl. 1997. "Conflict Management of Enduring Rivalries: Frequency, Timing and Short-Term Impact of Mediation." *International Interactions* 22: 299–320.

Bercovitch, Jacob, and Patrick Regan. 1994. "Managing Enduring International Conflicts: Theoretical Issues and Empirical Evidence." Paper presented at the annual meeting of the American Political Science Association, New York.

Berkowitz, Leonard. 1992. *Aggression: Its Causes, Consequences, and Control.* New York: McGraw-Hill.

———. 1994. "On the Escalation of Aggression." Pp. 33–42 in *The Dynamics of Aggression: Biological and Social Processes in Dyads and Groups*, ed. Michael Potegal and John F. Knutson. Hillsdale, N.J.: L. Erlbaum.

Best, Geoffrey. 1994. *Law and War Since 1945.* Oxford: Clarendon.

Blainey, Geoffrey. 1973. *The Causes of War.* New York: Free Press.

Blechman, Barry, and Stephen S. Kaplan. 1978. *Force Without War.* Washington, D.C.: Brookings.

Blight, James G., and Welch, David A. 1989. *On the Brink.* New York: Hill & Wang.

Bliss, Harry, and Bruce Russett. 1998. "Democratic Trading Partners: The Liberal Connection, 1962–1989." *Journal of Politics* 60: 1126–47.

Bloch, Jean de. 1903. *The Future of War.* Boston: Ginn.

Boehmer, Charles. 1998. "Economic Growth and the Onset of Militarized Interstate Disputes." Paper delivered at the thirty-second North American meeting of the Peace Science Society (International), Rutgers, N.J.

Borsi, Umberto. 1916. "Ragione di guerra e stato di necessita nel dritto internazionale," *Rivista di dritto internazionale* 10: 157–94.

Botero, Giovanni. 1965. *The Reason of State*, trans. P. J. and D. P. Waley. New Haven, Conn.: Yale University Press.

Boulding, Kenneth E. 1956. *The Image: Knowledge in Life and Society.* Ann Arbor: University of Michigan Press.

———. 1962. *Conflict and Defense.* New York: Harper.

Bowman, Isaiah. 1946. "The Strategy of Territorial Decisions." *Foreign Affairs* 24: 177–94.

Brams, Steven J. 1985. *Superpower Games: Applying Game Theory to Superpower Conflict.* New Haven, Conn.: Yale University Press.

———. 1994. *Theory of Moves.* New York: Cambridge University Press.

Brams, Steven J., and Jeffrey M. Togman. 1996. "Camp David: Was the Agreement Fair?" *Conflict Management and Peace Science* 15: 99–112.

Braumoeller, Bear F. 1999. "Incorporating the Logic of Multiple Causal Paths into Statistical Research in International Relations." Paper presented at the annual meeting of the International Studies Association, Washington, D.C.

Brecher, Michael, ed. 1980. *Studies in Crisis Behavior.* New Brunswick, N.J.: Transaction.

———. 1984. "International Crises, Protracted Conflicts." *International Interactions* 11: 237–98.

———. 1993. *Crises in World Politics: Theory and Reality.* Oxford: Pergamon.

———. 1999. "International Studies in the Twentieth Century and Beyond: Flawed Dichotomies, Synthesis, Cumulation." *International Studies Quarterly* 43: 213–64.

Brecher, Michael, with Benjamin Geist. 1980. *Decisions in Crisis: Israel 1967 and 1973.* Berkeley: University of California Press.

Brecher, Michael, and Patrick James. 1988. "Patterns of Crisis Management." *Journal of Conflict Resolution* 32: 426–56.

Brecher, Michael, Patrick James, and Jonathan Wilkenfeld. 1990. "Polarity and Stability: New Concepts, Indicators and Evidence." *International Interactions* 16: 49–80.

Brecher, Michael, and Jonathan Wilkenfeld. 1988. *Crises in the Twentieth Century: Handbook of International Crises.* Oxford: Pergamon.

———. 1989. *Crisis, Conflict and Instability.* Oxford: Pergamon.

———. 1997a. "The Ethnic Dimension of International Crises." Pp. 164–93 in *Wars in the Midst of Peace: The International Politics of Ethnic Conflict,* ed. David Carment and Patrick James. Pittsburgh: University of Pittsburgh Press.

——— 1997b. *A Study of Crisis.* Ann Arbor: University of Michigan Press.

———. 2000. *A Study of Crisis* (CD-ROM). Ann Arbor, University of Michigan Press.

Brehm, Jack W. 1996. *Psychological Reactance: A Theory of Freedom and Control.* New York: Academic Press.

Bremer, Stuart A. 1980. "National Capabilities and War Proneness." Pp. 57–82 in *The Correlates of War II. Testing Some Realpolitik Models,* ed. J. David Singer. New York: Free Press.

———. 1982. "The Contagiousness of Coercion: The Spread of Serious International Disputes, 1900–1976." *International Interactions* 9: 29–55.

———. 1992. "Dangerous Dyads: Conditions Affecting the Likelihood of Interstate War, 1816–1965." *Journal of Conflict Resolution* 36: 309–41.

———. 1993a. "Advancing the Scientific Study of War." *International Interactions* 19: 1–26.

———. 1993b. "Democracy and Militarized Interstate Conflict, 1816–1965." *International Interactions* 18: 231–49.

———. 1995a. "Advancing the Scientific Study of War." Pp. 1–33 in *The Process of War: Advancing the Scientific Study of War,* ed. Stuart A. Bremer and Thomas R. Cusack. Luxembourg: Gordon & Breach.

———. 1995b. "Final Words," Pp. 259–73 in *The Process of War: Advancing the Scientific Study of War,* ed. Stuart A. Bremer and Thomas R. Cusack. Luxembourg: Gordon & Breach.

———. 1996. "Power Parity, Political Similarity, and Capability Concentration: Comparing Three Explanations of Major Power Conflict." Paper presented at the annual convention of the International Studies Association, San Diego, Calif.

Bremer, Stuart A., and Thomas R. Cusack, eds. 1995. *The Process of War.* Amsterdam: Gordon & Breach.

Broder, John M. 1999. "Russian Premier Warns U.S. against Role as Policeman." *New York Times,* 28 July, p. A8.

Brodie, Bernard. 1946. *The Absolute Weapon.* New York: Harcourt Brace.

Brown, Michael E., Sean M. Lynn-Jones, and Steven E. Miller, eds. 1996. *Debating the Democratic Peace.* Cambridge, Mass.: MIT Press.

Buckle, Henry Thomas, 1857–61. [1913]. *History of Civilization in England.* New York: Hearst's International Library.

Bueno de Mesquita, Bruce. 1975. "Measuring Systemic Polarity." *Journal of Conflict Resolution* 19: 77–96.

———. 1978. "Systemic Polarization and the Occurrence and Duration of War." *Journal of Conflict Resolution* 22: 241–67.

———. 1980. "An Expected Utility Theory of International Conflict." *American Political Science Review* 74: 917–32.

————. 1981a. "Risk, Power Distributions, and the Likelihood of War." *International Studies Quarterly* 25: 541–68.

————. 1981b. *The War Trap.* New Haven, Conn.: Yale University Press.

————. 1982. "Where War Is Likely in the Next Year or Two." *U.S. News and World Report,* 3 May, p. 30.

————. 1996. *Red Flag over Hong Kong.* Chatham, N.J.: Chatham House.

————. 1999. "Realism's Logic and Evidence: When Is a Theory Falsified?" Paper presented at the annual meeting of the International Studies Association, Washington, D.C.

Bueno de Mesquita, Bruce, and David Lalman. 1988. "Empirical Support for Systemic and Dyadic Explanations of International Conflict." *World Politics* 41: 1–20.

————. 1990. "Domestic Opposition and Foreign War." *American Political Science Review* 84: 747–66.

————. 1992. *War and Reason.* New Haven, Conn.: Yale University Press.

Bueno de Mesquita, Bruce, and J. David Singer. 1973. "Alliances, Capabilities, and War: A Review and Synthesis." *Political Science Annual* 4: 237–81.

Bueno de Mesquita, Bruce, and Randolph Siverson. 1995. "War and the Survival of Political Leaders." *American Political Science Review* 89: 841–55.

————. 1996. "Inside-Out: A Theory of Domestic Political Institutions and the Issues of International Conflict." Unpublished manuscript, Hoover Institution and Stanford University.

————. 1997. "Nasty or Nice? Political Systems, Endogenous Norms, and the Treatment of Adversaries." *Journal of Conflict Resolution* 41: 175–99.

Bueno de Mesquita, Bruce, James D. Morrow, Randolph M. Siverson, and Alastair Smith. 1999. "An Institutional Explanation of the Democratic Peace." *American Political Science Review.* 93: 791–807.

Bueno de Mesquita, Bruce, Randolph Siverson, and Gary Woller. 1992. "War and the Fate of Regimes." *American Political Science Review* 86: 638–46.

Bull, Hedley. 1966. "International Theory: The Case for the Classical Approach." *World Politics* 18: 361–77.

————. 1977. *The Anarchical Society: A Study of Order in World Politics.* New York: Columbia University Press.

Burke, Edmund. 1899. "A Vindication of Natural Society." Pp. 1–66 in *The Works of the Right Honorable Edmund Burke,* vol. 1 Boston: Little, Brown.

Burkhart, Ross E., and Michael S. Lewis-Beck. 1994. "Comparative Democracy: The Economic Development Thesis." *American Political Science Review* 88: 903–10.

de Callières, François. 1963. *On the Manner of Negotiating with Princes.* South Bend, Ind.: Notre Dame University Press.

Carment, David. 1993. "The International Dimensions of Ethnic Conflict: Concepts, Indicators, and Theory." *Journal of Peace Research* 30: 137–50.

Carment, David, and Patrick James. 1995. "Internal Constraints and Interstate Ethnic Conflict: Toward a Crisis-Based Assessment of Irredentism." *Journal of Conflict Resolution* 39: 82–109.

————. 1997. "Secession and Irredenta in World Politics: The Neglected Interstate Dimension." Pp. 194–231 in *Wars in the Midst of Peace,* ed. David Carment and Patrick James.

Carr, E. H. 1946. *The Twenty Years' Crisis, 1919–1939: An Introduction to the Study of International Relations.* 2d ed. London: Macmillian.

Cashman, Greg. 1993. *What Causes War?* New York: Lexington.

Cassels, Lavender. 1984. *The Archduke and the Assassin.* New York: Dorset.

Chacko, Joseph C. 1958. "India's Contribution to the Field of International Law Concepts." *Recueil des cours* 93: 132–40.

Chan, Steve. 1984. "Mirror, Mirror on the Wall . . . : Are the Freer Countries More Pacific?" *Journal of Conflict Resolution* 28: 617–48.

———. 1997. "In Search of Democratic Peace: Problems and Promise." *Mershon International Studies Review* 41: 59–91.

Chanteur, Janine. 1992. *From War to Peace,* trans. Shirley Ann Weisz. Boulder, Colo.: Westview.

Chari, P. R. 1995. *Indo-Pak Nuclear Standoff: The Role of the United States.* New Delhi: Manohar.

Chay, Jongsuk, ed. 1990. *Culture and International Relations.* New York: Praeger.

Checkel, Jeffrey T. 1997. "International Norms and Domestic Politics: Bridging the Rationalist-Constructivist Divide." *European Journal of International Relations* 3: 473–95.

———. 1999. "Norms, Institutions, and National Identity in Contemporary Europe." *International Studies Quarterly* 43: 83–114.

Cheng, Bin. 1987. *General Principles of Law as Applied by International Courts and Tribunals.* Cambridge: Grotius.

Choucri, Nazli. 1972. "In Search of Peace Systems: Scandinavia and the Netherlands, 1870–1970." Pp. 239–99 in *Peace, War, and Numbers,* ed. Bruce M. Russett. Beverly Hills: Sage.

Choucri, Nazli, and Robert C. North. 1975. *Nations in Conflict.* San Francisco: Freeman.

———. 1989. "Lateral Pressure in International Relations." Pp. 289–326 in *Handbook of War Studies,* ed. Manus Midlarsky. Boston: Unwin Hyman.

Church, William F. 1972. *Richelieu and Reason of State.* Princeton, N.J.: Princeton University Press.

Cicero, Marcus Tullius. 1991. *De Officiis,* trans. Margaret Atkins, Cambridge: Cambridge University Press.

Cioffi-Revilla, Claudio. 1998. "The Political Uncertainty of Interstate Rivalries: A Punctuated Equilibrium Model." Pp. 64–97 in *The Dynamics of Enduring Rivalries,* ed. Paul F. Diehl. Urbana: University of Illinois Press.

Claude, Inis L., Jr. 1962. *Power and International Relations.* New York: Random House.

Clausewitz, Karl von. 1962. *On War,* trans. E. Colins. Chicago: Regnery.

Clinton, David W. 1996. *The Two Faces of National Interest.* Baton Rouge: Louisiana State University Press.

Coates, A. J. 1997. *The Ethics of War.* Manchester: Manchester University Press.

Cohen, Raymond. 1980. "Rules of the Game in International Politics." *International Studies Quarterly* 24: 130–31.

———. 1996. "On Diplomacy in the Ancient Near East: The Amarna Letters." *Diplomacy and Statecraft* 7: 246.

Coleman, James. 1964. *Introduction to Mathematical Sociology.* New York: Free Press.

Collins, Edward, Jr., and Martin A. Rogoff. 1990. "The Caroline Incident of 1837, the McLeod Affair of 1840–1841, and the Development of International Law." *American Review of Canadian Studies* 20: 88–89, 92.

Condorcet, Marquis de. 1795. *Sketch for a Historical Picture of the Progress of the Human Mind.* London: Weidenfeld and Nicholson.

Coplin, William D. 1970. "Current Studies of the Functions of International Law." Pp. 149–207 in *Political Science Annual: An International Review,* ed. James A. Robinson, vol. 2. Indianapolis: Bobbs-Merrill.

Coser, Lewis A. 1964. *The Functions of Social Conflict.* New York: Free Press.

Cox, D. R., and David Oakes 1984. *Analysis of Survival Data.* London: Chapmann & Hall.

Creel, H. G. 1953. *Chinese Thought: From Confucius to Mao Tse-Tung.* New York: Mentor.

Crescenzi, Mark J. C., and Andrew J. Enterline. 1999. "Ripples from the Waves? A Systemic, Time-Series Analysis of Democracy, Democratization, and Interstate War." *Journal of Peace Research* 36: 75–94.

Cusack, Thomas, and Wolf-Dieter Eberwein. 1982. "Prelude to War: Incidence, Escalation and Intervention in International Disputes, 1900–1976." *International Interactions* 9: 9–28.

Cusack, Thomas, and Richard Stoll. 1990. *Exploring Realpolitik.* Boulder, Colo.: Rienner.

Damasio, Antonio. 1994. *Decartes' Error: Emotion, Reason, and the Human Brain.* New York: Putnam's.

Dawisha, Adeed I. 1980. *Syria and the Lebanese Crisis.* London: Macmillan.

Dawisha, Karen. 1984. *The Kremlin and the Prague Spring.* Berkeley: University of California Press.

Dawson, Doyne. 1996. *The Origins of Western Warfare: Militarism and Morality in the Ancient World.* Boulder, Colo.: Westview.

Dessler, David. 1991. "Beyond Correlations: Toward a Causal Theory of War." *International Studies Quarterly* 35: 337–55.

Deutsch, Karl W., and J. David Singer. 1964. "Multipolar Power Systems and International Stability." *World Politics* 16: 390–406.

Devlin, Keith Goodby. 1997. *Decartes: The End of Logic and the Search for a New Cosmology.* New York: Wiley.

DiCicco, Jonathan M., and Jack S. Levy. 1999. "Power Shifts and Problem Shifts: The Evolution of the Power Transition Research Program." *Journal of Conflict Resolution* 42: 675–704.

Diehl, Paul F. 1983. "Arms Races and Escalation: A Closer Look." *Journal of Peace Research* 20: 205–12.

———. 1985a. "Arms Races to War: Testing Some Empirical Linkages." *Sociological Quarterly* 26: 331–49.

———. 1985b. "Contiguity and Military Escalation in Major Power Rivalries, 1816–1980." *Journal of Politics* 47: 1203–11.

———. 1991. "Geography and War: A Review and Assessment of the Empirical Literature." *International Interactions* 17: 11–27.

———. 1992. "What Are They Fighting For? The Importance of Issues in International Conflict Research." *Journal of Peace Research* 29: 333–44.

———, ed. 1998. *The Dynamics of Enduring Rivalries.* Urbana: University of Illinois Press.

Diehl, Paul F., and Mark Crescenzi. 1998. "Reconfiguring the Arms Race–War Debate." *Journal of Peace Research* 35: 111–18.

Diehl, Paul F., and Gary Goertz. 2000. *War and Peace in International Rivalry.* Ann Arbor: University of Michigan Press.

Diehl, Paul F., Jennifer Reifschneider, and Paul R. Hensel. 1996. "United Nations Intervention and Recurring Conflict." *International Organization* 50: 683–700.

Dixon, William. 1994."Democracy and the Peaceful Settlement of International Conflict." *American Political Science Review* 88: 14–32.

———. 1996a. "Democracy and the Management of International Conflict." *Journal of Conflict Resolution* 37: 42–68.

———. 1996b. "Third-Party Techniques for Preventing Conflict Escalation and Promoting Peaceful Settlement." *International Organization* 50: 653–82.

Dobrynin, Anatoly. 1995. "Dobrynin's Cable to the Soviet Foreign Ministry, 27 October 1962." Pp. 79–80 in *Cold War Crises: Cold War International History Bulletin* (CWIHB), No. 5. Washington, D.C.: Woodrow Wilson International Center.

Donaldson, Peter S. 1988. *Machiavelli and the Mystery of State.* Cambridge: Cambridge University Press.

Donnelly, Jack. 1992. "Twentieth Century Realism." Pp. 85–111 in *Traditions of International Ethics,* ed. Terry Nardin and David R. Mapel. Cambridge: Cambridge University Press.

Doran, Charles F. 1971. *The Politics of Assimilation: Hegemony and Its Aftermath.* Baltimore: Johns Hopkins University Press.

———. 1983. "Power Cycle Theory and the Contemporary State System." Pp. 165–82 in *Contending Approaches to World System Analysis,* ed. William R. Thompson. Beverly Hills: Sage.

———. 1985. "Power Cycle Theory and Systems Stability." Pp. 292–312 in *Rhythms in Politics and Economics,* ed. Paul M. Johnson and William R. Thompson. New York: Praeger.

———. 1989. "Systemic Disequilibrium, Foreign Policy Role, and the Power Cycle: Challenges for Research Design." *Journal of Conflict Resolution* 33: 371–401.

———. 1991. *Systems in Crisis: New Imperatives of High Politics at Century's End.* Cambridge: Cambridge University Press.

———. 1995. "The 'Discontinuity Dilemma' of Changing Systems Structure: Confronting the Principles of the Power Cycle." Paper presented at the annual meeting of the International Studies Association, Chicago.

Doran, Charles F., and Wes Parsons. 1980. "War and the Cycle of Relative Power." *American Political Science Review* 74: 947–65.

Downing, David. 1980. *An Atlas of Territorial and Border Disputes.* London: New English Library.

Dowty, Alan. 1984. *Middle East Crisis: US Decision-Making in 1958, 1970, and 1973.* Berkeley: University of California Press, 1984.

Doyle, Michael. 1986. "Liberalism and World Politics." *American Political Science Review* 80: 1151–70.

Durkheim, Emile. 1895. *The Rule of Sociological Method.* New York: Free Press.

East, Maurice, and Philip M. Gregg. 1967. "Factors Influencing Cooperation and Conflict in the International System." *International Studies Quarterly* 11: 244–69.

East, Maurice, and Charles F. Hermann. 1974. "Do Nation-Types Account for Foreign Policy Behavior?" Pp. 269–303 in *Comparing Foreign Policies,* ed. James N. Rosenau. New York: Wiley.

Eberwein, Wolf-Dieter. 1982. "The Seduction of Power: Serious International Disputes and the Power Status of Nations, 1900–1976." *International Interactions* 9: 57–74.

Eldredge, Niles, and Stephen J. Gould. 1972. "Punctuated Equilibria: An Alternative to Phyletic Gradualism." Pp. 82–115 in *Models in Paleobiology*, ed. Thomas J. M. Schopf. San Francisco: Freeman, Cooper.

Elfstrom, Gerard. 1990. *Ethics for a Shrinking World.* New York: St. Martin's.

El-Gamasy, Marshall A. G. 1993. *The October War: Memoirs of Field Marshall El-Gamasy of Egypt.* Cairo: American University in Cairo Press.

Elman, Miriam Fendius, ed. 1997. *Paths to Peace: Is Democracy the Answer?* Cambridge, Mass.: MIT Press.

Enterline, Andrew J. 1996. "Correspondence: Driving While Democratizing." *International Security* 20: 183–96.

———. 1998a. "Fledgling Political Systems: Communities, Regimes, Authorities, and Interstate Conflict, 1816–1992." Ph.D. dissertation, State University of New York at Binghamton.

———. 1998b. "Regime Changes and Interstate Conflict, 1816–1992." *Political Research Quarterly* 51: 385–409.

———. 1998c. "Regime Changes, Neighborhoods, and Interstate Conflict, 1816–1992." *Journal of Conflict Resolution* 42: 804–29.

Erasmus, Desiderius. 1997. *The Education of a Christian Prince,* trans. Lisa Jardine, Cambridge: Cambridge University Press.

Eriksen, Thomas Hylland, and Iver B. Neumann, 1993. "International Relations as a Cultural System: An Agenda for Research." *Cooperation and Conflict* 28: 233–64.

Ewald, François. 1991. "Norms, Discipline, and the Law." Pp. 138–61 in *Law and the Order of Culture*, ed. Robert Post. Berkeley: University of California Press.

Faber, Jan, Henk W. Houweling, and Jan G. Siccama. 1984. "Diffusion of War: Some Theoretical Considerations and Empirical Evidence." *Journal of Peace Research* 21: 277–88.

Farber, Henry S., and Gowa, Joanne. 1995. "Polities and Peace." *International Security* 20: 123–46.

——— 1997. "Common Interests or Common Polities: Reinterpreting the Democratic Peace." *Journal of Politics* 59: 393–417.

Fearon, James D. 1994. "Signaling Versus the Balance of Power and Interests: An Empirical Test of a Crisis Bargaining Model." *Journal of Conflict Resolution* 38: 236–69.

———. 1995. "Rationalist Explanations for War." *International Organization* 49: 379–414.

Fearon, James D., and David D. Laitin. 1996. "Explaining Interethnic Cooperation." *American Political Science Review* 90: 715–35.

Feierabend, Ivo K., and Rosalind L. Feierabend. 1969. "Level of Development and International Behavior." Pp. 135–88 in *Foreign Policy and the Developing Nation*, ed. R. Butwell. Lexington: University of Kentucky Press.

Finnemore, Martha, and Kathryn Sikkink. 1998. "International Norm Dynamics and Political Change." *International Organization* 52: 887–917.

Forsythe, David P. 1992. "Democracy, War and Covert Action." *Journal of Peace Research* 29: 385–95.

Friedrich, Carl. J. 1957. *Constitutional Reason of State.* Providence, R.I.: Brown University Press.

Fukuyama, Francis. 1992. *The End of History and the Last Man*. New York: Free Press.

Gaddis, John Lewis. 1987. "The Long Peace: Elements of Stability in the Postwar International System." Pp. 215–46 in *The Long Peace: Inquiries into the History of the Cold War*, ed. John Lewis Gaddis. Oxford: Oxford University Press.

Galtung, Johan. 1964. "A Structural Theory of Aggression." *Journal of Peace Research* 1: 95–119.

Gambetta, Diego. 1988. "Can We Trust?" Pp. 213–37 in *Trust: Making and Breaking Cooperative Relations*, ed. Diego Gambetta. Oxford: Blackwell.

Garner, James Wilford. 1920. *International Law and the World War*, vol. 1. London: Longmans, Green.

Garnham, David. 1976a. "Dyadic International War, 1816–1965: The Role of Power Parity and Geographical Proximity." *Western Political Quarterly* 39: 231–42.

———. 1976b. "Power Parity and Lethal International Violence, 1969–1973." *Journal of Conflict Resolution* 20: 379–94.

Garrett, Stephen. 1996. *Conscience and Power: An Examination of Dirty Hands and Political Leadership*. New York: St. Martin's.

Gartzke, Erik, and Michael Simon. 1998. "A General Test of Alliance Theory." Unpublished manuscript, Penn State University.

———. 1999. "Hot Hand: A Critical Analysis of Enduring Rivalries." *Journal of Politics* 63: 777–98.

Gaubatz, Kurt T. 1996. "Democratic States and Commitment in International Relations." *International Organization* 50: 109–30.

Geller, Daniel S. 1985. *Domestic Factors in Foreign Policy*. Cambridge, Mass.: Schenkman.

———. 1988. "Power System Membership and Patterns of War." *International Political Science Review* 9: 365–79.

———. 1990. "Nuclear Weapons, Deterrence, and Crisis Escalation." *Journal of Conflict Resolution* 34: 291–310.

———. 1992a. "Capability Concentration, Power Transition, and War." *International Interactions* 17: 269–84.

———. 1992b. "Power Transition and Conflict Initiation." *Conflict Management and Peace Science* 12: 1–16.

———. 1993. "Power Differentials and War in Rival Dyads." *International Studies Quarterly* 37: 173–93.

———. 1996. "Relative Power, Rationality, and International Conflict." Pp. 127–43 in *Parity and War: Evaluations and Extensions of The War Ledger*, ed. Jacek Kugler and Douglas Lemke. Ann Arbor: University of Michigan Press.

———. 1998. "The Stability of the Military Balance and War among Great Power Rivals." Pp. 165–90 in *The Dynamics of Enduring Rivalries*, ed. Paul F. Diehl. Urbana: University of Illinois Press.

———. 1999. "Status Quo Orientation, Capabilities, and Patterns of War Initiation in Dyadic Rivalries." Paper presented at the Military Operations Research Society, 67th symposium, U.S. Military Academy, West Point, N.Y., 22–24 June.

Geller, Daniel S., and J. David Singer. 1998. *Nations at War: A Scientific Study of International Conflict*. Cambridge: Cambridge University Press.

Gelpi, Christopher. 1997. "Crime and Punishment: The Role of Norms in Crisis Bargaining." *American Political Science Review* 91: 339–60.

George, Alexander et al. 1983. *Managing US-Soviet Rivalry: Problems of Crisis Prevention.* Boulder: Westview.

George, Alexander, and Richard Smoke. 1974. *Deterrence in American Foreign Policy.* New York: Columbia University Press.

Gibbs, Brian H. and J. David Singer. 1993. *Empirical Knowledge on World Politics: A Summary of Quantitative Research, 1970–1991.* Westport, Conn.: Greenwood.

Gibler, Douglas M. 1996. "Alliances that Never Balance: The Territorial Settlement Treaty." *Conflict Management and Peace Science* 15: 75–97.

———. 1997a. "Control the Issues, Control the Conflict: The Effects of Alliances That Settle Territorial Issues on Interstate Rivalries." *International Interactions* 22: 341–68.

———. 1997b. "Re-conceptualizing the Alliance Variable: An Empirical Typology of Alliances." Ph.D. dissertation, Vanderbilt University.

———. 1998. "Identifying Revisionist States." Mimeo., University of Kentucky.

———. 1999a. "Counterpoint: East or Further East?" *Journal of Peace Research* 36: 627–37.

———. 1999b. "An Extension of the Correlates of War Formal Alliance Data Set: 1648–1815." *International Interaction,* 25: 1–28.

Gibler, Douglas M., and John A. Vasquez. 1998. "Uncovering the Dangerous Alliances, 1495–1980." *International Studies Quarterly* 42: 785–807.

Gilpin, Robert. 1981. *War and Change in World Politics.* Cambridge: Cambridge University Press.

Ginther, Konrad. 1995. "Reflections on International Law in Respect to African Customary Law." Pp. 71–88 in *Recht zwischen Umbruch und Bewahrung,* ed. Ulrich Beyerlin, Michael Bothe, Rainer Hofmann, and Ernst-Ulrich Petersmann. Berlin: Springer.

Gleditsch, Nils Petter. 1992. "Democracy and Peace." *Journal of Peace Research* 29: 369–76.

Gleditsch, Nils Petter, and Havard Hegre. 1997. "Peace and Democracy: Three Levels of Analysis." *Journal of Conflict Resolution* 41: 283–310.

Gleditsch, Nils Petter, and J. David Singer. 1975. "Distance and International War, 1816–1965." Pp. 481–506 in Proceedings of the International Peace Research Association (IPRA) Fifth General Conference. Oslo, Norway: IPRA.

Gobineau, Joseph Arthur de. 1874. *Les Pleiades.* 1928. Reprint, New York: Knopf.

Gochman, Charles S. 1990a. "Capability-Driven Disputes." Pp. 141–59 in *Prisoners of War? Nation-States in the Modern Era,* ed. Charles S. Gochman and Alan N. Sabrosky. Lexington, Mass.: Lexington.

———. 1990b. "The Geography of Conflict: Militarized Interstate Disputes since 1816." Paper presented at the annual meeting of the International Studies Association, Washington, D.C.

———. 1991. "Interstate Metrics: Conceptualizing, Operationalizing, and Measuring the Geographic Proximity of States since the Congress of Vienna." *International Interactions* 17: 93–112.

———. 1993. "The Evolution of Disputes." *International Interactions* 19: 49–76.

Gochman, Charles S., and Russell J. Leng. 1983. "Realpolitik and the Road to War." *International Studies Quarterly* 27: 97–120.

Gochman, Charles S., and Zeev Maoz. 1984. "Militarized Interstate Disputes, 1816–1976: Procedures, Patterns, and Insights," *Journal of Conflict Resolution* 28: 585–616.

Goertz, Gary. 1995. "Enduring Rivalries and the Study of Deterrence." Draft manuscript.

Goertz, Gary, and Paul F. Diehl. 1992a. "The Empirical Importance of Enduring Rivalries." *International Interactions* 18: 151–63.

———. 1992b. *Territorial Changes and International Conflict*. London: Routledge.

———. 1992c. "Toward a Theory of International Norms: Some Conceptual and Measurement Issues." *Journal of Conflict Resolution 36*: 634–64.

———. 1993. "Enduring Rivalries: Theoretical Constructs and Empirical Patterns." *International Studies Quarterly* 37: 147–71.

———. 1994a. "International Norms and Power Politics." Pp. 101–22 in *Reconstructing Realpolitik*, ed. Frank W. Wayman and Paul F. Diehl. Ann Arbor: University of Michigan Press.

———. 1994b. "Toward a Theory of International Norms: Some Conceptual and Measurement Issues." *Journal of Conflict Resolution 36*: 634–64.

———. 1995a. "The Initiation and Termination of Enduring Rivalries: The Impact of Political Shocks." *American Journal of Political Science* 39: 30–52.

———. 1995b. "Taking 'Enduring' Out of Enduring Rivalry: The Rivalry Approach to War and Peace." *International Interactions* 21: 291–308.

———. 1997. "Connecting Risky Dyads: An Evaluation of Relations between Enduring Rivalries." Pp. 132–60 in *Enforcing Cooperation:"Risky" States and the Intergovernmental Management of Conflict*, ed. Gerald Schneider and Patricia Weitsman. London: Macmillan.

———. 1998. "The Volcano Model and Other Patterns in the Evolution of Enduring Rivalries." Pp. 98–127 in *The Dynamics of Enduring Rivalries*, ed. Paul F. Diehl. Urbana: University of Illinois Press.

Goldstein, Joshua S. 1988. *Long Cycles: Prosperity and War in the Modern Age*. New Haven, Conn.: Yale University Press.

Gowa, Joanne S. 1994. *Allies, Adversaries, and International Trade*. Princeton, N.J.: Princeton University Press.

———. 1999. *Ballots or Bullets: The Elusive Democratic Peace*. Princeton: Princeton University Press.

Gowa, Joanne, and Edward Mansfield. 1993. "Power Politics and International Trade." *American Political Science Review* 87: 408–20.

Gray, Colin S. 1993. "Force, Order, and Justice: The Ethics of Realism in Statecraft." *Global Affairs* 8: 1–17.

Guetzkow, Harold. 1950. "Long Range Research in International Relations." *American Perspective* 4: 421–40. Reprint, pp. 67–75 in *Classics of International Relations,* ed. John Vasquez. 3d ed. Upper Saddle River, N.J.: Prentice Hall, 1996.

———. 1968. "Some Correspondences Between Simulation and Realities in International Relations." Pp. 202–69 in *New Approaches to International Relations,* ed. M. Kaplan. New York: St. Martin's.

Gulick, Edward V. 1955 *Europe's Classical Balance of Power*. New York: Norton.

Gurr, Ted Robert. 1974. "Persistence and Change in Political Systems." *American Political Science Review* 68: 1482–504.

———. 1989. *Polity II: Political Structures and Regime Change, 1800–1986*. Inter-University Consortium for Political and Social Research, Ann Arbor, Mich.

———. 1993. *Minorities at Risk: A Global View of Ethnopolitical Conflicts*. Washington, D.C.: United States Institute of Peace Press.

Haas, Peter. 1989. "Do Regimes Matter? Epistemic Communities and Mediterranean Pollution Control." *International Organization* 43: 377–403.

Habicht, Max. 1931. *Treaties for the Pacific Settlement of Disputes*. Cambridge, Mass.: Harvard University Press.

Halberstam, David. 1969. *The Best and the Brightest*. New York: Random House.

Harre, Rom. 1970. *The Method of Science*. London: Wykeham.

Harvey, Frank P. 1995. "Rational Deterrence Theory Revisited: A Progress Report." *Canadian Journal of Political Science* 28: 403–36.

Hempel, Carl G. 1966. *Philosophy of Natural Science*. Upper Saddle River, N.J.: Prentice Hall.

Hensel, Paul R. 1994. "One Thing Leads to Another: Recurrent Militarized Disputes in Latin America, 1816–1986." *Journal of Peace Research* 31: 281–98.

———. 1995. "Political Democracy and Militarized Conflict in Evolving Interstate Rivalries." Paper presented at the annual Meeting of the American Political Science Association, Chicago.

———. 1996a. "Charting a Course to Conflict: Territorial Issues and Militarized Interstate Disputes, 1816–1992." *Conflict Management and Peace Science* 15: 43–73.

———. 1996b. "The Evolution of Interstate Rivalry." Ph.D. dissertation, University of Illinois, Urbana.

———. 1997. "What Do They Do When They Are Not Fighting?: Event Data and Non-Militarized Dimensions of Interstate Rivalry." Unpublished manuscript, Florida State University.

———. 1998a. "Domestic Politics and Interstate Conflict." Paper presented at the annual meeting of the American Political Science Association, Boston.

———. 1998b. "Evolutionary Perspectives on Recurrent Conflict and Rivalry." Paper presented at the Conference on Evolutionary Perspectives on International Relations, Bloomington, Ind.

———. 1998c. "Interstate Rivalry and the Study of Militarized Conflict." Pp. 162–204 in *Conflict in World Politics: Advances in the Study of Crises, War, and Peace*, ed. Frank Harvey and Ben Mor. London: Macmillan.

———. 1999a. "Contentious Issues and World Politics: The Management of Territorial Claims in the Western Hemisphere." (4 August).

———. 1999b. "The Evolution of the Franco-German Rivalry." Pp. 86–123 in *Great Power Rivalries*, ed. William R. Thompson. Columbia: University of South Carolina Press.

Hensel, Paul R., and Paul F. Diehl. 1994a. "It Takes Two to Tango: Non-Militarized Response in Interstate Disputes." *Journal of Conflict Resolution* 38: 479–506.

———. 1994b. "Testing Empirical Propositions About Shatterbelts, 1945–1976." *Political Geography* 13: 33–52.

Hensel, Paul R., Gary Goertz, and Paul F. Diehl. 2000. "The Democratic Peace and Rivalries." *Journal of Politics*, forthcoming.

Hensel, Paul R., and Sara McLaughlin. 1996. "Power Transitions and Dispute Escalation in Evolving Interstate Rivalries." Paper presented at the annual meeting of the American Political Science Association, San Francisco.

Hensel, Paul R., and Thomas Sowers. 1998. "Territorial Claims, Major Power Competition, and the Origins of Enduring Rivalry." Paper presented at the joint meeting of the

International Studies Association and the European Standing Group on International Relations, Vienna.

Hermann, Charles F. 1969. *Crises in Foreign Policy.* Indianapolis: Bobbs-Merrill.

———. 1972. "Threat, Time, and Surprise: A Simulation of International Crisis." Pp. 187–216 in *International Crises,* ed. Charles F. Hermann. New York: Free Press.

Hersh, Seymour H. 1993. "On the Nuclear Edge." *New Yorker,* 29 March, pp. 56–73.

Hewitt, J. Joseph, and Jonathan Wilkenfeld. 1997. "Dyadic or Monadic? Democracies in Crisis." Paper presented at the annual meeting of the International Studies Association, Toronto.

Hill, Norman. 1945. *Claims to Territory in International Relations.* New York: Oxford University Press.

Hobbes, Thomas. 1651 [1946]. *Leviathan,* ed. Michael Oakeshott. Oxford: Blackwell.

Hoffmann, Steven A. 1990. *India and the China Crisis.* Berkeley: University of California Press.

Holsti, Kalevi J. 1991. *Peace and War: Armed Conflicts and International Order 1648–1989.* Cambridge: Cambridge University Press.

———. 1996. *The State, War, and the State of War.* New York: Cambridge University Press.

Holsti, Ole. 1972. *Crisis Escalation War.* Montreal: McGill-Queens University Press.

———. 1989. "Crisis Decision Making." Pp. 8–84 in *Behavior, Society, and Nuclear War,* vol. 1, ed. Phillip. E. Tetlock, Jo L. Husbands, Paul C. Stern, and Charles Tilly. New York: Oxford University Press.

Holsti, Ole R., Richard A. Brody, and Robert C. North. 1965. "Measuring Affect and Reaction in International Reaction Models: Empirical Materials from the 1962 Cuban Crisis." *Peace Research Society (International)* Papers 2: 170–90.

Holsti, Ole R., Robert C. North, and Richard A. Brody 1968. "Perception and Action in the 1914 Crisis." Pp. 123–58 in *Quantitative International Politics,* ed. J. David Singer. New York: Free Press.

Holsti, O. R., P. T. Hopmann, and J. D. Sullivan. 1973. *Unity and Disintegration in International Alliances.* New York: Wiley.

Hopf, Ted. 1991. "Polarity, the Offense-Defense Balance, and War." *American Political Science Review* 85: 475–94.

Houweling, Henk W., and Jan G. Siccama. 1981. "The Arms Race-War Relationship: Why Serious Disputes Matter." *Arms Control* 2 : 157–97.

———. 1985. "The Epidemiology of War, 1816–1980." *Journal of Conflict Resolution* 29: 641–63.

———. 1988a. "Power Transitions as a Cause of War." *Journal of Conflict Resolution* 32: 87–102.

———. 1988b. *Studies of War.* Dordrecht, The Netherlands: Martinus Nijhoff.

———. 1991. "Power Transitions and Critical Points as Predictors of Great Power War: Toward a Synthesis." *Journal of Conflict Resolution* 35: 642–58.

———. 1993. "The Neo-Functionalist Explanation of World Wars: A Critique and an Alternative." *International Interactions* 18: 387–408.

Howard, Michael. 1991. "British Grand Strategy in World War I." Pp. 21–41 in *Grand Strategy in War and Peace,* ed. Paul Kennedy. New Haven, Conn.: Yale University Press.

Hudson, Valerie M., ed. 1997. *Culture and Foreign Policy.* Boulder, Colo.: Rienner.

Huntington, Samuel P. 1958. "Arms Races: Prerequisites and Results." *Public Policy* 8: 41–86.

———. 1996. *The Clash of Civilizations and the Remaking of World Order.* New York: Simon & Schuster.

Huth, Paul K. 1988. *Extended Deterrence and the Prevention of War.* New Haven, Conn.: Yale University Press.

———. 1996a. "Enduring Rivalries and Territorial Disputes, 1950–1990." *Conflict Management and Peace Science* 15: 7–41.

———. 1996b. *Standing Your Ground.* Ann Arbor: University of Michigan Press.

Huth, Paul, D. Scott Bennett, and Christopher Gelpi. 1992. "System Uncertainty, Risk Propensity, and International Conflict Among the Great Powers." *Journal of Conflict Resolution* 36: 478–517.

Huth, Paul, Christopher Gelpi, and D. Scott Bennett. 1993. "The Escalation of Great Power Militarized Disputes: Testing Rational Deterrence Theory and Structural Realism." *American Political Science Review* 87: 609–23.

Huth, Paul, and Bruce Russett. 1984. "What Makes Deterrence Work? Cases from 1900 to 1980." *Journal of Conflict Resolution* 36: 496–526.

———. 1993. "General Deterrence between Enduring Rivals: Testing Three Competing Models." *American Political Science Review* 87: 61–73.

Hwang, Peter, and William P. Burgers. 1999. "Apprehension and Temptation: The Forces Against Cooperation." *Journal of Conflict Resolution* 43: 117–30.

Inglehart, Ronald. 1990. *Culture Shift.* Princeton, N.J.: Princeton University Press.

———. 1997. *Modernization and Post-Modernization.* Princeton, N.J.: Princeton University Press.

Ingram, Edward. 1999. "Great Britain and Russia." Pp. 269–305 in *Great Power Rivalries*, ed. William R. Thompson. Columbia: University of South Carolina Press.

Intriligator, Michael D., and Dagobert L. Brito. 1989. "Richardsonian Arms Race Models." Pp. 219–36 in *Handbook of War Studies*, ed. Manus I. Midlarsky. Boston: Unwin Hyman.

Iriye, Keishiro. 1968. "The Principles of International Law in the Light of Confucian Doctrine." *Recueil des cours* 120: 33, 45.

Isocrates,1929. *On the Peace*, trans. George Norlin. London: Heinemann.

Jacquin, Dominique, Andrew Oros, and Marco Verweij. 1993. "Culture in International Relations: An Introduciton to the Special Issue." *Millennium* 22: 375–77.

Jaggers, Keith, and Ted Robert Gurr. 1995. "Tracking Democracy's Third Wave with the Polity III Data." *Journal of Peace Research* 32: 469–82.

James, Patrick. 1988. *Crisis and War.* Montreal: McGill-Queen's Univesity Press.

James, Patrick, and Lui Hebron. 1997. "Great Powers, Cycles of Relative Capability and Crises in World Politics." *International Interactions* 23: 145–73.

James, Patrick, Eric Solberg, and Murray Wolfson. 1999. "An Identified Systemic Model of the Democracy-Peace Nexus." *Defence and Peace Economics* 10: 1–37.

James, Patrick, and Jonathan Wilkenfeld. 1984. "Structural Factors and International Crisis Behavior." *Conflict Management and Peace Science* 7: 33–53.

Janis, Irving. 1982. *Victims of Groupthink.* 2d ed. Boston: Houghton Mifflin.

Jarosz, William W., and Joseph Nye. 1993. "The Shadow of the Past: Learning from History in National Security Decision Making." Pp. 126–89 in *Behavior, Society, and International Conflict*, Vol. III, ed. Phillip E. Tetlock et al. New York: Oxford University Press.

Jayatilleke, K. N. 1968. "The Principles of International Law in Buddhist Doctrine." *Recueil des cours* 120: 445–567.

Jervis, Robert. 1970. *The Logic of Images in International Relations*. Princeton, N.J.: Princeton University Press.

————. 1976. *Perception and Misperception in International Politics*. Princeton, N.J.: Princeton University Press.

————. 1997. *System Effects: Complexity in Political and Social Life*. Princeton: Princeton University Press.

Joll, James. 1984. *The Origins of the First World War*. London: Longman.

Jones, Daniel M., Stuart A. Bremer, and J. David Singer. 1996. "Militarized Interstate Disputes, 1816–1992: Rationale, Coding Rules, and Empirical Patterns." *Conflict Management and Peace Science* 15: 163–213.

Jones, Karen. 1996. "Trust as an Affective Attitude." *Ethics* 107: 4–21.

Jones, Susan and J. David Singer. 1972. *Beyond Conjecture in International Politics: Abstracts of Databased Research*. Itasca, Ill.: F. E. Peacock.

Jukes, Geoffrey. 1985. *Hitler's Stalingrad Decisions*. Berkeley: University of California Press.

Kacowicz, Arie M. 1994. *Peaceful Territorial Change*. Columbia: University of South Carolina Press.

————1995. "Explaining Zones of Peace: Democracies as Satisfied Powers?" *Journal of Peace Research* 32: 265–76.

Kahn, Herman. 1965. *On Escalation: Methaphors and Scenarios*. New York: Praeger.

Kaiser, David. 1990. *Politics and War: European Conflict form Philip II to Hitler*. Cambridge, Mass.: Harvard University Press.

Kaplan, Morton. 1957. *System and Process in International Politics*. New York: Wiley.

Kegley, Charles W., Jr., and Gregory A. Raymond. 1981. "International Legal Norms and the Preservation of Peace, 1820–1964: Some Evidence and Bivariate Relationships." *International Interactions* 8: 171–87.

————. 1982. "Alliance Norms and War: A New Piece in an Old Puzzle." *International Studies* Quarterly 26: 572–95.

————. 1986. "Normative Constraints on the Use of Force Short of War." *Journal of Peace Research* 23: 213–27.

————. 1990. *When Trust Breaks Down: Alliance Norms and World Politics*. Columbia: University of South Carolina Press.

————. 1994. "Networks of Intrigue: Realpolitik, Alliances, and International Security." Pp. 185–203 in *Reconstructing Realpolitik*, ed. Frank W. Wyman and Paul F. Diehl. Ann Arbor: University of Michigan Press.

————. 1999. *How Nations Make Peace*. New York: Worth/St. Martin's.

Kelsen, Hans. 1952. *Principles of International Law*. New York: Rinehart.

Kemp, Anita. 1977. "A Path Analytic Model of International Violence." *International Interactions* 4: 53–85.

Kennan, George F. 1991. "Morality and Foreign Policy." Pp. 59–76 in *Morality and Foreign Policy: Realpolitik Revisited*, ed. Kenneth M. Jensen and Elizabeth P. Faulkner. Washington, D.C.: United States Institute of Peace Press.

Kennedy, Paul. 1987. *The Rise and Fall of the Great Powers*. New York: Random House.

Khong, Yuen Foong. 1992. *Analogies at War: Korea, Munich, Dien Bien Phu, and the Vietnam Decision of 1965*. Princeton, N.J.: Princeton University Press.

Kim, Samuel S. 1997. "China as a Great Power." *Current History* 96: 246–56.

Kim, Woosang. 1991. "Alliance Transitions and Great Power War." *American Journal of Political Science* 35: 833–50.

———. 1992. "Power Transitions and Great Power War from Westphalia to Waterloo." *World Politics* 45: 153–72.

———. 1996. "Power Parity, Alliance, and War from 1648 to 1975." Pp. 93–105 in *Parity and War: Evaluations and Extensions of The War Ledger*, ed. Jacek Kugler and Douglas Lemke. Ann Arbor: University of Michigan Press.

Kim, Woosang, and James D. Morrow. 1992. "When Do Power Shifts Lead to War?" *American Journal of Political Science* 36: 896–922.

King, Gary, Robert O. Keohane, and Sidney Verba. 1994. *Designing Social Inquiry*. Princeton: Princeton University Press.

Kinsella, David. 1994a. "Conflict in Context: Arms Transfers and Third World Rivalry During the Cold War." *American Journal of Political Science* 38: 557–81.

———. 1994b. "The Impact of Superpower Arms Transfers on Conflict in the Middle East." *Defence and Peace Economics* 5: 19–36.

———. 1995. "Nested Rivalries: Superpower Competition, Arms Transfers, and Regional Conflict, 1950–1990." *International Interaction* 15: 109–25.

Kirby, Andrew, and Michael Ward. 1987. "The Spatial Analysis of Peace and War." *Comparative Political Studies* 20: 293–313.

Kocs, Stephen. 1995. "Territorial Disputes and Interstate War, 1945–1987." *Journal of Politics* 57: 159–75.

Köhler, Gernot. 1975. "Imperialism as a Level of Analysis in Correlates of War Research." *Journal of Conflict Resolution* 19:48–62.

Kremenyuk, Victor A. 1994."The Cold War as Cooperation." Pp. 3–25 in *From Rivalry to Cooperation: Russian and American Perspectives on the Post–Cold War Era*, ed. Manus I. Midlarsky, John A. Vasquez, and Peter V. Gladkov. New York: HarperCollins.

Kroeber, Alfred, and Clyde Kluckholn. 1952. *Cultures: A Critical Review of Concepts and Definitions*. New York: Random House.

Kruzel, Joseph. 1994. "More a Chasm Than a Gap, but Do Scholars Want to Bridge It?" *Mershon International Studies Review* 38: 179–81.

Kugler, Jacek. 1984."Terror Without Deterrence: Reassessing the Role of Nuclear Weapons," *Journal of Conflict Resolution* 28: 470–506.

Kugler, Jacek, and Douglas Lemke, eds. 1996. *Parity and War*. Ann Arbor: University of Michigan Press.

———. 2000. "The Power Transition Research Program: Assessing Theoretical and Empirical Advances." Pp. 129–63 in *Handbook of War Studies II*, ed. Manus I. Midlarsky. Ann Arbor: University of Michigan Press.

Kugler, Jacek, and A. F. K. Organski. 1989. "The Power Transition: A Retrospective and Prospective Evaluation." Pp. 171–94 in *Handbook of War Studies*, ed. Manus I. Midlarsky. Boston: Unwin Hyman.

Lakatos, Imre. 1970. "Falsification and the Methodology of Scientific Research Programmes." Pp. 91–196 in *Criticism and the Growth of Knowledge*, ed. Imre Lakatos and Alan Musgrave. Cambridge: Cambridge University Press.

Lake, David. 1992. "Powerful Pacifists: Democratic States and War." *American Political Science Review* 86: 24–37.

Lapid, Yosef, and Friedrich Kratochwil, eds. 1996. *The Return of Culture and Identity to IR Theory.* Boulder, Colo.: Rienner.

Larson, Deborah Welch. 1999. "The US-Soviet Rivalry." Pp. 371–89 in *Great Power Rivalries,* ed. William R. Thompson. Columbia: University of South Carolina Press.

Lasswell, Harold. 1958. *Politics: Who Gets What, When, How.* New York: Meridian.

Lebow, Richard Ned. 1981. *Between Peace and War: The Nature of International Crisis.* Baltimore: Johns Hopkins University Press.

———. 1985. "Miscalculation in the South Atlantic: The Origins of the Falklands War." Pp. 89–124 in *Psychology and Deterrence,* ed. Robert Jervis, Richard Ned Lebow, and Janice Gross Stein. Baltimore: Johns Hopkins University Press.

Leech, H. Brougham. 1877. *An Essay on Ancient International Law.* Dublin: Ponsonby & Murphey.

Lehman, Edward. 1982. "On the Concept of Culture: A Theoretical Reassessment." *Social Forces* 50: 361–70.

Lemke, Douglas. 1993. "Multiple Hierarchies in World Politics." Unpublished manuscript, Vanderbilt University.

———. 1995. "The Tyranny of Distance: Redefining Relevant Dyads." *International Interactions* 21: 23–38.

———. 1996. "Small States and War: An Expansion of Power Transition Theory." Pp. 77–91 in *Parity and War: Evaluations and Extensions of The War Ledger,* ed. Douglas Lemke and Jacek Kugler. Ann Arbor: University of Michigan Press.

Lemke, Douglas, and William Reed. 1996. "Regime Types and Status Quo Evaluations: Power Transition Theory and the Democratic Peace." *International Interactions* 22: 143–64.

Lemke, Douglas, and Suzanne Werner. 1996. "Power Parity, Commitment to Change, and War." *International Studies Quarterly* 40: 235–60.

Leng, Russell. J. 1983. "When Will They Ever Learn? Coercive Bargaining in Recurrent Crises." *Journal of Conflict Resolution* 27: 379–419.

———. 1980. "Influence Strategies and Interstate Conflict." Pp. 124–57 in *The Correlates of War II: Testing Some Realpolitik Models,* ed. J. David Singer. New York: Free Press.

———. 1988. "Crisis Learning Games." *American Political Science Review* 82: 179–94.

———. 1993. *Interstate Crisis Behavior, 1816–1980: Realism vs. Reciprocity.* Cambridge: Cambridge University Press.

———. 1994. "Interstate Crisis Escalation and War." Pp. 307–32 in *The Dynamics of Aggression: Biological and Social Processes in Dyads and Groups,* ed. Michael Potegal and John. F. Knutson. Hillsdale, N.J.: Erlbaum.

———. 2000. *Bargaining and Learning in Recurring Crises: The Soviet-American, Egyptian-Israeli, and Indo-Pakistani Rivalries.* Ann Arbor: University of Michigan Press.

Leng, Russell J., and J. David Singer. 1988. "Militarized Interstate Crises: The BCOW Typology and Its Applications." *International Studies Quarterly* 32: 155–73.

Leng, Russell J., and Hugh Wheeler. 1979. "Influence Strategies, Success and War." *Journal of Conflict Resolution* 23 (December): 655–84.

Levy, Jack S. 1981. "Alliance Formation and War Behavior: An Analysis of the Great Powers, 1495–1975." *Journal of Conflict Resolution* 25: 581–613.

———. 1983a. "Misperception and the Causes of War." *World Politics* 36: 76–99.

———. 1983b. *War in the Modern Great Power System, 1495–1975.* Lexington: University of Kentucky Press.

———. 1984. "Size and Stability in the Modern Great Power System." *International Interactions* 11: 341–58.

———. 1985. "The Polarity of the System and International Stability: An Empirical Analysis." Pp. 41–66 in *Polarity and War,* ed. Alan Sabrosky. Boulder: Westview Press.

———. 1986. "Organizational Routines and the Causes of War." *International Studies Quarterly* 30: 193–222.

———. 1987. "Declining Power and the Preventive Motivation for War." *World Politics* 40: 82–107.

———. 1988. "Domestic Politics and War." *Journal of Interdisciplinary History* 18: 653–73.

———. 1989a. "The Causes of War: A Review of Theories and Evidence." Pp. 209–333 in *Behavior, Society, and Nuclear War*, vol. 1, ed. Philip E. Tetlock, Jo L. Husbands, Robert Jervis, Paul C. Stern, and Charles Tilly. New York: Oxford University Press.

———. 1989b. "Quantitative Studies of Deterrence Success and Failure." Pp. 98–133 in *Perspectives on Deterrence*, ed. Paul Stern, Robert Axelrod, Robert Jervis, and Roy Radner. Oxford: Oxford University Press.

———. 1990/91. "Preferences, Constraints, and Choices in July 1914." *International Security* 15: 151–86.

———. 1994a. "The Democratic Peace Hypothesis: From Description to Explanation." *Mershon International Studies Review* 38: 352–54.

——— 1994b. "Learning and Foreign Policy: Sweeping a Conceptual Minefield." *International Organization* 48: 279–312.

———. 1998. "The Causes of War and the Conditions of Peace." *Annual Review of Political Science* 1: 139–65.

Levy, Jack, and Salvatore Ali. 1998. "From Commercial Competition to Strategic Rivalry to War: The Evolution of the Anglo-Dutch Rivalry, 1609–1652." Pp. 29–63 in *The Dynamics of Enduring Rivalries,* ed. Paul F. Diehl. Urbana: University of Illinois Press.

Levy, Jack S., and T. Clifton Morgan. 1984. "The Frequency and Seriousness of War: An Inverse Relationship?" *Journal of Conflict Resolution* 28: 731–49.

———. 1986. The War-Weariness Hypothesis: An Empirical Test. Pp. 126–48 in *Persistent Patterns and Emergent Structures in a Waning Century*, ed. Margaret P. Karns. New York: Praeger.

Levy, Jack S., and Lily I. Vakili. 1992. "Diversionary Action by Authoritarian Regimes: Argentina in the Falklands/Malvinas Case." Pp. 118–46 in *The Internationalization of Communal Strife*, ed. Manus I. Midlarsky. New York: Routledge.

Licklider, Roy. 1995. "The Consequences of Negotiated Settlements in Civil Wars, 1945–1993." *American Political Science Review.* 89: 681–90.

Lind, Michael. 1999. *Vietnam: The Necessary War.* New York: Free Press.

Liska, George. 1962. *Nations in Alliance.* Baltimore: Johns Hopkins University Press.

Londregan, John B., and Keith T. Poole. 1996. "Does High Income Promote Democracy?" *World Politics* 49: 1–30.

Luard, Evan. 1970. *The International Regulation of Frontier Disputes.* New York: Praeger.

————. 1976. *Types of International Society*. New York: Free Press.

————. 1986. *War in International Society*. New Haven: Yale University Press.

Lueder, Carl. 1898. *Voelkerrecht*. Freiburg: Mohr.

Machiavelli, Niccolò. 1950. *The Prince,* trans. Luigi Ricci New York: Random House.

Mackie, J. L. 1977. *Ethics: Inventing Right and Wrong*. Harmondsworth, England: Penguin.

Mandel, Robert. 1980. "Roots of the Modern Interstate Border Dispute." *Journal of Conflict Resolution* 24: 427–54.

Mandell, Brian S., and Brian W. Tomlin. 1991. "Mediation in the Development of Norms to Manage Conflict: Kissinger in the Middle East." *Journal of Peace Research* 28: 54.

Mansbach, Richard W., and John A. Vasquez. 1981. *In Search of Theory: A New Paradigm for Global Politics*. New York: Columbia University Press.

Mansfield, Edward D. 1988. "Distributions of War over Time." *World Politics* 41: 21–51.

————. 1994. *Power, Trade, and War*. Princeton, N.J.: Princeton University Press.

Mansfield, Edward D., and Jack Snyder. 1995a. "Democratization and the Danger of War." *International Security* 20: 5–38.

————. 1995b. "Democratization and War." *Foreign Affairs* 74: 79–97.

————. 1996. "Correspondence: The Effects of Democratization on War." *International Security* 20: 196–207.

Maoz, Zeev. 1982. *Paths to Conflict: International Dispute Initiation, 1816–1976*. Boulder, Colo.: Westview.

————. 1983. "Resolve, Capabilities, and the Outcomes of Interstate Disputes, 1816–1976." *Journal of Conflict Resolution* 27: 195–229.

————. 1984. "Peace by Empire?: Conflict Outcomes and International Stability, 1816–1976." *Journal of Peace Research* 21: 227–41.

————. 1989. "Joining the Club of Nations: Political Development and International Conflict, 1816–1976." *International Studies Quarterly* 33: 199–231.

————. 1990. *Paradoxes of War: On the Art of National Self-Entrapment*. Boston: Unwin Hyman.

————. 1995. "National Preferences, International Structures, and Balance-of-Power Politics." *Journal of Theoretical Politics* 7: 369–93.

————. 1996. *Domestic Sources of Global Change*. Ann Arbor: University of Michigan Press.

————. 1997a. "The Debate over the Democratic Peace: Rearguard Action or Cracks in the Wall?" *International Security* 32: 162–98.

————. 1997b. "The Strategic Behavior of Nations, 1816–1986." Unpublished manuscript, Jaffee Center for Strategic Studies, Tel-Aviv University.

————. 1998. "Realist and Cultural Critiques of the Democratic Peace: A Theoretical and Empirical Reassessment." *International Interactions* 24: 3–89.

————. 2001. "Democratic Networks: Connecting National, Dyadic, and Systemic Perspectives in the Study of Democracy and War." In *War in a Changing World*, ed. Zeev Maoz and Azar Gat. Ann Arbor: University of Michigan Press.

Maoz, Zeev, and Nasrin Abdolali. 1989. "Regime Types and International Conflict, 1817–1976." *Journal of Conflict Resolution* 33: 3–35.

Maoz, Zeev, and Ben Mor. 1995. "Satisfaction, Capabilities, and the Evolution of Enduring Rivalries, 1816–1990: A Statistical Analysis of a Game-Theoretic Model." Paper presented at the annual meeting of the American Political Science Association, Chicago.

———. 1996. "Enduring Rivalries: The Early Years." *International Political Science Review* 17: 141–60.

———. 1998. "Learning, Preference Change, and the Evolution of Enduring Rivalries." Pp. 129–64 in *The Dynamics of Enduring Rivalries*, ed. Paul F. Diehl. Urbana: University of Illinois Press.

———. forthcoming. "International Hate Affairs: The Evolution of Enduring Rivalries." Ann Arbor: University of Michigan Press.

Maoz, Zeev, and Bruce Russett. 1992. "Alliance, Contiguity, Wealth, and Political Stability: Is the Lack of Conflict Among Democracies a Statistical Artifact?" *International Interactions* 17: 245–67.

———. 1993. "Normative and Structural Causes of Democratic Peace, 1946–1986." *American Political Science Review* 87: 624–38.

Marantz, Paul. 1995. "Eduard Shevardnadze and the End of the Soviet System: Necessity and Choice." Pp. 195–212 in *Ethics and Statecraft: The Moral Dimension of International Affairs*, ed. Cathal J. Nolan. Westport, Conn.: Praeger.

Marshall, Monty G. 1999. *Third World War: System, Process, and Conflict Dynamics*. Lanham, Md.: Rowman & Littlefield.

McClelland, Charles A. 1972. "The Beginning, Duration and Abatement of International Crises: Comparisons in Two Conflict Areas." Pp. 83–111 in *International Crises,* ed. Charles Hermann. New York: Free Press.

McClelland, David, and David Winter. 1981. *A New Case for Liberal Arts*. San Francisco: Jossey-Bass.

McElroy, Robert W. 1992. *Morality and American Foreign Policy*. Princeton, N.J.: Princeton University Press.

McGinnis, Michael. 1990. "A Rational Model of Regional Rivalry." *International Studies Quarterly* 34: 111–35.

McGinnis, Michael, and John Williams. 1989. "Change and Stability in Superpower Rivalry." *American Political Science Review* 83: 1101–23.

McLaughlin, Sara. 1996. "Endogeneity and the Democratic Peace." Paper presented at the annual meeting of the Peace Science Society (International), Houston, Tex.

Meinecke, Frederich. 1965. *Machiavellism: The Doctrine of Raison d'Etat and Its Place in History*. New York: Praeger.

Melville, Herman. 1979. *Moby Dick*. Berkeley: University of California Press.

Merton, Robert K. 1963. "Singletons and Multiples in Scientific Discovery." *Proceedings of the American Philosophical Society*, pp. 470–86.

Midlarsky, Manus I. 1975. *On War: Political Violence in the International System*. New York: Free Press.

———. 1988. *The Onset of World War*. Boston: Unwin Hyman.

———. 1993. "Polarity and International Stability." *American Political Science Review* 87: 173–77.

———. 1994. "Polarity, the Learning of Cooperation, and the Stability of International Systems." Pp. 26–39 in *From Rivalry to Cooperation: Russian and American Perspectives on the Post–Cold War Era*, ed. Manus I. Midlarsky, John A. Vasquez, and Peter V. Gladkov. New York: HarperCollins.

————. 1995. "Environmental Influences on Democracy: Aridity, Warfare, and a Reversal of the Causal Arrow." *Journal of Conflict Resolution* 39: 224–62.

————. 1998. "Democracy and Islam: Implications for Civilizational Conflict and the Democratic Peace." *International Studies Quarterly* 42: 485–511.

————. 1999. *The Evolution of Inequality: War, State, Survival, and Democracy in Comparative Perspective.* Stanford, Calif.: Stanford University Press.

————, ed. 1989. *Handbook of War Studies.* Boston: Unwin Hyman.

————, ed. 2000a. *Handbook of War Studies* II. Ann Arbor: University of Michigan Press.

————. 2000b. "Identity and International Conflict," in *Handbook of War Studies II*, ed. Manus I. Midlarsky. Ann Arbor: University of Michigan Press.

Mihalka, Michael. 1976. "Hostilities in the European State System, 1816–1970." *Peace Science Society Papers* 26: 100–16.

Mishra, Aneil K. 1996. "Organizational Responses to Crises: The Centrality of Trust." Pp. 264–69 in *Trust in Organizations: Frontiers of Theory and Research*, ed. Roderick M. Kramer and Tom R. Tyler. London: Sage.

Mitchell, Sara McLaughlin, and Brandon C. Prins. 1999. "Beyond Territorial Contiguity: Issues at Stake in Democratic Militarized Interstate Disputes." *International Studies Quarterly* 43:169–83.

Modelski, George. 1972. *Principles of World Politics.* New York: Free Press.

————. 1983. "Long Cycles of World Leadership." Pp. 115–39 in *Contending Approaches to World System Analysis*, ed. William R. Thompson. Beverly Hills: Sage.

————. 1999. "Enduring Rivalry in the Democratic Lineage: The Venice-Portugal Case." Pp. 153–71 in *Great Power Rivalries*, ed. William R. Thompson. Columbia: University of South Carolina Press.

Modelski, George, and William R. Thompson. 1989. "Long Cycles and Global War." Pp. 23–54 in *Handbook of War Studies,* ed. Manus I. Midlarsky. Boston: Unwin Hyman.

Moore, John N. 1995. "Remarks in Honor of R. J. Rummel." Paper presented at the annual meeting of the International Studies Association, Chicago.

Moore, Omar K. 1952. "Nominal Definitions of 'Culture.' " *Philosophy of Science* 19: 245–56.

Mor, Ben. D. 1993. *Decision and Interaction in Crisis: A Model of International Crisis Behavior.* Westport, Conn.: Praeger.

Morgan, T. Clifton. 1994. *Untying the Knot of War: A Bargaining Theory of International Crises.* Ann Arbor: University of Michigan Press.

Morgan, T. Clifton, and Kenneth Bickers. 1992. "Domestic Discontent and the External Use of Force." *Journal of Conflict Resolution* 36: 25–52.

Morgan, T. Clifton, and Valerie Schwebach. 1992. "Take Two Democracies and Call Me in the Morning." *International Interactions* 17: 305–20.

Morgenthau, Hans J. 1946. *Scientific Man vs. Power Politics.* Chicago: University of Chicago Press.

————. 1948, 1960, 1967. *Politics among Nations: The Struggle for Power and Peace.* 1st, 3rd, and 4th eds. New York: Knopf.

Morgenthau, Hans J., and Kenneth W. Thompson. 1985. *Politics among Nations: The Struggle for Power and Peace.* 6th ed. New York: Knopf.

Morrow, James D. 1989. "A Twist of Truth: A Reexamination of the Effects of Arms Races on the Occurrence of War." *Journal of Conflict Resolution* 33: 500–29.

———. 1991. "Alliances and Asymmetry: An Alternative to the Capability Aggregation Model of Alliances." *American Journal of Political Science* 35: 904–33.

———. 1993. "Arms versus Allies: Tradeoffs in the Search for Security." *International Organization* 47: 207–33.

Most, Benjamin, and Randolph Siverson. 1987. "Substituting Arms and Alliances, 1870–1914: An Exploration in Comparative Foreign Policy." Pp. 131–57 in *New Directions in the Study of Foreign Policy,* ed. Charles F. Herman, Charles W. Kegley, and James N. Rosenau. Boston: Allen & Unwin.

Most, Benjamin A., and Harvey Starr. 1989. *Inquiry, Logic and International Politics.* Columbia: University of South Carolina Press.

Most, Benjamin, Harvey Starr, and Randolph Siverson. 1989. "The Logic and Study of the Diffusion of International Conflict." Pp. 111–39 in *Handbook of War Studies*, ed. Manus Midlarsky. Boston: Unwin Hyman.

Moul, William B. 1988a. "Balance of Power and the Escalation of Serious Disputes among European Great Powers, 1815–1939: Some Evidence." *American Journal of Political Science* 32: 241–75.

———. 1998b. "Great Power Nondefense Alliances and the Escalation to War of Conflicts Between Unequals, 1815–1939." *International Interactions* 15: 25–43.

Mousseau, Michael. 1998. "Peace in Anarchy: Democratic Governance and International Conflict." Ph.D. dissertation, State University of New York, Binghamton.

Mousseau, Michael, and Yubang Shi. 1999. "A Test for Reverse Causality in the Democratic Peace Relationship." *Journal of Peace Research* 36: 639–63.

Moynahan, Brian. 1994. *The Russian Century.* New York: Random House.

Mueller, John E. 1989. *Retreat from Doomsday: The Obsolescence of Major War.* New York: Basic Books.

———. 1993. "The Essential Irrelevance of Nuclear Weapons." Pp. 45–69 in *The Cold War and After: Prospects for Peace*, ed. Sean M. Lynn-Jones and Steven E. Miller. Cambridge, Mass.: MIT Press.

Muncaster, Robert, and Dina Zinnes. 1993. "The Phenomenology of Enduring Rivalries." Paper presented at the Workshop on Processes of Enduring Rivalries, Bloomington, Ind.

Murphy, Alexander. 1990. "Historical Justifications for Territory Claims." *Annals of the Association of American Geographers* 80: 531–648.

Nevin, John. 1996. "War Initiation and Selection by Consequences." *Journal of Peace Research* 33: 99–108.

Newman, David. 1999. "Real Spaces, Symbolic Spaces: Interrelated Notions of Territory in the Arab-Israeli Conflict." Pp. 3–34 in *A Road Map to War: Territorial Dimensions of International Conflict*, ed. Paul F. Diehl. Nashville, Tenn.: Vanderbilt University Press.

Nie, Norman. 1991. "Model vs Data Driven Science: A Corrective Prescription for the Evolution of Social Sciences." Distinguished Lectures in the Social Sciences. DeKalb: Northern Illinois University.

Niou, Emerson, Peter Ordeshook, and Gregory Rose. 1989. *The Balance of Power.* Cambridge: Cambridge University Press.

North, Robert, Ole Holsti, and Richard Brody. 1964. "Some Empirical Data on the Conflict Spiral." *Peace Research Society (International) Papers* 1: 1–14.

Nys, Ernest. 1894. *Les Origines du droit internationale.* Brussels: Castaigne.

Olson, Mancur, and Richard Zeckhauser. 1966. "An Economic Theory of Alliances." *Review of Economics and Statistics* 48: 266–79.

Oneal, John R. 1988. "The Rationality of Decision Making during International Crises." *Polity* 20: 598–622.

Oneal, John R., Frances H. Oneal, Zeev Maoz, and Bruce Russett. 1996. "Liberal Peace: Interdependence, Democracy, and International Conflict." *Journal of Peace Research* 33: 11–28.

Oneal, John R., and James Lee Ray. 1997. "New Tests of the Democratic Peace: Controlling for Economic Interdependence, 1950–85." *Political Research Quarterly* 50: 751–75.

Oneal, John R., and Bruce Russett. 1997a. "The Classic Liberals Were Right: Democracy, Interdependence, and Conflict, 1950–1985." *International Studies Quarterly* 41: 267–94.

———. 1997b. "Escaping the War Trap: Evaluating the Liberal Peace Controlling for the Expected Utility of Conflict." Paper delivered at the annual meeting of the International Studies Association, Toronto.

———. 1999. "Assessing the Liberal Peace with Alternative Specifications: Trade Still Reduces Conflict." *Journal of Peace Research* 36: 423–42.

Oren, Ido 1990. "The War Proneness of Alliances." *Journal of Conflict Resolution* 34: 208–33.

Organski, A. F. K. 1958. *World Politics*. New York: Knopf.

Organski, A. F. K., and Jacek Kugler. 1980. The *War Ledger*. Chicago: University of Chicago Press.

Osgood, Charles E. 1965. "Escalation as a Strategy in War." *War/Peace Report* 5: 12–14.

Osgood, Robert E. 1967. "The Expansion of Force." Pp. 41–120 in *Force, Order, and Justice*, ed. R. E. Osgood and R. W. Tucker. Baltimore: Johns Hopkins University Press.

Ostrom, Charles W., Jr. 1977. "Evaluating Alternative Foreign Policy Decision-Making Models." *Journal of Conflict Resolution* 21: 235–66.

———. 1978. "A Reactive Linkage Model of the U.S. Defense Expenditure Policymaking Process." *American Political Science Review* 72: 941–57.

Ostrom, Charles W., Jr., and Francis W. Hoole. 1978. "Alliances and War Revisted: A Research Note." *International Studies Quarterly* 22: 215–36.

Paul, T. V. 1994. *Asymmetric Conflicts: War Initiation by Weaker Powers*. Cambridge: Cambridge University Press.

Patchen, Martin. 1998. "When Does Reciprocity in the Actions of Nations Occur?" *International Negotiation* 3: 171–96.

Pateman, Carole. 1971."Political Culture, Political Structure, and Political Change." *British Journal of Political Science* 1: 291–305.

Paul, T. V. 1994. *Asymmetric Conflicts: War Initiation by Weaker Powers*. Cambridge: Cambridge University Press.

———. 1995. "Nuclear Taboo and War Initiation in Regional Conflicts." *Journal of Conflict Resolution* 39: 696–717.

Pavithran, A. K. 1965. *Substance of Public International Law: Western and Eastern*. Bombay: Tripathi.

Philipson, Coleman. 1991. *The International Law and Custom of Ancient Greece and Rome*, vol. 2. London: Macmillan.

Pillitu, Paola Anna. 1981. *Lo Stato di necessità nel diritto internazionale*. Perugia: University di Perugia.

Pinker, Steven. 1997. *How the Mind Works*. New York: Norton.

Pollins, Brian. 1989. "Does Trade Still Follow the Flag?" *American Political Science Review* 83: 465–80.

Popper, Karl. 1959. *Logic of Scientific Discovery*. New York: Basic Books.

Pouncey, Peter R. *The Necessities of War: A Study of Thucydides' Pessimism*. New York: Columbia University Press.

Powell, Robert. 1996. "Uncertainty, Shifting Power, and Appeasement." *American Political Science Review* 90: 749–64.

Prados, John. 1996. *Presidents' Secret Wars*. Chicago: Dee.

Princen, Thomas. 1992. *Intermediaries in International Conflict*. Princeton, N.J.: Princeton University Press.

Pruitt, Dean G., and Jeffrey Z. Rubin. 1986. *Social Conflict: Escalation, Stalemate, and Settlement*. New York: Random House.

Przeworski, Adam, and Fernando Limongi. 1997. "Modernization: Theories and Facts." *World Politics* 49: 155–83.

Putnam, Robert D. 1988. "Diplomacy and Domestic Politics: The Logic of Two-Level Games." *International Organization* 42: 427–60.

Quetelet, Adolphe. 1848. *Du Systeme Social et des Lois qui le Regissent*. Paris: Guillaumin.

Quintilian. 1921. *Institutio Oratoria*, trans. by H. E. Butler. Cambridge, Mass.: Harvard University Press.

Ragin, Charles C. 1987. *The Comparative Method: Moving beyond Qualitative and Quantitative Strategies*. Berkeley: University of California Press.

Raknerud, Arvid, and Havard Hegre. 1997. "The Hazard of War: Reassessing the Evidence for the Democratic Peace." *Journal of Peace Research* 34: 385–404.

Randle, Robert F. 1987. *Issues in the History of the International Relations*. New York: Prager.

Rapisardi-Marabelli, Andrea. 1919. "Breve nota critica in tema di 'stato di necessità' nel dritto internazionale." *Rivista Italiana per le scienze giuridiche* 62: 170.

Rapoport, Anatol. 1960. *Fights, Games, and Debates*. New York: Harper.

Rapoport, Anatol, and Melvin Guyer. 1966. "A Taxonomy of 2×2 Games." *General Systems* 11: 203–14.

Rasler, Karen A., and William R. Thompson. 1994. *The Great Powers and Global Struggle, 1490–1990*. Lexington: University Press of Kentucky.

———. 1998. "Explaining Rivalry Escalation: The Contiguity Factor in the Major Power Subsystem." Paper presented to the Third Pan European International Relations Conference/Joint Meeting with International Studies Association, Vienna.

Ray, James Lee. 1982. "Understanding Rummel." *Journal of Conflict Resolution* 26: 161–87.

———. 1990. "Friends as Foes: International Conflict and Wars between Formal Allies." Pp. 73–91 in *Prisoners of War?*, ed. Charles S. Gochman and Alan Ned Sabrosky. Lexington, Mass.: Lexington.

———. 1991. "The Future of International War." Paper presented at the annual meeting of the American Political Science Association, Washington, D.C.

———. 1995. *Democracy and International Conflict*. Columbia: University of South Carolina Press.

———. 1997. "The Democratic Path to Peace." *Journal of Democracy* 8: 49–64.

———. 1998. "R. J. Rummel's Understanding Conflict and War: An Overlooked Classic?" *Conflict Management and Peace Science* 16: 125–47.

———. 1999. "A Lakatosian View of the Democratic Peace Research Programme: Does It Falsify Realism (Or Neorealism)?" Paper presented at the annual meeting of the International Studies Association, Washington, D.C.

Ray, James Lee, and J. David Singer. 1973. "Measuring the Concentration of Power in the International System." *Sociological Methods and Research* 1: 403–37.

Raymond, Gregory A. 1980. *Conflict Resolution and the Structure of the State System: An Analysis of Arbitrative Settlements*. Montclair, N.J.: Allenheld, Osmun.

———. 1994. "Democracies, Disputes, and Third-Party Intermediaries." *Journal of Conflict Resolution* 38: 24–42.

———. 1996. "Demosthenes and Democracies: Regime-Types and Arbitration Outcomes." *International Interactions* 22: 1–20.

———. 1997a. "Neutrality Norms and the Balance of Power." *Cooperation and Conflict* 32: 123–146.

———. 1997b. "Problems and Prospects in the Study of International Norms." *Mershon International Studies Review* 41: 205–45.

———. 1998/99. "Necessity in Foreign Policy." *Political Science Quarterly* 113: 673–88.

———. 1999. "Duties beyond Borders? Appeals to Moral Necessity in Statecraft." Pp. 667–80 in *Proceedings of the Fourth International Conference of the International Society for the Study of Argumentation*, ed. Frans H. van Eemeren et al. Amsterdam: Stichting Internationaal Centrum voor de Studie van Argumentatie en Taalbeheersing.

Raymond, Gregory A., and Charles W. Kegley, Jr., 1985. "Third Party Mediation and International Norms: A Test of Two Models." *Conflict Management and Peace Science* 9: 33–51.

Reed, William 1997. "Alliance Duration and Democracy: An Extension and Cross Validation of 'Democratic States and Commitment in International Relations.'" *American Journal of Political Science* 41: 1072–78.

Reiter, Dan. 1996. *Crucible of Beliefs*. Ann Arbor: University of Michigan Press.

Reuveny, Rafael, and Heejoon Kang. 1996. "International Trade, Political Conflict/Cooperation, and Granger Causality." *American Journal of Political Science* 40: 943–70.

Reynolds, H. T. 1983. *Analysis of Nominal Data*. 2d ed. Newbury Park, Calif.: Sage.

Richards, Diana, et al. 1993. "Good Times, Bad Times, and the Diversionary Use of Force." *Journal of Conflict Resolution* 37: 504–35.

Richardson, James. 1994. *Crisis Diplomacy*. Cambridge: Cambridge University Press.

Richardson, Lewis. 1939. "Generalized Foreign Policies." *British Journal of Psychology Monographs Supplement* 23.

———. 1960a. *Arms and Insecurity*. Pacific Grove, Calif.: Boxwood.

———. 1960b. *Statistics of Deadly Quarrels*. Pacific Grove, Calif.: Boxwood.

Richelieu, Cardinal [Armand Jean de Plessis]. 1961. *The Political Testament of Cardinal Richelieu*, trans. by H. B. Hall. Madison: University of Wisconsin Press.

Riker, William. 1962. *The Theory of Political Coalitions*. New Haven: Yale University Press.

Rioux, Jean Sebastien. 1996. "The Reputation-Building Behavior of States, 1918–1988." Ph.D. dissertation, Florida State University.

———. 1997. "U.S. Crises and Domestic Politics: Crisis Outcomes, Reputation, and Domestic Consequences." *Southeastern Political Review* 25: 219–29.

———. 1998. "A Crisis-Based Evaluation of the Democratic Peace Proposition." *Canadian Journal of Political Science* 31: 263–83.

Rivier, Alfonse. 1896. *Principes du droit des gens.* Paris: Rosseau.

Röling, Bert V. A. 1975. "The Significance of the Laws of War." Pp. 133–55 in *Current Problems of International Law*, ed. Antonio Cassese. Milan: Giuffrè.

Rosen, Steven. 1972. "War Power and the Willingness to Suffer." Pp. 167–84 in *Peace, War, and Numbers*, ed. Bruce M. Russett. Beverly Hills: Sage.

Rothman, Rozann. 1981. "Political Symbolism." Pp. 285–340 in *The Handbook of Political Behavior*, ed. Samuel L. Long. New York: Plenum.

Rousseau, David, Christopher Gelpi, Dan Reiter, and Paul Huth. 1996. "Assessing the Dyadic Nature of the Democratic Peace, 1918–88." *American Political Science Review* 90: 512–33.

Rubin, Jeffrey Z., Dean Pruitt, and Sung Hee Kim. 1994. *Social Conflict: Escalation, Stalemate, and Settlement.* 2d ed. New York: McGraw-Hill.

Rule, John C. 1999. "The Enduring Rivalry of France and Spain ca. 1462–1700." Pp. 31–59 in *Great Power Rivalries*, ed. William R. Thompson. Columbia: University of South Carolina Press.

Rummel, Rudolph J. 1968. "The Relationship between National Attributes and Foreign Conflict Behavior." Pp. 187–214 in *Quantitative International Politics: Insights and Evidence*, ed. J. David Singer. New York: Free Press.

———. 1977. *Understanding Conflict and War*: Vol. 3, *Conflict in Perspective.* Beverly Hills, Calif.: Sage.

———. 1979. *Understanding Conflict and War*: Vol. 4, *War, Power, Peace.* Beverly Hills, Calif.: Sage.

———. 1983. "Libertarianism and International Violence." *Journal of Conflict Resolution* 27: 27–72.

———. 1995. "Democracies *Are* Less Warlike Than Other Regimes." *European Journal of International Relations* 1: 457–79.

———. 1997. *Power Kills.* New Brunswick, N.J.: Transactions.

Russett, Bruce. 1983. *The Prisoners of Insecurity.* San Francisco: Freeman.

———. 1990. "Economic Decline, Electoral Pressure, and the Initiation of Interstate Conflict." Pp. 123–40 in *Prisoners of War?* ed. Charles S. Gochman and Alan Ned Sabrosky. Lexington, Mass.: Lexington.

———. 1993. *Grasping the Democratic Peace.* Princeton, N.J.: Princeton University Press.

———. 1995. "Correspondence: And Yet It Moves." *International Security* 19: 164–75.

———. 1998. "A Neo-Kantian Perspective: Democracy, Interdependence, and International Organization in Building Security Communities. Pp. 368–94 in *Security Communities,* ed. Emanuel Adler and Michael Barnett. Cambridge: Cambridge University Press.

Russett, Bruce, and William Antholis. 1992. "Do Democracies Fight Each Other? Evidence from the Peloponnesian War." *Journal of Peace Research* 29: 415–43.

Russett, Bruce, John Oneal, and David R. Davis. 1998. "The Third Leg of the Kantian Tripod for Peace: International Organization and Militarized Disputes, 1950–1985." *International Organization* 52: 441–68.

Russett, Bruce M., J. David Singer, and Melvin Small. 1968. "National Political Units in the Twentieth Century: A Standardized List." *American Political Science Review* 62: 932–51.

Russett, Bruce M., and Allan C. Stam. 1998. "Courting Disaster: An Expanded NATO vs. Russia and China." *Political Science Quarterly* 113: 361–82.

Russett, Bruce M., and Harvey Starr. 2000. "From Democratic Peace to Kantian Peace: Democracy and Conflict in the International System." Pp. 93–128 in *Handbook of War Studies II*, ed. Manus I. Midlarsky. Ann Arbor: University of Michigan Press.

Sabrosky, Alan Ned. 1985. "Alliance Aggregation, Capability Distribution, and the Expansion of Interstate War." Pp. 145–89 in *Polarity and War*, ed. A. Sabrosky. Boulder, Colo.: Westview.

Salmore, Steven A., and Charles F. Hermann. 1969. "The Effect of Size, Development and Accountability on Foreign Policy." *Peace Science Society Papers* 14: 16–30.

Sample, Susan G. 1996. "Arms Races and the Escalation of Disputes to War." Ph.D. dissertation, Vanderbilt University.

———. 1997. "Arms Races and Dispute Escalation: Resolving the Debate." *Journal of Peace Research* 34: 7–22.

———. 1998a. "Furthering the Investigation into the Effects of Arms Buildups." *Journal of Peace Research* 35: 122–26.

———. 1998b. "Military Buildups, War, and Realpolitik: A Multivariate Model." *Journal of Conflict Resolution* 42: 156–75.

Sanders, David. 1986. *Lawmaking and Co-Operating in International Politics: The Idealist Case Re-examined*. New York: St. Martin's.

Sandler, Todd 1993. "The Economic Theory of Alliance." *Journal of Conflict Resolution* 37: 446–83.

Schampel, James H. 1993. "Change in Material Capabilities and the Onset of War: A Dyadic Approach." *International Studies Quarterly* 37: 395–408.

Schelling, Thomas C. 1960. *Strategy of Conflict*. Cambridge, Mass.: Harvard University Press.

———. 1966. *Arms and Influence*. New Haven, Conn.: Yale University Press.

Schjolset, A. 1996. "Are Some Democracies More Peaceful Than Others?" Thesis for the Cand. Polit in Political Science, Norwegian University of Science and Technology, Trondheim.

Schlesinger, Arthur M., Jr. 1973. *The Imperial Presidency*. Boston: Houghton Mifflin.

Schroeder, Paul. 1976. "Alliances, 1815–1945: Weapons of Power and Tools of Management." Pp. 227–62 in *Historical Dimensions of National Security Problems*, ed. Klaus Knorr. Lawrence: University Press of Kansas.

Schroeder, Paul W. 1999. "A Pointless Enduring Rivalry: France and the Habsburg Monarchy, 1715–1918." Pp. 60–85 in *Great Power Rivalries*, ed. William R. Thompson. Columbia: University of South Carolina Press.

Schultz, Kenneth A. 1998. "Domestic Opposition and Signaling in International Crises." *American Political Science Review* 92: 829–44.

Senese, Paul D. 1996. "Geographical Proximity and Issue Salience: Their Effects on the

Escalation of Militarized Interstate Conflict." *Conflict Management and Peace Science* 15: 133–61.

———. 1997a. "Costs and Demands: International Sources of Dispute Challenges and Reciprocation." *Journal of Conflict Resolution* 41: 407–27.

———. 1997b. "Dispute to War." Paper delivered at the annual meeting of the International Studies Association.

Sherman, Frank. "SHERFACS: A Cross-Paradigm, Hierarchical and Contextually Sensitive Conflict Management Data Set." *International Interactions* 20: 79–100.

Shlaim, Avi. 1983. *The United States and the Berlin Blockade, 1948–1949: A Study of Crisis Decision-Making.* Berkeley: University of California Press.

Signorino, Curtis S. 1999. "Strategic Interaction and the Statistical Analysis of International Conflict." *American Political Science Review* 93: 279–97.

Simmons, Beth. 1999. "See You in 'Court'? The Appeal to Quasi-Judicial Legal Processes in the Settlement of Territorial Disputes." Pp. 205–37 in *A Road Map to War: Territorial Dimensions of International Conflict*, ed. Paul F. Diehl. Nashville, Tenn.: Vanderbilt University Press.

Simon, Herbert. 1969. *Science of the Artificial.* Cambridge, Mass.: MIT Press.

Simon, Julian. 1969. *Basic Research Methods in Social Science.* New York: Random House.

Simon, Michael W., and Erik Gartzke 1996. "Political System Similarity and the Choice of Allies: Do Democracies Flock Together, or Do Opposites Attract?" *Journal of Conflict Resolution* 40: 617–53.

Singer J. David. 1961. "The Levels of Analysis Problem in International Relations." Pp. 77–92 in *The International System: Theoretical Essays*, ed. Klaus Knorr and Sidney Verba. Princeton, N.J.: Princeton University Press.

———. 1968. "Man and World Politics: The Psycho-Cultural Interface." *Journal of Social Issues* 24/3: 127–56.

———. 1972a. "The 'Correlates of War' Project: Interim Report and Rationale." *World Politics* 24: 243–70.

———. 1972b. "Theorists and Empiricists: The Two Culture Problem in International Politics." Pp. 80–95 in *The Analysis of International Politics*, ed. James N. Rosenau, Vincent Davis, and Maurice A. East. New York: Free Press.

———. 1979. *The Correlates of War I: Research Origins and Rationale.* New York: Free Press.

———. 1988. "The Making of a Peace Researcher." Pp. 213–29 in *Journeys through World Politics,* ed. Joseph Kruzel and James N. Rosenau. Lexington, Mass.: Lexington.

———. 1990. "Reconstructing the Correlates of War Data Set on Material Capabilities of States, 1816–1985." Pp. 53–72. in *Measuring the Correlates of War*, ed. J. David Singer and Paul F. Diehl. Ann Arbor: University of Michigan Press.

———. 1991a. "Peace in the Global System: Displacement, Interregnum, or Transformation?" Pp. 56–84 in *The Long Postwar Peace: Contending Explanations and Projections,* ed. Charles W. Kegley, Jr. New York: HarperCollins.

———. 1991b. "Toward a Behavioral Science of World Politics." Pp. 131–47 in *Perspectives on Behavioral Science,* ed. Richard Jessor. Boulder, Colo.: Westview.

———, ed. 1980. *The Correlates of War II: Testing Some Realpolitik Models.* New York: Free Press.

Singer, J. David, Stuart Bremer, and John Stuckey. 1972. "Capability Distribution, Uncertainty, and Major Power War, 1820–1965." Pp. 19–48 in *Peace, War, and Numbers*, ed. Bruce M. Russett. Beverly Hills: Sage.

Singer, J. David, and Thomas Cusack. 1981. "Periodicity, Inexorability, and Steeresmanship in Major Power War." Pp. 404–22 in *From National Development to Global Community*, ed. Richard Merritt and Bruce Russet. Boston: G. Allen & Unwin.

Singer, J. David, and Jeffrey Keating. 1997. "Military Preparedness, Weapon Systems and the Biosphere: A Preliminary Impact Statement" *New Political Science* 21: 325–43.

Singer, J. David, and Melvin Small. 1966. "Formal Alliances, 1815–1939: A Quantitative Description." *Journal of Peace Research* 3: 1–32.

———. 1968 "Alliance Aggregation and the Onset of War, 1815–1945." Pp. 247–86 in *Quantitative International Politics: Insights and Evidence*, ed. J. David Singer. New York: Free Press.

———. 1972. *The Wages of War, 1816–1965: A Statistical Handbook*. New York: Wiley.

Singer, J. David, and Richard Stoll, eds. 1984. *Quantitative Indicators in World Politics: Timely Assurance and Early Warning*. New York: Praeger.

Singer, J. David, and Michael Wallace, eds. 1979. *To Augur Well*. Beverly Hills, Calif.: Sage.

Singer, Max, and Aaron Wildavsky. 1993. *The Real World Order: Zones of Peace, Zones of Turmoil*. Chatham, N.J.: Chatham House.

———. 1996. *The Real World Order: Zones of Peace, Zones of Turmoil*. 2d ed. Chatham, N.J.: Chatham House.

Singh, Nagendra. 1989. "The Machinery and Method for Conduct of Inter-State Relations in Ancient India." Pp. 845–53 in *International Law in a Time of Perplexity*, ed. Yoram Dinstein and Mala Tabory. Dordrecht: Martinus Nijhoff.

Siverson, Randolph M. 1995. "Democracies and War Participation: In Defense of the Institutional Constraints Argument." *European Journal of International Relations* 1: 481–89.

Siverson, Randolph, and Bruce Bueno de Mesquita. 1996. "Inside-Out: A Theory of Domestic Political Institutions and the Issues of International Conflict." Paper presented at the annual meeting of the American Political Science Association.

Siverson, Randolph, and Juliann Emmons. 1991. "Birds of a Feather: Democratic Political Systems and Alliance Choices in the Twentieth Century." *Journal of Conflict Resolution* 35: 285–306.

Siverson, Randolph, and Joel King. 1979. "Alliances and the Expansion of War." Pp. 37–49. in *To Augur Well*, ed. J. David Singer and M. Wallace. Beverly Hills, Calif.: Sage.

———. 1980. "Attributes of National Alliance Membership and War Participation, 1815–1965." *American Journal of Political Science* 24: 1–15.

Siverson, Randolph J., and Harvey Starr. 1990. "Opportunity, Willingness, and the Diffusion of War." *American Political Science Review* 84: 47–67.

———. 1991. *The Diffusion of War: A Study of Opportunity and Willingness*. Ann Arbor: University of Michigan Press.

———. 1994. "Regime Change and the Restructuring of Alliances." *American Journal of Political Science* 38: 145–61.

Siverson, Randolph M., and Michael R. Tennefoss. 1984. "Power, Alliance, and the Escalation of International Conflict, 1815–1965." *American Political Science Review* 78: 1057–69.

Small, Melvin. 1980. *Was War Necessary?* Beverly Hills: Sage.

Small, Melvin, and J. David Singer. 1970. "Patterns in International Warfare, 1816–1965." *Annals* 391: 145–55.

———. 1976. "The War Proneness of Democratic Regimes." *Jerusalem Journal of International Relations* 1: 49–69.

———. 1982. *Resort to Arms: International and Civil Wars, 1816–1980*. Beverly Hills, Calif.: Sage.

Smith, Alastair. 1995. "Alliance Formation and War." *International Studies Quarterly* 39: 405–26.

———. 1996. "To Intervene or Not to Intervene: A Biased Decision." *Journal of Conflict Resolution* 40: 16–40.

———. 1998. "A Summary of Political Selection: The Effect of Strategic Choice on the Escalation of International Crises." *American Journal of Political Science* 42: 698–701.

Smith, Theresa C. 1980. "Arms Race Instability and War." *Journal of Conflict Resolution* 24: 253–84.

Snyder, Glenn D. 1984. "The Alliance Dilemma in World Politics." *World Politics* 36: 461–95.

Snyder, Richard C., H. W. Bruck, and Burton Sapin. 1962. *Foreign Policy Decision-Making*. New York: Free Press.

Snyder, Glenn, and Paul Diesing. 1977. *Conflict among Nations*. Princeton, N.J.: Princeton University Press.

Solingen, Etel. 1996a. "Democracy, Economic Reform, and Regional Cooperation." *Journal of Theoretical Politics* 8: 79–114.

———. 1996b. "Democratization in the Middle East: Quandaries in the Peace Process." *Journal of Democracy* 7: 139–53.

Somit, Albert, and Stephen Peterson. 1997. *Darwinism, Dominance and Democracy*. Westport, Conn.: Praeger.

Sorokin, Gerald L. 1994. "Alliance Formation and General Deterrence: A Game Theoretic Model and the Case of Israel." *Journal of Conflict Resolution* 38: 298–325.

———. 1997. "Patrons, Clients, and Allies in the Arab-Israeli Conflict." *Journal of Strategic Studies* 20: 46–72.

Sorokin, Pitirim A. 1937. *Social and Cultural Dynamics*. New York: American.

Spanier, John W. 1980. *American Foreign Policy since World War II*. New York: Holt, Rinehart, & Winston.

Spiezio, K. Edward. 1990. "British Hegemony and Major Power War, 1815–1939: An Empirical Test of Gilpin's Model of Hegemonic Governance." *International Studies Quarterly* 34: 165–81.

Spiro, David E. 1994. "The Insignifance of the Liberal Peace." *International Security* 19: 50–86.

Stam III, Allan C. 1996. *Win, Lose, or Draw: Domestic Politics and the Crucible of War*. Ann Arbor: University of Michigan Press.

Starr, Harvey. 1974. *The Reliability of Alliances*. Lexington, Mass.: Heath.

———. 1992. "Why Don't Democracies Fight One Another? Evaluating the Theory-Findings Feedback Loop." *Jerusalem Journal of International Relations* 14: 41–59.

Starr, Harvey, and Benjamin Most. 1978. "A Return Journey: Richardson, Frontiers, and War in the 1945–1965 Era." *Journal of Conflict Resolution* 22: 441–62.

————. 1991a. "Democratic Dominoes: Diffusion Approaches to the Spread of Democracy in the International System." *Journal of Conflict Resolution* 35: 356–81.

————. 1991b. "Joining Political and Geographic Perspectives: Geopolitics and International Relations." *International Interactions* 17: 1–9.

Stoll, Richard. 1984. "From Frying Pan to Fire: The Impact of Major Power War Involvement on Major Power Dispute Involvement, 1816–1975." *Conflict Management and Peace Science* 7: 71–82.

Stinnett, Douglas, and Paul F. Diehl. 1998. "The Path(s) to Rivalry." Paper presented at the annual meeting of the American Political Science Association, Boston.

Sullivan, Michael. 1978. *International Relations: Theories and Evidence.* Upper Saddle River, N.J.: Prentice Hall.

Taoka, Ryoichi. 1978. *The Right of Self-Defense in International Law.* Osaka: Osaka University of Economics and Law, Institute of Legal Study Research.

Tetlock, Philip E. 1989. "Methodological Themes and Variations." Pp. 334–86 in *Behavior, Society, and Nuclear War,* vol. 1, ed. Philip E. Tetlock, Jo L. Husbands, Paul C. Stern, and Charles Tilly. New York: Oxford University Press.

Thompson, William R. 1983a. "Cycles, Capabilities, and War: An Ecumenical View." Pp. 141–63 in *Contending Approaches to World System Analysis*, ed. William R. Thompson. Beverly Hills: Sage.

————. 1983b. "Succession Crises in the Global Political System: A Test of the Transition Model." Pp. 93–116 in *Crises in the World-System,* ed. Albert Bergesen. Beverly Hills: Sage.

————. 1986. "Polarity, the Long Cycle, and Global Power Warfare." *Journal of Conflict Resolution* 30: 587–615.

————. 1988. *On Global War: Historical-Structural Approaches to World Politics.* Columbia: University of South Carolina Press.

————. 1992. "Dehio, Long Cycles and the Geohistorical Context of Structural Transition." *World Politics* 45: 127–52.

————. 1995. "Principal Rivalries." *Journal of Conflict Resolution* 39: 195–223.

————. 1996. "Democracy and Peace: Putting the Cart Before the Horse*?" International Organization* 50: 141–74.

————. 1999. "The Evolution of a Great Power Rivalry: The Anglo-American Case." Pp. 201–23 in *Great Power Rivalries*, ed. William R. Thompson. Columbia: University of South Carolina Press.

————. 2000. "Whither Strategic Rivalries?" Talk given at Vanderbilt University, January.

Thompson, William R., and Richard Tucker. 1997. "A Tale of Two Democratic Peace Critiques." *International Studies Quarterly* 41: 428–54.

Tieya, Wang. 1991. "International Law in China: Historical and Contemporary Perspectives." *Recueil des cours* 221: 196–369.

Toft, Monica Duffy. 1997. "Nations, States, and Violent Ethnic Conflict: Territory as Subject and Object." Paper presented at the annual meeting of the American Political Science Association, Washington, D.C.

Truman, Harry S. 1956. *Memoirs: Years of Trial and Hope.* Vol. 2. Garden City, N.Y.: Doubleday.

Ullman, Richard. 1999. "The US and the World: An Interview with George Kennan." *New York Review of Books* 46: 4–6.

United States Department of State. 1990. *Current Policy No. 1293*. Washington, D.C.: Bureau of Public Affairs.

Vasquez, John. 1976. "A Learning Theory of the American Anti-Vietnam War Movement." *Journal of Peace Research* 13: 299–314.

———. 1987. "The Steps to War: Toward a Scientific Explanation of Correlates of War Findings." *World Politics* 40: 108–45.

———. 1991. "The Deterrence Myth: Nuclear Weapons and the Prevention of Nuclear War." Pp. 205–23 in *The Long Postwar Peace*, ed. Charles W. Kegley, Jr. New York: HarperCollins.

———. 1993. *The War Puzzle*. Cambridge: Cambridge University Press.

———. 1995a. "Developing a Strategy for Achieving Greater Cumulation in Research." Pp. 241–49 in *The Process of War: Advancing the Scientific Study of War*, ed. Stuart Bremer and Thomas Cusack. Luxembourg: Gordon & Breach.

———. 1995b. "Why Do Neighbors Fight? Territoriality, Proximity, or Interactions." *Journal of Peace Research* 32: 277–93.

———. 1996a. "Distinguishing Rivals That Go to War from Those That Do Not." *International Studies Quarterly* 40: 531–58.

———. 1996b. "When Are Power Transitions Dangerous? An Appraisal and Reformulation of Power Transition Theory." Pp. 35–56 in *Parity and War: Evaluations and Extensions of* The War Ledger, ed. Jacek Kugler and Douglas Lemke. Ann Arbor: University of Michigan Press.

———. 1997a. "The Realist Paradigm and Degenerative versus Progressive Research Programs: An Appraisal of Neotraditional Research on Waltz's Balancing Proposition." *American Political Science Review* 91: 899–912.

———. 1997b. "War Endings: What Science and Constructivism Can Tell Us." *Millennium* 26: 651–78.

———. 1998a. "The Evolution of Multiple Rivalries Prior to the Second World War in the Pacific." Pp. 191–223 in *The Dynamics of Enduring Rivalries*, ed. Paul F. Diehl. Urbana: University of Illinois Press.

———. 1998b. *The Power of Power Politics: From Classical Realism to Neotraditionalism*. Cambridge: Cambridge University Press.

———. Forthcoming. "Mapping the Probability of War and Analyzing the Possibility of Peace." Presidential Address to the Peace Science Society (International). *Conflict Management and Peace Science*.

Vasquez, John A., and Marie T. Henehan. 1999. "Territorial Disputes and the Probability of War, 1816–1992." Unpublished manuscript, Department of Political Science, Vanderbilt University.

Viroli, Maurizio. 1992. *From Politics to Reason of State: The Acquisition and Transformation of the Language of Politics 1250–1600*. Cambridge: Cambridge University Press.

Visscher, Charles de. 1917. "Les lois de la guerre et la théorie de la nécessité." *Revue générale de droit international public* 24: 74–108.

Viswanatha, S. V. 1925. *International Law in Ancient India*. London: Longmans, Green.

von Pufendorf, Samuel. 1749. *The Law of Nature and Nations,* 5th ed., trans. Basil Kennet. London: Bonwicke.

Vyasa. 1964. "Kanika's Advice," in *Comparative World Politics*, ed. Joel Larus. Belmont, Calif.: Wadsworth.

Wagner, R. Harrison. 1994. "Peace, War, and the Balance of Power." *American Political Science Review* 88: 593–607.

Walker, Thomas Alfred A. 1899. *History of the Law of Nations*, vol. 1. Cambridge: Cambridge University Press.

Wallace, Michael. 1971. "Power, Status, and International War." *Journal of Peace Research* 8: 23–35.

———. 1972. "Status, Formal Organization, and Arms Levels as Factors Leading to the Onset of War, 1820–1964." Pp. 49–69 in *Peace, War, and Numbers,* ed. Bruce M. Russett. Beverly Hills: Sage.

———. 1973 "Alliance Polarization, Cross-Cutting, and International War, 1815–1964." *Journal of Conflict Resolution* 17: 575–604.

———. 1979. "Arms Races and Escalation: Some New Evidence." *Journal of Conflict Resolution* 23: 3–16.

———. 1980. "Some Persisting Findings: A Reply to Professor Weede." *Journal of Conflict Resolution* 24: 289–92.

———. 1982. "Armaments and Escalation: Two Competing Hypotheses." *International Studies Quarterly* 26: 37–56.

Wallensteen, Peter. 1981. "Incompatibility, Confrontation, and War: Four Models and Three Historical Systems, 1816–1976." *Journal of Peace Research* 18: 57–90.

———. 1984. "Universalism vs. Particularism: On the Limits of Major Power Order." *Journal of Peace Research* 21: 243–57.

Wallensteen, Peter, and Margareta Sollenberg. 1998. "Armed Conflict and Regional Conflict Complexes, 1989–97." *Journal of Peace Research* 35: 621–34.

Wallerstein, Immanuel. 1984. *The Politics of the World-Economy*. Cambridge: Cambridge University Press.

Walt, Stephen. 1987. *The Origins of Alliances*. Ithaca, N.Y.: Cornell University Press.

———. 1996. *Revolution and War*. Ithaca, N.Y.: Cornell University Press.

———. 1997. "The Progressive Power of Realism." *American Political Science Review* 91: 931–35.

Waltz, Kenneth N. 1959. *Man, the State, and War*. New York: Columbia University Press.

———. 1979. *Theory of International Politics*. Reading, Mass.: Addison-Wesley.

———. 1981. *The Spread of Nuclear Weapons: More May Be Better*. Adelphi Paper No. 171. London: Institute for Strategic Studies.

———. 1997. "Evaluating Theories." *American Political Science Review* 91: 913–17.

Wang, Kevin, and James Lee Ray. 1994. "Beginners and Winners: The Fate of Initiators of Interstate Wars Involving Great Powers since 1495." *International Studies Quarterly* 38: 139–54.

Ward, Michael D. 1982. *Research Gaps in Alliance Dynamics*. Beverly Hills: Sage.

Wayman, Frank Whelon. 1982. "Power Transitions, Enduring Rivalries, and War, 1816–1970." Paper presented at the meeting of the Institute for the Study of Conflict Theory and International Security, Urbana-Champaign, Illinois, September.

———. 1984a. "Bipolarity and War." *Journal of Peace Research* 21: 61–78.

———. 1984b. "Voices Prophesying War." Pp. 153–85 in *Quantitative Indicators in World Politics*, ed. J. David Singer and Richard Stoll. New York: Praeger.

———. 1989. "Power Shifts and War." Paper presented at the joint meeting of the International Studies Association and the British International Studies Association, London.

———. 1990. "Alliances and War: A Time-Series Analysis." Pp. 93–113 in *Prisoners of War? Nation-States in the Modern Era*, ed. Charles Gochman and Alan Sabrosky. Lexington, Mass.: Lexington.

———. 1993. "The Role of Rivalries in the Explanation of International Conflict." Paper presented to the Workshop on Processes of Enduring Rivalries, Indiana University, Bloomington, Ind., 1–2 May.

———. 1995. "Purpose, Process, and Progress in the Study of War." Pp. 251–58 in *The Process of War*, ed. Stuart Bremer and Thomas Cusack. Luxembourg: Gordon & Breach.

———. 1996. "Power Shifts and the Onset of War," Pp. 145–62 in *Parity and War: Evaluations and Extensions of* The War Ledger, ed. Jacek Kugler and Douglas Lemke. Ann Arbor: Univeristy of Michigan Press.

———. Forthcoming. *War and Theory in World Politics.*

Wayman, Frank Whelon, and Paul Diehl, eds. 1994. *Reconstructing Realpolitik.* Ann Arbor: University of Michigan Press.

Wayman, Frank Whelon, and Daniel M. Jones. 1991. "Evolution of Conflict in Rivalries." Paper presented at the annual meeting of the International Studies Association, Vancouver.

Wayman, Frank W., Meredith R. Sarkees, and J. David Singer. 1997. "Inter-State, Intra-State, and Extra-Systemic Wars, 1816–1995: A New War Typology, with Trends in Modern Warfare." Unpublished manuscript, University of Michigan.

Wayman, Frank Whelon, and J. David Singer. 1990. "Evolution and Directions for Improvement in the Correlates of War Project Methodologies. " Pp. 247–67 in *Measuring the Correlates of War*, ed. J. David Singer and Paul F. Diehl. Ann Arbor: University of Michigan Press.

Wayman, Frank Whelon, J. David Singer, and Gary Goertz. 1983. "Capabilities, Allocations, and Success in Militarized Disputes and Wars, 1816–1976." *International Studies Quarterly* 27: 497–515.

Weart, Spencer R. 1998. *Never at War: Why Democracies Will Not Fight One Another.* New Haven, Conn.: Yale University Press.

Weede, Erich. 1970. "Conflict Behavior of Nation-States." *Journal of Peace Research* 7: 229–37.

———. 1975. "World Order in the Fifties and Sixties: Dependence, Deterrence, and Limited Peace." *Peace Science Society Papers* 24: 49–80.

———. 1976. "Overwhelming Preponderance as a Pacifying Condition among Contiguous Asian Dyads, 1950–1969." *Journal of Conflict Resolution* 20: 395–411.

———. 1980. "Arms Races and Escalation: Some Persisting Doubts." *Journal of Conflict Resolution* 24: 285–87.

———. 1984. "Democracy and War Involvement." *Journal of Conflict Resolution* 41: 649–64.

———. 1994. "Constraints, States, and Wars." *European Journal of Political Research* 26: 171–92.

———. 1996. "Correspondence." *International Security* 20: 180–83.

Welch, David A. 1993. *Justice and the Genesis of War.* Cambridge: Cambridge University Press.

Werner, Suzanne, and Jacek Kugler. 1996. "Power Transitions and Military Buildups: Resolving the Relationship between Arms Buildups and War." Pp 187–207 in *Parity and War: Evaluations and Extensions of The War Ledger,* ed. Jacek Kugler and Douglas Lemke. Ann Arbor: University of Michigan Press.

Wheaton, Henry. 1845. *History of the Law of Nations in Europe and America.* New York: Gould, Banks.

White, Ralph K. 1970. *Nobody Wanted War: Misperception in Vietnam and Other Wars.* Garden City, N.Y.: Anchor.

Wilkenfeld, Jonathan, and Michael Brecher. 1988. *Crises in the Twentieth Century: Handbook of Foreign Policy Crises.* Oxford: Pergamon.

Williams, Bernard. 1993. *Shame and Necessity.* Berkeley: University of California Press: 72–74.

Wills, Garry. 1999. "Lincoln's Greatest Speech?" *Atlantic Monthly* 284 (September): 60–70.

Witte, John, Jr., and Michael Bourdeaux. 1999. *Proselytism and Orthodoxy in Russia: The New War for Souls.* Maryknoll, N.Y.: Orbis.

Worchal, Stephen. 1974. "The Effects of Three Types of Arbitrary Thwarting on the Instigation to Aggression." *Journal of Personality* 42: 300–18.

Wright, Quincy. 1942. *A Study of War* [1964 abridged ed.] Chicago: University of Chicago Press.

Yamamoto, Yoshinobu, and Stuart A. Bremer. 1980. "Wider Wars and Restless Nights: Major Power Intervention in Ongoing War." Pp. 85–119 in *The Correlates of War,* vol. 2, ed. J. D. Singer. New York: Free Press.

Yost, Charles W. 1968. "How It Began." *Foreign Affairs* 46: 304–20.

Zagare, Frank C. 1987. *The Dynamics of Deterrence.* Chicago: University of Chicago Press.

Zinnes, Dina. 1976. "The Problem of Cumulation." Pp. 161–66 in *In Search of Global Patterns,* ed. James Rosenau. New York: Free Press.

Zinnes, Dina, Robert C. North, and H. E. Koch. 1961. "Capability, Threat, and the Outbreak of War." Pp. 469–82 in *International Politics and Foreign Policy,* ed. James Rosenau. New York: Free Press.

Zinnes, Dina, Joseph L. Zinnes, and Robert D. McClure. 1972. "Hostility in Diplomatic Communication: A Study of the 1914 Case." Pp. 139–62 in *International Crises,* ed. Charles Hermann. New York: Free Press.

Zinnes, Dina, and Jonathan Wilkenfeld. 1971. "An Analysis of Foreign Conflict Behavior of Nations." Pp. 167–213 in *Comparative Foreign Policy,* ed. Wolfram Hanrieder. New York: McKay.

Subject Index

"Alert" crisis (1973), 243–44
alliances: definition of, 113–12; duration
  of, 124–28; findings on, 115–17, 119–
  20, 125–28, 307, 341–42, 356–57, 367;
  formation of, 111–24. 130–34, 148–49,
  154–62, 170–78, 265, 346; and friends
  as foes, 149, 300, 369n4; types of, 71,
  113, 148, 150–54, 159–62, 214, 324,
  342, 367; and war, 19, 26, 111–12,
  128–38, 145–48, 341–44. *See also* democracies, alliance behavior
Anglo-American rivalry, 213–15
Anglo-Dutch rivalry, 207–11
Anschluss crisis (1938), 245
arms races, controversy over, 166–68. *See*
  also escalation process, military
  buildups
authoritarian states and war, 47, 50, 102–
  103, 109, 301–304, 310, 314, 321,
  352–53

balance of power, 114, 124, 147–48, 213,
  263–65, 271, 274–75, 320, 329. *See*
  also unstable balances
bargaining, crisis, 27, 351; findings on, 49–
  50, 350–51, 367
basic rivalry level (BRL), 202–3, 206–7,
  212, 215–16
Berlin crises, 188
border conflicts, 60, 63, 70, 79, 92–93,
  104, 220, 230, 265, 333, 340
bullying, 27, 37, 208, 242, 351

capability, 25, 209–10, 214, 320; and alliances, 114–16, 120, 123, 125–28,

131–32; and crisis, 244, 246–47, 256;
  dyadic level patterns, 262–71; findings
  on, 29–30, 47, 49, 172–73, 210, 260–
  62, 264–70, 272–74, 354–59, 367; state
  level patterns, 259–62; system level
  patterns, 271–75. *See also* military
  capabilities
causes of war, xiii, xvii, 12–13, 30–33,
  197, 213, 321, 323, 333
chance and war, 17, 33–34
Cold War, 185–93
compromise, 59, 105–108, 210, 243, 291
confounding variables, 300, 307
Congress of Vienna, 292
contagion, 19, 295
contiguity, 68–69, 77–79, 229–30, 322–
  23, 333, 337–38; findings on, x, xvii,
  6–8, 21, 64–67, 72–73, 79, 137, 190,
  300, 306–7, 337–38
correlates of war, x, xvii, 6–8, 21, 137,
  190, 367
Correlates of War project, x, 225, 339; history of, xiii, 6, 220
crisis, definition of, 39–40
crisis escalation, 37, 48, 224–25, 333; data
  list, 53–54; findings on, 41–48, 67,
  237–38, 243, 246–47, 256, 272, 336–
  37, 350, 353. *See also* arms races, bargaining, escalation process
Cuban Missile Crisis, 188, 191, 242–43,
  252–56
cultural factors, 19, 27–28
cycles, 17–18

decision processes, 13–16, 31–32, 129,
  274–75, 322

407

Name Index

Abdolali, Nasrin, 300, 311, 362
Achilles, 296n3
Ajax, 296n3
Ali, Salvatore, 207, 211, 213–14
Alker, Hayward R., 11
Allison, Graham, 224, 226
Altfeld, Michael F., 111, 113, 129, 167
Amenhotep IV (Akhenaten), 295n1
Anderson, Paul A., 201, 210, 266, 268, 270–71, 358
Andromache, 286
Angell, Robert, G., 6
Anglin, Douglas G., 51n2
Anzilotti, Dionisio, 285
Archer, John, 236
Aristotle, 32
Aron, Raymond, 4, 224, 246
Asterion, 288
Axelrod, Robert A., 188, 257n15, 291
Azar, Edward, 202
Azevedo, Jane, 12

Babst, Dean V., 362
Barbieri, Katherine, 28, 315n3, 316n12, 320, 327n9
Barkun, Michael, 290
Barnett, Michael, 163n3
Baron, Robert A, 237
Bates, Robert H., 324
Baumgartner, Frank R., 202
Beck, Nathaniel, 139, 143n5, 144n12, 315n9, 325–26
Bennett, D. Scott, 124, 127–28, 212, 215, 217n12, 267, 269–70, 349, 357

Benoit, Kenneth, 301
Ben Yehuda-Agid, Hemda, 43, 46, 336, 352
Bercovitch, Jacob, 212, 228, 349
Berkowitz, Leonard, 235, 237
Best, Geoffrey, 281
Bickers, Kenneth, 327n14
Bismarck, Otto von, 292
Blainey, Geoffrey, 15, 17, 30, 237, 263
Blechman, Barry M., 232
Blight, James G., 254, 258n24
Bliss, Harry, 307
Bloch, Jean de, 5
Boehmer, Charles, 30
Boulding, Kenneth E., 4, 6, 25, 61
Bourdeaux, Michael, 332
Bowman, Isaiah, 59–60
Brams, Steven J., 79, 257n4, 324
Braumoeller, Bear F., 325–26
Brecher, Michael, xiv, xviin1, 39–46, 51nn2–3, 52n5, 52n7, 52n11, 60, 87–88, 91, 94, 201, 225, 236, 272–73, 333, 336, 347–48, 350–52, 369n10, 370n14
Brehm, Jack W., 237
Bremer, Stuart A., x, xiv, 17–18, 24–29, 49–50, 64–65, 67–68, 72–74, 76–77, 83n12, 87, 90, 94, 99, 128, 133, 139, 146–47, 149–51, 153–54, 219–22, 224, 229, 244, 260, 266, 274, 289, 300, 304, 308, 315n2, 322, 326n3, 332, 335, 337, 341, 346, 351, 354–55, 357, 368, 369n4
Brito, Dagobert L., 185
Broder, John M., 332
Brodie, Bernard, 182

411

About the Contributors

Michael Brecher is R. B. Angus Professor of Political Science at McGill University.

Stuart A. Bremer is Professor of Political Science at Pennsylvania State University.

Paul F. Diehl is Professor of Political Science and University Distinguished Teacher/Scholar at the University of Illinois at Urbana-Champaign.

Daniel S. Geller is Professor of Political Science at the University of Mississippi.

Douglas M. Gibler is Assistant Professor of Political Science at the University of Kentucky.

Gary Goertz is Assistant Professor of Political Science at the University of Arizona.

Paul R. Hensel is Assistant Professor of Political Science at Florida State University.

Paul K. Huth is Professor of Political Science at the University of Michigan.

Patrick James is Professor of Political Science at Iowa State University.

Russell J. Leng is James Jermain Professor of Political Economy and International Law at Middlebury College.

Jack S. Levy is Board of Governors' Professor of Political Science at Rutgers University.

Zeev Maoz is Professor of Political Science at Tel Aviv University.

Manus I. Midlarsky is Moses and Annuta Back Professor of International Peace and Conflict Resolution at Rutgers University.

James Lee Ray is Professor of Political Science at Vanderbilt University.

Gregory A. Raymond is Professor of Political Science and Director of the Honors College at Boise State University.

Susan G. Sample is Assistant Professor at the School of International Studies at the University of the Pacific.

J. David Singer is Professor of Political Science at the University of Michigan and founder-director of the Correlates of War project.

John A. Vasquez is Professor of Political Science at Vanderbilt University.

Frank Whelon Wayman is Professor of Political Science at the University of Michigan at Dearborn.

Jonathan Wilkenfeld is Professor and Chair of the Department of Government and Politics at the University of Maryland.